# Social Policy and the
# Conservative Agenda

*To Darlaine Gardetto and Donna DiDonato*

# Social Policy and the Conservative Agenda

Edited by

*Clarence Y. H. Lo
and Michael Schwartz*

Copyright © Blackwell Publishers Ltd 1998

First published 1998

2 4 6 8 10 9 7 5 3 1

Blackwell Publishers Inc.
350 Main Street
Malden, Massachusetts 02148
USA

Blackwell Publishers Ltd
108 Cowley Road
Oxford OX4 1JF
UK

*Library of Congress Cataloging-in-Publication Data*

Social policy and the conservative agenda/edited by Clarence Y. H. Lo
and Michael Schwartz.
   p.    cm.
   Includes bibliographical references and index.
   ISBN 1-57718-119-0. — ISBN 1-57718-120-4 (pbk.)
   1. United States—Social policy—1980-1993. 2. United States—
Social policy—1993–. 3. Social problems—United States.
4. Conservatism—United States.    I. Lo, Clarence Y. H.
II. Schwartz, Michael, 1942–.
HN59.2.S626   1998
361.6′1′0973—dc21                           97-19087
                                                   CIP

*British Library Cataloguing in Publication Data*

A CIP catalogue record for this book is available from the British Library.

Typeset in 10 on 12 pt Ehrhardt
by Ace Filmsetting Ltd, Frome, Somerset
Printed in Great Britain by MPG Books Ltd, Bodmin, Cornwall

This book is printed on acid-free paper.

# Contents

# Contributors

**Patrick Akard** teaches sociology at Skidmore College. He has just completed a book on the politics of US economic policy from 1974 to 1994, which is part of a larger study of the postwar political economy. He is currently examining the role of ideology and the media in framing public policy debates in the United States.

**J. Kenneth Benson** is a Professor of Sociology at the University of Missouri-Columbia. He has published a number of articles on organizations, interorganizational networks, and policy analysis. He is currently conducting a study of industrial policy initiatives of the Clinton administration.

**Cynthia J. Bogard** is Assistant Professor of Sociology at Hofstra University, New York. She received a Ph.D. in sociology from the State University of New York at Stony Brook in December, 1995. She is currently working on several projects involving homelessness and the construction of social policy.

**Zillah Eisenstein** is Professor of Politics at Ithaca College. She is the author of many books, the most recent being *The Color of Gender* (University of California Press, 1994) and *Hatreds* (Routledge, 1996). She presently is working on a book, *Cyberfantasies and Reconstructions of Gender and Knowledge*. She continues to be active in welfare politics and AIDS activism.

**Gregory Hooks** is Associate Professor of Sociology at Washington State University. He is the author of *Forging the Military-Industrial Complex* (University of Illinois Press, 1991), which examines the origins of the military-industrial complex during World War II. His current research continues to examine the many facets of US militarism. With Greg McLauchlan he is exploring post-World War II science policy. He is also examining the regional impact of the defense program over the last 50 years and the changes underway in the post-Cold War era.

**Carole Joffe** is a Professor of Sociology and Women's Studies at the University of California, Davis. She is the author of *Doctors of Conscience: The Struggle to Provide Abortion Before and After Roe v. Wade* (Beacon Press, 1995). Her current research includes medical responses to physician-assisted suicide.

**Jerry Lembcke** is Associate Professor of Sociology at Holy Cross College. His book *The Spitting Image: Myth, Memory, and the Legacy of Vietnam* is forthcoming with NYU Press.

**Clarence Y. H. Lo** is Associate Professor of Sociology at the University of Missouri at Columbia. He is the author of *Small Property versus Big Government: Social Origins of the Property Tax Revolt* (University of California Press, 1990; expanded edition, 1995) and articles about theories of the state and conservative social movements. He is writing a book about media representations of public opinion polls on social policies and budgets, and has been a consultant to political campaigns against tax-cutting ballot initiatives.

**Ann Markusen** is State of New Jersey Professor of Urban Policy and Planning at Rutgers University and Senior Fellow at the Council on Foreign Relations in New York. Her books include *Dismantling the Cold War Economy* (Basic Books, 1992), *Trading Industries, Trading Regions* (Guilford, 1995), and the forthcoming *Arming the Future* and *Second Tier Cities*. Her current research is focused on international defense conversion, technology policy, and regional economic development.

**J. Jeff McConnell**, former Field Director of the federal evaluation of the Transitional Housing Demonstration Project for homeless families in New York State, is a doctoral candidate at the State University of New York at Stony Brook. His dissertation analyzes communities of the suburban, street-dwelling homeless, and focuses on the social organization and "career" trajectories accounting for their survival and perseverance.

**Gregory McLauchlan** is Associate Professor of Sociology at the University of Oregon. His recent work on the relationship between the state, military institutions, and science and technology has appeared in *Political Power and Social Theory*, *Sociological Inquiry*, and the *Sociological Quarterly*. He is currently studying community resistance to globalization in the semiconductor industry.

**Beth Mintz** is Professor of Sociology at the University of Vermont. She is the author of *The Power Structure of American Business* (with M. Schwartz; University of Chicago Press, 1985), editor of *Corporate Control, Capital*

*Formation, and Organizational Networks* (with T. Takuyoshi and M. Schwartz; University of Chuo Press, 1996), and author of numerous articles including contributions to the *American Sociological Review*, *Social Problems*, *Theory and Society*, *Sociological Methodology*, and *Social Science History*. She is currently studying capital formation within the healthcare sector.

**Harvey Molotch** is Professor of Sociology at the University of California, Santa Barbara. In his chapter in this volume, he draws from his book with John Logan, *Urban Fortunes* (University of California Press, 1987), which won the Robert Park Award and was named Distinguished Contribution to the Discipline (1990) by the American Sociological Association.

**Morris Morley** is an associate professor of politics, Macquarie University, Sydney, Australia. He is the author of *Washington, Somoza and the Sandinistas* (Cambridge University Press, 1994) and co-author of *Empire or Republic?* (Routledge, 1995). He is currently researching a study of US policy toward Chile during the 1960s.

**Nick Paretsky** is a graduate student in sociology at the University of Missouri-Columbia. He is currently completing a doctoral dissertation entitled "Industrial Policy and the Council on Foreign Relations, 1974–1994."

**James Petras** is Professor of Sociology at the State University of New York, Binghamton. His most recent book (co-authored) is *Empire or Republic?* (Routledge, 1995). Forthcoming is *Neoliberalism and Class Conflict in Latin America* (Macmillan).

**Frances Fox Piven** is on the faculty of the Graduate Center of the City University of New York. She is co-author with Richard Cloward of *Regulating the Poor* (Vintage, 1971, updated 1993), *Poor People's Movements* (Pantheon, 1977), *The New Class War* (Pantheon, 1982), and *Why Americans Don't Vote* (Pantheon, 1988). She is currently working on a book on the historical episodes of expansion and contraction of the social contract.

**Jill Quadagno** is Professor of Sociology at Florida State University, where she holds the Mildred and Claude Pepper Eminent Scholar Chair in Social Gerontology. She is the author of seven books on aging and social policy issues, including *The Transformation of Old Age Security* (University of Chicago Press, 1988), *States, Labor Markets and the Future of Old Age Policy* (ed., Temple University Press), and *The Color of Welfare: How Racism Undermined the War on Poverty* (Oxford University Press, 1994). She is presently engaged in a study of the effect of downsizing on the health, income security, and savings behavior of older workers.

**Michael Schwartz**, Professor of Sociology at the State University of New York at Stony Brook, has published over fifty articles and five books, including the widely acclaimed *Radical Protest and Social Structure* (Academic Press, 1976), a pioneering work in historical sociology and social movement analysis; *The Power Structure of American Business* (with Beth Mintz; University of Chicago Press, 1985), an award-winning analysis of American business structure; and *The Structure of Power in America: The Corporate Elite as a Ruling Class* (with 13 others, Holmes and Meier, 1988),

which presents a Marxist interpretation of the American state. His current work includes *The Rise and Fall of Detroit*, a historical analysis of the collapse of the American automobile industry; and a four-year, longitudinal study of homeless families in Westchester County, New York.

**Judith Stacey**, the Streisand Professor of Contemporary Gender Studies and Professor of Sociology at the University of Southern California, has written and lectured extensively on the politics of family change. Her publications include: *In the Name of the Family: Rethinking Family Values in the Postmodern Age* (Beacon Press, 1996); *Brave New Families: Stories of Domestic Upheaval in Late Twentieth Century America* (Basic Books, 1990); and *Patriarchy and Socialist Revolution in China* (University of California Press, 1983). She is a founding member of the Council on Contemporary Families, a group committed to challenging the research and politics behind contemporary campaigns for family values.

**Ronald Walters** is Professor in the Afro-American Studies Program and the Government and Politics Department and is Senior Scholar in the Academy of Leadership at the University of Maryland, College Park. He has written extensively on issues of presidential politics and public policy. His book *Black Presidential Politics in America* (Wayne State University Press, 1988) won the Ralph Bunche Prize given by the American Political Science Association.

# Introduction: What Went Right?

## Why the Clinton Administration Did Not Alter the Conservative Trajectory in Federal Policy

 ★ *Michael Schwartz* ★

## Introduction

Conservatism is the ideology of the times. Fewer than 30 years ago, it was almost discredited, that even traditional Republicans felt compelled to modify it with adjectives like "responsible" or "moderate." But when Ronald Reagan was elected president in 1980, it marked the end of this period of eclipse.

The depth of this rebirth's effects could not be fully appreciated until Bill Clinton ascended to the presidency. Before 1992, it was unclear whether the policies enacted under Reagan and Bush reflected the (possibly temporary) Republican presence in the White House, or deeper trends that would impose themselves on policy trajectories without regard to the political complexion of incumbent executives. But as early as 1994 – before the Contract with America and the election of a Republican-led Congress – even journalistic accounts could appreciate the continuities between the Clinton Administration and its immediate predecessors.

While it is tempting to offer a facile explanation for such matters by referencing the winds of public opinion, this continuity demands an understanding of the deep structures in American politics that produced this change in the political complexion of government activity. We need to develop a systematic analysis of the forces that root out long-standing policies and replace them with new laws, new policies and new structures that embody a radically different perspective.

Looking back over the last 17 years and looking forward into the unknowable future, one gets a feeling of inevitability about this policy trajectory. It is as though an agenda was set in 1980, and we are destined to follow it until the adjournment of this era in American politics. The overall profile of the agenda is apparent: dramatic cutbacks in social spending, withdrawal of government from business regulation, sustained military superiority, aggressive, interventionist foreign policy, and an overarching commitment to deficit reduction.

For the most part, the many observers of this trend have focussed on the often fascinating (and challenging) details of the enacted programs. Particularly since Clinton formalized his abandonment of the traditional Democratic policy posture, the battles over these specifics have been fierce, and their outcomes have never been easy to predict. But these analyses have left the larger and far more significant questions unanswered.

The chapters in this collection take a very different approach. They seek to understand the forces that underpin the underlying trend and that therefore ensure conservative policy postures even when the commitments and interests of political incumbents should lead in a more liberal direction. And the Clinton Administration provides an ideal opportunity for such analyses, because so many observers, scholarly and journalistic, had expected Clinton to resist the conservative trend. No one was interested in why George Bush did not change the trajectory of American politics, because we had no reason to expect him to try. In this sense, Clinton was more like Reagan: His entry into office was accompanied by a general sense that he would attempt to alter the existing tendencies, to seek out new methods of addressing the vexing problems facing the American political economy, and to push at the constraints that most observers agree limit the government's capacity to adapt to a rapidly changing international and internal landscape.

But this expectation was actually the expression of two underlying assumptions made by most observers – from ordinary citizens to high-powered political theorists – that government policy is largely determined by the intermingling of two vectors: the policy impetus that flows from public opinion through elections and into the commitments of public officeholders, and the momentum and inertia of state structures that tend to resist any change in existing policy and administrative profile.

Clinton's presidency thus becomes a sort of social experiment that tests the validity of this implicit model by forcing us to take a close look at these assumptions, and to evaluate whether government trajectories are actually determined by these forces. And, since Clinton has already "failed," this means that we have a negative case to begin with.

But what is the nature of his failure? Certainly, he can only be a failure if he was "trying" to change the direction of government policy, that is, if he was trying to alter the existing policy profile. We assume he was because we know from the 1992 electoral campaign that he called for a large number of changes in most of the activities of govern-

ment (with the possible exception of foreign affairs). Our expectations therefore derive from a sense that electoral promises and campaign platforms are *at least* an expression of intention, and that we can rely on them as indicators of what a successful candidate will try to do.

## The Stages of Government Policy Formation

Electoral promises are a good starting place for reviewing the chapters in this collection, because most of them reference Clinton's Democratic Party legacy, and the electoral promises he made regarding the policy area they explore. Implicitly, they all follow a pattern of detection – each looks for the process by which these electoral promises were undermined, transformed, or disregarded in establishing, launching, or sustaining Clinton's presidency. To understand the patterns that emerge from the book as a whole, this introduction will outline the various moments at which such promises can (and did) go astray. We will then review those moments in light of the chapters in this collection, pointing to the places in which the expectations of change in the various policy realms reviewed here were modulated, eliminated, or defeated.

### Elections

At one level, elections are the ultimate filter, since they determine which candidates will reach office and therefore be in a position to articulate policy. But there is a much less visible way in which elections create filters, even for successful candidates. This refers to the process by which candidates recruit ideas and financial support for their campaigns. At the less sinister level, experts are recruited to help formulate polices that will appeal to both the electorate and potential backers. These advisers, who may themselves be significant political actors, bring with them a set of pre-dilections and a history of association with certain policy orientations. In the context of the campaign, therefore, the candidate's choice of advisers becomes a further constraint on the policies that he or she will advocate as part of the election campaign.

At the more sinister level lies the interests of financial backers. While Clawson and his collaborators (as well as many other authors) have emphasized that most campaign contributions do not carry policy strings in any overt sense, the chapters in this collection make clear that contributions nevertheless require candidates to make public utterances that reassure the community of backers.[1] These statements, which often presage policy orientation after election, serve notice to activist segments of the business and financial community that the candidate will be solicitous of their articulated needs and interests.

## Enunciation

Once candidates are elected there is no guarantee that they will pursue all the policies they advocated during the campaign. In fact, it is quite inevitable that many policies will never be enunciated as part of the official package, in part because there is simply too much to do and in part because most successful candidates have advocated contradictory programs that cannot be simultaneously enacted.

It is therefore important to focus on which ideas become part of the new official's formal statements of intentions, the programs that he or she advocates at or near the beginning of his or her term of office. This is the first moment when policies developed in the campaign can disappear from the set of policies to be pursued.

In the case of chief executives (particularly the president, but also governors and even mayors), a key to the enunciated profile of programs is the selection of high-ranking aides. Though the official version of such appointments is always that the new department head will be a "team player" loyal to whatever programs the chief decides are appropriate, in fact observers are correct in analyzing these appointments as significant indicators of policy direction. (Domhoff, in particular, has documented this in the context of tracing the pedigree of officials who championed key new programs back into the business-sponsored policy-planning groups that developed them.)[2] The absence of advocates of a particular viewpoint in the top councils of a new incumbent is a virtually certain indicator that this viewpoint will be neglected in the creation and pursuit of policy initiatives.

## Policy proposals

Little attention has been given to the disjunction between enunciated ideals and actual proposals, but the chapters in this collection make it clear that there is a long and troubled road to travel between these two policy-formation moments. Many programs that are advocated by newly elected presidents and their newly appointed top advisers are never converted into formal bills or executive orders.

This disjunction calls our attention to the understudied infighting that goes on in all executive branches of government, but which is particularly salient in presidential administrations. At the federal level there has always been bureaucratic inertia to deal with, in this case as it intrudes into the process by which legislation is formulated. This aspect of the problem has, at least, attracted the attention of state-centered theorists, who have made it a central factor in their understanding of government behavior.[3]

But less attention has been paid to the simple process of coalition formation within administrations. Once the appointments are made, a sort of positional warfare begins over both specific policies and the broad profile of programs that will be proposed. This process has not been placed at center stage because most analysts are tyrannized by what one might call the "electoral assumption" – that this infighting is resolved by comparing the several alternatives to the electoral platform and/or the (often shifting) condition of public opinion. But this is at least exaggerated, if not wholly inaccurate. The power wielded by individual cabinet officials and other agency heads is at least partially independent of the will of the president, and the ability of certain agencies to outmaneuver others is at least well understood in the popular press. As appointments are made, it is the secretaries of state and treasury that are seen as most significant, not only because these domains are so important, but also because they will be seen as the most influential advisers in the area of overall strategy.

We need to know more about this process, and the chapters in this collection are a good beginning.

## Enactment

This is certainly the most studied of the various policy moments, even more so than elections. This reflects the conjunction of most theories – with the notable exception of the class-power theorists led by Domhoff – that the Congress still exercises vast influence over which executive proposals will finally become law. C. Wright Mills's relegation of Congress to the secondary levels of power did not convince most observers of the American political scene.

But. this near consensus is simply a thin veneer over a deeper and more abiding disagreement that takes us back, once again, to the question of elections and public opinion. The observers of congressional behavior, particularly those who focus on its role in enacting, modifying, or defeating presidential initiatives (or those of the Congress itself), divide between the yea-sayers who assert the consonance of outcomes with the desires of

voters, and the nay-sayers who see these actions as serving special interests, usually those of large corporations, at the expense of the interest of voters. It is critical, therefore, in following the path of enunciated proposals through the legislative process, that this crucial divide be in the foreground. The chapters in this collection give special attention to these matters, and we return to a more thorough discussion of them in the conclusion.

## Execution

The process of executing enacted policies has never received the attention it deserves. Most observers have assumed not only that appointed officials simply followed the letter and spirit of an elected candidate's policy attitudes, but also that the executive branch enforces legislation, even when the new legislation varies drastically from its policy preferences. And, at a deeper level, the government bureaucracies are usually assumed to be obedient servants of legislative and executive will, rather than independent agencies capable of systematically altering or sabotaging the intent of enacted policy.

Here again the state-centered theorists (following the lead of the structuralists) have applied a useful corrective, forcing us to consider the possibility that execution will be at least a refracted version (if not an overt reformulation) of the original legislation. But beyond this, we should be sensitive to the ability of the executive branch, including appointed officials, to systematically redirect policy during the execution process. Such redirection can be much more than bureaucratic inertia, it can be actual policy formation under the guise of implementation. In the Clinton Administration, this effect has been particularly large, since this was a principle vehicle through which the conservative legacy of the Bush and Reagan administrations was transmitted into the policy process of Clinton's regime.

The remainder of this introduction will be devoted to a detailed consideration of each of these policy moments, relying on the chapters in this collection to illuminate the specific fate of Clinton's electoral promises. Before we begin this review, however, we need to address a key issue that derives from our common-sense understanding of current trajectories in American politics.

## How Does the Current Conservative Climate Impact on Policy Formation?

This is certainly a key issue, and the typology just enunciated seems to leave this as an aside. Partly this is true: We believe that ideology – even conservative ideology – has little life of its own until and unless it is embedded in policy. In fact, as many of the chapters in this collection demonstrate, the ideas that we have come to associate with the recent conservative ascendancy were created *in the process* of creating policy, and even their characterization as conservative is partly a consequence of the spin put on them as these policies have been developed. Sometimes, as exemplified by the creation of homelessness policy, there is even a struggle over whether what emerges is to be called "conservative" or "liberal," and this ambiguity extends into the long-term analysis of its impact. In other times, policies enacted in an apparently non-ideological context (such as the 1980 rescue of social security) emerge later as key moments in the enactment of conservative ideology.

And perhaps most significantly, the ideology of the American electorate is fully buried by the policy-formation process. If one theme emerges from all these chapters, it is that the attitudes of American citizens – liberal or conservative – enter into the equation only in very narrow ways and only under strictly de-limited circumstances.

But ultimately, ideology emerges as the abiding theme of Clinton's first administration, even if it operates within much narrower boundaries than popular imagery suggests. In reviewing the policy moments of the Clinton Administration, we reference both the role of public opinion and the enactment of conservative ideology as one element of the ongoing process. When we are done, we will revisit this issue to briefly summarize the large role of ideology in Clinton's regime and in American politics more generally.

## The Fate of Electoral Promises in the Clinton Administration

What is clear to the naked eye, halfway through the Clinton presidency, is that virtually all of the programs enunciated during the electoral campaign were defeated or are doomed, and that whatever emerges from his time in office will be at best refractions of the original proposals. But we need to understand this failure more analytically, and the five key moments listed above provide a lens through which to view it. At each moment, programs can be compromised or defeated: They can fail to proceed to the next step, they can be significantly modified, or they can be transformed. We can therefore ask a series of interesting questions:

1. Have Clinton's programs been progressively eroded from one step to another, or have they been swallowed up by the resistance at a single step?
2. Has Clinton had better success with certain moments (e.g. enunciation), but less success with others (e.g. enactment)?
3. Have the same forces defeated all of Clinton's programs, or have there been different oppositional configurations for different defeats?

The chapters in this collection allow us to formulate the beginning of an answer to these queries, and in doing so, gain insight into the more general processes that condition policy formation within the government. To understand them, let us briefly review some of the interesting results offered here.

## Elections as a policy-formation process

Too often journalists and scholars look at elections as a process by which candidates seek out positions that please voters or backers, without appreciating the ways in which this creative process impacts on later policy development. Patrick Akard (chapter 10) alerts us to some of the ways in which this occurs by tracing the intellectual background of key advisers to the 1992 Clinton campaign. By bringing Laura Tyson, Robert Reich, and other highly visible academic policy analysts into the campaign, Clinton purchased more than their ability to enunciate ideas with electoral appeal. He also purchased their intellectual biographies and their style of analysis. As the election proceeded, they sought to find those aspects of their ideas that would work as election tools, and this meant that Clinton's public pronouncements were colored with their ideology. For example, though Robert Reich and Laura Tyson were recruited because Clinton embraced their ideas about job creation, their internationalism became embedded in their proposals – though it is doubtful that this was an explicit mandate of campaign strategy.

In another world, Clinton might have recruited money for his campaign without public pronouncements on matters dear to the hearts of the business community. But because the job-creation liberals successfully impacted on the policies advocated during the campaign, many business backers became edgy about Clinton's intentions. In order to ensure that his business supporters were securely on board, he therefore felt compelled to recruit campaign advisers who had good reputations with the business, and particularly the financial, community. These deficit hawks, mostly drawn from moderate Democratic congressional circles, had established themselves as committed to deficit reduction above all else – the policy most favored by Wall Street and other major sectors of the business community. These new advisers, like the job-creation liberals, arrived with policy orientations and convictions that became embedded in Clinton's public platform and in the less public assumptions within the campaign about how to fulfill them.

Clinton's 1992 election campaign was therefore self-contradictory in a very familiar way. Clinton proposed different policies for different audiences, and did not attempt to develop an overarching platform that resolved the incompatibilities of these perspectives. In many campaigns – and 1992 was one of them – such a resolution is not attempted until after the election. But this does not mean that these campaign promises had no consequences for the future posture of the Clinton presidency. The campaign advisers who authored them were destined to inhabit the upper reaches of the executive branch, where they would seek to implement their favorite programs. The implicit contradictions of campaign rhetoric were therefore destined to become the explicit friction of the sitting administration.

It is important to note that this sort of implicit sparring during a campaign is not the only modality by which campaigns influence subsequent policy. As Zillah Eisenstein (chapter 14) demonstrates in her review of Clinton's second (1996) campaign, the absence of central issues (the personalities of the candidates were the center of controversy, while policy disputes were relegated to trivial details of proposed or already enacted legislation) – does not imply that elections are really apolitical. The popular image of such elections is that the candidates, once elected, will be uncommitted to *any* policy orientation and therefore responsive to public opinion as it crystallizes around arising issues. But, as Eisenstein demonstrates, this is a profoundly misleading image. The underlying reality of personality politics is that the policy choices are simply made outside the public view – before, during, and after the campaign. In 1996, this meant that the crucial decisions about abandoning state entitlements for poor people and sustaining state entitlements for rich corporations had already been made, that there would be no effort to give the Family Leave Act teeth by making it paid instead of unpaid, and that there would be no effort to extend access to abortion to all those desiring it. In fact, because the 1996 campaign avoided *any* issue that would actually generate dispute and therefore benefit from public debate, it guaranteed that decisions on these issues would be made without the benefit of public discourse.

One enduring pattern that emerges is that electoral campaigns are not self-contained efforts to attract votes and money. The texture of the campaign is influenced greatly by the policy baggage that the candidates and their advisers bring with them. And these pre-existing predilections are not the random intellectual meanderings of spaced-out academics and "wand in the wind" politicians. They are part of a system of ideas and political commitments held by savvy political actors who are seeking a method to enact those programs they believe in. Beyond this, these policy pronouncements may be further modified by the issues raised by other politicians, who alert backers to key controversies and force candidates to take stands on matters they might prefer were not a part of the discourse. But even when issues are not raised at all – and this is the increasing pattern in American politics – the sifting process is proceeding within the councils of the campaign.

What is finally said by the candidate is a seamless mixture of decisions about which things to advocate or to leave unraised, the pre-existing predilections of the advisers who craft the ideas, and the issues that are forced upon then candidate by other politicians.

## *Official appointments and the policy process*

The moment Clinton was declared the winner in 1992, a winnowing process began which profoundly affected the ultimate policy profile of his administration. This was not simply a matter of post-campaign decision making by the new president and his top advisers. There was a coercive substructure that is neatly revealed by Patrick Akard, who focusses our attention on the abrupt drop in stock and bond prices that accompanied Clinton's victory. Though candidate Clinton had responded to the challenge of D'Amato and others by recruiting advisers and enunciating policies that reassured Wall Street, the post-election reality brought new factors into the equation.

Fred Block introduced the concept of "business confidence" into the language of political analysis, and Akard's account of the immediate post-election period certainly illustrates the ways in which the absence of such confidence can threaten the viability of an administration, even before it ascends to office.[4] But even more significantly, it reveals the standard procedure by which a new official can generate business confidence, even before he or she takes office. This involves the selection of cabinet officers and White House advisers who have the confidence of the business fraction that the candidate wishes to reassure. As Akard shows, Clinton sought out the same deficit hawks who had first made their appearance during the campaign – individuals who had a long record of advocating deficit reduction as the number one priority of government policy. In Clinton's estimation, this was necessary to forestall what might have been a business crisis even before he was inaugurated. But it also constituted a more-or-less irrevocable commitment to act on these matters once he arrived in Washington.

It is important to note both the continuity and the discontinuity between the election process and this critical moment of selecting the executive team. The continuities arise because those who participated in the policy development process during the campaign have first claim on the post-election appointments. For that reason, Clinton's appointment of deficit hawks did not seem altogether out of place: His earlier use of deficit hawks to develop pro-Wall Street rhetoric that reassured his backers about the financial crises dovetailed with this new effort, and made his appointments appear to be a continuation of the already established effort to court and win Wall Street.

But there were discontinuities as well. This was reflected not only in the ascension of outsiders with Wall Street pedigrees, but also in the relative positioning of the job-creation liberals and the deficit hawks. Whereas the campaign had emphasized job creation – in keeping with this as the primary concern of voters – and made the financial crisis a decidedly secondary issue, the selection of officials abruptly shifted the emphasis. As the essays by Akard and by Morris Morley and James Petras, (chapter 6) both demonstrate, the key policy-making positions (secretaries of the treasury, state, etc.) went to the deficit hawks, while the job-creation liberals got nothing larger than the secretary of labor. To close observers, this became the first indication of a major shift in Clinton's policy posture.

But there is an even deeper and less visible part to this appointment process. As Cynthia Bogard and J. Jeff McConnell point out (chapter 4), the – virtually inevitable – appointment of local Democratic politicians to the Department of Housing and Urban Development (HUD) (notably Andrew Cuomo, his second-term secretary) appeared at first to be

a decided commitment to liberal policy making in this area. But beneath this surface was the commitment of these appointees to the programs they had developed during the conservative era of Bush and Reagan. Since these programs had been designed to be compatible with the conservative tenor of the times, these appointments assured that the Clinton era housing programs – and most notably the showcase homelessness polices – would be extensions of those developed in the earlier administrations.

And Judith Stacy (chapter 15) reveals another facet of the same process in the broader area of "family policy." The appointment of a particular brand of adviser meant that the neo-conservative defense of the two-parent, father-headed family would have privileged access to the policy-formation process, excluding those who supported less conventional (but actually more common) single-parent, same-gender, and extended families as reasonable adaptations to modern American life. These appointments made it almost inevitable that Clinton would abandon many of the key constituencies that had won him the election in the first place.

Once these appointments were announced, and particularly after the appointees took office, they began developing and enunciating a set of policy objectives. Like the advisory process during the campaign, these pronouncements reflected the broader decisions made by the Clinton team, but they also reflected the policy agendas of the appointees themselves. The contradictory profile of Clinton's cabinet choices therefore ensured that the enunciated programs would contain contradictions of at least three types: Different appointees would advocate contradictory policies; his appointees would advocate policies that contradicted the enunciated positions of the campaign; and his appointees (and ultimately the president) would advocate policies that contradicted the desires of his most fervent supporters.

During the free-for-all that characterized the early days of the administration, implicit and even explicit contradictions among various policy pronouncements were inevitable, as they are in most administrations. And, as in most administrations, these contradictory pronouncements became the beginning of the struggle between the major factions within the executive branch. This much was visible to the popular press. Less visible was the fact that the profile of appointments established the administrative power and the visibility of the combatants. The struggles that ensued between these factions would be colored both by the very different responsibilities that inhered in their different positions (and therefore the administrative clout that these appointments conferred), and by their visibility to the outside world. To put the matter bluntly: The secretary of the treasury can access the media and the attention of those who monitor government much more easily and much more regularly than the secretary of labor can. In conflictual circumstances, that access, combined with the greater administrative clout that inheres in the major ministries, confers upon their incumbents a decided advantage.

For some policies, therefore, the appointment/enunciation process was the definitive moment. As Gregory Hooks and Gregory McLauchlan (chapter 8) demonstrate, the Clinton promise to civilianize scientific research died aborning during the enunciation process. The commitment to the policy of "dualism" – in which scientific research and development projects would simultaneously serve military and civilian ends – ensured that there would be no substantial civilianization. It meant that the military would continue to control the lion's share of the scientific research budget, modulated by a mandate to develop non-military applications in conjunction with maintaining US superiority in military technology. Hence, the fundamental trajectories would inevitably be determined by current military imperatives, while potentially fruitful civilian scientific initiatives with no military applications would remain unfunded and undeveloped.

Here, then, is an example in which the enunciation stage spelled the definitive demise of a Clinton Administration initiative. But it also points toward some important and still unanswered questions. If the pattern traced by Hooks and McLauchlan is a more general one, the key to this defeat was the choice of appointed officials to administer the military research and the military more generally. Without understanding the process by which they ascended to these positions, we cannot fully understand why dualism became the one and only option enunciated.

Judith Stacey's chapter raises much the same point. Despite the fact that there was a well-established social science establishment that supported more tolerant policies toward "non-traditional" families, Clinton chose his advisers from a narrow group of "right"-thinking scholars, thus assuring that policy pronouncements from his administration would be indistinguishable from those of his predecessor administrations.

Harvey Molotch (chapter 3) makes this point also, but in a context that indicates the coercive legacy of the Bush and Clinton administrations. Clinton's recruitment of Henry Cisneros, the former mayor of San Antonio, guaranteed that his key adviser on urban policy would be opposed to the sort of federal intervention in local politics that liberal presidents have traditionally practiced. But this was not so much a choice as an inevitability: At the time Clinton ascended to office, there were virtually no traditional liberals who could have been treated as worthy candidates for such positions – the Reagan/Bush era had effectively purged them from national and local office. That is, all the viable candidates for positions in HUD were individuals who had made their careers by building and exploiting the sort of government-business alliances that preclude Federal intervention into urban social problems. This contrasts with the examples of science policy and family policy – in which the key question becomes the reasons for choosing appointees from a particular camp. In this case, Clinton's abandonment of traditional Democratic urban policy was made inevitable by the structural change in Democratic Party leadership during the 15-year conservative era.

The enunciation of policy at the beginning of an administration is simultaneously the culmination of the appointment process and the definitive break with the direct impact of public opinion on government words or deeds. As the chapters in this collection amply demonstrate, public opinion rapidly recedes into the deep background once the appointments are completed and the new administration sets to work. While public opinion is a matter of concern, it no longer has even the modest coercive power that it achieves during elections. Instead, it becomes an object of manipulation, rather than a force to be reckoned with.

## The struggle over official policy proposals

The official process of policy development began only after the appointments were made, the new administration ascended to power, and the various executive appointees staked out their policy areas. At that moment, the newly appointed officials began pressing for commitments to the policies they advocated. During the election campaign – and to a lesser extent during the period of enunciation – implicit or even explicit contradictions among advocated policies were acceptable and perhaps even advantageous. But these disagreements were unacceptable as official proposals, and the vast contradictions among the various orientations become a major issue once actual policies began to be crafted. Most notably, the job-creation liberals sought to implement programs that would utilize the resources of the federal government to create an industrial policy that would nurture promising industries, and a job-training program that would create the workforce needed to sustain them. But since this involved massive infusions of federal money, it conflicted directly with deficit-reduction programs, advocated by deficit hawks, that focussed on a pay-as-we-go approach to new spending.

The jockeying for policy advantage during the first months of the Clinton Administration allows us to better understand the intimate connection between appointments and the development of official policy proposals. Because the deficit hawks had won the key positions, they now were able to speak with greater authority within the administration and to the outside world. This gave them a strong initial advantage that was reflected in the initial set of policy proposals emanating from the Clinton White House.

Morris Morley and James Petras, in their review of the Clinton Administration policy profile, offer a succinct summary of the fate of the programs favored by job-creation liberals. The job-creation program itself – the centerpiece of the campaign – was halved as compared to election promises; the proposed program (subsequently defeated in Congress) would not have absorbed the new entries into the workforce for the year 1993–4, let alone have made a dent in the accumulated unemployment of the Reagan/Bush years. The education/job-training budget – another prominent campaign issue – fared even worse; Clinton's initial budget actually decreased expenditures by 2–3 percent, as compared to the final Bush budget. And repairs to the public infrastructure – yet another prominent campaign proposal – were not addressed at all; Transportation Secretary Pena ultimately made a gesture at them by offering an almost casual proposal that the $290-billion repair bill for the nation's decaying bridges and highways be managed by privatizing some or all of them.

This initial advantage of the deficit hawks was significantly enhanced by the reinfusion of outside forces. Once again the matter of business confidence raised its ugly head, this time around the struggle itself. Unlike elections, which occur only periodically, market declines, capital flight, export of capital, and potential bankruptcy can occur at any time. The threat of declining business confidence therefore became a part of the struggle over official proposals. This strengthened the hand of the deficit hawks and weakened the job-creation liberals still further. The policies that the Clinton Administration ultimately proposed to Congress reflected this, and this became the most significant point of departure from electoral promises. As J. Kenneth Benson and Nick Paretsky (chapter 9) demonstrate, this constituted the moment when "industrial policy" (in the sense in which it was originally enunciated) was abandoned.

This did not, of course, put an end to the struggle. As long as the job-creation liberals retained a beachhead in the administration, they continued to press their agenda. This was reflected in the industrial programs that were ultimately enunciated, in their efforts to modify and even reform other policy proposals, and in their implementation of policies for which they were responsible. In some sense, once such a conflict becomes embodied in administration appointments, it continues until one side is removed from positions with leverage or the administration ends. And so, this friction did continue through the entire first administration, but died out in the second, when the job-creation liberals left or were pushed out of the Cabinet.

Jill Quadagno's discussion (chapter 5) offers further insight into the ways in which such internal friction is resolved, by focussing on the as yet unfinished debate over social security. The debate derived from the original crisis in the early years of the Reagan Administration, which undermined the 50-year-old image of social security as a "trust fund" that simply held people's money until their retirement. Over the years since then, the trust fund imagery has competed with another one in which "we" (the middle-class taxpayers) support "old folks." By devolving social security into just another welfare program, this imagery laid the foundation for a redefinition of the fiscal viability of social security. Until the 1990s, funding for social security was administratively and politically segregated – and its viability was judged in terms of the ability of the separate social security tax to cover the cost of the program. But in the 1990s, the deficit hawks defined this as just another income stream, to be utilized in the most fiscally responsible fashion. From that perspective, social security funding became part of the more general question of how much total "welfare" the government could afford. Once that total was established, social security could simply compete with other programs for the total welfare dollar. Or, to put it more bluntly, the social security debate would devolve into the traditional one over whether this beneficiary of federal "largesse" is worthy of our support – whether its social security recipients were the "deserving elderly" being repaid for a lifetime of hard work, or "greedy geezers" grabbing an unearned subsidy from the already overburdened middle class.

By the end of Clinton's first administration, all of the important issues about social security were settled. The debates between Clinton and the Republican Congress masked the victory of the deficit hawks, since both sides embraced the devolution into "fiscal responsibility." Social security would no longer have a privileged place among federal programs, and would instead be subject to the vicissitudes of either the funding process or the stock market or both. In other words, like income transfer programs, old age insurance would be subject to debate in each funding cycle, and could not be seen as real social insurance.

Too often journalists and scholars have brushed past the policy enunciation process as a simple reflection of presidential ideology, and have failed to focus on its momentous impact on policy trajectories. Presidential administrations are complicated structures involving a form of collective decision making that is hard to penetrate and easy to ignore. The pushing and shoving begin even before the Cabinet is sworn in, and it constitutes the political equivalent of the famous "permanent floating crap game" immortalized in the musical *Guys and Dolls*: The players are forever coming and going, the sites of debate are constantly shifting, and the stakes are always high. During each undemarcated period, the winners accumulate greater resources with which to play the next round, while the losers stagger away seeking a new stake before they can re-enter the fray.

By determining the policies that would be submitted for enactment, the policy enunciation process also determined what was possible in the Clinton administration. And because the fiscal hawks won most of the early rounds, they also guaranteed that the later debates would fall well within boundaries they were comfortable with. Ultimately this – more than any other policy-making moment – created the profile of Clinton Administration policy.

## Enactment as fine tuning

In *The Power Elite*, C. Wright Mills declared that, in the post-World War II reality of American politics, Congress had only a secondary and reactive role in the policy-formation process.[5] Subsequent analyses of the process of enactment have provided a partial substantiation of this conclusion. Though there has been little work on failed campaign promises, there is now a vast literature on the formulation process of successful legislation, particularly the sort of major legislation under consideration here. The origins of such

major initiatives demonstrate that the active creational process routinely occurs long before congressional consideration begins. This is one of the few points of agreement between class theorists like Domhoff, who emphasize the role of elite policy-planning groups as the crafters of significant policy; and state-centered theorists like Skocpol, who focus upon the government bureaucracies and ad hoc commissions that ultimately enunciate policy. But this agreement conceals a larger disagreement: Whereas Domhoff sees the origins of proposals in the needs and articulated interest of the capitalist class, the state theorists find these origins in a complex of power centers, not the least of which lies ultimately with the voters. In the eyes of the state-centered theorists, the looming power of Congress as a veto group therefore plays a key role in the formulation process, even if most of the work is done before legislation arrives there. We address this issue more fully in the conclusion.

The first Clinton Administration appears to challenge the point on which these perspectives agree. The activist GOP Congress, which pushed through its Contract with America and seized the initiative from Clinton in 1994, appeared to make itself the center of policy formation, reducing the Clinton-led executive branch to the reactive role usually reserved for Congress.

But the chapters in this collection demonstrate that the popular image of Congressional policy making is overdrawn. As Morris Morley and James Petras demonstrate in their review of the actual policies enacted, most of the damage had already been done in the first two years of the Clinton Administration, when the policy-enunciation process determined which proposals Clinton would advocate; that is, before the GOP took control of Congress. The well-publicized clashes during the tumultuous 1995 and 1996 sessions over the Contract with America certainly resulted in a flurry of high-profile legislation; but this legislation did not differ fundamentally from proposals presented by Clinton in 1993 and 1994. Two very different examples exemplify this pattern.

First, consider welfare policy, ably analyzed in this volume by Frances Fox Piven (chapter 1) and Ronald Walters (chapter 2). These chapters demonstrate that the ferocious encounter between Clinton and Congress was epiphenomenal at best, and that the fundamental changes in welfare were decided upon even before the 1994 Congress was elected. In fact, the Clinton welfare plan, so soundly defeated by Congress even before the Contract was formulated, had already abandoned the key principle of economic instrumentalism that had informed the welfare system since its inception in the New Deal. It was Clinton's welfare taskforce that introduced the idea of time limits on benefits and that proposed the devolution of policy initiative to localities, thus allowing for ratcheting down benefits according to local fiscal logic. And these proposals had been germinating for at least 10 years within the Democratic Party, and particularly in the southern Democratic Party that nurtured Bill Clinton.

But even more profoundly, Clinton's plan constituted the definitive break with welfare as a system that presented itself as serving the entire working population, by allowing the unemployed to stay out of the labor market until and unless new and decent jobs were created. His "job-training" program was simply a poorly disguised effort to force welfare recipients into the already overcrowded market, and therefore undermine the wages and job security of those already employed. Despite its sometimes generous prose about job creation, the absence of an industrial policy meant that the program could accomplish nothing more than an increase in the pressure on wages.

And the deeper substructure of this policy is fully continuous with events in the 1980s that recentered American welfare politics on a racist foundation. Clinton embraced this characterization in his campaign and then re-emphasized it with the texture and tone of his subsequent policy pronouncements.

By the time 1994 rolled around, the die was cast, and the Contract with America simply embraced what Clinton's Welfare Task Force had already developed. The debates, however ferocious, were devoted to the details of implementation. And while these details were crucial to many of the participants in the debates (since they determined which businesses and which governments would most directly benefit from the changes being contemplated), they were not about the fundamental policy profile.

Second, consider the case of health care. While Beth Mintz (chapter 11) does not challenge the role of Congress in blocking passage of the Clinton in health plan, this defeat is well within Congress' traditional role as a veto group. And this spectacular defeat should not obscure the fact that it has been the president, not the Congress, that has set the trajectory for subsequent changes. As Mintz demonstrates, even before the bill arrived at Congress, Hillary Clinton's Task Force, following the lead of the Jackson Hole Group, opted for managed care as the principle vehicle for health coverage, abandoning the Canadian single-payer model, which most experts argued was the only sensible method of financial organization. In the very important changes that have occurred since the defeat of the bill, single-payer plans have never again reared their pretty heads, and managed care has become the de facto national policy, as insurers and large health-care companies have enacted it through consolidations and through contracts with major employers. As in the welfare case, the original Clinton plan already embodied conservative principles.

In both of these crucial cases of congressional power, then, the most significant policy decisions occurred before the policies were proposed; key choices had been made that

severely delimited both the terms of the debate and, therefore, the role of Congress in
creating and sustaining policy trajectories.
Even in this era of newfound congressional
activism, C. Wright Mills's relegation of Congress to the "second tier of power" still reveals more than it conceals.

### Execution as a policy formation moment

All policies, regardless of their policy-formation pedigree, are given over to the executive
branch for implementation. We must therefore be sensitive to the degree to which such
implementation is yet another occasion for
vitiating or altering the thrust of policy. And
we should also be prepared to find policies
that simply emanate from the executive
branch, working within the already enacted
guidelines of existing legislation.

Historically we can discern three patterns
by which enacted policy is drastically altered
during the implementation process. The most
visible derives from the failure of government
to successfully impose such policies on target
populations. Easy examples of this can be
found in the failure of the policy of pacification in Vietnam, in which the Vietnamese
people (with substantial help from American
citizens) simply refused to cooperate, using a
vast array of peaceful and violent means to
resist.

But one need not look at world historical
events like the Vietnam war to find examples
of unsuccessful execution. Collective protest
has been successful in resisting and ultimately
altering all manner of government policy, from
the colonists' resistance to the Stamp Acts to
the civil rights movement's assault on legal
segregation. Even unorganized mass action can
substantially undermine policy, as the boot-
legging industry during prohibition and the
recent tidal wave of unauthorized immigration amply demonstrate. And beyond this,
there is the day-to-day resistance offered to
all manner of legislation – from petty income
tax fraud practiced by prosperous citizens
(which regularly yields changes in the tax law
itself) to evasion of pure food and drug laws
by food processing and pharmaceutical companies (which result in altered or even transformed regulatory profiles).

Ann Markusen's chapter (chapter 7) in this
collection provides a pungent example of this
sort of resistance, which has matured into
identifiable policy during the Clinton Administration. Cuts in defense spending were part
of the "peace dividend" that Clinton spoke of
so frequently during his campaign, and these
– unlike many of his promises – appeared to
be enacted during his first administration,
when defense spending was displaced from
its historical trajectory. This displacement was
largely temporary because of the threat of
economic crises in localities dependent upon
the defense industry. The key to avoiding these
local depressions was the conversion of
defense-dependent firms to civilian production. But, for the most part, such conversion
did not take place; the contractors either failed
to attempt it or failed to execute it. Instead,
they sought to survive the threat to their profits by gobbling each other up in friendly and
unfriendly acquisitions, while intensifying their
lobbying efforts for sustained production of
the systems that they depended upon. Almost immediately, this strategy bore its initial fruit; the Clinton Defense Department
itself invested in facilitating overseas sales of
weapons, thus ensuring the short-term survival of key firms. In the medium term, the
administration found numerous budgetary
loopholes to support companies that remained
strictly weapons suppliers. But these measures, while rescuing key firms, also ensured
that they would only survive in the long run
if they received new infusions of government
support, to update old systems and/or develop new weapons systems. This, in effect,
perpetuated the old system of developing
weapons systems in order to keep major sup-

pliers profitable. This phenomenon was even observed in the *New York Times*, which commented during the 1995 budget struggle: "The Pentagon is expected to get billions of dollars worth of weapons it did not request, in part because they provide work for an otherwise idle military industry" (August 30, 1995, P. D1). In effect, defense contractors, by resisting the transition to civilian production, reversed the "peace dividend" that Clinton promised; by the 1996 campaign it had disappeared from the political firmament.

Here again, it is important to note the intrusion of "outsiders" into government processes. In this case, military contractors have become a recognized part of the military effort, and their needs and interests are seamlessly integrated into the logic of military policy. Moreover, as Markusen demonstrates, the national financial community played a key role in pressing for an ongoing commitment to specialized weapons companies. Even within the bureaucratic labyrinth of the executive branch, government decision making is semi-permeable. Outside actors – virtually always representatives of one or another business fraction – have privileged access to and/or institutional leverage on the key officials who determine the profile that policy will take. We further develop this theme in the conclusion.

The second type of change that takes place during implementation has to do with the creative role that implementing bureaucracies can and do play during the enforcement process. The great bureaucratic "black box" is another one of those understudied aspects of government, insulated from research scrutiny by the well-worn image of the Weberian bureaucracy that faithfully enforces directives from above. The inadequacy of this image is demonstrated by Cynthia Bogard and J. Jeff McConnell's tracing of homelessness policy into the nether world of local social service agencies. It was here that creative administrators figured out how to use funds designated for earthquakes and other disasters to house the homeless – first to pay for the notorious "welfare hotels" and then to create "supportive housing" that has become the chief holding institution for homeless families. And this new creation facilitated access to Medicaid funding – to cure the various dependencies (drug and psychological) that purportedly caused the homelessness in the first place. Eventually, these creative extensions of existing programs matured into the only high-profile social service legislation in the last 15 years – the McKinney Act; and it became the signature program of Clinton's Department of Housing and Urban Development.

The third modality through which the executive branch modifies enacted policy lies in the bureaucracy itself, which coerces policy simply through its capacity or lack of capacity to take certain actions. This is exemplified by Harvey Molotch's chilling analysis of urban policy as a whole. There were no Clinton Administration policy initiatives in this area, no well-publicized friction with the Republican Congress, and no controversial reversal of campaign promises. Instead, Clinton simply advanced and amplified the policy legacy bequeathed to him by Bush and Reagan, and, in doing so, consolidated the conservative thrust of the 1980s.

We have already mentioned the origins of this drift in Clinton's selection of key officials in HUD. And, while the big controversy over abolishing the agency was played out in public, these appointed officials inscribed their philosophy onto the ongoing activities of the agency. At the broadest level, as Molotch demonstrates, this involved ongoing devolution of initiative from the Federal agency to local agencies that explicitly coordinated their actions with local growth machines. This has left the federal government – and the American population more generally – with limited capacity to resist the interests of the local commercial and industrial firms that dominate municipal decision making. In Molotch's view, we may be definitively undermining the capacity of government to act as a countervailing force to the worst abuses of the profit nexus.

## What About Public Opinion?

Press coverage of the great confrontations between Clinton and Congress always referenced the battle for public opinion, and carefully analyzed the role of public opinion in determining the nuances of the resulting compromises. Yet the analyses presented in this volume offer a different portrait, in which public opinion rarely shows its face.

The contradiction is not nearly as palpable as it first appears. Even for journalists, public opinion only impacts on policy disputes that are played out in public. For the bread-and-butter issues that are routinely handled without dispute – foreign policy, industrial policy, homelessness policy, housing policy, and the rest – elected and appointed officials simply "do their job." It is only occasionally that the disputes erupt into public view and then, as the contributions to this volume indicate, they may be around minor aspects of a much larger (and undebated) consensus.

But even when public opinion is part of the decision-making process it does not necessarily represent the intrusion of democracy into the policy process. The chapters by Jerry Lee Lembcke (chapter 13) and Clarence Y. H. Lo (chapter 12) illustrate a very different relationship between policy makers and public opinion than the one which the media celebrate as part of the daily routine of government.

Lembcke explores the what can only be called the manipulation of public opinion in order to gain support for military adventures overseas. What is crucial to extract from this is that *public opinion did not coerce policy – the initial opposition of Americans to the Gulf War did not deter Bush from pursuing it*. All that was created was the necessity of reversing public opinion before the war could proceed.

Similarly, Lo demonstrates that a considerable component in the defeat of Clinton's health plan was persuading the general population that a fundamentally popular plan did not have strong public support. That is, *the popularity of the plan was not a force for enacting it*. Instead, this popularity became an incentive to create the impression that the plan was unpopular. And even when public opinion was constructed as negative it did not "get its way." The key axes around which this opposition was constructed were, as Beth Mintz points out, fears of "limited choice of physicians and limited access to high tech treatment" – in short, cost cutting managed care. Nevertheless, once the bill was defeated, internal industry evolution yielded up exactly this profile for the bulk of the country – managed care systems that severely limited physician choice and deprived patients of the most modern techniques when they were deemed cost-ineffective.

In both of these cases, public opinion created no policy imperatives – it was simply a barrier to be overcome on the way to enacting policies whose profile was determined by other forces. Instead of a coercive expression of popular will and the key symptom of democracy, public opinion becomes an annoyance that policy makers must deal with in order to pursue their own ends.

But why deal with the annoyance at all? Why not just ignore it? This fascinating question is beyond the scope of this volume, but it appears that this is one enduring legacy of the protests of the 1960s. Government officials are painfully aware of the dangers of unmanipulated public opinion. If negative attitudes are allowed to fester, they can mature into forceful protest that impinges on the officials' discretionary space. The safer road is to work hard to gather public opinion around a policy before enacting or revealing it, and therefore to foreclose the possibility of potentially effective opposition, disruption, or protest.

## How Typical is the Clinton Debacle?

Few presidents have been as publicly unsuccessful as Clinton was in his first term. But this should not obscure the more enduring patterns that his administration shares with those of his predecessors. These patterns can be briefly summarized in several observations.

First, there is no one moment at which policies are definitively undermined. There appears to be an incremental process for most of Clinton's failures, beginning even during the election campaign, when contradictory promises were embraced and campaign advisers were recruited whose policy agendas were incompatible.

Second, virtually all of the damage was done before policies reached Congress. This is a surprising result, considering the vast attention that the popular media have given to Clinton's inability to create a working majority in Congress, even before the 1994 election. Because of this focus on Congress, the pattern of early demise has not received the attention it deserves, and it should become the focal point for future scholarship. The chapters in this collection are a significant beginning.

Third, at each point in the vitiation process, "outside" forces, notably the financial community and other business groupings, played a key role in determining both the changes and the consistencies in policy profile. Government decision making is not insulated from business: It is responsive both to the possibility that government action will undermine corporate viability and to the vast interdependence of government agencies and private enterprise. This set of relationships lays the foundation for the creation and sustenance of ongoing consultations at all stages of the policy process, and therefore ensures ongoing access for the business world. We take up this theme in more detail in the conclusion to this volume.

Fourth, public opinion, though a constant referent during the electoral season, fades as a coercive mechanism once elections are over. Unlike the influence of business, public opinion cannot promise the immediate sanctions – such as the collapse of the banking system or the disabling of the military procurement system – that animate the responsiveness of government to business factions. This transforms concern with public opinion from a coercive policy vector into a matter of social control – a force to be molded and manipulated so that it will be manageable in the next election.

Other recent presidencies, despite apparently vast differences, reflect the same patterns. Reagan's administration, for example, was much more successful in enacting its enunciated policy package, but the pattern of changes and consistencies is quite similar. The package that was passed did not replicate his earliest platform. By the time he was nominated by the Republican Party, Reagan had already added "responsible conservatives" to his team, and once his appointments were made, right-wing Republicans were saying that Reagan was "no longer a Reaganite." Thus, the vitiation process appears to have operated in the early stages in much the same way as it did in the Clinton presidency: Campaign advisers and Cabinet appointees carried with them the changes and the consistencies of policy that would frame the ultimate proposals. The big contrast occurred in the comparison between enunciated policy proposals and the bills introduced into Congress; there was much less alteration during this stage in the Reagan Administration. But once the official proposals emerged from Reagan's White House, they passed through a Democratic Congress relatively unscathed, a remarkable achievement considering the gross contradictions between Reagan's program and that advocated by the Democratic leadership.

And, to a considerable degree, the policy profile was undermined during the enforcement stage. Reagan's programs were designed to reduce both the deficit and the size of the government – yet the years of his administration saw record increases in both the budget and the national debt.[6]

In sum, the same process was involved in Clinton's failure and Reagan's success. Moreover, the policies that have emerged from Clinton's administration are strikingly similar to those of Reagan: deficit reduction as

the major emphasis, implemented by severe budget cutting through attacks on domestic programs, and complemented by the sustenance of a strong military. It appears that the process of policy formulation cranks out the same policies, regardless of the political complexion of the president.

This leads us back to the premise upon which the expectation that Clinton would alter policy trajectories rested. It derived from the implicit assumption that electoral promises animate post-election policy formation and enactment. This close look at the policy process under Clinton suggests a drastic reinterpretation of the electoral assumption: Elections and campaign promises have little to do with the policies that emerge from a presidential administration, even a successful one like Reagan's.

## Notes

1  Dan Clawson, Alan Neustadtl, and Denise Scott, *Money Talks* (New York: Basic Books, 1992).

2  See, for example, G. William Domhoff, *The Higher Circles* (New York: Random House, 1970) and *State Autonomy or Class Domination* (New York: Aldine De Gruyter, 1996).

3  See, for example, Theda Skocpol, *Protecting Soldiers and Mothers* (Cambridge MA: Harvard University Press, 1992).

4  Fred L. Block, *Revising State Theory* (Philadelphia PA: Temple University Press, 1988).

5  C. Wright Mills, *The Power Elite* (New York: Oxford University Press, 1956).

6  Bennet Harrison and Barry Bluestone, *The Great U-Turn: Corporate Restructuring and the Polarizing of America* (New York: Basic Books, 1988).

# Part I
# Welfare, Social Security, and the State of Austerity

# 1

# Welfare and the Transformation of Electoral Politics

## ★ *Frances Fox Piven* ★

## Introduction

In August, 1996, as the election campaign heated up, President Clinton signed a bill that terminated the 60-year-old Aid to Families with Dependent Children (AFDC) program. This was another move in the several-years'-long contest among Democrats and Republicans, national and state politicians, all trying to position themselves as the front runners in the campaign against welfare.

Not that this was an entirely new development. For nearly two decades, Republican campaigners for the presidency regularly homed in on welfare as if the burgeoning rolls were a main problem confronting the country. And defensive Democrats have tried to ward off the challenge by reciting their belief in "work not welfare," and proposing a variety of schemes which would presumably put recipients to work. Meanwhile, state-level anti-tax campaigns, beginning with the Proposition 13 crusade to slash property taxes in California, also helped make the issue focal by advertising out-of-control welfare costs as a main reason to cut taxes and thus brake state spending.

But it was the 1992 presidential campaign that brought welfare to center stage. As has become customary, George Bush bashed welfare in his January, 1992, State of the Union message. And then, during the campaign, Bill

Clinton tried to take the initiative and steal the issue for the Democrats by ratcheting up the rhetoric and promising to "end welfare as we know it" with reforms that would mean "two years and off to work."[1]

With that, the race was on. At first the Clinton Administration talked of new programs in job training and job creation, health care and day care, all of which would presumably make it possible for mothers to work. However, such programs cost big money, much more than the current AFDC program. As the dollar estimates mounted, the services and job-promotion side of the plan shrank. In the end, the most important feature of the Clinton proposal was a two-year lifetime limit on cash assistance.

After the 1994 congressional election, it was inevitable that the victorious Republicans would try to go the president one better. Almost immediately, they proposed eliminating federal responsibility for cash assistance to poor mothers and children in favor of block grants, which would give the states less federal money over time, but broader latitude in deciding how that money should be spent, or whether it should be spent at all. And should a state be inclined toward generosity, other provisions would impose rigid work requirements on mothers, as well as strict time limits on the receipt of aid over a lifetime, but without funding for the child care, job training, or job creation that would be needed. Similar restructuring was proposed for the Medicaid program – big funding cuts combined with the devolution of responsibility to the states – and sharp cuts were also proposed for food stamp and other nutritional programs, for low-income housing, child protection, and so on. The president vetoed two early versions of the bill, which the Republican congressional leadership thought gave them an advantage as the election approached, and the final bill was not significantly different. In some ways it was worse. It barred the use of federal funds for aid to legal immigrants, and to large numbers of disabled children, and it also restricted food stamp aid to low-wage workers and some of the unemployed.

Meanwhile, state politicians pioneered their own battery of welfare reforms. Indeed, not only did a number of state politicians play a large role in bringing the issue to a boil by campaigning on the promise to slash welfare and then forging ahead with grant cuts and time limits,[2] but they invented some of the symbolically potent features of congressional welfare reform proposals. Douglas Besharov and Karen Gardiner from the American Enterprise Institute reported (approvingly) that two-thirds of the states have adopted "behavior-related" welfare rules.[3] The formula for these rules is simple: Family benefits are cut if a woman or her children misbehave, if the child truants from school, for example, or if the mother gives birth while on welfare. As a result of these various state-level initiatives, many of which had to be approved by the Clinton Administration before they were implemented, AFDC caseloads were already dropping rapidly, even before the new federal cutbacks were legislated. In July 1995, national caseloads were down 6.4 percent from the 1994 average, and some states had dropped much more. Indiana was down 18.4 percent, Massachusetts 15.8 percent, Michigan 14.3 percent, and this at a time when child poverty was increasing.[4] And then in early 1996, the nation's governors announced a bipartisan compromise on welfare reform that would allow huge cuts in welfare and the food-stamp programs, impose time limits on the receipt of benefits, and rip away federal support for additional spending when need increases.

Why is this happening? Why is welfare being trumpted as somehow a major and growing problem of American society when Aid to Families of Dependent Children is in fact a relatively small program, however it is measured? Fewer than five million adults are on the rolls, and except for the recent recession, the number has not risen since the early 1970s. Measured as a proportion of the poor, or as a proportion of single-parent households, the numbers on the rolls have in fact shrunk. And program costs are modest, to say the least, amounting to about 1 percent of the federal budget.

So, why the uproar? The question is highlighted when we also consider that the incessant talk about welfare by politicians simply does not fit the dominant view of how elections are won or lost in the United States. For more than half a century, both political scientists and pundits have taken for granted that voters were moved by "pocket-book" issues. There were debates, of course, about whether voters responded to general economic conditions or to their personal economic condition, about whether they voted in response to past economic troubles or simply to their current economic standing. But whatever the specific variants, it was assumed that economic conditions dominated modern elections, indeed that electoral outcomes could virtually be read off the economic indicators. Consistent with this view, incumbents campaigned by trying to deliver economic improvements as the election approached, and candidates campaigned with promises to do the same or better if the voters put them in office.

The preoccupation with welfare contradicts this model of electoral economism. While

AFDC is a small program, the "reforms" proffered by all contenders, along with proposed cuts in other means-tested programs including Medicaid and social services, will inevitably mean not only benefit cuts for the poor, but massive public-sector job losses, and downward pressure on wages among a huge number of less skilled workers in the private sector who will find themselves competing with the increasingly desperate people who lose their public jobs or benefits. In effect, instead of competing with promises of economic improvement, politicians are competing with proposals to worsen economic conditions for wide swaths of the voting public.

In this chapter I will try to explain these developments. My main argument is that the rise of welfare politics is symptomatic of the weakening of the electoral economism, or political Keynesianism, that has described American politics reasonably well since the New Deal. This development is often shrugged off as an inevitable reflection of the inability of government to deliver economic concessions as a result of the globalization of the economy. I think this argument about globalization is altogether too sweeping and, in any case, less applicable to the United States than to other advanced industrial nations. American politicians, especially Democratic politicians, are less inclined to campaign with economic appeals not because the measures that would be required are beyond the reach of government, but because they are pinioned by activated and politicized business interests. But either way, whether the causes lie in the penetration of global markets or in the politics of the capitalist class, the mode of electoral mobilization by means of economic appeals characteristic of the industrial era has weakened. And for the moment at least, a very American kind of fundamentalist irrationalism is taking its place, which the obsession with welfare signifies. In other words, the rise of welfare politics in the late twentieth century US reveals aspects of the twisted dynamics of the transition from industrial to postindustrial electoral politics in America.

## The Usual Explanations

But before I turn to this broader argument, I need to deal with more familiar explanations, some of which do indeed have some bearing on the rise of welfare politics. One is that the drive for tax cuts is forcing welfare spending cuts. Another is that politicians are merely responding to the fact that Americans detest welfare.

First, tax cuts and spending cuts: The assault on the means-tested programs can be viewed simply as an expression of the greed of organized and mobilized business interests and the politicians they fund. This part of the story goes back at least to 1981. One of Reagan's first initiatives was a round of tax cuts, skewed toward business and the affluent. The cuts were huge, reducing federal revenues by about $750 billion in the first Reagan term. And the tax cuts were coupled with rapid increases in military spending. Of course, the deficit widened, which, as we later learned from David Stockman, was not exactly unintentional.[5]

The expectation was that the growing deficit would generate powerful pressures for reductions in spending on social programs. In the 1980s, however, the Congress resisted these attempted cuts (and in 1983 went along with a social security tax increase that fell on working people instead).

After the election of 1994, the new Republican majority in the Congress proposed another round of huge tax cuts, again tilted to benefit the most affluent, who stood to realize a windfall through cuts in capital gains and estate taxes. This time the plan to make up for the forfeited tax revenues with cuts in programs for the poor and the elderly was on the table. The earned income tax credit, which benefits low-income working families, would be slashed, and big cuts were proposed in all of the means-tested programs, and in student loans and Medicare as well.[6] But the program singled out for the biggest cuts was AFDC, which would lose an estimated 57 percent of its federal funding over the seven-year projected budget (compared to Congressional Budget Office forecasts in 1995 of projected spending if there were no changes in the program). The reason for this tilt against programs for the poor seems transparent. The well-off want more big tax cuts. The easiest way to get them is to take them from the poor, who generally have neither lobbyists nor beholden politicians to defend them. Indeed, one suspects that if there were more money in the budget for means-tested programs, the Congress would shy away from attempting cuts in better-defended programs like Medicare altogether.

Still, greed could not be the whole of it. After all, the politicians leading this campaign are elected. They need voter support. And the polls do show popular support, both for the attack on government in general, and for the attack on programs for the poor. Why these animosities?

An obvious answer is that Americans, bred to a market culture that celebrates individual self-reliance and material success, just do not like welfare or the poor who rely on it. Longstanding and widely shared convictions about the virtue of self-reliance and material success, and antipathy toward the poor, might thus also be part of the explanation for the meanness of current welfare policy initiatives. This possibility gains weight when we add that welfare policies and practices have always worked to reinforce such antipathies. Think, for example, of the meanings communicated by ancient practices for dealing with the supplicant poor, including the lash, the brand, and other rituals of public humiliation; or think of the nineteenth-century poor law system, with its elaborate arrangements

for consigning the supplicant poor to hell-holes called "houses of industry."

It is easy to recognize these practices as Durkheimian rituals for defining the poor as the marginal Other. They are not, however, only features of poor relief. They are also embedded in contemporary American relief practices. Thus the intricately different programs divide people into intricately differentiated categories – the able-bodied unemployed, impoverished adults without children, poor single-parent families, the aged or disabled poor, the "insured" aged or disabled – helping to construct different identities, and different interests. And then, each of these program-constructed categories of people is dealt with differently: Each program confers different rights on prospective beneficiaries, subjects them to different procedures for determining and maintaining eligibility, and provides beneficiaries with different levels of economic support.

By segregating the poor into different programs, American welfare policy reinforces the separation of the poor from working- and middle-class Americans, and also creates sharp divisions among the poor. And once categorized by the programs, the poor are then denigrated by the treatment accorded them. Benefits in the poor-serving programs are less likely to be a matter of right and more likely to be discretionary, subject to the successful hurdling of bureaucratic inquisitions and runabouts, and continuing bureaucratic surveillance, all of which shape the understandings both of the people who endure this treatment, and of the people who in a sense are the public audience for these rituals. Finally, and very importantly, recipients receive benefits which keep them poor, ensuring their marginalization in an affluent and materialistic society.

So, there is something to the argument that attributes welfare cutbacks to the voters' antipathy to the program.[7] However, by definition, American cultural antipathies toward welfare and the poor are long-standing, and the policies and practices which reinforce them are long-standing as well.[8] But the zeal and stridency of the contemporary campaign for welfare reform are relatively new. While there are deep currents of dislike for the poor and the "dependent" in American culture, we still have to understand why they have welled up now. This is, I think, the big question. And a thoughtful answer will consider the broad developments that have contributed to the feebleness of electoral economism in contemporary American politics.

## The Decline of Electoral Economism

Conditions would seem to be ripe for economic appeals to the electorate. The enormous changes sweeping through the American economy are clearly generating discontent and anxiety, perhaps even terror. Wages are falling, for most people, despite the fact that worktime is lengthening.[9] And as the old mass-production industries shrink, new and onerous forms of work are spreading, in chicken-processing or garbage-recycling plants, for example, where the pace is hard and the work filthy, or in speeded-up service-sector businesses where computers monitor strokes or bathroom breaks. Sweatshops again cluster in the older cities.

Meanwhile, inequalities are widening at a dizzying pace, as income and wealth shift from workers to owners and managers of capital, and their corps of experts.[10] One measure captures the change: In the mid-1970s, chief executives earned 41 times the average wage; now the multiplier has increased to 225.[11] Meanwhile, the concentration of wealth in the United States has reached historic levels, with the top 1 percent claiming ownership of 42 percent of total assets, up from 33.7 percent in 1983, and up from 19 percent in 1976.[12]

Naturally, there is discontent. But why does

it take such a perverse form? Why is popular ire now directed not to demands for economic reform, but instead against programs which provide at least some minimum security for the most vulnerable? And why, in the 1994 election, were there heavy Democratic losses to the Republicans – who promised such program cuts – among less-educated whites, who are among the big losers from labor-market change, and are themselves at risk when income support programs are cut?[13]

The first thing to notice is the failure of political leaders, Democrats and Republicans alike, to articulate rational solutions to the economic hardships and insecurities that pervade the popular mood. F.D.R., J.F.K. to an extent, and L.B.J. all talked to voters about broad economic and social conditions, promised public action, and in that context were even able to talk about the marginalized poor, and to build voter support for public action to ameliorate poverty. Clinton did the reverse. True, he campaigned in 1992 with "It's the economy, stupid," although he coupled that with welfare bashing and a good deal of rhetoric about family values and individual responsibility. More important, he did not deliver on his economic promises. He allowed a weak economic stimulus package to fail, never pushed hard for a restoration of the buying power of the minimum wage,[14] did not promote legislation to stem the losses of the bleeding unions, and instead joined with the Republicans to become a champion of free trade and promoted the deregulation of international markets under NAFTA and GATT. Of course, there were economic promises: Once international markets were unfettered, a golden era of economic growth would ensue, a *laissez faire* utopia.[15] In fact, a Democratic president presided over an economic upturn in which productivity and profits moved up briskly, but wages stagnated, part-time and temporary work expanded, and earnings for the less educated continued to fall. And as the 1996 campaign began, Clinton was

artfully echoing the Republican budget-balancing, tax-cut, and spending-cut proposals.[16]

One explanation for this impasse is virtually a commonplace, quick to spring to the
lips of analysts and voters alike. The key fact
about our era is said to be the rise of global
economic competition that has fatally weakened the ability of nation states to control
their economies. Government has suddenly
been made helpless before markets, as Clinton
seems to be helpless before the financial markets. I do not think this explanation is entirely wrong. The penetration of goods, labor,
and capital from abroad is a real factor in the
economy, and especially in some industries.
But the argument is deployed so sweepingly
as to be misleading. And whether right or
wrong, the explanation itself has become a
political force, helping in the creation of the
institutional realities it purportedly merely
describes.

There are variations on the globalization
theme. Some two decades ago the emphasis
was on the flight of production from the older
industrialized countries to the low-wage areas on the periphery of developed capitalism.
Later the emphasis shifted from actual plant
relocation to the expansion of trade, a development facilitated by new communication and
transportation technologies. Either way,
whether plants were actually relocated, or
whether goods made elsewhere claimed an
increasing share of American markets, the
consequence was to pit the organized and
better-paid workers of the United States
against vulnerable workers everywhere. Enlarging flows of migration from Asia and Latin
America had similar consequences. And finally, in its most contemporary and fearsome
variant, economic globalism takes the form of
the vastly accelerated movement of financial
capital, pinning entire economies to the wall
and rendering governments helpless to intervene as, in the words of a *Barron's* columnist,
"capital market vigilantes [roam] the globe in
search of high returns at relatively low risk."[17]

Whatever the emphasis, all of these explanations lead to a common, and chilling, conclusion. The influence of voters in a democracy
rests on their ability to influence the uses of
state power. But if the state has been rendered helpless to regulate markets, then so
are democratic publics helpless to influence
economic conditions. Economic globalization
seems to open unlimited options for capital
to flee the scope of uncongenial state authority, whether through the relocation of production, or accelerated trade, or capital
mobility. The implication is stark: Economic
decisions are now beyond the reach of government and democratic publics.

But is globalization the problem it is said
to be? Is international penetration of the
American economy increasing significantly,
relative to the increased scale of economic
activity? While particular industries have
clearly been sharply affected by international
competition, there is reason to wonder about
the broad generalizations drawn from this
experience. Some years ago, David Gordon
argued that many of the economic data which
are taken as evidence of the international penetration of the American economy can be read
as evidence that we are on the downswing of
a long-wave economic cycle.[18] More recent
evidence underlines Gordon's queries.
America is still far less exposed to international economic currents than Western Europe is, and than most less-developed nations
are. The ratio of imports and exports to GDP
stands at 21 percent, unchanged since 1980.
Foreign investment in US stocks and bonds
has risen, but even so, in 1993 it accounted
for only 6 percent of US stocks, and 14 percent of corporate bonds.[19]

The issue can be examined in a more
commonsensical way. If indeed capital, goods,
and labor are circulating the globe with increasing velocity, how can German workers
continue to earn – if social benefits are included – nearly twice what workers earn in
the United States (or indeed eleven times what

workers earn in Thailand)? And how can the German economy continue to grow at a brisk rate, with corporate profits soaring? How, if international markets are in command, can there even be much of a German economy? *Business Week's* Bonn bureau chief answers that Germany is "sleepwalking." But that is merely to reassert the imperatives of global competition despite the evidence. Or, to ask the question more generally, why does there continue to be such large and enlarging variation among capitalist economies in the rewards to labor, in public expenditures, and in profit margins, if international markets are in command?

Thus, while labor unions remain vital in most of Europe,[20] the US leads advanced capitalist countries in measures of labor weakness, membership having fallen from about 35 million two decades ago to 15 million today.[21] After more than a decade in which the regulatory and social protection programs of the US welfare state were whittled back, a new round of huge cutbacks is underway. And while inequality is on the rise in all industrial countries, the US is the leader again, as real earnings fall steadily, especially for the unskilled, real poverty increases sharply, and the concentration of wealth reaches historic levels. While these trends are often read as symptoms of the impact of globalization, international trade explains relatively little of the growth in wage inequality, as Gary Burtless shows.[22] Indeed, patterns in wage inequality and job loss are not much different in industries affected by trade than in those that are insulated from trade.

This point made, I should also say that there is a good deal of capital mobility in the United States, which may lend a public credibility to arguments about globalization. But much of this mobility is within the US's own borders. In fact, important inter-regional shifts of industrial production began more than a century ago with the movement of the textile industry from New England to the south. Still today, most plant relocations have been from the old industrial centers of the northeast and the midwest to the sunbelt and the new cities. In other words, so far at least, most productive capital has remained within national borders. The importance of this point cannot be overstated. So far as markets are concerned, the national government retains the capacity to regulate the economy.

In fact, new production methods which facilitate outsourcing and reliance on less-skilled workers may have more to do with the alarming contemporary trend of increasing productivity and stagnant or declining wages than international competition has.[23] But this argument has none of the politically eviscerating implications of the globalization argument. For one thing, technological change and the changes in production methods they make possible are hardly unprecedented. From the replacement of the putting-out system with the factory to the introduction of the assembly line to the current explosion of computer-based technologies, the history of industrial capitalism has been the history of wrenching transformations. For another, and this is the important point for my argument, the consequences of such innovations are entirely susceptible to government regulation, and therefore as much a question of political determination as of market determination.

In short, while American political leaders have turned away from voter mobilization through economic appeals, it is not because the American government is helpless to regulate the economy. Most other industrial nations are far more exposed to international trade and capital movements than the United States. Yet no other rich democratic nation has been so hard hit by the traumas which are widely attributed to globalization, including the evisceration of unions, enormous wage cuts, the slashing of the public sector, and the extremes of poverty and wealth concentration. Something is missing in the argument.

I think a good deal of light can be cast on the preoccupation with globalization if we shift attention away from markets and market determinisms and turn to the politics associated with globalization. A series of economic changes associated with postindustrialism, including not only increasing international circulation, but the introduction of "lean production" methods made possible by the new information technology, have paved the way for a much more aggressive capitalist class politics. Put another way, capital is pyramiding the leverage it gains from the increased mobility of goods and capital – or perhaps from the spectre of increased mobility – as well as from the insecurities generated by downsizing, in a series of vigorous political campaigns to achieve its preferred public policies.

To understand the paralyzing impact of fears of internationalism in the United States, we have to attend not only or mainly to the economic data, which are ambiguous, but to politics, and particularly to business politics during the past two decades. Beginning in the 1970s, large employers became much more belligerent toward unions, stridently resisting new organizing efforts, and working to roll back earlier union gains. At the same time, business organized to change public policies, especially regulatory and tax policies. Of course, particular firms and industries had always worked to promote their interests in politics. But in the past 20 years, business political ambitions have expanded, and so have business strategies. Near dormant business trade groups were revived and new peak business coalitions were created and honed for political action. Business representatives and business money moved into the Republican Party and electoral politics, developing sophisticated campaign techniques and the tight organization that money makes possible. And big business developed and perfected a political agenda, funding new national think tanks to do the work that, after the 1960s, universities could not be relied upon to do.

With organization and agenda in formation, business groups mounted a formidable ideological campaign;[24] they launched an *argument* about the natural and inevitable primacy of markets over politics and the state (no matter that organized business was itself using politics and the state to secure enormous new advantages, and not least to create some of the conditions for international penetration which were then described as natural and inevitable). The argument was, of course, in essence a revival of nineteenth-century *laissez faire*, of the theory that market processes reflected the unfolding of the law of supply and demand. If there were social costs as a consequence of the unfettered operation of this species of natural law, if there was suffering, it was because people or places failed to meet the implacable tests of the market. Political interference with natural law only risked calamity. The new end-of-twentieth-century twist on nineteenth century doctrine was that market law now operated on an international scale. Capital and goods now circled the globe in search of local markets where costs were lowest and profits highest, and these processes were beyond the reach of nation states whose authority was limited to their sovereign territories.

Americans have always been more susceptible to *laissez faire* doctrine than Europeans have. For reasons much discussed in the literature on American exceptionalism, features of American culture, especially the emphasis on individualism, reinforced by racism and sectionalism, worked against class consciousness.[25] Moreover, this culture coexisted with and in some ways nourished institutional arrangements which inhibited class politics, including a fragmented and decentralized state structure and widespread disenfranchisement. When worker power did become important in the 1930s, the welfare state programs that emerged were themselves fragmented and decentralized, and heavily marked by racism, with the consequence that they continued to nourish the ideological biases which had blunted working-class influence in the first place.

Still, this large argument about the distinctiveness of American political culture notwithstanding, interpretations of the relationship of state and market in the contemporary United States seem remarkably fluid. After all, the experience of the Great Depression and the tutelage of Franklin Delano Roosevelt – who talked of "strong central government as a haven of refuge to the individual" – weakened if it did not shatter *laissez faire* convictions.[26] And until very recently, belief in the responsibility of government for popular economic well-being continued to hold sway, even in the United States. Popular opinion remains volatile, and susceptible to counter-arguments, whether mounted by oppositional political leaders, or by social movements that have yet to emerge.

But ideology does not merely reflect experience. It can also be a powerful force in the politics which shapes the institutions which in turn mold experience. A process like this helps to account for the institutional changes – the dismantling of Bretton Woods, the creation of the IMF – which facilitated international capital mobility, and the new institutions such as GATT and NAFTA which are now encouraging the expansion of trade. In these instances, a hegemonic ideology about the necessity and inevitability of the free movement of capital and goods helped to create the institutional conditions which then contributed to making the free movement of capital and goods a reality.[27]

In parallel fashion, the Republican juggernaut in Washington, tutored no doubt by business-backed think tanks, is undertaking a series of changes in American political arrangements which could well make the ideology of globalism "true," in the sense that people will come to experience the world in a way that confirms the ideology. The Contract with America features new constraints on the national government that if enacted will indeed make government helpless to regulate markets.

Of course, the Contract is many things. It is, for example, propaganda, as suggested by the baldly rhetorical titles of its legislative planks: the American Dream Restoration Act; the Personal Responsibility Act; the Legal Accountability Act. Even the use of the language of contract can be seen as an argument, a symbolic importation of a market idea into political relations between the state and its citizenry. And behind the fog created by this sort of rhetoric, the Contract is also a set of tax and spending measures that accelerate the redistribution of income and wealth from the poor to the rich.

But I want to direct attention to another and important feature of this legislative program. Taken as a whole, it would strip the national government of the capacity to do what contemporary governments do (or did) to reduce the extremes of inequality, regulate economic instabilities, and curb business excesses. One large way to limit government is to limit its ability to spend. The proposal for a balanced budget amendment to the Constitution was intended to put a brake not only on spending by the national government, but on its ability to raise taxes as well, by requiring super-majorities for the passage of tax increases in the Congress. The process of constitutional amendment is extremely cumbersome, and the amendment for the time being has been shelved, although the simplistic balanced-budget rhetoric invoking images of thrift and good housekeeping has clearly not receded. In the absence of a constitutional amendment, a new House rule requires 60 percent majorities on measures to raise taxes. Another severe limit on spending restricts the imposition by the federal government of unfunded mandates on state or local governments. Other bills would impede the federal government's ability to regulate business by requiring obstructive review procedures, or extravagant

compensation to private owners for losses due
to regulation. And still other measures are
designed to discourage citizens from turning
to the courts to resolve grievances against
corporations. Finally, there are the proposals
to radically slash and restructure federal
means-tested programs.

Viewed together, these proposals suggest a
pattern: The decentralized structure of the
America state is being reinforced. As the national government is less and less able to do
what governments do, responsibilities will
devolve to the states, and in some program
areas, federal funds will be transferred to the
states as well.

The banner hoisted to explain these changes
is that state governments are "closer to the
people."[28] The slogan resonates with the convictions of the late eighteenth-century anti-
federalists who fought the original constitution
because they feared a remote central government would become the instrument of elites.
But in the twentieth century, it is the state
governments that are more sensitive to business political pressures, simply because state
(and localities) are far more vulnerable to the
threat of disinvestment.[29]

This has been true for a long time. Early
in this century, for example, efforts to pass
state worker-compensation laws were stymied
by business threats to move to other states –
until, that is, manufacturers themselves, prod-
ded by multiplying damage suits in the courts,
decided to back model and modest legislation.[30]

But if state governments have always been
more susceptible to the bribe and threat of
business investment and disinvestment, they
are far more susceptible now, when capital is
increasingly mobile, and when even a single
corporate relocation can devastate a community.[31] This, together with the fact that most
movement of American business still takes
place within the national borders, as plants
move from Massachusetts to South Carolina,
from Michigan to Tennessee, makes the fis-

cal and regulatory powers of the federal government more important than ever. And this
may well be why congressional Republicans
are working to cripple those powers.

In sum, a mobilized business class allied
with a resurgent Republican Party is both
invoking the threat of capital mobility that
appears to weaken state power, and taking
large steps to make that threat real. Whether
this agenda will actually be realized remains
to be seen, of course. If it is, the ideology of
neo-*laissez faire* will have contributed to the
construction of institutional arrangements
which do indeed make the state nearly helpless before markets.

Everywhere in the world, when people are
blocked from dealing with the problems of
livelihood, community, respect, and security
through politics, they become more susceptible to fundamentalist appeals. When institutional reforms seem impossible, frustrated
publics are more likely to respond to calls for
a politics of individual moral rejuvenation,
typically coupled with calls to mobilize against
some vulnerable group. This group becomes
the Other, embodying a kind of moral pollution that is somehow to blame for the problems people experience in daily life.

Something like this seems to be underway
in the United States. Politician appeals are
directing popular political attention away from
the issues of wages and jobs, for example,
which had been taken for granted as the dominant preoccupations of electoral politics since
the New Deal, to a politics of individual responsibility and "values." At the same time,
and relatedly, political leaders are pointing to
minorities and the poor, and especially poor
women, as the miscreants, the polluters, whose
transgressions of core values are responsible
for contemporary troubles.

To be sure, these manipulative appeals draw
on real anxieties generated by a culture in
flux. Not least important, sexual and family
mores are changing, eroding a world in which

men are men, women are women, and the rules for mating and family life are clear. Changes of this sort can generate a distinctive terror, perhaps because the meanings they challenge are so deeply imprinted in early childhood. These cultural insecurities clearly helped to fuel the rise of the Christian right and its entry into Republican politics. But fundamentalist appeals are not restricted to the Christian right. They have become central to the electioneering of both Democrats and Republicans, as suggested by the "family values" theme of the Clinton 1996 State of the Union message.

The campaign against welfare plays a central part in this electioneering. Indeed, the relentless public charges leveled by politicians and conservative think-tank experts are as much an argument about what is wrong with America as an argument about welfare policy. And the heart of the argument is the idea that big American problems – deepening poverty, the breakdown of family and community, a kind of demoralization overtaking the society – are centered on poor and minority women. These women are said to contradict all of the old Protestant virtues of industry and self-reliance, of chastity and self-restraint. And their moral turpitude is perversely encouraged by government welfare programs.

The availability of welfare, the argument goes, allows young women to quit school or work and have out-of-wedlock babies. And once on the dole, these women become trapped and dependent, unable to summon the initiative to get a job, indeed unable even to raise their children properly. As a consequence, children raised on welfare turn into school dropouts and delinquents, and then into welfare users themselves. Welfare, in short, is encouraging the spread of a moral rot in American society. The solution is not hard to see: Eliminate the perverse incentives. This "tough love" will deter young women from having babies in the first place, and those who already have will be forced to go to work

to support their child or children. There may be some hardship along the way, but this is the only way to make poor women moral and self-reliant.

This litany is by now so familiar that it has worn ruts in our minds. But familiar or not, the argument does not stand up to scrutiny. What sense does it make to force women into the labor market if there are not jobs out there for unskilled women with child-rearing responsibilities that pay enough to support a family? Even during this economic upturn, the labor market is saturated, with 8 million officially unemployed, and some 25 million part-time and temporary workers, many of whom would prefer regular full-time work if they could get it.[32] Real wages for the unskilled and the young continue to fall, and fewer of these jobs pay health or pension benefits. Simply slashing welfare will not create jobs or raise wages. In fact, it will make the working conditions of those who have jobs worse, for welfare cutoffs will crowd the low-wage labor market with millions of desperate women, ready to work at any wage and under any conditions.[33]

The documented results of actual efforts to end welfare by sending these women "off to work" also argue their absurdity as policy, if not as political talk. We have in fact been "solving" the welfare problem for 25 years with a series of much-heralded welfare-to-work programs, all premised on the idea that what welfare mothers need is a little training and a big shove to make it in the job market. And for 25 years we have been evaluating the results of these reforms, called WIP or WIN or GAIN or JOBS or whatever. The results are trivial, or non-existent. The programs increase the job success of women by tiny percentages, when they increase job placement at all, and they have a similarly negligible effect on earnings. Even tiny percentages produce a few smiling and successful women for the TV talk shows. But no TV host invites the women who could not make it in the jobs they got and had to return to welfare. And no one invites the mothers who suffer the harassment of being hustled from one foolish work-preparedness scheme to another, and who are then perhaps sanctioned with slashed benefits if they do not cooperate. Nor, needless to say, is there research to measure this harassment, because researchers study the questions that government or foundation funders want answered.

The political talk about welfare causing a tide of "illegitimacy" is even more potent than the talk about work and dependency. The polemics get very excited, as when Charles Murray announced in the *Wall Street Journal* in 1993 that illegitimacy was "the most important social problem of our time," driving poverty, crime, drugs, illiteracy, homelessness, and so on. But while out-of-wedlock births are indeed increasing, they are increasing in all strata of the society and not only among welfare recipients or potential recipients. Indeed, they are increasing in all western countries. This is almost certainly the result of epochal changes in sexual and family mores, and not the result of the American AFDC program. Both divorce rates and single parenthood have skyrocketed throughout the west in the past two decades.

To be sure, the United States does have more single-parent families than other western countries. But this very fact suggests that welfare is not significantly related to single-parent family formation, since most other rich countries provide far more generous assistance to single mothers.[34] Other facts also argue against this familiar "welfare causes illegitimacy" argument. Most obviously, welfare benefits have declined sharply over the past two decades, but out-of-wedlock births have not.[35] Nor is there a discernible relationship between the level of state welfare benefits and out-of-wedlock birth rates.

Moreover, the all-too-familiar view that welfare is the cause of illegitimacy among black women does not stand up. The non-marital birth rates of black women have in fact not changed in two decades. What has changed is that marital birth rates have declined, for the reason that there are fewer men in black communities who have the income or stability to be reasonable husbands. In any case, the percentage of single mothers collecting welfare has actually declined over time, which would not be the case if women were having babies to get welfare.

So much for the facts. But this sort of argument is not won or lost with facts, and certainly not with facts alone. Opinions are too excited and inflamed. They evoke preoccupations deeply etched in American culture, including an age-old dislike of the poor, especially the supplicant poor, racial antipathies, and the strange American obsession with sexual transgression memorialized in the figure of Hester Prynne. And they draw finally on the awful vulnerabilities that people experience as their familiar worlds collapse, for the "the dynamic force of otherness . . . [is] the projection of the *internal* other as a defense against one's own vulnerability."[36]

Will the invocation of these ancient American devils continue to distract majorities of American voters? Or rather, will it distract them enough to allow governing elites to continue to ignore economic issues, especially declining wages and spiraling inequalities? The evidence so far is not definitive. A sitting Democratic president continues to talk mainly about family values, and his Republican challengers try to ease economic discontents with incantations about balanced budgets and tax cuts. And both sides compete to rouse support with calls for welfare reform that tell a story of American decline and demoralization that singles out welfare mothers as the main culprit.

So, what are likely to be the political consequences of the implementation of draconian cutbacks in means-tested programs, coupled with continued rhetorical assaults on the poor? The palpable consequences will accumulate, in child beggars on the streets, women and babies huddled over grates, already devastated urban slums turned into medieval wastelands. But these cruelties by no means guaranteee a reversal of course. To the contrary, the visible and deepening impoverishment of poor women and children may well only confirm the corruption imputed to the Other in the story of welfare reform.

We can spin the scenario out. Economic insecurity continues and worsens, and so does the degradation of the worst off, feeding fundamentalist calls for individual moral rejuvenation and the purging of the Other. This sort of politics is not, after all, entirely alien to the American experience. It recalls episodes of murderous hate politics that have swept through the country before, as when Chinese immigrants were stoned, their homes torched; or black newcomers to the cities were murdered by enraged white crowds; or impoverished whites in the south expressed their rage in the lynch mob and in a system of terror that sustained the southern caste order for more than a century. All such episodes drew on economic grievances. Yet all channeled economic discontent into a crazed politics of scapegoating. Pat Buchanan, with his appeals that stir economic anger but suggest no program beyond a fierce hostility to a government that gives hard-earned tax dollars to welfare moms; the rise of the paranoid militias and their doctrine of national and racial purity; the Christian Right and their preoccupation with sexual morality: all of these recent developments argue that fundamentalism is flourishing in American politics.

But other parts of American history suggest that hate politics will not work forever,

and maybe not for long. For one thing, the actual program cutbacks planned under the banner of "welfare reform" will have very wide reverberations. It will not only be poor women and their babies who will huddle over the grates. The huge take-backs contemplated are not mainly in welfare spending, but in Medicaid, housing, and social service programs. These cuts will mean enormous job losses in the public and voluntary sector, with potentially devastating effects on working-class urban neighborhoods, and on the landlords and small businesses that depend on poor and working-class consumers. And, of course, as the consequences of "welfare reform" spread, dragging down broader swaths of the population, the raw and simple politics of victim blaming becomes less persuasive. Even now, the polls show that, among voters, the pocketbook issues, which receded in the din of propaganda about welfare, crime, and immigration, are surging to the fore again.[37]

Earlier periods of aggressive and reckless business mobilization, in the 1890s and 1920s, helped precipitate the popular mobilizations and electoral convulsions that made possible the great political reforms of the twentieth century. First in the Progressive era, then again during the New Deal, social movements combined with electoral instability to force the forging of new government initiatives which tempered business excesses and reduced the extremes of inequality.

No one has ever successfully predicted the moments when ordinary people find their footing, discover new capacities for solidarity and power, and new visions of the possible. Still, American democracy depends on the perennial emergence of popular revolt, now more than ever.

## Notes

Portions of this article were first published in the *New Left Review* (no. 213, September/October,

1995), in the *Progressive* (February, 1995), and in *Dissent* (Fall, 1996). A slightly different version of the article was published in Frances Fox Piven and Richard A. Cloward, *The Breaking of the American Social Compact* (New York: New Press, 1997).

1 Many Democratic pundits applauded Clinton's welfare initiatives, arguing that it would bring defecting middle-class Democrats back to the party. See for example the afterword on the 1992 election in Thomas Byrne Edsall with Mary D. Edsall, *Chain Reaction* (New York: Norton, 1992).

2 Some 22 states had imposed some type of time limit on benefits, according to the Health and Human Services Department, as reported in the *Washington Post* (February 3, 1996).

3 Donglas J. Besharov and Karen N. Gardiner, "Paternalism and Welfare Reform," *Public Interest* 122 (Winter, 1996).

4 Center for Law and Social Policy, "AFDC Caseload Declines: Implications for Block Grant Planning" (Washington DC: Center for Law and Social Policy, 1995).

5 David Stockman, *The Triumph of Politics: Why the Reagan Revolution Failed* (New York. Harper and Row, 1986); Gary Wills, "It's His Party," *New York Times Magazine*, August 11, 1996.

6 The Center on Budget and Policy Priorities reports that entitlement programs for the poor, which account for one-quarter of entitlement spending, were slated by the Congress to absorb 50 percent of entitlement cuts. Non-entitlement programs for the poor, which account for 12 percent of federal spending for non-entitlement programs, were targeted for 62 percent of funding cuts. Center on Budget and Policy Priorities, "Only High-Income Households have Recovered Fully from the Recession," (Washington DC: Center on Budget and Policy Priorities, October 24, 1995).

7 David Ellwood, who later became a Clinton adviser and the architect of the Clinton welfare proposals, thought strict time limits on the receipt of cash benefits would appease public hostility and make other worthwhile reforms possible. David Ellwood, *Poor Support* (New York: Basic Books, 1988).

8 In fact, while Americans do not like welfare, they express little hostility toward the poor children who constitute two-thirds of the welfare roles. A New York Times/CBS poll in

December 1994 found that only 9 percent favoured cuts in spending for poor children, while 47 percent favored an increase. See Edward Herman, "The Balanced Budget Ploy," *Z Magazine*, (February, 1996).

9 On this point, there are of course numerous sources. See for example L. Mishel and J. Bernstein, "America's Continuing Wages Problems: Deteriorating Real Wages for Most and Growing Inequality," in L. Mishel and J. Schmitt, eds, *Beware of the U. S. Model: Jobs and Wages in a Deregulating Economy* (Armonk, NY: Economic Policy Institute, 1996); Sheldon Danziger and Peter Gottschalk, *America Unequal* (Cambridge, MA: Russell Sage Foundation and Harvard University Press 1995).

10 Income gaps are at their widest point since the Census Bureau began collecting these data in 1967.

11 The estimate, by executive compensation expert Graef Crystal, is cited in *U.S. News and World Report* (January 22, 1996). Crystal elsewhere estimates that CEOs at the biggest U.S. companies earn on average six times what their Japanese counterparts earn, and four times what their German counterparts earn. See the *New York Times* (March 9, 1996).

12 Edward N. Wolff, "How the Pie is Sliced: America's Growing Concentration of Wealth," *American Prospect* (Summer, 1995); Edward N. Wolff, "Time for a Wealth Tax," *Boston Review* (February/March, 1996).

13 Ruy Texiera and Joel Rogers, "Who Deserted the Democrats in 1994?", *American Prospect* 18 (Summer, 1994). Duane Swank identifies a suggestively parallel pattern in Western Europe, where marginal workers and postindustrial economic change contribute to the fortunes of radical right parties. Duane Swank, "Right-Wing Populism in Western Europe," paper prepared for delivery at the 1995 Annual Meetings of the American Political Science Association, August 31–September 3, Chicago, Illinois.

14 Clinton proposed a modest 90-cent-an-hour increase in the minimum wage at the end of 1994 (and reiterated his support for an increase in his 1996 State of the Union message). But while his proposal would prevent the minimum from dipping to its lowest level in 40

years, it would by no means restore it to the levels of 25 years ago.

15 Polanyi characterized nineteenth-century convictions about the unregulated free market as a utopian and disastrous ideology. Karl Polanyi, *The Great Transformation* (Boston: Beacon Press, 1957).

16 The polls clearly reflected these political maneuvers. In 1992, a whopping 51 percent of those surveyed said the economy and jobs were the country's most pressing problems. By 1996, the polls showed overwhelming dissatisfaction with "the way things are going," and intense personal economic insecurity. But reducing the deficit had replaced jobs as the most important political issue. See the *New York Times* (January 23 and February 1, 1996).

17 See "Back in the Soup," an interview with William H. Gross, *Barron's* (June 19, 1995).

18 David Gordon, "The Global Economy: New Edifice or Crumbling Foundations?," *New Left Review* 168 (March/April, 1988).

19 Robert J. Samuelson, "Global Mythmaking," *Newsweek* (May 29, 1995).

20 There have been modest downturns in union membership in Europe in recent years, but the losses are modest compared to those in the US, and in any case, comparative analysis suggests that it is mainly political factors that explain variations in the downturn, particularly the extent of union decentralization and the strength of left parties. Bruce Western, "Union Decline in Eighteen Advanced Capitalist Countries," *American Sociological Review* 60 (2) (April, 1995).

21 Strike levels fell as well, from hundreds of major strikes each year in the 1970s to 31 strikes in all of 1995. See the *New York Times* (March 8, 1996).

22 Gary Burtless, "Widening U. S. Income Inequality and the Growth in World Trade," paper prepared for the September 1995 meeting of the Tokyo Club in Dresden, Germany.

23 For a discussion, see Simon Head, "The New, Ruthless Economy," *New York Review* (February 29, 1996). Jason DeParle reports an informal poll at a meeting of 18 prominent economists at the end of 1994 at the Federal Reserve Bank in New York. They attributed, on average, only 10 percent of increased wage inequality to international trade. A far larger factor, they thought, was technological change. Jason DeParle, "Class is No Longer a Four-Letter Word," *New York Times Magazine* (March 17, 1994).

24 Edward Herman, "The Market Attack on Dissent," *Z Magazine* (March, 1996).

25 For one of the more recent excursions into this huge literature, see Seymour Martin Lipset, *American Exceptionalism: A Double Edged Sword* (New York: W. W. Norton, 1996).

26 The quotation is from a speech to the Commonwealth Club in 1932. See Aaron Singer, ed., *Campaign Speeches of American Presidential Candidates* (New York: Unger, 1976) cited in Ronald Schurin, "A Party Form of Government," PhD dissertation completed at the Graduate School and University Center of the City University of New York (1996). Schurin argues that this definition of the role of government was a strong and consistent theme in F.D.R.'s public addresses.

27 On this point, see G. William Domhoff, *State Autonomy or Class Dominance?: Case Studies on Policy Making in America* (New York: Aldine de Gruyter, 1996).

28 The *New York Times*, in an article entitled "The States Won't Be Cruel" on February 9, 1996, quotes Governor William Weld of Massachusetts: "We're closer and more directly answerable to our citizens than the cloud-dwellers in Washington are."

29 This generalization should be tempered by another: Business interests play the federal system, using multiple and overlapping sources of authority opportunistically, or even parlaying them against each other. Thus Goldberg points out that business interests are turning to national government to override state product liability and environmental standards, rhetorical assaults on big government notwithstanding. Lenny Goldberg, "Come the Devolution," *American Prospect* (Winter, 1996). For a general discussion of the political uses of centralization and decentralization, see Frances Fox Piven and Roger Friendland, "Public Choice and Private Power," in Andrew Kirby, Paul Knox and Steve Pinch, eds, *Public Service Provision and Urban Development* (New York: St Martin's Press, 1984).

30 F.D.R. seemed to understand the problem well in 1936 when, in a Chicago speech, he likened corporate financiers to "kidnappers and bank robbers [who] could in high-powered cars speed across state lines" and for that reason had to be controlled by federal law. B. D. Zevin, *The Selected Addresses of Franklin Delano Roosevelt* (Boston: Houghton Mifflin, 1946) pp. 63–4.

31 Howard Chernick and Andrew Reschovsky, "Devolution in Federalism: Prospects and Policy Responses," paper prepared for Economic Policy Institute Conference on Devolution in Federalism, Washington DC (November 27, 1995).

32 Lester Thurow estimates the number of job seekers by including contingent workers and those who drop out of the normal economy. He concludes that real unemployment is about one-third of the workforce. Lester Thurow, "The Crusade that's Killing Prosperity," *American Prospect* (March–April, 1996).

33 Mishel and Schmitt estimate the impact of welfare recipients pushed into the low-wage labor market could be nearly 12 percent nationally, and much higher in states with large welfare populations. Lawrence Mishel and John Schmitt, "Cutting Wages by Cutting Welfare: The Impact of Reform on the Low-Wage Labor Market," Briefing Paper, Economic Policy Institute, (Washington DC, 1996).

34 According to McFate et al., the US lifts fewer single-parent families out of poverty through income transfers than any of seven western industrial nations studied. In the Netherlands, Sweden, and the United Kingdom, at least 75 percent of all single-parent families in poverty were lifted out of poverty; in France about half; in West Germany a third; in Canada a fifth; in the US 4.6 percent. K. McFate, R. L. Lawson, and W. J. Wilson, "Poverty, Inequality and the Crisis of Social Policy: Summary of Findings," Joint Center for Political and Economic Studies, (Washington DC, September, 1996).

35 For recent reviews of the evidence on out-of-wedlock births, see Sara S. McLanahan, "The Consequences of Single Motherhood," *American Prospect* (Summer, 1994); Hilary Williamson Hoynes, "Does Welfare Play Any Role in Female Headship Decisions?" Institute for Research on Poverty Discussion Paper No. 1078–95 (Madison, Wisconsin, 1996). For a more general review of data on welfare utilization. Twentieth Century Fund, *Welfare Reform: A Twentieth Century Fund Guide to the Issues* (New York: Twentieth Century Fund Press, 1995).

36 Rob Crawford, "Reflections on Health, Culture and Aids," *Social Science Medicine* 39 (10) (1994).

37 In a *U. S. News* survey in the winter of 1996, pocket-book issues were cited as the biggest problem facing the nation by 47 percent of those polled, up from 21 percent in early 1995. *U. S. News and World Report* (January 22, 1996). And a *Washington Post*, Kaiser Family Foundation and Harvard University Poll found that 38 percent of Americans believe the economy is getting worse, while only 16 percent think it is getting better. See *Washington Post* (January 30, 1996). A recent *New York Times* poll showed that 10 percent of those surveyed said they had experienced a "major crisis" as a result of a layoff, and 78 percent of these believed that Congress could do something about job loss. The *Times* characterizes these people as "politically available." The question is, for what? *New York Times* (March 8, 1996).

# 2

# The Democratic Party and the Politics of Welfare Reform

★ *Ronald Walters* ★

## Introduction

In his 1992 Campaign for President, Bill Clinton made welfare reform one of the tenets of his platform, and after he became president, he took the position that the failure of the welfare system was "perhaps the most pressing social problem we face in our country."[1] This amazing statement completed the historical transmigration of the Democratic party leadership in its approach toward the welfare issue since at least 1968, toward convergence with the more conservative attitudes of the public.

In this chapter, I will attempt to describe the tortuous journey of this issue to the right of the political spectrum and its effect upon the Democratic party.

My argument is that by the end of the decade of the 1960s, the welfare program had grown to contain a substantial number of blacks, and the reaction to that, together with the black politics of the 1960s, led to the emergence of a strongly conservative political movement, which utilized the welfare program as an icon of those things it found abhorrent about the Democratic Party. Because of the increasing association of the public's negative image of welfare with the Democratic Party, party leaders moved steadily in the direction of revising the traditional focus on income maintenance to pursue a much

stronger version of workfare. The effect on the Democratic Party has been divisive, since the treatment of this issue has paralleled others associated with the African American community in particular.

In outline, I will briefly define the welfare/racial association, the shift in the liberal content of welfare reform in the Democratic Party toward workfare, the Clinton Administration's enhancement of the conservative direction in welfare policy, and the response of black leaders to this direction. I will conclude with some notions of why it has been difficult for Clinton to enact his version of welfare reform.

## Politics and Attitudes Toward the Poor

While it is true that a Democrat, Franklin Roosevelt, was president when the AFDC program was created, it is far from true that his action was associated with a liberal attitude in the development of this social policy. Although he is more widely known for using the formidable resources of government to pull the country out of an economic recession through the formation of a series of programs such as Works Progress Administration (WPA), Civilian Conservation Corps (CCC), and others, less known is his cautionary attitude toward state involvement in social policy, which was observed in a January 1935 speech, in which he said: "continued dependence upon government . . . includes a spiritual and moral disintegration fundamentally destructive to the national fibre. To dole out relief in this way is to administer a narcotic, a subtle destroyer of the human spirit . . . [the federal government] must quit this business of relief."[2] Thus, even though Roosevelt's action amounted to an admission that capitalism could not provide the economic security needed for all classes of Americans, he evidenced the distrustful attitude of the economic elite toward the state assuming responsibility for a permanent role in relief. Thus, government-sponsored social programs of this era were developed, without the intention that they would become permanent government relief programs.

Nevertheless, in 1935, Roosevelt's program moved toward the establishment of a systematic approach to dealing with the problem of public assistance as part of the Social Security Act of 1935. The welfare program established included aid to the poor elderly over 65, the blind, and dependent children. Almost immediately the latter aspect became politicized, as localities still operating under the older, Victorian attitude toward the poor imposed harsh parameters governing their approach to dependent families, such as limiting aid to the children of mothers with criminal records or modest amounts of property, and setting up standards of "suitable homes," the combination of which eliminated many poor and black potential recipients. In particular, the prohibition of poor blacks from public financial support was but one aspect of the naked racism which governed their exclusion from many such private and public programs, especially in the south.

## The Modern Era of Black Dependency

The modern debate about "dependency" has contained the notion that dependent populations such as blacks have enjoyed persistent support from government. Therefore, the notion continues that because of government intervention these groups have become inescapably dependent, such that it must be broken if independence is to be established. Such a view was propounded by George Gilder:

welfare, by far the largest economic influence in the ghetto, exerts a constant, seductive, erosive pressure on the marriages and work habits of the poor, and over the years, in poor communities, it fosters a durable "welfare culture." Necessity is the mother of invention and upward mobility; welfare continuously mutes and misrepresents the necessities of life that prompted previous generations of poor people to escape poverty through the invariable routes of work, family and faith.[3]

Gilder, writing in the early 1980s of a "welfare boom" that did not occur, also misrepresented welfare as the largest economic factor in the black community, since 70 percent of black men and 56 percent of black women were in the labor force, according to the census of 1980.[4]

Black dependency however was not, and should not be conceptualized as, dependence on government as such, but a manifestation of black socio-economic status in relation to American society itself an outgrowth of slavery. The migration of blacks from the rural areas of the south simply extended much of the dependent population of those areas to the northern cities.[5] In the new residences, blacks suffered legal segregation and both public and private discrimination by whites. This effectively made it difficult to acquire jobs or capital and social status equal with whites. The result was that even by 1960, 95 percent of blacks did not make the average family income.[6] Thus, one of the objectives of the civil rights movement was to raise the income of blacks, who were a disproportionately welfare-eligible population. As this happened, negative attitudes of whites toward blacks extended to their presence on the welfare rolls.

One indication of negative attitudes toward the black portion of the welfare population came from Louisiana, which had a 35-percent black population. When the welfare rolls began to accept a significant number of blacks, a provision was passed by the state legislature in 1960 eliminating 23,500 children, a group that was disproportionately black, from the rolls because their mothers had had an illegitimate child since entering the welfare program.[7] Indeed, at this time, the Welfare Advisory Committee of the Department of Health Education and Welfare indicated that "millions legally entitled to benefits were denied them."[8] This response was relatively widespread in other states, as moral rules were utilized to exclude blacks as welfare became more and more identified with the black poor.

The emergence of the National Welfare Rights Organization (NWRO) in the late 1960s, led by George Wiley, a militant black former professor at Syracuse University, was supported by a national group of black welfare mothers. They demanded not only a guaranteed income, but that, instead of the welfare system being administered to correct a defect in the black family, the system itself, which had maintained blacks in near serfdom, had to change. This had been Wiley's basic demand at the White House Conference on civil rights held on November 17, 1965.[9]

The leadership of the civil rights movement reciprocated by taking up this theme, as by 1967 Dr Martin Luther King Jr had come to believe that a guaranteed income should be enacted, that it should be pegged to the median income not the minimum wage, and that it should be dynamic in that it in-

creased over time with the standard of living. He thought, as most of those in the movement did then, that one could and should fight poverty with "the weapon of cash" in a way that was conceived not as a "civil rights" struggle, but as one of human rights. He felt that such a struggle would unite the black and white lower-income classes and help all poor people, two-thirds of whom at that time were white.[10]

However, many of the more radical reforms championed by the NWRO and Wiley could not succeed in the growing conservative atmosphere, which demanded during Richard Nixon's first term the emergence of "workfare," or that mothers be made to work for receiving welfare benefits, a mandate eventually written into the law.

By the end of the 1960s, the coincidence of the fact that the welfare rolls were just over 40 percent black with the high visibility of the civil rights movement enhanced both anti-black and anti-welfare sentiment as joined issues. The negative content is found in research on the emergence of the language used to describe the welfare population by Joseph Feagin. He found that the black poor, were often referred to as "Nigger bums"; welfare mothers became "welfare queens"; black automobiles became "welfare Cadillacs," and so on.[11] His study, based on surveys of racial attitudes on welfare in the mid-1970s, showed that a sample of attitudes from ordinary whites (he called them "Average Americans" about those on welfare produced the most vitriolic combination of negative racial stereotypes, resembling those toward blacks in society as a whole.[12]

Thus, the juxtaposition of race and welfare dependency in the public imagination enhanced the perspective that black welfare recipients were the "undeserving poor," fostering images of laggard, lazy, dull welfare recipients on the "dole" who deserve punishment to be visited upon them because they constitute a drag upon the economy and a

Table 2.1  Black percentage of the AFDC caseload, 1969–91

| May 1969 | Jan. 1973 | May 1975 | Mar. 1979 | 1983 | 1986 | 1988 | 1990 | 1991 | 1996 |
|---|---|---|---|---|---|---|---|---|---|
| 45.2 | 45.8 | 44.3 | 43.1 | 43.8 | 40.7 | 39.8 | 39.7 | 38.8 | 36.6 |

Data for 1983–96 are for the federal fiscal year, October through September. Percentages are based on the average monthly caseload during the year. Hawaii and the Territories are not included in 1983. Data after 1987 include the Territories.
*Source*: "Overview of Entitlement Programs: The 1993 Green Book," Committee on Ways and Means, US House of Representatives, Washington, DC (July 7, 1993), pp. 696–7; HHS Research Division (1996)

blot upon the moral image of the nation. This concept, part of the ancient staple of distorted and negative attitudes of the elite toward the poor in general, has been most recently popularized by Michael Katz, who, in his work *The Undeserving Poor*, illustrated how those on welfare, whose crime in most cases was only being poor were characterized as immoral and attacked accordingly.[13] And where once this concept was held by the elite, because of its convenient linkage to ancient poverty stereotypes, it has been generalized into views held by a substantial segment of whites in society, including a significant sector of the white working-class population who use it as an instrument of racial competition. As such, this issue would begin to have a significant impact upon the Democratic Party, which was the party of the working class.

## The black welfare "crisis"

The pretext for welfare reform was the declaration of a so-called "welfare crisis." Professor James Jennings concluded from an analysis of 1970s public opinion data that the so-called "crisis" of social welfare was created by a few vocal leaders (such as Governor Ronald Reagan and others in the conservative movement).[14] There was substantial growth in the welfare caseload from 1965 to 1975, the highest period of black enrolment, though still only one-third of poor blacks were on welfare rolls. In the period from 1965 to 1975, the welfare caseload grew by

237 percent, adding two million households to reach 3.5 million by 1975.[15] Ben Wattenberg says of the growth of black welfare the following:

In 1971 of the 10.6 million on welfare, 43 percent were Negro – 4.5 million. The black population in 1971 was 23 million. The percentage of blacks on AFDC, then, was 19% – up from 8% eleven years earlier.

Those rates . . . are reflective not only of human tragedy, but of political poison. Over this same time frame, the phrases "welfare mother" and "relief chiseler" became political buzz-words that clearly also meant black.[16]

And as table 2.1 shows, the black proportion of welfare recipients began to decline after 1973. Nevertheless, the voices declaring a "welfare crisis" became more vocal as the conservative movement became more prominent.

In another sense, the so-called welfare crisis was a function of the growth of poverty in America. For as the black contingent on public assistance was declining slightly in the 1970s, the amount of spending was increasing. In the 1980 Census, there were 29.6 million people officially classified as poor: white 20 million, black 8.5 million, and Hispanic 3.5 million. The national poverty rate was 13.2 percent: whites 10 percent, blacks 32 percent, and Hispanics 26 percent.[17] By 1992, the total number in poverty had grown to 14.5 percent, or 36 million: whites 24.5 million (11.6 percent), blacks 10.6 million (33.3 percent), and Hispanics 6.6 million (29.3 percent).[18] This meant that the national poverty rate had grown by 1.2 percent, to include 7 million more Americans in total, and while the black and white rate had grown concomitantly, the Hispanic rate had climbed by more than 3 percent.

As a consequence of the increase in poverty, federal spending on all public aid programs increased from $9.6 billion to $48.7 billion between 1970 and 1980.[19] The effect of this spending in the 1970s, social analyst Dorothy Newman said, was the following: "The public perception has been that idle black welfare recipients lived on Easy Street, despite the fact that in the only terms that count – money – welfare took only a little over 10 percent of the black households . . . out of poverty, but two times as many of the whites."[20]

Still, in the mid-1970s the national expenditure on welfare was less than 1 percent, and it grew to only 1 percent by the late 1980s. Thus, there is a question of what can explain the fervor in the massive public attention given to a federal program which constituted just 1 *percent* of the national budget. It must be concluded that much of the venom directed toward welfare recipients is generated by a traditional set of attitudes directed toward the poor, but increasingly at blacks in general.

### Black reaction to welfare debate

The black community was understandably sensitive to the racial cast of the welfare issue, reflected in views such as those preferred by Gilder cited above. An indication of this is contained in the largest-circulation black magazine:

Say the word "welfare" and immediately the image of the lazy Black welfare queen who breeds for profit surfaces in the minds of those who have come to believe the hideous stereotype. It is a myth that persists despite government figures and authoritative studies showing that Whites overwhelmingly reap the lion's share of the dole.[21]

However, blacks supported the incomes aspect of welfare in the 1970s, because of the depth of the income pressure on black families.

At the start of the civil rights movement in 1959, the rate of official black poverty was 48 percent, although it has been cut almost in half, falling to 28 percent in 1969 by a combination of economic growth, federal "Great Society" programs, and access to income maintenance programs.[22] Illustrating the income pressure another way, in 1974, average white family income was $13,356, but only 25 percent of black families made as much or better in that year.[23] Still, regardless of the fact that public assistance income made up only *3 percent* of the total income of black families below the poverty level, by 1969 welfare added to black income a stable base for the poor.[24]

Blacks, therefore, believe that racial stereotypes are a manifestation of white racism, as a part of the infrastructure of their oppression. Martin Luther King Jr, for example, chided "the white man," saying that "Day in and day out he violates welfare laws to deprive the poor of their meager allotments," and called for a "revolution" against the unjust structure which maintained people in poverty.[25]

The race–welfare linkage was also confirmed in research by Gerald C. Wright Jr. His line of reasoning was as follows:

If white racism is a major factor accounting for why a disproportionate number of blacks are poor, and therefore on welfare, then racism can also reasonably be expected to influence those policies ostensibly aimed at alleviating that poverty.

Where the political climate is more favorable toward Blacks whether as a result of successful black demands or from racial liberalism among whites – support for welfare is likely to be greater.[26]

Wright's research substantiated the high negative correlations among variables such as a state's a high AFDC payments with a low percentage of black population and a lack of civil rights liberality and, therefore, lends great weight to the presumption of a racial dynamic in welfare policy. And if his conclusion holds that in a favorable political climate support for welfare is likely to be greater, then the obverse may also be true.

Black politicians, it was clear, supported the incomes maintenance concept of welfare. In 1980, black Democratic politicians gathered for an agenda conference in Richmond, Virginia, and in the resulting document's section on "Income Maintenance," they recommended to both presidential candidates that: "1. A Universal income maintenance program should be a guaranteed minimum with 25% of a decent standard of living as defined by the BLS. [Bureau of Labor Statistics]."[27] These recommendations were passed to the Platform Drafting Committee of the Democratic Party.

There followed from the creation of a racialized "welfare crisis" the worsening of public attitudes toward welfare in the late 1970s and 1980s. In the process, the focus on poverty was lost as policy moved from the stance of eliminating poverty, to containment, to penalizing the poor by vilifying the programs which protected them from poverty. The result was that welfare policy was moving toward convergence with the Republican approach of eliminating it altogether.

### Growing party convergence

Since the presidential campaign of Barry Goldwater, Republicans have claimed a mandate to force the slothful to work and thereby to break the intergenerational cycle of dependence.[28] However, the conservatives were not then the majority in the party, and they were said to be "horrified" when Nixon adopted the guaranteed-income concept as part of his Family Assistance Plan approach.[29] They would work with the conservative Democrats from that point to overturn it.

The changing issue field had an impact upon policy such that perhaps the critical point in the changing attitude of the nation toward the black welfare population was the policy assault upon the system in the late 1960s. Although Lyndon Johnson was known as a champion of civil rights, on January 2, 1968, he signed into law a bill pushed by Wilbur Mills, an Arkansas Democrat who headed the House Ways and Means Committee, which froze welfare payments, stopped the expansion of the program, and required work and job training for mothers with children more than 16 years old who were not in school.[30]

Moreover, in his reference to black welfare recipients as "brood mares," Mills's attitude exhibited negative bias to the point that Senator Robert Kennedy, a leading liberal Democrat, would consider this bill to be "the most punitive measure in the history of the country." And while this gave impetus to the Poor People's Campaign launched by Martin Luther King Jr, the struggle against poverty by the civil rights movement never materialized, largely because of King's assassination.[31]

Another key moment was the legislative conflict over the Family Assistance Plan (FAP) in 1969, which was defeated by Southern Democratic conservatives despite support from Northerners and the NWRO. It was after this loss that the welfare problem was considered "out of control" and having to be contained.[32] Here, an important role was played by Senator Herman Talmadge (a Democrat from Georgia) in attaching workfare amendments to the 1972 version of FAP.[33]

The period of the 1970s was also one of increasing black mobilization within the Democratic Party institution itself. However, that mobilization was set against a growing wariness of the party establishment, which had lost the elections of both 1968 and 1972. With the election of Jimmy Carter, the McGovernite "New Democrat" insurgents within the party had not been extinguished and the growth of the black elite had highlighted the race and welfare issues.

Table 2.2 Unemployment and poverty rates for blacks, 1973–83

|              | 1973 | 1974 | 1975 | 1976 | 1977 | 1978 | 1979 | 1980 | 1981 | 1982 | 1983 |
|--------------|------|------|------|------|------|------|------|------|------|------|------|
| Unemployment | 8.9  | 9.3  | 14.5 | 13.1 | 14.7 | 13.2 | 12.6 | 13.4 | 15.9 | 18.9 | 21.0 |
| Poverty      | 31.4 | 30.3 | 31.3 | 31.1 | 31.3 | 30.6 | 31.0 | 32.5 | 34.2 | 35.6 | 35.7 |

*Sources*: Handbook of Labor Statistics, Bureau of Labor Statistics, US Department of Labor (1985), pp. 169–71, Bulletin 2217; Leatha Lamison-White, "Income, Poverty, and Wealth in the United States: A Chart Book," P-60, No. 179. Bureau of the Census, US Department of Commerce (July, 1992), table 7, "Poverty Status of Persons, by Age and Race: 1959 to 1990," P.B-3.

The administration of Ronald Reagan (1980–8) was the next period which saw a major attack on the welfare system. As governor of California, Ronald Reagan, in a 1966 telecast, played upon the theme of the "undeserving poor," arguing for a work requirement for all able-bodied welfare recipients in his state.[34] As president, he continued this attack, offering policy recommendations designed to reduce dependency by reducing errors and abuse in welfare eligibility, reducing fraud and waste, tightening workfare requirements, requiring step-parents to assume more responsibility for children, increasing the responsibility for absent fathers to pay child support, and thus giving benefits only to the "truly needy."[35]

By referring to female recipients as "welfare queens" Reagan also sought to inferiorize welfare recipients, and his policy attempted to separate the "deserving poor" from the "undeserving poor." This conclusion is suggested by a credible group of analysts who found that real dependency was reduced only slightly by these measures.[36]

The underlying concept in both the Reagan and Bush administrations was that adequate employment existed and that individuals just had to have the tenacity to find it. This is a continuation of the misplaced faith in capitalism's ability to solve all of the structural problems of the economy that produce poverty. However, there is the irony that as the economy has produced millions of jobs in the high-growth late 1980s and the first half of the 1990s, the transition to a service economy in the context of global economic competition has placed a downward pressure on the wage rate of the average family. The average service job yields about half of the former wage rate of industrial jobs.

One major reason why poverty, and thus the necessity for welfare programs, did not decline is the growth of the wage gap, resulting in the decreasing share of income by the lowest quintile of income earners. This characteristic was enhanced by the Reagan Administration. For example, census data indicated that the income to poverty ratio had not changed much between 1967 and 1992 for the poorest families (0.91–0.97) while that of the wealthiest had increased substantially (6.06–8.43).[37] The editors of the *Harvard Business Review* confirm the existence of wage stagnation over time with the view that: "data for total compensation per hour worked . . . shows a 4% real decline for all workers in the private sector between March 1987 and March 1994."[38]

This descent into structural poverty has been more pronounced for a sector of the African American community. Historically two-parent families have performed much better than single-female-headed households, but between 1980 and 1990, black two-parent families dropped from 48 percent to 37 percent of all black families, affecting average black family income in the process.[39] For about the same period, poor African American children grew as a proportion of all poor African Americans from 41 percent in 1981 to 48 percent in 1987.[40] The sum total of this deepening poverty is also reflected in the fact that the unemployment level of African Americans was rising, as indicated in table 2.2.

Two things stand out in these data. The first is that black unemployment more than doubled in the decade between 1973 and 1983, rising to its highest point in the Reagan Administration. The second is that if one compares the data at table 2.1 with this set, one finds the anomaly that as the black presence on the AFDC rolls decreased from the highest point in 1973 (45.8 percent) to 1983 (43.8 percent and 40.7 percent the following year), blacks were simultaneously experiencing more unemployment and an increase in the poverty rate. Although the pursuit of this issue is beyond the scope of this chapter, the point is supported that blacks, therefore, have maintained concrete reasons for wanting to retain a strong version of the social safety-net complex of welfare programs, including AFDC, as a buffer against cyclical changes in the economy.

## The Impact on Democratic Politics

The workfare direction upon which Wilbur Mills, a Democrat, launched welfare policy in the late 1960s was kept through the Nixon Administration, and adopted by Jimmy Carter in his own welfare policy. One observer said that Carter's directions to Joseph Califano, Secretary of Health, Education and Welfare, were clear: that he should develop a plan that was "prowork" and "profamily" and which rewarded work by giving additional assistance to the working poor. The working poor were, in many cases, worse off because they had no health care, such that Carter wanted work or job-training incentives created, but at no additional cost.[41] Eventually pieces of his plan were adopted that focussed on mild workfare requirements.

However, proof of the division within the

party was illustrated by the results of a panel Carter had appointed in October of 1979. There were eight panels, given the mandate to design an agenda for the 1980s. This group of mostly Democrats was to be a mechanism that would provide the President-elect and the new Congress with the views of 45 Americans drawn from diverse backgrounds outside government. One panel dealt with the subject of Government and the Advancement of Social Justice: Health, Welfare, Education and Civil Rights and was led by Benjamin Hooks, head of the National Association for the Advancement of Colored People (NAACP) and had membership from the party's labor, women, blacks liberal and business wings. It eventually issued a Report and in the section devoted to AFDC, made a strong case for Income Maintenance as the proper objective of the new administration and Congress.[42] Thus, there appeared to be an equally strong sentiment within the party that struggled for the continuance of the Kennedy, NWRO, liberal line of welfare reform, in contravention of the opposite sentiment that was evolving.

By the mid-1980s, most American whites had grown to believe that most blacks could do without welfare if they tried, an issue of race and welfare, cloaked in an anti-big government stance, that fueled the Reagan landslide of 1984, and caused a change in the Democratic Party.[43] The most immediate change was that a new organization, the Democratic Leadership Council (DLC), was created in 1985 as a result of both Reagan victories. Led by Democratic conservatives or "moderates" such as Governor Bill Clinton of Arkansas, Congressman Richard Gephardt of Missouri, Governor Lawton Chiles of Florida, Senators Charles Robb of Virginia, Sam Nunn of Georgia, and others, it pledged "vigorous" welfare reform.[44]

This was a change from the Democratic Party stance on this issue, which, by 1984, had begun to move in the direction of work rather than cash assistance. For example, in 1972, the section on social justice in the "Blue Book" platform of the Democratic Party contained a statement urging a positive disposition of welfare in support of the poor.[45] Likewise, in 1976, the Democratic Advisory Council of the Democratic National Committee published its policy priorities for the campaign. In the section on urban policy, it included the statement that it was important for the party:

No. 3. To provide for federal financing of total welfare costs. The logic for federal financing of total welfare costs would simply recognize that the causes of dependency are national, not local, and the removal of this burden would make it possible for local government to concentrate their resources on genuinely local needs.[46]

By 1984, however, the Democratic Party campaigned on a platform with respect to welfare which counseled, in the section of the platform on job training and transitional assistance, that:

We will also launch meaningful training programs that lead to job placement for women who receive public assistance, in order to break the cycle of dependence and to raise their standard of living. Instead of punitive reductions in AFDC and other benefits for women who seek training and employment while receiving such assistance, beneficiaries should be given a transition period during which they are permitted to earn income in a formal training program while receiving full benefits.[47]

This transition in the attitude toward the welfare issue was set by 1986, as seen in a party document, "New Choices in a Changing America," authored by the Democratic Policy Commission. It was important that the membership of this commission was essentially comprised of Democratic elected officials at all levels, who supported a new, moderate change in approach to the welfare issue toward workfare.

Governor Bill Clinton was an Arkansas politician in the line (though not strictly speaking the ideology) of Wilbur Mills, and a southern politician in the line of Jimmy Carter. He thus had a similar burden of reconciling the conservative political leanings of his region toward the welfare system with the party's traditional liberal constituency, and moved decidedly toward the center of a more conservative electorate.

Clinton's impact as a governor was being felt in the mid-1980s on the changing policy posture of this issue in the party, as his example of investing in education in the State of Arkansas was cited in the "New Choices" document as the lead-off paragraph in the section on investing in people. Moreover, this is cited in the context of the welfare issue; the section reads:

Welfare policies in many states penalize parents who work. These policies act as a disincentive for two-parent families to form and stay together. That is wrong. For parents of all ages, we must build ladders from welfare to work in a way that strengthens families and supports poor people in finding, getting, and keeping the job so many of them want. That is another reason why we need to invest in people.[48]

This direction in policy, supported by Democratic governors and party leaders, was symptomatic of the changing attitudes in the party toward racial issues in general. It caused Congressman John Conyers, a leading black politician, to observe in July of 1983 that, "the tweedle Dee and Tweedle Dum politics practiced by both Democrats and Republicans has ceased to furnish the answers to the real problems of jobs, justice, and peace that afflicts so many citizens."[49] Professor Lucius Barker went on to observe that this sentiment, widespread among black political leaders, was an important impetus to the presidential campaign of the Rev. Jesse Jackson in 1984.[50] Jackson had mounted his campaign on behalf of the poor, "the boats stuck on the bottom of life," but had not embraced an explicit economic policy that embraced or called for a radical enhancement of welfare. Rather, his policy sought to return to the methodology of John F. Kennedy, by raising all of the boats through a policy that focussed on job creation through "full employment," by rebuilding the infrastructure of America.[51] Moreover, it is clearly indicated in the data cited above reflecting the growth in black unemployment in the mid-1980s, that Jackson drew considerable support from those who felt that unemployment was a critical issue that "mattered in voting."[52]

## The Clinton campaign and administration welfare policy

Clinton in 1992 broke decidedly with the party's liberal wing and pushed strongly in the direction of eliminating welfare by campaigning on the theme of "Ending Welfare as We Know it."[53] His proposal encompassed giving people the skills through job training and education to get off welfare; then after two years they were to find a job, preferably in the private sector, but if not there a government-generated job. They would retain medical benefits for a period while being trained and while in the first stages of a job.[54]

By moving toward the conservative consensus in the public on the welfare issue, Clinton had coopted one of the Republican issues. A CBS/New York Times poll taken in December of 1994 found a relatively standard response which indicated that 48 percent of those polled felt welfare spending should be cut, and only 13 percent urged any increase. However, when the focus was changed to public assistance for children, 47 percent advocated increases and only 9 percent advanced cuts.[55] Clinton repeated this theme of ending welfare in his speech accepting the Democratic nomination for president by suggesting that "welfare should be a second chance, not a way of life."[56]

This proposal was championed by the DLC,

which published a governing agenda known as "Mandate for Change" in 1993, containing the following elements:

– Replace permanent welfare with a two-year transitional program.
– Shift public subsidies from welfare to work.
– Assure all Americans access to health care.
– Create social insurance for children through guaranteed child support.
– Offer people who cannot find private jobs work in community service.
– Expand welfare-to-work efforts by nonprofit groups and businesses.[57]

These proposals went far beyond Ronald Reagan's actions, which were designed to restrict eligibility for welfare and cut its cost, but not to eliminate the program altogether.

In July of 1993, President Clinton announced the formation of an interagency Working Group on Welfare Reform, headed by David Ellwood, Bruce Reed, and Mary Jo Bane. Ellwood and Bane, both Harvard Kennedy School professors, had done substantial research on welfare issues.

Clinton's January 15, 1994, State of the Union message carried forward a campaign pledge to "change welfare as we know it," and his subsequent proposals contain such features as: limiting public assistance to two years – thereafter recipients must accept a job or job-training program; providing resources for day care; confiscating the driver's license of fathers delinquent on child support; and others. Although Republican proposals were somewhat more liberal, the dominant consensus was for the short-term utilization of welfare, after which a work requirement ensues. By June of 1994, the welfare reform proposals of the Clinton Administration were released, and although they were only to cover 8 percent of welfare recipients by 1999, they mirrored in many respects the "two-years-and-off" provisions of his campaign approach.

In fact, the lead of the Clinton campaign emboldened the Republicans to go beyond Clinton and to propose eliminating welfare altogether after a period, with no substantive financial support for job training and education. They also wanted to cut food programs and benefits for immigrants. This would be evident in the welfare policy generated by the radical Republican Congress created by the landslide of 1994, a policy which was contained in the contract with America. In brief, their legislative proposal, entitled the "Personal Responsibility Act," aimed to: "Discourage illegitimacy and teen pregnancy by prohibiting welfare to minor mothers and denying increased AFDC for additional children while on welfare, cut spending for welfare programs, and enact a tough two-years-and-out provision with work requirements to promote individual responsibility."[58]

The Clinton welfare reform bill was substantially similar to that drafted by the Republicans:

*Clinton*
- Requires teen parents to live at home
- Child born to a family already on welfare: state can place a family cap
- Two-parent families: states can pay benefits each month if found necessary
- Paternity must be established
- Limit: 2 years
- Beyond 2 years: Recipient would go into a transitional employment program, public or private, 15 to 35 hours, for minimum wage

*Republicans*
- Requires teen parents to live at home
- Child born to a family already on welfare: forbids states from paying additional benefits, unless legislature passes exemption
- Two-parent families: option of extending benefits to six months
- Paternity must be established
- Limit: 2 years

- Beyond 2 years: Recipients would be required to work 35 hours per week for benefits

## *The policy conundrum*

The Clinton proposals led to conflict on every side of the Democratic Party coalition. Debates within the Working Group itself over the plan, which would cost $15 billion for the first five years, leaked out concerning paying for it by cutting other standard aspects of AFDC. Ellwood, for example, advocated removing 250,000 children from AFDC, saving $800 million by eliminating the $200-per-month stipend for households, for instance, run by grandparents who take in a child whose mother has a drug problem. Critics of this approach argued that eliminating family support, already inadequate, would be counterproductive to the other objectives.[59] Moreover, Liberals, Senator Daniel Patrick Moynihan, Marion Wright Edelman's Children's Defense Fund, the Republican budget cutters in the House, and others complicated Clinton's path to the smooth acceptance of his welfare reform package, creating a considerable policy and political quagmire.

*Democrats* Senator Moynihan was highly critical of Clinton for what he believed was his manufacturing of a national health-care crisis when there was a welfare crisis. However, when he saw Clinton's plan, he considered it too simplistic and essentially "boob bait for Bubbas."[60] The senator, who is a recognized legislative expert on the welfare issue, was shocked when it was intimated that the administration was considering agreeing with the Republican plan, because it contained far less financial support for job training and day care than would be required to place dependent women on the road to self-sufficiency.

In May of 1995, Senator Carol Moseley Braun attended an administration meeting on the Clinton welfare reform bill and pointed to a report by the Department of Health and Human Service itself that four million children would be eliminated from federal welfare benefits if a five-year hard limit was placed on payments.[61]

*Republicans* Ultimately, when the radical conservative House passed its version of welfare reform in H. R. 4, the Personal Responsibility Act of 1995, it contained proposals for adjustments in federal welfare spending which were projected to save $69 billion between fiscal years 1996 and 2000. The issue with critics was how those savings were achieved, the largest of which were in the categories of cash assistance ($11.4 billion), restricting welfare for immigrants ($13.8 billion), changes in eligibility and administration of the Food Stamp Program ($23.2 billion), and SSI reform ($13.4 billion).

An analysis of this legislation by the Clinton Administration revealed that the burden on children would be exceedingly harsh, since 80,000 would be denied cash benefits because of being born to unwed mothers under 18 years of age, 2.2 million because of being born to mothers already receiving AFDC benefits; and 4.8 million because of being born to mothers who had received AFDC benefits five years or longer.[62]

*Liberals* Liberals such as the Children's Defense Fund have pointed out to the administration as well that 2 million children would be dropped from the welfare rolls who are eligible because the amounts invested in day care are insufficient. The estimates of the amounts of funding necessary for job training and day care run into at least $6 billion to $8 billion.

Moreover, they said that there is no guarantee that states will meet federal obligations to welfare clients should the funds be structured into a block grant and given to the states. They point, for example, to the fact that 21

states are under one form of court supervision or another for failing to administer effective programs to protect abused and neglected children or to run foster-care facilities.[63] This does not build confidence that other aspects of the child welfare system can be administered more efficiently.

*Blacks* Blacks have monitored the proposals of both the administration and the Republicans, and while they are generally in favor of positive changes in the welfare system, they are also keenly sensitive to the negative affect of any reductions in cash benefits on a community which already has one-third of its members in poverty. Therefore, to the extent that any of the plans do not contain enough funding for job training and day care, they have been opposed. In February of 1996, responding to a new welfare reform by the National Governors' Association, groups such as the National Council of Negro Women, the National Black Caucus of Local Elected Officials, the National Congress of Black Churches, and the NAACP opposed it, saying: "Genuine welfare reform must provide more for education, training and child care."[64]

This is a sensitive issue, for if cash benefits are severely reduced, that would push additional blacks into the status of the working poor, a group that is already high. For instance, the percentage of black workers who did not make the average family income was 42 percent in 1994.[65] Thus, an analysis by the Congressional Black Caucus Research Institute found that if AFDC block grants had been in effect in the financial year of 1988, based on 1987 funding levels, the impact on black children by the financial year of 1993 would mean 617,321 black children having been eliminated from the caseload, causing families to lose $1,555.6 billion.[66]

*Analysts* Perhaps E. J. Dionne has said it best in referring to the reasons why Carter's attempt failed to have a comprehensive version of welfare reform enacted:

Carter's basic problem was that prowork welfare reform is inevitably *more expensive* than the current system. Providing jobs and job training for welfare recipients and lifting the incomes of the working poor – all essential ingredients to a program that would encourage and reward work – will require new spending and shifts in the tax code that will cost the government revenue. To have a system that promotes *conservative* values would require more *liberal* spending.[67]

There is some support for this point of view from conservative welfare researcher Lawrence Mead, whose analysis of the welfare data from the state of Wisconsin suggested that a paternalistic version of welfare system "means continued big government, not an escape from it."[68] His view was that the dramatic reduction in the welfare rolls of the state of Wisconsin, of 23 percent in the period 1987–94, was achieved through a program administered by a resource-rich bureaucracy.

## Conclusion

Although President Clinton signed the Republican welfare reform bill in August, 1996, the issue will probably benefit Republicans rather than Democrats, Continuing a trend from past years.[69] A *Washington Post/ABC News* poll indicated the public's confidence that the Republicans (51 percent to 38 percent) would be better at "reforming the welfare system" than would Democrats.[70] This is despite the fact that the Clinton Administration has given 23 waivers to governors, most of them Republicans, to enact local variations of welfare reform with federal dollars, most of which move in the direction of the conservative orthodoxy.

The fact that Clinton once vetoed the House Republican welfare reform bill would appear to give him credit with which to rally a segment of his traditional Democratic constituency of liberals, blacks, and Hispanics. However, if Clinton fails to provide the necessary economic underpinnings to make the transition from welfare to work feasible, then there could be a significant political fallout from minorities and liberals.

Otherwise, the emergence of a "two-years-and-you're-off" welfare policy has acted as a symbol of a series of racial slights visited upon the liberal wing of the party, especially blacks, that has included such acts as Clinton embarrassing Jesse Jackson in the 1992 campaign with an attack on Sister Souljah, a rap star who was attending Jackson's policy conference; the rejection of black law professor, Lani Gunier, as a member of his administration for her views; the firing of Dr Joycelyn Elders from the post of surgeon general; the elimination of the $1.6-billion-dollar contract set-aside program, the largest in the federal government; his recalcitrance on the equalization of the cocaine sentencing guidelines; his support of "three-strikes-and-you're-out" sentencing for a greatly expanded array of federal crimes; his adoption of a "one-strike-and-you're-out" policy for federal housing tenants; and many other such actions.

These actions, however, which have generally used the black community as a foil for establishing the conservative content of the "new politics" of the Clinton administration, have established some distance from the liberal policy positions of the administration on race-valued issues. Whether the repositioning will be perceived to be enough by the public or the Democratic leadership can be assessed by what happens to welfare policy in the future.

# Notes

1 "Progress is Reported on Welfare Overhaul," *New York Times* (January 29, 1995), p. 20.
2 James T. Patterson, *America's Struggle Against Poverty, 1900–85* (Cambridge: Harvard University Press, 1986), p. 59.
3 George Gilder, *Wealth and Poverty* (New York: Basic Books, 1981), p. 122.
4 "Summary Characteristics of the Black Population for States and Selected Counties and Places: 1980, Bureau of the Census," 1980 Census of Population, PC80-21 US Department of Commerce (January, 1987), p. 17.
5 See Nicholas Lemann, *The Promised Land* (New York: Vintage/Random House, 1992). Also, see my "Du Bois" 'The Philadelphia Negro': 100 Years Later," *Journal of Blacks in Higher Education* 11 (Spring, 1996), pp. 83–4.
6 "The Social and Economic Status of the Black Population in the United States: An Historical View, 1790–1978," CPR, Special Studies, p-23, No. 80, Bureau of the Census, US Department of Commerce, pp. 31–2.
7 Patterson, *America's Struggle*, p. 88.
8 Nick Kotz and Mary Lynn Kotz, *A Passion for Equality* (New York: W. W. Norton, 1977), p. 196.
9 Kotz and Kotz, *Passion for Equality*, pp. 165–6.
10 Martin Luther King Jr, *Where Do We Go from Here: Chaos or Community?* (Boston: Beacon Press, 1967), pp. 164–5.
11 Joseph Feagin, *Subordinating the Poor: Welfare and American Beliefs* (New York: Prentice-Hall, 1975), p. 9.
12 Ibid., pp. 5–11.
13 Michael Katz, *The Undeserving Poor: From the War on Poverty to the War on Welfare* (New York: Pantheon Books, 1990).
14 This section has benefited greatly from Professor Jennings analysis. James Jennings's, *Understanding the Nature of Poverty in Urban America* (Westport: Praeger, 1994), pp. 31–53. He cites the work of James Monroe (*The Democratic Wish: Popular Participation and Limits of American Government*), who says that between the Roosevelt era and that of Lyndon Johnson, poverty became a "black problem." Monroe says specifically that, "*poverty* became an ironic political euphemism for *black*" (p. 32).
15 Thomas Byrne Edsall and Mary D. Edsall, *Chain Reaction: The Impact of Race, Rights, and Taxes on American Politics* (New York: W. W. Norton, 1991), p. 106.
16 Ben Wattenberg, *The Real America* (New York: Capricorn, 1976), p. 138.
17 "Money Income and Poverty Status of Families and Persons in the United States: 1981," Bureau of the Census, US Department of Commerce (July, 1982), pp. 20–1.
18 "Poverty in the United States: 1992," Bureau of the Census, US Department of Commerce (September, 1993), pp. 2, 3.
19 "Statistical Abstract of the United States," Bureau of the Census, Economics and Statistics Administration, US Department of Commerce (September, 1991), p. 356.
20 Dorothy K. Newman, ed., *Protest, Politics, and Prosperity* (New York: Pantheon Books, 1978), p. 255.
21 "Who Gets Welfare?," *Ebony* 58 (2) (December, 1992), p. 55.
22 "Social and Economic Status of the Black Population in the United States," p. 50.
23 Ibid., p. 32.
24 Ibid., p. 54.
25 Martin Luther King Jr, *The Trumpet of Conscience* (New York: Harper, and Row, 1968), pp. 8, 60.
26 Gerald C. Wright Jr, "Racism and Welfare Policy in America," *Social Science Quarterly* 57 (4) (March, 1977), p. 719.
27 "The National Black Agenda for the '80s; Richmond Conference Recommendations," Joint Center for Political Studies, Washington, DC (1980), p. 2A.
28 Richard Rubin, *Party Dynamics: The Democratic Coalition and the Politics of Change* (New York: Oxford University Press, 1976), pp. 125–6.
29 Mary C. Brennan, *Turning Right in the Sixties: The Conservative Capture of the GOP* (Chapel Hill: University of North Carolina Press, 1995), p. 135.
30 Kotz and Kotz, *Passion for Equality*, p. 249
31 Ibid.
32 Evelyn Brodkin, "Ending Welfare," *Dissent* (Spring, 1995), p. 214.

33 Ibid.
34 Feagin, *Subordinating the Poor*, p. 6.
35 William Gorham, "The Social Welfare Objectives of the Reagan Administration," in D. Lee Bauden, ed., *The Social Contract Revisited* (Washington, DC: Urban Institute, 1984), p. 6.
36 Ibid.
37 "Press Briefing on 1992 Income, Poverty and Health Care Coverage Results," Bureau of the Census, US Department of Commerce, p. 9.
38 "Real Income: The Wage Gap Doesn't Tell the Whole Story," Briefings from the Editors, *Harvard Business Review* (November–December, 1994), p. 11.
39 Michael Fabricant and Steve Burghardt, *The Welfare State Crisis and the Transformation of Social Service Work* (New York: M. E. Sharpe, 1992), p. 16.
40 Ibid., p. 19.
41 E. J. Dionne, *Why Americans Hate Politics* (New York: Simon and Schuster, 1991), p. 135.
42 "Government and the Advancement of Social Justice: Health, Welfare, Education and Civil Rights in the Eighties," President's Commission for a National Agenda for the '80s Washington, DC (1980), pp. 63–6.
43 Paul Sniderman, Philip Tetlock, and Edward Carmines, eds, *Prejudice, Politics, and the American Dilemma* (Stanford: Stanford University Press, 1993), p. 146.
44 James MacGregor Burns, William Crotty, Louis Lovelace Duke, and Lawrence D. Longley, eds, *The Democrats Must Lead: The Case for a Progressive Democratic Party* (San Francisco: Westview Press, 1992), p. 67.
45 *The Official Proceedings of the Democratic National Convention 1972* (Washington DC: Democratic National Committee, 1972), p. 254.
46 "Ibid., p. 30.
47 "Democrats: Building America's Future," 1984 Democratic National Platform, Democratic National Committee (1984), p. 15.
48 "New Choices in a Changing America," Democratic Policy Commission, Democratic National Committee, Washington DC (1986), p. 17.
49 Cited in Lucius J. Barker and Ronald Walters, eds, *Jesse Jackson's 1984 Presidential Campaign: Challenge and Change in American Politics* (Chicago: University of Illinois Press, 1989), p. 12.
50 Ibid.

51 Ronald Walters, "The Issue Politics of the Jackson Campaign," in Lorenzo Morris, ed., *The Social and Political Implications of the 1984 Jesse Jackson Presidential Campaign* (New York: Praeger, 1988), p. 39. See Robert S. Browne, "The Economic Policy of the Jackson Candidacy," in Morris, *Social and Political Implications*, pp. 91–7.
52 William Crotty, "Constituency Attitudes and Political Outcomes," in Barker and Walters, *Jesse Jackson's Campaign*, table 6, p. 82. Although all primary election candidates drew substantially from those indicating that unemployment was an important voting issue, Jackson had the highest score: Jackson 47 percent, Mondale 44 percent, Hart 41 percent.
53 *Putting People First*, The Clinton–Gore Campaign for President and Vice President (Washington DC 1992), p. 165.
54 Ibid.
55 Jason DeParle, "Despising Welfare, Pitying its Young," *New York Times* (December 18, 1994), p. E5.
56 Paul Quirk and Joseph Hinchliffe, "Domestic Policy: The Trials of a Centrist Democrat," in Colin Campbell and Bert Rockman, eds, *The Clinton Presidency: First Appraisals* (Chatham, NJ: Chatham House Publishers, 1996), p. 279.
57 Democratic Leadership Council, *Mandate for Change* (Washington DC, 1993), pp. 218–19.
58 Ed Gillespie and Bob Schellhaus, eds, *Contract With America* (New York: Times/Random House, 1994), p. 9–10.
59 Jason DeParle, "Welfare Planners Struggle Over Final Sticking Points," *New York Times* (March 21, 1994), p. 4.
60 Quirk and Hinchliffe, "Domestic Policy," p. 280.
61 Robert Pear, "Senate Welfare Plan Cuts $41 Billion over 7 Years," *New York Times* (May 26, 1995), p. A18.
62 "Summary Impact Analysis of H. R. 4," US Department of Health and Human Services (April 7, 1995).
63 Robert Pear, "Many States Fail to Meet Mandates on Child Welfare," *New York Times* (March 17, 1996), p. 30.
64 Robert Pear, "Governors' Plans on Welfare Attacked," *New York Times* (February 14, 1996), p. A12.

65  Bureau of the Census, US Department of Commerce, Division of Racial Statistics (1996).

66  "The Personal Responsibility Act II – House Republicans Latest Welfare Reform Proposal," H. R. 4, Backgrounder #2, CBCF Working Group (February 17, 1995).

67  Dionne, *Why Americans Hate Politics,* p. 136.

68  Lawrence Mead, "Growing a Smaller Welfare State: Wisconsin's Reforms Show that to Cut the Rolls, You Need More Bureaucrats," *Washington Post* (December 3, 1995), p. C4.

69  Robert Pear, "Clinton Vetoes the Republicans' Welfare Plan," *New York Times* (January 11, 1996), p. B8.

70  Richard Morin, "Public Growing Wary of GOP Cuts: More Now Trust Clinton to Help the Middle Class, Poll Finds," *Washington Post* (March 21, 1995), p. A1, *Washington Post/ABC News* poll.

# 3

# Urban America

## Crushed in the Growth Machine

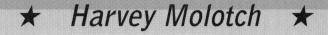 **★ *Harvey Molotch* ★**

## Introduction

US domestic policy has long been drifting away from one of the fundamental tenets of the New Deal: The federal government must provide a minimum standard of life for both individuals and communities; one's fate should not be overwhelmed by the economy's fluctuations or by where one happens to live. In regard to a specifically "urban policy," whatever else that ambiguous term might mean, it must mean that besides limiting inequalities among individuals, government should ameliorate intense inequalities among communities and regions. Something like this was Aristotle's vision of what it takes for a society to be decent and lasting, a vision shared by many Americans over our history. When rural poverty was prevalent during the Great Depression, the federal government aided poor rural areas directly with farm support systems, rural electrification, and cheap irrigation. As the proportion of Americans living in cities increased and urban poverty rates grew, the central cities became the focus – evidenced most notably in Lyndon Johnson's Great Society programs. The case for geographically focussed aid is not just that it is a convenient way of finding the poor, but also that concentration of poverty creates special problems for those caught in a web of mutually reinforcing disadvantages. Besides the hopelessness and suffering that result, it disunites what otherwise would be a more coherent body politic across the vast US landscape.

Geographically focussed federal intervention has also helped insulate residents from the worst aspects of local decision making, like provision of impure water or failure to immunize children or protect people from racist violence. Especially in the rural south, this meant, over the generations, reining in the almost medieval power of corrupt and backward regimes. Poor southern blacks (and most blacks, until World War II, were southern poor) came under the domination of these same insiders as well as that of the poor whites venting their own frustration. As a result of the 1960s civil rights movement and the political power of urban politicians in the north, federal authority and resources brought the deviant south into America, providing blacks with the vote, due process, and de jure integration.

Today, the rural population is virtually gone from everywhere; postwar economic development, including vast defense expenditures in the south and migrations in both directions, have shrunk differences between that region and the rest of the country, in both race relations and economic standing. It is the central cities that most depart from the US norms in terms of capacities to provide for their populations and also in the concentration of racial minorities – most notably African Americans.

The conflict between the south and the rest of the country has been replaced by a national schism between whites and blacks – and to a lesser degree Hispanics. The relation between local regimes and the impoverished is more subtle than in the old days of chains and poll taxes, but it is still highly problematic to leave people to the mercies of locals. Removing federal responsibility sinks the cities, especially their poor, and most disproportionately the black poor. Because of the kind of people who control them, the goals they work toward, and the kinds of situations they get locked into, there are systematic reasons that make contemporary state and local governments unlikely to befriend those without resources. That is why the Republicans have been so enthusiastic about developing power downward. The Democrats' challenge was whether or not to go along to get along.

To understand what is occurring, I need first to set out the political conditions that most affect Clinton's urban policies – how he was closed in by his Republican opponents. Then we can see how the administration bought into the idea that the local is good and that Washington is bad. To evaluate this proposition, we need to see what the "local" actually looks like: who runs the state and city governments, for what purpose, and what they are likely to do when they gain greater control over resources. That understood, we can finally critique programs, Clinton's or anyone else's, that takes power from the national level. We will try to understand what the Democrats have done and why they have done it.

## Bending in the Wind

The Clinton people, unlike myself and other critics, are the ones who had to contend with the House of Gingrich and all its support structures in the right-wing think tanks and conservative media. HUD, created at the crescendo of the civil rights movement in 1965, saw its budget cut from $26 billion to $20 billion over two years; Congress threatened to shut it down altogether and has not been bashful about declaiming the programs it finds especially obnoxious. All this during a time of budget-balancing fetishism that permits no new taxes; initiatives need to be cheap and palatable. Mandates are a special no-no, in part because the president signed the 1995 Unfunded Mandates Reform Act which made them difficult to enact.

Also a part of the HUD inheritance (as with other government agencies) has been the continuous discouragement of "competition" with the private sector, as happens when the government builds housing, for example. There is also the heritage of corruption in the prior Republican regime that, not believing in the HUD mandate at all, could at least use it to line the pockets of insiders. Government shut-downs also do little to make government more efficient; mail fails to go out, tasks build up, and deadlines are missed. Attacks on the national government as a failure become a self-fulfilling prophecy when there is utter disrespect for its mission. When it comes to HUD, the anti-urban sentiment blows hard in the wind, which is to say a sentiment that holds that the disadvantaged deserve nothing.

The right wing successfully connects "big" not just to amount of spending, but to the governmental level that does the spending: Washington is most evil, the states next worst, counties and towns least nefarious (although still not good). Besides its resonance with mythic traditions of English home rule, New England town meetings, and the frontier spirit, the chorus of bringing government back to "the people" connects with residues of 1960s movement rhetoric, surviving in country and western song lyrics if nowhere else, that "the people, yes" and the national establishment "no." Small town Babbitt, site of traditional values as well as small business, is the hero and updated to "entrepreneur" transmutes into corporations and state-level development agencies.

The Clinton HUD's response was to tack, picking through policies that could preserve the agency and at least have the potential, in the HUD collective view, for doing some good. HUD fights segregation by race and income, in part through striving to locate new public housing outside already impacted zones of poverty and minority concentration. There are also efforts at stricter enforcement of laws against residential racial discrimination, a just cause as well as one Republicans cannot easily complain about since the affirmative action demon does not come into play. HUD has made strong appointments of competent and progressive people to exact as much benefit as possible out of the available slack. But it would have been, as a HUD official told me, "the end of HUD" to have continued the status quo. In this context, devolution becomes a viable option – one of the few openings for action and one with consequences sufficiently vague to encourage the hope that it will probably end up OK.

Hence, HUD embraced programs that move authority "down" – the favored direction of the day. In each case of adjustment, there is ambiguity as to whether the Democrats have appropriated the language of the right to sustain their own goals or have themselves been coopted in pursuit of simple bureaucratic survival. Here is the rundown of how HUD, at least as read from its official policy statements, has embraced devolution and other elements of conservative talk:

• *Deregulation.* HUD's statements and policies support "removing unreasonable tax and regulatory barriers"[1] (although not "indiscriminate" deregulation) and "reducing significantly the regulatory burdens that have enmeshed states, local governments, and private firms in the webs of micro-

management and uncompensated costs."[2] HUD aspires to provide "waivers from federal requirements concerning job training, community development, and 'safety net' programs."[3] Commenting on the higher costs of doing business in large metropolitan areas compared to small towns, HUD Secretary Cisneros indicates that high city wages are part of the reason, but that "I am quite sure that in many of America's most important urban agglomerations, costs are higher than they need to be." He then stresses the need to "revamp the local regulatory environment – labyrinthine and uncertain approval processes are among the most certain turnoffs to potential investors . . . [and to] examine local tax structures to be sure that, in comparison to other areas, local tax burdens are no higher than they need to be."[4]

• *Entrepreneurialism.* HUD calls its "empowerment zones" and "enterprise communities" its "flagship" program[5] – and one that Vice-President Gore celebrated in his televised campaign debate with rival candidate and former HUD secretary Jack Kemp (you proposed it, we did it, Gore crowed). Under the zone strategy, companies in certain disadvantaged places receive special benefits and regulatory relief. HUD pushes "niche marketing" for communities in which each place will build on its own particular advantages, for example grants to Harlem to use its artistic and show-business history to build tourism – a born-again Harlem Renaissance. HUD calls this strategy for generating resources "asset-based" rather than "needs-based"; mayors will turn in their tin cups and go for market share.[6] Another face of entrepreneurialism is HUD's blessing of so-called "private–public partnerships" in which local governments join in development ventures with private businesses, putting up some of the money and taking on some of the risk.

- *Housing vouchers.* As it encourages localities to get in to commercial development, HUD moves away from constructing public housing; rather than build new units (or funding others to do so) it embraces vouchers – the federal government subsidizes rents in privately owned buildings for eligible persons. Vouchers do not add to the *permanent* stock of housing units available to the poor,[7] but they play to conservative ideology by operating through private markets. In weak housing markets, they also increase profits for landlords who have units they otherwise can not rent. On the plus side, the program can help deconcentrate the poor and desegregate minorities if recipients are able to use their vouchers in suburbs where they otherwise would not be. Combined with the abandonment of high-rise housing projects (including blowing some of them up), HUD's goal is to lessen voter hatred of public housing and thereby of the welfare policies with which it is so identified.
- *Voluntarism and religion.* HUD supports engaging local groups, especially churches (a.k.a. "faith communities") in its programs to leverage both the funding capacities and volunteer workpower of these groups. HUD encourages non-profits to participate in the construction of housing, voucher programs, and investment in empowerment zones and enterprise communities. The administration has also made care of the homeless another realm in which non-profits are increasingly to be put in control. Making coalition with local non-profits is another form of devolution, one which – especially in the case of religious-based ones – helps deflect right-wing attack.
- *Individual responsibility.* HUD talks about individual responsibility and pushes programs that encourage it. Church groups and other community associations, increasingly playing a role in aid programs, are

more free than the federal government to make religious and moral virtue a criterion for receipt of services. In the public housing realm, HUD policies now call for elimination of trouble-making tenants from its programs. HUD is also fighting crime by encouraging "defensible spaces" in neighbourhoods through physical barriers and *cul-de-sacs* to keep out undesirables.[8]

# The Growth Machine System and Place Competition

Students of urban power know that the real people who play the key roles below the federal level are not a random group of citizens or volunteers from the churches and non-profits, but business activists. These are the actors ready to catch the devolution bouquet. At the scale of cities, the metropolis, and to a degree the states, those with economic interest in land and buildings are, along with others linked to local growth, the key players.[9] This special business segment makes money off infrastructure projects and, as a more general matter, the future of their own wealth depends on how many more residents and business investors are around to bid up the price of their holdings. United on growth for the metropolis overall, they have their periodic internal squabbles over the specific distribution of that growth (who gets the airport nearby, your land or mine?), and these sometimes become public issues that give an exaggerated appearance of internal conflict. The precise conditions of that development – taxes, subsidies, utility access – cause them to expend the energy and funds to influence outcomes. Whereas other political players come and go, they are omnipresent in the political structure, participating almost daily on matters that affect their projects, as well as on larger-scale issues such as approval of general plans and initiating new programs of urban redevelopment, water projects, acquiring ball-team franchises, and attracting defense and manufacturing plants. In effect, they turn the city itself – its agencies and departments – into a "growth machine." This is not new; it is the American "booster" tradition that, in the nineteenth century, led towns and cities to finance canals, railroad lines, and highways that bankrupted many of them but also made many of their leaders rich.[10] Then as now, the growth entrepreneurs include local media (whose revenues depend on aggregate growth) and members of professions and specialties like land-use lawyers, accountants, and construction engineers.

The growth machine system is clothed in public-welfare terms – the idea that growth will better local residents in general, that additional industry and increases in population will yield greater prosperity across the board. The city is anthropomorphized into a unitary being with a common interest; growth floats all the ships and tugboats alike – bringing jobs, revenue for social, services, and a way to "clean up" slums. Growth is also framed in terms of civic pride – a "greater" metropolis is a better one; rising numbers are the metric of goodness and progress. Under growth-machine logic, any particular project nets gains for the local private economy, its tax base, as well as the aggregate public good. "Helping the cities" can easily transmute into helping the businesses that develop it. A corollary is that a "good business climate" must be maintained, and this means low taxes and going easy on safety and environmental regulation. It also is said to mean keeping workers from becoming too strident and welfare from being too generous. The last thing any locality needs is to be a "magnet" for poor who will drain the tax coffers and physically blight the shopping and tourist economies. Growth entrepreneurs are the linchpin of this consensus as they link the local scene to larger corporate and political forces.

The growth-machine system bleeds into all realms of urban life. If we want to know why city governments do so little for their poor, or fail to be preoccupied with the sometimes desperate need of, say, single mothers, we need to understand what is instead filling the urban action space. Increasingly, both in the US and to a degree in Europe as well, any policy must justify itself in terms of growth strategy. Sport is not a matter of spreading recreational activities among young people but of investing millions in facilities for professional teams that will, in turn, mark the place as "big league" and draw crowds to boost business. Museum directors document that their institutions attract foot-traffic that stimulates retail sales and office economy expansion. For this they bring in blockbuster shows, on more or less conventional themes (anything by Cezanne, or "the flower through history"). Universities intensify their links with entrepreneurs to justify state support. Even the central city as a whole is "sold" – by the Cisneros HUD at least – as something useful because it is said, on very thin evidence, to be the real basis of growth in the whole metropolis.[11] Regardless of function or its scale, the development agenda tail wags the institutional dogs, even those not directly part of the growth-machine apparatus. In the process, cities are thwarted from basic actions that might enhance ordinary day-to-day life; if welfare happens, it must come indirectly through the growth process that will trickle its benefits down.

Just as the system now moves responsibilities to the local level, it also manipulates what counts as "local" for particular purposes. Since most important growth-machine activists are from businesses with metropolitan spread (not just central cities), they think in terms of the larger unit for many purposes. Development in the suburbs works fine since media, utilities, banks, and large construction firms cover at that scale. So a new stadium project is "ours" at the metroplex or even state-wide level, thus helping generate support well be-

yond the central city boundaries for such
projects. While the central city is usually the
unit that has to pay the environmental and
fiscal costs, the cheers come from all around.
Clinton position papers rather wistfully encourage suburbs to share their revenues with
the central cities. Suggestions are also made
for some form of metropolitan government;
"flexible borders" is the term being used to
denote that suburbs could opt into sharing
costs for certain area-wide benefits, like sta-
dia and city museums, as has occurred under
local initiatives in Denver and the Minnesota
Twin Cities.[12]

Running cities to help them grow is historically bipartisan even if some prominent
Democrats have tended to favor environmen-
talist and other positions contrary to growth-
machine goals. Many liberal Democrat
contributors have come from the developers'
ranks, some of whom have been ardent supporters of civil liberties and other cultural
positions aligned with the left. Well before
the Clintons, Democrat regimes sponsored
monsters like urban renewal and other unfor-
tunate redevelopment mechanisms that came
out of the state houses and city halls. Trying
to block the decline of property values threatening downtowns as well as the movements
of minorities too close to elite institutions,
urban renewal was a way for cities to be saved
through vast subsidies from the federal government. The old statistic is worth trotting
out once again: At great taxpayer cost, urban
renewal – which was supposed to aid the slum
poor – destroyed more housing than it created.[13] It also eliminated some wonderful ar-
chitectural and social resources, the loss of
which continues to yield only a void in the
heart of some cities. Urban renewal essentially worked like block grants in that cities
initiated their urban-renewal programs without much by way of meaningful federal restrictions. Only in the later stages of urban
renewal did the national government thwart
localities from dislocating the poor, but at that

point enthusiasm for the program (not coin-
cidentally) began its decline. Again, the contrast is with the War on Poverty initiatives
(Head Start and community organizing),
which bypassed city governments and thus
the growth interests.

The subsequent advent of urban redevelopment, the "son" of urban renewal, brought
initiatives back to the control of state and
local governments (federal funds were less
directly involved). This program, because it
razed or gentrified so many single-room oc-
cupancy buildings, greatly contributed to current homelessness.[14] Its funding mechanism,
"tax increment financing" allows cities to put
any tax increment that occurs within its redevelopment area into a separate fund, usually to be used to subsidize development
projects. This means that even when tax in-
crements occur only because of property inflation (as wildly occurred in California during
the 1980s), none of the new revenue goes to
schools or city general funds. Redevelopment
usually subsidizes business and downtown
amenities. Urban policy, whether under
Democrats or Republicans, has always been
at war within itself, between programs that
might actually help the poor and other ordinary city dwellers, and those that bolstered
business, especially real estate. The tension
remains. Mr and Mrs Clinton themselves
flirted, quite dangerously as it turns out, with
real estate as a way to get rich in their sleep.

In part because of the ideological track they
have inherited, the Clintonites have done little, in either policy or rhetorical terms, to
alter the system. The liabilities of continued
(much less enhanced) decentralization have
hardly been mentioned in policy statements,
much less from the bully pulpits. As is well
known by the HUD analysts, America is rich
and its urban areas are rich; the inner cities
are kept poor because they lack ways to tap
into the wealth that surround them and to
some degree was created in them. But those
building affluent suburbs and edge-city

office parks will resist (along with residents, to be sure) sharing their tax base or absorbing welfare responsibilities for the larger whole. Such fiscal and social integration risks raising taxes on their holdings as well as making them less attractive to tenants and investors. The idealistic aspects of the voucher system, to break up inner-city concentrations of the poor, will not be welcomed by suburban town governments and landlords, likely to do what they can to sabotage move-ins from central cities (never mind the need to enthusiastically welcome folks who are reluctant to leave neighborhoods of friends and family). Metropolitan concern for real central-city problems, as opposed to whether or not there is a sports team, is not likely.

One reason for the great suburban spread outward and the hollowing of the central core is the place competition that causes localities to sponsor leapfrog development, no matter how inefficient and costly to service. Place entrepreneurs with suburban investments in what will become auto malls, shopping centers, and high-tech installations gain zoning changes and utility hookups as needed. This then facilities in-fill of remaining parcels as the metropolis expands into the hinterland – exacerbating ecological damage and infrastructure costs, and further distancing inner-city from the edge of job creation. The spread to the suburbs means that the volume of urbanized land grows at a rate far greater than population increase because newly urbanized land is used less intensively than urban land overall. Thus, although Chicago's metropolitan population, for example, grew by only 4 percent between 1970 and 1990, land used for housing increased 46 percent and for commercial development by 74 percent.[15] Such numbers are cited by HUD policy makers[16] as the seeds of environmental problems (as well as social problems). But not much discussion takes places on the ecological consequences of leaving power at this local level, and indeed, this mode of urban expansion is

still supported by such federal measures as interstate highway funding, mortgage financing, and cheap gas policies.

## Partnerships: Games Cities Play

The old-style growth boosterism that built America and its cities has become more complex and professionalized. As part of their general competition for new business, city governments now formally create joint projects in which they put up cash or grant tax and other types of subsidy to private companies they want to attract. Under some conditions, like enterprise zones and other variants of the Clinton-type special zone designations, this also means regulatory relief, as for example from pollution regulations or certain safety standards. Controls for these types of programs have varied from state to state, and usually amount to very little in the sense that cities can designate even very wealthy neighborhoods and business districts, for example, as redevelopment zones eligible for special treatment. These partnerships altered the status quo in which business came of its own accord to one in which business will only come under inducement. The "partnership" is a change in that local government takes on greater liability than government ordinarily engages in (if the new hotel or shopping center goes under, the city takes part of the loss), and gains less in revenues than under the prior status quo (because of the up-front subsidies it grants). The justification is usually that there will be more tax revenues than if the project goes elsewhere, although those revenues will be less than if the project had come in the old-fashioned way. Whereas in the past city regimes may have been the indirect instruments of growth elites, the two realms have become officially conjoined as development syndicates. Because the city becomes as vulnerable as the private business to potential failure of the enterprise (now it loses not just tax revenue, but ability to pay back bonds and recoup its investment), it must pursue the growth and business agenda *as an institutional fact*.

HUD Secretary Cisneros was a partisan of partnership (as is his successor, Andrew Cuomo). Cisnero's own political success in San Antonio derives in part from successful promotion of high technology (biotechnology in particular) in the far north of the city — quite distant from his Hispanic political base. Cisneros also, most famously, carried forward the growth of the downtown. "Riverwalk" tourist constellation of hotels, shops, and restaurants. The pleasantness of such developments notwithstanding, their commercial success does not demonstrate even fiscal gains for their cities, much less net income gains for their needy residents. These projects are all products of the growth-machine system and its list of troubling characteristics:

- *The zero-sum game.* Local growth coalitions compete with one another but there is only so much development to go around. Competition distributes activity from one place to another; it does not add value to the country's output or jobs to its labor force. Conventions that take place in San Antonio do not take place in Chicago. Certainly at the national level, it makes little sense to foster redistribution of economic activity from one place to another. The possibility that the growth involved will come from affluent suburbs (rather than a competing central city or poor suburb) goes without empirical test. The hope that central city workers will gain the good jobs that growth may bring is also an open empirical proposition, which has, as I will show, much evidence against it.
- *The zero-zero game.* Especially if it is accomplished with subsidies, place competition simply lowers the benefit that the national public gains from economic ac-

tivity within the country's borders. Compared to an era when hotel developers paid full taxes in all the cities in which they built, the new system lowers the full tax take to the country as a whole. If firms move from one district to another as a result of a new and better deal, they may be leaving an infrastructure that will go disused to a new area in which new infrastructure has to be built. This is fiscal and ecological waste.
- *Winners can be the biggest losers.* Places that "win" may gain dubious victories. The costs of servicing new developments can be more than the promised bounty of the new projects, at times disastrously more. Other rewards may also not compensate for the subsidies and tax breaks bestowed, especially likely for towns and cities most disadvantaged in the first place because they will have to give the most to gain the least. Bidding wars have the potential of making the poor poorer.

## Research Results: Deals, Subsidies, and the Spoils of Growth

A substantial research base now explains the costs and benefits of specific projects as well as growth overall. In terms of using growth to solve local unemployment problems, as a first example, the thrust of research indicates that development schemes often yield no new jobs and that when new jobs do result, they are swamped by more migrants and cost so much in subsidies that it would be cheaper just to pay people to stay home. According to one series of studies, places with rapid growth (measured in a variety of ways) experience no lower rates of unemployment than places with less rapid development.[17] Some evidence suggests curvilinear effects, with both high rates of growth and absolute losses of population or economic activity as detrimental.

Scholars studying "dreams cases" of robust urban growth in individual cities come up with troubling results. There is the prominent case of Atlantic City, new Jersey – a scenario of vigorous redevelopment under the aegis of the gambling industry – but with the jobs captured by migrants and suburbanites, not the struggling residents in whose name the casino projects had been launched.[18] Some of the same dynamics were likely behind the failure of Baltimore to do much for its people despite a vast array of handsome public–private growth partnership in its inner core. Dubbed the "Cinderella City" for its tourist developments, high rise office complexes, and successful bids for ball team franchises, Baltimore did far worse than average even among other frost belt cities in terms of population losses and growth in poverty rates during its 1970s downtown boom years. Even in fiscal terms, accordingly to one estimate, the gain has been a loss: Downtown redevelopment expenses annually amount to $17 million more than the revenue the projects generate.[19]

Generally in terms of budgetary health, the data tend to be consistently negative:[20] Growth generates costs to a greater degree that it adds to the tax base, even when no public subsidies are involved. The *kind* of growth does matter in that rich people pay more taxes than the poor and some industries generate net benefits – especially if their workers can be caused to live (and draw on services) in a different jurisdiction. Local taxing powers also matter; California's laws make it virtually impossible to maintain positive revenue streams. Ambiguities and refinements aside, the research picture does not demonstrate growth to be a net economic benefit. This murkiness of growth benefits contrasts with its more clear-cut environmental and life-quality costs.

Several careful studies have compared places defined as having good business climates – low taxes, weaker environmental controls, fast growth rates, pro-business "receptivity" – based primarily on rankings from within the business world itself, such as those from *Inc.* magazine, Fantus, and Grant companies. The sociologist William Freudenburg's comparison of states' economic performance determined that, if anything, a good business climate predicted weaker economic growth in subsequent years (based on the three major rankings).[21] Another study, by the economist Charles Skoro, using a slightly different methodology, came up with the similar conclusion that business climate indicators "are useless as predictors . . . [and] worse than useless as guides to state and local government action."[22] Still another scholar, MIT political scientist Stephen Meyer, remarks after presenting his comparable data analysis on the effects of state differences in environmental protection: "we can conclude that shifts in environmental policy, whether intended to extend environmental control or reduce it, have no discernible effect on state economic performance."[23]

Economists have tried to determine impacts on manufacturing and trade caused by social regulations and environmental restrictions among countries – e.g. whether or not industries, especially polluting ones, escape to "pollution havens." The repeated findings is that the costs of complying with environmental controls are simply not sufficiently consequential to impact on corporations' locational behavior.[24] Costs for things like labor and raw materials swamp environmental considerations, which means, according to still additional studies, that firms' location decisions likely have little to do with levels of environmental controls.[25] As economists Cropper and Oates summarize the policy implications: "there is little force to the arguments that we need to relax environmental policies to preserve international competitiveness."[26]

Some studies use corporate officials' own survey responses to specify whether or not pollution abatements, regulatory relief, and other forms of assistance make a difference in their location decisions. Developers are the most vociferous in telling researchers "horror stories" of what they had to pay to satisfy local authorities.[27] Surveys of other types of corporate executives (e.g. manufacturers, service businesses) tell a more ambiguous tale, quite significant given the ongoing ideological commitment of the business community to weak regulation and a fondness for special measures to attract them. Eisinger summarizes the literature regarding tax and financial incentives – often thought to be the most powerful form of inducement – by saying there is "little warrant in these various studies to argue that [these incentives] play a role of much, if any, significance in plant-location decisions," although "some evidence" does suggest that a favorable overall tax structure on business may have some effect.[28]

Other studies using towns as the units of analysis (instead of states) indicate the local governments' efforts to attract projects are usually ineffective.[29] The plants they get would have come anyway, or localities spend money and effort to gain projects for which they were never really in the running. Case studies of particular "winning" projects, like the city of Detroit's $250 million subsidy of General Motors' "Poletown" factory, and Flint, Michigan's, public – private investments in convention and amusement facilities (its "Auto World" project), show very unhappy financial results for their respective cities.[30] The Flint attraction had to close down for lack of customers; the Poletown subsidies for each created job were astronomical and did nothing to prevent GM from moving its far more significant headquarters functions out of central-city Detroit and into suburban Macomb County and Manhattan.[31] As the examples imply, the larger research findings are that disadvantaged cities must invest more, with less hope of success, and with greater cost and risk when "success" manages to come.[32]

Enterprise zones, with their tax abatements, public subsidies of new hires, and relief from regulation, in effect, focus the attributes of a so-called good business climate on a delimited needy area of cites; this should provide another test of how well growth schemes work. The research indicates the enterprise zones create only trivial numbers of jobs, with few being taken up by local residents.[33] Under one version, any resident of the designated area who worked for a firm in the same area would count in a firm's list of "new jobs"; consultants sometimes went through company payrolls to gain subsidies on the basis of people hired in ignorance of the program by companies that never had plans to move. These programs can cost government quite a lot; in one current variant, employers are given up to $3,000 annually per employee, as well as tax credits for their property investments and access to tax-exempt facility bond financing.

Enterprise zone programs may merely "cream" the inner-city investment potential ("bringing in" firms that would have come anyway). In other cases, the enterprise zone causes a relocation, perhaps from just outside, that then adds to the depression in the sending area while beefing up the enterprise zone statistics. Some so-called successes are so marginal they are likely to collapse once subsidies fall away (sometimes there is a patchwork of subsidies that draw on governments as well as on foundations and non-profits). Even so, it needs to be reiterated, the numbers of new dollars and jobs are small no matter how projects are evaluated; very little has been accomplished.[34]

The Clinton HUD version does contain elements aimed at warding off some mistakes of the past. For example, for an area to qualify for zone status, it must meet criteria as being truly depressed; various community stakeholders, including churches, neighborhood leaders, and the non-profit sector, have to be "at the table" in the planning process. There can be no obvious signs of "piracy" in which one locality gains at the expense of another. But the history of private–public partnerships is replete with "indigenous" neighborhood people in visible roles, selected because they do not make demands inconsistent with business needs. Sometimes they have been mere window dressing on enterprise as usual. Similarly, it is virtually impossible to know of, much less preclude, the use of public funds to pirate enterprise from other areas or subsidize business that would be coming anyway.

City mayors making their reputations through alliances with business are especially benefited by edifices downtown, shining and concrete signs of urban success, even as the central-city periphery deteriorates more rapidly than the heralded rejuvenation at the center takes place (which has been the experience of most cities that have gone the redevelopment route). But the mayor has "done something" to get the city moving, a fact duly celebrated by media and business notables. Bonds grow between Democrat mayors, the local business establishment, and national politicians, like Clinton, who also gain a feather in their cap for HUD's own participation. Whereas in the past the big-city political machines, particularly the ethnic-based ones, merely worked with local business elites in what at times was fragile or even conflictful relationship, now local governments, even those controlled by minorities, are tied directly into the growth-machine apparatus. The harder they work, especially if it is "all together," the worse it becomes.

## Schizoid Urbanism

One of the sources of the predicament is that it is so difficult in the US to speak openly about systematic ways to helping people. Using the term "communist" (even "socialist") could cost you your job if not your life; the very word "collective" is anathema. The polls must have told the Republicans that even "liberal" was a pejorative that could safely be used as scarlet stigma. Hence the retreat to terms like "progressive" or, most relevant here, the "city", "central city," or "urban." These geographical terms are euphemisms for the most important domestic issue in any society: inequality and suffering; but they are so inexact that they allow aid and effort to widely miss their mark. Programs oriented toward "the city" can be massively inefficient in actually helping the poor, since some poor (at least a few) are rural and because some rich (more than a few) are in the city. The geographic zone designation also means that help can be directed to all sorts of things that come within city borders, like fuel for the growth infrastructures that make so little sense. The word "urban" implies housing (but for which class?), economic infrastructure (but for whose benefit?), transport (of what sort?), and communications (for whose access?). There is thus much room for directing resources to the "urban" with little positive impact on people's lives.

While many liberals (or whatever you want to call them) may be pushing for more "urban," other governments agencies can be far more crucial for their goals. Commerce influences trade policies, which, in turn, distribute jobs both geographically and across the class structure, and the Federal Reserve (FED) and Treasury Departments arguably fix the unemployment rate in a very precise way. Defense lays down criteria for military careers and deploys contracts and job-rich installations. Even "out-of-the-way" departments like Energy and Interior impact pollution standards and fuel costs that determine access to transportation and healthful environments – especially important for the urban poor, who most depend on public transit and deal with noxious effluents and land uses.[35]

Of all the devolution schemes, the most radical and most consequential for city dwellers and the texture of urban life is the 1996 welfare bill, which comes under Health, Education, and Welfare (HEW) rather than HUD.

Beyond cutbacks and access elimination for legal immigrants, the president's acquiescence to block grants breaks new ground. While previous block grant programs gave the states money for bricks, mortar, and payrolls (also a part of Clinton programs), welfare was left under federal control. The Clinton precedent raises the scourge of the magnet effect as places decide, in the context of the ongoing growth competitions, how *in detail* they will spend their welfare allocation. Some states – Maryland was already in motion within weeks of the bill's signing – will likely further devolve block grants to their counties where the magnet effect will be even more of a factor in ideological play ("Wouldn't *you* take a short bus ride," critics will argue, "to get a higher benefit? a free lunch? a bench to sit on?").

Devolution, whether in welfare or more specifically urban programs (like vouchers), means also a devolution in corruption opportunities, record keeping, and evaluation studies. The federal government has had more sophisticated methods for understanding how caseloads rise and fall with changes in the economy and the differential impacts of changes in benefits on groups (by income, location, gender, age, and race), and for assessing the value of interventions (although years of GOP rule and cutbacks have hurt federal capacities as well). States and localities will be weaker in all these regards, making it hard for expenditures to be well spent even if the will should be there.[36]

With only weak federal standards and performance measures, local governments will finagle what counts as welfare. What is a better way to get people off welfare: give them money for food or have another insipid anti-drug program? Who will the deserving poor be: pregnant women or those demonstrating chastity? Which geographic zones will receive the most real money: central cities or affluent suburbs that, after all, have their problems too? It will make sense, in growth-machine logic, to bend "welfare" in the direction of economic development, under the premise that a vibrant local economy is the best welfare program of all. Indeed, President Clinton, in an election year speech to the country's governors, advised them to use their block grants to take money from food stamps for able-bodied men and direct it to employers for hiring welfare recipients in new jobs. He told the governors that this sort of job subsidy program "should be the center" of every state's use of its block grant.[37]

Once the money is out into the states and localities, it will be hard for federal authorities to force adherence to whatever guidelines are still left or which later may come to "fix" the problems. State and local governments will attack federal efforts as more big government interference, taking advantage of the very rhetoric that Clinton's people have joined in sustaining. If a conservative Republican should win the White House, there will not even be the motivation to force compliance with original guidelines. This is what occurred when Nixon followed Johnson and Reagan followed Carter, both eliminating the targeting of block grants to cities with the most pressing needs to the advantage of affluent towns and suburbs which were cut in on the federal largess.[38]

Compared to other welfare cutbacks which decrease benefit amounts or tighten eligibility rules, welfare block grants create an institutional change that will be difficult to reverse. Many local officials will howl, some just on the grounds of jurisdictional autonomy, if the national government tries to renege. Some states are entertaining proposals to turn the welfare function over to commercial operators who will design and administer the programs on a for-profit basis. This will then replicate the American system of medical care, which will create a permanent lobby of private corporations that will be there as a further block against going back to a "single-payer" system. As perhaps a worst-case scenario, block grants could be eliminated altogether with no substitute allocation of funding at either the federal or the state level. Granted for vaguely unpleasant purposes anyway, these would not be cuts in particular programs. It is not like saying there will be cutbacks in "Head Start" or "Medicare" or "the environment" – just elimination of what will be for most people a tedious bureaucratic abstraction.

Again we have precedent: the deinstitutionalization of the mentally ill – another non-urban program with intense urban consequences. The US ended mental health care as we knew it, but the community-based care systems that were supposed to fill the void never materialized. We now have a small army of mentally ill people wondering the city streets and costing quite a bit in emergency medical care and police attention. The 1996 welfare cutbacks will cast out still more desperate bodies to fend for themselves and, especially as the follow-through state cutbacks develop, yield still more expensive and humanly destructive outcomes of crime, drug use, disease, and violence. While permission to do this comes from Washington, localities will have to respond with some mix of cruelty and expenditure because the localities are where the bodies will be. This too is devolution.

## Going Up

Two idiosyncrasies of US governance – weak commitment to welfare and dispersion of responsibility for it – are related in that decentralization not only generates uneven social and environmental provision across places but also encourages each place to hold down benefits lest it scare off business investment. Stated nowhere as a goal by HUD or any other government agency, this in fact has long been the basis of the country's urban system and the heart of its urban policy – a dual competition among places to attract business

and constrain benefits. It follows that a fundamental policy goal must be to combat the growth-machine system as a mechanism for allocating people and resources across settlements. A progressive program would remove the nexus between the local tax take and development, as well as the nexus between the local tax take and the amount available for local welfare expenditures. A national takeover of welfare, health, and education costs – as is common in Europe – would be a significant step toward undermining the growth-machine apparatus.

Short of such a major transformation in government organization, there are more modest tactics. One is to end state and local governments' capacity to spend tax money to compete with one another for development. If it would be politically better to argue on legal principles, the lawyers might say that use of local government authority to lure business from other localities is an "interference" in interstate commerce. It certainly interferes in the market; on the occasions when incentives do work, as when investments are moved across adjacent jurisdictions – the most likely scenario – it means government has been used to locate facilities away from places where efficiency and traditional location determinants (proximity to markets, etc.) would otherwise cause them to be. The US may need a constitutional amendment to provide a more perfect federalism (and market) by banning such maneuvers.

More modestly still, the federal government should stop the common practice of using tax-exempt government bonds to subsidize private development – a major cost for the federal treasury. The national government should similarly prevent tax-increment financing as a means of redevelopment, at minimum restricting it only to depressed communities – a point also made by Henry Cisneros. Indeed, if there are to be government–business "partnerships" of any sort, the logic has to be reversed. As with any deal making, the first step for a good bargainer is to enter under advantaged conditions – it must at least be made to appear that they need you more than you need them. And that means, at times, holding out and even letting deals go by – all of them, if they are bad deals. In the urban context, this means government entering development negotiations under the supposition that it controls a rare resource – access to land and infrastructure – that business needs. Localities rather than business play coy and wait for business to offer the kind of package that will deliver the largest public benefit given the access being requested. The partnership makes the business responsible for more, rather than less, than it otherwise would have to provide. In a context of shrinking government largesse at state and federal levels and tax ceilings in some states, this means government must gain, at minimum, the full long-term external net costs of business's presence. Projects must be hit when they "open" for their full stream of net costs – fiscal, social, and environmental – over their entire life.

One route for localities to understand these true costs is the environmental review process, which, if properly expanded in both frequency and analytic depth, could yield a qualitative shift in public knowledge and the political environment. At present, the review procedures initiated by the 1970 federal environmental quality act are applied unevenly across places, even among jurisdictions which share the same labor and housing markets and bioregion. Some jurisdictions – the Boulders and Palo Altos – demand high-quality analyses that do not assume, as many such reports naïvely do, that virtually any hiring of workers means a drop in local unemployment. Similarly, some local governments take it upon themselves to publicize findings of environmental reviews, while others put the reports on shelves to gather dust. Better environmental reviews would enhance any efforts at moderating the growth-machine dynamic by inform-

ing local citizens of development consequences, such that linkages could be increased and projects could internalize their liabilities.

Some localities have embraced at least the principle that, in effect, developers are partners in providing for the public good and hence must bear the external liabilities of their projects. These cities, operating with little help from the Clintonites, point toward the solutions the feds should take seriously. Usually involving amalgams of environmental and social justice activists, they have been sufficiently strong at the polls (and in raising campaign funds) to give growth coalitions a run for their money. The Santa Monica case is one well-told instance,[39] but there are parallel stories from other US cities – most of them small-scale, often with universities – Boulder, Palo, Alto, Eugene, Ann Arbor, Santa Barbara, and Santa Fe among them. Oppositional groups have also had policy consequence in some big cities, San Francisco and Boston being the two prime examples.[40] Such places are advantaged in that they have high amenities for residence and are rich in the kind of cultural and human capital that high-technology, finance, and information firms especially desire. During the heyday of Boston's downtown office building boom, when nearly $1 billion per year was being invested in downtown structures, the city leveraged about $50 million for affordable housing and job training – a modest total, but undertaken at a time when other cities, like New York, were in effect *paying* developers to make their investments.[41]

Some towns and cities have used growth control, in particular, to generate economic and social benefits. By limiting the *amount* of growth, governments can grant exceptions (innumerable if desired) for projects that most enhance environmental and social goals. In regard to affordable housing, for example, the so-called "no-growth" cities have (at least in California) led the way compared to nongrowth control places in using government to leverage below-market housing.[42] Santa Monica used linkage to support homeless services (quite controversially, even there) as well as, and here the case is more common across the country, backing for the arts. Very often, linkages involve provision of recreational facilities, restoration of natural habitats, or open-space set-asides for aesthetic or ecological values. It is a mistake to minimize the significance of these linkages on the grounds that these are privileged places with special bargaining resources. The bargains they strike set the outer limit of standards. The higher those standards and the more projects they turn down, the stronger the negotiating position of places lower in the hierarchy.[43]

For all jurisdictions, reform in campaign contribution laws would be enormously useful. Other aspects of this complex issue aside, special rules on development and real estate could be demarcated. If elected officials were banned from voting on development projects in which their own campaign contributors had an interest, a hole would be blown in the current apparatus (Boston's Mayor Flynn refused to take contributions from developers with projects pending before city agencies).[44] The president and his party could speak out and help finance crusades to bring about the reform – hardly one that voters would find repulsive (although some of his contributors might).

Pushing the joys of big government was perhaps just not in the cards during the first Clinton term. But the Clinton government sometimes went overboard in stressing the glories of the local and not even bringing up the liabilities. Other than being maneuvered into the true innovation of welfare block grants, the Clinton White House has simply not moved the country's urban policies beyond the nostrums of prior years. Even during its first two years of mounting large-scale and controversial initiatives (health care, gay

rights), the administration was silent on the need to reform the place-competition system. The Clintonites exacerbated places' competition to do themselves in – the race to the bottom.[45] Most dangerously, the discourse has been to pose the country's overall economic well-being as the sum of the growth of its parts – hence falling into the growth-machine moloch.[46] Absorbed with "globalism" as an inexorable force that makes even a country like the US little more autonomous than a Kentucky hamlet trying to lure an automobile plant, the policy prescription has been to grow the localities as a component of growing the USA, the reasoning so falsely goes. The Clinton people have fed the development mongers, passing along the "grow" verb as something every patriot can get behind, regardless of the geographic level, the substantive ends, or the nonsense that ensues. The president's talky-talk may well last in the public memory and thwart future progressive action.

The policies over the first term weakened the national government's capacity to act competently, not just because of the Republicans' assaults, but also by acquiescing to devolution. In an era when the relevance of government institutions is being questioned in both political talk and sophisticated intellectual discourse, it is important to assert that not only is the state worth bringing in, but the precise institutional locus of authority is also important. That is why it has, historically, been a site of intense conflict. Whether naively or through the realpolitik at which the group is so adept, the Clinton people appear to not see the issue very clearly. It has been painful to watch the Clinton watch. Its operatives – honorable women and men many – have fed a self-sustaining mechanism that increases inequality, stigmatizes the dispossessed, and destroys much of what is left of American nature.

## Notes

1  Henry Cisneros, "Urban Entrepreneurialism and National Economic Growth," US Department of Housing and Urban Development (Washington, DC, September, 1995), p. 6 of my printout from the HUD Website.

2  US Department of Housing and Urban Development, Office of Policy Development and Research, "Empowerment: A New Covenant with America's Communities: President Clinton's National Urban Policy Report," (July, 1995), p. 58; see also p. 64.

3  HUD, "Empowerment," p. 64; see also Cisneros, "Urban Entrepreneurialism," p. 2 of my printout from HUD Website.

4  Cisneros, "Urban Entrepreneurialism," p. 10 of my printout from HUD Website.

5  Personal conversation with HUD official.

6  See John L. McKnight and John P. Kretzmann, "Building Communities from the Inside Out: A Path Toward Finding and Mobilizing Community Assets," (Evanston IL: Center for Urban Affairs and Policy Research, Northwestern University, 1993).

7  Vouchers cost less per unit per move-in because the government is, in effect, only paying the difference between the market rate and the amount a poor family can pay. But because the units never become government property (or that of the tenant), the payment must continue infinitely. This also threatens housing stability for families; if the programs are cut back they could be out. Another worry with vouchers is that they may, especially in the tight housing markets where housing assistance is most needed, merely push up the costs of local housing markets, given the influx of dollars chasing a relatively inelastic supply of units.

8  Keeping them out of some neighborhoods means, of course, concentrating them in others – a less talked about feature.

9  This argument has been worked out in many dozens of theoretical statements and empirical studies. For examples, see Harvey Molotch, "The City as a Growth Machine," *American Journal of Sociology* 82(2) (1976); John Mollenkopf, *The Contested City* (Princeton, NJ: Princeton University Press, 1983); John Logan and Harvey Molotch, *Urban Fortunes* (Berkeley

CA: University of California Press, 1987); G. William Domhoff, *Who Rules America Now?* (Englewood Cliffs, NJ: Prentice-Hall, 1983); Todd Swanstrom, *The Crisis of Growth Politics: Cleveland, Kucinich, and the Challenge of Urban Populism* (Philadelphia: Temple University Press, 1985); Clarence N. Stone, *Regime Politics: Governing Atlanta, 1946–88* (Lawrence, KA: University Press of Kansas, 1989; Ronald K. Vogel and Bert E. Swanson, "The Growth Machine Versus the Antigrowth Coalition: The Battle for Our Communities," *Urban Affairs Quarterly* 25 (1) (1989), pp. 63–85. See also the collection of critical essays in Andrew Jonas and David Wilson, eds, *The Urban Growth Machine: Critical Perspectives Twenty Years Later* (Albany, NY: State University of New York Press, forthcoming).

10  Harry N. Scheiber, "Urban Rivalry and Internal Improvements in the Old Northwest, 1820–60," in Alexander Callow Jr, ed., *American Urban History*, 2nd edn. (New York: Oxford University Press, 1973), pp. 135–46.

11  The evidence is a positive correlation between economically strong central cities and economically strong metropolitan areas. This correlation may be an artifact of regional effects; central cities and their suburbs alike prosper in the same region, not because of interaction between them but because of factors affecting both. For the positive argument, but not the critique, see Michael Stegman and Margery Turner, "The Future of Urban America in the Global Economy," *Journal of the American Planning Association* 62 (2) (1996), pp. 157–62; Larry Ledebur and William R. Barnes, *"Toward a New Political Economy of Metropolitan Regions"* (Washington DC: National League of Cities, 1993); H. V. Savitch, David Collins, Daniel Sanders, and John P. Markham, "Ties that Bind: Central Cities, Suburbs, and the New Metropolitan Region," *Economic Development Quarterly* (November, 1993), pp. 341–58.

12  Allen D. Wallis, "The Third Wave: Current Trends in Regional Governance," *National Civic Review* (Summer–Fall, 1994).

13  Scott Greer, *Urban Renewal and American Cities* (Indianapolis: Bobbs-Merrill, 1965).

14 Christopher Jencks, *The Homeless* (Cambridge MA: Harvard University Press, 1994).

15 "Cities: Onwards and Outwards," *The Economist* (October 15, 1994), as cited in HUD, "Empowerment," p. 11.

16 HUD, "Empowerment," p. 11 of my printout from HUD Website.

17 Richard Appelbaum, *Size, Growth, and US Cities* (New York: Praeger, 1978); see also George Sternlieb and James W. Hughes, *The Atlantic City Gamble* (Cambridge MA: Harvard University Press, 1983); David Fasenfest, "Cui Bono?" in Charles Craypo and Bruce Nissen, eds, *Grand Design: The Impacts of Corporate Strategies on Workers, Unions, and Communities*, (Ithaca NY: ILR Press, 1993); David Fasenfest, "Community Politics and Urban Redevelopment: Poletown, Detroit, and General Motors," *Urban Affairs Quarterly* 22(1) (September, 1986), pp. 101–23. For a different conclusion, see Thomas Muller, *Growing and Declining Urban Areas: A Fiscal Comparison* (Washington DC: Urban Institute, 1975).

18 Sternlieb and Hughes, *The Atlantic City Gamble*; Elizabeth A. Williams, "The plan to Save Atlantic City: Consequences of Community Disarticulation on Central City Revitalization," paper presented at annual meeting of the American Sociological Association, Washington DC (August 19–23, 1995).

19 For the Baltimore story, see Marc V. Levine, "Downtown Development as an Urban Growth Strategy," *Journal of Urban Affairs* 9 (2) (1987), pp. 18–37; Bernard L. Berkowitz, "Rejoinder to Downtown Development as an Urban Growth Strategy: A Critical Appraisal of the Baltimore Renaissance," *Journal of Urban Affairs* 9 (2) (1987), pp. 38–43 Marc V. Levine, "Response to Berkowitz," *Journal of Urban Affairs* 9 (2), (1987), pp. 44–7. For an excellent summary of this and other cases, see Dennis R. Judd and Todd Swanstrom, *City Politics: Private Power and Public Policy* (New York: Harper Collins, 1994), pp. 346–50.

20 Appelbaum, *Size, Growth, and US Cities*; Michael Danielson and James Doig, *New York: The Politics of Urban Regional Development* (Berkeley CA: University of California Press, 1982), p. 44; Peter K. Eisinger, *The Rise of the Entrepreneurial State* (Madison: University of Wisconsin Press, 1988).

21 William Freudenburg, "A 'Good Business Climate' as Bad Economic News," *Society and Natural Resources* 3 (1993), pp. 313–30.

22 Charles L. Skoro, "Rankings of State Business Climates: An Evaluation of their Usefulness in Forecasting," *Economic Development Quarterly* 2(2) (1988), pp. 138–52; quoted from p. 151.

23 Stephen M. Meyer, *Environmentalism and Economic Prosperity* (Cambridge MA: MIT Press, forthcoming), p. 10.

24 H. Jeffrey Leonard, *Pollution and the Struggle for the World Product* (Cambridge: Cambridge University Press, 1988); James A. Tobey, "The Impact of Domestic Environmental Policies on International Trade," PhD dissertation, Department of Economics, University of Maryland, College Park (1989); James A. Tobey, "The Effects of Domestic Environmental Policies on Patterns of World Trade: An Empirical Test," *Kyklos* (2) (1990), cited in Maureen L. Cropper and Wallace E. Oates, "Environmental Economics: A Survey," *Journal of Economic Literature*, (June, 1992), pp. 675–740.

25 Virginia D. McConnell and Robert M. Schwab, "The Impact of Environmental Regulation in Industry Location Decisions: The Motor Vehicle Industry," *Land Economics* 66 (February, 1990), pp. 67–81; Timothy Bartik, "The Effects of Environmental Regulation on Business Location in the United States," *Growth and Change* 19 (3) (Summer 1988), pp. 22–44.

26 Cropper and Oates, "Environmental Economics: A Survey," p. 699.

27 Examples include Bernard Frieden, *The Environmental Protection Huslte* Cambridge, MA: MIT, 1980); Sidney Plotkin, *Keep Out: The Struggle for Land Use Control* (Berkeley CA: University of California Press, 1987).

28 Eisinger, *Rise of the Entrepreneurial State*, p. 220.

29 Craig R. Humphrey and Richard Krannich, "The Promotion of Growth in Small Urban Places and its Impact on Population Change, 1975–78," *Social Science Quarterly* 61 (3/4) (1980), pp. 581–94; Gene F. Summers, "Small Towns Beware: Industry Can Be Costly," *Planning* 42 (May, 1976), pp. 20–1.

30 Fasenfest, "Community Politics and Urban Redevelopment".

31 For a series of cases, see George D. Squires, ed., *Unequal Partnerships: The Political Economy of Urban Redevelopment in Postwar America* (New Brunswick NJ: Rutgers University Press, 1989).

32 I. S. Rubin and H. J. Rubin, "Economic Development Incentives – the Poor (Cities) Pay More," *Urban Affairs Quarterly* 23 (1) (1987), pp. 37–62; Helga Leitner and Eric Sheppard, "Transcending Urban Individualism: Conceptual Issues, and Policy Alternatives in the European Union," in Jonas and Wilson, *Urban Growth Machine*.

33 Virginia Battle and Jack Underhill, "Coming to Grips with the US Enterprise Zone Experiment: A Summary of Ten Case Studies," *Enterprise Zone Notes*, US Department of Housing and Urban Development (Fall, 1986), pp. 11–14; Eisinger, *Rise of the Entrepreneurial State*, pp. 194–9; David E. Dowall, Marc Beyeler, and Chun-Cheung Sidney Wong, "Evaluation of California's Enterprise Zone and Employment and Economic Incentive Programs," Berkeley, California Policy Seminar, University of California (1994). For other reviews of enterprise zone experience, see Robert Guskind, "Enterprise Zones: Do They Work?" *Journal of Housing* 47 (January–February, 1990); Rochelle Stanfield, "Battle Zones," *National Journal* 24 (1992), pp. 1348–52; Jill Zuckman, "All About Enterprise Zones," *American Caucus* (August 31–September 13, 1992), p. 1.

34 Parallel to the lack of impact of government efforts aimed at growing the local economy, there is a good basis in the literature for suggesting that efforts to limit growth, in either economic or residential terms, also have little by way of measurable effects. See John Logan and Min Zhou, "The Adoption of Growth Controls in Suburban Communities," *Social Science Quarterly* 71 (1) (1990), pp. 118–29. See also: John Landis, *Do Growth Controls Work?: An Evaluation of Local Growth Control Programs in Seven California Cities*, Berkeley, California Policy Seminar, University of California (1992); Kee Warner and Harvey Molotch, "Growth Control: Inner Workings and External Effects," Berkeley, California Policy Seminar, University of California (1992).

35 That the poor, particularly the African American urban poor, bear the brunt of noxious land uses is documented in Robert Bullard, *Dumping in Dixie: Race, Class, and Environmental Quality* (Boulder: Westview Press, 1990), and in Robert D. Bullard, ed., *Unequal Protection: Environmental Justice and Communities of Color* (San Francisco: Sierra Club Books, 1994).

36 I am grateful to Chester Hartman for making this point to me in conversation (October 14, 1996).

37 I watched his speech, complete, on CSPAN. (C. Thursday, September 12, 1996). Under the Clinton program the same jobs can be subsidized for as long as 10 years even if the first person employed leaves the post – just so long as new workers are taken off welfare.

38 Marshall Kaplan, "Urban Policy: An Uneven Past, An Uncertain Future," *Urban Affairs Review* 30 (5) (May, 1995), pp. 662–80.

39 Derek Shearer, "How the Progressives Won in Santa Monica," *Social Policy* 12 (3) (Winter, 1982), pp. 7–14; Pierre Clavel, *The Progressive City* (New Brunswick NJ: Rutgers University Press, 1986); Stella Capek and John I. Gilderbloom, *Community Versus Commodity: Tenants and the American City* (Albany NY: State University of New York Press, 1992).

40 R. E. DeLeon, *Left Coast City: Progressive Politics in San Francisco, 1975–91* (Lawrence KA: University Press of Kansas, 1992); Peter Dreier, "Ray Flynn's Legacy: American Cities and the Progressive Agenda," *National Civic Review* (Fall, 1993), pp. 380–403.

41 "Raymond L. Flynn, "America's Cities: Centers of Culture, Commerce, and Community – or Collapsing Hope?" *Urban Affairs Review* 30 (5) (May, 1995), pp. 365–640.

42 Madelyn Glickfeld and Ned Levine, *The New Land Use Regulation Revolution: Why California's Local Jurisdictions Enact Growth Control and Management Measures* (Los Angeles: University of California at Los Angeles, 1990).

43 See e.g. Helga Leitner, "Cities in Pursuit of Economic Growth: The Local State as Entrepreneur," *Political Geography Quarterly* 9 (2) (1990), pp. 146–170.

44 Peter Dreier, "Ray Flynn's Legacy: American Cities and the Progressive Agenda," *National Civic Review* (Fall, 1993), pp. 380–403.

45 See Brecher and Costello in Jeremy Brecher

and Tim Costello, *Global Village or Global Pillage: Economic Reconstruction from the Bottom Up* (Boston: South End Press, 1994). See also Molotch, "The City as a Growth Machine"; John Cumberland, "Efficiency and Equity in Interregional Environmental Management," *Review of Regional Studies* 10 (2) (Fall, 1981), pp. 1–9.

46 For Cisneros's discussion of this point, see his "Urban Entrepreneurialism."

# 4

# Rhetoric, Recision, and Reaction

## The Development of Homelessness Policy

 *Cynthia J. Bogard*
*and J. Jeff McConnell*

## Introduction

When a "new" American homelessness came to public attention in the early 1980s experts and the public alike seemed surprised. Fifteen years later, it has become clear that the political response to homelessness itself contained political surprises, surprises we consider here.[1] Perhaps the most notable of these surprises occurred during the Reagan and then Bush administrations, when a new social program to care for the homeless with almost a billion federal dollars attached was implemented across the nation in the form of the Stewart B. McKinney Homeless Assistance Act of 1987. This appeared to be an unprecedented incident in the Reagan/Bush era's generally successful commitment to rolling back public spending on poverty programs. And another almost as notable surprise came when the program was adopted with almost no modification under the Clinton Administration. Though Democrats have a long historical record of developing new poverty programs, the homelessness policy Clinton inherited from his predecessors appeared to be a conservative response to homelessness.

From 1991 to 1995 we directed the federally mandated outcome evaluation of New York State's AFDC Transitional Housing Demonstration Project (consisting of two homeless family shelters) located in Westchester County, an area of New York State directly north of New York City. The evaluation consisted of a three-wave, three-year longitudinal study of 340 families. Virtually all families becoming homeless in the county in 1992 were tracked through their stays in shelters and, in most cases, back into permanent housing. As program evaluators of this national model for addressing family homelessness, we became integrated into the county, state and – to some extent – the federal, political milieux where family homeless policy was produced both before and after Clinton's election. Our collaboration with implementation evaluators additionally gave us access to the political history of the model programs dating to the mid-1980s.[2] As these programs developed in New York State they involved political figures of considerable influence who would define family homeless policy for the nation: New York Senator Daniel Patrick Moynihan, long a powerful and controversial figure in Democratic poverty politics; New York State Governor Mario Cuomo and his son Andrew, an up and coming political figure in his own right; and Republican Westchester County Executive Andrew O'Rourke, who had once run against the elder Cuomo for the governor's office. At the core of this chapter, then, is a case study of homeless family policy in Westchester County and of the country's model homeless family shelter, which opened in 1991. The analysis extends to the political context in which the model program developed under the Reagan administration, as well as the process of its institutionalization that ensured its continuation under the Clinton Administration.

We have found the language of constraint and discretion, as developed by Beth Mintz and Michael Schwartz in *The Power Structure of American Business*, useful in understanding the interplay of political limitations and opportunities that generated and then perpetuated homelessness policy. Although originally developed to understand American business structure, the model devised by Mintz and Schwartz is ideally suited to unraveling the political dynamics of the homelessness process as it developed in the 1980s and continued through the Clinton years.[3]

We begin by examining the constellation of factors that constituted both the sources of constraint and those of discretion in the process of developing homeless family policy at the national level. First, we examine the political context in which homelessness emerged. Though family homelessness demanded government intervention, the conservative agenda of the 1980s severely limited possibilities for policy formation on an issue which would necessarily be tied to social welfare spending. We then look at how the conservative fiscal policy agenda of the time, and the concomitant political rhetoric, presented themselves as an opportunity for the Democrats to forge a new national policy based on a resource acquisition strategy. We pursue these themes in our case study of Westchester County by delineating how, at the local level, the constraints of a conservative politics were answered with a bipartisan project that accessed resources to build a new homeless family shel-

ter bureaucracy. Political necessity mandated that the new shelter programs incorporate an agenda for homeless families that fit conservative rhetoric surrounding the poor. This bipartisan effort transformed homeless family policy in the country and linked Democrats and Republicans in a joint effort that permeated federal, state, county, and municipal governments. Finally, we find that, faced with an institutionalized homeless family policy that had been engineered largely by Democrats under the constraints of conservative administrations, Clinton was obliged to persist with this quasi-conservative agenda.

## Sources of Constraint: The Political Context

By the end of the 1980s, media-driven middle-class compassion for homeless children had created a new category of the "worthy poor" that would help to legitimate continued public spending for homeless families. Public sentiment by itself, however, is an insufficient explanation for the creation of a new welfare industry in the mid-1980s aimed specifically at homeless families. Instead, the politically untenable specter of children and their families living in the streets combined with the financially expensive alternative proposition of housing homeless families on an ad hoc basis in welfare motels. Family homelessness was expensive, both politically and economically, for the Reagan Administration, and these factors combined to force the conservative Reagan Administration to act. In addition, policy to deal effectively with family homelessness could draw upon existing institutional mechanisms, particularly that of AFDC.

### Constraints and the new fiscal conservatism

A long-standing legal public commitment to caring for destitute children existed in the form of the joint federal and state-funded Aid to Families with Dependent Children (AFDC). Despite the declining value of AFDC assistance since the early 1970s and the resulting meager support it provided families, it had long been cast as an expensive and ineffectual program and was a political target of fiscal conservatism. The mid-1980s, however, gave rise to a new cause for alarm, when increasing numbers of poor families declared themselves homeless and were provided "temporary" emergency housing through departments of social services. The portion of the AFDC family grant allotted for housing could be inflated by almost ten times to cover emergency accommodations. In New York State, for example, about $4,500 was provided per year to an AFDC family of three to cover housing. When the same family became homeless, approximately $45,000 per year would be paid to house them in motels or hotels.[4] The expense of family homelessness, then, made it an issue ripe for major legislative attention despite Reagan's early resistance.[5]

Such was not the case for the vast majority of the homeless of the 1980s–single men. Single impoverished adults, sometimes women but mostly men, had never had a very significant hold on social welfare in the US. By the 1980s public assistance available to this population consisted of a patchwork of programs such as unemployment and disability insurance, veterans' benefits, Medicaid, general assistance, Supplemental Security Income (SSI) and Social Security Disability Income (SSDI), and food stamps. Eligibility requirements for these programs, which, ironically, often included having a permanent address, precluded many of the street-dwelling homeless and sheltered singles from successfully accessing public support. Put simply, unlike the situation for families with children, it did not cost the government much, either politically or financially, to have homeless singles living on the streets and so there was less need for or interest in a federally coordinated

policy to do anything about them.[6]

From the start, however, homeless policy development was constrained by Washington's determination not to initiate spending on public programs, by its refusal to build public service infrastructure, and by its insistence upon dismantling what structure existed. While Democrats may have been more prone to initiate progressive social spending historically, they were certainly constrained in the 1980s both by the essentially conservative political rhetoric of the time and by the very real electoral strength of the Republicans.

The resulting federal homelessness plan – the Stewart B. McKinney Act of 1987 – is a product of these political realities. In the McKinney Act, relatively little attention was given to the street-dwelling population. Rather, the act put in place a policy that would coordinate a national effort to rehouse homeless families, which at the time was a small (though growing) minority of the homeless, visible mostly to the welfare bureaucracy responsible for answering their requests for expensive emergency housing.[7]

Reflecting on the conservative interests behind the McKinney Act and the projects it sponsored, in 1991 a program supervisor from Health and Human Services (HHS) told us, "the Federal Government wants to get out of the homelessness business." The single demand HHS, still responsible to the Bush Administration at that time, had of the fledgling programs and their evaluators was a cost-benefit analysis showing that the federally sponsored homelessness policy that grew out of the McKinney Act reduced the cost of family homelessness compared with the welfare motel dumping policies then prevalent around the nation.

## Constraints and the new rhetoric about the poor

Accounting for poverty under the new conservatism of the 1980s saw the culture of poverty revisited once again in American political discourse. These ideas would be extended to the new homeless, but the divergent meanings they once had for conservative or liberal policies would be blurred as the two camps faced family homelessness together. As Michael Katz argues, the culture of poverty thesis was "amputated" from its intellectual and liberal origins almost upon its appearance on the horizon of American political discourse. But as he also notes, "[t]he idea of such a culture, however, did not disappear."[8]

Though the culture-of-poverty thesis showed itself equally adept at serving either liberal or conservative political perspectives, originally, common assumptions about the cultural basis of poverty were read by conservatives and liberals as indicating almost opposite agendas for policy. Generally, proponents of the thesis believed that the transmission of attitudes and behaviors from generation to generation accounted for the perpetuation of poverty.[9] For liberals, who tended to conceive of these behaviors as pathologies, this meant that the cycle of poverty could best be broken through social-work intervention, retraining, and therapy. Large-scale social programs and spending were called for. Conservatives have long been more likely to interpret the cultural dimensions of poverty as the result of moral failings on the part of the poor. They therefore viewed social spending as encouraging and supporting the essentially immoral behaviors and lifestyles that commit the poor to perpetuating their own poverty.[10]

Various elements of the culture-of-poverty argument persist as fundamental organizing ideas in American poverty politics today.[11] Despite significant research on the structural roots of homelessness, for example, major state and federal policy initiatives on the issue have all proceeded from the assumption of problematic characteristics or character on the part of its victims.[12] It is within the culture of poverty rhetoric, then, that 1980s homelessness policy was conceived, negotiated, and presented to the public.

The new wave of conservative rhetoric that swept into prominence with the Reagan Administration concentrated attention on three ideas about social life that had an influence on how homelessness was defined and how programs to treat it developed. First, old Democratic principles which spoke of individual rights in terms of economic and social justice and equality were replaced in the mainstream political discourse by a conservative rhetoric. This successful new rhetoric highlighted the right of the individual to pursue economic gain unencumbered by burdensome taxes and the regulations of what was characterized as a mostly unnecessary. "big government" headed up by a faceless horde of "Washington bureaucrats."[13] Although cuts to public spending on social programs were never as deep as the Reagan Administration promised or portrayed, and became even more muted during the Bush Administration, they were significant.[14] More importantly, downsizing government, especially federal government, became a popular slogan and political goal of the 1980s and continued under a different rhetorical scheme – "reinventing government" – under the Clinton Administration in the 1990s.

Second, to some degree, the history of anti-poverty programs in the US was reinterpreted. Large-scale programs for the poor begun in the 1930s and reorganized during the War on Poverty had drastically reduced poverty rates among the elderly, and had provided some measure of relief in the form of food stamps, housing, and cash assistance to impoverished families. These efforts had enjoyed varying degrees of public commitment – especially adamant in the 1960s – which was gradually overtaken, in the 1980s, by a pervasive clamoring for "individual responsibility" among the poor.[15] According to this 1980s reformulation, the non-elderly poor, through bad decision making, laziness, and personal defects brought on by moral lapses, were responsible for their own plight, and efforts to aid them through public funds only doomed them to a cycle of poverty and dependence. Democrats supplied their own version of the same logic albeit in the language of illness and therapy. Senator Daniel Patrick Moynihan, a sociologist by training and a Democratic politician by trade, had coined the phrase "tangle of pathology" in the 1960s to describe the lifestyles that kept the poor impoverished.[16] By the 1980s, receipt of welfare itself – increasingly referred to as "welfare dependency" – was considered by a growing number of liberals to be a part of the tangle of pathology that caused poverty's continuation. This conceptual shift proved a death knell to traditional liberal anti-poverty programs that would play itself out finally in the dismemberment of the federal AFDC program at the hands of the Democratic Clinton Administration in 1996.

The final element in conservative political discourse that was relevant to the development of programs for treating the homeless was the emphasis on the threat to "the family." New conservative rhetoric claimed that the nuclear family was becoming subverted by the decline of culture in general, which in turn was brought on by moral lapses among some individuals.[17] Impoverished mother-only minority families, headed by single women who were accused of refusing work and reproducing thoughtlessly, were often cited as the exemplars of this new cultural and moral decline.[18] Here again, Democratic political rhetoric has not been far from the conservative position. Moynihan's early work on *The Negro Family* in the 1960s, for example, and his continuing public commentary on the declining American family and the dangers of single-mother parenting, did not provide a substantially alternative cultural view. Additionally, throughout the 1980s, the politics of racial division constituted a crucial undercurrent that helped to sever traditional Demo-

cratic alliances.[19] The success of a politics centered on shoring up the declining American family came full circle during the 1996 presidential campaign when the Clinton Administration wholeheartedly adopted "family values" as a re-election theme.

The rhetoric of the 1980s, then, increasingly stressed that society should not have compassion for those who – according to conservatives – *would* not support themselves. The public institutions that served the poor were attacked while the same rhetoric encouraged compassion for taxpayers, whose burden of filling the public coffers was excessive, who all too often had to face bureaucrats employed to thwart their every efforts, and who were also made – against their will – to support lazy and sexually suspect single mothers who did not control their fertility and would not work for a living or get married. The racial overtones of this rhetoric were also readily apparent. Compassion for adults was reserved for those who (in President Clinton's version of this same argument) "worked hard and played by the rules." Though his own running commentary on the poor contributed to this shift, Senator Daniel Patrick Moynihan has called this recasting of the poor by conservatives – and the change in the perception of the poor that has seemingly resulted – "the great rhetorical inversion."[20]

Homelessness therefore emerged as a prominent social problem in the mid-1980s just as conservative and liberal cultural interpretations of poverty converged in a fashion that could support a bipartisan policy framework for addressing homelessness that focussed on individual failure as its cause and intervention – eliminating immoral behaviors and remedying personal pathologies – as its solution. A solution to the constraints on policy formation posed by conservative victim-blaming rhetoric presented itself to the largely Democratic homeless policy makers. But the task remained for policy makers to design an intervention that appeared to meet the demands of fiscal conservatism as well.[21]

## Sources of Discretion: Public Sympathy and a Dispersed Strategy for Acquiring Resources

Economic trends of the 1980s helped to ensure continued homelessness, but concomitant political trends precluded addressing this resurgent social problem through direct public spending. A progressive solution to the problem would have been a formidable task in any case. At the least it would have required the creation of affordable housing units, which had long been declining due to the process of urban and suburban housing-market restructuring.[22] But as the new conservative rhetoric explained, social ills just could not be solved by "throwing money at a problem."[23] This contention belied the outcomes of many past government programs, including social security, which successfully protects the elderly from poverty; the GI bill, which educated a nation of young men in the post-World War II era and enabled them to buy homes as well; and Medicaid, which, as it functioned in most states, enabled the very poor to have better health care than the ineligible working poor.[24] Nevertheless, unlike the political contexts that gave birth to either the New Deal or the War on Poverty. Reagan Administration priorities and the conservative milieux of the 1980s seemingly precluded the direct creation of a new government bureaucracy to deal with the problems of the now discredited poor.[25]

Homelessness, however, was a social problem ripe for just such government intervention. First, though public opinion had largely turned against sympathetic notions of the poor, homelessness proved an exception. In poll after poll, the public expressed sympathy for those who were disenfranchised from the American dream to the extent that they had to live in public doorways, on subway grates, and in train stations. Though the single women with their children who became homeless were, for the most part, the exact same unwed mothers who were scorned as lazy welfare cheats, once homeless, these same women proved an exception to the shift in compassion trends of the 1980s.[26] Reagan's claim that "people choose to be homeless" notwithstanding, people felt sorry for them and categorized them as victims.[27]

Perhaps because the homeless still evoked sympathy, and also because of the actions of advocates for the homeless such as Mitch Snyder, the press took an interest in reporting on the conditions the homeless were forced to endure. Between 1982 and 1992, the *New York Times* ran 2,303 articles about homelessness, many of them exposés revealing the deplorable conditions homeless families were subjected to once they were placed in welfare motels.[28]

Eventually, public pressure and hard-lobbying advocates for the homeless, mixed with an astute perception by liberal Democrats that homelessness was one of few opportune issues for expanding public resources for the poor, converged to create the political space in which Democrats could exercise policymaking discretion on the homelessness issue. The flexible infrastructure for dealing with homelessness that emerged took note of compassion trends, the new call for individual responsibility among the poor, attitudes towards government programs, and real fiscal constraints on public funding that characterized the 1980s.

The two factors mentioned earlier were also critically important in the successful effort to construct homelessness policy that focussed on families. Homeless families already had some resources available to them: primarily AFDC, food stamps, and Medicaid, but also other helpful programs such as the Women, Infants and Children (WIC) nutrition supplement program, and the Head Start pre-school program. All of these programs had relatively uniform eligibility requirements, all of which could be met by a destitute mother living with her children. As far as government programs for the poor were concerned, these were routine and easy to access – at least with the help of experienced and motivated social workers. Most significantly, the welfare hotel system was enormously expensive, and liberals could propose a plan that would appear to cap the overall cost of family homelessness and still result in the development of a substantial new program for the poor.

Developing programs to aid homeless families, however, was still a delicate undertaking. Because of inflamed attitudes against the poor, and reluctance to spend public funds on social ills, policy implements had to create programs that suited the "rhetoric of inversion" and yet funneled significant resources to homeless families. The result was the creation of the McKinney Act, which President Reagan reluctantly signed into law in 1987. In general, the McKinney Act contained the seed money for a brand new bureaucracy to aid the homeless poor. In 1988 the act was amended specifically to provide the monies for demonstration supportive housing projects. Provisions in the bill involved $589 million over a two-year period for temporary shelters, including $180 million for "demonstration projects" such as the West HELP facilities we studied. The fact of its passage in the midst of a substantial shift in the redistribution of wealth from the poor to the wealthy must be acknowledged as a first-rate legislative coup.

The idea of "supportive housing" around which these expenditures were organized was equally clever. First, it effectively fused the once divergent conservative and liberal readings of the culture of poverty into an intervention strategy that would be palatable to both sides. Second, it aimed the new monies

squarely at the expansion of programs like Andrew Cuomo's temporary housing projects for homeless families in New York City (HELP), which had established a respectable track record of serving homeless families under the constraints of the conservative era. By further supporting such Democratic-backed programs, liberal Democrats would accrue political capital around the issue of family homelessness policy, upon which the Clinton Administration would necessarily eventually draw. Westchester County's supportive housing program and its funding structure illustrate the political consequences of Democratic policy making in the midst of an era dominated by conservatism.

## Westchester County, New York: A Case Study

The interplay of constraint and discretion around the issue of family homelessness would produce a flexible addition to the welfare bureaucracy even in the face of general public-sector downsizing. In Westchester County, a demonstration model of supportive housing was built that put the county and, by cooperative association, New York State at the forefront of family homelessness policy formation. The county's story also directly involved some of the key political figures who initiated the process and would see it proliferated nationally. A HUD study of 450 similar projects around the nation released in 1994 indicates that, fueled by McKinney Act seed money, the model that emerged in Westchester County had been successfully and widely replicated.[29]

What would later become known as "supportive housing" started as small-scale, grassroots efforts to comprehensively aid homeless families in New York's metropolitan area. Andrew Cuomo observed these grassroots efforts, modified them, and implemented them on a much broader scale in New York City, where they proved to be a more humane and less costly alternative to the use of welfare hotels. Supportive housing has as its defining characteristics the provision of moderately long-term supervised housing, the provision of care and schooling for homeless children, and a simultaneous focus on the rehabilitation of homeless parents from whatever is deemed to have caused their homelessness initially. Supportive housing then differs markedly from the focus on "emergency housing" that characterized early efforts to deal with the growing problem of homelessness. These earlier efforts provided only basic shelter of uncertain duration and left other needs of homeless parents and children to go unmet. Supportive housing, in contrast, took its structure from residential drug and alcohol-addiction rehabilitation facilities; it proved to be a comprehensive and cost-effective alternative that was politically popular as well. Supportive housing was quickly becoming an accepted practice for dealing with family homelessness in New York City when this framework was enfranchised by the federal McKinney Act in 1987.

### A Republican dilemma: the structure of local constraints

By the mid and late 1980s Westchester County had the fastest growing population of homeless families in the nation.[30] As in other districts with burgeoning homeless populations, the local department of social services first dealt with homeless families by placing them in welfare motels. In Westchester's case, these motels were not only the same sort of seedy environments excoriated by Johnathan Kozol and other critics, they were also mostly out of Westchester County – at times, even out of New York State. Soon, Westchester's local press and the *New York Times* began covering the deplorable situations many Westchester homeless families endured. Lengths of stays in

welfare motels had climbed to an average of 18 months, so that young children were spending appreciable portions of their lives in pest-infested, drug-ridden, poorly maintained motels at such a distance from schools as to make regular attendance all but impossible. To make matters worse, the county was spending vast sums on motel placements: In 1989, each placement averaged $104 per day per room – a total of $56,160 for a family's average stay of one and one half years.[31]

Aside from bad press, this treatment of homeless families became a thorny legal issue. After 1987, federal law required that the county provide transportation so homeless children could attend school in their previous district. With no budget to cover these costs, housing families out of county became prohibitively expensive. Further legislative mandates requiring special services for homeless children appeared impossible to implement at most of the welfare motels that were leased by the county. In addition, many cities where the seamy motels leased by the county were located instituted legal proceedings meant to end welfare dumping in their jurisdictions. Soon, it seemed, Westchester's homeless families would have nowhere to go.[32]

### Democratic discretion: resource acquisition and HELPing homeless family management in Westchester County

The strategy for dealing with Westchester's burgeoning homeless population came in the form of a collaborative effort of Democrats and Republicans that bridged the federal, state, and county political arenas and therefore involved a wide array of political figures who would have otherwise been at odds about social welfare policy.

At the federal level, the Stewart B. McKinney Act of 1987 – legislation authored, passed, and amended by the Democratic Congress with substantial influence from New

York liberals Senator Moynihan and Representative Downey – had become the articulation of the Reagan Administration's homelessness agenda. Homelessness policy on the state level was influenced informally by Governor Mario Cuomo's son, Andrew Cuomo, who since 1981 had made constructing family homeless shelters a personal priority. In doing so, he and his agency, HELP, Inc., had accumulated substantial expertise in the planning, implementing and administering of family homeless shelters. It was no wonder then that Westchester's Republican county executive sought the help of the younger Cuomo in addressing homelessness in Westchester County even before New York State was awarded the grant for the demonstration programs that would fund new shelters in the county. With funded federal legislation designed to funnel money to local start-up programs, a governor sympathetic to policy expansion in this social welfare area, and an expert on homeless policy development in the form of the Democratic governor's son, the Westchester county executive's move to enlist the help of Andrew Cuomo wove together Democratic and Republican political interests. By doing so, once contradictory policy agendas were fused into a single initiative, and eventually into a single institution.

As utilizing out-of-county welfare motels grew more and more untenable, Westchester County officials began negotiations with Cuomo's organization, HELP, which was already the largest provider of housing for the homeless in the state.[33] It had its own central staff in New York City, had politically influential supporters, and could draw on often impressive pro bono help. In addition, HELP promoted itself as a program that could provide the homeless with better temporary housing and increased services less expensively and more conveniently than the alternatives available to the county.

Contracting with HELP essentially allowed the county to hire the administrative apparatus to implement a new family homelessness policy without expanding – and perhaps even with shrinking – county government. Moreover, Cuomo had the political connections and prior expertise to enable the State Department of Social Services to successfully apply for and receive a portion of new federal monies allocated for model demonstration programs under the federal Stewart B. McKinney Homeless Assistance Act. In part because of HELP's superior political connections, New York State and Westchester County social services administrators gave the HELP initiative their full support. Another important reason for the state throwing its weight behind a HELP demonstration project for Westchester County was the already very high per diem motel rates the county was paying. By 1990, emergency housing rates paid to for-profit motels were running as high as $125 per room per day – a monthly rate of $3,500. HELP offered to provide improved services and substantially better housing for $2,600 per month. Though actual costs eventually were only slightly less than $100 per day, even this figure appeared to clearly offer savings to the state.[34] New York State Department of Social Services eventually received one of three sizable federal demonstration project grants awarded nationwide with the intent of using it for Westchester's proposed HELP program. In part because of his abilities to marshall resources, Andrew Cuomo's HELP program quickly became the most viable prototype for meeting demands for homeless services in Westchester County.

By the time the county executive announced his "Westchester County Emergency Housing Plan for Homeless Families" in June, 1990, a new HELP, Inc., facility was under construction and was touted as the flagship for a new way to deal with homeless families – through service-intensive supportive housing.[35] The siting of the new facility in the prosperous Westchester bedroom community of

Greenburgh occurred despite a vocal and well-organized opposition.[36] Yet HELP's advantages as a mechanism for retooling the county's inadequate policies toward the homeless caused state and county social services officials to back the proposed new shelter programs.[37] Eventually, these forces prevailed and HELP, Inc., came to Westchester County.

*Discretionary dollars: how HELP was financed* The attraction of Andrew Cuomo's model for dealing with family homelessness was a resource-acquisition strategy that would neither offend nor threaten any of the political interests involved in the venture, because it combined separate, but already existing, resource streams. Later, most of these devices were used by other non-profits to establish similar facilities elsewhere in the county.

The construction of the new shelter structures was accomplished with $12.3 million of tax-free municipal bonds, under an agreement that the buildings would be returned to the county after a period of ten years. Financing the project this way and amortizing the construction costs provided a physical plant that would not be reflected in the demonstration project budgets.

Through its contract with Westchester County, HELP accessed federal and state AFDC allotments and Title IVA federal emergency housing funds that are the mainstay of HELP and all other family shelters, including welfare motels. Of particular importance to program viability were the addition (via sub contracts) of those agencies which provided mostly Medicaid-billable services, notably drug and alcohol rehabilitation services, mental health services, and general health care. Medicaid has been a relatively stable source of public funding, and provider agencies brought with them their reputations of being well-financed, stable, and effective private non-profits.

Federal McKinney demonstration project funds supplied start-up monies for programs that were not Medicaid-reimbursable or cost more than could be financed through Medicaid. Five separate program areas were funded through this grant, including enhanced alcohol and drug-treatment services, a mental health program, on-site child care, educational programs, and a support program for families after they had returned to permanent housing.

The existence of many different services at this and other model homeless shelters can best be explained by examining the economic value of such programs to the maintenance of this new social-service sector. First, funding made available through the offering of services are important resource streams needed by the shelter program. Importantly, offering services by subcontracting them to other organizations also interests numerous other non-profits in the survival of the shelter program. Reflecting on the success of the strategy in 1994, a Westchester Department of Social Services official told us: "We teased a few more people into ownership of homeless issues and we got other disciplines interested in community services."

In tenuous times for programs that serve the poor, these links among service agencies can prove crucial to agency survival. Perhaps most critically, the interlocking of key organizations, which occurs through negotiating and maintaining subcontracts with each other, helps all non-profits justify their existence.[38] If funds are threatened, each organization can list others dependent on it as a reason why its funding must be maintained. The HELP program established an especially resilient interdependence with other agencies because it encompassed so many services.

Together, these resource streams enabled the creation of two new shelters, a 35-family shelter (WestHELP Mt Vernon) located in an urban area with substantial numbers of homeless families, and HELP's flagship shelter, WestHELP Greenburgh, a 108-family, brand new, condominium-like facility located in a wooded area adjacent to a community college. Together, these shelters housed over 40 percent of the county's homeless families.

*The institutional product: a flagship facility for homeless families* West HELP-Greenburgh consisted of eight residential complexes and one service complex, arranged on a six-acre site around a large lawn featuring a modern playground of slides, swings, and climbing structures. Mature trees surrounded the complex; a circular drive and a number of flags completed the condominium look of this facility. Inside there was a spacious and well-equipped child-care center, a health clinic, modern offices for social workers and administrators, conference rooms, classrooms, and a large community center. Individual apartments consisted of a living room with a convertible couch, a fully equipped kitchen and bathroom, and a bedroom. There were laundry facilities on site and a van to take residents grocery shopping. The program offered was a mixture of services and regulations, often poorly differentiated from one another. Elsewhere, we have referred to this way of managing the poor as "therapeutic incarceration."[39]

*The therapeutic element* The services offered at HELP included health services such as medical care; mental-health counseling; substance-abuse assessment and ongoing individual and group treatment; education services such as educationally enriched child care; a host of educational programs for adults including Graduate Equivalency Diploma (GED) preparation, English and literacy classes, basic math classes, and a two-year college program called Mothers on the Move (located right next door at the community college); other specialized classes in AIDS education and alcohol- and drug-abuse education; life skills training, which emphasized budgeting, housework and checkbook keeping; and parenting classes. In fact, the offering of services on site was one of the crucial factors said to make HELP a potential model program – offering services which were located conveniently was predicted to (and did in fact) markedly increase usage rates. Supportive housing epitomized the therapeutic bread and butter of the liberal welfare package.

*Incarceration and moral regulation* Several features of this facility, however, served to differentiate it from a modern apartment complex or stereotypic therapeutic community. The security guards at the entrance signed in visitors and residents; residents' handbags and packages were checked for alcohol and drugs before they entered. No visitors were allowed past the entrance hall or beyond the gaze of the security guards; there was no in-room visiting or overnight visiting, even by non-resident fathers or partners. A wrought-iron fence surrounded the compound; it was topped with several strands of barbed wire.

At WestHELP, new residents had to sign a four-page regulations sheet shortly after arrival that outlined behaviors that were prohibited by the shelter (drinking, drug use, violence, possession of a weapon, any illegal activity, returning late in the evening, excessive stays off site, leaving children unattended) and listed a host of other "suggested" behaviors (cooperation with social workers and other office and advocacy staff, at least 20 hours per week of program attendance, room cleanliness, proper supervision and care of children, initial visits to health care and assessment personnel). Although parents were not legally required to engage in any services or even the assessment process, the regulations sheet was written in such a way that participation in these activities was understood by residents to be required. In addition, residents were threatened with various punishments, such as expulsion from the shelter, exclusion from child-care services, or being thought of as less than "housing ready" – therefore delaying eligibility for placement in permanent housing.[40]

Movement toward "self-sufficiency" and "independence" was also a stated goal and implied requirement of the program. This can be measured by participation in services, such as substance-abuse treatment and education programs thought to enhance employability. Thus the shelter adopted a "get tough" attitude toward homeless parents – one in keeping with currently prevalent attitudes about the poor that claimed that it was their personal deficiencies that were responsible for their homelessness and that a redoubled effort at self-improvement would deliver them from their situation.

To middle-class observers, the message was clear – these people would be required to reform themselves in exchange for the largesse made possible through tax dollars; homeless mothers (unlike, as popular perceptions had it, mere welfare mothers) would not get "something for nothing."

Under the political conditions of the 1980s and early 1990s, maintaining at least a portion of homeless families in highly regulated shelter programs was probably a critical element in the successful construction and maintenance of this new welfare industry. Maintaining the incarceration aspects of the shelter increased its chances of surviving the new politics of poverty and spoke to the moralizing elements of conservative interests; maintaining the therapeutic component increased its chance of financial survival and spoke to the liberal interests in social work and therapy.

## Replicating the HELP model

By the time Clinton took office in 1992 the county had made tremendous strides in making all of its major shelter programs resemble

HELP as much as possible. Although no other shelter replicated West HELP-Greenburgh's gorgeous physical plant, all the other large shelters in the county had developed more-or-less comprehensive on-site services, including even the most notorious welfare hotel, which gradually added on-site services provided by agencies subcontracting with the county.

This practice of offering seemingly appropriate and useful services to homeless families through subcontracting with other provider agencies resulted in the establishment of a dense web of organizations which had a stake in treating homeless families. Overtly, however, there was no net expansion of "government bureaucracy." In 1995, after five years of active expansion, the county's Housing Services Unit still consisted of a very small number of staff in modest accommodations. Since this new bureaucracy was run through subcontracting, it could theoretically be dismantled almost instantly; however, because there were so many subcontractor organizations with an interest in the treatment of homeless families, it was not likely to be dismantled at all. Indeed, through the subcontracting process and the many coordinating meetings made necessary to ensure the shelter programs' smooth operation, the HELP program had served to unify the social-service community during a political period when its members might otherwise have been motivated to compete with each other for shrinking public funding. Thus by adopting HELP's financial and organizational strategy, the county also created a new social-welfare industry with substantial political clout without creating a new government bureaucracy.

At the outset of Clinton's presidency, this model of family homelessness policy had already established deep roots extending to municipal governments and local service agencies across the nation.

## Discretion Constrained: Family Homelessness and Supportive Housing Under Clinton

The McKinney Act was written and funded with a HELP-like supportive housing model in mind. Because of this, the process that occurred in Westchester County was replicated nationwide. Between 1987 and 1990, HUD awarded 535 transitional housing grants totaling $340 million. By the time the Clinton Administration came to Washington in 1992, 94 percent of these projects were in operation. Virtually all were engaged in constructing a dense network of local service providers and using McKinney funds to leverage local resources on behalf of local supportive housing initiatives. HUD estimates that for every federal dollar used to help acquire facilities or rehabilitate them, state and local entities contributed $5.50 for a total of $202 million nationwide. Likewise, for every dollar HUD spent on social services, local community organizations contributed $2.50 for a total of $89 million.[41]

Supportive housing was a policy idea conceived by Democrats under the constraints of a Republican administration which was determined not only to make significant cuts to poverty programs but to hobble the structural capacity for government to engage in large-scale poverty programs. Yet, despite these adverse conditions, in the five years between the signing of the McKinney Act and the election of a Democrat to the presidency, this program had developed into an entrenched bureaucracy, replete with funding sufficient to provide seed money for numerous initiatives around the nation.

The Clinton Administration, then, inherited an initiative it found easy to support. But even more significantly, there were many factors which worked against modifying it, particularly in a liberal direction. First, supportive housing benefited many local Democratic constituencies. By encouraging the leveraging of substantial local resources for providing housing and services to the homeless, and by providing substantial federal back-up funding, the McKinney Act institutionalized a decade of social-work activism, initiative, and program expansion on behalf of the homeless. Those who had constructed these programs, like Andrew Cuomo, were local Democratic functionaries and activists. Clinton could not tamper with their handiwork without risking an antagonistic response.

Second, the mechanisms through which these new initiatives were funded made the new homelessness industry less vulnerable to demise even if additional federal budget cutbacks should occur. Since many local agencies and many sources of funding at various levels of government were combined to create family-shelter programs, this program initiative offered non-profit organizations and other local government agencies promise of a stable poverty-related mission that was in welcome contrast to the era of constant threats of cutbacks they had recently suffered through. Supporting these programs as they already existed, then-satisfied an important liberal constituency without necessitating any additional political action on the part of the Clinton Administration.

Third, though the policy fit well with an expected reinvigoration of interest in anti-poverty activities under the new Democratic administration, it did so without appearing to expand government bureaucracy – a new mandate for policy success inherited from a dozen years of Republican leadership in Washington. Indeed, no new federal bureaucracy has been created in support of this new industry. Instead, supportive housing provided HUD, an already existing but threatened federal agency, with a new mission.[42] This came at a time when federal sponsorship of public housing projects, HUD's past priority policy for the poor, was out of favor in the new era of smaller government and market-based solutions to housing problems.

Fourth, the policy was resilient enough to withstand a political climate that called for the poor to transform themselves into respectable citizens. Democrats had expended considerable energy in ensuring that demonstration supportive housing programs were viewed as successful, at least those in New York built on the Cuomo model.[43] While constructing a Democratic Party poverty initiative was an important victory during the constraining times of the Reagan/Bush administrations, constructing policy without expanding the welfare state was a priority under a Clinton Administration which sought to avoid conservative charges of "tax-and-spend" liberalism. In addition, since the policy had been written and signed during the Reagan Administration and with the cooperation of many Republicans, there was little chance of a Republican attack on it. Indeed, since it was a time-limited program aimed at reducing dependency and making the homeless self-sufficient, the new Democratic administration could claim that this was a program in keeping with conservative goals for the poor.

Finally, family homelessness policy had been forged by important liberals, a group still crucial to Democratic success in Congress. To do other than support the policy would mean discrediting what had been largely a Democratic initiative as well as the Democrats who sponsored it. When it came time for the Clinton Administration to make political appointments, the only Democrats who had accrued any expertise or political capital on this new social issue were those who had done so formulating Republican-friendly programs. In the process of forging policy thus constrained, they had repositioned themselves in precisely the fashion that would later come to characterize the Clinton Administration's approach to poverty policy more generally. In other words, liberals working on the prob-

lems of poverty constrained by the conservative rhetoric and funding goals of the 1980s had invented poverty policy that well suited the agenda of the "New Democrats" of the 1990s. In particular, this policy fit well with the "work and responsibility" agenda the Clinton Administration would promote as its own vision for transforming poverty policy. It could be further argued that Democratic repositioning, made necessary by the fact of a dozen years of a Republican White House, had been one crucial factor in forcing the creation of the centrist New Democrats.[44] Thus, the Clinton Administration found it unproblematic to cement its commitment to supportive housing policy by appointing one of its chief promoters and designers, Andrew Cuomo, as "homelessness czar" – Assistant Secretary to the Department of Housing and Urban Development.[45]

In the initial months of the new Democratic administration, the McKinney Act was substantially amended, and it was superseded by the Housing and Community Development Act of 1992. This act made supportive housing initiatives for the homeless, which had previously operated as demonstration projects only, into permanent programs. In addition, the new legislation expanded funding for other supportive services and relaxed requirements for the use of supportive housing funds. In March of 1993, an interim rule further expanded the scope of supportive housing funding by providing for the renewal of grants for projects originally funded under the McKinney Act whose funding had expired. Congress significantly increased funding for supportive housing from $150 million in the fiscal years of 1992 and 1993 to $334 million for the fiscal year of 1994.[46]

By expanding and solidifying commitment to a short-term dependency-reducing model of supportive housing, however, the Clinton Administration and local program administrators found themselves constrained from engaging in traditionally liberal and Democratic approaches to poverty policy, such as expanding public housing or strategically intervening in structural problems confronting the poor. In other words, on the homeless front at least, liberal Democrats enacted the long-sought conservative agenda for dealing with poverty and, in doing so, disabled government's capacity to provide sufficient housing for homeless families.

The discretion liberal Democrats had exercised in the conservative Reagan/Bush era had come fully around to confront them as constraints on their own traditional policy agenda for the poor in the new Clinton Administration. Clinton, himself a product of a similar strategic repositioning for survival in more conservative times, was no longer able to re-enact, or interested in re-enacting, old liberal redistribution-of-wealth policies. Ironically, however, in order for supportive housing to truly accomplish its mission, it would come to rely on the very sorts of liberal subsidy programs that Democrats now had a stake in repudiating.

### Housing homeless families: facing the realities of a shortage of affordable housing

Despite its success at program expansion and stabilization, the rehabilitative model enfranchised in the McKinney Act as supportive housing was not able to make housing more affordable or accessible. Because Westchester County, like many other areas of the northeast, suffers from a chronic shortage of low-cost family housing, the county had one irreducible problem in its treatment of homeless families: There was very little permanent affordable housing available.[47] In Westchester County, even homeless families who had successfully completed every rehabilitative requirement still faced a high-priced, racially segregated housing market with a low vacancy rate.[48]

The adoption of policy based on individual rehabilitation precluded even an acknowledge-

ment of this problem, since the public ideology declared that, once rehabilitated, the homeless would be able to take care of their own problems – that is, they would be self-sufficient. Indeed, the federal supportive housing policy strategy made no government-led provision for the permanent rehousing of homeless families.[49] It instead claimed that rehabilitated families would now have increased access to housing presumed to be already available on the free market. Because of the constraints imposed on program administrators by the policy model, local policy makers had to employ semi-covert methods to access or create subsidized housing for program graduates, even after a Democratic administration came to Washington.

In Westchester, two methods were employed. First, the county actively sought Section 8 certificates (an ongoing federal housing subsidy) for the graduates of all its shelter programs, and many families did exit the emergency housing system through obtaining a Section 8 certificate.

A second solution involved the creation of scattered site Emergency Housing Units (EHUs). EHUs are, quite simply, ordinary one-, two- and three-bedroom apartments that are rented by Westchester County Department of Social Services for former residents of congregate homeless shelters. Administratively, they are not very different from a shelter, in that they are funded by AFDC emergency Title IVA funds through contractual arrangements with non-profit organizations that negotiate rental arrangements with private landlords. However, they are much less expensive – at about half the price – than either the old welfare hotels or shelters in which the homeless are placed for rehabilitation. To homeless families, these apartments appear identical to permanent housing. Often EHU families reside in these units until their name comes up on the Section 8 list; and then these apartments are administratively converted to Section 8 apartments. During the study time, EHU placements in the county grew more than any other type of emergency housing.

Without the cover of high-profile rehabilitative congregate shelters, the county could probably not have developed this "housing policy by stealth" system at all. Indeed, early in our evaluation of the county's programs, state-level social-service administrators cautioned us against mentioning EHUs to the McKinney grant administrators in Washington, fearing that using Title IVA emergency housing funds in this way would be viewed as inappropriate or even illegal by federal administrators. It was only when it was revealed that all three states receiving McKinney demonstration grants used funds for EHU-type programs that New York State officials felt comfortable admitting this policy.

Eventually, under the Clinton Administration, a federal legislative investigation was undertaken to determine the legality and viability of using Title IVA emergency funds more widely to support EHU-type housing. Increased coordination of Section 8 allotments to graduates of homeless programs is also a proposal taken under consideration by HUD officials.[50] Both these methods of making family-sized apartments available and affordable to homeless families had proven to be essential components to making supportive housing appear successful.

Without quiet access to a federally funded method for reducing the cost of housing to these low-income families, the free-market approach to locating family housing would be revealed as an untenable proposition in a county where little housing was available. Ironically, it seemed a major program outcome had become the distribution of an ongoing federal housing subsidy – a complete contradiction of the central program goal of reducing family dependency on the public dole. As small-scale, semi-covert placement programs, finding Section 8 certificates and creating EHU placements for program graduates was an effective means to both provide

affordable permanent housing and keep length of stays in congregate facilities at a reasonable length. Providing families with subsidized housing would seem a reasonable solution to family homelessness on a wider scale in areas where there is an obvious shortage of affordable housing. For two reasons, however, it is unlikely that the expansion of either of these methods for rehousing homeless families will become an overt component of poverty policy.

The first can best be discussed by citing an example that helps illustrate the effects of a constriction in the availability of adequate and affordable housing in some areas. In 1990, New York City for a time prioritized homeless families for one quarter of the 8,000 Section 8 certificates available to the city, in order to move families out of the shelter system more rapidly. After shrinking the average time spent in shelter from nine to three months, city officials realized that the short wait was luring some families into the system in order to jump to the top of the 189,000-person Section 8 waiting list. The length of the list itself speaks volumes about the inadequacy of the affordable housing stock in the city. The policy was quickly changed after New York experienced a rapid rise in numbers appealing to the city for shelter – from 10,370 to 11,290 between 1990 and 1991. Giving subsidized housing priority to homeless families appeared even more ludicrous in the wake of a *New York Times* report in which parents called their cost-free stay in emergency housing "the best way to get a place of my own."[51]

Expanding timely placements to permanent housing as a solution to family homelessness, then, expands the number of customers desiring the service, especially in tight and expensive housing markets.[52] In New York City, many families were still willing to wait nine months to get an affordable place of their own. In Westchester, where the housing crisis is even more severe, families willingly remained in emergency shelters for well over a year.[53]

For the same reason, it is unlikely that direct creation of EHUs would have been possible without the cover of HELP and other congregate family shelters. The county made limited casework and other services available to EHU residents in part to keep EHUs within the framework of a temporary rehabilitative placement. But for residents in EHUs, there are virtually no special apartment rules and no special regulations, overt or implied, regarding participation in rehabilitative activities. Instead, by virtue of their homelessness, they appear to get "something for nothing"—a subsidized apartment. This becomes a problem for policy administrators because directly expanding the stock of public or subsidized housing lost credibility in the last decade as a viable public idea for the treatment of the poor. Moreover, in constructing a family homelessness policy that overtly denies any need for increased amounts of affordable housing, Democrats lost the cachet they needed to argue for government intervention in rehousing the homeless, even under a Democratic administration. It is unlikely, then, that the county, much less the nation, could have constructed a system for rehousing homeless families based strictly or even primarily on giving homeless families a subsidized apartment, even if there were some objective way to determine a family's need for housing.

A shrinking amount of affordable housing stock at first produces what has been termed a "musical chairs" result for families.[54] Those family heads who have mental or physical health problems, drug or alcohol addictions, or other problems that make it difficult to access rent money regularly tend to be the first to lose their place in a tight housing market. HELP and other shelter programs based on similar models presume most homeless families fail to keep housing for these types of reasons. The persistence of extremely limited amounts of affordable housing in locations such as Westchester County, however, eventually prices many other poor families

out of the housing market as well. These families may well have limited need for the services offered at shelters built on the therapeutic model; more affordable housing is their primary need. EHUs are an effective strategy for meeting the needs of these families, who may well eventually constitute the vast majority of homeless families in areas where there is a persistent shortage in affordable housing.

EHUs as a replacement for group supportive housing projects, however, are financially vulnerable in a way that congregate shelter programs are not. They have no network of non-profits interested in their survival; no flagship facility, no model program attached to them. At best, then, permanently rehousing homeless families directly is a policy that can only be pursued as a secondary measure, with the majority of families being assigned to congregate supportive housing first. In this way, the homelessness industry manages to constrain the potential numbers of homeless families and also keeps public opinion at bay. Homeless families must be willing to put up with much inconvenience, close personal supervision, many behavioral rules, and long waits in order to access housing through the homelessness system. By endorsing a rehabilitative model that is less vulnerable to federal poverty program cuts, Democrats have markedly reduced the federal government's ability to directly provide housing to homeless families, even when they themselves control the presidency and/or Congress.

## Conclusion

The supportive housing program continued by the Clinton Administration was the result of a successful struggle on the part of liberal Democrats to develop and maintain a new poverty initiative that was relatively immune to the threats of spending reductions for poverty programs that characterized the 1980s. Because widespread homelessness and its policy response emerged in a time when sympathy for the poor was minimal, the initiative of necessity stressed short-term rehabilitation and reduction in dependency on the public dole. The case of homeless policy well represents the consequences of years of successful attacks on large, traditional Democratic redistribution-of-wealth programs, attacks which have made these programs, such as public housing, increasingly viewed as unacceptable by the taxpaying public. In an effort to salvage the political advantages of traditionally Democratic poverty initiatives, if not the programs themselves, Democrats have turned to what Clarence Lo elsewhere in this volume terms "flexible economizing."[55] In this case, a program of providing short-term housing for homeless families that reduced the obscene costs of welfare hotels, while embracing the victim-centered philosophy of conservatives, enabled liberal Democrats to claim that they had actively forged policy for a sympathetic subset of the poor. By 1987, the McKinney Act institutionalized nationally what had become a juggernaut of densely connected local social-work departments and non-profit organizations. Though these organizations were deeply rooted in the Democratic Party and its history of provision for the poor, the constraints of the 1980s had transformed their agenda for the homeless into one that closely resembled a conservative vision.

By the time the Clinton Administration came to power in 1992, the trajectory of homeless policy response had been firmly established. Because homelessness policy was clearly a creation of liberal Democrats, Clinton would have alienated an important part of his constituency if his administration had attempted to undo what had been accomplished by Democrats under the previous Republican administrations. In addition, the growing problem of homelessness was one of the few poverty-policy areas where Democratic national leadership had been nurtured during the dozen years of Republican domination of the White House.

Though the homeless family policy that resulted and its proponents were infused with the more conservative tenor of the times, few other nationally credentialed alternative Democratic leaders in this area existed. Thus, the only alternative for the new Democratic administration was to continue homelessness policy constructed under the Republican administrations and appoint its proponents to official roles in the federal policy bureaucracy.

This approach to homeless families, however, hid the real need for increases in publicly financed or subsidized housing. There was little social margin within the context of this poverty strategy for liberal Democrats to advocate direct housing-subsidy programs. By conceding that family poverty's worst excess is the fault of each individual parent, adherents of this policy strategy helped slam the already closing door on public-housing programs, even under a Democratic administration and even though there is covert acknowledgment that the free market has not provided adequate amounts of housing at affordable prices. Instead, Democrats have committed themselves to a family homelessness policy that claims the sufficiency of market forces to provide housing for the poor. Democrats, liberals, and other advocates for the poor have paid a high price for authoring and enacting policy that is relatively immune from conservative attack.

The 1987 McKinney Act foreshadowed the 1996 Welfare Reform Act, with its similar emphasis on short-term, market-based solutions to the problem of family poverty. Ironically, as a program of last resort for impoverished families, supportive housing may well become the "poverty policy by stealth" of the Welfare Reform Act. Though many families may be found ineligible for the new, time-limited, state-sponsored public-assistance programs, the national welfare industry that has grown up around family homelessness may find itself filling the role that the national entitlement AFDC program once provided – the safety net of last resort for impoverished families.

## Notes

1 Mark Stern, "The Emergence of the Homeless as a Public Problem," *Social Service Review* 58 (1984), pp. 291–301.

2 The most complete account of this history was documented in the implementation evaluation team's draft of the first project interim report, which considerably informs this chapter. The draft was deemed too controversial and politically dangerous by New York state officials, however, and only a severely shortened version ever reached a wider audience. This occurred despite the officials' inability to find significant factual errors in the original document. Robert T. Nakamura, Christopher M. McMahon, and Michael C. Gizzi, "AFDC Homeless Evaluation Draft Interim Report, Implementation Study," Graduate School of Public Affairs, State University of New York at Albany (1993), typescript. For the official version, see Richard P. Nathan, Richard Pulice, Robert T. Nakamura, and Michael Schwartz, "The New York State McKinney AFDC Transitional Housing Demonstration Project, Final Evaluation Report", unpublished report of the Nelson A. Rockefeller Institute of Government, State University of New York at Albany (1995).

3 Beth Mintz and Michael Schwartz, *The Power Structure of American Business* (Chicago: University of Chicago Press, 1986).

4 The actual breakdown for Westchester County welfare hotels included an average per unit monthly cost of $3,315 for rent, $232 restaurant allowance (because there were no kitchens in the hotels), and $240 for social services. The annual yearly average per family cost in 1990 then was $45,444. New York State Department of Social Services, "Emergency Services and Shelter AFDC Transitional Housing Demonstration Program," proposal submitted to the US Department of Health and Human Services for funding under Section 903 of the Stewart B. McKinney Homeless Assistance Ammendments Act of 1988 (1990), p. 33.

5 Joel Blau, *The Visible Poor: Homelessness in the United States* (London: Oxford University Press, 1992).

6 Obviously, unemployment insurance is a limited program that most benefits those who were recently employed on the books, particularly in well-paying jobs. Few of the street-dwelling homeless we studied received other benefits for which they may have been eligible, partly because the application process was difficult, especially for those tenuously housed or already living on the streets. Many of the homeless believed not having a permanent address disqualified them from benefits like food stamps and Medicaid; those who did get these benefits had generally done so through advocacy services from non-profit agencies. See Ellen Granovetter, "Homelessness on Long Island: The Intersection of Lives and Policy," unpublished report of the Robert Sterling Clark Foundation (New York, NY, 1992). For a discussion of the other barriers to street dwellers accessing benefits like SSI, see Dalton Clark Conley, "Getting it Together: Social and Institutional Obstacles to Getting Off the Streets," *Sociological Forum* 11 (1996), pp. 25–40.

7 For example, the federal Stewart B. McKinney Homeless Assistance Act of 1987 earmarks $180 million for demonstration programs for homeless families. In contrast, only $70 million was earmarked for subsidies for homeless singles. These funds are to be used only for those with permanent mental or physical disabilities – a minority of homeless singles. For an additional justification of the need to house homeless families, see Ralph DaCosta Nunez, *Hopes, Dreams, and Promise: The Future of Homeless Children in America* (New York: Institute for Children and Poverty, Homes for the Homeless, 1994).

8 Michael B. Katz, *The Undeserving Poor: From the War on Poverty to the War on Welfare* (New York: Pantheon, 1989) p. 29.

9 Ibid., p. 28.

10 Linda Gordon, *Heroes of their Own Lives: The Politics and History of Family Violence, Boston 1880–1960* (New York: Viking Press, 1988), pp. 99–108; Katz, *Undeserving Poor*, pp. 29–35; Andrew J. Polsky, *The Rise of the Therapeutic State* (Princeton NJ: Princeton University Press, 1991); Charles Murray, *Losing Ground: American Social Policy 1950–80* (New York: Basic Books, 1984).

11 Charles Murray, "Does Welfare Bring More

Babies?," *The Public Interest* 115 (1994), pp. 17–30; Lawrence M. Mead, *Beyond Entitlement: The Social Obligations of Citizenship* (New York: Free Press, 1986); George Gilder, *Wealth and Poverty* (New York: Basic Books, 1981); Christopher Jencks, *The Homeless* (Cambridge MA: Harvard University Press, 1994); Elijah Anderson, "Neighborhood Effects on Teenage Pregnancy," in Christopher Jencks and Paul E. Peterson, eds, *The Urban Underclass* (Washington DC: Brookings Institution, 1991) pp. 375–98.

12 For examples, see Jamshid Momeni, ed., *Homelessness in the United States: Data and Issues* (New York: Prager, 1990); Ellen L. Bassuk. "The Homelessness Problem," *Scientific American* 251 (1984), p. 40; Ellen L. Bassuk, Linda Rubin, and Alison Lauriat, "Is Homelessness a Mental Health Problem?," *American Journal of Psychiatry* 141 (1984) pp. 1546–50; Alice S. Baum and Donald Burnes, *A Nation in Denial: The Truth about Homelessness* (Boulder: Westview Press, 1993); Pamela J. Fischer "Mental Health and Social Characteristics of the Homeless: A Survey of Mission Users," *American Journal of Public Health* 76 (1986) pp. 519–24; and a review of such articles specifically about family homelessness, Kay Y. McChesney, "A Review of the Empirical Literature on Urban Homeless Families since 1980," paper presented at the American Sociological Society annual meeting, Los Angeles (August, 1994).

13 Michael Weiler and W. Barnett Pearce, eds, *Reagan and Public Discourse in America* (Tuscaloosa: University of Alabama Press, 1992).

14 For a brief review, see Michael B. Katz, *In the Shadow of the Poorhouse: A Social History of Welfare in America* (New York: Basic Books, 1986), pp. 274–91.

15 Frances Fox Piven and Richard A. Cloward, *The New Class War: Reagan's Attack on the Welfare State and its Consequences* (New York: Pantheon, 1982); Michael B. Katz, *Improving Poor People: The Welfare State, the "Underclass," and Urban Schools as History* (Princeton NJ: Princeton University Press, 1995).

16 Lee Rainwater and William L. Yancey, *The Moynihan Report and the Politics of Controversy: A Transaction Social Science and Public Policy*

*Report* (Cambridge MA: MIT Press, 1967).

17 David T. Ellwood, *Poor Support: Poverty in the American Family* (New York: Basic Books, 1988); Mark Green and Gail MacColl, *Reagan's Reign of Error: The Instant Nostalgia Edition* (New York: Pantheon, 1983); Dan Quayle, *Standing Firm* (New York: HarperCollins, 1994), p. 319; Weiler and Pearce, *Reagan and Public Discourse.*

18 Although this argument about family life was not uncommon before the 1980s, public criticism of alternative family forms and the supposed causes behind them (moral lapses, the hippie movement, the gay and lesbian movement, and the feminist movement, to name a few) revisited the public discourse most forcefully at the 1992 Republican national convention. Dan Quayle's 1992 "Murphy Brown" speech is another famous example of public moralizing about the nuclear family on the part of the new conservatives. See also Baum and Burnes, *A Nation in Denial;* Gilder, *Wealth and Poverty;* Mead, *Beyond Entitlement;* Murray, *Losing Ground;* Richard P. White, *Rude Awakenings: What the Homeless Crisis Tells Us* (San Francisco: ICS Press, 1992); David Popenoe, *Disturbing the Nest: Family Change and Decline in Modern Societies* (New York: A. de Gruyter, 1988).

19 Robin Toner, "The New Bipartisanship. Resolved: No More Bleeding Hearts," *New York Times* (July 16, 1995), sec. 4, p. 1; Daniel Patrick Moynihan, *Family and Nation* (New York: Harcourt Brace Jovanovich, 1986); Anderson, "Neighbor Effects;" M. W. Edelman and L. Hihaly, *Homeless Families and the Housing Crisis in the United States* (Washington DC: Children's Defense Fund, 1989); William J. Wilson, *The Truly Disadvantaged: The Inner City, the Underclass, and Public Policy* (Chicago: University of Chicago Press, 1987); Christopher Jencks, *The Homeless* (Cambridge MA: Harvard University Press, 1994).

20 Toner, "New Bipartisanship."

21 For another articulation of this social policy agenda, see, Gordon Berlin and William McAllister, "Homelessness," in Henry J. Aaron and Charles L. Schultze, eds, *Setting Domestic Priorities* (Washington DC: Brookings Institution, 1992).

22 The inevitable development of homelessness as a result of these trends has been widely documented. See, for example, Kim Hopper, Ezra Susser, and Sarah Conover, "Economies of Makeshift: Deindustrialization and Homelessness in New York City," *Urban Anthropology* 14 (1985), pp. 183–236; Douglas S. Massey, and Nancy A. Denton, *American Apartheid: Segregation and the Making of the Underclass* (Cambridge MA: Harvard University Press, 1993); Blau, *Visible Poor.*

23 Weiler and Pearce, *Reagan and Public Discourse.*

24 Katz, *Undeserving Poor.*

25 John O'Conner and Michael Lewis, "Turning the Tide: Reagan and Social Welfare Policy," paper presented at the American Sociological Association annual meeting, Washington DC (August, 1995).

26 Bruce Link, Sharon Schwartz, Robert E. Moore, Jo Phelan, Elmer Struening, Ann Stueve, and Mary Ellen Carter, "Public Knowledge, Attitudes, and Beliefs About Homeless People: Evidence for Compassion Fatigue?," unpublished manuscript (Columbia University and New York Psychiatric Institute, New York, 1993).

27 These sentiments about the homeless continued to be expressed by President Reagan through the end of his presidency. See, for example, Ronald Reagan and David Brinkley, *A Farewell Interview, ABC News* (December 22, 1988). During this interview, Reagan expressed the view that "a large percentage" of the homeless were "retarded" people who had voluntarily left institutions that would have cared for them. In Lou Cannon, *President Reagan: The Role of a Lifetime* (New York: Simon and Schuster, 1991), p. 24.

28 In 1982, the *New York Times* ran only one article about homelessness. The next year, however, the issue had exploded into public view and 81 articles were printed. Peak interest in homelessness occurred in 1987, when the *New York Times* printed 350 articles in a single year on the issue. Interest continued for the next five years, when over 200 articles on the subject appeared each year. *New York Times* Index.

29 Paradoxically, while the HUD study ostensibly reflected the "success" of programs insti

tuted under the Reagan and Bush administrations, it then served the democratic HUD leadership and the Clinton Administration in perpetuating and refunding these policies. Office of Policy Development and Research, *Review of Stewart B. McKinney Homeless Programs Administered by HUD,* HUD-1505-PDR (Washington DC: US Department of Housing and Urban Development, 1995). We return to this point later.

30 Jane Wagner, New York State AFDC Transitional Housing Demonstration Program Briefing Report (August 16, 1994).

31 Jonathan Kozol, *Rachel and Her Children* (New York: Crown, 1988); Eric Schmitt, "Westchester Homeless Linger in a Connecticut Hotel," *New York Times* (November 13, 1989), sec. B, p. 1; Michael Winerip, "For Homeless, Short Bus Ride to Stove and Bed," *New York Times* (July 24, 1990), sec. B, p. 1.

32 The adjoining county of Putnam was one local jurisdiction to take such actions; others were towns within Westchester's own borders – the city of White Plains, the village of Elmsford, and the town of Mamaroneck. *New York Times* (April 26, 1986).

33 James Feron, "A Plan to House Westchester's Homeless," *New York Times* (October 9, 1987), sec. B, p. 1.

34 Proposal submitted to the US Department of Health and Human Services for funding under Section 903 of the Stewart B. McKinney Homeless Assistance Amendments Act of 1988 (1990), p. 33.

35 A second, smaller site in the city of Mt Vernon was also renovated and operated by HELP Inc.

36 See, for example, James Feron, "Homeless Project is Rejected," *New York Times,* (December 18, 1989), sec. B; Michael Winerip, "The Homeless Head for Suburb and Suits Follow," *New York Times* (July 24, 1990), sec. B, p. 1. For a more thorough discussion of the siting dispute, see Nathan et al., "New York State Report."

37 The plan was further justified and legitimated by a report published by a New York City commission on homeless policy, chaired by Andrew Cuomo, that also called for a HELP-type system for aiding homeless families. See New York City Commission on the Homeless

(David Dinkins, Mayor; Andrew Cuomo, Chairman), *The Way Home: A New Direction for Social Policy*, Report, New York City Mayoral Office (1992).

38 Richard Pulice, Robert T. Nakamura, LuAnn McCormick, and Christopher McMahon, "Where Does this Policy Come From? Placing Approaches, Strategic Implementation Decisions, and Organizational Choices," unpublished manuscript, School of Social Welfare, State University of New York at Albany (1994).

39 Naomi Gerstel, Cynthia J. Bogard, J. Jeff McConnell, and Michael Schwartz, "The Therapeutic Incarceration of Homeless Families," *Social Service Review* 70 (1996), pp. 543–72.

40 We saw the term "housing ready" develop as service providers learned to justify extended stays in service-oriented shelters in the county. It supposedly meant families had been prepared by the onslaught of services to graduate from supportive housing back into independent permanent housing of their own. It actually had at least as much to do with the availability of such placements, however. When one shelter's access to subsidies for so placing families was temporarily cut off, for example, the director told us "We'll have to concentrate on making families housing ready." But when renovations in the shelter began shortly afterwards and the number of available rooms was drastically reduced, about half of the families suddenly became "housing ready" within a couple of months and were placed in subsidized housing.

41 Mark L. Matulef, Scott B. Crosse, and Stephan K. Dietz, *National Evaluation of the Supportive Housing Demonstration Program*, HC-5836 (Washington DC: US Department of Housing and Urban Development, 1995).

42 Under the direction of Secretary Henry G. Cisneros, appointed by President Clinton to head HUD, its homeless policy during the Clinton Administration was articulated in a fashion that was very consistent with the emergence of policy and practice forged during the 1980s. HUD policy under Clinton is outlined in the United States Inter-Agency Council, *Priority Home: The Federal Plan for Rehousing the Homeless* (Washington DC: US Government Printing Office, 1994). This document details the advantages of the McKinney Act funding structure and advocates a HELP-like rehabilitative shelter program structure to aid homeless families, referred to in the document as the Continuum of Care (p. 73). Andrew Cuomo was the Assistant Secretary appointed to forge national policy for homelessness during this period. Thus the Westchester County model became enfranchised as HUD's new mission to aid the homeless.

43 The two other demonstration programs, in Massachusetts and New Jersey, fared considerably less well, although they offered interesting alternatives to some of the more negative elements of the HELP model. The Massachusetts projects, for example, employed scattered-site apartments at the outset, thus avoiding some of the incarcerative elements of HELP. Without the strong Democratic support at the state level, however, the Massachusetts projects disintegrated administratively and the New Jersey projects were severely attacked by HHS officials for being unable to provide a favorable cost-benefit analysis. As evaluators of the New York projects, the cost analysis we provided was not, incidentally, entirely positive. Also, we were under considerable political pressure to provide an overall positive evaluation, while we were not likewise encouraged to engage in a critical assessment of the programs.

44 The other factor that forced Democratic repositioning, and one that is particularly salient to Clinton's political history, is southern realignment and the wholescale defection of white southern voters, particularly men, to the Republican ticket.

45 In 1996 Andrew Cuomo was promoted to Secretary of the Department of Housing and Urban Development, a cabinet-level position.

46 Matulef et al., *National Evaluation*.

47 Cynthia J. Bogard, "No Place Like Home: Rehousing Homeless Families in an Age of Declining 'Family Values'," doctoral dissertation, State University of New York at Stony Brook, Department of Sociology (December, 1995).

48 Over two-thirds of Westchester County's homeless family population is African American (69

percent), though African Americans comprise only 13.8 percent of the county's overall population.

49 There are provisions in the McKinney Act for permanent housing stock increases, but these are only for disabled individuals.

50 Matulef et al., *National Evaluation.*

51 Celia W. Dugger, "Benefits of System Luring More Families to Shelters," *New York Times* (September 3, 1991), sec. A, p. 1; Hopper et al., "Economies of Makeshift;" Kim Hopper and Jim Baumohl, "Held in Abeyance: Rethinking Homelessness and Advocacy," *American Behavioral Scientist* 34 (1994), pp. 522–52; M. E. Stone, *One-Third of Nation: A New Look at Housing Affordability in America* (Washington

DC: Economic Policy Institute, 1990).

52 Jencks, *Homeless*, pp. 102–6.

53 Gerstel et al., "Therapeutic Incarceration"; Cynthia J. Bogard, J. Jeff McConnell, Naomi Gerstel, and Michael Schwartz, "Selecting for Homelessness: Gender and Dependence," paper presented at the Eastern Sociological Society annual meeting, March, Philadelphia PA (1995).

54 See Kay Young McChesney, "Family Homelessness: A Systemic Problem," *Journal of Social Issues* 46 (1992) 191–205; Marybeth Shinn, "Homelessness: What is a Psychologist to Do?," *American Journal of Community Psychology* 20 (1992) 1–24.

55 Clarence Y. H. Lo, Conclusion to this volume.

# 5

# Social Security Policy and the Entitlement Debate

## The New American Exceptionalism

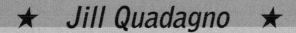 **★ *Jill Quadagno* ★**

## Introduction

The most memorable act of President Clinton's first term is likely to be his signing of the welfare reform bill crafted by the Republican Congress. In turning over responsibility for the welfare of poor mothers and children to the states, Clinton departed dramatically from his own party's New Deal heritage. Although renouncing the federal government's commitment to the poor may have resonated with public disdain for welfare recipients, it did nothing to resolve the issue that dominated debate for most of his first term in office, balancing the federal budget. AFDC had great symbolic significance. As a program that consumed only 1 percent of federal spending, however, its fiscal significance was minimal. Notably absent was any action on the three welfare state programs that consume nearly half of the federal budget – social security, Medicare, and Medicaid. Indeed, neither the Republican nor Democratic proposals for balancing the federal budget by 2002 included any mention of social security.[1] Its absence was particularly puzzling given that throughout 1994, an entitlement frenzy consumed the attention of

Congress. It began in the House of Representatives with an "A to Z" spending-cut plan for across-the-board cuts in all entitlement programs and gathered momentum with news accounts of progress by the Bipartisan Commission on Entitlement and Tax Reform.[2] Yet the Entitlement Commission failed to agree on any recommendations, and by 1995, entitlements no longer dominated the media. In the 1996 election campaign, neither party was willing to make cuts in entitlement programs an issue, and although President Clinton's 1996 budget plan included cuts in Medicare and Medicaid, social security remained off the table.

In part, the unwillingness of politicians of either party to recommend cuts in social security reflects the strength of public support for this program. A 1986 survey by Cook and Barrett found that 97.3 percent of respondents favored maintaining (40 percent) or increasing (57.3 percent) social security benefits.[3] A 1994 Gallup poll found that 70 percent of the public opposed a reduction in social security benefits.[4] And 84 percent of respondents to a 1994 poll conducted by the American Association of Retired Persons (AARP) agreed that social security benefits were "very important," while 88 percent opposed cutting benefits to reduce the federal deficit.[5]

The failure of Clinton and Congress to even consider cutting social security benefits also reflects the stabilizing effect of the institutional structure of the social security program itself. Social security includes two components, income redistribution and income replacement. In the former case, social security transfers income from the lifetime rich to the lifetime poor. In the latter case, it reallocates income over the life course by collecting payroll taxes when one works and distributing benefits when one retires.[6] It is this feature that distinguishes the American program of public pensions from that of other capitalist democracies, which typically have a two-tier system of universal flat benefits for the aged and an earnings-related social insurance tier. Combining income redistribution and income replacement into a single program has expanded the constituency for social security and made the program politically untouchable.

The battle over the budget and the attention directed at entitlement spending have had an effect, however, for they have eroded public confidence in social security. By 1993, only 30 percent of the public felt confident that social security benefits would be paid throughout their retirement. Lack of confidence is especially acute among young people.[7]

The disparity between support and confidence, the fear that social security will not "be there," partly reflects a pervasive distrust of government. Trust in government has steadily eroded from 75 percent in 1958 to only 30 percent by 1994.[8] According to a 1993 Gallup survey, 88 percent of the public believe that the federal government routinely mismanages money, 80 percent that many elected officials are dishonest, and 70 percent that government employees are dishonest.[9] If people believe that government is incompetent and government officials corrupt, it is not surprising that 81 percent believe that "fraud and waste in the Social Security sys-

tem will reduce [their] retirement benefits."[10]

Public apprehension about social security's long-range viability reflects more than general distrust in government. It also reflects confusion generated by a public dialogue about such technocratic issues as the integrity of the trust fund as well as broader ideological questions about equity between generations. This dialogue has undermined public faith in the social insurance imagery that has sustained the program and introduced what William Gamson terms a "counter theme" for defining social security.[11]

The public dialogue about social security has its origins in conservative arguments about the effect of the welfare state on the economy. It began in the early 1970s when conservative economist Martin Feldstein charged that the social security system had reduced private saving and undermined economic growth, and it has remained a persistent criticism among conservatives.[12] In recent years, however, the conservative critique of the welfare state has gained wider credence in light of declining economic growth and the specter of population aging.

## Theorizing Welfare State Retrenchment

Throughout the 1980s the main problematic for political theorists of the welfare state was explaining cross-national variations in the timing and quality of benefits and in analyzing through detailed case studies the processes of welfare-state development.[13] As the era of expansion gave way to belt-tightening, attention has shifted to processes of retrenchment.[14] Although theories of welfare-state expansion represent a natural starting point, it is questionable whether they can adequately explain variations in patterns of welfare-state retrenchment. What is different now is that the welfare state itself has created new constituents who may be more important in determining the outcome than the actors who played so central a role in development theories – labor, capital, or even federal officials.

Public support for the welfare state emanates from what Esping Anderson labels "middle class universalism":

The formula was to combine universal entitlements with high earnings-graduated benefits, thus matching welfare-state benefits and services to middle-class expectations. For the average worker as social citizen, the result was an experience of upward mobility. For the welfare state, the result was the consolidation of a vast popular majority wedded to its defense. "Middle class universalism" has protected the welfare state against backlash.[15]

All social-welfare benefits represent a transfer of tax dollars to some defined population according to certain eligibility criteria. What distinguishes programs imbued with a sense of middle-class universalism from traditional welfare is a moral claim of entitlement. Anyone who qualifies on the basis of his or her work history automatically has an earned right to benefits without the stigma that accompanies "welfare."[16] In this regard, social security is the program that most clearly has generated "middle class universalism." As a result, the actors that have become featured in the defense of the welfare state are (1) the American public, whose will can only be determined by voting patterns and public opinion polls, and (2) the interest groups that represent a vocal constituency protecting their programs.

Because of the mobilization of the middle class, retrenchment is unlikely to develop easily. For one thing a government seeking to expand benefits differs fundamentally from one seeking to take those benefits away. In the former case, reformers can take credit for the benefits produced, while in the latter case, politicians have to figure out how to impose concrete losses on voters in return for diffuse and uncertain gains. The dilemma is how to transform program cuts into an electorally

attractive proposition, or at least minimize the costs involved. In this context, efforts to minimize widespread opposition become crucial or retrenchment will be blocked.[17]

One solution has been to employ indirect strategies whose consequences will only be felt in the long run. Another solution is to devise proposals that lower the visibility of changes or obscure responsibility. Indirect strategies also include "institutional reforms that strengthen the hands of budget cutters, policies that weaken the government's revenue base, and efforts to undermine the position of pro-welfare state interest groups."[18] "New federalism," for example, represents an effort to strengthen budget cutters and weaken the government's revenue base. In the early 1970s, President Nixon's new federalism reduced federal responsibilities for the welfare state through block grants and the adoption of revenue sharing with the states. Then during the Reagan Administration funds for block grants were cut substantially. As Estes notes, "Reagan administration policies diminished federal grants-in-aid to state and local governments as a percentage of GNP from 3.4 percent in 1980 to 2.4 percent in 1989."[19]

While indirect strategies may have major long-term effects, the strength of public support for social security makes it difficult to make any kind of change with a short-term impact. The decline in confidence in social security, however, reflects the success of a strategy by right-wing opponents of the welfare state to transform the image of the elderly as deserving, undermine public support, and thus pave the way for future cuts. The ideological war being waged over social security illustrates what political theorists clearly recognize: that power struggles are a matter not merely of who gets what, when, and how but also of who defines what, when, and how. In an era of mass-mediated political realities, skillful orchestration of symbolic messages by "image managers" and the resultant manipulation of mass public perceptions are as forma-

tive in shaping political outcomes as the more
tangible realities of economic conditions, group
resources, and demographic change.

The question of "who defines," and of who
will be in a position to frame public debates
over social issues and determine which interpretations are appropriate to place on the nation agenda for public consumption, reflects
what political scientists call "symbolic politics." In any emergent national "crisis," "scandal," or "social problem," there exist
competing definitions and a variety of solutions.[20] These competing definitions and accompanying solutions attempt to rationalize
and institutionalize the relative advantages of
counterpoised groups and classes through
policies that will ultimately be legislated to
solve the socially defined problem or crisis.

In the United States, the moral claim behind the social security program lies in the
concept of "social insurance." Social insurance
has provided the hegemonic paradigm for defining social security in the twentieth century.
The social security program has remained remarkably impenetrable to cuts. What has taken
place, however, has been a reconstruction of
public discourse. Instead of being defined as a
social insurance program that provides income
security across the life course, social security
has become part of an "entitlement crisis" that
threatens to destroy the American dream and
undermine the future of the next generation.
This ideological reconstruction of social security has been the primary weapon of program
opponents in the past decade. As a result, the
imagery of social insurance, which inspired
public support for the program since its inception, has now made social security vulnerable to critics who use aspects of this imagery
to develop an oppositional counter-theme that
resonates with the broader political culture.
This counter-theme draws upon the central
elements of welfare-state "crisis," the fiscal
consequences of expanding public budgets, and
the inability of the welfare state to protect
young families.[21]

## The social construction of social insurance

Since its inception the image defining the
social security system has been that of social
insurance. The idea of social insurance was
transported to the United States at the turn
of the century by European immigrants.[22] The
concept became part of President Roosevelt's
strategy for gaining public support for the
Social Security Act of 1935. Crucial to public
acceptance of a national welfare program on
so massive a scale was the distinction between
social security and "welfare" in the traditional
sense. Whereas "welfare" targetted benefits
to the poor through means-testing, social insurance programs accorded an earned right
to workers who paid "contributions" into a
trust fund. The contributions gave "contributors a legal, moral and political right to collect their pensions."[23]

In the postwar period, Americans understood social insurance to be equivalent to a
private insurance plan. They believed they
were making contributions into a trust fund
and that they had separate accounts in their
own names, similar to a private annuity,
which they would draw down at retirement.
In reality income and outgo to the trust funds
were ledger entries.[24] Income was recorded
by posting federal securities to them, outgo
by deleting securities.[25] In reality "contributions" were payroll taxes. In reality, retirees
of all income levels received "returns" that
far exceeded their contributions to their accounts. In an era of high levels of economic
growth and continuing improvements in living standards, it made no difference how the
accounts were kept, whether contributions
were really taxes, and what return wage earners received on their "investment." Payroll
taxes were low relative to income taxes, benefits were paid on time, and most of the
labor force was guaranteed a stable retirement income.

## *The growth of middle-class universalism*

During the 1950s and 1960s labor productivity grew at 2.5–3.5 percent a year and the extra output provided the margin for higher wages.[26] Economic prosperity allowed the nation to expand its commitment to income security for the aged. Between 1950 and 1972 Congress extended social security coverage to farm workers and to other occupations that were previously excluded, granted workers the right to retire at age 62 with reduced benefits, raised benefit levels substantially, and in 1972 provided automatic costs-of-living adjustments (COLAs) as protection against inflation.[27]

As social security improved, public support grew. So did the number of organizations representing the interests of the aged. Just a scattering of organizations was formed between 1940 and 1970. Then the number of old-age interest groups exploded. As Pratt notes, "In purely numerical terms, the organizational wave in the 1970s and 1980s was extraordinary, its scale probably exceeding that of any previous wave of its kind in American history."[28]

In 1977, the gray lobby first exerted its clout when President Carter considered cutting social security benefits as a solution to declining reserves in the trust fund. Save Our Security (SOS), a coalition of senior citizen groups, was formed to protect social security benefits from being cut. SOS members lobbied Congress and helped prevent any cuts in social security benefits. Then in 1981 President Reagan proposed a 10-percent cut in future benefits, a 31-percent cut in early-retirement benefits, and a tightening of the rules regulating eligibility for disability benefits. Days after his proposal appeared, his public-approval rating dropped 16 points.[29] SOS, which had been dormant for several years, came to life. SOS members wrote thousands of letters to Congress protesting the proposed cuts. New organizations were formed, and by 1994 there were 61 national organizations representing the interests of the elderly.

Although the old-age lobby receives much attention from the media, there has also been a phenomenal growth of lobbyists representing business association. Those centered in Washington DC increased by 32 percent between 1971 and 1990. In addition to trade associations, representatives of domestic and foreign corporations, think tanks, and public interest groups all have representatives in the nation's capital. In 1993 about 69,000 people worked for trade and membership organizations in the greater Washington area. The number of American corporations with offices in Washington grew from under 100 in 1950 to more than 500 in 1990. Of the 50 largest multinational corporations, two-thirds have offices in Washington. In this context, then, the influence of the organizations representing older people is just one component of a much larger phenomenon.[30]

## *The decline of prosperity*

For one hundred years, from 1870 to 1972, the American economy grew at an annual rate of 3.4 percent after inflation.[31] In 1971 the United States experienced the first trade deficit of the century, an indicator that the nation was losing the competitive advantage it had enjoyed in the postwar period. Then in 1973 the first OPEC oil price increase led to recession and inflation. These events inaugurated a new era of declining economic growth and reduced living standards. Economic growth slowed to only 2.3 percent a year, and incomes grew by less than one-third the previous growth rate.[32]

Declines in the rates of growth of individual incomes were accompanied by changes in the family. Between 1960 and 1990 the proportion of married mothers with jobs rose from 26 percent to nearly 70 percent. The entry of women into the labor force initially compensated for the loss of male earning power so that family incomes remained stable. But rising divorce rates and increasing numbers of children born to single mothers created more female-headed households and more child poverty. By 1991 child poverty rates were at 22 percent, about their 1965 level.[33] These factors – declining real wage growth and the increasing vulnerability of young families, especially those headed by women – precipitated both a programmatic and an ideological crisis for social security.

## The crisis in social security

The programmatic crisis followed in the wake of the high unemployment associated with the stagflation of the 1970s, which reduced contributions flowing into the trust fund to pay for social security benefits. Between 1974 and 1983, the trust fund was repeatedly plagued with threats of insolvency. In 1977 Congress enacted amendments to the Social Security Act. The amendments increased future payroll taxes from their then current level of 12.26 percent to 15.3 percent, to begin in 1990.[34] Double-digit inflation continued to drain the reserves, however, and by early 1983, the trust fund had sufficient reserves to pay only one month's benefits. If no legislation had been passed, the trust fund would have been exhausted in August.[35] That year Congress passed new amendments that accelerated the effective dates of the 1977 payroll tax increases and enacted benefit cuts to be gradually phased in. The cuts included an increase in the retirement age for full benefits from 65 to 67, a six-month delay in the COLA, and the taxation of 50 percent of benefits for higher-income recipients.

Ideologically, the trust fund crisis provided conservative critics of the welfare state with empirical evidence to attack social security.

The attack originated in the early 1970s as part of the business community's response to a rise in the payroll tax and a series of benefit increases enacted between 1968 and in 1972. Then, in the late 1970s and early 1980s, an outpouring of books and articles from conservative think tanks, many supported by corporate donations, declared that social security was near bankruptcy.[36] When the 1983 amendments solved the problem, however, critics were forced to devise a new critique. The new counter-theme of generational equity played upon the empirical realities of the weak state of the economy and the declining fortunes of young families. Articles declared generational warfare centered on a futuristic battle between young and old "over the remains of a shrinking economy."[37] The economy was shrinking, the deficit rising, and savings rates dropping, critics contended, because of overspending on the welfare state, and especially on social security. Peter Peterson, an investment banker and founder of the Concord Coalition, an organization dedicated to deficit reduction, declared in a 1987 *Atlantic* magazine article that the US "has let its infrastructure crumble, its foreign markets decline, its productivity dwindle, its savings evaporate, and its budget and borrowing burgeon."[38]

The counter-theme of generational equity focused primarily on social security, the most popular American welfare program, and the program with the most firmly entrenched sense of middle-class entitlement. As it became clear that the public was unmoved by depictions of generational warfare, critics employed a revised counter-theme. The attack on social security was now incorporated into a broader "entitlement crisis," which combined the theme of generational equity with dire predictions about the deficit, the erosion of family income, and the future of the economy.

1963 mandatory spending 29.6%

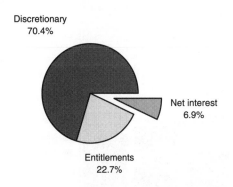

Discretionary
70.4%

Net interest
6.9%

Entitlements
22.7%

1973 mandatory spending 45.0%

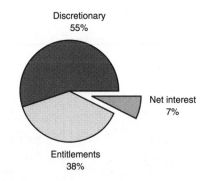

Discretionary
55%

Net interest
7%

Entitlements
38%

1983 mandatory spending 56.3%

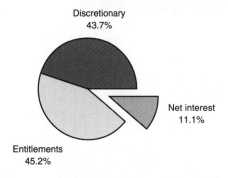

Discretionary
43.7%

Net interest
11.1%

Entitlements
45.2%

1993 mandatory spending 61.4%

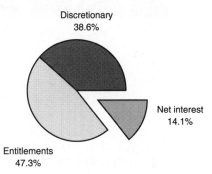

Discretionary
38.6%

Net interest
14.1%

Entitlements
47.3%

2003 (projected) mandatory spending 72.0%

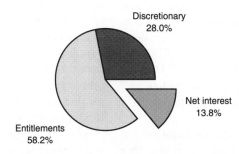

Discretionary
28.0%

Net interest
13.8%

Entitlements
58.2%

Figure 5.1 Growth of mandatory spending in the federal budget, 1963–2003
*Source*: Bipartisan Commission, *Interim Report*, 1994

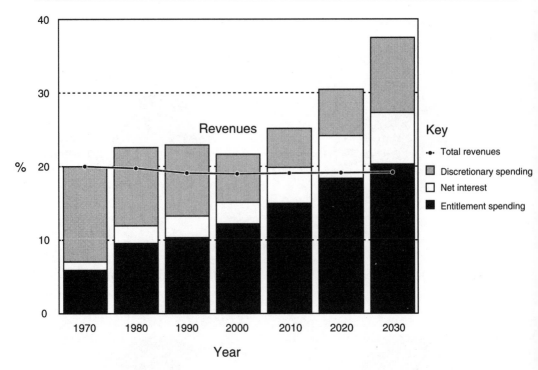

Figure 5.2  Federal outlays as a percentage of GDP, 1970–2030
*Source*: Bipartisan Commission, *Interim Report*, 1994

## Budget Politics and the Entitlement "Crisis"

The concept of an entitlement grew out of the "new property" movement in legal thought in the 1960s, when the courts ruled in regard to AFDC that social-welfare benefits were not gratuities that could be denied at will. Rather, according to the court decision, "beneficiaries have something akin to property rights in them and therefore have a right to due process in their distribution."[39] One element of an entitlement, then, meshes with common understanding. It features the right to benefits.

Formally, however, what distinguishes entitlements from other programs is that they are governed by formulas set in law and not subject to annual appropriations by Congress. In other words, entitlements are on automatic pilot. Individuals who are eligible for payments simply apply for funds.[40]

In the federal budget there are more than 100 entitlement programs, with the three largest being social security, Medicare, and Medicaid. Entitlements stand distinct from two other federal budget categories: discretionary spending, which includes domestic and defense spending, and net interest on the debt.[41] Although components of the entitlement crisis have been a part of public dialogue for more than two decades, it was not fully articulated into a single theme until the Bipartisan Commission on Entitlement and Tax Reform gave it political legitimacy and media attention.

The commission was established on November 5, 1993, by President Clinton "to recommend potential long-term budget saving measures involving statutory entitlement and other mandatory programs, and recommend alternative tax reform proposals."[42] According to journalist Bob Woodward, the commission was a trade-off between President Clinton and Senator Bob Kerrey for Kerrey's vote on the 1993 budget. Kerrey had indicated he would vote "no" because the plan did not solve the entitlement problem, so the commission was his gift from the president.[43] The commission, which was co-chaired by Senator Kerrey and Senator John Danforth, consisted of 32 members. It included ten senators and ten members of the House of Representatives, equally divided between Democrats and Republicans. The 12 persons from the private sector, who had "experience and expertise in the areas considered by the Commission,"[44] included longtime social security critic Pete Peterson, two CEOs, and Richard Trumpka, President of the United Mine Workers.

Three public commission meetings were held during the summer of 1994. The Clinton Administration remained aloof from but watchful of the proceedings. At the third meeting, Congressional Budget Office (CBO) Director Robert Reischauer testified that:

the country now has a more generous set of entitlement commitments than it seems willing to pay for . . . But the nation has been unwilling to raise taxes to match the growth in the costs of entitlement programs . . . Entitlement spending is not expected to surge before the retirement of the baby-boom generation some 15 years from now, so a precipitous policy response is not required now.[45]

From Reischauer's remarks, it seemed clear that Clinton would not consider a dramatic change of course.

After much behind-the-scenes negotiation over defining the "problem," the majority of the commissioners agreed to a list of "findings" in an *Interim Report to the President*. The hold-out was Trumpka, who refused to vote "yes" on the statement of the problem.

The *Interim Report* succinctly summarized the entitlement crisis. In the report the crisis consists of two distinct problems. The first, as shown in figure 5.1, is that entitlement spending is consuming a disproportionate share of the federal budget and crowding out funds for other social needs.[46] The second, as illustrated in figure 5.2, is that current trends are not sustainable, that entitlements will consume all federal revenues by 2030. Both the present-oriented and the futuristic message are drawn from broader themes about the state of the economy and the declining fortunes of young families.

## Greedy entitlements

According to figure 5.1, the share of federal spending devoted to entitlements increased from 22.7 percent in 1963 to 47.3 percent by 1993. This present-oriented message – that entitlements are crowding out spending for domestic programs – is viable because of the rising deficit, which doubled between 1981 and 1985 from $784 billion to $1,499 billion.[47] As a *Fortune* magazine article declared:

Want to pin a face on America's persistent deficit and savings crisis? Forget those hoary clichés – the welfare queen, lazy bureaucrat, greedy businessman, weapons-crazed general or rich Third World potentate living off U.S. aid. Reach instead for a photograph of your mom and dad. That's because the main engine driving federal spending ever upward is the explosive growth in entitlements, programs that churn out benefits aimed mostly at older middle- and upper-middle Americans. Indeed, you could eliminate all discretionary spending right now – shut down Congress, the federal agencies, the national parks, the Pentagon; wipe out waste, fraud and abuse – and thanks to the spending programmed to pour automatically through the entitlement spigot, the budget would be gushing red ink again by 2012.[48]

The implication is two-fold. First, both entitlements and discretionary spending cannot continue to increase because they will drive up the deficit. Second, even if discretionary spending is drastically cut, no deficit reduction will occur because of wasteful entitlement spending.

There are two problems with figure 5.1. The first is that entitlement spending has not experienced explosive growth but rather has been stable for more than a decade. The second is that shrinking domestic spending is the result not of entitlement growth but rather of tactics by conservatives to reduce the welfare state.

Is not an increase from 22.7 to 47.3 percent in entitlement spending explosive growth? As the Interim Report stated, "to ensure that funds are available for essential and appropriate government programs, the nation cannot continue to allow entitlements to consume a rapidly increasing share of the federal budget."[49] The problem with this message is that the bulk of the growth occurred between 1965 and 1975, a result of the start-up costs associated with Medicare, which was passed in 1965. In the ten years between 1983 and 1993 entitlement spending increased by just 2 percent of federal expenditures, from 45.2 percent to 47.3 percent. The more valid measure of expenditure growth, that used by most economists and in all government documents, is the percent of GDP. By this measure, entitlement spending has shown almost *no* growth; it was 11.3 percent of GDP in 1976 and 11.9 in 1994.[50] Social security, the real target of this charge, has also remained steady at just over 4 percent of GDP since 1975. It will remain at this level until 2010, when it will rise by 2 percent of GDP as the baby-boom generation begins to retire. If there was an entitlement crisis due to rapid growth, it ended in 1975.

By 2030, US spending still will be low compared to that of other countries. At present the percentage of GDP spent on public pensions ranges from 15.03 in Austria to 11.87 in Sweden to 3.75 in Australia and 4.97 in Japan. The average for OECD countries is 7.52. Even at an estimated 6 percent in the future, US expenditures will remain considerably less than what most European countries presently spend.[51]

What is real is the decline in discretionary spending. Figure 5.1 accurately shows that it declined from 43.7 percent of federal spending in 1983 to just 38.6 percent by 1993. If entitlement spending growth is not the cause of declining funds for discretionary programs, then what is? The lack of funding is the result of two explicit tactics by conservatives to reduce the welfare state, Reagan's Economic Recovery Tax Act of 1981 (ERTA), which substantially cut taxes for individuals and corporations, and the Bush Administration's Budget Enforcement Act (BEA) of 1990, which placed caps on spending for discretionary programs.[52] These tactics strengthened the hands of budget cutters and weakened the revenue base for social spending.

ERTA's major provisions included cumulative across-the-board reductions in individual income tax rates of 1.25 percent in 1981, 10 percent in 1982, 19 percent in 1983, and 23 percent in 1984, and a reduction in the top marginal rate from 70 percent to 50 percent. ERTA also reduced the maximum tax rate on long-term capital gains to 20 percent and indexed income-tax brackets to increases in the consumer price index. Corporate tax rates declined from 17 percent on the first $25,000 of taxable income to 16 percent in 1982 and 15 percent in subsequent years. Taxes on the next $25,000 were reduced by 2 percent.[53]

As general revenue funds declined, the costs were borne solely by domestic programs, while defense spending rose. Figure 5.3 shows the distribution of discretionary spending from 1980 to 1988, the years of the Reagan Administration, and then for 1993 when President Clinton's first budget went into effect. Domestic spending declined from 22 percent of federal expenditures in 1980 to 14.8 percent in 1988. Nearly all the decline occurred in social programs for the poor. Reagan's Omnibus Budget Reconciliation Act of 1981

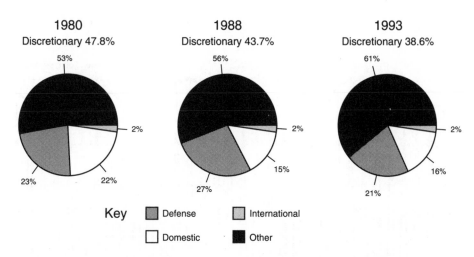

Figure 5.3 Distribution of discretionary spending, 1980, 1988, 1993
*Source*: Congressional Budget Office, *Economic and Budget Outlook 1995–1999*

eliminated the entire public-service jobs program, removed 400,000 individuals from the food-stamp program, and reduced or eliminated AFDC and Medicaid benefits for the working poor. Residents of public housing were now required to pay 30 instead of 25 percent of their income toward rent.[54] The cuts were real. Domestic spending declined from 4.9 percent of GDP in 1980 to 3.3 percent of GDP by 1987 and remained at approximately 3.3 under the Bush Administration.[55]

In that same period defense spending more than doubled from $144 billion to $295 billion and from 22.9 percent of federal expenditures to 27.3 percent.[56] By 1991 defense spending was $319 billion. Thus, one could argue that rather than a deficit-financing crisis, there existed a defense-spending crisis.

One of the major and unheralded accomplishments of the Clinton Administration was to reduce defense spending, a potential benefit of the "peace dividend" available after the fall of the Soviet Union. Between 1992 and 1995 President Clinton reduced defense spending in real dollars to $273 billion. Defense spending also declined in percent of GDP from a peak of 6.3 percent in 1986

to 3.8 percent of GDP in 1995, a postwar low.[57]

Clinton also reversed the decline in domestic spending. Between 1991 and 1995 domestic spending rose from $193.9 billion to $252 billion. It also increased slightly in its share of GDP from 3.3 to 3.5 percent. However, Clinton could not return domestic spending to 1980 levels in terms of share of GDP because of technocratic rules that have placed a lid on total discretionary spending. The BEA of 1990 established discretionary spending limits by placing caps on the amount of discretionary appropriations that can be enacted each year.[58] If spending is increased on one program, a cut must occur in another. Thus, domestic spending growth has been halted by the combination of the 1981 tax cut and the rules of the BEA, not because it has been squeezed out by rising entitlements. As a result domestic programs have received no benefit from the peace dividend.

A puzzle remains. Figure 5.4 shows that yearly federal revenues did not decline following ERTA but remained stable. Why did a large tax cut fail to reduce federal revenues? The explanation is that revenues from the

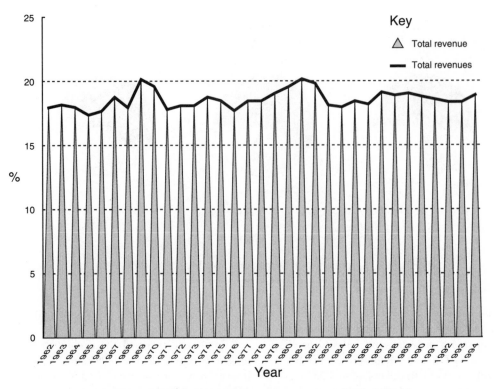

Figure 5.4 Federal revenues as a percentage of GDP, 1962–94
*Source*: Congressional Budget Office, *Economic and Budget Outlook 1996–2000*

payroll tax increase enacted in 1983 replaced revenues lost from ERTA. As figure 5.5 shows, following the 1981 tax cut *general revenues* did drop sharply, but payroll tax revenues began rising. It was payroll tax revenues that financed the defense build-up and that are presently paying for a significant share of domestic programs.

The payroll tax hikes were intended to restore solvency to the social security trust fund, not to build up a reserve. As one member of the National Commission on Social Security Reform recalls, "the building up of a huge fund that would peak in the midst of the baby boomers' retirement was a coincidence – or at most, an unintended by-product of the recommendations."[59] Nonetheless, the reserve grew, providing an alternative source of revenues for discretionary programs.

## The unsustainable future

A message with widespread public appeal is that of preserving the American dream for future generations. As one Republican pollster explained:

Your challenge is to create "The New America," the post-welfare state vision as powerful to Americans as the New Deal was 60 years ago ... Remember that many Americans perceive the key challenge ahead in moral terms rather than economic terms ... Put the budget debate in terms of the "American Dream" and "our Children's Future."[60]

With no immediate crisis in sight, conservative critics of the welfare state have used the saleable message of protecting the American dream for the next generation to describe a future crisis. This crisis is depicted in figure

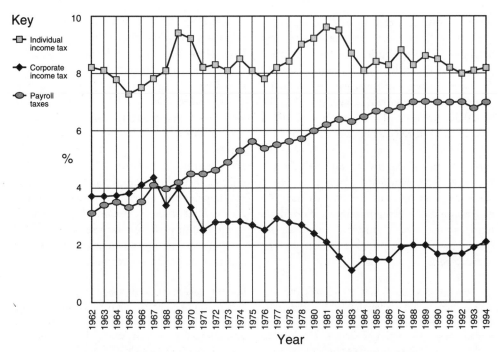

Figure 5.5  Revenues by major source as a percentage of GDP, 1962–94
*Source*: Congressional Budget Office, *Economic and Budget Outlook 1996–2000*

5.2 with the *Interim Report* "finding" that "current trends are not sustainable." The "finding" is based on 30-year projections for social security, Medicare, Medicaid, federal employees' retirement benefits, and more than 100 other entitlements. The accuracy of the finding depends upon the validity of the projections.

The model for such long-term projections is social security, which itself is subject to a variety of inevitable inaccuracies as well as political manipulation. The social security actuaries yearly make long-term actuarial projections about the long-range solvency of the social security trust fund.[61] These projections are based on assumptions about future economic and demographic trends. Their purpose is to estimate whether the system's resources and expenditures are somewhat aligned.[62]

According to present projections, the social security trust fund will be insolvent by

2030.[63] These long-term projections have now become the grist for a new crisis, which combines fears about the economy with concern for future generations. As the National Taxpayers' Union warns, we face "a huge financing gap that must be closed if tomorrow's promised benefits are to be paid at all."[64] The problem with this message is that a crisis 30 years in the future may undermine confidence in the program, but it is unlikely to create sentiment for change, especially when experts explain that modest changes would restore the social security system to long-range actuarial balance. As David Walker, Public Trustee of Social Security and Medicare, states, social security "can be sustained for the 'baby boom' generation and beyond with modest reforms."[65] With a social security crisis a dubious political weapon, critics have instead rolled these estimates into a larger entitlement crisis: an unsustainable future.

The severity of the crisis depends on the

accuracy of the projections. The entitlement spending-growth estimates depicted
in figure 5.2 are modeled after actuaries'
predictions for social security and Medicare.
As noted earlier, social security is predicted
to increase by less than 2 percent of GDP
by 2010, a matter of concern but hardly a
crisis. Health-care costs have been rising rapidly, so the crisis must be in the two health-
care programs, Medicare and Medicaid.
However, the Medicaid projections were
based on a set of assumptions that have no
programmatic or economic basis. The Medicaid estimates for figure 5.2 are based on
the following assumptions made in the *Interim Report*:

Medicaid outlays are assumed to follow CBO estimates through 2004 from the 1994 budget outlook. After 2004, Medicaid spending is projected
using a simplified outlay model. The model as-
sumes that Medicaid costs per member of specific
population groups (e.g. persons 65 to 84, persons
85 and over, and the disabled) grow in proportion
to the projected increases in Medicare costs (after
adjustment for demographic change). The model
adjusts total Medicaid costs to reflect projected
changes in the demographic composition of the
population from the 1994 Social Security Trustees Report.[66]

Medicaid is projected to rise in concert with
Medicare even though the two programs cover
different population groups, pay for different
services, and have different patterns of past
growth. Medicare is a federal program that
pays for inpatient hospital services and physician services for people over age 65, the
disabled, and victims of chronic kidney disease. Medicaid is a federal–state health-insurance program for low-income persons who
are aged, blind, disabled, members of families with dependent children, and poor pregnant women and children. Medicaid eligibility
is linked to eligibility for two means-tested
welfare programs, AFDC and SSI. It also pays
for nursing home care for the elderly and

disabled.[67] In the past there has been no correlation in growth between the two programs.
From 1966 to 1993 Medicare spending increased much more rapidly than Medicaid
spending. During the 1980s Medicaid spending remained stable at 0.6 percent of GDP
while Medicare spending rose from 1.4 to 2.0
percent of GDP.[68] If program costs were not
correlated in the past, why should they be
correlated in the future?

Even if the Medicaid projections rested on
programmatically plausible assumptions, which
they do not, there is reason to question the
validity of any 30-year estimates. The CBO
provides numerous warnings regarding the
accuracy of even ten-year projections:

[G]reat uncertainties surround such long-range
extrapolations. The economy's performance is a
big question mark; these projection are predicated
on continued growth in real GDP of 2.3 percent
annually in 2000 through 2004, on inflation of 3.1
percent, and on short-term and long-term interest
rates (specifically, rates on three-month Treasury
notes and 10-year Treasury notes) of 4.7 percent
and 6.2 percent, respectively. The economy is
bound to deviate from these assumptions in ways
that cannot be anticipated. And other major uncertainties abound, most notably about future trends
in health care spending and about other open-ended
commitments.[69]

The warning is well made. The 1993 budget
projections made by the General Accounting
Office for President Clinton's 1994 budget
was off by 23 percent in less than two years.[70]
How much faith can one place in 35-year
projections that combine all entitlement spending in one category?

## The Discourse of
## Retrenchment

The build-up of the trust fund reserve and
legitimate concerns about the long-range solvency of the trust fund have allowed con-

servative critics of the welfare state to expound three counter-themes: that the trust fund is full of worthless IOUs, burdening future generations; that there is an unfair distribution of the tax burden; and that future workers will not receive their "money's worth" from their payroll tax contributions.

## The defunct trust fund

According to one critic of social security, former Commissioner Dorcas Hardy, "there are no real dollars in the social security trust funds . . . The trust funds are, in effect, merely a growing stack of IOUs that will need to be redeemed in the future in order to meet program obligations."[71] Paul Hewitt of the National Taxpayers' Union Foundation, a conservative think tank, echoes this charge: "The vaunted Social Security 'surplus' consists entirely of IOUs from the Treasury that Congress has agreed to repay by raising taxes on workers in the next century."[72]

To protect social security against such claims, program advocates have adopted a counter-strategy, that of declaring the trust fund "off-budget." The 1983 National Commission on Social Security Reform recommended removing social security from federal budget calculations "in order to insulate this trust fund from budgetary politics."[73] The 1983 amendments to the Social Security Act specified that beginning in 1993, income and expenditures from social security and Medicare would be *excluded* from the budget totals of the president and Congress. Then, in 1990, the Omnibus Budget Reconciliation Act moved up the date, removing all calculations of the social security trust funds from the federal budget. The purpose was to prevent the surplus in the social security trust fund from masking the extent of the deficit.[74] Although social security became officially off-budget in 1990, payroll taxes continued to be deposited in the general treasury with the appropriate crediting of securities to the trust

funds, and benefits continued to be paid out of the general treasury.

The outcome of the struggle over whether social security was off-budget or part of a unified budget has allowed various interest groups to portray the trust fund and its relationship to the deficit in totally contradictory ways. Program advocates have used the off-budget status of social security to claim that it operates independently from other federal spending. It is self-financing, with contributions stored in a separate trust fund. This position has been articulated by many of the senior advocacy organizations. It was clearly summarized by the National Committee to Preserve Social Security and Medicare in response to the "finding," depicted in figure 5.1, in the *Interim Report* of the Bipartisan Commission on Entitlement and Tax Reform:

Social Security is self-financing with a dedicated payroll tax and generates a substantial surplus, which is a source of borrowing for deficit spending in the general fund . . . the findings erroneously suggest that Social Security contributes to the deficit and the increase in national debt.[75]

Critics deride this position. In a response to a statement by AARP regarding social security's off-budget status, Entitlement Commission member Peter Peterson charged:

AARP attempts to get around these unwelcome numbers by dividing all revenues into two categories: "social insurance" revenues and "non-social insurance" revenues. . . . My first reaction to this peculiar bifurcation of tax types is to point out that it has found little acceptance among economists or budget analysts – either in this country or elsewhere in the world. The reason is obvious: A tax is a tax. FICA taxes, like all other kinds of taxes, are involuntary; their payment does not give the payer any contractual (or even customary) right to any specific benefit; FICA revenues are commingled with other federal revenues from the moment they are collected; and – through "borrowing" and "lending" through paper "trust funds" – there is no practical constraint on what these revenues may be used for.[76]

Proponents of the welfare state have sought to protect social security by weakening possibilities for program cuts. Programmatically, this tactic has succeeded, but ideologically, it has provided critics with a new counter-theme. The ensuing debate has contributed to public confusion over the status of the trust fund and further undermined confidence in the program.

## The inequitable tax burden

The definition of payroll taxes as "contributions" sustained the social security system for its first 40 years. However, this image has become increasingly ineffectual, because of the shifting distribution of the federal tax burden. Since 1977, as mentioned above, Congress has enacted eight major tax bills as well as the Social Security Amendments of 1977 and 1983.[77] These changes in the law have resulted in a very different tax structure than before 1980. The income tax rate is flatter and lower and many tax preferences for individual income have been tightened or eliminated. On the other hand, the base for payroll taxes is wider and rates are higher. As a result, federal taxes became less progressive between 1977 and 1985. Effective rates rose for low-income families and fell for high-income families. In 1977 payroll taxes accounted for 30 percent of federal revenues; by 1994, 37 percent. Thus, regressive payroll taxes came to replace income taxes as the major revenue source, especially for lower-middle- and middle-income families.

Clinton reversed this trend. By 1994 the *distribution of federal taxes among income groups was more progressive than it had been since 1977.*[78] The shift was due to his 1993 Omnibus Budget Reconciliation Act, under which much of the payroll tax burden for low-income families was offset by the Earned Income Tax Credit (EITC), which refunds to working families with children all of their payroll taxes and some of their income taxes.[79]

Still, the claim that increased payroll taxes have shifted the tax burden to low- and moderate-income families is a strong criticism of social security. And the response that taxes overall are more progressive now than at any time since 1977 poses new difficulties for program advocates. One problem is that responding in kind forces advocates to abandon the language of "contributions" and concede that payroll taxes are indeed taxes. A second problem is that advocates have to admit that all taxes – payroll taxes and general revenues – are part of the same general pool. This depiction negates the claim that the trust funds represent a sacred and separate part of the federal budget and challenges conventional understanding about how social security operates.

## The "money's worth" debate

An essential component of the American version of social insurance is income redistribution. The payroll contributions of high earners subsidize the benefits of low earners. Because of this redistributory component, workers have never received back in benefits exactly what they paid in taxes. From 1942 when benefits were first paid out until the present, however, all contributors have received more back in benefits than they paid in payroll taxes. For example, a low-wage single male worker born in 1905 would receive a lifetime rate of return on payroll taxes of 8.25 percent, a high wage earner 5.19 percent. In the future workers will not get back the same return. A low-wage single male born in 1985 will receive a rate of return of only 2.07 percent, a high-wage single male just −0.03.[80] Conservative critics of social security have used future rates of return to expand the idea of inequity between generations. They contend that whereas the elderly in the past received "windfall" benefits, future generations will not get their money's worth.

The calculation of rates of return has become part of the conservative agenda for introducing the idea of privatizing social security. The idea of privatization first appeared in a bill circulated in Congress in the early 1980s, designed by the Insurance Company of North America. A similar plan was promoted by the right-wing Cato Institute in the mid-1980s. Another plan, promoted by the National Federation of Independent Business, would have turned social security into a two-tier system more amenable to cuts. Then in 1986 Rep. Newt Gingrich developed a plan to eliminate the payroll tax and have workers under 40 contribute to individual retirement accounts (IRAs).[81] All privatization proposals are justified by the "money's-worth" argument.

In response to the criticism that future generations will not get their money's worth from their contributions, program advocates have attempted to resurrect the social insurance theme. According to AARP, "Social Security was established by the government to provide income protection to workers and their families if the wage earner retires, becomes disabled or dies."[82] Other advocates have been baited into using metaphors that compare social security to private investments. Kingson argues, "Even the well-off should have a reasonable return on their Social Security investment."[83] If high earners begin to question the value of their benefits, middle-class support for the program may dwindle.

## Clinton's Social Security Politics

In terms of any public stance, the debate over entitlement spending and social security has taken place around, not within, the Clinton Administration. Members of the administration remained aloof from the Entitlement Commission. The only clue to the administration's thoughts on the subject came in the form of a secret memo from Alice Rivlin, which was leaked to the press. Although Republicans attempted to use the memo to claim that Clinton secretly planned to cut social security, the actual memo simply contained a list of options that had already been aired in a variety of forums. In the memo, entitled "Big Choices," Rivlin noted that "Decisions must be made soon . . . about our response to the Kerrey–Danforth commission report." After listing options under review by the Commission, Rivlin suggested that one policy choice is to "address the looming problems of Social Security in a way that both restores the long-run fiscal balance of the system and frees some resources in the nearer term for deficit reduction or even investment."[84] The moderate tone of the position in the secret document echoed the public testimony of Reischauer.

No decision on how to respond to the Commission was needed, however, for the Commissioners failed to reach consensus on a set of specific policy objectives. Instead of a final report with policy recommendations, the commissioners published a laundry list of options. Among them was a proposal for means-testing social security and thus making it equivalent to welfare in the traditional sense. Another proposal, endorsed by Senator Kerrey and Senator Alan Simpson and subsequently introduced in the Senate as the Personal Investment Plan Act of 1995, would allow workers the option of diverting 2 percent of their payroll taxes to their own personal investment plans. Employees would be allowed to invest their contributions either in an investment fund or in an Individual Retirement Account.[85] It was nearly midnight the night before the final commission meeting in November, 1994, before Senator Kerrey could even get a majority to sign a vaguely worded letter to the president about "Broad principles to be used when crafting solutions to our fiscal problem."[86] The non-signers were a renegade group of liberal Democrats who opposed the options for cutting entitlements. They included John Dingell (Democrat,

Michigan), Daniel Patrick Moynihan (Democrat, New York), Martin Sabo (Democrat, Minnesota), Richard Trumpka, and former Congressman Thomas Downey. Another non-signer was conservative Bill Archer (Republican, Texas), who felt the *Final Report* did not go far enough in addressing the problem.

President Clinton has never addressed the actuarial predictions of a future trust fund deficit. Nor has he taken a public stance on the recommendations of the 1996 Advisory Council on Social Security, which split among its members' recommendations for dealing with the impending depletion of the social security trust fund. Two of the Advisory Council recommendations involve the privatization of social security, the most radical proposal being the replacement of the present social security system with a flat benefit of $5,000 a year (in 1996 dollars) for all retirees and the investment of 5 percent of the current payroll tax in "personal security accounts."[87] Although it was reported in *U.S. News and World Report* that Clinton had stated he would be willing to test a partial privatization of social security as part of a plan to shore up the system's finances, Donna Shalala, Secretary for Health and Human Services, subsequently denied Clinton had made such a statement.[88]

Although no policy change has occurred in social security, the Entitlement Commission has had an indirect impact on the policy debate. The charts and measures used to define the entitlement crisis have not only become embedded in public debates, they have also become accepted estimates in official government documents. As a 1994 report by the General Accounting Office (GAO) notes regarding Medicaid projections:

The Medicaid program presents a major estimating challenge. Each state makes different program choices. Further, eligibility is hard to predict, benefits are not cash, implementation and financing are shared among multiple parties and levels of government, and interactions with other programs are complex.[89]

Nonetheless the GAO used the Entitlement Commission's Medicaid estimates unquestioningly for its long-term simulation model of future mandatory spending.[90]

## Conclusion

In his first term in office, Clinton initially emphasized progressive measures. He reduced defense spending and increased discretionary social spending. He began a second term in office with a new legacy, a welfare reform bill that signified the undoing of the New Deal and two recommendations from the Advisory Council on Social Security that would mandate an equally dramatic departure from the New Deal in regard to the nation's core public-pension program. Although the public remains adamantly opposed to cutting social security, the lack of confidence in the program, especially among people aged 25–34, suggests that the conservative shift from a direct attack on social security to a more fundamental undermining of the program's image has succeeded at some level.[91]

If Clinton has learned from his predecessors that social security remains politically untouchable, at least for the present, he has also learned that programs aimed at the poor and the disreputable are easy targets for budget cutters. What is still to be determined is whether the transformation of the deserving elderly into "greedy geezers" will erode public support sufficiently to make possible dramatic program restructuring. The exemplar of AFDC shows that such a scenario is indeed possible.

In cross-national research on the growth and development of welfare states, the US has stood out as a "laggard." It was slow to legislate national programs of social protection for the elderly, the unemployed, and the poor; the programs it did implement were less generous than those of other nations; and it never legislated the full array of social programs other nations offered.[92] Typically, American exceptionalism has been explained in terms of structural variables such as the strength of organized labor or the nature of the state. Yet the US appears to be on the verge of becoming a welfare-state leader in undoing the core programs of the New Deal and moving toward privatization of income security in old age – a new form of American exceptionalism.

Should such a scenario emerge, it will suggest that ideological factors must be incorporated into theories of welfare-state retrench-ment. Understanding this paradigm shift requires a departure from analysis solely on the socio-economic and political-institutional features of the welfare state. It also requires an analysis of the discursive structures that have sustained it. Recent evidence on the entitlement debate suggest that struggles over policies are not only over concrete options but also over meaning and interpretation.[93] The outcome of these struggles organizes the political terrain and limits the options for the future.

## Notes

This research was supported by a John Simon Guggenheim Memorial Fellowship, an American Council of Learned Societies Fellowship, and a Congressional Fellowship from the American Sociological Association. I would like to thank Chris Howard, Theda Skocpol, Hans Reimer, Eric Kingson, James Orcutt, and the editors, Michael Schwartz and Clarence Lo, for their comments on a previous version of this chapter.

Portions of this chapter were first published in "Social Security and the Myth of the Entitlement Crisis," the *Gerontologist* 36 (1996), pp. 391–9.

1 Congressional Budget Office, *The Economic and Budget Outlook: Fiscal Years 1997–2006* (Washington DC: US Government Printing Office, 1996).

2 "A to Z Spending Cut Team, Summary of Proposal by Rob Andrews (D-NJ) and Bill Zeliff (R-NH)" (June 21, 1994) Author's files.

3 Fay Lomax Cook and Edith J. Barrett, *Support for the American Welfare State: The Views of Congress and the Public* (New York: Columbia University Press, 1992), pp. 62–5.

4 Virginia Reno and Robert Friedland, "Strong Support but Low Confidence: What Explains the Contradiction?" in Eric Kingson and James Schulz, eds, *Social Security for the 21st Century* (New York: Oxford University Press, 1996).

5 "Public Opinion on Entitlement Programs," Research Report from AARP Research Division, unpublished typescript (1994).

6 Joseph Quinn, *Entitlements and the Federal Budget: Securing Our Future* (Washington DC: National Academy on Aging, 1966).

7 Robert Friedland, "When Support and Confidence are at Odds: The Public's Understanding of the Social Security Program," National Academy of Social Insurance (1994), p. 5. For other surveys of public opinion, see Theodore Marmor, Jerry L. Mashaw, and Philip Harvey, *America's Misunderstood Welfare State* (New York: Basic Books, 1990); Sally Sherman, "Public Attitudes toward Social Security," *Social Security Bulletin*, 52 (December, 1989), pp 2–16.

8 Theda Skocpol, "Why it Happened: The Rise and Resounding Demise of the Clinton Health Security Plan," paper presented at the Brookings Institution, conference on "The Past and Future of Health Reform," Washington DC (January 24, 1995), p. 21.

9 Friedland, "When Support and Confidence are at Odds" p. 32.

10 Robert Friedland, "Social Security: Public Support and Public Confidence," paper presented at the National Academy of Social Insurance, Washington DC (January 25, 1994).

11 William Gamson, *Talking Politics* (Cambridge: Cambridge University Press, 1992), p. 11.

12 Martin Feldstein, "Social Security, Induced Retirement and Aggregate Accumulation," *Journal of Political Economy* 82 (September–October, 1974), pp. 905–25.

13 Jill Quadagno, "Theories of the Welfare State," *Annual Review of Sociology* 13 (1987), pp. 109–28.

14 John Myles and Jill Quadagno, "Recent Trends in Public Pension Reform: A Comparative View," in Keith Banting, ed., *Reform of the Retirement Income System* (Ottawa: Avebury, 1997).

15 Gosta Esping-Anderson, *The Three Worlds of Welfare Capitalism* (Princeton NJ: Princeton University Press, 1990), p. 69.

16 Ibid., p. 65.

17 Paul Pierson, *Dismantling the Welfare State: Reagan, Thatcher, and the Politics of Retrenchment* (Cambridge: Cambridge University Press, 1994), pp. 6–7.

18 Ibid. pp. 6–7.

19 Carroll Estes, "The Reagan Legacy: Privatization, the Welfare State, and Aging in the 1990s," in John Myles and Jill Quadagno, eds, *States, Labor Markets and the Future of Old Age Policy* (Philadelphia PA: Temple University Press, 1991), p. 65.

20 Murray Edelman, *Constructing the Political Spectacle* (Chicago: University of Chicago Press, 1995).

21 My analysis is based on my participant-observer research experience as a staff member on the Bipartisan Commission on Entitlement and Tax Reform from June, 1994, to December, 1994. As a senior policy analyst my tasks were to provide background briefings for commission members, to write up summaries of all the social programs under the jurisdiction of the commission, and to analyze various options for reducing spending in those programs. During this period, I recorded my experiences in a diary and kept detailed files of all memos, notes, staff meetings, and copies of documents that arrived in the office. I also conducted interviews with policy makers and representatives of interest groups, attended hearings on various legislative proposals, and went to meetings of the Advisory Council on Social Security as well as its technical panels.

22 Ann Orloff, *The Politics of Pensions: A Comparative Analysis of Britain, Canada, and the United States, 1880–1940* (Madison: University of Wisconsin Press, 1993), p. 9.

23 Arthur Schlesinger, *The Coming of the New Deal* (Boston: Houghton Mifflin, 1958), pp. 308–9.

24 Social security is the largest of 167 federal trust fund programs. In 1989 it accounted for 69 percent of all revenues and 58 percent of all spending for trust fund programs. Trust fund income consists of specific taxes and premiums levied on segments of the populations to help cover the program's expenditures; trust funds also receive "income" from the government, i.e. "credit" from one government account to another – what is in essence paper income. No resources are moved; no actual money is collected. In the case of social security, these government payments represent interest on federal securities, the government share of the payroll tax as an employer, and a small amount for special payments. See David Koitz, Gene Falk, and Philip Winters, "Trust Funds and the Federal Deficit," Congressional Research Service, Washington, DC Library of Congress (February 26, 1990), p. 1.

25 These securities are non-marketable, meaning they can not be sold to the public. Typically, they are called special issues. The trust fund is credited with payroll tax receipts, income from taxes levied on benefits, and interest income on the securities held. The credit is provided in the form of federal securities, not in the form of cash. The trust fund securities represent "spending authority" for the programs involved, a promise of future funding. Thus, the trust fund was a government accounting device, to which receipts were simply credited.

26 Frank Levy and Richard Michael, *The Economic Future of American Families: Income and Wealth Trends* (Washington DC: Urban Institute, 1991), p. 8.

27 John Myles, "Postwar Capitalism and the Extension of Social Security into a Retirement Wage," in Margaret Weir, Ann Shola Orloff, and Theda Skocpol, eds, *The Politics of Social Policy in the United States* (Princeton NJ: Princeton University Press, 1998) pp. 265–91; Gerald Nash, Noel Pugach, and Richard Tomasson, *Social Security: The First Half-Century* (Albuquerque: University of New Mexico Press, 1988).

28 Henry J. Pratt, *Gray Agendas: Interest Groups and Public Pensions in Canada, Britain and the*

*United States* (Ann Arbor: University of Michigan Press, 1993), pp. 178–9.

29 Paul Light, *Artful Work: The Politics of Social Security Reform* (New York: Random House, 1985), p. 124.

30 Kevin Phillips, *Arrogant Capital: Washington, Wall Street and the Frustration of American Politics* (New York: Little Brown, 1994), p. 61.

31 Angus Maddision, *Dynamic Forces in Capitalist Development* (New York: Oxford University Press, 1991), pp. 50–3.

32 Levy and Michael, *Economic Future*, p. 9.

33 Lawrence Mishel and Jared Bernstein, *The State of Working America* (Washington DC: Economic Policy Institute, 1993).

34 Eugene Steuerle and Jon Bakija, *Retooling Social Security for the Twenty-First Century* (Washington DC: Urban Institute Press, 1994), p. 51.

35 Robert Myers, "Two Current Widespread Myths about Social Security Financing," *Generational Journal* (1988), p. 4.

36 Jill Quadagno, "Interest Group Politics and the Future of U.S. Social Security," in Myles and Quadango, *States, Labor Markets and the Future of Old Age Policy*, p. 43.

37 Ibid., p. 44.

38 Peter Peterson, "The Morning After," *Atlantic Monthly* (October, 1987), p. 43.

39 Kent Weaver, "Controlling Entitlements," in John Chubb and Paul E. Peterson, eds, *The New Direction in American Politics* (Washington DC: Brookings, 1985), p. 308.

40 Congressional Budget Office, *The Economic and Budget Outlook: Fiscal Years 1995–99* (Washington DC: US Government Printing Office, 1994), p. 39.

41 The discretionary category includes spending for defense, education, training and social services, the environment, health research, medical care for veterans, aid to other countries, and numerous other government activities. Congressional Budget Office, *Economic and Budget Outlook 1995–99*, p. 39.

42 Charter of the Bipartisan Commission on Entitlement and Tax Reform, Executive Order 12878 (November 5, 1993). Author's files.

43 Bob Woodward, *The Agenda: Inside the Clinton White House* (New York: Simon and Schuster, 1994), pp. 307–8.

44 Charter of the Bipartisan Commission. Author's files.

45 Statement of Robert Reischauer, Director, Congressional Budget Office on Entitlement and Tax Reform (July 15, 1994).

46 Bipartisan Commission on Entitlement and Tax Reform, *Interim Report to the President* (Washington DC: Superintendent of Documents, 1994).

47 Committee on Ways and Means, *Green Book: Overview of Entitlement Programs* (Washington, DC: US Government Printing Office, 1994), p. 1271.

48 Ann Reilly Dowd, "Needed: A New War on the Deficit," *Fortune* (November 14, 1994), p. 191.

49 Bipartisan Commission, *Interim Report* p. 10.

50 Congressional Budget Office, *The Economic and Budget Outlook: Fiscal Years 1996–2000* (Washington DC: Government Printing Office, 1995).

51 *New Orientations for Social Policy* (Paris: Organization for Economic Co-operation and Development, 1994), p. 59.

52 ERTA was not the only tax legislation in this period. Since 1977 Congress has enacted eight major tax bills: the Revenue Act of 1978, the Economic Recovery Act of 1981, the Tax Equity and Fiscal Responsibility Act of 1982, the Deficit Reduction Act of 1984, the Tax Reform Act of 1986, the Omnibus Budget Reconciliation Act (OBRA) of 1989, the OBRA of 1990, and most recently, OBRA, 1993. Congressional Budget Office, *Economic and Budget Outlook 1995–99*, p. 52.

53 Staff of the Joint Committee on Taxation, "General Explanation of the Economic Recovery Tax Act of 1981," H. R. 4242, 97th Congress; Public Law 97–34, December 29, 1981 (Washington DC: US Government Printing Office, 1981), pp. 5, 9.

54 Jill Quadagno, *The Color of Welfare: How Racism Undermined the War on Poverty* (New York: Oxford University Press, 1994).

55 Congressional Budget Office, *Economic and Budget Outlook*, pp. 140–1.

56 Congressional Budget Office, *Reducing the Deficit* (Washington, DC: US Government Printing Office, 1994), p. 11.

57 Congressional Budget Office, *Economic and Budget Outlook 1996–2000*, pp. 98–9.

58 Although initially established for 1990–5, the BEA, with some changes, was extended through 1998 in the Omnibus Budget Reconciliation Act of 1993 (OBRA 93). James Edwin Kee and Scott V. Nystrom, "The 1990 Budget Package: Redefining the Debate," *Budgeting and Public Finance* (Spring, 1991), pp. 3–24.

59 Robert Myers, "Two Current Widespread Myths about Social Security Financing," *Generational Journal* (October, 1988), pp. 1–2.

60 "Attention! All Sales Reps for the Contract with America," *New York Times* (February 5, 1995), p. 10B.

61 Board of Trustees of the Federal Old Age and Survivors Insurance and Disability Insurance Trust Fund, *1994 Annual Report* (Washington DC: US Government Printing Office, 1994).

62 David Koitz, "Social Security: Its Funding Outlook and Significance for Government Finance," Congressional Research Service, Library of Congress (June 1, 1986), p. 31.

63 David Koitz and Geoffrey Kollmann, "The Financial Outlook for Social Security and Medicare," CRS Report for Congress (April 27, 1995), p. 1.

64 Neil Howe and Richard Jackson, *Entitlements and the Aging of America* (Washington DC: National Taxpayers' Union Foundation, 1994), Chart 4–30.

65 Testimony of David Walker before the Bipartisan Commission on Entitlement and Tax Reform (July 15, 1994), p. 4. Author's files.

66 Bipartisan Commission, *Interim Report*, p. 20.

67 Committee on Ways and Means, *Green Book*.

68 Congressional Budget Office, *Economic and Budget Outlook 1996–2000*, p. 97.

69 Congressional Budget Office, *The Economic and Budget Outlook: Fiscal Years 1996–99*, Report to the Senate and House Committees on the Budget (Washington DC: Congressional Budget Office, January, 1994), p. 28.

70 General Accounting Office, *Fiscal Year 1994 Budget Estimates and Actual Results*, Report to the Chairman, Committee on the Budget, House of Representatives (April, 1995).

71 Dorcas Hardy, "The Social Security Trust Funds: Myth or Reality?," United Seniors Association (August, 1993), p. 2. Author's files.

72 Paul Hewitt, "Are the Elderly Benefitting at the Expense of Younger Americans?," in Leonard Kaye and Andrew Scharlach, eds, *Controversial Issues in Aging* (Greenhaven Press, forthcoming).

73 Letitia Chambers and James A. Rotherham, *Social Security Financing* (Washington DC: National Committee to Preserve Social Security and Medicare, 1994), p. 7.

74 David Koitz, "Social Security's Treatment under the Federal Budget: A Summary," Library of Congress (Washington DC: Congressional Research Service, January 26, 1995), p. 2.

75 Letter from Martha McSteen, President, National Committee to Preserve Social Security and Medicare, to Senator Robert Kerrey (July 14, 1994). Author's files.

76 Memo from Peter G. Peterson to Members of the Bipartisan Commission on Entitlement and Tax Reform, Re: Statement submitted to the Commission by the AARP (September 23, 1994), p. 7. Author's files.

77 Congressional Budget Office, *Economic and Budget Outlook 1995–99*, p. 52.

78 One could argue that if payroll taxes had not grown in importance, the federal tax system might have become even more progressive, because their increased weight in revenue totals has dampened the overall move toward greater progressivity. On the other hand, the increase in the payroll tax may have prevented other kinds of tax increases. There is no way to know.

79 Steuerle and Bakija, *Retooling Social Security*, p. 160.

80 Rates of return are calculated in 1993 dollars. Ibid. table A.3.

81 David Koitz, *Ideas for Privatizing Social Security*, CRS Report for Congress, Library of Congress (June 5, 1996), pp. 3–4.

82 American Association of Retired Persons, "Public Opinion on Entitlement Programs," Research Report from AARP Research Division, unpublished typescript (1994), p. 17. Author's files.

83 Eric Kingson, "Testing the Boundaries of University," *Gerontologist* 34 (6) (1994), p. 740.

84 Memo from Alice Rivlin, "Big Choices" (October 3, 1994). Author's files.

85 Bipartisan Commission on Entitlement and Tax Reform, *Final Report to the President* (Wash-

ington DC: US Government Printing Office, 1995).

86 Bipartisan Commission on Entitlement and Tax Reform, *Final Report*, p. vi.

87 Advisory Council on Social Security, "Report of the Advisory Council on Social Security" (Washington DC, 1996).

88 Susan Dentler, "Social Security: A Private Matter?," *U.S. News and World Report* (July 29, 1996). p. 53; Donna Shalala, presentation at the annual meeting of the American Sociological Association New York NY (August 18, 1996)

89 Committee on the Budget, House of Representatives, *Fiscal Year 1994 Budget Estimates and Actual Results*, Report to the Chairman

(Washington DC: General Accounting Office, April, 1995), p. 14.

90 *The Deficit and the Economy: An Update of Long-Term Simulations*, Report to the Chairman, Committee on the Budget, US Senate, and the Chairman, Committee on the Budget, House of Representatives (Washington DC: General Accounting Office, April, 1995), p. 23.

91 Reno and Friedland, "Strong Support but Low Confidence," p. 181.

92 Quadagno, *Color of Welfare*, p. 234.

93 Nancy Fraser, "Struggle Over Needs: Outline of a Socialist-Feminist Critical Theory of Late-Capitalist Political Culture," in Linda Gordon, ed., *Women, the State and Welfare* (Madison: University of Wisconsin Press, 1990).

# Part II
# Welfare–Warfare Spending, Technology, and the Global Economy

# 6

# Wealth and Poverty in the National Economy

## The Domestic Foundations of Clinton's Global Policy

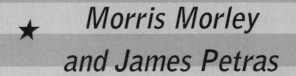

★ *Morris Morley* ★
*and James Petras*

## Introduction

The Clinton presidency has been a maze of contradictions: He talks to the poor and works for the rich. In 1992 he campaigned for the White House promising social reforms and to "rebuild America;" four years later, amid his bid for a second term, Clinton was being praised by thousands of corporate executives as the best business president of the century. Yet, in 1996, the US remained the only major industrialized country without a national health plan and within this group of nations the one with the greatest inequalities in wealth and income. What went wrong? Part of the answer is to be found in the political priorities and socio-economic backgrounds and committments of Clinton and his senior policy makers. You cannot promote booming corporate profits through tax write-offs, overseas investment, and cutbacks in social spending and expect improvements in workers' living standards. You cannot appoint corporate lawyers and Wall Street executives to

key domestic economic positions and expect them to impose new tax burdens on the wealthy to fund a national health program.

This chapter provides an overview of the Clinton Administration's domestic socio-economic policies within a global framework. It argues that this Democratic White House has promoted global capitalism at the expense of a revitalized domestic economy. It further contends that Clinton cannot serve two masters: the corporate rich and the working people of America. And here it documents Clinton's clear-cut choice: He has opted for higher profits for the Fortune 500 and skyrocketing earnings for their CEOs while providing empty inspirational speeches about personal responsibility for the rest of the citizenry. The Republicans lost the 1996 presidential election but their ideas will continue to govern the US. So who really "won" that election?

During the Reagan/Bush era, the US pursuit of global dominance and "leadership" increasingly depended on the appropriation of resources in the national economy: the re-programming of state funds from social programs to promoting overseas expansion; the lowering of domestic wages and living standards to sustain high rates of profitability and market share in the global arena; an elite-dominated political system that sustained externally oriented structures and shaped national policy priorities; a regressive tax structure that reconcentrated income at the top (in the hands of the global actors); and the creation of a two-tiered economy and society in which the majority were linked to decaying domestic institutions while a small, privileged elite pursued its accumulation drives within the global networks.

To facilitate this process, the executive branch and state institutions increasingly adopted an "enforcer" role, policing the violence and discontent of those excluded from the new axis of economic activity. For the globally oriented elite, maintaining the practice of diverting state resources and confronting the consequences was basically a political problem: building "police barriers" so that the disorganization and crime spawned by the two-tiered system did not spill over into their work sites or lifestyles; containing domestic social expenditures so that they would not impinge on the state's ability to bail out capitalist sectors in crisis (e.g. financial institutions); and ensuring a docile and politically impotent labor movement that posed no threat to the capacity of this elite to increase profits locally and appropriate home state resources in order to maximize expansion in the world economy.

Far from contesting the Republican order of priorities, Clinton embraced them from the outset. Promoting US overseas corporate activities became the core element of his administration's strategic economic planning: the needs of the domestic economy were purposefully subordinated to subsidizing high-tech, speculative, and overseas investors all seeking to take advantage – directly or indirectly – of highly lucrative profit opportunities in the world market. To facilitate this process, the US economy has been restructured while new investments in national industry have declined: The result has been a continuation during the 1990s of stagnating wage levels, the disappearance of millions of secure, well-paid, high-benefits jobs, the substitution of a more economically insecure, poorly paid, wage-working class witnessing a steady contraction of job benefits (health, holidays, etc.), and new cuts in welfare spending alongside lowered corporate taxes. Appeals to the demands of "global competitiveness" and the "imperatives of the world market" have served to legitimate this drive by the Democratic White House to lower the domestic social costs of production and maximize state incentives for America's overseas investors and traders – all the while deliberately undercutting the bargaining power and political clout of organized labor.

This chapter will trace Clinton's conversion from a rhetorician of the poor into a celebrant of the stock market. First, we detail the shifts in policy during Clinton's first two years in office: primarily the turn to the right and adoption of the Republican–Gingrich agenda. Then we document how the Democratic administration collaborated with conservative Republicans in Congress in dismantling the welfare state, even as the president resisted some of their more extreme proposals. As we point out, it was Clinton, not Newt Gingrich, who started it all by declaring the "end of welfare as we know it." We go on to discuss the social impact of Clinton's policies on wages, profits, and jobs. We argue that the president's Republican stance is creating a two-tiered society that disproportionately benefits the nation's globally oriented capitalist class at the expense of the domestic economy. The next section provides a global framework for understanding the problem of domestic decay – which it locates in Clinton's committment to overseas corporate expansion.

The concluding section provides a theoretical and empirical basis for understanding why corporate America was so willing to bankroll the 1996 Clinton re-election campaign – while most eligible voters either abstained, cast their ballot for a minor candidate, or held their nose in voting for the "lesser evil."

## Changing National Economic Priorities: "Democratic" Rhetoric, "Republican" Democrats, 1993–4

During his election campaign, President Clinton implicitly recognized that empire building abroad and the reconstruction of the domestic economy were incompatible. So too did a clear majority of voters, who preferred the Clinton emphasis on "rebuilding America" to Bush's preoccupation with "global leadership." Armed with an impressive mandate, Clinton entered the White House publicly declaring his intention to focus on the home front while accepting US global commitments in Central Europe, the Middle East, southern Africa, and elsewhere. Furthermore, he acknowledged that the most critical problems facing the US economy were "longer-term and structural."[1]

On taking office, however, he immediately proceeded to move in the opposite direction: Revitalizing urban America took a back seat to bailing out Yeltsin's Russia; a critical view of NAFTA gave way to an emphasis on expanding and fast-tracking the program; instead of significant cuts in military and intelligence spending programs, the projected Clinton defense budgets for 1994–8 indicated far more limited savings, while administration officials expressed their opposition to any major tampering with the spy budget. This shift reflected the institutional power of those economic forces that brought Clinton to power and were disproportionately represented in the highest echelons of his government. Clinton was a new breed of Wall Street populist, one who talked to the people but worked for the internationally oriented corporate elite.

There was perhaps no more striking illustration of Clinton's reversal of election priorities than his allocation of key economic and foreign policy positions to individuals who were oriented toward "global leadership": free traders and promoters of the multinational investment and banking community, and advocates of projecting American power abroad, including intervention in the Third World.

Asked to comment on the new administration's economic program, William Kristol, chief of staff of former Vice-President Dan Quayle, perceptively observed: "What is striking [about the program] is that there is this class warfare rhetoric, but what's creepy is how cynical it is ... He doesn't believe in this rhetoric. He has a cabinet full of millionaires."[2] Almost 80 percent to be precise (a figure higher than for the Reagan and Bush cabinets), most of whom accumulated their wealth during the speculator ("making money, not goods") decade of the 1980s.

Just as Clinton's personnel appointments ran counter to his campaign rhetoric about "rebuilding America," so too did the policies pursued during his first year in office – which conformed more to the structures of US power linked to empire building (and domestic decay) than to the requirements of the national economy.

Prior to, and following, the November presidential election, Clinton and his advisors stressed time and again that the Democratic administration would give top priority to "structural" problems (falling productivity, declining incomes, eroding industrial base, etc.) that plagued the American economy. "The big challenge," declared the newly appointed Secretary of Labor Robert Reich, was "to prevent the long-term structural agenda from being trumped by problems with the short-term business cycle."[3] As part of a "stimulus and investment" strategy, Clinton had promised to spend at least $30 billion to create new, well-paid jobs and repair the nation's decaying infrastructure. But after January 1993, the focus on long-term structural changes began to take a back seat to deficit reduction. This reflected the fact that, with the exception of Reich, all of Clinton's most influential economic advisers were "deficit hawks."

Clinton's 1994 budget proposals reflected this post–election shift: The economic stimulus package was almost halved to around $16 billion, to be divided roughly equally between "job retraining" and infrastructure investments. Analyzing the tax, spending, and investment proposals, economist David Gordon concluded that over the next four years "the balance favors net deficit reduction over new investments by a margin of nearly two to one."[4] Even if the package had not subsequently been filibustered to defeat by Senate Republicans, it would not have come close to keeping pace with the new additions to the work force in 1993–4 alone, or compensated for the hundreds of thousands of white-collar jobs that major corporations were in the process of shedding throughout the first twelve months of the Clinton presidency.

Finally, the allocation for education and training programs in the first Clinton budget made a mockery of his campaign pledge to "put people first." Not only did the share of the economy (GDP) devoted to federal investment programs fall by around 2–3 percent compared with the last year of the Bush Administration; education and training programs were set to experience the biggest single decline, of nearly 6 percent.[5]

The year-long focus on deficit reduction at the expense of investments, though, did not produce a national economic recovery. New York, California, Pennsylvania, and other key states were still in recession. During 1993, according to a *U.S. News and World Report* analysis, the ten states that experienced the most gains were responsible for a mere 11 percent of total economic activity while the ten states where economic revival had been weakest accounted for 40 percent.[6] The widening gap between Clinton's rhetoric and policy proposals led one commentator to astutely observe that he talks like Franklin Roosevelt but acts like Herbert Hoover.

The prevailing economic wisdom of the Reagan/Bush years was that the upward redistribution of wealth and income would result in greater investment in productive activities, creating more jobs and higher incomes for all. As we now know, nothing of the sort happened: The rich became richer, millions of well-paid jobs disappeared, and speculation flourished. Nonetheless, under Clinton a new version of "trickle-down" economics was touted, this time taking the form of a "trickle-down technology." According to Secretary of Labor Robert Reich, state subsidies to private businesses for technological development would create high-paying jobs and also make the US economy more globally competitive. The administration budgeted $17 billion over the next four years to subsidize state–industry cooperation with the basic aim of making state research centers the "incubators" of advanced technology for corporate profit making.

But one of the lessons of the 1980s is that the high-tech approach and tax subsidies did not create new, well-remunerated jobs. The introduction of new technologies enabled enterprises to increase productivity levels as they pared down their workforce. As demand picked up, however, the new technology combined with longer work hours and tighter discipline of labor meant that few, if any, new workers were hired. Productivity gains came at the expense of job creation.[7] This trend has shown no signs of reversal since Clinton entered the White House. And few, if any, areas of the economy have been exempt. For example, Intel, the world's leading semiconductor corporation, did record sales of $5.9

billion in 1992 and $8.8 billion in 1993 in an industry employing 34,000 fewer workers than it did in 1988.[8] In the automobile sector, Chrysler produced the same number of cars in 1995 (1.72 million) as it did in 1988 with 9,000 fewer employees.[9]

The 0.7-percent decline in the official unemployment rate during Clinton's first year in office (to 6.4 percent) was a deceptive indicator of any real improvement in the nation's job plight. The official rate count, for instance, excluded the 75–80 percent of black and Hispanic youths living in big cities who did not even bother looking for employment. Nor did it take account of the millions of self-employed workers who were underemployed, the victims of corporate layoffs, downsizing, and slashed budgets.[10] Furthermore, in the 28 months of "job recovery" after the 1990–1 recession, the net gain in payroll employment was only 563,000, compared with a 3.3 million figure for similar periods of previous postwar revivals.[11] On top of that, most of the new positions continued to be lower paying and less secure than the recession-lost jobs. Between January and July 1993, 60 percent of new hirings were part-time; during approximately the same period (January to September), the industrial-manufacturing sector laid off almost 450,000 full-time, well-remunerated workers – with major corporations such as Eastman-Kodak, Philip Morris, and NCR committed to eliminating thousands more such jobs over the course of the Clinton presidency.[12]

Real wage levels continued their downward trend under Clinton for almost all workers, with the lowest-paid sectors experiencing the most rapid loss of purchasing power. In the first half of 1993, real wages across the board declined by 0.6 percent compared with the first half of 1991, and 1.1 percent compared with the first six months of the Bush Administration.[13] In October, under White House pressure, the strongest advocate of an increase in the hourly minimum wage (whose real value

had declined from $4.25 to about $2.50 over the past decade), Labor Secretary Reich, agreed to put his campaign "on hold" until after Congress had voted on what promised to be a long-drawn-out debate on the administration's health-care reform package. At a time when a family of three living on a full-time minimum wage were earning $2,300 below the poverty line (the same worker earned $459 above it in 1979), a *Wall Street Journal* report noted that the current $4.25 an hour "provided an income so meager that welfare recipients often do better if they turn down jobs paying it."[14] Meanwhile, according to a survey of 26 major cities released by the United States Conference of Mayors, the number of families seeking food and shelter in 1993 increased by 30 percent; families jumped from 33 percent to 43 percent of the homeless population during the first year of the Clinton presidency.[15] So much for the election rhetoric about "putting people first."

By concentrating on capital-intensive, high-tech growth instead of labor-intensive and low-tech human social services (health, education, energy conservation, etc.), Clinton appeared to be sabotaging his own "stimulus and investment" strategy. The policy of "trickle-down technology" seemed to be further polarizing the nation's social structure, widening the gap between the rich, high-tech capitalists and the majority of workers in low-paid, part-time service jobs, alongside a significant proportion of the workforce who had no prospects of ever finding employment again.

The growth of low-paid jobs and the increase in the "working poor" is also linked to the Reagan, Bush, and Clinton promotion of speculative capital. On the one hand, this type of capital has aggressively financed "risk-taking" new ventures based on technological innovations which promise swift, highly profitable returns positing lower labor costs. On the other, speculative capital also serves to impoverish the American working class more indirectly, through growing amounts of investment overseas to take advantages of high rates of return, largely resulting from low wage rates. The latter, in turn, serves to create a downward pressure on wage levels at home; and rising imports produced by this movement of speculative dollars abroad accelerates the conversion of stable, well-paid manufacturing jobs into temporary or full-time, poorly remunerated jobs in retail shopping malls and the like. By 1994, the percentage of "working poor" (part- and full-time), together with the unemployed, accounted for a record 38.5 percent of the total labor force.[16]

Clinton's domestic policy reversals since entering the White House extended to the formulation of a new health-care policy: During 1993, the social rhetoric of the election campaign appeared to shift to a more "market"-oriented approach. The call for universal health care gave way to a focus on lowering the costs of the existing health-care program. To accommodate the powerful health-insurance industry, the administration watchword became "managed competition" – a health program to be funded through payroll tax and with the market accepting some form of government regulation. In the course of the evolving debate, agreement was reached on the need to correct some major inequities in the existing system, e.g. including a benefit package to cover the tens of millions of uninsured Americans. Nonetheless, there was little indication that the proposed new approach would stop giving preferential treatment to those with most ability to pay. In September, a Harvard Medical School expert remarked that, if passed in its present form, the health-care plan would be "really ratifying a multi-tiered health-care system."[17]

Meanwhile, throughout 1993 and the first half of 1994, Clinton steadily retreated from the idea of health-care reform based on universal coverage with an employer mandate to meet 80 percent of the premiums, capitulating to a ferocious, multimillion-dollar, indus-try lobbying "offensive." The heavily compromised legislation submitted to the Congress focussed, instead, on "regional health alliances" competing with local "health plans" or networks of doctors, hospitals, and insurance companies for the best medical care. Then, in August 1994, acknowledging that even this bill, which sought to accommodate the concerns of every powerful existing industry player, was doomed to failure on Capitol Hill, Clinton signalled a willingness to support a bill devised by Senate Majority Leader George Mitchell, which proposed 95-percent coverage by 2002 and employers paying only 50 percent of premiums after that date if Congress could not come up with some alternative plan.[18] This was at a time when corporate "downsizing" and the substitution of lower-paid jobs without employer-sponsored health-insurance coverage were increasing the number of Americans who lack any coverage whatsoever to 43 million in 1996 (up from 40 million in 1993).[19] Even this figure understates the severity of the problem: Another 28 million with private coverage are significantly underinsured.[20] The policies of the Democratic and Republican leaderships increasingly reflected a common purpose based on a profound "break" with the very notion of the welfare state and centered on the creation of a low-wage, job-competitive economy. Attacks on welfare and threats of incarceration had a specific goal: to coerce millions of "downsized" workers to compete with one another for the millions of newly created, less-remunerative positions in the labor force.

One of the key planks of the Clinton campaign platform was a commitment to major reductions in military spending and a comprehensive effort to reconvert military industry to civilian production. Given the disintegration of the Soviet empire, there seemed even less reason to maintain the mammoth 1980s spending levels. But the 1994 budget approved by Congress reflected little evidence of Washington's accommodation to the changed global context: The administration request of $263 billion, $0.5 billion less than the Pentagon's own budget recommendations, was only cut by $2.6 billion. The $261-billion authorization constituted a fairly incremental fall (approximately $12 billion) compared with the last Republican (Bush) defense budget.[21] Furthermore, Clinton proposed a $1.3-trillion diversion of funds to the military over the next five years, reflecting his strong support for the new Pentagon strategy of being able to fight two regional wars "nearly simultaneously."

Within a relatively short period of time, the Clinton Administration began redefining its political agenda on virtually every major issue of the day. Instead of social changes benefitting workers and the poor and a significant economic stimulus to revitalize industry, the emphasis shifted to a call for more "sacrifices" and a concern for deficit reduction and other deflationary policies. Instead of giving priority to enacting a universal health program, the emphasis shifted to squeezing health services in the interests of reducing the deficit. Instead of cutting taxes on wages and salaried workers, the beneficiaries of new tax concessions were real-estate developers and high-tech industries. Instead of promised large cuts in the military budget, projected spending levels were only marginally smaller than the Bush authorizations.

Entering 1994, the income disparity between rich and poor continued to widen, the purchasing power of all workers continued to fall, stable and well-paid jobs continued to disappear in the hundreds of thousands and to be replaced by temporary/part-time positions, and there were significantly more homeless families in America than a year earlier. The dislocating effect of these trends on the country's poor showed no signs of abating. And Clinton's response seemed remarkably similar to Reagan's and Bush's before him: Allocate more financial resources to incarcerate law breakers and impose "order." This took the form of support for a Crime Bill which earmarked billions for new prison construction and promised the hiring of 100,000 additional police.

The White House support for an anti-crime bill, combined with the president's call for "an end to welfare as we know it" and his proposal to Congress to overhaul welfare programs that included forced work requirements and a provision allowing states to "experiment" with a two-year time limit on benefits, helped establish the framework for the political and economic program promoted by the post-1994, Republican-dominated Congress, the so-called Contract with America. What was described as Clinton's "moderate" alternative was nothing of the kind. The Contract was based partly on a core principle already in place: that the reliance of the poor on government spending must be broken by submitting them to low-wage jobs as the only alternative to welfare cuts or the increased likelihood of incarceration. To make crime more costly for the poor and unemployed, the Congress also supported multibillion allocations for new prison construction as well as restrictions on prisoner appeals and the relaxation of evidentiary rules. The Contract, if enacted, also promised to further reconcentrate wealth upward through more tax concessions to large corporations and the very rich, and through new measures to ease regulatory constraints on capital accumulation, while simultaneously applying downward pressure on wage levels that had been falling since Clinton came into office.

The 1992 elections decisively repudiated the Bush Administration and a decade of free-market orthodoxy, and provided the victorious Clinton forces with a powerful mandate for social change, increased public investment in the nation's physical and human infrastructure, and redistribution of wealth and income from the rich to the middle and lower classes. But the Democratic White House revealed itself unwilling to come to grips with the fun-

damental causes of domestic decline that occurred during the Republican era.

## Bipartisan Politics: Clinton Unravels the Welfare State, 1995–6

The Clinton presidency has not been, strictly
speaking, a "conservative" period in the sense
of sticking with the status quo. Rather, it has
been a *reactionary* government, rolling back
50 years of social legislation. In the following
discussion we examine Clinton's dismemberment of the welfare state. Our main argument is that despite the surface clashes
between the White House and the Republican Congress, there were powerful similari-
ties between the conservative agenda of the
Contract with America and Clinton's policies.

At best, the Clinton administration has interspersed symbolic gratification to some
popular party constituencies along with substantive economic concessions to elite sectors,
mostly large contributors to the 1992 and 1996
presidential election campaigns. By 1995, nationwide polls indicated that a majority of
Americans no longer believed that either major party was capable of solving the country's
most pressing social and economic problems,
while an even larger percentage voiced dissatisfaction with the performances of both
Congress and the White House.[22]

During the latter part of his tenure, Clinton
presided over an expanding gap between rich
and poor, a more unequal distribution of
wealth and income, the continuing growth of
"poverty-level" jobs at the expense of well-
paid positions, an upward trend in the number
of homeless families, an exploding prison
population, the disintegration of the welfare
state, and an erosion of workplace and environmental safeguards – all the while refusing
to cut military spending much below Cold
War levels.

Among the more visible accompaniments
to the "globalization" of American capital over
the past decade has been the resurgence of
sweatshop labor in the national economy: part-
time workers earning poverty-level wages and
often exposed to all manner of on-the-job
dangers. The $86-billion garment industry is
a case in point: Thousands of mostly Latino
and Asian illegal immigrants are paid virtual
slave wages by employers who ignore health
and safety regulations, thereby avoiding billions of dollars in state and federal taxes. Like
its Republican predecessors, the Clinton administration has been extremely lax in pros-
ecuting those responsible for exploiting this
class of workers. Such foot-dragging has not
resulted from inadequate enforcement capacity but rather indicates the low priority given
this task. Stringent laws already on the books
to tackle the sweatshops "problem" have too
often been ignored.[23]

On of the by-products of growing income
inequalities has been growing homelessness
among American families. In the 29 cities
surveyed by the United States Conference of
Mayors during 1995, requests for shelter by
families increased by 15 percent over 1994;
and nearly two-thirds of the cities noted a
rise in the length of time people were homeless. The continuing lack of affordable housing also contributed to the problem. "The
waiting lines for subsidized housing are so
long," one expert on the subject commented,
"that many cities have actually stopped taking applications."[24] But if Clinton's policies
have failed to arrest the upward trend in homelessness, they have been far more successful
in filling the country's jails, in incarcerating
the poor. By the end of 1995, America had
overtaken Russia as the globe's leading jailer
with 565 out of every 100,000 citizens in
legal detention.[25]

In January, 1996, Clinton took the first of
a number of decisive steps toward repealing
the nation's welfare system, bowing to incessant Republican demands for a balanced

budget. Jettisoning an earlier 1996 budget proposal that contained no major deficit-reduction measures, he announced a plan to eliminate the deficit by 2002 the basis on of large cuts in entitlements and discretionary funding: $102 billion from Medicare (government insurance for the elderly); $52 billion from Medicaid (government insurance for the poor and disabled); and $295 billion from other domestic programs. Although the proposed cuts were "backloaded," as one analyst pointedly observed, by 2002 they will be "almost as draconian as those in the Republican plan."[26] Only weeks later, the White House increased to 38 the number of states issued with waivers of federal rules in order "to experiment with programs requiring or encouraging welfare recipients to work."[27] Then, in mid-May, Clinton publicly endorsed the more radical Wisconsin welfare plan that would abolish Aid To Families with Dependent Children (AFDC), replace it with wage subsidies to single mothers who work, and provide no guarantees that assistance to families would extend beyond five years.[28]

In June, Clinton submitted a revised plan to balance the budget over ten years, increasing combined Medicare–Medicaid cuts to $201 billion, together with a 20-percent cut in all discretionary spending (except education). Minimal cuts in federal subsidies to corporate America merely underscored the order of priorities: They were projected to reach a mere $6 billion annually by the end of the decade. The following month, the White House suspended enforcement of new rules restricting the traditional Health Maintenance Organization (HMO) practice of financially rewarding doctors who cut costs and controlled the use of services by Medicare and Medicaid patients, buckling under to an avalanche of protests from HMOs and their supporters.[29] On the eve of the November presidential vote, a *Washington Post* analysis of Clinton's six-year budget plan for Medicare revealed that the proposed cutbacks were only marginally smaller than those savings contained in the Republican proposal: The difference in total spending by 2002 would amount to only $15 billion.[30]

During his 1992 election campaign, candidate Clinton promised to "empower" people with education, training, and child care to enable them to escape poverty and the "dependency cycle." In his January 1995 State of the Union address to Congress, President Clinton declared that "we shouldn't cut people off [from welfare] just because they're poor, they're young, or even because they're unmarried."[31] By mid-1996, he had visibly retreated from these commitments. Some $3 billion in work-program aid to help people find employment had already been dropped[32] when in August 1996, he signed newly passed legislation that promised the most radical dismantling of the welfare state in more than half a century.

The new welfare bill cuts spending by more than $54 billion over six years, transfers most key programs to the states along with new powers to remove people from the rolls, and imposes unprecedented restrictions on aid eligibility: Cash payments will be terminated to individuals (and their families) who are unemployed for more than two years; benefits will be limited to five years; food stamps will be cut by $23 billion over six years; legal immigrants who are not citizens (minimum five years) will be denied welfare and medical benefits (approximately one-third of the proposed savings); women with children as young as 6 will be required to work even if they cannot afford child care; and single mothers may be refused benefits if they are under 18 and living with their parents or if they refuse to identify their children's fathers.[33]

The decision to target legal immigrants was not all that surprising given that they had some months earlier already felt the brunt of the administration's punitive domestic policies. In April, the president signed into law a new counter-terrorism bill which gave the Immigration and Naturalization Service the power to detain (without appeal) and deport legal permanent residents even if they have lived in the United States for at least seven years and were married to, or had children who were, American citizens.[34]

Policy shifts in other areas are also symptomatic of the Clinton Administration's order of priorities. Partly in response to White House efforts to "downsize" the federal government and cut "red tape," key public agencies responsible for workplace conditions, environmental standards, and product safety "have begun to fundamentally change the way they do their job." Funding cutbacks have forced the Occupational Safety and Health Administration (OSHA) to limit its on-site inspections; increased pressure on the Food and Drug Administration (FDA) has encouraged it to rush new products onto the market by slicing approval times; and the Department of the Interior has started "making it easier for developers to build on land that may have been off limits because of rules protecting endangered species."[35]

## Wages, Profits, and Jobs: The "Republican" White House and the Two-Tiered Society

Clinton's regressive social policies, embedded in his slashing of the welfare budget to lower taxes for the rich and provide subsidies for the corporations, is matched by his pro-business, anti-labor policies – leading to higher profits, lower wages, and the growth of low-paying jobs. In what follows, we argue that the result of Clinton's championing of the US multinational corporations and banks under the guise of promoting "global competitiveness" has been government acquiescence in the substitution of low-paying for well-remunerated jobs, plant relocations to low-wage areas, and greater income inequalities between workers and corporate CEOs.

Between 1983 and 1989, the share of marketable net worth held by the top 1 percent of the population increased from 34 per cent to 39 per cent, while the share accounted for by the bottom 80 percent fell from 19 percent to 15 percent.[36] This trend toward growing wealth inequality persisted during the Bush presidency, as the top 10 percent marginally increased their net worth while the rest of the population's share remained relatively static.[37] The Clinton White House, despite its populist rhetoric, has made no effort to halt this process of wealth concentration. Indeed, the contrary appears to be the case. The richest 10 percent of households accounted for 61.1 percent of the nation's wealth in 1989; by 1994, this figure had jumped to 66.8 percent. During this same period, the poorest 10 percent of the population went deeper into debt. Their net negative worth (debts over assets) increased from $4,744 to $7,075 (measured in 1996 dollars). A booming stock market, enabling wealthy families to reap high profits from financial investments, has further exacerbated the inequality gap.[38] In 1995, the market rose an estimated 35 percent, with the Dow Jones Industrial Average index cracking the 5,000 barrier for the first time; by October 1996, the index topped 6,000, and by June 1997 it approached 8,000, as the speculative bubble grew. The theoretical significance of this trend is clear: There is a direct relationship between corporate downsizing and stagnant wages and the rise of the Dow index. Given the highly concentrated nature of stock ownership, the prime beneficiaries of these price rises have been the very rich, not the poor or the "working poor" or the middle class whose investments, if they have any, are overwhelmingly tied up in home ownership.[39]

Under Clinton, the Reagan/Bush era trend of increasing profits at the expense of wages has accelerated. "Cost restructuring," rather than accelerated investments or productivity growth, pushed after-tax profit rates in 1994 and 1995 to their highest levels in 25 years, while wages were moving in the opposite direction.[40] In 1993–4, labor's share of corporate sector income plummeted to its lowest level since 1969; throughout the first half of the 1990s, the hourly wage of the median male and female worker steadily declined.[41] During this half decade, moreover, annual productivity increases (around 2 percent) outstripped the yearly growth in wage compensation (a minuscule 0.6 percent).[42] Profit-rich corporations have continued to accumulate large cash reserves and invest in high-tech equipment (computers, software, etc.) that promise increased productivity gains and profits without equivalent salary gains.

At the end of the third year of Clinton's presidency, *Business Week* reported that employers were also "chipping away at benefits as never before."[43] These efforts targetted paid holidays and health insurance. The loss of jobs due to corporate "downsizing," the re-hiring in new positions with less security of tenure, pay, and benefits, together with the growth of self-employed workers, are making annual holidays a thing of the past for an ever-increasing number of Americans. In 1995, 34 percent of families told pollsters they had no plans to take a vacation that year; in 1996 the figure jumped to 38 percent.[44] In the case of health insurance, where it has not been eliminated altogether more and more of the cost burden has been shifted onto workers themselves. This is at a time when the growth of low-wage, service-sector jobs has further compounded the difficulties faced by workers even paying for the dwindling benefits available to them. Despite record profits and rising productivity, total labor compensation (including wages and benefits) in the twelve months to September 1995 grew at the slowest rate since 1981.[45] "Workers in every industry you look at," observed the Economic Policy Institute's Lawrence Mishel in March 1996, "including those that are the most technologically advanced, have been losing ground

[since Clinton entered the White House]."[46]

The major beneficiaries of the 1990s surge in corporate profits (in 1994 the profits for the 900 companies on *Business Week*'s Corporate Scoreboard jumped by 40 percent)[47] have been the CEOs of many of the country's largest enterprises. The median increase in the total compensation for chief executives at 76 of the biggest 150 companies (salary, cash bonuses, stock options, etc.) rose 31 percent to nearly $5 million in 1995. For those CEOs who had held that position for the preceding two years, their 1995 financial rewards was almost double the 1994 figure and triple the amount received in 1993.[48] Moreover, while the annual increase in wages and salaries of American workers between 1990 and 1995 never exceeded 4 percent (and in 1995 was below 3 percent), the thousands of CEOs of publicly traded companies received average annual pay increases of close to 9 percent during this same period.[49] The ratio of the average CEO salary to that of the average wage worker during Clinton's presidency has reached unprecedented heights, even when compared with the Reagan/Bush era (141 to 1 in 1987–9 vs. 225 to 1 in 1992–4).[50]

Greater rewards for CEOs over and against worker salaries have also been paralleled not only by an increase in the average annual number of jobs lost under Clinton compared with his Republican predecessors,[51] but also by a significant increase in the disappearance of higher-paid, white-collar positions. According to Labor Department statistics, managerial and professional workers accounted for 24 percent of all permanent layoffs during 1991–3, almost double the percentage for the 1981–3 period. Since 1993, this trend has shown few signs of levelling off. Between 1991 and 1995, for example, job losses in the banking industry totalled 70,000, with another 450,000 positions expected to disappear over the next decade. In the telecommunications sector, similar developments are occurring. Entering 1996, the Clinton Administration had presided over the elimination of 140,000 jobs; in January, AT&T announced it was going to shed 40,000 positions (13 percent of its workforce) over the next three years.[52]

The surge in mergers and takeovers by "blue-chip" corporations and major banks has often involved the same institutions as are engaged in the biggest "downsizing" activities. The dollar volume of mergers reached its highest levels ever during 1994 ($347 billion) and 1995 ($363 billion from January to October) – typically associated with "cost-cutting" measures to increase short-term profits, which more and more take the form of shedding workers.[53] In its successful effort to acquire First Interstate Bankcorp of Los Angeles in late 1995, for example, First Bank Systems of Minneapolis claimed that it could produce annual cost savings of $500 million with no effect on revenue, partly though the elimination of 6,000 jobs. Some months earlier, in New York, Chemical Bank's purchase of Chase Manhattan was expected to "disappear" 12,000 jobs as a result of the merger.[54] Pressure from the banks to service debts accumulated by corporations engaged in merger activities has further compounded the pressure for "cost cutting" and savings on labor costs.[55] Finally, to compete with speculative capital for investments, productive capital has also been forced to introduce cost-savings labor practices such as more temporary employees, low-wage contract labor, and lower-paid full-time workers.

One of the reasons for corporate America's enthusiasm for "downsizing" well-paid jobs and refusal to reward its workers for productivity gains is the absence of a strong trade union movement. Membership in unions fell by an estimated 400,000 in 1995, and currently accounts for less than 15 percent of the total workforce.[56] And, not surprisingly, job losses, growing worker insecurity, and the manifest willingness of corporations to permanently replace striking employees have severely weakened labor's ability to press for improved wage and working conditions – in the absence of a powerful union movement to support their confrontations with capital. In 1995, there were only 32 strikes involving 1,000 or more workers, compared with double that number a decade earlier, at a time when the Reagan Administration was actively promoting an anti-union policy.[57] Workers' vulnerability and the power of capital were symbolized in the outcome of a three-day strike by 1,200 nursing-home workers in Pennsylvania in April 1996. The company, Beverly Enterprises, hired permanent replacements and sacked 350 of their striking employees.[58]

To the extent that the economy began to experience an upturn in 1995, it was based largely on the changing nature of the workforce, which provided greater profits for capital. While the official unemployment level declined modestly from 7.1 percent to 5.4 percent during Clinton's first three years in office, this was far less significant than the remarkable growth of a class of vulnerable, low-wage workers that composed such a large proportion of the millions of new jobs created in the 1990s. Only a distinct minority of the millions of "downsized" workers forced back into the labor market since 1993 have found new jobs that offer equal or improved wage remuneration. According to a Labor Department study, almost two-thirds of those who lost their jobs between 1993 and 1995 either did not find new positions by February 1996, obtained only part-time employment, or were displaced into jobs that paid below their previous earnings.[59] For a large majority, downward social and economic mobility has been the norm: displaced workers forced into less secure, more poorly paid, often part-time jobs below their educational and professional skills, and with few, if any, benefits. Not surprisingly, the competition for low-wage, low-skilled jobs intensified. In the inner cities, a recent study concluded that fast-food jobs have become "the object of fierce competition," with applicants consistently far outnumbering available positions.[60] The other side of this low-wage "coin" has been increasing concentration "at the top." Between 1993 and January 1996, the richest 5 percent of wage earners increased their percentage of national income from 18.1 to 21, a three-year rate of increase without precedent.[61]

The results of nationwide polls at the beginning of 1996 found that more than one-third of respondents expected the general economic situation and their own financial circumstances to worsen in the near future, while over one-quarter of those interviewed who worked full- or part-time articulated varying degrees of concern that they would lose their jobs before the end of 1997.[62]

Far from challenging the corporate sector's job-shedding, low-wage strategy, Clinton told a round-table conference attended by 100 CEOs in early 1996 that he understood the need for "downsizing" in a number of large firms, while his chairman of the Council of Economic Advisors, Dr Joseph Stiglitz, dismissed the very notion as a "myth" given the millions of new jobs created during the Clinton years.[63]

## "Domestic Decay" and Global Expansion: The Priorities of the Clinton State

Since 1980 there has been an historic shift taking place in the source of profits for American multinational corporations (MNCs). That year, 27 percent of the top 100 MNCs earned more than 50 percent of their profits overseas; by 1993, the number had risen to 33 percent. In 1980, only 5 percent of the largest MNCs earned over 75 percent of their profits abroad; by 1993, this figure had almost tripled to 13 percent.[64] The Clinton Administration's embracing of policies favoring overseas trade and investment expansion, reflecting a profound continuity with

his Republican predecessors, has been at the expense of, and taken precedence over, its commitment to reviving the domestic economy and maintaining the welfare state at home. Growing income and wealth inequalities, declining wage and welfare payments, the elimination of millions of full-time, well-remunerated, high-benefits jobs in favor of lower-paid, insecure, often part-time and minimum-benefits positions, and lowered corporate taxes have been the accompaniment to greater accumulations of MNC capital that can be exported abroad to earn higher rates of profit, and to the vigorous promotion of global and regional free-trade agreements. Under Clinton, the relationship between domestic economic "pain" and the diversion of state resources to subsidize the overseas capitalist class has become tighter than ever.

Given the rising importance of profits earned abroad for US corporations and the expansion of exports as a percentage of national output (from 7.2 percent of GDP in 1985 to 10.1 percent in 1994)[65] it is not surprising that in seeking to promote multicountry agreements that would open up economies and free markets around the world, the Clinton White House has increased the direct involvement of US state agencies in boosting US overseas investment. While the Commerce Department has played an important role in rationalizing and boosting trade promotion, involving greater emphasis on heavy-industry exports (automobiles, aircraft, electronics, etc.), the most striking feature of the Clinton strategy has been the use of State Department diplomats to "help close deals" and to lobby foreign governments to implement "structural changes" that increase market access for American exporters.[66] In mid-1993, Secretary of State Warren Christopher cabled all American embassies "making it clear that I expected each [Ambassador] to take personal charge of promoting our commercial interests –and to engage their embassies in a sustained effort to help the American business community."[67] Two years later, *Business Week* approvingly described these senior US diplomats as "unabashed peddlers in pinstripes, vigorously lobbying local officials on behalf of Corporate America."[68]

The Clinton trade-promotion strategy has been a mix of diplomacy and confrontation. US diplomats and corporate executives have negotiated amicably with host governments in such "big emerging markets" as India and Brazil over the elimination of barriers to market access.[69] At the same time, the White House has been more than willing to apply considerable and persistent pressure, including the threat or actual imposition of trade sanctions, against major trading partners. By early 1995, the US had become embroiled in numerous trade disputes with South Korea, severely stressing bilateral ties, and was preparing to impose protective tariffs affecting $2.8 billion in Chinese exports in retaliation for Beijing's pirating of US intellectual property such as movies, software, and tapes.[70]

But the chief target of Clinton's merchant diplomacy, almost from the beginning of his presidency, has been Japan.[71] After 15 months of acrimony, Japan agreed to open its insurance, glass, medical, and telecommunications markets to US products and services. In early 1995, the administration decided it was an opportune time to apply pressure on the Japanese automobile industry to open up its market to US vehicles and spare parts, especially since some domestic companies were in the red and Mazda Corporation was even in danger of going out of business.[72] Failing to make much headway in achieving its objective, Washington rapidly substituted threats for negotiation. Japan was given one month's notice of a decision to impose 100-percent tariffs on the country's very profitable luxury auto exports to the United States unless its government buckled under White House demands. Clinton's dollar diplomacy was aided by the stagnant Japanese economy, emerging from its worst recession in decades, and the earthquake at the port of Kobe, which fur-

ther contributed to Japan's economic troubles. As *Business Week* observed of the US trade negotiators: "They're determined to exploit the strong yen by provoking an all-out confrontation."[73]

On occasion, the interests of America's overseas capitalist class have been promoted by the Clinton White House not on the basis of global competition and conflict but through intercapitalist cooperation–although still at the expense of domestic producers and immobile national labor forces. This was never more evident than in the case of the GATT, signed in December, 1993, and enthusiastically supported by the American multinational community. Under the GATT, 117 nations agreed to cut their tariffs by an average of one-third. The magnitude of promised financial benefits was a powerful inducement to cooperation and compromises among the major "blocs" and their overseas capitals.[74] The agreement ensured that the Third World would become an even more lucrative arena for US and European exporters in particular. As Walden Bello trenchantly put it:

In signing on to GATT, Third World countries have . . . agreed to ban all quantitative restrictions on imports, reduce tariffs on many industrial imports, and promise not to raise tariffs on all other imports. In so doing, they have effectively given up the use of trade policy to pursue industrialization objectives . . . [Furthermore] the GATT agricultural regime – perpetuates state-subsidized American and European domination of world agricultural trade while abolishing what little subsidies and protective mechanisms there are for Third World agriculture.[75]

There is perhaps no better illustration of Clinton's pursuit of policies that fulfill the goals of multinational capital at the expense of the domestic economy than his unqualified support for NAFTA. Determined to hold onto its favored dominion of exploitation, profits, and interest payments, NAFTA became the centerpiece of a new economic strategy through which Washington hopes to use the hemisphere as a springboard for becoming more competitive in the world market: freeing markets, exploiting labor, seizing resources, and breaking down all barriers to US commerce and investment. The White House wheeling and dealing to secure congressional passage of the NAFTA legislation clearly demonstrated Clinton's anti-labor orientation; paving the way for American corporations to enter a low-wage country, thereby facilitating greater opportunities for profit making. Since NAFTA took effect in early 1994, tens of thousands of US manufacturing jobs have been lost as corporations moved their plants to Mexico to take advantage of cheap wage levels.[76]

The February 1995 bailout of the Mexican government following a major devaluation of the peso, brought about by trade deficits, capital flight, and political instability, provides additional evidence of the link between the growth of wealth/income inequalities at home and the US support of its overseas traders and investors. To forestall a Mexican government default on $58 billion in foreign debt due in 1995, and thereby prevent a financial collapse, the Clinton Administration coordinated a $50-billion assistance package with the IMF. The major beneficiaries of the US/IMF largesse were foreign, primarily American, investors in stocks, shares, and bonds (owed approximately $60 billion), whose value lost billions of dollars when the peso was devalued by 40 percent against the US dollar, and US private commercial banks, whose financial exposure exceeded $18 billion. The White House was also concerned to protect a $40-billion-a-year export market-the third largest market in the world for US goods and services sold abroad.[77]

The Clinton global vision has also demanded continuing support for bilateral and multilateral aid programs to the former Soviet bloc countries, conditional on the target government introducing "economic reforms" that include selling off public enterprises,

eliminating restrictions on capital flows, abolishing impediments to foreign takeovers, and facilitating raw materials' exploitation. In particular, this explains the sustained, often effusive support for the Yeltsin government in Russia, based on the rapid implementation of "market reforms" under the auspices of the IMF. This extended to Yeltsin's re-election in 1996, notwithstanding US disquiet over some of his electoral promises, which ran counter to the demand for "budget discipline." But at a summit meeting in Moscow in late April, Clinton downplayed any bilateral differences, and in the weeks leading up to the election he gave approval to a $10.2-billion IMF credit facility and to the disbursement of $1 billion prior to the vote, all the while describing Yeltsin as a Russian "reformer" who "represents the future."[78]

Measured by its contribution to expanding opportunities for US multinationals in the global economy, the success of the Clinton free-trade strategy has been undeniable: In 1993, one-third of the largest 100 US multinationals earned more than 50 percent of their profits overseas; in 1994, US companies earned about 20 percent of their profits from foreign sales; in 1995, US merchandise exports rose by close to 15 percent. CS First Boston's chief investment strategist, Jeffrey Applegate, calculates that by 1997 foreign earnings could reach one-third of total US corporate profits.[79]

Profits from US direct investments abroad have moved in a similar direction: In 1996, total profits jumped 30 percent compared with 1994, including a record $35 billion in Europe and a doubling to $3.7 billion in Japan. During the first quarter of 1996 this upward trend continued, as total profits rose 12 percent over the first three months of 1995. Europe and Japan were again the sites of major gains but were also accompanied by Mexico, where investment returns skyrocketed by 256 percent to $830 million.[80] Based on market value, share-price gains, sales, and profits, the number of US MNCs in *Business Week*'s 1,000

most valuable global corporations increased
from 396 in 1995 to 422 in 1996; American
overseas firms now account for 46 percent of
the value of the Global 1000, compared with
30 percent in 1988.[81]

But while the Clinton Administration has
aggressively maintained that free trade and the
unfettered movement of capital and commerce
across the globe are the cornerstone of its international economic policy, what explains its
relentless hostility toward Cuba, which stands
in sharp contradiction to the interests of global capital? Not satisfied with his role as the
driving force behind the 1992 Cuban Democracy Act, which bans subsidiaries of American
corporations abroad from trading with Cuba,
in July 1996 Clinton signed into law the Helms–
Burton bill, which seeks to bludgeon Washington's closest allies into preventing their
MNCs from doing business with Cuba. Clinton
has justified his policy approach on the basis
of Cuba's refusal to engage in major political
and economic reform. While the former is
unlikely as long as the "hardline," non-negoti-
ating White House posture persists it is a demand, incidentally, which had not been made
of other Third World "socialist" regimes, such
as China and Vietnam. Cuba's already significant recent opening to market forces suggests
a White House whose rhetoric belies its own
policy objectives.

Since 1993, Cuba has legalized the use of
foreign currency for domestic transactions and
allowed the emergence of a parallel "dollar
economy;" legalized self-employment and
converted state farms into agricultural cooperatives; decentralized economic decision
making, allowing for the emergence of profit-
driven trading companies; reintroduced free
markets for agricultural produce and some
industrial products; opened up the economy
to foreign investment (including the creation
of free-trade zones); and eliminated a range
of state subsidies on goods and services.

The magnitude of these changes have induced the European Community, Canada, and
Latin America to favor a conciliatory approach,
one that promotes additional reforms through
constructive engagement. For Washington,
however, Cuba still remains a potential threat
to its post-Cold War global economic vision,
particularly as it relates to Latin America. In
its drive for market share, the Clinton White
House has exhibited a determination to consolidate its economic hold on the region, reinforced by the fact that this is the only area
where the US has a favorable external account to compensate for its trade deficits elsewhere. Because Washington seeks to maintain
the hemisphere as a closed economic sphere
within an open world, a development strategy such as Cuba's gradualist, selective opening is deemed unacceptable. This is the
strategic importance of Helms–Burton: The
administration's preparedness to act uni-
laterally in violation of international law (the
doctrine of extraterritoriality) and trade agreements (GATT, NAFTA) to which it is a party
ultimately reflect a desire to eliminate any
possible alternative to the US free-market
model in Latin America. And despite its significant retreat from socialism, the Cuban
approach still envisages a continuing important role for the state and public sector. What
Clinton's hardline policy toward Cuba reveals
is a White House still refusing to jettison Cold
War politics in an era when the principle battle field is the world market.[82]

In the defense sphere, the level of military
spending continues to have more affinity with
"global leadership" and "empire building."
While the fiscal year of 1997 defense budget
request for $254.4 billion represents a decline
of 5.8 percent in real, inflation-adjusted dollars from the fiscal year of 1996 level, it "proposes no new cuts in troops levels and nearly
no elimination of major new weapons programs."[83] In real dollar terms, Clinton budgets "remain in the same range as the average
peacetime defense outlays during the Cold
War." And a re-elected president has no intention of implementing major defense cuts:

Budget outlays are projected to climb steadily between 1998 and 2002 to $287.4 billion.[84] What this suggests is the administration's failure to construct an alternative civilian economic program capable of absorbing the displaced workers from the military-industrial complex in states like California where high-level unemployment is rife in the aerospace and other defense related industries.

## Conclusion

Today, US global power needs to appropriate local resources because of the decline of US competitiveness in the world market of the 1990s. In an earlier period, immediately after World War II, the US as the sole capitalist economic superpower was able to dominate trade and investment markets, extract monopoly profits, and thus finance expansion from its overseas profits as well as domestic social programs and wage increases. This was partly the result of a lack of international competition which has a tendency to put downward pressure on profits. With the entry of new global competitors, US corporate profits came under increased pressure, and their capacity to extract above-average profit rates declined under Clinton. The large-scale, long-term financing to sustain international competitiveness has more and more revolved around appropriating national resources, intensifying the exploitation of traditional areas of hegemony (Latin America and Canada) through free-trade agreements, and mobilizing the US state to play a leading role in facilitating greater market and investment access for its multinationals on a global scale.

The Clinton Administration's policy choices have reflected the decisive power of the MNC within the US political economy.[85] The growing MNC demand for "equality" with global competitors is leading to greater "inequalities" in the domestic economy. State subsidies to enable the MNC to "compete" in the global market have gone hand in hand with a deregulated local economy, which has meant falling wages, disappearing benefits, declining services, and increased diversion of funds for policing purposes (an added cost for wage and salaried groups)– in practice, the transfer of income from the national workforce to outward-looking capital and the dismemberment of the welfare state. Combined with favorable regulatory and taxation policies, they have facilitated domestic accumulation for global expansion.

Since the 1970s, there has been a shift in political power toward the export and global elites at the expense of wage/salaried and domestic-oriented forces; representatives of global interest penetrate all levels of executive and legislative power. The structural links between "global empire builders" and the state is far more extensive and profound than what is commonly described as the "military-industrial complex." A growing proportion of profits of the largest corporations is earned in the world market; local producers are seen increasingly as a cost, not as consumers. The problem for the empire builders is how to reduce local costs (pensions, employment benefits, etc.) to ensure profits in international markets.[86]

The overseas investors do not need a large, healthy, and educated workforce to reproduce capital. Their needs are for an elite, specialized, skilled labor force – to provide financial services and staff-automated factories. Hence the deterioration of health, skills, and education does not greatly affect the export elites. As such they are unconcerned when Clinton proposes a 1997 budget with spending on education and training, infrastructure, and non-military research and development only two-thirds the amount allocated to these sectors in 1980 as a percentage of GDP, and almost one-third less as a percentage of the budget.[87] Payments for social services are seen as a cost, not as a potential benefit. So what is "bad for the country" or the national economy is not so for America's global elites.

## Notes

Parts of this chapter, particularly the first section, are drawn from pp. 114–19 and other paragraphs in the epilogue to James Petras and Morris Morley, *Empire or Republic: American Global Power and Domestic Decay* (New York: Routledge, 1995).

1 Quoted in David E. Rosenbaum, "Clinton Leads Experts in Discussion on Economy", *New York Times* (December 15, 1992), p. 1.
2 Quoted in Thomas L. Freidman, "Congress Listens, Waiting to See if the Plan Sells," *New York Times* (February 18, 1993), p. 16.
3 Quoted in Steven Pearlstein, "Clinton Advisers Still Stress New Economic Tack," *Washington Post* (December 9, 1992), p. A14.
4 David M. Gordon, "The Upsides and the Downsides," *Nation* (March 15, 1993), p. 344.
5 Tod Schaefer, "*Still Neglecting Public Investment*," Briefing Paper, Economic Policy Institute, Washington DC (September, 1993), p. 1.
6 "An Uphill Struggle," *U.S. News and World Report* (November 8, 1993), p. 64.
7 See Amy Kaslow, "Clinton's Job Plan: Ready! Train! Wait!," *Christian Science Monitor*, International Weekly Edition (March 26–April 1, 1993), p. 4.
8 "Roaring Back," *Los Angeles Times* (September 5, 1993), p. D4; John Dillon, "U.S. Work Force Hit Hard as Manufacturing Jobs Flee," *Christian Science Monitor* (October 7, 1993), p. 4; "The Party's Not Over Yet," *Business Week* (January 10, 1994), p. 83.
9 Louis Uchitelle, "We're Leaner, Meaner and Going Nowhere Faster," *New York Times* (May 12, 1996), p. E1.
10 See Doug Henwood, "Happy Days Again," *Nation* (February 21, 1994), p. 221; John Miller, "As the Economy Expands, Opportunity Contracts," *Dollars and Sense* (May/June, 1994), pp. 9–10; Dillon, "U.S. Work Force Hit Hard," p. 4; Steven Pearlstein, "Layoffs Become a Lasting Reality," *Washington Post* (November 6, 1993), p. A10; John Holusha, "10,000 Jobs to be Cut by Kodak," *New York Times* (August 19, 1993), p. D1; Steve Lohr, "More Cuts by 2 Big Companies," *New York Times* (November 25, 1993), p. D1.

11 Louis Uchitelle, "More are Forced into Ranks of Self-Employed at Low Pay," *New York Times* (November 15, 1993), p. 1, D2; Bob Herbert, "America's Job Disaster," *New York Times* (December 1, 1993), p. 23.
12 "Economic Trends," *Business Week* (September 27, 1993), p. 28.
13 Ibid.
14 Tony Horwitz, "The Working Poor: Minimum Wage Jobs Give Many Americans Only a Miserable Life," *Wall Street Journal* (November 12, 1993), p. 1.
15 "Homeless Families Increase in Cities," *New York Times* (December 22, 1993), p. 18.
16 Unpublished figures provided by the Bureau of Census, US Department of Commerce.
17 Quoted in Mark Jaffe, "Even With Reform, Money Talks," *Philadelphia Inquirer* (September 21, 1993), p. A10.
18 Adam Clymer, "Senate's Leader Unveils his Plan for Health Care," *New York Times* (August 3, 1994), pp. 1, 18.
19 "A Portrait of the Uninsured," *Washington Post Health Supplement* (October 29, 1996), p. 7.
20 David U. Himmelstein and Steffie Woolhandler, "U.S. Health Reform: Unkindest Cuts," *Nation* (January 22, 1996), p. 20.
21 Eric Schmitt, "$261 Billion Set for the Military," *New York Times* (November 7, 1993), p. 25.
22 See R. W. Apple Jr, "Polls Show Disenchantment with Politicians and the White House," *New York Times* (August 12, 1995), pp. 1,8.
23 See Alan Finder, "Despite Tough Laws, Sweatshops Flourish," *New York Times* (February 6, 1995) pp. 1, B4; William Branigin, "Sweatshop Instead of Paradise: Thais Lived in Fear as Slaves in L.A. Garment Factories," *Washington Post* (September 10, 1995), p. A1; "U.S. Apparel Groups to Target Sweatshops," *Washington Post* (September 13, 1995), p. A2.
24 Quoted in Marilyn Gardner, "No Home for the Holidays: Plight of Homeless Families," *Christian Science Monitor*, International Weekly Edition (December 22–8, 1995), p. 2. On United States Conference of Mayors' study, see ibid.
25 Ian Katz, "America Offers a Bull Market in Jails," *Guardian Weekly* (June 2, 1996), p. 13.

26 Robert D. Reischauer, "Time for the GOP to Declare Victory," *Washington Post* (January 25, 1996), p. A25. Also see Barbara Vobejda, "Revised Clinton Plan Makes Bigger Cut in Welfare," *Washington Post* (December 8, 1995), p. A18; Ann Devroy, "Clinton Submits 7-Year Budget Plan," reprinted from *Washington Post* in *Guardian Weekly* (January 14, 1996), p. 16.

27 Robert Pear, "Governor's Plan on Welfare Attacked," *New York Times* (February 14, 1996), p. 8.

28 Robert Pear, "Clinton Endorses the Most Radical of Welfare Trials," *New York Times* (May 19, 1996), pp. 1, 20; Judith Havemann, "Clinton Backs Proposal to Scrap Welfare," *Washington Post* (May 19, 1996), pp. A1, A8.

29 Martin Walker, "Clinton Summons up the Ghost of Ike," *Guardian Weekly* (June 25, 1996), p. 6; Robert Pear, "U.S. Shelves Plan to Limit Rewards to H.M.O. Doctors," *New York Times* (July 8, 1996), p. 1.

30 Steven Pearlstein and Clay Chandler, "Medicare: After the Rhetoric, a Reality Check," *Washington Post* (November 3, 1996), pp. H1, H2.

31 Quoted in Martin Walker, "Republicans Take Heat Off Clinton," *Guardian Weekly* (February 5, 1995), p. 6.

32 Peter Wilson, "Dubious Policy, Yes, but First-Rate Politics," *Australian* (August 2, 1996) p. 8.

33 Robert Pear, "Clinton Says He'll Sign Bill Overhauling Welfare System," *New York Times News Service* (July 31, 1996); Barbara Vobejda, "Welfare Bill Glides through Senate," *Washington Post News Service* (August 1, 1996); John F. Harris and John E. Yang, "Clinton to Sign Bill Overhauling Welfare," *Washington Post* (August 1, 1996), pp. A1, A6; Peter Wilson, "Clinton Bows to Hardline Welfare Cuts," *Australian* (August 2, 1996), p. 8.

34 Lena Williams, "Aimed at Terrorists, Law Hits Legal Immigrants," *New York Times* (July 17, 1996), p. 1. Also see Eric Schmitt, "Milestones and Missteps on Immigration," *New York Times* (October 26, 1996), pp. 1, 9.

35 Cindy Skrzycki, "Slowing the Flow of Federal Rules," *Washington Post* (February 18, 1986), pp. A1, A10.

36 Edward N. Wolff, *Top Heavy: A Study of the Increasing Inequality of Wealth in America* (New York: Twentieth Century Fund, 1995), pp. 10–11.

37 Richard W. Stevenson, "Rich are Getting Richer, but Not the Very Rich," *New York Times* (March 13, 1996), p. C1.

38 Keith Bradsher, "More Evidence: Rich Get Richer, and the Middle Class Makes Gains," *New York Times* (June 22, 1996), p. 31. Also see Steven A. Holmes, "Income Disparity Between Poorest and Richest Rises," *New York Times* (June 20, 1996), p. 1.

39 "The Down Run-Run," *The Economist* (February 17, 1996), p. 70; "Economic Trends," *Business Week* (March 18, 1996), p. 28.

40 Dean Baker and Lawrence Mishel, *Profits Up, Wages Down*, Briefing Paper, Economic Policy Institute, Washington DC (September, 1995), pp. 1–2.

41 "Plumper Profits, Skimpier Paychecks," *Business Week* (January 30, 1995), p. 86; Baker and Mishel, *Profits Up, Wages Down*, pp. 1–2.

42 "Winter of Discontent," *U.S. News and World Report* (January 22, 1996), p. 52. Also see Steven Pearlstein, "U.S. Find Productivity, but Not Pay, is Rising," *Washington Post* (July 26, 1995), pp. A1, A9.

43 "Benefits are being Pecked to Death," *Business Week* (December 4, 1995), p. 2.

44 See Edwin McDowell, "More Work or Less Work can Equal No Time Off," *Washington Post* (July 6, 1996), pp. 31, 33. Also see Juliet B. Schor, *The Overworked American: The Unexpected Decline of Leisure* (New York: Basic Books, 1991).

45 "Winter of Discontent," p. 48.

46 Quoted in Bob Herbert, "A Job Myth Downsized," *New York Times* (March 8, 1996), p. 31.

47 "Hot Damn, What a Year!," *Business Week* (March 6, 1996), pp. 98–100; "It Doesn't Get a Lot Better than This," *Business Week* (February 27, 1996), p. 43.

48 Louis Uchitelle, "1995 was Good for Companies, and Better for a Lot of C.E.O.'s," *New York Times* (March 29, 1996), p. 1.

49 Ibid.

50 "Winter of Discontent," p. 54.

51 See Louis Uchitelle and N. R. Kleinfield, "On the Battles of Business, Millions of Casualties,"

*New York Times* (March 3, 1996), p. 15.

52 "No Letup in U.S. Layoffs," *Business Week* (September 11, 1995), p. 26; "Winter of Discontent," pp. 50–1; Edmund L. Andrews, "Job Cuts at AT&T will Total 40,000; 13 percent of its Staff," *New York Times* (January 3, 1996), p. 1. Also see David M. Gordon, *Fat and Mean: The Corporate Squeeze of Working Americans and the Myth of Managerial "Downsizing"* (New York: Free Press, 1996); *New York Times, The Downsizing of America* (New York: Times Books/Random House, 1996).

53 Floyd Norris, "Latest Mergers Driven by Cost Cuts," *New York Times* (November 7, 1995), p. D1, D8.

54 Ibid., p. D8; N. R. Kleinfield, "The Company as Family, No More," *New York Times* (March 4, 1996), p. 10.

55 Stephanie Strom, "This Year's Wave of Mergers Head Toward a Record," *New York Times* (October 31, 1995), p. 1. Department of Labor statistics reveal that the rate of layoffs in the workforce during 1993–5 remained constant compared with the 1991–3 period. See Richard W. Stevenson, "Revised Data Show Layoff Rate Constant in the 1990s," *New York Times* (October 26, 1996), pp. 37, 38.

56 Steven Greenhouse, "Labor's Labor Not Lost," *New York Times* (May 12, 1996), p. 4E.

57 Steven Greenhouse, "Strikes Decrease to a 50-Year Low," *New York Times* (January 29, 1996), pp. 1, 12.

58 Greenhouse, "Labor's Labor Not Lost," p. 4E.

59 See "Downsized Workers Recovered No Ground," *New York Times* (October 20, 1996), p. 14E.

60 See "Economic Trends," *Business Week* (July 31, 1995), p. 30.

61 "Up, Down, and Standing Still," *The Economist* (February 24, 1996), p. 38.

62 See Richard Morin and Dan Balz, "In America, Loss of Confidence Seeps into All Institutions," *Washington Post* (January 28, 1996), p. A6.

63 See Martin Walker, "Dole Quits Senate and Goes for Broke," *Guardian Weekly* (May 26, 1996), p. 6.

64 See "The Largest 100 Foreign Companies," *Forbes* (July 18, 1980), pp. 99–102; "Getting the Welcome Carpet," *Forbes* (July 18, 1994), pp. 276–9.

65 Allen R. Myerson, "Looking Outward to Keep U.S. Economy Chugging," *New York Times* (January 8, 1995), p. 8F.

66 "Peddlers in Pinstripes," *Business Week* (May 1, 1995), p. 67.

67 Warren Christopher, "Supporting U.S. Business in Asia and Around the World," Speech to the American Business Council, Singapore (July 27, 1993), reprinted in US Department of State, *Dispatch* (August 2, 1993), p. 551.

68 "Peddlers in Pinstripes," p. 66.

69 See, for example, John F. Burns, "India Now Winning U.S. Investment," *New York Times* (February 6, 1995), pp. D1, D3; Stephen Engleberg, "Clinton to Ease Computer Sales," *New York Times* (October 2, 1995), pp. 1, 2.

70 On the conflict with China, see David E. Sanger, "U.S. Threatens $2.8 Billion of Tariffs on China Exports," *New York Times* (January 1, 1995), p. 14.

71 See, for instance, Andrew Pollack, "U.S. Steps Up the Pressure on Tokyo," *New York Times* (April 24, 1993), pp. 37, 38.

72 David E. Sanger, "Cars, Trade Sanctions and a Legacy of Frustration," *New York Times* (May 8, 1995), pp. 1, 2.

73 "Showdown Time for U.S.–Japan Trade?," *Business Week* (April 24, 1995), p. 48.

74 See Keith Bradsher, "Relying on the Irresistible Force of GATT's Appeal," *New York Times* (December 13, 1993), pp. D1, D5; "Gatt: Who Wins What," *Guardian Weekly* (December 26, 1993), p. 6.

75 Walden Bello, "The United Nations: Between Sovereignty and Global Governance?" paper presented to a conference on "The Bretton Woods Institutions and the Demise of the United Nations Development System," La Trobe University, Melbourne, Australia (July 2–6, 1995), pp. 11, 12.

76 See James Sterngold, "Nafta Trade-Off: Some Jobs Lost, Others Gained," *New York Times* (October 9, 1995), pp. 1, 13; Anthony DePalma, "For Mexico, Nafta's Promise of Jobs is Still Just a Promise," *New York Times* (October 10, 1995), pp. 1, 10; James L. Tyson, "NAFTA Fallout Irks Workers Across America," *Christian Science Monitor*, International Weekly Edition (January 5–11, 1996), p. 8; Paul Blustein,

"NAFTA: Free Trade Brought and Oversold," *Washington Post* (September 30, 1996), pp. A1, A10.

77 See Walker F. Todd, "Bailing Out the Creditor Class," *Nation* (February 13, 1996), p. 193; US General Accounting Office, "Mexico's Financial Crisis," Report No. GAO/GGD-96-95 (February, 1996), p. 114.

78 Quoted in Peter Wilson, "Outspoken Clinton Stands by His Man," *Australian* (June 15–16, 1996), p. 14. Also see Michael Dobbs, "Christopher Pursues Political Objectives by Economic Means," *Washington Post* (February 12, 1996), p. A14.

79 "Getting the Welcome Carpet," pp. 276–9; "Profits Haven't Peaked Yet," *Fortune* (February 20, 1995), p. 38; "Why Profits Will Keep Booming," *Fortune* (May 1, 1995), p. 35; "Economic Trends," *Business Week* International Edition (March 4, 1996), p. 8.

80 "Economic Trends," *Business Week*, International Edition (July 29, 1996), p. 11.

81 "The Globetrotters Take Over," *Business Week* International Edition (July 8, 1996), p. 48.

82 For a more detailed analysis, see James Petras and Morris Morley, "Clinton's Cuba Policy: Two Steps Backward, One Step Forward," *Third World Quarterly* 17 (2) (June, 1996), pp. 269–87.

83 Paul J. Graney, "Defense Budget for FY1997: Data Summary. Report for Congress, Congressional Research Service, Library of Congress, 96-288F (March 26, 1996), pp. 1, 18–19; Bradley Graham, "$242.6 Billion Sought for Defense in 1997," *Washington Post* (March 5, 1996), p. A4. The bill Clinton eventually signed totalled almost $257 billion. See Todd S. Purdum, "Clinton Signs Bill for $256.6 Billion for Armed Services," *New York Times* (September 24, 1996), p. 1.

84 Graney, "Defense Budget for FY1997," pp. 2, 19. "Black" (clandestine) military budgets under Clinton also have more in common with the Cold War era. Current identifiable funding for these purposes exceeds $14 billion, most of which is absorbed in research and development. Billions more are allocated for operations, support, and construction projects. These figures indicate that spending in this area remains close to the peak period of Reagan/Bush outlays. Bill Sweetman, "The Budget You Can't See," *Washington Post* (July 7, 1996), p. C3.

85 In part, this power derives from the dominant role that the corporate world plays in the funding of presidential and congressional election campaigns. The major contributors during the 1995–6 electoral cycle were the finance, insurance, real-estate, agricultural, and tobacco sectors. See Leslie Wayne, "Business is Biggest Campaign Spender Study Says," *New York Times* (October 18, 1996), pp. 1, 26. For a more detailed analysis of this subject, see Thomas Ferguson, *Golden Rule: The Investment Theory of Party Competition and the Logic of Money-Driven Political Systems* (Chicago: University of Chicago Press, 1995).

86 For additional data on the accelerated growth of a two-tiered American society and economy during the 1990s, see Donald L. Barlett and James B. Steele, *America: Who Stole the Dream?* (Kansas City: Andrews and McMeel, 1996); Lawrence Mishel and Jared Bernstein, *The State of Working America: 1996–1997* (Washington, DC: Economic Policy Institute, 1996).

87 See Robert L. Borosage, "The Politics of Austerity," *Nation* (May 27, 1996), p. 22.

# 7

# America's Military Industrial Make-Over

## ★ *Ann Markusen* ★

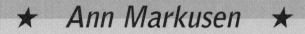

## Introduction

In a few short years after World War II, the American economy wrenched itself from being 40 percent defense-dedicated to become less than 10-percent so, defying the fears of economists. At the end of the Cold War, with much less far to fall, the defense budget has turned out to be surprisingly "sticky downwards." Spending remains in real terms above the post-Vietnam trough, when the Cold War was being waged. Much of it goes for Cold War systems that are patently obsolete. Supplyside resistance is a major cause, compounded by a befuddled Pentagon policy toward the post-Cold War defense industrial base.

The bogged-down defense budget brings with it worrisome security, competitive, and fiscal consequences. Inappropriate weapons systems and force structures undermine the efficiency of the military. Exports of surplus arms and, worse, leading-edge new systems like F-15 and F-16 fighters place American forces at risk in future conflicts. A large contingent of top scientific and engineering talent remains locked up in the US's nuclear weapons labs and defense plants, unavailable to the civilian economy. Public research dollars remain skewed toward esoteric military missions with little civilian payoff. Efforts to reduce the deficit are steered emphatically away from the defense budget and targetted

on "entitlements" as if there were no other options. In reality, Americans continue to borrow billions every year to finance Cold War-era outfitting.

The reason defense spending has proven so difficult to rein in and match to new security concerns lies in carefully orchestrated supplyside resistance. Over the past 50 years, a specialized set of firms, industries, regions, and occupations has emerged to serve the Cold War effort. Unlike the Fords and Bell and Howells of World War II, many possess no pre-existing commercial expertise to help them weather contract cancellations. Nor do they enjoy, as firms did in the 1950s, robust demand from consumers knowing exactly what they want (autos, appliances, housing). Their resistance is understandable. In a world of cut-throat competition where market niches are the best place from which to operate, they have theirs. Vigorous political efforts have been mounted to defend them.

But resistance alone is not enough to explain the persistence of military spending and weapons systems unwanted even by top military chiefs. Defense activity accounts directly for less then 5 percent of the economy. Despite an active caucus in the Congress, members with a really sizable chunk of defense receipts in their districts are a distinct minority.

Lack of executive branch leadership in overseeing conversion has encouraged supplyside intransigence. President Clinton's conversion strategy was half-hearted and has been further eviscerated by the most recent Congress. The Clinton departments of Defense and Energy undermined their own new dual-use and technology-transfer initiatives with large budget requests to purchase more Cold War-type technology. The Defense, State, and Justice departments have proven astonishingly acquiescent in approving and subsidizing both exports of leading-edge weaponry and mega-mergers among the largest defense-dependent contractors.

These mixed signals have thrown defense-dependent constituencies back on the tried and true. Those who at the outset of the decade welcomed dual-use technology grants, cooperative R&D agreements with weapons labs, procurement reform, and major new projects in energy, environment, and transportation concluded by mid-decade that too few real dollars are committed to them and that military sales, either here or abroad, are an easier mark.

A coherent defense industrial base policy and an effective conversion strategy are badly needed at this juncture. It is no use pretending that supplyside resistance is not at work. It will persist as long as new arms export and merger subsidies render defense-dedicated production highly profitable without making riskier conversion strategies, bound to generate higher returns in the longer run, more attractive. Perverse incentives should be dismantled, and new, more effective ones adopted to shift resources into civilian products and activities. The payoff will be a safer world and more rapid economic progress.

## How has Defense Spending Adjusted to Post-Cold War Realities?

Most recent accounts stress the fact that the defense budget has plummeted nearly 40 per-

cent in real terms since 1986. Indeed, the slide from the 1980s high has been relatively deep and rapid from the point of view of firms and communities forced to accommodate it. Contractors have faced real procurement cuts of nearly 70 percent. The number of Americans employed by the armed services and on military-related contracts will have fallen 7 million to 4.5 million by 1997. Most analysts agree that the US is probably only about two-thirds of the way through this round of budget cuts and their associated impacts.

But the hand-wringing over this downsizing is somewhat disingenuous, because it does not take into account the even more rapid buildup and accompanying industrial, regional, and financial distortions which took place under the Carter and Reagan administrations. Beginning in 1978 and accelerating through 1986, the US defense budget rose over 60 percent in real terms, to a level well in excess of $300 billion a year. The buildup was almost entirely deficit-financed. By at least one accounting, nearly half the entire national debt accrued by 1986 was attributable to the buildup.[1]

Placed in perspective, then, the post-Cold War cuts are meager and stuck at an inappropriately high level. Defense spending remains, in the mid-1990s, close to the 1970s post-Vietnam trough, despite the cessation of Cold War hostilities. Some districts in the military industrial complex have proven even more resilient than these figures show. The nation's three nuclear weapons labs (at $1 billion apiece, not included in the defense budget) enjoyed continued real spending increases up through 1993 and have had to cut back only modestly – on the order of 15 percent – since then.

Most analysts have concluded that U.S. military spending could be substantially cut without threatening US security.[2] Associated budget estimates for various alternative security regimes range from $87 to $246 billion annually. The range alone suggests just how uncertain defense-preparedness policy is and how much opportunity for debate exists.

Public opinion polls suggest that a majority of Americans, although they remain in favor of a strong defense, believe that defense spending cuts are both possible and desirable. Furthermore, when asked to make trade-offs among various types of spending, social and civilian categories best military ones consistently. In a recent poll asking Americans whether they favored more spending on research, for instance, only 40 percent throught the nation should spend more on military research while 80 percent favored spending more on health research.

Yet it has proved difficult to have a national debate about post-Cold War military preparedness and spending. Recently, pundits and politicians have found it easier to tackle entitlements, which possess a more amorphous and less well-organized constituency, than to suggest that defense spending might be slimmed down. Military supplyside resistance has proved formidable.

## Supplyside Resistance

It is generally not well understood how important the Carter/Reagan buildup was in deepening the dependency of firms in many sectors on military sales. In addition, since this spending bonanza incurred a large deficit, it hampered the ability of the federal government to use post-Cold War savings to invest in civilian initiatives like environmental or transportation technologies. Markets like those opened up for vulnerable firms by the debt-financed Marshall Plan and space programs in the 1940s and 1950s have not materialized for post-Cold War contractors.

The 1980s spending hike, unprecedented in a peacetime period, was devoted disproportionately to private-sector procurement, resulting in a dramatic expansion of the contracting sector and the regions hosting it.[3] A number of industries rapidly reoriented themselves to defense markets. The aircraft industry, for instance, increased military sales from 37 percent to 66 percent of output, while military dependency in shipbuilding rose from 61 percent to 93 percent. A number of critical machinery and parts industries dramatically shifted toward defense as well – machine tools, for instance, quadrupled their defense orientation from 8 percent to 34 percent.[4]

The impact on individual firms, occupations, and communities was quite remarkable. Coming as it did when the dollar was overvalued and international competition was on the rise, defense expansion induced many firms to abandon commercial lines altogether to concentrate on defense. Bath Iron Works, one of the two major yards building destroyers for the navy, was balanced about fifty/fifty between commercial and military shipbuilding projects in the early 1980s, but became 100 percent defense dependent within a few years as defense orders pre-empted capacity. Many smaller firms similarly lost civilian competence. By the late 1980s, many of the nation's defense contractors were more heavily dependent than they had been in any year since Vietnam.

The 1980s spending bubble only exacerbated a longer-term trend toward a separate military industrial sector which operated on one side of a "wall of separation" from the civilian economy. For decades, Cold War defense spending commandeered not only production lines, but research labs in many corporations, especially in high-tech industries like aircraft, electronics, computing, and communications equipment. In an average year, more than 80 percent of the aerospace industries' R&D funds originate in government, accounting for more than 54 percent of all federal R&D contracted out to the private sector.

Certain classes of workers have been particularly hard hit by defense cutbacks. In the 1980s, competition for the nation's scarce science and engineering talent was heightened by disproportionately large increases in military R&D. The national weapons labs each recruited hundreds of newly minted PhDS in nuclear physics, while engineers, mathematicians, and computer scientists were in high demand as well. By the mid-1980s, 69 percent of aeronautical engineers, 50 percent of oceanographers, and 34 percent of physicists and astronomers depended on government defense and space dollars, not counting additional demand from the nuclear complex and arms exports. Certain blue-collar occupations were also quite vulnerable – 51 percent of aircraft assemblers, 18 percent of electronics assemblers, and 11 percent of all machinists worked on defense projects.

Military industrial facilities and bases are remarkably concentrated geographically and have created a swath of constituencies across the "Gunbelt" that militantly opposes particular cuts or closings.[5] In the 1980s, military industrial cities in California boomed, while big federal receipts helped New England detach itself from the deindustrialization of the Middle Atlantic and Great Lakes states. In a typical defense-boom year like 1984, contractors in Los Angeles county won $14 billion in prime contracts, with another $4 billion awarded to Orange Country, $5 billion to Silicon Valley, and $5.5 billion to the Boston area.

A plethora of organizations – corporations, trade associations, trade unions, local and state governments – have organized to defend federal military receipts in the 1990s. In a mark of how hotly contested defense downsizing was to become, Congress decided to implement a Base Closures Commission process to deflect heat from individual members of Congress. Ironically, the commission's activities elicited an historically unprecedented expenditure of time and money on the part of local communities to plead their cases. Some argue that the commission itself ended up leaving far more bases only partially closed than is optimal. But the commission process did manage to shutter many bases.

Defense plants and national weapons labs have proved harder to eliminate. Even stronger political efforts have been mounted to preserve private-sector defense establishments, underwritten by contractor-retained earnings from the preceding boom. The lobbying effort has been targetted on liberalizing arms exports as well as maintaining defense budgets and sales to the US government.[6] The Aerospace Industries Association pushed for and won major new subsidies for arms exports under the Bush and Clinton administrations, computed by one researcher to amount to $7.6 billion in 1995.[7] Arms exports doubled over the first half of the decade, and although they have receded to more modest levels, the US share of the world market has risen substantially.

Paradoxically, despite the 60 percent cut in procurement budgets since 1986 and despite Pentagon incentives to close plants described below, very few military production lines have actually closed down, as demonstrated in a striking study by Sapolsky and Gholz.[8] They show that despite the fact that the nation owns 7,500 first-line fighters while the air force fields only about 2,000, the US retains eight lines producing military aircraft. The same capacity overhang has appeared in most major weapons systems. Still in business are six private yards assembling large warships, five helicopter companies fully dependent on military purchases, five satellite makers, and four missile manufacturers. Three aircraft lines remain open in the merged Lockheed/Martin/Loral amalgam, and nine plants producing aerostructures have survived the Northrop/Grumman/Voight combination.

Such obdurate capacity constitutes what Sapolsky and Gholz call the "private arsenal" problem. Over the postwar period, government arsenals and depots have methodically been eliminated in favor of private contractors with greater political clout. It has been difficult to shutter military bases, requiring the innovation of the Base Closing Commission, but it is proving even harder to shut down production lines. On an annualized basis, fewer defense plants have closed since the end of the Cold War than were shuttered during it.

## The Clinton Downsizing Strategy

The stickiness of the defense budget cannot be wholly laid to supplyside resistance. A forceful president, backed by strong public opinion, can succeed in overcoming congressional pork-barrelling impulses, as Nixon did in the 1970s. But in the post-Cold War era, both the Bush and Clinton administrations dragged their feet and failed to provide for an efficient and forward-looking reconfiguration of the defense industrial base. Bush was slow to bring spending down and repudiated conversion strategies as too interventionist. Clinton quickened the pace of defense cuts and initiated promising new conversion programs, but simultaneously capitulated to industry pressures to peddle arms for purely commercial purposes and allow a merger binge which has crowded out private-sector conversion efforts.

The Clinton departments of Defense and Energy, which preside over the conventional and nuclear industrial complexes respectively, have both taken bold steps to dismantle the "wall of separation" that kept security-related capacity cordoned off from civilian activity during the Cold War. Under Secretary William Perry, the Department of Defense has vigorously pursued procurement reform, cutting through regulatory red tape and buying large amounts of "off-the-shelf" commercial components.

President Clinton's Pentagon has also sought to integrate civilian and military technological capability with a multibillion-dollar Technology Reinvestment Program (TRP) awarding competitive grants to consortia of companies, universities, and other non-profit partners. Secretary Hazel O'Leary's Department of Energy allotted more than a billion dollars to Cooperative Research an Development Agreements (CRADAs) which pair company and consortia researchers up with national lab counterparts to explore technologies with potential for both defense and civilian uses. Where these programs have penetrated to the operations level, companies on both "sides" of the market report favorably on the changes.[9]

But both agencies have hedged their bets by forwarding weapons research and procurement budgets that would defend their size, staffing, and procurement budgets at accustomed Cold War levels. Conversion and dual-use initiatives are the casualties. The Department of Energy's Industrial Partnership program was traded off against the more saleable and pricier Stockpile Stewardship program, which commits more than $10 billion over the next decade to the construction and operation of one-of-a-kind facilities to simulate nuclear explosions. The late Secretary Les Aspin's eagerly awaited "Bottom-up Review" grandfathered in tens of billions of old Cold War weapons like the Seawolf submarine and the B-2 bomber. Under concerted Republican efforts, the current Congress added another $8 billion for such programs, while more or less zeroing out future funds for the TRP.

Of greater long-term import, the Clinton Department of Defense has actively facilitated a great leap forward in the size and global reach of American defense firms. Despite internal voices of caution, the department has acquiesced in the transformation of arms exports oversight from preoccupation with American security interest to promotion for commercial ends. The American share of a stagnant world arms market has risen from 35 percent to over 50 percent since the end of the Cold War, with billions of American taxpayer dollars footing the promotional bill.

These exports, especially of high-tech weaponry and components, pose a future security threat, especially when sold to regimes such as Turkey, Saudi Arabia, and Indonesia. Because they are highly profitable, such sales blunt the drive for companies to find civilian markets for their defense-bred technology. And, because more dual-use technologies are now sanctioned for export, the potential for conventional arms proliferation is enhanced.[10]

Furthermore, the department has not only welcomed but subsidized a rapid consolidation in the industry where the largest, most defense-dependent corporations are swallowing each other up. The recently approved Lockheed/Martin purchase of Loral creates a $30-billion-dollar-a-year defense contractor with more than 80 percent of its sales in weapons and accounting for 40 percent of the Pentagon's procurement budget. On the totally unproved grounds that it will save taxpayers money in the future, the Clinton Pentagon is now reimbursing companies billions of dollars for closing down lines (although this happens less often than anticipated) and laying off people (which happens in great numbers than expected). Lockheed/Martin expects to rake in $1 billion to complete its merger, just one of 30 reimbursement requests to the Pentagon.[11]

Enjoying such Pentagon largesse, it is not surprising that defense-company profits are soaring and defense-industry stocks are posting remarkably high price-to-earnings rations, historically unprecedented in a period of defense-spending cuts. It is unseemly and disturbing that these should be in large part attributable to Pentagon subsidies and indifference to whether workers and facilities retired from military projects are efficiently shepherded into new productive activities. Furthermore, the indulgence of mega-mergers is occurring without sober Pentagon evaluation of either security or economic consequences. Two former Pentagon officials in separate analyses have concluded that there

is absolutely no hard evidence on just how many production lines the future US defense effort will require, what the future taxpayer cost of rapidly evaporating competition might be, or whether past mergers have resulted in real gains for the country.[12]

Like the open door for arms exports, incentives favoring the creation of defense-dependent giants garble the pro-dual-use message of Pentagon. Fewer, more powerful (and needy) companies who have unusual access to top Pentagon decision makers will make it even harder to streamline and update the American arsenal and curb arms exports.

## Conversion in Fact

Meanwhile, despite Lockheed/Martin CEO Norm Augustine's famous quip that "our record at conversion is unblemished by success," a surprising amount of conversion is actually taking place. Large primes like Hughes, Raytheon, Rockwell, and TRW have ambitiously committed retained earnings and organizational resources to moving aerospace and communications technologies into civilian products for space, automotive, environmental, energy, and transportation management markets.[13] Hundreds of smaller contractors have followed suit. By and large, this is a response to the facts of life – Pentagon procurement dollars have shrunk by 30 percent since the heady days of the 1980s. And where conversion programs have reached companies, they help.

But not all defense contractors have taken this tack. Largely as a result of Pentagon bungling, some of the biggest have stubbornly defended their specialization and have sought to consolidate or expand their military-market positions. General Dynamics decided very early in the post-Cold War period to "stick to its knitting." It aggressively closed down lines, sold off others, and used its defense profits and proceeds from the sales of assets to buy back its stock. McDonnell Douglas has similarly focused on lobbying for existing weapons systems, staying aloof from merger activity, and more or less eschewing efforts at moving into civilian markets. Other companies, like Honeywell, spun off their defense divisions as stand-alone units (in this case, Alliant Systems), preferring to concentrate on their civilian activities.

A second set of firms has chosen to grow by acquiring and merging with other heavily defense-dependent companies. The recent Lockheed/Martin/Loral merger, creating a company with $30 billion a year in sales, is archetypal, but not singular – Northrop/Grumman is another. This strategy is driven by expected savings from consolidation of research and production capacity in a shrunken market and from the elimination of overhead associated with marketing to and complying with the regulations of the Pentagon. Perhaps even more important (and unacknowledged by current Department of Defense policy), merging firms hope to gain from greater market power and leverage with the monopsonistic defense buyer.

These disparate coping strategies on the part of large contractors have resulted in a substantial shake-out in the defense industrial base. The top-ranked contractors are now much larger and more defense dependent, and the gap in defense dependency between these and the more diversified corporations that remain large defense contractors in absolute terms has grown. The largest – Lockheed/Martin, McDonnell Douglas and Northrop/Grumman – remain more than 70 percent defense dependent, while TRW, Hughes, and Rockwell have lowered their military sales ratios to less than 40 percent. Remaining defense dedicated also appears to have a stultifying effect on firms' investment strategies. A study by Michael Oden finds that the more heavily defense-dependent firms invest significantly lower shares of their earnings in research and new equipment than do the more

aggressively diversifying firms.[14] Instead, these firms are focussing their efforts on lobbying for new systems and export sales and on yet more mergers, many of them with overseas counterparts.

## The Wall Street Connection

Because the Pentagon has no clear vision of a post-Cold War defense industrial base, much of the initiative for restructuring has by default passed to Wall Street. Following a decade of a "hands-off" posture towards military industrial firms – the GM purchase of Hughes Aircraft was the only major deal of the 1980s involving a large defense contractor – Wall Street investment banking houses have become very active in engineering the large deals like Lockheed/Martin and Northrop/Grumman of the 1990s. Their strategy is not only to match up former competitors in either market-deepening or market-widening mergers, but to convince more diversified companies like Rockwell, Texas Instruments, and TRW to sell off their military units, which would then become available for consolidation with other highly defense-dependent firms.

The pervasive view on Wall Street is that the "wall of separation" is a fact of business life, and that "pure-play" defense companies return better value to their stockholders than do conglomerates that attempt to operate across both types of market. It is difficult to evaluate these claims. "Pure-play" mergers are driven as much by expectations of short-term speculative gain as they are by longer-term real returns. Some skeptics see this as simply the Wall Street fad of the mid-decade. In addition, "pure-play" companies of any type may outperform their more diversified competitors on price/earnings ratios. But this may simply be the result of the greater transparency of "pure-play" companies and thus of higher, surer bids on their stock.

The evidence is not yet in on whether "pure-play" companies are actually more efficient or earn higher returns their diversified. Furthermore, if higher returns in the longer run are due to monopolistic profits and enhanced market power, what is good for stockholders is not equivalent to what is optimal for Americans as taxpayers and citizens. The Oden study suggests that those companies that are actively diversifying will be better positioned to compete in an economy with a permanently smaller military, and will be less heavily invested in lobbying for maintenance of defense-spending levels, arms-export permissiveness, and expensive, esoteric R&D projects with little spin-off potential.

## Conclusion

Private-sector supplyside resistance, well organized and heavily financed from past defense earnings, has sabotaged efforts to bring down defense spending, reconfigure the defense industrial base, and reverse conventional arms proliferation. But it has prevailed only because the Clinton Administration has proven unwilling to strategically manage defense downsizing. New permissiveness on exporting and merger fronts, peppered with massive new subsidies, has overwhelmed the ability of underfunded conversion programs and dual-use initiatives to take down the wall of separation.

Like any other transformation that is in the public interest, government ought to use appropriate carrots and sticks in this case, too. As it stands, the US has created lucrative new incentives in the form of arms export and merger subsidies, which are rendering defense-dedicated production highly profitable just when one would want the market to be madly signaling in favor of conversion. These should be eliminated. Instead, incentives should be crafted to encourage firm diversification, dual-use investments, and civilian

exports. Contractors and military facilities should be required to plan for smaller defense budgets and altered missions, just as they have long been asked to plan for new weapons systems and various mobilization scenarios. If payoffs and adjustment assistance are necessary to overcome resistance, that price should be paid – it is a lot cheaper than featherbedding for companies, bases, and projects over the long haul.

Estimates of what the United States really needs to spend on defense range from former Reagan-era official Lawrence Korb's $225 billion to Randall Forsberg's "defense only" force structure at $70 billion. The distance between these pegs and the current $260 billion the US spends (not including the nuclear weapons complex) represents an annual peace dividend that can be applied to other public investments, social programs, and deficit reduction. Expertise no longer employed on the B-2 bomber line or in futuristic weapons research labs could be freed up for American civilian competition. Restraint in arms sales would be a savvy investment in future security.

Though neither major party candidate made much of this opportunity in the 1996 election debate, in the years a head, it should prove irresistible. Poll after poll shows a majority of Americans favoring a strong defense but convinced that the nation spends too much and isn't spending it well. With security, economic prosperity, and lower deficits hanging in the balance, the glue that keeps defense budgets sticky downwards is likely to become brittle and ineffectual. The US enjoys an opportunity to remake the face of the defense economy not seen since after World War II.

United States leadership on defense downsizing and conversion would dampen supplyside resistance in other nations and embolden political leaders to follow suit, magnifying both security and economic payoffs. Conventional arms proliferation would be easier to restrain, and an expensive arms race among allies could be avoided.

# Notes

1  Michael Oden, "Military Spending, Military Power and U.S. Postwar Economic Performance", Ph D dissertation, Department of Economics, New School for Social Research, New York, (1992).

2  See, for instance, the chapter by John Steinbrunner and William Kaufman in Robert Reischauer, ed., *Setting National Priorities: Budget Choices for the Next Century* (Washington, DC: Brookings Institution, 1997).

3  Ann Markusen and Joel Yudken, *Dismantling the Cold War Economy* (New York: Basic Books, 1992).

4  David Henry and Richard Oliver, "The Defense Buildup, 1977–85: Effects on Production and Employment," *Monthly Labor Review* (August 1987), p 3–11.

5  Ann Markusen, Peter Hall, Scott Campbell, and Sabina Deitrick, *The Rise of the Gunbelt* (New York: Oxford University Press, 1991).

6  Project on Demilitarization and Democracy, *Hostile Takeover* (Washington DC: PDD, November, 1995).

7  William D. Hartung, *Welfare for Weapons Dealers: The Hidden Costs of the Arms Trade*. (New York: World Policy Institute, June, 1996).

8  Harvey M. Sapolsky and Eugene Gholz, "Private Arsenals: America's Post Cold War Burden," forthcoming in Ann Markusen and Sean Costegan, eds, *Arming the Future: A Defense Industry for the 21st Century*. (New York: Council on Foreign Relations).

9  Jay Stowsky, "America's Technical Fix: The Pentagon's Dual Use Strategy, TRP and the Political Economy of U.S. Technology Policy," in Markusen and Costegan, *Arming the Future*; Michael Oden, Gregory Bischak, and Christine Evans-Klock, *The Technology Reinvestment Project: The Limits of Dual-Use Technology Policy* (New Brunswick NJ: Rutgers University, Project on Regional and Industrial Economics, 1995).

10  Judith Reppy, "Dual Use Technology: Back to the Future," in Markusen and Costegan, *Arming the Future*.

11  Lawrence Korb, "Merger Mania," *Brookings Review* (Summer, 1996), pp. 22–5.

12  Ibid.; Kenneth Flamm, "Redesigning the Defense Industrial Base," in Markusen and Costegan, *Arming the Future*.

13  Michael Oden, Ann Markusen, Dan Flaming, Jonathan Feldman, James Raffel and Catherine Hill, *From Managing Growth to Reversing Decline: Aerospace and the Southern California Economy in the Post Cold War Era* (New Brunswick NJ: Rutgers University, Project on Regional and Industrial Economics, March, 1996).

14  Michael Oden, "Cashing-in, Cashing-out, and Converting: Restructuring of the Defense Industrial Base in the 1990s," in Markusen and Costegan, *Arming the Future*.

# 8

# Big Missions and Big Business

## Military and Corporate Dominance of Federal Science Policy

### *Gregory Hooks*

 ### *and Gregory McLauchlan*

## Introduction

Many of the policy issues examined in this book pit the "haves" against the "have-nots." However, science policy is the realm of elites. Well-educated scientists are paid by public institutions or private laboratories to conduct research on topics that are often obscure, and usually poorly understood by most of the citizenry. The losers in science policy debates rarely find themselves on the streets, they merely lose influence over the allocation of government resources to scientific endeavors. As such, the Clinton Administration's science policy, and more broadly US R&D policy (which encompasses basic and applied science and technology development), have not been in the forefront of public concern and criticism.

Despite the relative obscurity of science policy, developments in this arena reveal both the limitations of the Clinton Administration's initiatives and the constraints on reform in the late twentieth-century United States. This is especially the case when we consider that from World War II to the present, superiority in science and technology has provided both the material foundation of the US's glo-bal role as a military and economic super-power, and the cultural support for an American identity at the leading edge of modernity in a world where science and technology were viewed as the source of ongoing, progressive transformation of society. From the atomic bomb that destroyed Hiroshima to nuclear power reactors, earth satellites and intercontinental ballistic missiles (ICBMs), *Apollo* and men on the moon, microchips and the Internet, genetic engineering and the "biological revolution," stealth bombers, "star wars" and the space shuttle, state-led R&D projects have provided icons for the national culture and the investment and human capital for new growth industries.

We begin our examination with an overview of the heightened expectations following the 1992 Clinton–Gore victory. In the wake of this election and the lofty campaign rhetoric, hopes were high that science policy would be thoroughly re-evaluated with an emphasis on the demilitarization of science. These hopes were not realized. To fully understand the wide gap between the rhetoric and reality of the first Clinton Administration, we place the US R&D program in a larger historical and institutional context.

There have been two regimes of science in the postwar period: the Cold War regime, in which national security was the overriding concern, and a "competitiveness regime," in which the state has supported corporations with publicly funded research. Cold War science programs (military and civilian) were marked by a mission orientation (build a new weapon, go to the moon, etc.), government production of knowledge, and government consumption of the knowledge produced. In recent decades, especially since the end of the Cold War, the competitiveness approach to R&D policy has gained momentum. In this new regime, corporations (not the state) establish the goals of science, and the government is no longer the major producer and consumer of knowledge. The government's role is reduced to subsidization. We close our chapter with a consideration of the partisan differences over science policy. There are two important ones: the amount of emphasis to place on military objectives and the manner in which federal science policy boosts competitiveness. For Republicans, the majority of federal science spending should be allocated to national security. To the extent that federal research contributes to competitiveness, the subsidization of businesses should be indirect and accomplished through supporting basic research. The Clinton Administration advocates lower levels of defense spending and supports direct ties to businesses and funneling science spending toward "strategic" economic planning.

## The Unrealized Promise of the First Clinton Administration

More forcefully than at any time in the last 50 years, the end of the Cold War and the associated military downsizing raise fundamental questions about the broad priorities and institutional structure of the R&D program. This possibility for major reassessment and institutional change has been given added impetus by recent crisis tendencies in big science and technology. For example, nuclear disasters at Chernobyl and Three Mile Island, the *Challenger* explosion, the toxic legacy of the nuclear arms race, a fierce debate over a "star wars" ballistic missile defense, cancellation of the superconducting supercollider (SSC), and growing evidence of global climate change have given critics of Cold War R&D efforts renewed credibility.[1] During the 1992 campaign vice-presidential candidate Al Gore wrote the best-selling *Earth in the Balance: Ecology and the Human Spirit*, in which he called for a new Global Marshall Plan that would initiate "the rapid creation and development of environmentally appropriate technologies – especially in the fields of energy, transportation, agriculture, building construction, and agriculture," technologies that would then be "quickly transferred to all nations – especially those in the Third World."[2] As the first post-Cold War presidency, the Clinton Administration came into office at a unique conjuncture in the history of US science and technology policy, and candidates Clinton and Gore said much to fuel expectations of significant change.

During the 1992 campaign and in the first months of the new administration, Clinton spoke of the disproportionate spending on military R&D and relative underinvestment in civilian science initiatives.[3] Military R&D accounted for over 60 percent of all federal science and technology outlays, while economic rivals (especially Germany and Japan) invested a significantly larger share of their GDP in civilian R&D. Clinton set the goal of reducing the military's share of federal R&D to 50 percent or less, thereby increasing funds available to civilian initiatives.[4] The new administration made the case that the United States could not respond to the economic, social, medical, and environmental challenges it confronted by simply spending more money

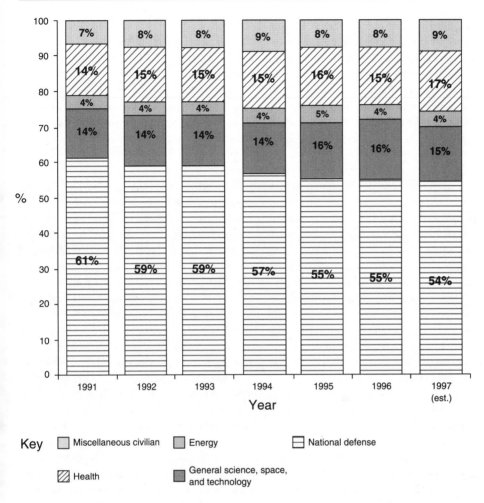

Figure 8.1 Shares of federal R&D expenditures by function, 1991–7

*Notes:* "National defense" includes Department of Defense and selected activities of the Department of Energy.

"Health" includes National Institute of Health and health-related efforts of other agencies.

"Energy" includes civilian-oriented efforts by the Department of Energy.

"General science, space and technology" includes allocations to NASA, the National Science Foundation, and general science efforts of federal agencies.

"Miscellaneous civilian" includes agricultural, natural resource, environmental, and transportation research conducted by the Department of Agriculture, Department of Transportation, Environmental Protection Agency, and other federal agencies.

*Source:* US office of Management and Budget, *The Budget of the United States Government, Fiscal Year 1997* (Washington DC: US Government Printing Office, 1996), table 9.8.

on R&D. Existing science institutions had been structured for and charged with meeting military objectives. Because "new missions" were contemplated, "new institutions" were needed.[5] Clinton's central objectives were: (1) shift resources away from military R&D and into civilian applications (i.e. the "peace dividend" for science); (2) pursue strategic R&D initiatives, including industrial planning efforts centered on the Department of Commerce, and a reorientation of some military R&D toward "dual use," i.e. military and civilian applications; and (3) expand biomedical research in support of the proposed overhaul of health care.

On each front, the first Clinton Administration fell far short of its goals. While reduced, military R&D remains the dominant national effort. The administration's proposed industrial planning efforts – and the attendant R&D efforts – were modest in scope, and these proposals were sharply cut back by the Republican Congress. Biomedical research, which enjoyed bipartisan support, was protected but not transformed. Figure 8.1 shows highlights of the R&D budget from 1991 through 1997.

Figure 8.1 reveals gradual changes over the period. Military R&D has fallen from the 60 percent range (1991–3) to approximately 55 percent of federal outlays in the most recent years. The biggest beneficiary of this decline has been health-related research, increasing from 14 percent of the total in 1991 to 17 percent in the estimated 1997 budget. All other categories of research have been largely unchanged over the period, with no indication that significant changes are on the horizon. Given the largely constant distribution of federal R&D spending among these functions, the overall commitment to R&D is an important issue. The president's shift from investing in infrastructural renewal (1993–4) to balancing the budget (1995–6) has impacted on the R&D budget. While science budgets were not targetted for the deepest cuts by the

Republicans in 1995, the president's own budget calls for significant and sustained cuts in science and R&D beginning in 2000 in an effort to balance the budget. As the editors of *Science* put it, "In essence, this nation is getting ready to run an experiment it has never done before – to see if we can reduce the federal investment in nondefense R&D by one-third and still be a world leader in the 21st century."[6]

The sharpest critics of Clinton's science policies have not been liberals concerned with his failure to deliver on promises. Rather, Republicans in Congress have been harshly critical of Clinton's agenda and have imposed obstacles on several fronts. Republicans assert that Clinton seeks to cut the military too deeply in a still dangerous world and have made repeated proposals to expand military R&D. The GOP has placed a special emphasis on reviving the Strategic Defense Initiative (renamed the Ballistic Missile Defense) and attendant science efforts. Concerning civilian initiatives, the GOP is adamantly opposed to industrial planning and to any initiative that may contribute to it. Congressional Republicans have proposed the complete elimination of the Department of Commerce and have repeatedly targetted for elimination R&D programs in which the government helps firms develop new products or subsidizes the commercialization of emerging technologies. Republicans have proposed eliminating the Department of Energy, transferring its weapons labs to the military, and closing down or privatizing all alternative energy research. While so far not prevailing on these fronts, the GOP did eliminate the Office of Technology Assessment, the congressional office that provided advice on science and technology issues, and severely cut back funding for environmental initiatives such as the National Biological Service, which is concerned with ecosystem management and endangered species. The GOP successfully blocked the overhaul of health care, and thus reduced the scope of the Clinton Administration's reorientation of biomedical R&D. In the era of tight federal budgets, the Republicans have advanced a science agenda that would largely restrict federal science to military R&D and "basic" research (i.e., with no connection to economic planning or overarching health-care policies).

## Big Missions, the Military and Cold War Science Policy

To gain a broader understanding of the continuity evident in the Clinton Administration, we examine the militarization of R&D from World War II through the end of the Cold War. This historical overview provides a context for considering the changes underway in the post-Cold War era. In recent years, both major parties have proclaimed an emphasis on harnessing science to maintain global leadership in military R&D while reorienting science policy to boost international economic competitiveness – they differ on specific programs to achieve these objectives.

### National security and big science

"World War II ushered in the modern era of government–science relations in the United States.[7] The advent of nuclear weapons in World War II not only revolutionized warfare and the international system, it brought a qualitatively new urgency to the military interest in science and technology during peacetime. During the Cold War, nuclear weapons were coupled with new global transport technologies (aircraft, then missiles) capable of delivering these weapons quickly enough to destroy a nation at the outset of a war. Thus, the World War II military strategy of mobilization, in which industrial resources (supported by science and technology) were mobilized over a period of years to wage

a war of production, was replaced by a strategy of deterrence. In the new regime, the emphasis was on qualitative advances in weapons and related systems developed on an ongoing basis during peacetime, to be available at the outset of war (and to deter large-scale war). Bruce Smith identifies the key elements of the postwar science compact: "Society (more precisely, the federal government) would for the first time assume the responsibility for supporting basic research (mainly, but not exclusively, in the universities). Basic research would be the engine driving the whole system. The progress of science would ensure national security, a healthy nation, and economic strength."[8]

While the federal government's commitment to basic research served as the foundation of military superiority, large mission-oriented efforts made use of basic scientific knowledge (often influencing the direction of basic science) and accounted for the dominant share of total R&D outlays. The widely held belief that the atomic bombings of Hiroshima and Nagasaki ended the war and "saved lives" provided legitimation for a postwar science-intensive military program. Atomic fission had only been discovered shortly before the war, and the first sustained nuclear chain reaction was not demonstrated until December 1942. But the unprecedented scale, organizational resources, and national effort of the Manhattan Project – it was the largest scientific or industrial project ever undertaken, and involved for the first time the vertical integration of large science corporations such as DuPont, major university laboratories, and the military – led from theory to operational weapons in only a few years. Thus, the Manhattan Project ushered in the nuclear age and was the archetype of large mission-oriented science programs.[9]

The nuclear revolution also accelerated the scale of military science and technology. For example, ICBMs and nuclear-powered missile submarines – both technologies explicitly designed to deliver nuclear weapons – became the weapon systems of choice. These required complex command, control, and communications infrastructures because the need for real-time information and decision making was paramount, and the risks of failure (e.g. accidental launch of nuclear missiles) were catastrophic. In short, the nuclear revolution placed a premium on developing technologies that were global in geographic range and had great speed, that integrated individual soldiers and operating weapons platforms in real time with the highest level in the chain of command, and that had previously unimagined reliability and performance specifications. Yet the major military advances flowing from science and technology laboratories only provided a *temporary* advantage to the nation that developed them – indeed, they were likely to stimulate the efforts of an adversary by showing what was possible. As a result, military scientists and engineers were in a perpetual race against time, where the *pace* of scientific R&D itself became a key factor in the definition of national security.[10]

Military dominance of the postwar science and technology agenda was facilitated by the military's political, budgetary, and organizational resources. The legacy of civilian state building from the New Deal was largely frozen by the wartime mobilization, and then eclipsed by the Cold War expansion of military institutions.[11] Thus, while Congress engaged in acrimonious debate over the establishment of a civilian National Science Foundation (NSF) after the war, the Office of Naval Research (ONR) and the Atomic Energy Commission (AEC) were well underway in funding a broad range of projects in basic research in the nation's universities and government laboratories.[12] Throughout the Cold War, the military services, the Department of Energy (the successor agency to the AEC), and NASA accounted for the majority of federally funded basic scientific research in the physical sciences in US universities and non-profit laboratories.[13]

Secrecy reinforced autonomy. In Executive Branch agencies and in the Congress, deliberations on military projects and atomic energy, and much of the Cold War R&D effort, were conducted in secret, while thousands of individuals working on military programs had to sign loyalty oaths and submit to security clearance investigations.[14] Secrecy was legitimized by the science and technology-intensive nature of the arms race, where information leaks or espionage regarding sensitive research or technical knowledge could give an adversary important knowledge, or reveal technical weaknesses in the nation's military arsenal. The two most sensationalized cases of alleged Cold War espionage and questionable loyalty – the conviction and execution of the Rosenbergs on charges of atomic espionage, and the security hearings that stripped J. Robert Oppenheimer of his security clearance and hence ability to participate in nuclear policy – symbolized successful efforts by the state to subordinate science and technology to the imperatives of national security.[15]

The Pentagon translated large budgets and its insular administrative authority into an ongoing R&D program that produced a steady stream of impressive – and not so impressive – weapon systems during the Cold War. Because military research and development was large-scale, highly capital-intensive, and pushed the limits of science and technology, the Pentagon fostered the growth of relatively few huge, highly specialized firms that dominated the defense sector and depended heavily on military versus civilian markets for their survival.[16] The Pentagon exercised a significant planning capacity in tailoring the development of key high-tech industries to military needs; it dominated the aeronautics industry and exercised great influence over the emerging electronics and computer industries in the first decades of the Cold War. It exercised such control by providing R&D funding, imposing military specifications for new technologies, and providing demand for industry end-products. Thus, for example, the government accounted for 75 percent of computer purchases in the 1950s, and the military consumed 70 percent of the microchips produced in the 1960s.[17]

The interlocking ties between the Pentagon, military-funded industries and laboratories, and key congressional leaders were the foundation for the military-industrial complex (MIC).[18] But, as Eisenhower observed when coining the term, the military-industrial complex was founded on science and technology: "This conjunction of an immense Military Establishment and a large arms industry is new in the American experience . . . [We] must guard against the acquisition of unwarranted influence whether sought or unsought, by the military-industrial complex" and "be alert to the . . . danger that public policy could itself become the captive of a scientific technological elite."[19]

### Moon rocks and public health

While national security efforts accounted for approximately two-thirds of all federal R&D outlays during the Cold War, the federal government's commitment to basic research and the generalized belief in science gave rise to science initiatives that were only partially or indirectly devoted to military objectives. Yet even many of these enduring civilian programs reflected the Cold War paradigm of large, government-run, and mission-oriented projects. The *Apollo* program is a good example: It incorporated characteristics of military projects, but was a "hybrid" project having both military and civilian aims. *Apollo* had Cold War origins and Cold War objectives.[20] It originated immediately after the Kennedy Administration's humiliations in the Bay of Pigs disaster in Cuba, and the Soviet success in putting the first person in earth orbit when

Yuri Gagarin circled the planet on April 12, 1961. The explicit aim of *Apollo* was to restore US prestige and pre-eminence on the frontiers of the Cold War project, where military high technology and civilian hypermodernity meet.

To accomplish its mission, *Apollo* was given resources few civilian projects could claim. With an unwavering presidential commitment, Project *Apollo* was carried out as a crash program and given sustained budgetary resources, costing some $25 billion over more than a decade. Personnel and resources were transferred wholesale from the military to NASA, the new civilian agency having centralized control and overall authority for the program. *Apollo* was begun at the pinnacle of US hegemony, when the US economy was far larger than those of the rest of the industrialized world.[21] Finally, like military R&D projects, *Apollo* was "mission-oriented" – it was focussed on a specific, highly visible technological goal, one that constituted a spectacular achievement and had during its undertaking widespread public support. Indeed, as Michael Smith argues, "the twelve year effort to put Americans on the moon constituted the most elaborate advertising campaign ever devised. Its audience was truly global. Eight hundred million people saw or heard the first men on the moon."[22]

The National Cancer Program (NCP) or "War on Cancer," launched by the Nixon Administration in the early 1970s, is a good example of a large-scale civilian effort. The NCP was managed by the largest civilian research and development agency, the National Institutes of Health (NIH). The history of the NCP shows how civilian R&D projects have adapted elements of the Cold War military model, as well as some of the organizational and political limitations of civilian R&D. The NCP was launched during the last part of US involvement in the Vietnam war and in the afterglow of *Apollo*, when the science and technology establishment was under increasing attack for its preoccupation with military objectives and its lack of attention to earthly needs. Interestingly, the early rhetoric of the War on Cancer was reminiscent of military programs, with frequent reference in congressional hearings to the need for a "Manhattan Project" to cure cancer and for a centralized, national mobilization with clear-cut objectives. Cancer would be conquered by the same kind of effort that had proved successful in the Cold War.

As was the case with mega-projects pursued under the banner of national security, the National Cancer Program dramatically accelerated the coordination of federal biomedical laboratory resources and left an enduring legacy, including the Human Genome Project and many of the research breakthroughs that ushered in the revolution in genetic research and the biotechnology industry. Indeed, the present US international leadership in biotechnology is seen by many to represent, outside the military arena, the central arena of US comparative advantage in science and thus the key area for large state investment in R&D. This perception helps explains in part why biomedical and genetic research and NIH budgets generally have fared well in the present climate of budget cutting (see figure 8.1).[23] But any idea that what is unquestionably a well-heeled "medical-industrial complex" will grow to rival the military R&D program in scale and command of resources should be met with some skepticism.

The War on Cancer also exhibits characteristics typical of large-scale R&D done by civilian agencies. It is difficult, if not impossible, to determine whether it has been a "success." In contrast, in the case of *Apollo* and military projects, success was easy to determine, even if the benefits of success might be ambiguous or short-lived. The NCP has not cured cancer (though it has brought significant advances in etiology, diagnosis, and treatment). Indeed, the idea of a "cure" for cancer has been increasingly displaced by the meth-

odology of risk assessment, which seeks to determine the number of deaths for a given rate of exposure to carcinogens in a population, resulting in regulation of exposure and rates of "acceptable" deaths. Here the public perception and political definition of "success" can be highly variable, and this can in turn affect the prospects for institutional consolidation and resources.[24] Combating cancer is not a discrete, mission-oriented goal, such as landing on the moon or building an atomic bomb. There are many kinds of cancer, resulting from different causes, and the NCP encompasses objectives in diverse areas including improving prevention, diagnosis, treatment, and follow-up care. Furthermore, many dimensions of these objectives are the primary responsibility of agencies other than the National Cancer Institute. The NCP must coordinate a program across a number of autonomous agencies and compete with a host of non-governmental entities to guide medical research, a sharp contrast with the centralized authority of NASA or military bureaucracies.

The postwar compact between science and the state was based upon the skills and knowledge scientists and engineers offered the military. By the same token, the federal government, especially military institutions, provided unprecedented benefits to the practitioners of science and technology: sustained budgets, unparalleled resources, centralized coordination, political authority, and relative autonomy.[25] If the current post-Cold War transition were simply a matter of redirecting financial allocations from military to civilian pursuits, a reorientation of national R&D priorities would be challenging. But, as the above discussion indicates, this challenge is made more daunting, for it involves, in part, the necessity of civilian agencies competing with national security agencies (especially the departments of Defense and Energy) that have a long track record of managing large science projects and strong allies in the Executive

Branch and the Congress. A dramatic post-Cold War transition would require the restructuring or dismantling of some of the national security institutions and the expansion of civilian sectors of the state. But the post-Cold War era has been marked by sharp budgetary constraints and challenges to the legitimacy of state-led initiatives. Instead of shifting power from military to civilian agencies, the end of the Cold War and the breakdown of the compact between science and the state have led to the diminution of the state's overall influence in the realm of science, and the augmentation of corporate control over the nation's R&D agenda.

## The Clinton Variation on Competitiveness R&D Policy

During the Cold War, a national security coalition, centered in the Department of Defense, Department of Energy, and NASA, concentrated on the development of nuclear weapons and the massive weapon systems to deliver these. Since the 1970s, a more fragmented but significant biomedical coalition (centered in the NIH and congressional committees) has supported research on selected diseases and in biotechnology. Whereas scientists often assert that scientific research is controlled by autonomous researchers seeking answers to "pure" intellectual dilemmas, these mission-oriented agencies controlled the federal science budget and influenced the production of scientific knowledge. Since 1971, these agencies (military and NIH) have distributed no less than 80 percent of federal R&D outlays, with a significant portion of these outlays designated as "basic" research; in 1991 their combined share of the US's R&D reached 86 percent. These same agencies have accounted for 80–5 percent of federal support for university research.

Even before the end of the Cold War, questions were being raised about the efficacy of funneling large investments in R&D to established national security agencies, laboratories, defense contractors, and defense-oriented university facilities. Instead of clearing the path – as the government's large science projects had done in earlier decades – critics contended that the government's science efforts were now lagging behind the private sector in a host of critical science and technology arenas. Moreover, the cost-plus contracting and secrecy that characterized national security R&D inflated the costs of scientific efforts while offering few incentives for scientists and laboratories to develop efficient or practical civilian and commercial applications.[26]

Critics of US militarism have long raised objections to the "military-industrial complex." However, it was not the critics of militarism that made these pivotal concerns in debates over science policy. In the 1970s and 1980s, prominent business executives and political leaders from both political parties began asserting that "competitiveness" was becoming the central challenge and scientific efforts should be harnessed to serve this end.[27] "The 'competitiveness' agenda was proposed as a basis for science and technology policy in the 1980s, during the Reagan and Bush administrations, and found an ardent and articulate champion in President Clinton."[28] The growing concern with competitiveness was focussed especially on the computing, telecommunications, and biotechnology sectors.

The competitiveness agenda seeks to channel the research efforts of federal agencies and universities toward issues that promise direct commercial benefit to US corporations. Even the National Science Foundation (NSF) has been under increasing pressure to fund research that promises pragmatic and profitable results.[29] The emerging competitiveness coalition is not novel for including business leaders to oversee and influence science policy. The national security science establishment included representatives of major defense contractors, and via the "revolving door" many employees of national security agencies and Congress were closely affiliated with leading defense firms. In the realm of biomedical research, pharmaceutical firms, hospitals, insurance companies, and physicians have exerted significant influence over the development and implementation of the federal medical research agenda. But to the extent that "competitiveness" becomes the driving force of government R&D, such elites gain even greater influence. Beginning in the 1970s and gathering momentum in the 1980s, the federal government's civilian research agenda and, to a far smaller extent, its military R&D have shifted away from its own missions (i.e. win the Cold War, go to the moon, or eradicate cancer) and toward support for the profitability and global market shares of US firms. With the state's own mission less salient and the private sector's concern with profitability ascendant, there is less need for the state to define and control science policy.

During the Cold War and thus most of the postwar period, any undue influence of business executives over science policy would have been seen as scandalous: National security might be compromised by the short-term interests and greedy actions of business leaders. In the ascendant science regime, the federal government has no higher mission than to assist firms. While critics of the emerging order find this rationale and structure to be scandalous, proponents argue the extensive involvement and influence of the business community in defining science policy is an essential component of the quest for global competitiveness.

Support for a competitiveness science policy has been growing in Congress for several decades. In 1980, Congress passed the Bayh–Dole Act which encouraged universities to pursue research for profit. This act permitted businesses and not-for-profit organizations – especially universities – to retain title to patents

and inventions made possible by federal funding. "The Bayh–Dole Act gave new and concrete meaning to the phrase 'commodification of knowledge.' The act enabled universities to enter the marketplace and to profit directly when universities held equity positions in companies built around the intellectual property of their faculty, as well as to profit indirectly when universities licensed intellectual property to private sector firms."[30] During the Reagan years, the goal of harnessing science to promote international competitiveness was promulgated by a number of influential policy analysts and business organizations. Despite President Bush's antipathy for any initiative that smacked of industrial policy, the Bush Administration abetted the shift of emphasis in science policy. "Under Bush, the President's Council of Advisors on Science and Technology (PCAST) began to articulate a competitiveness R&D policy. ... By the late 1980s, even the NSF began to promote a competitiveness R&D program."[31] The new science regime has received bipartisan support, and in the last two presidential elections all the major candidates – Clinton was an outspoken supporter – have endorsed the competitiveness science regime.

The Clinton Administration has placed emphasis on identifying "strategically" important civilian research in an effort to help US corporations compete in international markets.[32] Clinton and the Republicans agree that corporate profitability is the benchmark for gauging policy effectiveness and that the private sector will take the lead in identifying projects. Disputes between Clinton and the GOP center on the means to assist US corporations. President Clinton has charged the Department of Commerce with directing and harnessing federal science initiatives in support of US businesses, while mission-oriented agencies (especially NASA, the departments of Defense and of Energy, and NIH) have been mandated to enter into cooperative agreements with private firms to commercialize the scientific knowledge and technologies at their disposal. The administration's priorities for strategic economic initiatives include: new manufacturing technologies (including development of an environmentally friendly, "green" car); computing technologies, including expansion of the data superhighway; global climate and environmental change; and biotechnology.[33] The Clinton Administration has also expanded the funding and the mission of the National Institute of Standards and Technology (NIST), which is housed in the Department of Commerce. As the "favored child of the Clinton Administration," NIST initially saw a sharp increase in its funding with a primary emphasis on the Advanced Technology Program.[34] This program funds high-risk and commercially oriented industrial research. NIST is also playing a prominent role in disseminating information concerning new technologies among US firms.

It should be emphasized that these Clinton initiatives only command a small share of the total R&D budget, and none are large-scale by Cold War military project standards. Clinton is following the advice of science advisers who argue civilian science initiatives should be relatively small and that the demand for the product, especially by the private sector, should be considered at the outset.[35] Additionally, Republicans have attacked and in some cases significantly pared the funding of projects that seek to direct the market in terms of product development (such as a "green" car) or that have implications for industries that are traditional bastions of GOP support (e.g. the threat of global environment research to the oil, chemical, and coal industries). For example, some of the biggest losers at the hands of GOP congressional cuts between the financial years of 1995 and 1997 were the National Biological Service (cut from $162 to $138 million), the EPA's Environmental Technology Initiative (cut from $68 to $10 million), and the Advanced Technology Program (cut from $345 to $225 million).

But these examples can be viewed as skirmishes in light of a broader consensus on post-Cold War US science and technology policy. In a survey of the first Clinton Administration's R&D accomplishments, *Science* concluded that "The Administration has been very vocal in its support of high technology – often in the face of fierce Republican opposition – but has made few radical departures from the policies and programs of its predecessors."[36] The new competitiveness regime has not displaced a mission-oriented and military-dominated US science policy. On the contrary, the United States is pursuing both objectives despite the federal government's fiscal constraints.

## A Peace Dividend for Science?

In its budget statement for fiscal year 1997,[37] the Clinton Administration indicated its intention to continue modest reductions in defense spending through 2002. If these reductions are accomplished, this would represent an absolute level of defense spending comparable to the 1970s (in constant dollars) and the lowest share of resources going to the military since 1940. From this smaller total budget, the Clinton Administration projects significant spending to clean up the toxic legacy of the Cold War ($4.5 billion yearly) and on defense conversion ($3.3 billion yearly) in 1999.

The Clinton Administration's military initiatives have been premised on "dual-use" research and development, i.e. science and technology that can be used in both military and commercial applications. In part, this emphasis comes from defense planners committed to reforming defense procurement. Jacques Gansler,[38] a former Assistant Secretary of Defense, criticized the military's reliance on defense-oriented contractors (either defense-dependent corporations or subsidiaries specializing in defense work) to produce esoteric military end-items. Especially in computing, telecommunications, and other electronic goods, he asserts that commercial vendors are better able to produce reliable and affordable products – and have demonstrated a far better record of maintaining and replacing defective goods. Wherever possible, the Pentagon should buy "off the shelf" at competitive prices, and the federal government should actively encourage "spin-on," i.e. the development of commercial markets for technologies that are important to military applications. For example, federal subsidies to develop high-definition television (HDTV) are justified on the grounds that improved military surveillance is made possible by HDTV. If the Pentagon is obliged to foot the bill for developing HDTV and pay a premium price for televisions only used in the defense sector, this technology would be prohibitively expensive. However, the costs of deploying HDTV in satellites and other military applications will decline if major corporations pay a large portion of development costs and sell HDTV in large commercial markets.

The mission of the Defense Advanced Research Project Agency (DARPA) has changed to emphasize a strengthened commitment to dual-use technologies. President Clinton dropped "Defense" from the title and renamed it the Advanced Research Project Agency (ARPA) in 1993, but it is still housed in the Pentagon. Throughout its 35-year history, ARPA has received high marks for taking a long-range view of science and technology issues in the service of national defense. This agency played a role in identifying the military uses of "advanced computer architectures, packet-switched networks, and lightweight composite materials."[39] ARPA contributed to the early development of these technologies and facilitated commercial applications. ARPA is charged with playing a leadership role in identifying dual-use technologies and stimu-

lating their early development.

To transfer technologies to the commercial sector, the Clinton Administration has encouraged "cooperative research and development agreements" (CRADAs) between federal laboratories and private firms. For federal laboratories, especially the Department of Energy weapons laboratories, CRADAs are attractive because they offer the potential to demonstrate a new usefulness in the post-Cold War era and prospects of gaining access to corporate resources to aid research initiatives. Corporations are attracted to CRADAs because they defray the costs of high-risk research and development and, if successful, the corporation enjoys patent protection.[40] In federal weapons laboratories (Department of Defense and especially the Department of Energy), the Clinton Administration has emphasized CRADAs to resocialize the staff to incorporate more market-oriented thinking in R&D and to reallocate resources toward commercial applications.

But what became "CRADA-mania" in the early 1990s, with upwards of 500 new industry–Department of Energy agreements being signed in 1994 alone, has recently fallen on hard times, and in many of these cases "the marriage of entrepreneurial zeal and publically-funded expertise is on the rocks."[41] The number of new Department of Energy CRADAs fell to less than 100 in 1996, and the experience indicates the difficulty – both political and cultural – of shifting specialized weapons laboratories toward commercial endeavors.[42] In part the military labs went far afield looking for industrial partners in the search for new post-Cold War missions; nuclear weapons labs, for example, joined a consortium to improve textile manufacturing technologies. But the real attack on the CRADA movement came from conservative congressional Republicans. Robert Walker, chair of the House Science Committee, asserted that CRADAs were a form of corporate welfare and argued that "these are two very different cultures – labs and business – and I don't think they have found a way to work together."[43] Some critics also think major departures from the labs' military missions threaten to undermine US military superiority. The Republican-controlled Congress cut funding for CRADAs by 50 percent to $150 million in financial year 1997, and one result is that many corporations that entered into agreements have felt burned by the experience as the labs have had to pull out. In this area of direct industry–laboratory collaboration the future of the Clinton competitiveness agenda remains uncertain.

The Clinton Administration's push for dual-use technologies reflects the continuing emphasis on global military dominance. The administration has made modest changes in basic research; Department of Defense funding for basic research has declined over the last few years. Whereas Cold War science policy placed great emphasis on basic research performed in university laboratories, there is every indication that university researchers who have depended on military funding can look forward to even leaner budgets in the future. The emphasis has been on applied research and development to generate militarily useful innovations that corporations can profitably exploit. Moreover, many of these commercially oriented applications are defended to the national security establishment on the grounds that military agencies can procure cheaper and more reliable products from commercial firms than they can by financing esoteric military end-items produced by defense-dependent firms. Still, it should be emphasized that under "dual-use" policy the path of technological development is bounded by the requirement of demonstrating military applications. Thus scientific and technological development is being led by military agencies to complement the existing military technology base and to serve the Department of Defence's emerging technology agenda.[44] Instead of converting federal

and private facilities from military to civilian applications, critics contend the dual-use strategy constitutes a "Trojan horse" that perpetuates the overemphasis on defense production and underinvestment in civilian-oriented initiatives.[45]

Despite the lofty rhetoric about a "peace divided" for science, it is evident that "the White House had no stomach for putting existing military R&D programs out of business."[46] The United States remains committed to military dominance. The $208 billion (1987 dollars) the United States spent on defense in 1995 was greater than the defense spending of the rest of the world. Moreover, "with the cuts in active duty forces, many defense experts argue that it is vital to continue defense research as a hedge against rogue powers who may exploit high-tech weaponry to wreak havoc in the world."[47] Even as total defense outlays, and the share of federal outlays devoted to military research and development, shrink, the military's R&D effort is projected to remain in the $30–2 billion (1987 dollars) range – still larger than all other federal R&D combined and representing a level of absolute spending that has only been significantly surpassed at the height of the Cold War in the 1980s. While the overall defense budget is projected to shrink modestly in Clinton's second term, R&D will account for a growing share of it.

To the extent that there are identifiable defense-oriented science initiatives in the 1990s, we would call attention to two areas. First is a "counter-proliferation" initiative centering on developing "technology to counter weapons of mass destruction in the hands of potential enemies – whether nations or terrorists."[48] Whereas the nuclear arms race and the Strategic Defense Initiative emphasized spectacular high technology to counter a large and potent nuclear adversary, post-Cold War planning anticipates the dangers of a myriad of lower-level threats. The diffusion of knowledge and the wide availability of necessary materials makes it likely that a host of nations and political organizations can acquire lethal biological, chemical, and nuclear weapons. The task of monitoring the activities of so many states and political organizations, and the diversity of the weapons available (the vast majority of these developed and produced in large quantity by the United States and Soviet Union), makes the challenge a daunting one. This science initiative is quietly redirecting military research and development toward efforts such as detection of biological and chemical weapons (in the United States and elsewhere), non-nuclear means of destroying underground weapons and storage facilities, rapid development and production of vaccines against biological weapons, safe disposal of weapons of mass destruction, and developing protection for US soldiers to survive and fight in contaminated areas.

The second area involves the Department of Energy's nuclear "stockpile stewardship" program, a long-range initiative to monitor, test (through computer simulation), and potentially redesign the several thousand strategic warheads that remain in the arsenal after the Strategic Arms Reduction treaties. The recently enacted Comprehensive Test Ban treaty prohibits nuclear testing, so the labs are in a transition from an applied science and engineering model that involved building and testing weapons to a new era where what is needed is sophisticated computer hardware and software to conduct massive computer simulations of nuclear weapons characteristics. According to *Science*, this effort to create what might be considered a "virtual" weapons industry is now nearly a $4-billion-per-year program and includes plans by the weapons labs "to build bridges to U.S. universities on a scale not seen since the start of the Cold War."[49] Over the next several years the Department of Energy labs intend to channel significant funding into academic areas that are key to this initiative, such as nuclear engineering and radiochemistry, and more importantly, to involve many university computer scientists in research on a new generation of supercomputers at the weapons labs. The combination of these initiatives with looming cuts in basic civilian research funding is not lost on university administrators: "For universities facing a squeeze on funding, having a new suitor – even one regarded as unsavory in some circles – is a happy prospect."[50]

From our vantage point, the post-Cold War transformation is best seen as the deindustrialization of the US military, and not a substantial conversion to civilian pursuits. The deindustrialization that occurred in the rustbelt during the 1970s and 1980s did not convert these economies to a new and vibrant postindustrial economy; it merely shut down industrial facilities that no longer served corporate interests. In a similar vein, the current disinvestment in the conventional military forces and baroque nuclear arsenal of the Cold War era is closing down facilities that no longer serve strategic priorities. In large measure, this disinvestment is undertaken to reallocate resources to capital and science-intensive military force structures and initiatives.

## Future Prospects

In both the military and civilian sectors, science policy presents a confusing front. Throughout the Cold War, critics of mega-projects objected to scientists and policy makers entrenched in well-funded initiatives removed from public scrutiny and accountability. Even if this approach to policy making and administration were efficient, it creates tensions and may be inconsistent with democracy.[51] Critics objected that mega-projects did not respond to society's needs, but took on a life of their own. Scientists advanced their careers by securing a niche in large and insulated projects, not by developing the skills to serve social needs.

Although the realities are far removed from the populist concerns voiced by critics of Cold War-era mega-projects, the emerging competitiveness regime is often advanced under the banner of reform. The Clinton Administration lacks the will, legitimacy, and discretionary spending to advance a grand science project. There is little danger of a mega-project taking on a life of its own. Instead, basic science is being channeled and small projects are being undertaken in the quest for competitiveness. The competitiveness regime has eroded the insulation of scientists that had troubled populist critics of Cold War science initiatives. However, scientists are not responding to the "will of the people" as a populist would hope; scientists and universities are under pressure to document their direct contribution to the profitability of firms. Profit-seeking corporations – often the largest and most powerful – are placed in a position to define society's needs and the role that science can play in meeting these needs. Populist critics longed for the day that scientists would operate with less insulation and with greater accountability. That day has arrived – but because the benchmark for accountability is in terms of commercial viability and profitability, science policy has not become democratic.

In the realm of military science, there is little reason to believe that the Clinton Administration's policies will civilianize science. Instead, these policies protect the national security establishment's ability to channel public and private scientific resources toward military goals. However, if compared to the science policy advanced by Republicans in Congress, science is less militarized under the Clinton Administration. Among the proposals under favorable consideration by Republicans are: (1) concentrating weapons development in several national laboratories, transferring these to the Department of Defense, selling off or closing the remaining laboratories, and abolishing the Department of Energy; (2) phasing out all civilian science and technology that could contribute to industrial planning (including all dual-use and NIST planning; (3) placing lower priorities on "basic" research in environmental, social, and AIDS/HIV research; and (4) reducing the overall civilian science budget to balance the federal budget.[52] Although science was militarized throughout the Cold War, the Reagan Administration's commitment to the Strategic Defense Initiative significantly and dramatically increased this emphasis on military objectives. In a similar fashion, partisan differences in the current period center on the degree of militarization, not its presence or absence.

For much of the Cold War period, critics of defense spending have relied on a "guns versus butter" theme.[53] By demonstrating that the diversion of a significant share of social and economic resources is being devoted to warmaking, advocates of conversion hoped to demonstrate that it was in the self-interest of US citizens to reduce militarism. In the current era of fiscal austerity, insecure employment, and wage stagnation experienced by the majority of US workers, the "guns versus butter" theme may continue to resonate. But we expect it to do so less and less in coming years. Military spending represents the smallest share of federal spending and GDP since World War II. While it is true that national security claims on science remain above 50 percent of all federal science outlays, the military's share is at a postwar low point. Moreover, by stressing dual-use technologies, the "guns versus butter" theme will be less compelling still. Defenders of US militarism will claim that the United States is no longer forced to choose between military or civilian, as dual-use policies make it possible for the US to achieve civilian goals by investing in scientific initiatives in weapons laboratories.

By concentrating on the self-interest of US citizens, the "guns versus butter" theme does not draw attention to the unique moral responsibility of the US state and its citizens. By harnessing science to wage "spectator sport" wars,[54] the US military reduces the risk to US citizens and forestalls war resistance based on "guns versus butter" or anti-conscription sentiments. A cursory review of the eighteenth- and nineteenth-century Indian Wars reveals that the US confronted little resistance to a series of wars against adversaries who were completely overwhelmed by the technological advantages of US military forces. These wars were frequently in direct violation of existing treaties, but the enfranchised citizens of the United States often benefitted directly from the confiscation of lands and exploitation of mineral resources made possible by them. Because the self-interests of US citizens were either served or at a minimum not directly harmed, opponents of these militaristic policies had little success in articulating a powerful critique of these wars.

Fifty years ago, the United States became the only nation to ever use atomic weapons (a decision that was met with an 85-percent approval rating at the time). Like a spectator sport war, a nuclear war that pits two great nuclear powers against one another would require little active participation by the citizenry. However, unlike a spectator sport war in which the citizenry are protected from harm, a nuclear war places the entire population at immediate risk.[55] But the United States has been working to perfect spectator sport wars on a smaller scale. The invasions of Grenada and Panama in 1980s were followed by the overwhelming military defeat of Iraq in the 1990s. The United States suffered minimal casualties in these military adventures and the popularity of political leaders was – if only temporarily – enhanced. Thousands of Iraqi soldiers were killed and injured. Moreover, tens of thousands of Iraqi civilians were killed or injured during the bombing campaign, and even more are dying of disease and starvation that are a result of the deliberate destruction of the nation's infrastructure. From the atomic bomb through the current high-tech "conventional" wars, science has been harnessed to set the United States in a class by itself. Even if the relative balance of military and civilian science spending were to shift more toward civilian initiatives – and thereby significantly redress the "guns versus butter" imbalance – the United States would continue to lead the world in military spending and be able to overwhelm most potential adversaries. Under these circumstances, spectator sport militarism would still be a viable option.

The challenge is to redefine the debate over militarism to better examine the controlled spectator sport wars the United States has been waging over the last 15 years. The neo-liberal and populist attacks on the state may reflect the deep discontent felt because 50 years of heavy investment in military science and technology has created weaponry that must not be consumed, but has had few (if any) positive effects on everyday life. Civilizing science is impeded by 50 years of institution building that reinforces military objectives and by the US's continuing emphasis on military superiority. Partisan differences influence the manner in which these impediments are managed, but neither of the major political parties is proposing policies to directly challenge the continuing militarization of science. Only by confronting directly the scientific, technological, and institutional legacy of 50 years of World War and then Cold War will a public imagination starved for ideas and a vision of social reconstruction be revived. This challenge must be mounted in social movements and by political leaders committed to a thorough reassessment of where US science policy has been, and of where this policy can and should be going.

# Notes

In this chapter, the discussion of NASA and NIH during the Cold War is based on Gregory McLauchlan and Gregory Hooks, "The Last of the Dinosaurs? Big Weapons, Big Science, and the American State from Hiroshima to the End of the Cold War," © *The Sociological Quarterly* 36, 4 (1995), pp. 755–8.

1  We elaborate on these issues in "Last of the Dinosaurs? Big Weapons, Big Science, and the American State from Hiroshima to the End of the Cold War," *Sociological Quarterly* 36(4), pp. 749–76.

2  Al Gore, *Earth in the Balance: Ecology and the Human Spirit* (New York: Penguin, 1992), p. 306.

3  Lewis Branscomb. "The National Technology Debate," L. Branscomb, ed., *Empowering Technology: Implementing a U.S. Strategy.* (Cambridge MA: MIT Press, 1993), pp. 1–35.

4  US Office of Technology Assessment, *Defense Conversion: Redirecting R&D* (Washington DC: US Government Printing Office, 1993), p. 5.

5  US Office of Technology Assessment, *Defense Conversion*, p. 37.

6  Neal F. Lane. "Science and the American Dream," Editiorial, *Science*, (271) (February 26, 1996), p. 1037.

7  Bruce L. R. Smith. "The United States: The Formation and Breakdown of the Postwar Government–Science Compact," in Etel Solingen, ed., *Scientists and the State: Domestic Structures and the International Context* (Ann Arbor: University of Michigan Press, 1990), pp.33-61, quoted from p. 38. See also McLauchlan and Hooks, "Last of the Dinosaurs?"

8  Smith, "United States," p. 41.

9  Richard G. Hewlett and Oscar E. Anderson Jr, *The New World, 1939–1964. Vol. 1: A History of the United States Atomic Energy Commission* (University Park: Pennsylvania State University Press, 1962); Gregory McLauchlan, "The Advent of Nuclear Weapons and the Formation of the Scientific-Military-Industrial Complex in World War II," in Gregg Walker, David Bella, and Richard Clinton, eds, *The Military-Industrial Complex: Eisenhower's Warn-*ing Three Decades Later . (New York: Peter Lang, 1992), pp. 125–50.

10  McLauchlan. "Advent of Nuclear Weapons."

11  Gregory Hooks, *Forging the Military-Industrial Complex: World War II's Battle of the Potomac* (Urbana: University of Illinois Press, 1991).

12  Daniel Kleinman, *Politics on the Endless Frontier* (Durham NC: Duke University Press, 1995); Smith, "United States."

13  Paul Forman, "Behind Quantum Electronics: National Security as the Basis for Physical Research in the United States, 1940–1960." *Historical Studies in the Physical and Biological Sciences* 18 (1985), pp. 149–229. Stuart Leslie, *The Cold War and American Science: The Military-Industrial-Complex at M.I.T. and Stanford* (New York: Columbia University Press, 1993).

14  G. H. Clarfield and W. M. Wiecek, *Nuclear America* (New York: Harper and Row, 1984); Forman, "Behind Quantum Electronics."

15  See, for example, H. F. York, *Race to Oblivion: A Participant's View of the Arms Race* (New York: Simon and Schuster, 1970).

16  Gregory Hooks and William Luchansky, "Warmaking and the Accommodation of Leading Firms: Defense Procurement and Corporate Growth, 1939–1959," *Political Power and Social Theory* 10 (1995), pp. 3–38.

17  John K. Galbraith, *The New Industrial State* (Boston: Houghton Mifflin, 1967); Gregory Hooks, "The Rise of the Pentagon and U.S. State Building: The Defense Program as Industrial Policy," *American Journal of Sociology* 96 (1990), pp. 358-404; David Noble, *Forces of Production: A Social History of Industrial Automation* (New York: Knopf, 1984).

18  Gordon Adams, *The Iron Triangle: The Politics of Military Contracting* (New York: Council on Economic Priorities, 1981); Ann Markusen and Joel Yudken, *Dismantling the Cold War Economy* (New York: Basic Books, 1992).

19  Dwight Eisenhower, "Farewell Address to the Nation," in Walker, Bella, and Clinton, *Military-Industrial Complex*, pp. 361–67.

20  Walter McDougall, *The Heavens and the Earth: A Political History of the Space Age* (New York: Basic Books, 1985).

21  Gregory Hooks and Gregory McLauchlan,

"The Institutional Foundation of Warmaking: Three Eras of U.S. Warmaking, 1939–1989," *Theory and Society* 21 (1992), pp. 757–88.

22 Michael Smith, "Selling the Moon: The U.S. Manned Space Program and the Triumph of Commodity Scientism," in Richard Wightman Fox and T. J. Jackson Lears, eds, *The Culture of Consumption* (New York: Pantheon, 1983), pp. 175–210, quoted from p. 17.

23 Richard Kerr, "Congress: Biomedical Research Wins Big," *Science* 274 (1996), pp. 27–8.

24 Mark Rushefsky, *Making Cancer Policy* (Albany NY: State University of New York Press, 1986).

25 Markusen and Yudken, *Dismantling the Cold War Economy.*

26 Ibid.

27 Jacques Gansler. *Defense Conversion: Transforming the Arsenal of Democracy* (Cambridge MA: MIT Press, 1995); Robert Johnston and Christopher Edwards, *Entrepreneurial Science: New Links between Corporations, Universities and Government* (New York: Quorum Books, 1987); Laura D'Andrea Tyson, *Who's Bashing Whom? Trade Conflict in High-Technology Industries* (Washington DC: Institute for International Economics, 1992).

28 Sheila Slaughter and Gary Rhoades, "The Emergence of a Competitiveness Research and Development Policy Coalition and the Commercialization of Academic Science and Technology," *Science, Technology, and Human Values* 21 (1996), p. 304.

29 Ibid., p. 307.

30 Ibid., p. 318.

31 Ibid., p. 315.

32 Tyson, *Who's Bashing Whom?*, p. 289.

33 Deborah Shapely, "Clintonizing Science Policy," *Bulletin of the Atomic Scientists* (December, 1993), p. 42.

34 Jeffrey Mervis, "Clinton Holds the Line on R&D," *Science* 267 (1995), p. 782.

35 Branscomb, "National Technology Debate."

36 Andrew Lawler, "Clinton's R&D Achievements Tilt Toward Technology," *Science* 271 (February 23, 1996), p. 1046.

37 US Office of Management and Budget, *Budget of the United States Government, Fiscal Year*

*1995* (Washington DC: US Government Printing Office, 1994), pp. 440–3.

38 Gansler, *Defense Conversion.*

39 US Office of Technology Assessment, *Defense Conversion*, p. 121.

40 Ibid.

41 Andrew Lawler, "DOE to Industry: So Long, Partner," *Science* 274 (October 4, 1996), pp. 24–8.

42 Branscomb, "National Technology Debate."

43 Lawler, "DOE to Industry," p. 26.

44 Jeffrey Mervis, "Defense Conversion Comes to Campus," *Science* 263 (1994), pp. 1676–8; Gary Taubes, "The Defense Initiative of the 1990s," *Science* 267 (1995), pp. 1096–1100.

45 James Raffel, "The 1991 Conversion Program: An Update," *New Economy* 3 (1992), pp. 7–8.

46 Shapely, "Clintonizing Science Policy," p. 41.

47 Ibid.

48 Taubes, "Defense Initiative of the 1990s," p. 1096.

49 Peter Weiss, "Weaponeers Cultivate Academics," *Science* 274 (November 8, 1996), p. 914.

50 Ibid.

51 See for example Dorothy Nelkin, "Science and Technology Policy and the Democratic Process," in James Petersen, ed., *Citizen Participation in Science Policy* (Amherst MA: University of Massachusetts Press, 1984).

52 Andrew Lawler, "Walker Unveils R&D Strategy," *Science* 266 (1994), p. 1938; Lawler, GOP Plans Would Reshuffle Science," *Science* 268 (1995), pp. 964–7; Lawler, "Republicans Split Over Fate of the Department of Energy," *Science* 268 (1995), p. 1559.

53 Seymour Melman, *Pentagon Capitalism: The Political Economy of War* (New York: McGraw-Hill, 1970); John Tirman, "The Defense-Economy Debate," in J. Tirman, ed., *The Militarization of High Technology* (Cambridge MA: Ballinger, 1984).

54 For a discussion of "spectator sport militarism," see Michael Mann, "The Roots and Contradictions of Modern Militarism," in *States, War, and Capitalism* (New York: Blackwell, 1988).

55 Martion Shaw, *The Dialectics of War: An Essay in the Social Theory of Total War and Peace* (London: Pluto Press, 1988).

# 9

# Active-Competitive Industrial Policy

## From Elite Project to Logic of Action

 *J. Kenneth Benson and Nick Paretsky*

## Introduction

In the last 20 years the United States government has moved toward a new kind of industrial policy. This movement began with the recommendations of elite policy councils linked to large and powerful capitalist interests. The movement succeeded in enacting several programs of recent presidents – Reagan, Bush, and Clinton. In this chapter we first analyze elite councils and their influence on policy making since 1980. Then we examine the industrial policies of the first Clinton Administration.

American governments have, for most of the postwar period, pursued scattered and somewhat incoherent policies toward specific industries. The government granted protective tariffs, price supports, and occasional bailouts to particular industries.[1] The government financed facilities and investments in research and development in a few industries, particularly agriculture and health care. And, of course, defense and space-related industries were extensively interlocked with the federal government through financing, R&D,

selection of production goals, and many other ways.[2]

Recently the US government developed new kinds of programs and initiatives which we call "active-competitive industrial policy." These programs were active in the sense that government acts directly to shape industrial development rather than providing only a context within which market forces are allowed to determine outcomes. The policies are competitive in their focus on improving the capability of particular sectors to compete in global markets and against international firms in the American markets. The new policies are intended to enhance the overall performance of the American economy by selecting particular industries for government actions.[3]

In this chapter we intend to account for the emergence of the active-competitive industrial policy and its embodiment in particular programs. On the first level, we seek the origins of the active-competitive policy in the recommendations of elite policy councils. These councils formed a "project" to produce an active-competitive policy. On the second level, we analyze the actual industrial policies of the Clinton Administration. We also try to understand the linkage between these levels. We intend to explain why the industrial policy innovations occurred and why they took specific forms.

The policy stance of the Clinton Administration was based on a particular logic of action that grew out of the elite project and was refined by the political process. The logic of action is a framework of reasoning which provides the basis for the development of specific programs and initiatives. The Clinton Administration argued the need for an active-competitive industrial policy and then developed an extensive array of programs and initiatives to implement that logic. The logic was built into the programs and initiatives so that it concretized the organizational and programmatic embodiment of those ideas.

For the Clinton Administration, an active-competitive policy orientation included not only government investments in industry, but also reorganizations of a large array of government programs to focus them increasingly on industrial competitiveness. Established domains and work paradigms of programs and agencies were challenged. Active-competitive policies created organizational contradictions across a wide spectrum of government actions. Such policies challenged and were challenged by a number of alternative logics, some deeply entrenched and some connected to alternative visions of the future. In pursuing active-competitive policies and grappling with contradictions, the Clinton Administration and its opponents created an extensive but eventually narrowly circumscribed array of programs and initiatives.

We argue that the move toward active-competitive industrial policy grew out of the debates among elite policy councils of the capitalist class. Particular capitalist-class fragments, especially high-tech companies and some segments of finance capital,[4] made active-competitive industrial policy their "policy project." They created a political context in which industrial policy became possible. They helped legitimate state activism in the investment decisions of private companies, and worked out specific strategies answering the puzzle of how to expand state capacity in a limited way that leaves the investment prerogatives of capitalists largely intact. Their ideological, financial, and organizational interventions created an opening for politicians to link their political careers to the expansion of state capacities.

The connection between the elite segments and the political actors is dialectical, not one-way. Policy intellectuals, politicians, government officials, and others have shared in the development of the elite policy project. Some academics formulated solutions to America's competitiveness problems, helped elite policy councils to form ideas and eventually took positions in government where those ideas could be implemented. Politicians sometimes presented their ideas to industrialists and financiers, and sought endorsements and contributions. Out of these interchanges came a series of elite-sponsored proposals, which in turn shaped the policies of several presidential administrations.

The elite policy project contained three general elements. First, the state must lead the innovation process by targeting public and private investments in R&D on technologies crucial to the future competitiveness of key segments of American industry. Second, the state must encourage the reorganization of the private ownership structure of particular industries through the formation of joint ventures, partnerships, and consortia. This would permit the industry to deal flexibly with technological change. Third, the state's actions would be limited or constrained by several considerations: (1) it would make investments to stimulate private investments, not to replace those permanently; (2) it would form partnerships with the private sector, not act autonomously; (3) it would not engage in profit-making production, but would turn the resulting new technologies over to the private sector for commerical production; and (4) it would take action only in those industries or sectors where investments needed to secure competitiveness would not be made by the private sector alone.

## Policy Councils: Constructing Active-Competitive Industrial Policy

Active-competitive industrial policy was the agenda of a broad coalition of high-tech companies from industries such as semiconductors, computers, telecommunications, aerospace, and pharmaceuticals, along with some elements of finance capital. Major capitalist policy-planning groups – chiefly the Council on Foreign Relations (CFR) and the Committee for Economic Development (CED) – helped formulate and advocate the agenda. Domhoff and others have argued that these organizations, which are at the center of a network of think tanks, university research institutes, and foundations, are important in shaping the class-wide rationality of the ruling class[5]. Fennema and Pijl argue that these organizations can be viewed as "forums by which diverse fractions attempt to reach a common perspective and course of action."[6] The resulting positions become the basis for recommendations to state policy makers, who themselves are often recruited from these organizations.[7] Their leaders are drawn from the corporate "inner circle," the small group of business leaders whose connections to several companies, via directorships and stock ownership, enable them to adopt a class-wide perspective and act as a political vanguard for the business community as a whole.[8]

High-tech business executives began to mobilize during the early 1980s, in response to growing competitive pressures from for-eign producers supported by the industrial policies of their home governments. Trade associations such as the American Electronics Association and the Semiconductor Industry Association were important here. But multi-sector organizations, representing diverse high-tech industries, as well as some more traditional sectors such as auto and chemicals, also came into existence to push for industrial policy. The most important was the Council on Competitiveness (CoC), formed in 1986 by Hewlett-Packard president John Young. During its first decade, the Executive Committee of the CoC was composed largely of the heads of other large technology companies, such as IBM, Xerox, Intel, Motorola, Boeing, Kodak, and Pfizer, with a few chief executives from basic manufacturing firms such as Ford and BF Goodrich. From banking, the chairman of Chase Manhattan served on the executive committee. The council was an outgrowth of earlier efforts by the Business–Higher Education Forum,[9] an organization of top executives and university presidents, and the President's Commission on Industrial Competitiveness,[10] formerly chaired by Young.

A crucial grouping of policy intellectuals involved in producing the industrial policy agenda came from the University of California-based think tank, Berkeley Roundtable on the International Economy. BRIE was formed in the early 1980s to "express a West Coast perspective" on high-tech competitiveness with a business advisory board that included the heads of Intel, National Semiconductor, Apple, and other Silicon Valley firms.[11] University of California faculty members involved in BRIE included political science professor John Zysman, economics professor Laura D'Andrea Tyson, and Stephen Cohen, a professor of planning. BRIE advanced arguments for the US to adopt sectoral industrial policies to aid high-tech industries.[12] Members such as Zysman and Tyson were advisers to the President's Commission on Industrial

Competitiveness, and Tyson was a consultant to Motorola and the CoC.[13]

The CoC warned of the erosion of the US edge in industrial technology,[14] which it argued was in part the result of foreign industrial policies that "combine funding with extensive public–private collaboration."[15] According to the council, "Many in the private sector believe ... that they cannot compete overseas against foreign government–industry alliances unless they have a more cooperative relationship with the US government."[16] It called for the president to "increase dramatically the percentage of federal R&D expenditures allocated to support for critical generic technologies" and to "direct key technology agencies" such as DARPA "to work with industry to advance US leadership in critical generic technologies" and to ensure "the federal laboratories' contribution to US technological leadership and competitiveness."[17] The council advocated more government-backed industry consortia such as the Pentagon-funded semiconductor consortium SEMATECH,[18] but drew the line for subsidies at "precompetitive, generic technologies"; "[f]unding for the production and commercialization of consumer products ... should always be industry's responsibility."[19]

The CFR actively advocated industrial policy, linking to the need for the foreign-policy community to focus on the economic dimensions of national security, in a post-Cold War world of intensifying economic rivalries between capitalist powers formerly united by the common Soviet threat. Thus, CFR chairman Peter Peterson, chairman of the Blackstone investment bank, writing for a joint CFR–American Assembly project on "Rethinking American Security," argued that "economic constraints are beginning to influence, if not dictate, America's relations with others ... US national security interests must include the development of policies that will increase our economic strength and domestic stability." Viewed from this perspective, "na-

tional security threats" included "a loss of technological leadership in cutting-edge industries, and a general decline in our global competitiveness."[20] Elsewhere, Peterson wrote that "civilian-sector R&D [is] arguably a key to post-Cold War economic security."[21]

More specifically, CFR argued that the US military had come to depend both on foreign suppliers for many key technical components of weapons systems and on civilian US industry, as the difference between civilian and military components eroded. "As a result," argued CFR director Bobby Inman, former deputy director of the CIA and the head of the National Security Agency, and CoC executive vice-president Daniel Burton, writing for the CFR-American Assembly project, "the national security debate is increasingly preoccupied with issues related to technology and industrial competitiveness."[22] And, in "High-Tech is Foreign Policy," CFR director Harold Brown, former secretary of defense and a partner with the Warburg, Pincus venture capital firm, called for a "high technology industrial policy" to help counter the rise of Japan as an industrial and potential military power.[23]

Prominent members of the CFR board helped craft specific proposals for government technology investment. Brown chaired a panel of the National Academy of Sciences and Engineering, which recommended a $5-billion Civilian Technology Corporation to finance industry R&D projects through loans and direct investments.[24] Inman, himself an electronics executive, championed making the Pentagon into an American version of MITI[25] and chaired a panel of the Carnegie Commission on Science, Technology and Government, a group strongly tied to the CFR which advocated transforming DARPA "into a National Advanced Research Projects Agency" to support dual-use technologies with "potentially high payoff" in the commercial sector.[26] Inman was also closely involved with the CoC, first serving on its executive committee and then becoming senior adviser for the group.

The CED also endorsed a more active government role in developing commercial technology. In a 1992 policy statement on post-Cold War international economic strategy, the CED called for the federal government to "shift resources [from defense] to financing the development of technologies for civilian use," which "may require changing the mission of federal research agencies." The report stated that "Small federal investments . . . can also help convene industry-wide consortiums," and called for the federal labs to be "redirected toward commercial use."[27] The CED had been slow to support such measures and opposed proposals for the targeting of government investments on specific industries, worrying that "selective intervention would fall prey to pork barrel politics" and arguing that the market remains a better allocator of resources than government bureaucrats.[28]

In contrast, a number of CFR-linked forums supported targeting, among them the Institute for International Economics, a think tank whose board was chaired by CFR chairman Peterson and included numerous current and former council directors and members, such as Paul Volcker and CFR chairman emeritus David Rockefeller. The institute's director, Fred Bergsten, an economist long active in CFR circles, proposed "direct help for key industries," and argued that "Thoughtful sector-specific domestic policies can assist the development of crucial industries, as in the past with respect to agriculture and commercial aircraft and numerous other defense-related products."[29] The institute had also published a book by BRIE research director Laura Tyson, herself a CFR member, which advocated targeting.[30] In its preface Bergsten stated that "Our goal in publishing it" was to help "start developing a consensus on the proper course for policy in the future.[31]

The governing bodies of the CFR and CED overlap significantly and interlock closely with the executive committee of the CoC. But there are some differences in the composition of the CFR and CED leadership which may partly explain the divergence on targetting. From the late 1980s into the early 1990s, there was an influx onto the CFR board of high-tech business leaders seeking federal assistance, including the chairmen of Xerox, AT&T, and Corning. Further, all the industrial firms represented on the CFR board were from high technology; some of the financial capitalists at the core of its leadership apparently had a strong stake in this sector. In contrast, high-tech influence in the CED was less profound; although a large number of high-tech executives were on the CED's policy committee, their influence was diluted by the greater mix of sectors represented, including textiles, oil, retail, services, and real estate.

Specific initiatives of the Clinton Administration can be traced to the recommendations of the CFR and CoC. At the level of administrative innovations, the National Economic Council, which was to play an important coordinating role in the technology policy, was recommended by a commission on government reorganizations sponsored by the Institute for International Economics and the Carnegie Endowment for International Peace. CFR director Richard Halbrooke of Shearson-Lehman (who became a state department official) chaired the commission, which included CFR chairman Peterson, CFR president Peter Tarnoff (who also went into the state department), Fred Bergsten, Bobby Inman, and other CFR figures. A memorandum to President-elect Clinton by the commission stated the need for a "shift of priority and resources away from national security, as traditionally defined, and toward the broader problems of making America competitive in a global economy." It recommended creating an "Economic Council . . . your instrument for assuring that economic policy gets attention equal to traditional national security."[32]

These elite forces also shaped the major role of the Commerce Department and its National Institute of Standards and Technology (NIST) in the administration's policy. The Carnegie Commission on Science, Technology and Government had recommended that NIST "have a central responsibility for supporting generic and pre-competitive research and development not within the missions or R&D programs of other departments and agencies," through the Advanced Technology Program (ATP), discussed in greater detail below.[33] The CoC had proposed providing "adequate funding" for NIST and the ATP "to give them a chance to succeed."[34]

A number of key personnel who implemented the administration's policy came out of the CFR–CoC network. A central figure in the administration's efforts was BRIE's Laura Tyson, first head of the Council of Economic Advisers and later chair of the NEC whose nomination to head the CEA was supported by the CoC and the Institute for International Economics.[35] The director of the Office of Science and Technology Policy, John Gibbons, had been a member of the CFR, the CFR-linked Aspen Institute, and the Carnegie Commission on Science, Technology and Government.[36] The Defense Department started to increase support for dual-use technologies under the leadership of William Perry, a former Silicon Valley investment banker and department official in the Carter administration who had been a member of the Carnegie Commission on Science, Technology and Government and had chaired a commission panel on defense support for technology.[37]

So policy organizations sponsored by capitalist elites formulated a detailed agenda for directly involving the state in industrial development. Their reports and the placement of personnel in high government positions transmitted the agenda to government policy makers. Now we examine how the Clinton Administration actually implemented it.

## Clinton Administration: The Logic of Active-Competitive Industrial Policy

The Reagan and Bush administrations had given grudging support to the active-competitive policy and had enacted specific policies in a piecemeal fashion; by contrast, the Clinton team made a large and obvious commitment to the policy orientation and sketched out its development in a wide range of programs. The administration initially projected large outlays of funds for these to convert the abstract principles of the policy council recommendations into the logics of action of specific programs and initiatives.

By "logics of action" we mean the particular rationality underlying and infusing a set of programs and initiatives. The "logic of action" was quite clearly articulated by the actors,[38] as in many of Bill Clinton's and Al Gore's 1992 campaign speeches and as refined and restated in several early statements and reports. Technology was seen as one of the main causes of economic change and of the levels of competitiveness of firms, industries, and nations: Nations with higher levels of investment in new technologies were expected to be more competitive than others, so an important objective was to increase public and private-sector investments in new technologies.

The Clinton Administration formulated a coherent framework as a basis for its active-competitive industrial policy,[39] including the assumption that globalization of production necessitated reforms and investments to make the American economy compete in future world markets. It justified an important but limited role for government in producing the needed change, particularly in directly supporting and even selecting wide-ranging business innovations that would presumably enhance competitiveness.[40]

The administration also reasoned that organizational arrangements prevailing in particular firms, industries, and nations affect their competitiveness. In general, it argued that contemporary international competition requires flexible labor–management relations in order to deploy new technologies, introduce new products, and move production into new regions. Even the relations among firms must be more flexible, permitting alliances and joint ventures to form, dissolve, and reform quickly to take advantage of opportunities to introduce new products, exploit new technologies, and gain control of new markets.

Some governments, such as Japan's were said to have greater capacity to coordinate economic interests than others, so a practical implication of this logic was to enhance the US government's capacity to identify promising technological innovations and to bring together interorganizational coalitions to develop them. State action would stimulate the formation of such linkages, which in turn would provide a social basis for forming new alliances in the future; so the administration pushed partnership as the organizational means of carrying out its industrial policy objectives. The partnerships included private firms, public agencies, and non-profit organizations.

Government was to form the alliances and to participate in the needed projects.[41] Some needed investments were said to be too large for private firms to undertake; and some industries include so many competitors that particular firms cannot be sure of reaping the profits from the needed investments because the resulting technological innovations will spill over quickly to other firms in the sector.

At the same time, the role of government would normally be circumscribed, restricted for the most part to "generic technologies" at a "precommercial" or "precompetitive" stage of development.

These proposals always assumed that private investment is more important in determining competitiveness, so the government role was to stimulate and create situations fa-

vourable to private investment, not to replace it; innovations created with public investments would be turned over to private enterprise for profit-seeking production.

The administration linked this logic to many other agendas; that is, instead of focussing on the specific problem of technology R&D investments, it branched out and developed a number of policies held together loosely by the competitiveness problem and the call for government activism to address it, by, for example, revising regulatory and tax regimes. The tax code revisions were to create incentives for investment in new technology R&D while the regulatory changes were to eliminate inflexibilities restricting the use of new products and technologies and the formation of new alliances. These regulations tend to institutionalize an interorganizational division of labor and to make certain kinds of linkages illegal. At least three arenas were targeted: anti-trust, environment, and management–labor relations.

The administration argued also that government must make investments in job training and infrastructure, targetted at the specific areas of needed technological innovation. Preparing workers for new technologies would help to make American firms competitive and investments in them attractive, and infrastructural investments targetted on new technologies would improve efficiency in transport and communication. One such area was the Information Superhigheay or National Information Infrastructure.

Concerted government action on trade issues was to enhance the competitiveness of American industry. Generally, the administration argued for free trade and opposed protection, supporting NAFTA and the extension of the GATT in steps that clearly signalled a rejection of protectionist sentiment. But the administration also argued for tough negotiating positions in bilateral negotiations where foreign practices unfairly disadvantaged American industries.[42]

Contradictions – opposing tendencies which limit an emerging line of organizing activity,[43] – were important in shaping the policy process. Active-competitive industrial policy challenged other reform agendas and a number of logics already established in the government, including organizational and policy paradigms. It became a basis for launching new programs, reorganizing existing agencies, rearranging funding priorities, and constructing new coordination centers. We propose here a particular way of reading the field of contradictions while recognizing that different readings are possible and even plausible.

- *Deficit reduction versus public investments.* The Clinton Administration advocated both deficit reduction and investments in technology R&D and job training; and it struggled internally over the dilemma in early 1993. Concerns about interest rates, the bond market, and Perot voters apparently prevailed. Later the Republican-controlled Congress pushed to speed up deficit reduction and a balanced budget, and the technology and job-training investments originally planned by the administration were severely cut back.[44]
- *Public investments versus private investments.* The logic of active-competitive industrial policy pushed toward increased government involvement in investment decisions on technology R&D, challenging the established domain divisions between public and private organizations. Some agencies previously confined to infrastructural support of industry were thrust into selective R&D investments, while some that had supported primarily basic science were pushed into applied R&D work close to the commercialization stage, and new agencies investing in public–private R&D partnerships began to compete for funds and authority with established, old-line ones. Resistance to the technology R&D investments came

from many quarters, foremost among them some conservative Republicans in Congress, who attacked programs like the ATP which implemented the investments. These Republicans generally argued that private capitalists are better able to select technologies for R&D investments and that government should not invest close to the commercialization stage, because such actions require government to select among firms and sectors. After the 1994 elections the Republican leadership in the Congress tried to abolish the offending programs.[45]

- *Civilian versus defense R&D.* The administration's program challenged the previously strong link of government R&D to military technologies,[46] since the logic of active-competitive industrial policy demanded that the percentage of R&D going to strictly military uses be reduced. Defense Department and Energy Department laboratories devoted to weapons research were challenged to take on civilian R&D projects in conjunction with private-sector partnerships.
- *Competitive versus protective policy.* The administration concentrated on making American industries competitive rather than protecting them. This involved refocusing government expenditures, cutting back protective payments, and increasing support for changing technologies, ownership structures, and marketing strategies. The administration's reorganization program, "Reinventing Government," had the specific objective of reducing the payments and policies intended to protect domestic industries from international competition,[47] since many industries and firms were already receiving tariff protection from foreign competition, government guarantees of support payments, government assistance in the export of products, and the like. One prominent example was the maritime industry, including shipping

and shipbuilding. Efforts to cut back such subsidies and protections were resisted by firms, unions, congressional representatives, communities, and federal agencies administering the programs,[48] while within the administration a battle over "corporate welfare" was waged.[49]

- *Competitive policy versus environmental protection regimes.* The Clinton Administration examined the rules governing environmental protections, anti-trust, and labor–management relations, seeking efficiencies to enhance competitiveness.[50] It funded studies of environmental regulations in particular industries looking for changes to make new environmental technologies more economical, and proposed a holistic assessment of a full range of environmental and competitiveness problems, industry by industry. So the administration's reorganizing drive to some degree contradicts the existing environmental protection paradigm of mandating and enforcing standards for each pollution source without regard to competitiveness.

- *Competitive policy versus labor-management regimes.* The active-competitive policy tends to challenge established labor-management regimes, as technology innovations and the emphasis on flexible organizational structures run up against the established order. For example, the administration initiated studies of existing relationships, which tend to be adversarial, and sought more flexible and adaptive labor relations.[51] Pressure from both management and labor interests seems to have stimulated the re-examination of the National Labor Relations Board (NLRB) and other rules and statutes; one specific problem was labor-management committees in some companies, challenged by unions as "company unions."

- *Technology R&D versus training.* Investments in new technologies and associated flexible ownership and control structures tend to destabilize existing jobs and to generate inequalities. To counter these tendencies the administration also promoted job and apprenticeship training programs, seeing these as complementary. It pushed training programs which would prepare workers for the new technologies and retrain them when displaced by industrial change, and managed the contradiction at the political level by pushing both sides of it. But the contradiction is deeply rooted in the labor process. Various nation states have tried to manage this tension; the Clinton team tried to combine active industrial policy with active labor market policy, as for example, did Sweden.[52]

The logic of action and its contradictions thus shaped the issues and the mobilizations of political interests. The social constructions of the issues and the strengths of the political forces then affected policy outcomes, with the administration trying to define issues to overcome or manage contradictions and so weld together a political alliance supporting the agenda. Some opposing interests heightened the contradictions, and generally, the array of policies was marked by political struggles. But the matrix of contradictions could have produced different outcomes. Capitalist firms, many of which directly benefitted from the programs, might have offered stronger support for the agenda and helped more to manage the contradictions, or policies challenging the current limits of the American capitalist system might have been more successful.

Now we turn to a summary and analysis of the programs and initiatives actually produced.

## Programs and Initiatives: Implementing the Logic

The Clinton Administration initiated, revised, and/or expanded many programs based on the logic of active-competitive industrial policy. Program designs provided for a more active government role in shaping economic activity and yet restricted the intrusion of the state into investment decisions. The administration fought to increase and then to defend funding for path-breaking programs in the face of ideologically based opposition, despite which some programs that challenged the previous limits of American policy were expanded, and new programs were established.

The Clinton team set up several mechanisms for initiating, guiding, and coordinating its scattered initiatives. It established the National Economic Council, strengthened the Office of Technology Policy, and created the National Science and Technology Council with coordinating committees in particular fields. The National Economic Council, headed first by Robert Rubin and later by Laura Tyson, also had the responsibility of formulating plans and bringing them to the president for action. Issues of economic competitiveness, thus, were given a stronger position in policy debates. Beyond this, there were two basic categories of programs and initiatives: civilian technology programs and job-training programs (including apprenticeships).

## Civilian technologies

A number of strategies for civilian technology development were embodied in the Clinton initiatives. Here we identify five distinct types, with examples of each.[53]

1  *Generic Investing in R&D.* Government investments in civilian R&D were the most challenging to the established paradigm. Not surprisingly, they also encountered the most resistance on ideological grounds, since they directly confronted the rules of American capitalism. These programs funded interfirm cooperation in firms developing civilian technologies close to com-

mercialization. The Advanced Technology Program (ATP) in the Commerce Department is the principal exemplar.

It identified certain program priorities for R&D funding based on assessments of the promise of particular technologies and production arenas, invited project proposals from partnerships and others, and selected the proposals to be supported through a merit-based review process conducted by experts who judged both the scientific significance and the business promise of the proposals. Though ATP was started under the Bush Administration, it was expanded during Clinton's first term and was clearly the centerpiece of the Clinton Administration's civilian technology plans. In 1993, the administration had projected 1997 spending of $750 million for ATP;[54] actual funding went from $40 million in 1992 up to $345 million in 1995, then, under the impact of Republican sponsored budget cuts, fell to $225 million for 1997.[55]

The Technology Reinvestment Project (TRP) in the Defense Department was similar to ATP but focussed on "dual-use" projects (though even this distinction is not clean, since some "dual-use" projects were also funded in ATP). TRP began in March, 1993, and its initial funding was much larger than ATP's; but by 1996, funding levels were similar. TRP was then phased out in favour of a new program, the Dual Use Application Program (DUAP).[56]

These programs' structure reduced the challenge to established rules. Government identified broad areas of needed innovation but left the selection of specific projects to a process by which firms and partnerships could propose projects and have them evaluated on merit. The government could then claim that it was not selecting specific technologies or companies but only prioritizing some general areas of technological development and facilitating the selection of specific R&D projects by the private sector. Moreover, a requirement – that one-half of the funding for ATP projects come from the coalitions of firms – provided assurance that the selected projects were based on the priorities of private business.

2   *Selective investing in R&D.* Some technology R&D investment programs were more selective of particular companies and technologies, and some initiatives identified specific industries where technological innovations were needed and established public–private partnerships with the relevant companies. The Partnership for a New Generation of Vehicles (PNGV), established in 1993, linked government laboratories to the "big three" American automakers in a bid to invent new technologies leading to more fuel-efficient (80-miles-per-gallon) automobiles. The PNGV involves selecting a particular industry, allying with particular companies, developing specific product goals in order to enhance competitiveness of the selected industry vis-à-vis foreign competition, and selecting specific innovations and companies to undertake them. Its government funding reached well over $200 million per year.[57]

The Civilian Aeronautics Initiative in NASA, which seems similar to the PNGV on these dimensions, was intended to produce a new generation of civilian airplanes through R&D investments and laboratory collaboration with industry.[58]

Similar selectivity occurred in other technology programs. The Flat Panel Display Consortium was intended to create a US capability to manufacture flat-panel display screens that could be used in a variety of military and civilian products – televisions, computers, radars, and others. As in PNGV, the program linked government laboratories with civilian companies to pursue a specific manufacturing objective.

The administration also continued funding for SEMATECH, a public – private consortium begun in 1987 to establish a US semiconductor manufacturing industry.[59]

The size of the R&D initiatives was curtailed by the drive toward deficit reduction and by conservative opposition to the direct participation of government in investment decisions. ATP and TRP became targets for budget cuts and even elimination. Indeed, some conservatives called for the elimination of the entire Commerce Department, in part because of the ATP. It is significant that the programs survived at modest levels.

3   *Disseminating technology innovations.* The Clinton Administration revised and expanded the Manufacturing Extension Partners Program (MEP) in the Commerce Department. An extension program for small manufacturers, it reached funding levels of around $100 million per year.[60] Other programs with an extension-dissemination function were Intelligent Transportation Systems (ITS), National Information Infrastructures grants programs and Educational Technology.[61]

4   *Manipulating regulatory regimens.* The administration also facilitated technological change by altering regulations in particular industries. The Environmental Technology Initiative (ETI) in the Environmental Protection Agency is perhaps the clearest example. It targeted existing regulatory regimes of environmental protection as impediments to the rapid deployment of new technologies and thus also as a barrier against private investment in R&D on new environmental technologies.[62] The new technologies were expected to create an advantage for US companies in the emerging environmental technology market while improving

environmental quality. Funding for ETI reached $72 million per year;[63] regulatory regimes were often the focus of the funded projects.[64]

The administration supported deregulating the telecommunications industry with similar logic; indeed, it sometimes spoke of creating a single industry by breaking down the compartmentalized structure sustained by regulation, arguing that new technologies already available and some in process would make possible wholesale changes in the vast telecommunications arena. Deregulating legislation was passed by the Congress and signed by President Clinton in 1996.

5   *Combining strategies.* Some programs combined several approaches. The exemplar was the High Performance Computing and Communication Initiative (HPCCI), expanded by the Clinton Administration.[65] HPCCI seeks to develop new computing capabilities through basic and applied research and to encourage their use in government, schools, libraries, and other settings.[66] From 1994, the Clinton Administration linked the HPCCI to the development of the Information Superhighway; funding reached over $1 billion per year by 1995. The HPCCI is a coordinated activity extending into many departments.

## Job Training

The Clinton Administration established the School to Work Opportunities Program and expanded and reorganized other training programs, meant to enhance the competitiveness of American industry by providing a workforce skilled in the new technologies, while combating the inequalities these potentially generated. We concentrate here on two programs.

●   *Apprenticeship training.* The School-to-Work Opportunities Program (STWOP) is an apprenticeship program linking high-school students to work. Students participate during their last two years of high school, with some continuing for two additional years.

The Clinton Administration proposed this program, which passed both houses of Congress in 1994 with bipartisan majorities. It was assigned equally to Education and Labor and passed as a short-term intervention with a 2001 sunset. The program channeled grants to local partnerships including schools, businesses, non-profits, and others.[67] Funding reached $400 million for 1997.[68]

●   *Dislocated Worker Training.* The administration substantially increased funding for and coordination of training programs for workers who lose their jobs. These were intended to help displaced workers learn new skills that would make them employable, and funding for Adult/Dislocated Worker Training was $2.2 billion in 1995.[69] The administration and Congress also created One Stop Career Centers to coordinate a large and complicated array of previously established job training and placement programs,[70] funding the centers program at $150 million for 1997.[71]

On the whole it appears that the capacity of the state to guide industrial development was strengthened by the enactment of some new programs, the reorganization of others, and the increased funding of most. But this increased capacity was limited in scope and scale. Scope was limited by restrictions on state action that protect the capitalist investment process. Government selectivity was restricted by rules requiring the state to act only where private investment fails and implementing interventions through the active participation of capitalist firms. The re-examination of regulatory regimes did get underway. The scale of the whole effort was restricted by the deficit reduction agenda and by the resistance of the defense establishment to the diversion of R&D funds into civilian technologies. Certainly the whole effort fell far short of the original Administration goals.

## Conclusion

In the 1980s and 1990s, some leading circles of the capitalist class and important segments of industry proposed to change fundamental features of the American political economy. Specifically, they tried to strengthen the state capacity to influence the investment process in the area of technology development. High-tech interests were important in pushing this project, but some components of finance capital were also supportive. Their project was partly successful. The Reagan and Bush administrations moved grudgingly in the proposed direction, and the Congress enacted some supportive legislation in those years.

The Clinton Administration at first advocated the elite project very strongly. Although forced into retreat, it managed to establish a number of modestly funded initiatives, which established foundations in the bureaucracy upon which an expanded industrial policy might be built. The administration did so by expanding and/or establishing an array of scattered programs tied together by the logic of active-competitive industrial policy. It also established coordinating structures where the implications of the logic are worked out and new initiatives invented and implemented. The nature of these initiatives and their degrees of success were negotiated in a complex matrix defined by the active-competitive logic of action and its contradictions.

In short, the whole elite project and logic of action affirmed basic capitalist rules while modifying some specific features of American capitalism. Indeed the whole project drew the state more directly and openly into the capitalist rationalization process. Barriers like anti-trust laws and environmental protection were revised. New technologies and even entire new industries were created and opened to capitalist production.

The rationalizing agenda encountered strong opposition; and this generated conflicts and political resistance across a wide range of issues. The previous limits on state action contradicted the emerging policies. Active-competitive industrial policy requires new state capacities, i.e. competencies that have not been developed in the American political system, particularly, if the state is to select industries and technologies, make investments that enhance competitiveness, and coordinate these activities across the public and private sectors. These capabilities might be developed to some extent by reorienting and expanding existing government programs and administrative structures, but new programs are probably necessary too. And beyond these administrative changes lie expansions of domains of legitimate activity by the government as a whole and by specific agencies. These domain changes would, in turn, require the restructuring of coordination mechanisms to integrate new functions and overcome traditional bureaucratic resistance within the agencies.

The experience of the Clinton initiatives demonstrates that successful active-competitive industrial policy must enable and alter integral parts of the American model of capitalism. Under existing conventions, the state can regulate investments, provide tax incentives for them, construct infrastructure to support them, oversee the ownership structures governing production, control the uses of labor power, and restrict the uses of the physical environment. In many important ways, therefore, it already hedges in the capitalist investment process. But active-competitive industrial policy moves the state directly into the making of investment decisions – choosing technologies, funding specific R&D projects, picking specific companies to run those projects, and so on. It also involves purposeful changes in the ownership structures governing production, most significantly encouraging joint ventures, partnerships, and innovative ownership arrangements. Ordinarily the American model of capitalism allows the state such a direct role in investment only within highly circumscribed arenas, such as defense procurement and health-care provision.

Although deeply rooted ideologically and strongly defended, these limits are sometimes examined and revised. It seems that the Clinton Administration initiated an era in which they were evaluated from the standpoints of effectiveness and efficiency. Even so, the active-competitive policy sought to redefine the boundaries between public and private action to only a limited degree. The domains of the public agencies carrying the policy were precisely limited; and the participation of private capitalists in the investment decisions was guaranteed. And even these narrowly limited intrusions were hotly contested in the Congress and starved of funds.

The agenda for rationalizing capitalism was combined in the Clinton Administration with measures combating the inequality generated by technology investments and reorganization. The Clinton Administration supported job training and apprenticeships, pushed for equal access to the information superhighway, and mobilized capitalist firms to provide new information and communication technology to schools. It passed a minimum wage increase, searched for new ways to facilitate worker participation in industry, and saw the whole project as a way of maintaining high-wage employment.

At the beginning of Clinton's second term, the outcomes of active-competitive industrial policy remained uncertain. The reproductive tendencies of American capitalism limited the scope of the innovations, and the deficit reduction agenda limited their size, leaving the state with inadequate powers to shape industrial development. The programs intended to direct investment seemed likely to develop into conduits of public funds placed at the disposal of private capitalists. Effective state steering of industrial investment seemed unlikely, with private steering of public investment a more probable outcome.

## Notes

The authors' names are listed alphabetically to indicate equal contributions to the chapter. The section on the formation of the elite project in the business policy councils was researched and first drafted by Paretsky and is based on his doctoral dissertation, in progress at the University of Missouri-Columbia. The sections on the active-competitive policy of the Clinton Administration are based mainly on research by Benson and were first drafted by him. Both authors have participated in putting the sections together, the formulation of the overall argument, and revisions. The authors wish to thank a number of people who have helped with the collection of information, including Rhonda Glazier, Zoey Heyer-Gray, Mary Grigsby, Michael Rebstock, Nancy Turner, Dan Thompson, and several librarians in the Government Documents Sections of the Ellis Library, University of Missouri-Columbia. They also thank Kelli Simmons and Kathy Yardley for preparation of the final text. Clarence Lo provided insightful critiques on several drafts. Gregory Hooks and Harland Prechal also made helpful comments.

1  John L. Campbell, J. Rogers Hollingsworth, and Leon Lindberg, eds, *Governance of the American Economy* (Cambridge: Cambridge University Press, 1991).
2  Otis Graham, *Losing Time: The Industrial Policy Debate* (Cambridge MA: Harvard University Press, 1992).
3  On industrial policy variations, see Sharon Zukin, ed., *Industrial Policy: Business and Politics in the United States and France* (New York: Praeger, 1985). For a treatment of the recent trend toward competitiveness in US policy see

Sheila Slaughter and Gary Rhodes, "The Emergence of a Competitiveness Research and Development Policy Coalition and the Commercialization of Academic Science and Technology," *Science, Technology and Human Values* 21 (Summer, 1996), pp. 303–39.

4 The concept "elite project" is similar to Jessop's 'hegemonic project'. Bob Jessop, *State Theory, Putting the Capitalist State in its Place* (University Park PA: Pennsylvania State University Press, 1990), pp. 197–219.

5 G. William Domhoff, *Who Rules America Now?* (New York: Simon and Schuster, 1983); Domhoff, *The Powers That Be* (New York: Vintage, 1978); Joseph Peschek, *Policy-Planning Organizations* (Philadelphia PA: Temple University Press, 1987).

6 M. Fennema and Kees van der Pijl, "International Bank Capital and the New Liberalism," in Mark S. Mizruchi and Michael Schwartz, eds, *Intercorporate Relations: The Structural Analysis of Business* (Oxford, New York: Cambridge University Press, 1987), pp. 300–1.

7 Domhoff, *Who Rules America Now?* Domhoff, *The Powers That Be.*

8 Michael Useem, *The Inner Circle* (Oxford, New York: Oxford University Press, 1984), pp. 70–4.

9 Business–Higher Education Forum, *America's Competitive Challenge: The Need for a National Response* (Washington DC: Business–Higher Education Forum, 1983).

10 President's Commission on Industrial Competitiveness, *Global Competition: The New Reality*, 2 vols (Washington DC: US Government Printing Office, 1985).

11 United States House Committee on Banking, Finance and Urban Affairs, "Industrial Policy," Part I, 98th Congress, 1st Sess (Washington DC: US Government Printing Office, 1983), p. 456.

12 See, for example, Stephen Cohen and John Zysman, *Manufacturing Matters: The Myth of the Post-Industrial Economy* (New York: Basic Books, 1987).

13 United States Senate Committee on Banking, Housing, and Urban Affairs "Nomination of Laura D'Andrea Tyson," 103rd Congress, 1st Sess, (Washington DC: US Government Printing Office, 1993), p. 79.

14 Council on Competitiveness, "Gaining New Ground: Technology Priorities for America's Future" (Washington DC: Council on Competitiveness, 1991); Council on Competitiveness, "Picking Up the Pace: The Commercial Challenge to American Innovation" (Washington DC: Council on Competitiveness, 1988).

15 Council on Competitiveness, "Gaining New Ground," p. 2.

16 Council on Competitiveness, "Roadmap for Results: Trade Policy, Technology and American Competitiveness" (Washington DC: Council on Competitiveness, 1993), p. 12.

17 Council on Competitiveness, "Gaining New Ground," p. 4.

18 Council on Competitiveness, "Roadmap for Results," p. 24; Council on Competitiveness, "Picking up the Pace," p. 50.

19 Council on Competitiveness, "Roadmap for Results," p. 49.

20 Peter Peterson and James K. Sebenius, "The Primacy of the Domestic Agenda," Graham Allison and Gregory Treverton, eds, *Rethinking America's Security: Beyond Cold War to New Order* (New York W. W. Norton, 1992), pp. 58, 61.

21 Peter Peterson, *Facing Up* (New York: Simon and Schuster, 1993), p. 200.

22 B. R. Inman and Daniel F. Burton, "Technology and US National Security," in Allison and Treverton, *Rethinking America's Security*, p. 118.

23 Harold Brown, "High-Tech is Foreign Policy," *SAIS Review* (Summer–Fall, 1989), p. 15.

24 Committee on Science, Engineering, and Public Policy, "The Government Role in Civilian Technology: Building a New Alliance" (Washington DC: National Academy Press, 1992).

25 B. R. Inman, "Reformers Seek Broader Military Role in Economy," *Science* (August 1, 1988), p. 780.

26 Carnegie Commission on Science, Technology and Government, *Technology and Economic Performance: Organizing the Executive Branch for a Stronger National Technology Base* (New York: Carnegie Commission on Science, Technology and Government, 1991), p. 7. One of the co-chairs of the Commission was Rockefeller University professor Joshua Lederberg, a CFR director. The commission was created by the Carnegie Corporation, whose board of

trustees included CFR vice-chairman Warren Christopher; David Packard and other high-tech business leaders were also members.

27 Committee for Economic Development, *The United States in a New Global Economy: A Rallier of Nations*, (New York: CED, 1992), p. 78.

28 Ibid., p. 24.

29 C. Fred Bergsten, "The World Economy after the Cold War," *Foreign Affairs* 3, (Summer, 1990), p. 105; Bergsten, "The Primacy of Economics," *Foreign Policy* 87 (Summer, 1992), p. 14.

30 Laura D'Andrea Tyson, *Who's Bashing Whom? Trade Conflict in High-Technology Industries* (Washington DC: Institute for International Economics, 1992).

31 Fred Bergsten, "Preface," in Tyson, *Who's Bashing Whom?*, p. XIV

32 Carnegie Endowment for International Peace and the Institute for International Economics, "Special Report: Policymaking for a New Era," *Foreign Affairs* 5 (1992/3), pp. 175, 181.

33 Carnegie Commission on Science, Technology, and Government, *Technology and Economic Performance*, p. 23.

34 Council on Competitiveness, "Gaining New Ground," p. 46.

35 United States Senate Committee on Banking, Housing, and Urban Affairs, "Nomination of Laura D'Andrea Tyson," pp. 150–1, 152.

36 United States Senate Committee on Commerce, Science, and Transportation, "Nomination of John H. Gibbons to be Director of the Office of Science and Technology Policy," 103rd Congress, 1st Sess (Washington DC: US Government Printing Office), pp. 11–12.

37 Carnegie Commission on Science, Technology, and Government, *New Thinking and American Defense Technology* (New York: Carnegie Commission on Science, Technology and Government, 1990).

38 The concept of "logic of action" is drawn from the works of several organization theorists. Lucien Karpik, ed., "Organizations, Institutions and History", in Karpik, ed., *Organization and Environment* (London: Sage, 1978), pp. 15–68; Michel Callon and Jean-Paul Vignolle, "Breaking Down the Organization: Local Conflicts and Societal Systems of Action," *Social Sci-*

*ence Information* 16 (1977), pp. 147–67; J. Kenneth Benson, "A Dialectical Method," In Gareth Morgan, ed., *Beyond Method* (Beverly Hills CA: Sage, 1983), pp. 331–46.

39 Some early sources on the Clinton initiatives are *New York Times* (November 10, 1992), p. B5, (November 23, 1992), p. A1 (November 18, 1992), p. C1 (November 25, 1992), p. A1, (November 13, 1992), p. A9, (November 26, 1992), p. A1, (November 21, 1992), p. A19.

40 Some important statements of the policy stance include: President William J. Clinton and Vice-President Albert Gore Jr, *Technology for America's Economic Growth: A New Direction to Build Economic Strength* (February 22, 1993); *Technology for Economic Growth: President's Progress Report*, (November, 1993) (Washington, DC: Office of the President, US Government Printing Office); Clinton and Gore, *Science in the National Interest*, (Office of Science and Technology Policy, August, 1994). Some elements of the logic were already in place in the closing years of the Bush Administration. Executive Office of the President, *Science and Technology* (Washington, Office of Science and Technology Policy, January, 1993), pp. 141–81.

41 Laura Tyson was an important advocate of these selective policies within the elite policy councils and then within the Clinton Administration. Bruce Stokes "By the Numbers," *National Journal* 25 (January 30, 1993), pp. 285–7; Tyson, *Who's Bashing Whom?*

42 Bruce Stokes, "Wary Partners," *National Journal* 25 (April 10, 1993), pp. 868–72.

43 On organizational contradictions, see Wolf Heydebrand, "Organizational Contradictions in Public Bureaucracies: Toward a Marxian Theory of Organisations," *Sociological Quarterly* 18 (Winter, 1977), pp. 83–107; J. Kenneth Benson, "Organizations: A Dialectical View," *Administrative Science Quarterly* 22 (March, 1977) pp. 1–21.

44 Paul Starobin, "Weak Link," *National Journal* 26 (January 29, 1994), pp. 231–4; William Schneider, "Wooing Ross Perot's Voters for 1996," *National Journal* 25 (January 16, 1993) p. 166. On Clinton's links to Wall Street interests, see "An Affair to Remember?" *National Journal* 25, (January 16, 1993), pp. 120–4. The struggle within the administration over deficit re-

duction versus investments has been described well by Bob Woodward, *The Agenda: Inside the Clinton White House* (New York: Simon and Schuster, 1994), and more recently by Robert Reich, *Locked in the Cabinet* (New York: Alfred Knopf, 1997).

45 Graeme Browning, "Tense Days Down in the Lab," *National Journal* 27 (April 22, 1995), p. 1005; Ben Wildavsky, "On the Block," *National Journal* 27 (July 22, 1995), pp. 1880–84.

46 Otis Graham, *Losing Time: The Industrial Policy Debate* (Cambridge MA: Harvard University Press, 1992); James Kitfield, "The New Partnership," *National Journal* 26 (August 6, 1994), pp. 1840–5.

47 Eliza Newlin Carney, "Still Trying to Reinvent Government," *National Journal* 26 (June 18, 1994), pp. 1442–4.

48 *New York Times* (October 3, 1996), p. 1A.

49 Kirk Victor, "Takin' on the Bacon," *National Journal* 27 (May 6, 1996), pp. 1082–6; Victor, "Anchor's Away?" *National Journal* 25 (September 11, 1993), pp. 2180–3.

50 On labor relations see Kirk Victor, "Labor's New Deal," *National Journal*, 25 (April 24, 1993), pp. 978–88.

51 Commission on the Future of Worker–Management Relations, *Reports and Recommendations* (Washington, DC: US Department of Labor, 1994).

52 Jonas Pontusson, *The Limits of Social Democracy: Investment Politics in Sweden* (Ithaca NY: Cornell University Press, 1992).

53 An overview of early proposals for technology policy is available in Vivecka Novak, "Spending Spree?" *National Journal* 25 (February 27, 1993), pp. 508–18. See also "Graeme Browning "A Glossy, Familiar Plan," *National Journal* 25 (February 27, 1993), pp. 518–19.

54 *Technology for Economic Growth: President's Progress Report.*

55 Budget figures are drawn from several sources including *Budget Supplement: Budget of the United States Government, Fiscal Year 1997* (Washington, DC: US Government Printing Office, 1996), p. 98; reports on the World WideWeb Home Page of the ATP.

56 Internet Web Page for DUAP reports only $185 million available for grants in 1997. *The Budget of the US Government for 1998* (Washington,

DC: US Office of Management and US (Government Printing Office, 1997), p. 79, listed $181 million in estimated 1997 spending for DUAP. In 1993 TRP "distributed $472 million in federal matching research grants," according to US/OTP Highlights," Office of Technology Policy news release (December, 1996). See also Graeme Browning, "Why the Techies Aren't Smiling," *National Journal* 26 (April 23, 1994) p. 984.

57 Peter H. Stone, "Detroit's Smooth Ride," *National Journal*, 26 (May 21, 1994), pp. 1176–81. Some advocates of technology investments thought the money should have gone to smaller, more innovative companies. See Graeme Browning, "Why the Techies Aren't Smiling," p. 984.

58 *Budget Supplement 1997*, pp. 98, 100.

59 *Technology for Economic Growth: President's Progress Report* (November, 1993); Kitfield, "New Partnership," pp. 1840–5.

60 *Budget Supplement 1997*, p. 98.

61 Ibid.

62 *Budget Supplement 1997*, p. 99.

63 The Clinton Administration policy on environmental technologies and regulations was set out in *Technology for a Sustainable Future* (National Science and Technology Council, July, 1994); *Bridge to a Sustainable Future* (National Science and Technology Council, April, 1995). See also *Budget Supplement 1997*, p. 99.

64 ETI program description on the Web at http:www. epa. gov/oppe/eti. html.

65 For a general description of HPCCI, see *High Performance Computing and Communications: Technology for the National Information Infrastructure*, Supplement to the President's Fiscal Year 1995 Budget (Washington, DC: US Government Printing Office, 1994).

66 HPCCI began with a presidential initiative by President Bush. Executive Office of the President, *Science and Technology*, pp. 158–9. It was strengthened by the passage of the High Performance Computing Act of 1991 (PL102–194), which President Bush signed on December 9, 1991. In 1992 Bush established a coordinating Office for HPCCI.

67 Rochelle L. Stanfield, "Hire Learning," *National Journal*, 25 (May 1, 1993), pp. 1042–7; Bruce Stokes and Kirk Victor, "A Higher Mini-

mum Wage," *National Journal*, 25 (May 8, 1993), pp. 1122–3.

68 *Budget of the US Government for Fiscal Year 1998* (Washington DC: US Government Printing Office, 1997), pp. 415, 707.

69 *Appendix, Budget of the United States Government, Fiscal Year 1998* (Washington DC: US.

Government Printing Office, 1997), p. 76.

70 Anon., "At a Glance: A Weekly Checklist of Major Issues," *National Journal*, 26 (January 22, 1994), p. 197; Kirk Victor, "New Jobs for Old," *National Journal*, 26 (January 1, 1994), pp. 6–10.

71 Data retrieved from the Web at http.www. usbudget.com.

# 10

# Where Are All the Democrats?

## The Limits of Economic Policy Reform

## ★ *Patrick Akard* ★

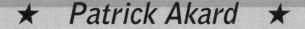

*Where are all the Democrats? . . . I hope you're all aware we're all Eisenhower Republicans . . . We're Eisenhower Republicans here, and we are fighting the Reagan Republicans. We stand for lower deficits and free trade and the bond market. Isn't that great?*

Bill Clinton to his economic policy staff[1]

*Harry Truman said it best: When the voters have a choice between a Republican and a Republican, they'll pick the Republican every time.*

Robert Kuttner[2]

## Introduction

Since the late 1970s, the "reform" of US economic policy has involved reducing the fiscal and administrative capacities of the state to ameliorate market-driven economic outcomes. By 1992, however, conditions appeared to favor a change in direction. In the wake of a recession and long-term economic restructuring, voters were fearful about their economic futures and impatient with the policy inertia of the Bush Administration. Avoiding the political mistakes of the three previous Democratic candidates for president, Bill Clinton ran on a "growth" platform that promised the expansion of economic opportunities. While distancing itself from the "redistributive" liberalism of the past, Clinton's "New Democrat" campaign included an activist economic agenda of public investment in education, infrastructure, research, and technological development; tax incentives for private investment; and major health-care reform. But by the end of 1993 it was clear that economic

policy options were limited to those promoting slow growth, lower deficits, free trade, and the confidence of financial markets. In spite of a nominally Democratic president and Congress, policy outcomes were strikingly similar to those of the previous Republican regime.

This chapter accounts for this outcome by tracing the history of the Clinton economic program from the 1992 campaign to the passage of the Omnibus Budget Reconciliation Act of 1993. It is important to emphasize that the conservative measures enacted in this agreement were not responses to the demands of a democratic electorate. While much was made of public opinion on "big government," "balanced budgets," and other abstract notions, the *specific* measures that resulted reflected elite interests, not the policy preferences of the majority. The most salient issues of the 1992 campaign – jobs, stagnant wages, and growing economic inequality – were not addressed directly by administration policy.

The first Clinton budget was rooted in the past; not that of traditional New Deal liberalism, but the more recent past of fiscal conservatism and pro-market philosophy that dominated the 1980s. It also established a foundation for the future; the limits on government activism that were extended in 1993 will constrain policy makers for years to come. How do we explain this policy inertia given the economic concerns and political climate of 1992? Several interrelated factors must be considered.

1   First, of course, there was the budget deficit, an issue that received the lion's share of attention from political elites and the media that cover them. This legacy of the Reagan Administration imposed a major fiscal constraint on economic policy and was wielded as an ideological hammer by both conservatives and "moderate" policy elites. However, neither existing economic conditions nor structural deficits automatically called forth one particular policy response. There was much disagreement among economists as to whether deficit reduction should be the top economic priority, and it was not the preference of the general public. Within these broad constraints, there were several policy options, including tax increases of various types to reduce the deficit and perhaps finance crucial public investments, economic stimuli of various types to foster economic growth, and so on. The resulting policy outcomes were not inevitable, but a product of several other converging institutional and political forces.

2   Among the most potent of these forces was the power of financial markets and the Federal Reserve to determine the macro-economic limits within which economic policy could be constructed. In the absence of countervailing power elsewhere within the state, the markets and the Fed set the parameters of budget policy by default. This, in turn, contributed to an economic policy driven by the perpetual fear of inflation and "excessive" growth and a demand for deficit reduction.

3   Complementing these institutional constraints was a consensus on economic priorities among conservative and "moderate" policy intellectuals in elite universities and major think tanks, especially on the benefits of free trade, free markets, and deficit reduction. This was another institutional factor that had its roots in the previous decade, when the Keynesian assumptions of the 1960s were challenged by a revival of neo-classical economics within the dominant policy establishment.

4   Economic policy reform was further limited by the fiscal conservatism of the Democratic Party and the ideological composition of Congress. In particular, the increasing fragmentation of the national Democratic Party and its dominance by conservatives (both old-style southern conservatives and increasingly prominent "neo-liberals" or "New Democrats") undermined support within Congress for even a mildly activist economic program by the Clinton Administration.

5   Another important factor shaping the Clinton program as it moved through Congress was the extensive political mobilization by business groups. The organizational capacities of major corporate interests to act together to shape policy had developed substantially in the previous decades and were employed to great effect in 1993. In the early Clinton Administration, corporate mobilization was especially crucial in influencing legislation favoring free trade and deficit reduction and in opposing corporate tax increases, especially a proposed energy tax that was to provide revenues for the "investment" side of the administration's economic program.

6   Last but not least, however, we must con-

sider the political and ideological limitations of the Clinton regime itself. Given its major financial supporters and its dominant economic philosophy, there is little evidence that the new administration was predisposed to mediate the effects of global economic restructuring that were of most concern to the electorate. This, in fact, will be our starting point as we consider the first-year economic program of the Clinton Administration. In spite of the liberal hopes that were fired by the 1992 election, the conservative policy outcomes were predictable from the beginning.

## Economic Policy and the Clinton Campaign

### Business ties and economic philosophy

Bill Clinton's rise to the top of the political world was aided by his contacts with a variety of overlapping elite networks in academia, business, politics, and the media, which he developed as a college student at Georgetown, as a Rhodes Scholar at Oxford, at Yale Law School, and through connections forged during his career as governor of Arkansas. He has often been linked to a "liberal elite" of friends in academia, the media, and the entertainment industry,[3] especially by conservative critics. However, in tracing the sources of Clinton's economic policy, it is more relevant to note the strong ties he cultivated with influential sectors of business and finance. After some initial confrontations during his first term as governor, Clinton was able to establish significant support from the business community in Arkansas. He began his campaign for the presidency with an established base of local business support. Among his most important backers were Warren Stephens, CEO of the Little Rock

investment bank Stephens Inc.,[4] Tyson Foods, Murphy Oil, Wal-Mart (which included Hillary Rodham Clinton on its board of directors), and Beverly Enterprises.[5]

However, the business backing of Clinton's candidacy extended considerably beyond the borders of his home state. To a much greater extent than other Democratic challengers, he was able to raise money and support from key Wall Street backers and major corporate executives who had supported Republicans in the past. Wall Street contributors supplied about a quarter of Clinton's total campaign funds. Another quarter was received from the network of Washington law and lobbying firms that often supported Democratic candidates but tended to represent large corporate clients.[6]

Clinton developed many of his most important Wall Street connections through the Democratic Leadership Council (DLC), an organization founded in 1985 by conservative Democrats (including then Governor Clinton) to wrest the national Democratic Party away from "liberal" influence.[7] A core of Wall Streeters associated with the business wing of the Democratic party through the DLC provided much of the crucial financial and advisory support for Clinton during the 1992 campaign and gave his "New Democrat" agenda legitimacy in the corporate community. Goldman Sachs was an especially important backer, in both money and personnel. The firm had prior connections to Governor Clinton as a chief underwriter for major bond issues in Arkansas, and as a lead underwriter for Wal-Mart. Goldman had earlier supported Clinton's 1990 governor's race. In the presidential campaign, Clinton received $112,000 in campaign contributions from 135 Goldman Sachs employees and spouses.[8] Goldman co-chair Robert Rubin was an adviser to Clinton during the campaign, serving as an influential "moderate" voice of the financial community. Rubin would later head the National Economic Council, created to coordinate economic policy in the new administration. Clinton's key New York fund-raiser was Kenneth Brody, also a Goldman Sachs partner. Another important Wall Street connection was Roger Altman, an old friend and classmate from the governor's undergraduate days at Georgetown, who was vice-chair of the influential Blackstone Group. Altman would be appointed Deputy Treasury Secretary in the new administration.[9] In Clinton, these supporters saw a gifted politician who could speak the language of the people but who also understood the economic realities of the business world. As Paul Starobin of the *National Journal* noted, the support of the DLC-connected Wall Streeters was premised on "loyalty, on Clinton's part, to a core set of philosophical principles – namely, the policies of free trade, free markets, and fiscal discipline advocated by the DLC and its think tank, the Progressive Policy Institute (PPI). This, the Wall Streeters insist, is what attracted them to Clinton in the first place, above and beyond his other winsome qualities."[10] Clinton also forged important ties with the big business community beyond a handful of Wall Street investment bankers. By late September, 1992, the Clinton – Gore campaign could boast a list of 400 top corporate executives endorsing the Democratic ticket, including the heads of such prominent corporations as Apple Computer, Hewlett-Packard, Xerox, and Sarah Lee.[11] Clinton also gained support, or at least conciliatory praise, from business organizations like the US Chamber of Commerce (USCOC) and the National Association of Manufacturers (NAM).[12]

While the Clinton campaign was able to attract corporate money not available to other Democrats, the Bush – Quayle campaign was lagging behind its 1988 pace. A significant factor in Clinton's success seemed to be corporate disillusionment with the Bush Administration over its inability or unwillingness to deal with the recession and the trade and budget deficits. Some monied interests were

also uncomfortable with the prominence of the extreme right wing within the Republican Party, especially after its performance at the 1992 Republican National Convention.[13]

We should not overstate the degree of business support for the Clinton campaign. Even though Clinton had greater access to corporate money than his fellow Democrats, his support was relatively narrow, especially in comparison to Democratic candidates in the pre-Reagan era. Compared to Jimmy Carter, for example, he relied more on investment bankers, a few high-tech and communications companies, and some large retailers, and less on old line-manufacturing interests.[14] After an active courtship, Clinton had gained the endorsement of some important high tech firms, especially in economically depressed California. These companies had soured on Bush's lack of action on the economy and were attracted to Clinton's support of an investment tax credit for new businesses, government funding for research and development, and trade promotion.[15] The majority of corporate donors still favored Bush.[16] Corporate backers of Clinton were cautious, and always wary of his succumbing to the pressure of traditional "liberal" constituents within the Democratic Party who favored an interventionist or redistributive policy agenda.[17] Nevertheless, compared to other Democratic candidates, Clinton was able to convince important segments of finance and industry that he was committed to a sound and "realistic" economic policy.

### Campaign economic policy: the two "new democrat" strategies

In its statements on economic policy, the Clinton campaign walked a fine line between praise of market principles and a willingness to utilize a more activist government strategy where necessary to stimulate growth, investment, and economic efficiency. Clinton sought to avoid the fatal mistakes of previous Democratic candidates who had tried to counter the "economics of joy" of the Reagan era with "responsible" assessments of the need for austerity and fiscal discipline. Unlike Carter, Mondale, and Dukakis, the Clinton team played down the rhetoric of "limits" for a positive-sum message of growth, to be achieved through their own investment-oriented program.

On the other hand, from the outset the campaign stressed its differences with traditional Democratic liberalism. Clinton was campaigning as a "New Democrat," and he distinguished his policies from the interventionist and redistributive policies of past Democratic regimes. However, within the campaign there were two general orientations representing competing – and somewhat contradictory – versions of the New Democrat economic strategy. One stressed the need for significant public investment in education, job training, research, and other infrastructure development – the "investment" approach favored by the more activist members among Clinton's economic advisers, such as Robert Reich, Ira Magaziner, and Derek Shearer. The other emphasized deficit reduction as the first economic priority, and would be referred to as the "financial markets" strategy because its positive economic effects would supposedly follow from the indirect benefits of lower interest rates and a favourable market response to a lower deficit. Among Clinton's policy advisers more inclined to fiscal conservatism and market-oriented strategies were Robert Shapiro, chief economist of the Progressive Policy Institute (the DLC think-tank), and Wall Streeters Altman and Rubin.[18]

Developments throughout 1992 led the Clinton campaign to emphasize the activist side of its economic agenda. First, instead of running against traditional Democrat Mario Cuomo, as expected, Clinton found his main competition for the Democratic nomination was Massachusetts Senator Paul Tsongas. Tsongas was a fiscally conservative neo-liberal who was preaching "realism" and "responsibility" on economic issues. More important, however, as the economy continued to sputter, voters were increasingly concerned with the issues of jobs, wages, and economic growth.[19] This led Clinton to emphasize economic growth as the primaries progressed.

As Clinton moved closer to the Democratic nomination, the campaign began working on a major economic policy statement directed against Bush. The revised economic plan, introduced in a speech to the US Conference of Mayors on June 22, reflected the changing political context. Deficit reduction was de-emphasized. The new focus was on economic growth through new public and private investment, and major health-care reform. Titled "Putting People First," the new plan called for nearly $220 billion in new spending over four years. These proposals, coupled with the absence of a clear plan to reduce the deficit, immediately drew fire from the economic policy establishment that had been insisting on deficit reduction as the top priority.[20] On the other hand, a proposed middle-class tax cut that was featured earlier was quietly reduced in prominence. Although still mentioned as a policy goal, it was no longer a central element and was much scaled back from the 10-percent across-the-board cut announced in January.[21] A tax increase on the wealthy remained a major part of the plan, with a proposal to impose a fourth tax bracket of 36–8 percent on taxpayers with incomes over $200,000.

Negative news about the economy continued throughout 1992, with growth sluggish and unemployment rates remaining stubbornly high. In addition, major studies by the Congressional Budget Office and other reputable sources were released documenting that the wealthiest Americans had benefitted from the economy and economic policies of the 1980s, while the majority saw their standard of living stagnate or decline. Throughout the year, polls consistently showed that the economy was the most salient issue for potential voters. This was bad news for George Bush; by many measures, the US economy had performed worse during his administration than at any time since World War II.[22]

## But what did the "people" want? Interpreting the 1992 election

Clinton won the November election with a shaky 43 percent of the popular vote. Independent candidate Ross Perot had captured a significant 19 percent, demonstrating the degree of voter disillusionment with both major parties. Clinton won an actual majority of the votes in only 98 congressional districts; almost all of these had a heavily minority population or were liberal enclaves such as university districts or urban neighborhoods of relatively affluent liberal professionals. Significantly, this core of the most loyal supporters of the Democratic Party – minorities, liberals, and also the elderly – were mainly ignored by the DLC and the business wing of the campaign. They preferred to emphasize the importance of former Republican voters. This included a significant number of "Reagan Democrats" among urban ethnic groups and working-class voters, especially those in the upper Midwest who were hurt badly by the recession and industrial restructuring. Clinton was also supported, for varying reasons, by independents, the young, suburban professionals, and in the rural heartland and the economically troubled west.[23]

Polls showed clearly that the overwhelming factor in Clinton's victory over Bush was the economy. But beyond this obvious point, what were the *specific* issues of most concern to the voters? In a September Gallup survey asking respondents for the most important problem facing the country, the top answer had been "the economy in general" (37 percent), followed by unemployment (27 percent). The most important "non-economic" problems cited were poverty and homelessness (13 percent), health care (12 percent),

and education (10 percent). Only 9 percent of the respondents listed the federal budget deficit as the most important economic problem.[24] These findings were no surprise to Clinton campaign strategists, who had tailored their emphasis on growth and jobs to their own similar poll results. In a November Gallup survey soon after the election, when asked what the top policy priority of the incoming administration should be, respondents overwhelmingly cited "creating jobs" (49 percent) over cutting the deficit (17 percent) or health care (14 percent).[25] Further, when they were asked which policies should go first if a choice was required between postponing deficit reduction, raising taxes, or cutting entitlements, 49 percent favored postponing deficit reduction, versus 24 percent who favored cutting entitlements and 22 percent who favored raising middle-class taxes. Similar results were found in a December poll that asked respondents directly which was more important, deficit reduction (33 percent) or stimulating the economy (57 percent).[26]

One other poll result is relevant for the development of the Clinton economic program. While the population tended to oppose tax increases in general, a very solid 80 percent favored raising federal income taxes on individuals making over $200,000 a year. Only 17 percent were opposed.[27] This was related to a perception of the unfairness of the tax system and growing inequality. This progressive measure would be the one element of Clinton's economic agenda that remained constant from the beginning, and the one element that would make it through Congress unscathed.

## The Clinton Transition: Triumph of the Deficit Hawks

Bill Clinton won in 1992 by taking a page from Ronald Reagan's book: appearing to be all things to all people and offering a version of the "politics of joy" that promised jobs, corporate investment incentives, health-care reform, public spending, *and* deficit reduction. Like Reagan, Clinton could also run against the dismal performance of the economy under his predecessor. But after the election, populist rhetoric had to confront political and economic realities. The policy establishment of politically connected economists, prominent think-tanks, and the mainstream press immediately converged on the deficit issue. This included not only the business press and conservative intellectuals, but the "moderate" representatives of the liberal policy establishment as well. Elizabeth Sawhill of the Urban Institute checked in as a deficit hawk, as did Charles Schultze of the Bookings Institution. Major reports issued by the influential Committee for Economic Development (CED) and the Organization for Economic Cooperation and Development (OECD) stressed the necessity for immediate deficit reduction.[28] The policy establishment also took pains to criticize the public-investment alternatives favored by some progressives and put forward in moderate form by the Clinton campaign. Researchers from the OECD, John Tatom of the St Louis Federal Reserve, and Clifford Winston of the Brookings Institution, among others, developed economic projections critical of a public-investment strategy for promoting growth. The investment strategy was now denigrated as the Democratic version of "supply-side economics" by deficit hawks in the economic policy establishment,[29] even though earlier in the year a large group of prominent economists had endorsed the investment strategy as the best means for stimulating economic growth.[30] In a phenomenon that would be repeated over the issue of free trade during the NAFTA debates, the national press conveyed the impression that anyone with real economic knowledge understood the neces-

sity for deficit reduction, and that the overwhelming majority of economists and economic policy officials accepted this as the unavoidable reality. But this was not the case. While nearly everyone agreed that deficit reduction was *a* desirable goal, the evidence cited to justify making it the top priority was contestable. Neither economic theory nor empirical evidence concerning the effects of high interest rates, the response of investment to lower rates and deficit reduction, and so on, were conclusive, and the goal was challenged by many in the economics profession and elsewhere.[31] In other words, neither public opinion nor the preponderance of "scientific" evidence supported the argument that deficit reduction had to be the first economic priority. Rather, this was the opinion of the narrow, but very influential, economic policy establishment.

More important politically than the views of policy intellectuals, the financial community also demanded a "responsible" economic program from the incoming Clinton regime. In an article appropriately titled "Time to Get Real," Paul Starobin spelled out the dilemma faced by the new administration:

The massive federal debt hangs like a dark cloud over Little Rock, and it will follow Clinton to Washington in January. Almost 44 million voters put Clinton into office, but now he has to pass muster with a new group of judges, many of whom are not even U.S. citizens: investors in government securities and other dollar-denominated assets, including stocks, corporate bonds, and dollars themselves.[32]

Major corporate leaders were also part of the elite consensus on deficit reduction. This was reflected in the proposals of the CED, whose membership was dominated by Fortune 500 executives. It was also indicated in a *Fortune* magazine poll of top CEOs, which found that their number-one economic policy priority was "a credible long-term deficit reduction agree-

ment, including cuts in entitlement spending," which was favored even over "new tax
incentives for investment" and "more investment in infrastructure."[33]

Clinton wasted little time signaling his
awareness of the "hard choices" that had
to be made. He quickly appointed staunch
deficit hawks with strong ties to Wall
Street and Congress to the key economic
policy positions in his administration. Influential conservative Democrat Lloyd
Bentsen, chair of the Senate Finance Committee, was appointed Secretary of the
Treasury. Bentsen was a respected fiscal
conservative who had the trust of Wall Street
and the corporate community in general.
Wall Street financier Roger Altman was
named Bentsen's deputy. Former House
Budget Committee chair Leon Panetta,
known as a deficit superhawk in Congress,
was named to head the Office of Management and Budget (OMB). His second in
command would be Alice Rivlin, former
head of the Congressional Budget Office,
currently housed at the Brookings Institution. Rivlin was also widely respected among
the policy and financial elite as a hard-nosed
budget analyst and forceful advocate of deficit reduction. Another Wall Streeter,
Goldman Sachs's Robert Rubin, was named
to head Clinton's new National Economic
Committee (NEC), which would coordinate
economic policy among the various agencies and departments of the Executive
branch.[34]

News of Clinton's top economic appointments generated a favorable response in the
bond markets. Key Republican leaders such
as Bob Dole and Pete Domenici also praised
the choices as "responsible."[35] They were
viewed as a sign that Clinton had moved away
from "his starry eyed buddies from the 1960s"
and made the "realistic" decision to go with
"Washington and Wall Street insiders with
whom capitalists and fiscal conservatives feel
comfortable."[36]

## The Original Clinton
## Economic Program

Once the Clinton team began to hammer out
their first economic program, they had to sort
out their priorities from among the many
promises announced at various stages of the
campaign. Throughout January, there were
debates on the economic plan and a tug-of-
war between deficit hawks like Panetta, Rivlin,
and Bentsen and officials like Labor Secretary Robert Reich and CEA chair Laura
D'Andrea Tyson, who while supporting deficit
reduction, were stronger advocates of a more
activist growth strategy.[37] The eventual result was a compromise of sorts, though by
the time the plan was announced there was a
clear concern to project a commitment to fiscal "responsibility."

The administration introduced its economic
proposals to a national television audience on
February 15, 1993, followed by a formal presentation to Congress two days later. Included
in the plan were deep spending cuts and major tax increases on energy users, affluent social security recipients, and the wealthy. The
program was based on three distinct but interrelated strategies. The first was a $130-
billion economic stimulus package which
included $16.3 billion in spending and $12
billion for business tax cuts, loans, and other
investment incentives. This was designed to
provide a quick boost to the economy and
was projected to create around 500,000 new
jobs. The second element was a five-year,
$230-billion program of tax breaks and spend-
ing programs to provide for longer-term business investment and the development of
infrastructure, education, expanded child care,
and job-training opportunities. This was promoted as a response to the public "investment deficit" of the Reagan/Bush years. The
third strategy was a deficit reduction package. The administration proposed approximately $473 billion in deficit reduction over

five years through a roughly equal proportion of spending cuts and tax increases.[38]

To pay for new public investment and deficit reduction, new revenues of $357 billion over five years were to come from several sources. A new top rate of 36 percent was to be added to the federal income tax for individuals making over $115,000 a year and couples making over $140,000. In addition, those with taxable income over $250,000 would face a 10 percent tax surcharge, resulting in a marginal tax rate of 39.6 percent. The top rate on capital gains income, however, would remain at 28 percent as an incentive to investment. High-income social security recipients (individuals making over $25,000 and couples making over $32,000) would have the percentage of their benefits subject to taxation increased from 50 percent to 85 percent. Caps on wages subject to the Medicare payroll tax would be removed as well.[39]

Another crucial source of new revenue in the economic program was a proposal for a broad-based energy tax based on the heat content, or Btu output, of various forms of energy use. The administration was attracted to the Btu tax because of its broad revenue base among various industries, its environmental correctness (it would provide a disincentive to energy consumption), and its supposed political feasibility versus other tax options. In addition, the top tax rate on corporations was to be raised from 34 percent to 36 percent. In a move to increase the fairness of the tax system at the bottom end, the Clinton Administration proposed an expansion of the earned income tax credit (EITC) which provided tax credits for the working poor.[40]

On the spending side, the Clinton plan proposed to cut defense expenditures by $112 billion over five years. Entitlements were to be reduced by a total of $144 billion over the same period. This included the $29-billion tax increase on high-income social security recipients, and a reduction in Medicare payments. The smallest proportion of spending cuts came from non-defense discretionary spending – $73 billion over five years – which the administration argued had taken most of the hits during the previous Republican regimes.

## The Corporate Response to the Clinton Plan

A major reason for Clinton's victory in November was the voters' desire for action on the economy. When the plan was unveiled, public opinion was largely favorable. According to a CNN/*USA Today* poll, 79 percent of the public favored the plan, and only 16 percent were opposed.[41] But the responses of major industrial and financial leaders were less enthusiastic. Administration officials Rivlin and Rubin were sent to New York shortly after the economic program was announced to gauge Wall Street reaction. There they met with executives from the nation's largest banks, investment firms, and corporations at the New York Stock Exchange. Most media accounts of this meeting emphasized the strong backing of Clinton's deficit reduction efforts by the business community.[42] But behind the scenes, there was much criticism of what the executives saw as Clinton's "soak-the-rich" populist rhetoric in announcing the upper-income tax increase in the February 15 television address. Rivlin and Rubin heard the same criticisms that evening at a meeting with top corporate executives hosted by CBS chair Laurence Tisch, where they were warned that the "class warfare" rhetoric would scare off investors and erode business confidence.[43]

The administration did get one powerful vote of confidence, however. Although the stock market dropped sharply after the Clinton speech, the crucial long-term bond market reacted favorably, with interest rates on 30 year bonds falling to a 16-year low.[44] The "financial markets" strategy seemed to be working at the outset. This was reinforced by an even more important source, Fed chairman Alan Greenspan, who endorsed the plan as a serious first step toward significant deficit reduction in an appearance before the Senate Banking Committee on February 19.[45] A favorable comment by the cautious Greenspan was invaluable for convincing markets of the efficacy of the Clinton proposal.

After Rubin's report of corporate unease with the president's "populist" speech, Clinton toned down public criticism of corporate and wealthy benefactors of the 1980s Republican policies. In fact, he mobilized administration officials with the closest ties to the business community to go out and gather visible business support for his economic plan. An extensive lobbying effort resulted in a February 25 White House gathering of corporate leaders willing to express public support for Clinton's program. There were still numerous concerns by the business community over NAFTA, labor-law reform, health care, and other issues. But the assembled CEOs were generally supportive of the administration's focus on deficit reduction, investment, job training and infrastructure development. Many took the pragmatic position that with both the White House and Congress under Democratic control, it was better to try and shape policy from the inside than simply throw stones from the outside.[46] Among the business organizations taking a publicly conciliatory attitude was the traditionally antagonistic US Chamber of Commerce, which angered more ideologically pure conservatives and business groups.

Many old line-manufacturers remained strongly opposed to the Clinton program, however. They felt that their industries would be the hardest hit by both the proposed energy tax and the hike in corporate tax rates. Fear of tax increases led some companies that had been among the most politically active in the recent past – including DuPont, IBM, Kellogg, and Procter and Gamble – to re-

activate the Tax Reform Action Committee (TRAC), the corporate ad hoc coalition that had fought for the Tax Reform Act of 1986. Small business organizations were also leery of the plan. The National Federation of Independent Business (NFIB) was especially vehement in its criticism. It opposed the higher tax rates on affluent individuals which would affect many of its members. It was also fearful of many proposals that were not in the Clinton budget plan but that were being considered by the administration, such as mandatory health insurance funded primarily by employers, or a higher minimum wage.[47]

Sectors of the business community reacted to specific elements of the Clinton plan according to their particular interests. Nearly all business representatives favored action on deficit reduction. A survey of over 500 top CEOs by the Conference Board found the three issues of greatest concern to be skyrocketing health-care costs, the continued burden of federal regulations, and the budget deficit. Joining with the academic policy establishment and Wall Street, the executives in the Conference Board study felt that rapid movement to reduce the deficit was crucial to future economic health. A majority favored large spending cuts to accomplish this, especially in farm programs, welfare, defense, and foreign aid. Not surprisingly, they supported general reductions in business taxes, though there was little enthusiasm for a temporary or incremental Investment Tax Credit (ITC) proposed by the administration. There was also corporate support for infrastructure investment and even for a mild economic stimulus package – provided that these were accompanied by a credible plan to reduce the deficit.[48]

There was much resistance to some aspects of the Clinton plan, especially on the revenue side. Most major corporations opposed raising the top corporate tax rate to 36 percent. TRAC was especially upset by this proposal. But the element of the Clinton plan that drew the most corporate attention was the proposed energy tax. This was perceived as especially threatening by energy producers, and by high energy-consuming industries such as steel and aluminum. Alcoa chairman Paul O'Neill predicted that if enacted, the administration's Btu tax would force plant closings and relocation outside the United States to keep costs competitive with those of foreign producers. Like many large manufacturers, O'Neill favored a gasoline tax or a broad-based consumption tax that would help reduce the deficit without threatening profits and productive investment. However, heavy users of gasoline (agribusiness, trucking) were strongly opposed to a gas tax, and retailers were opposed to a consumption tax that would affect their business directly.[49]

For the banking and financial community, the deficit was the central concern. Although uncomfortable about parts of the Clinton plan, they were favorably disposed toward the steps leading to deficit reduction,[50] and many in the financial community were not particularly bothered by an energy tax if the added revenues were applied to deficit reduction.

## Conservative Constraints in the Congressional Budget Process

By the time the Clinton Administration presented its official fiscal 1994 budget on April 8, 1993, Congress had already passed its own general budget outline in the form of a non-binding Congressional Resolution as required by congressional budget procedures (H Con Res 64). The Democratic Congress followed the general guidelines of the original administration proposal and was able to stave off most Republican modifications. But conservatives had insisted on lower caps on spending than were required by law or desired by the administration. Republicans and many conservative Democrats had grumbled loudly about the ratio of tax increases to spending

cuts in the original Clinton plan, demanding less of the former and more of the latter.[51] The zero-sum budget environment meant that the domestic spending plans of the administration would have to be scaled back, or paid for through cuts in existing programs, any of which had the strong support of some coalition in Congress.

An important factor in the subsequent political struggle was the total intransigence of congressional Republicans. In the House, the Republicans had debated submitting their own plan, which included some tax increases. But the House Republican Committee decided instead to endorse a resolution against any tax increases, which effectively removed them from any positive contribution to the budget process. Ultimately, the GOP would not provide a single vote in favor of the fiscal 1994 budget in committee or on the floor, in either chamber. This meant that the administration and Democratic congressional leaders had to rely completely on Democratic votes, which in turn gave blocs of conservative Democrats the veto power to force more spending cuts and fewer tax increases at several points in the legislative process. This would also give corporate lobbyists extra leverage over Congress by allowing them to focus resources on influencing a few key Democratic members.[52]

The Conference Committee version of the first Congressional Budget Resolution was passed by the House on March 31 by a 240–184 vote, and cleared the Senate 55–45 on April 1. The general reaction of the media and the public response of the administration was to declare it a major victory for Clinton and the Democrats over a unified Republican opposition. But in private, administration officials recognized that the budget resolution represented at least a partial *defeat* for the administration. The deficit hawks within the administration were delighted that Congress had actually added more deficit reduction than the original administration proposal. But the activists among Clinton's advisers were dismayed to discover that the extra spending cuts had occurred at the expense of the investment side of the plan, as a result of conservative pressures and caps on discretionary spending that had been imposed by the budget agreement of 1990. The new investment had been reduced to a mere $1 billion in 1994 and about $6 billion in 1995. Panetta blamed this setback on "deficit mania" in Congress.[53]

It is important to consider the source of this "mania," however. Establishment economists had provided the academic rationale for the deficit reduction offensive with their arguments about saving, investment, "crowding out," and interest rates. Members of Congress had justified their action by citing the "Perot" factor and public opinion. As noted above, both arguments were fallacious. The economic evidence for the "financial markets" strategy was ambiguous at best.[54] And the evidence on public opinion was clear. The "people" did favor deficit reduction in general, and as a symbol of their dissatisfaction with government (the real "Perot factor"). But polls consistently showed that they *preferred* a stimulative economic strategy to promote growth and job creation over deficit reduction, and by large margins. "Deficit mania" was the legitimation used by various political elites to translate ambiguous expressions of public discontent into specific policy outcomes that reflected their own preferences. Making deficit reduction the top economic priority reflected the power of the conservative bloc in Congress and the dominant views of the conservative and "moderate"policy elites in academia, the think-tank network, and the Clinton Administration. It also represented the priorities of big business and Wall Street. It did *not* reflect the policy preferences of the "general public."

## Defeat of the stimulus package

A second setback for the Clinton administration – one that was more visible to the media

and the public – followed closely on the heels of the first when the short-term economic stimulus package was defeated by Republican filibuster in the Senate in April. Originally, the administration had planned to introduce the stimulus plan first, before dealing with the budget resolution. The rationale was that the stimulus would provide a quick economic jolt to keep the fledgling economic recovery going, while the more long-term measures for investment and deficit reduction would be handled in the more complex budget process. But conservative Democrats in Congress insisted on dealing with the budget first. They did not want to vote on new spending proposals before they had a chance to vote for budget cuts.[55]

The stimulus package was introduced separately from the rest of Clinton's economic program as a $16.3 billion supplemental appropriations bill for fiscal year 1993 (HR 1335). The administration proposed it as an emergency spending measure so it would not be subject to existing budget caps on discretionary spending. The bill included public-works projects, summer jobs programs for youth and the unemployed, social programs for the poor, and accelerated government purchases of high-tech equipment. The Democratically controlled House approved the stimulus measure quickly. But in the Senate, the bill met stiff resistance from Republicans and conservative Democrats. They expressed concerns about the deficit and new "liberal" spending. Some of the targetted programs drew special criticism from conservatives, in particular a proposed $2.5-billion increase in block grants to cities. The tactics of Senate Appropriations Committee chair Robert Byrd also angered conservative opponents. Rather than negotiate a compromise in the Senate, Byrd pledged to deliver the president's bill intact. Assuming the Republicans would not filibuster a jobs bill, he used several parliamentary tricks to forestall amendments. The strategy did not work. A united Republican Party led a successful filibuster, which survived four closure votes. Finally, the bill was stripped of everything except a $4-billion emergency appropriation for extended unemployment benefits, which quickly passed and was signed on April 23.[56]

## The Omnibus Budget Reconciliation Act of 1993

By the time Congress began deliberations on the actual budget, the Clinton Administration had already seen its original plan modified considerably. The stimulus package was dead, and spending constraints in the first budget resolution had limited planned public investments. The Republicans had decided on a strategy of total resistance and began an intensive public relations campaign focussing especially on the purported negative effects of the energy tax and tax increase on social security benefits.[57] Most Republicans also opposed the income tax increases on the wealthy, but strong public support for this particular measure kept their opposition low-key.

In the three months since its introduction, a growing conservative and business opposition had organized against specific elements of the Clinton program, especially on the tax side. By May, the National Association of Manufacturers and the American Farm Bureau Federation had brought together a coalition of over 900 corporations and trade associations to fight the energy tax. This coalition, which would eventually be called the American Energy Alliance, also included the American Petroleum Institute, the American Dairy Products Institute, and the 600,000-members NFIB.[58]

Corporate lobbyists found it easy to generate "grassroots" opposition to the energy tax. The tax was so broad in scope (one of its original attractions to the Clinton Administration) that it affected a wide range of industries and business. In addition, the ad-

ministration had made some significant early concessions to selected interests, including farm states, airlines, and the steel and aluminum industries, to increase support. This had the unintended (but in hindsight quite predictable) consequence of encouraging lobbyists for other industries and regions to fight even harder for their own special protections. The USCOC had come under intense criticism from other conservative and business organizations for their initial conciliatory stance. By early May, the USCOC had joined the lobbying effort against the Btu tax and higher corporate tax rates. TRAC was also well into a multimillion dollar campaign against both the corporate tax increase and higher individual rates on the wealthy.[59]

## Compromise in the House

The major responsibility for shaping the budget bill in the House was with the Ways and Means Committee, chaired by Illinois Representative Dan Rostenkowski. Rostenkowski sought to copy the successful tactics of the 1986 Tax Reform Act in creating a core of corporate supporters, or at least neutralizing the most powerful corporate opponents, by offering a number of pro-business concessions on the tax side of the bill such as selected concessions on the Btu tax, a reduction in the corporate tax increase, generous write-offs for "passive losses" on rental property for the real-estate industry, and so on.[60] By moving to appease major business interests, Rostenkowski was able to enlist a number of corporate supporters after the revised bill was passed by the Ways and Means Committee on May 13. The concessions led TRAC to withdraw its active opposition to the Clinton plan.[61] Small business opposition remained strong, however, led by the ever-intransigent NFIB. This was in spite of the fact that, at the urging of Clinton, the committee had raised from $10,000 to $25,000 the amount small businesses could write off for machinery and equipment purchases to increase incentives for investment.

By making several concessions to business and the regional interests of key Democrats, the Ways and Means Committee was able to pass a budget bill that retained the income tax increases on the wealthy and kept the broad outlines of Clinton's corporate and energy taxes. But on the House floor, the plan ran into more resistance by conservatives, led by the so-called "Mainstream Forum," the coalition of DLC members in the House led by Oklahoma Representative Dave McCurdy. Given the unified Republican opposition, every Democratic vote was important, and the Mainstream Forum was a crucial obstacle. Final passage of the bill was only possible when the administration promised to make major modifications in the energy tax and consider further cuts in entitlement programs when the Senate considered the bill in June.[62]

## Defeat of the energy tax in the Senate

In spite of the pacification of some major corporations by Rostenkowski's concessions, an ever-expanding coalition of business and conservative organizations kept up pressure on the Clinton proposals, especially on the broad-based energy tax. By June, the American Energy Alliance (AEA) included 1650 organizations.[63] Financed and organized mainly by the USCOC, NAM, and the American Petroleum Institute, the AEA spent between $1 million and $2 million to stir up "grassroots" opposition to the energy tax. They relied heavily on local television advertisements, radio talk shows, staged news events like rallies and protests, and patch-through phone networks which allowed lobbyists to select suitably angry citizens and link them up directly to the office of relevant members of Congress.[64] The AEA was joined by conservative organizations like Citizens for a Sound Economy, a Washington-based lobbying group led by former

Reagan official James C. Miller III. Dedicated to the reduction of government, Citizens for a Sound Economy began raising money and plotting strategy to oppose the Clinton economic plan in December 1992, before there was even a plan to oppose! This indicates the rather narrow possibilities for "compromise" faced by the administration. This organization also staged public protests, and sent out detailed "information packets" on the dire consequences of the tax for business and jobs, especially in key energy-producing states like Oklahoma, Texas, and Louisiana.[65]

The lobbying effort against the energy tax was led by big business organizations fearful of reduced profits, and by conservative groups that sought the reduction of government on principle. But their strategy was to paint the energy tax as a broad "middle-class" tax increase that was contrary to Clinton's campaign promise to cut middle-class taxes and that would force industries to shut down plants and/or relocate to other countries. As *Fortune* magazine observed in a cogent summary of the anti-Btu tax campaign,

Opponents used the most effective argument against any legislative proposal today: that it would cost jobs ... As long as the NAM and the American Petroleum Institute were the only visible BTU critics, they got nowhere. But when they organized more than 2,000 small and medium-size companies, farm organizations, and consumer groups into the American Energy Alliance, what had once appeared a typical big-business lobby was transformed into a grassroots movement. Coalition leaders then used local rallies, press conferences, phone banks, fax machines, TV and print ads, and appearances on radio talk shows to generate an avalanche of calls and letters to swing Senators. In the end, even Clinton's attacks on the oil industry for "trying to wiggle out of its contribution" could not stand up to angry constituents.[66]

This underscores a major political liability for the Clinton Administration. They could not counter this play on the real fears of lost jobs with a job-creation strategy of their own. Their economic program relied primarily on austerity and favorable financial markets in hopes that, indirectly, economic growth and expanded employment opportunities would result. This was especially true after the defeat of the stimulus plan. The administration promised economic expansion and a new wave of high-tech, high-pay jobs as the eventual result of their program. But in the meantime, deficit reduction provided little to capture the imagination or political support of the electorate.

The Democrats held a slim 11–9 majority on the Senate Finance Committee. Moreover, several of these Democrats were conservatives representing farm or energy-producing states. The Clinton budget could not move without major revisions. The unyielding opposition to the Btu tax by conservative Democrat David Boren of Oklahoma made its passage in the Finance Committee impossible (it was also opposed by John Breaux of Louisiana). But if the energy tax was dropped, then the Finance Committee would have to find some way to replace the huge revenue shortfall – estimated to be $71.5 billion over five year – or make large additional spending cuts to maintain the deficit reduction features of the package. After extensive debate and much argument, the committee finally agreed to replace the Btu tax with a 4.3-cent-per-gallon increase in the federal tax on gasoline and other fuels. This was a much more regressive source of revenue, but one which would elicit much less organized opposition from business. Unfortunately, it would also bring in much less revenue, around $24.2 billion according to staff estimates. With no other politically feasible sources of new revenue, the committee was forced to cut back even more on Clinton's proposed expenditures. They trimmed the administration's proposed tax breaks for business investment and urban development, and reduced the EITC for the working poor. They also included higher cuts

in Medicare than the administration had recommended.[67]

On the Senate floor, the complex bill ran into more resistance. Supporters of tax incentives for business investment were angry that these had been dealt away to pay for the abolition of the energy tax. Liberal members were angered that Medicare cuts were increased and tax breaks for the poor reduced to make up for the shortfall. To buy support, the Senate leadership gave up $17 billion in deficit reduction to allow for smaller Medicare cuts and some investment incentives for small business. Even so, every Republican and six Democrats voted against the bill, and Vice-President Gore was required to break a 49–49 tie on June 25, a sign of how fragile support was for Clinton's increasingly modest economic program.

## The final conference agreement

On July 15, a huge Conference Committee of over 200 members began the heated negotiations to bring the House and Senate versions of the budget plan together. The most important conflicts concerned the tax aspects of the plan. The level of new revenue allowed would determine whether any of the Senate cuts in social programs could be restored. Some members favored increasing the top corporate tax rate to make up for revenue losses on the failed energy tax. But tax committee chairs Rostenkowski and Daniel Patrick Moynihan of the Senate Finance Committee quickly locked in the 35-percent maximum corporate rate worked out by Rostenkowski in the compromise with corporate lobbyists, which shut off one source of extra revenue. Conservative Democrats would not reconsider a broad-based energy tax and would not go higher than 4.3 cents per gallon on the gasoline tax. The Senate's became the final version of the energy tax.[68]

The budget process was shaped under the tight political constraints of a unified Republican opposition and a fragmented Democratic Party. Moreover, this political contest was occurring within a broader set of constraints imposed by the Federal Reserve and the financial community. Their demands were even represented by a numerical line in the sand. After consultations with Wall Street and Fed chairman Greenspan, administration deficit hawks determined that only a deficit reduction goal of at least $500 billion over five years would appear credible to financial markets. This credibility was now crucial to the Clinton economic strategy. With the short-term stimulus gone and the long-term investments weakened, the administration relied on deficit reduction to spur falling interest rates, which, it was hoped, would stimulate investment and economic growth. Greenspan reinforced this general viewpoint when he warned in testimony before a House Banking subcommittee on July 20 that any further rollback of the deficit reduction aspects of the economic package would likely have a negative impact on interest rates.[69] Thus beyond the political contest in Congress, setting the fiscal parameters within which distributive decisions would have to be made were the financial markets.

The final Conference Committee agreement reflected these political and economic constraints. The net deficit reduction for fiscal years 1994 through 1998 was set at $496 billion, close enough to the magic half-trillion mark to be taken seriously by the Fed and the financial community. The major source of new revenue was the increase in individual income tax rates for the affluent, with a new top marginal rate of 36 percent and a 10-percent surcharge on taxable income over $250,000. As in the president's original proposal, the top rate on capital gains remained at 28 percent, a major loophole for the affluent, who could shift income to capital gains, but justified by the administration as a stimulus to new investment. Even though the higher marginal tax rate was resisted by some con-

servatives and business groups, it was the one element of the program that remained intact straight through the political process and had no trouble clearing both houses of Congress. One other progressive element remained in the plan that was also widely popular: the expansion of the EITC for the working poor. Liberals liked the progressive aspects of the measure, and ideological conservatives generally favored rewarding people for work as an alternative to welfare.[70] Clinton had originally proposed an expansion of the EITC that would have cost $28.3 billion; Congress passed a $20.8 billion increase.

The Conference Committee raised the top corporate tax rate 1 percent, to 35 percent, the level represented in both the House and Senate versions of the budget. They also agreed to increase the proportion of social security benefits for upper-income recipients that would be subject to taxation from 50 percent to 85 percent. However, they set the point at which this tax bite would take effect higher than Clinton or either chamber had originally proposed ($34,000 a year for individuals and $44,000 for couples).

The conference bill also included a good portion of the Medicare cuts that had been approved by the Senate. Growth in Medicare spending was to be trimmed by $55.8 billion over five years (versus $58 billion in the Senate bill and $50 billion in the House version). Tax incentives for small business, and for investment in special urban "empowerment" zones, survived, but were scaled back from Clinton's original proposals.[71]

The increasingly fragile budget agreement finally passed the House by the slimmest of margins, 218–216, on August 5. Forty-one Democrats and all House Republicans voted against the measure. The minimum number of conservative Democrats were persuaded to vote for the budget only when the administration promised to send another bill to Congress in the fall that would attempt to cut 1994 appropriations further, and to allow consideration of other fiscally conservative measures as well, including entitlement review. Even then, it took every bit of lobbying skill and appeals to party interest by the administration to save the bill.[72]

It was the same story in the Senate. Once again, Vice-President Gore was required to break a 50–50 tie to get the budget passed. Senator Boren, who had reluctantly voted for the earlier Senate version after extracting significant concessions, voted against the conference bill. This forced the administration to convert one of the six Democrats who had voted against the earlier Senate bill. Clinton succeeded in convincing Senator Dennis DiConcini of New Mexico to switch his vote in exchange for raising the threshold levels for the higher social security tax, and by establishing a "deficit-reduction trust fund" to ensure that all new tax revenues and spending cuts would go to deficit reduction rather than program expansion.

## Summation: Lower Deficits, Free Trade, and the Bond Market

The first Clinton budget agreement illustrates the degree to which economic policy options had narrowed by 1993. The presence of a Democrat in the White House presiding over a Democratic Congress provided a test case of sorts for the possibility of an "activist" economic program. The eventual results of the Omnibus Budget Reconciliation Act of 1993 were strikingly similar to the 1990 budget agreement of the Bush administration,[73] demonstrating the constraints on economic policy regardless of the nominal party in power.

With the defeat of the short-term stimulus bill, and with other spending and tax incentives to promote investment reduced, the Clinton Administration placed its economic hopes on the "financial-markets" strategy. The continued reduction of the fiscal capacities of

the state marked the continued demise of a crucial component of traditional Democratic politics since the New Deal: the ability to reward constituents through government action, especially those constituents who are disadvantaged by the operation of a market economy. This capacity is now severely constrained, and the party is dominated by conservative and neo-liberal "reformers" who share the economic views of the policy establishment. The "party of the people" no longer has the capacity to protect them from the vagaries of the market.[74]

The narrow ideological boundaries within which economic policy was formulated are nicely illustrated in an interview given by CEA chair Laura D'Andrea Tyson to *Challenge Magazine* editor Richard Bartel in early 1994. Considered one of the most liberal of Clinton's policy officials, Tyson spent most of the interview praising the 1993 deficit-reduction package as if her only audience was the bond market and Alan Greenspan. She even defended Greenspan's moves to tighten monetary policy in *anticipation* of inflation at several points in the interview. She also acknowledged that the budget agreement would act as a "fiscal drag" on the economy in 1994 and 1995,[75] which of course was why it was originally popular with the bond market. When Bartel pointed out that this seemed to place all of the burden of sustaining economic growth on the monetary policies of the Fed, Tyson replied by reciting the assumptions of the "financial-markets" strategy:

I would put it differently although with the same implication. The whole macroeconomic strategy here is predicated on the notion that, if you change the government's borrowing needs in a significant way, you allow for a climate in which financial markets offer more attractive, lower costs of capital to private business.[76]

Pressed on the Fed's seemingly excessive concern with inflation, Tyson responded as follows:

Clearly, the Administration and the Federal Reserve share the concern that inflation is a possible development in the future that might undermine the economic expansion. Under our current institutional arrangements, the Fed has an independent responsibility to read the economic evidence and to formulate and carry out monetary policy accordingly. The Administration can't do that, and *it's not our responsibility to comment on it.*[77]

Not only must the administration adhere to the dictates of financial markets in its economic strategy, but it cannot even comment about Fed policy! Why was the Clinton administration so cautious? Tyson continued:

In fact, if we were to comment on Federal Reserve actions, it would probably cause much more concern and instability in the financial markets than if we had remained silent. We are all – the Administration and the Fed – trying to communicate a clear signal to the markets that we share the same concern about inflation. The Administration did that in its fiscal strategy and the Fed is doing that in its monetary policy.[78]

When the interview turned to the employment issue, Tyson made a general statement about jobs being "the central concern" of the Clinton administration. Yet it was clear that these jobs would have to be created in the private sector. Government would not or could not provide them; there was no jobs program on the Clinton agenda. Further, the administration's fiscal policy would admittedly slow economic growth. All hope was placed on the indirect stimulus of lower interest rates. Yet by the time of the interview, the Fed had taken steps to *raise* rates in anticipation of "inflationary" economic growth (this would continue throughout 1994). And the chair of the CEA was afraid of even commenting on this situation, lest the markets get even more nervous. Rarely is the "veto power" of capital over economic policy illustrated so clearly.

The administration placed its hopes for economic growth not only on lower interest rates, but also on the positive stimulus of global expansion. In an interview with *Fortune* magazine just prior to the battle over NAFTA in 1993, President Clinton made it clear that an export-oriented economic policy was to be our economic salvation, and promotion of free trade was to be a primary means to this end. Clinton stressed the crucial importance of both the NAFTA and GATT agreements for promoting growth and job creation in the United States. When *Fortune* pointed out that most corporate CEOs, while favoring these agreements, did not share this optimistic vision of America's employment future, Clinton envoked the rhetoric of neo-classical economics popular among business lobbyists and the economic policy establishment:

a lot of big companies will continue to restructure and downsize . . . indeed, I'm trying to get the federal government to do some of the same.

But most of the new jobs will be generated by a resurgent manufacturing sector, which I think you will see, particularly if we get the GATT agreement reducing tariffs on manufacturing products. Unlike NAFTA, there is virtually no disagreement that the agreement we reached in Tokyo with the G-7 on manufactured products will create hundreds of thousands of jobs on its own.[79]

It is interesting to compare this optimistic prediction with those of the business press, representing the views of the companies that would create these new jobs. While nearly unanimous in their support of free trade, the corporate community did not see this as leading to significantly higher wages or the creation of a large number of high-wage jobs. More attuned to the harsh realities of global competition than the abstractions of market economics, the business press has repeatedly issued sober warnings about the future, projecting the continued disappearance of high-paying industrial and professional jobs, and an increase in low-pay, part-time employment.[80]

By the end of 1993, the limits of US economic policy were clear. Whatever the original policy goals of the Clinton Administration, the policy of "free trade, free markets, and fiscal discipline" advocated by the business community, the DLC, and the intellectuals of the mainstream economic policy establishment had prevailed in a Democratic regime.

## Conclusion: Where Are All the Democrats?

The first Clinton budget further institutionalized the pro-capital orientation that has dominated economic policy since the late 1970s. This has meant, and will mean, relatively slow growth and relatively high unemployment. It is this prospect that explains the favorable reactions in the stock and bond markets when such austerity measures are announced; expectations of rapid economic growth or employment expansion would have the opposite effect.[81] This elementary point is rarely noted by mainstream media accounts or deficit-obsessed politicians, but it has important political implications. An economic environment of slow growth, low inflation, and high unemployment is most advantageous to those who own capital (especially in the form of flexible financial instruments). While nobody prefers excessive inflation, moderately inflationary growth generally provides a mild redistributive effect and benefits a substantial segment of the population below the top rungs.

Presenting the financial-markets strategy as if everyone benefits equally from it is an exercise in ideology. The immediate beneficiaries are the minority of individuals and institutions that own the majority of financial assets. For most people, a more directly beneficial policy would be one leading to more rapid economic growth and job creation, especially of skilled jobs at reasonable wages. Increasingly, this appears to be beyond the capacity of government.

In fact, the great non-issue of the Clinton Administration has proven to be employment, and the related issues of stagnating wages and growing inequality in an era of economic transition. It can reasonably be argued that this contributed to the political weaknesses of a nominally Democratic administration. The success of conservative and business groups in shaping policy in 1993 often depended on "grassroots" lobbying. For example, the anti-Btu tax effort relied on a strategy of tying the interests of big business to those of the "people" by fostering fears of higher taxes, higher prices, and, especially, lost jobs. As *Fortune* magazine noted, in the current economic climate:

Generating public pressure seems easier than ever. People are worried, particularly about the economy, and thanks to Ross Perot, Rush Limbaugh, and Clinton himself, people seem more willing to speak their minds to Washington ... The lesson for business from the first months of the Clinton era is clear: Go directly to the people, and persuade them with pocketbook logic and tug-at-the heartstrings emotion that U.S. jobs are at stake, and you can move Congress and the President.[82]

This is perhaps the greatest irony in the policies of the early Clinton Administration, and a lesson on the ideological limits of current economic discourse. Conservatives, Republicans, and business lobbyists were using jobs and the economy at will against a Democratic administration at a time when unemployment and restructuring in the private sector were major concerns – and the administration could not effectively respond. Its pro-capital, market-oriented policies included no jobs program, other than the hope that the market would provide for all. In the US today, the struggle over class-relevant economic issues occurs in the absence of class-based politics. Existing political institutions and dominant modes of public discourse do not allow articulation of these issues along class lines. Rather, all "realistic" positions fall safely within the bounds of a pro-market consensus. In the energy-tax battle, it was the conservative–business coalition that successfully mobilized "populist" fears in their favor, as they have often done since the 1970s. This is easier when there is nowhere else for the "people" to go.

It is perhaps instructive to recall the fate of the last Democratic president. Jimmy Carter was elected as a "populist" outsider reflecting the people's disgust with "business as usual" in Washington and their impatience with the conservative economic policies of a Republican predecessor. By the end of his tenure, Carter had pushed for a pro-capital policy agenda favored by powerful business and financial interests that alienated him from most of the traditional Democratic constituency. In the even more restricted political environment of the 1990s, Bill Clinton did the same thing in his first year in office. It is worth noting that after extracting as many concessions as possible from a Democratic administration, business deserted Carter in 1980 for an even more agreeable Republican regime. For a while, it looked as though Clinton might suffer the same fate. By October 1994, *Business Week* was explaining "Why Business Hates Clinton"[83] in spite of his generally pro-business economic policies. One month later, the people rejected the Democratic Party en masse as the Republicans took over Congress in an historic mid-term election landslide.

The conventional political wisdom on the travails of the Democratic Party holds that it is perceived as too "liberal" by the electorate and must move ideologically to the right if it is to remain viable. This same argument explains the victory of Clinton over Bob Dole in 1996 as an effect of his moving to the "center" and away from his "liberal" tendencies, just in time. There is a grain of truth to this argument if it refers to the ability of policy elites to focus public discourse on social issues like "getting tough" on criminals, welfare cheats, and minority groups. The

distortions of fact and injustices imposed in these policy areas are well documented elsewhere in this volume. But in terms of economic policy, it seems much more logical – even obvious – that the main problem with the Democrats today is that they are much too conservative, indeed that they offer no real alternative to the traditional Republican program.[84] They have not addressed the economic concerns of the 70–80 percent of the population whose incomes and standard of living have stagnated or declined since the 1970s and whose lives are not linked through high-tech job skills or flexible financial assets to the great "postindustrial" run-up of the economy. Is there any support for the audacious suggestion that the Democrats must move to the *left* to be politically viable? Consider the lack of enthusiasm for the conservative, "financial-markets" orientation by the general public. Consider also that the two elements of Clinton's 1993 economic program that had solid popular support were the two progressive components – the income tax increase on the wealthy, and the expansion of the EITC for the working poor. This suggests a possible base of support for more "redistributive" economic measures, provided they are perceived as fair. There has also been consistent popular support for public investment in job training, education, and infrastructure, which was a part of the "activist" agenda of the first Clinton Administration that has so far come to little. Much of the policy of the first Clinton term hurt the most loyal constituents of the Democratic Party directly, and did little for the working-class or middle-class "swing" voters. This was not entirely the administration's fault. But given the large disparity between the economic concerns of the electorate and the policy priorities of the administration and many Congressional Democrats, perhaps Harry Truman's warning bears repeating: When the voters have a choice between a Republican and a Republican, they'll pick the Republican every time.

# Notes

1 As attributed to Bill Clinton by Bob Woodward in *The Agenda* (New York: Simon and Schuster, 1994), p. 165.

2 Robert Kuttner, *The Life of the Party* (New York: Viking, 1987), p. 5.

3 For example, Jacob Weisberg, "Clincest," *New Republic* (April 26, 1993). On Clinton's background and social ties, see Paul Starobin, "Aspiring to Govern," *National Journal* (May 9, 1992), pp. 1103–10; David Maraniss, *First in his Class: A Biography of Bill Clinton* (New York: Simon and Schuster, 1995).

4 Clinton received contributions of around $50,000 from Stephens family members and employees of family-owned businesses such as Arkansas–Oklahoma Gas Co. and Worthen Bank Corp. See *Business Week*, "Bill Clinton, the Terror and Toast of Wall Street" (April 6, 1992), p. 83.

5 Thomas Ferguson, "The Democrats Deal for Dollars," *Nation* (April 13, 1992), p. 476; see also Michael Kelly, "The President's Past," *New York Times Magazine* (July 31, 1994), pp. 20–9.

6 *Business Week*, "Bill Clinton"; William Greider, "Who's Pulling Bill Clinton's Strings?," *Rolling Stone* (April 30, 1992), pp. 33, 35.

7 Thomas Ferguson and Joel Rogers, *Right Turn: The Decline of the Democrats and the Future of American Politics* (New York: Hill and Wang, 1986); Kuttner, *Life of the Party*; Paul Starobin, "An Affair to Remember?," *National Journal* (January 16, 1993), pp. 120–4.

8 Starobin, "An Affair to Remember?," p. 121.

9 Ibid., p. 123.

10 Ibid., p. 120.

11 Stephen Labaton, "Angry at Bush, Republican Contributions are Helping Clinton," *New York Times* (September 22, 1992), p. A24; Kirk Victor, "The Long Hello," *National Journal* (December 12, 1992), pp. 2829–32.

12 Victor, "Long Hello," p. 2829.

13 Labaton, "Angry at Bush," p. 1992.

14 Ferguson, "Democrats Deal for Dollars."

15 Victor, "Long Hello," p. 2831.

16 Thomas Ferguson, "Who Bought Your Candidate and Why," *Nation* (April 6, 1992), pp. 441–4.

17 Victor, "Long Hello," p. 2831.

18 *Business Week*, "Clinton's Economic Brain Trust" (August 10, 1992), pp. 54–5.

19 Greider, "Who's Pulling Bill Clinton's Strings?," p. 33.

20 John Cranford, "Clinton Makes Priorities Clear in Revised Economic Plan," *Congressional Quarterly Weekly Report* (June 27, 1992), p. 1899; Bill Clinton and Al Gore, *Putting People First: How We Can All Change America* (New York: Times Books, 1992).

21 Cranford, "Clinton Makes Priorities Clear," p. 1900.

22 Paul Starobin, "Confusing Signals," *National Journal* (November 30, 1991), p. 2910.

23 See the analysis in Rhodes Cook, "Clinton Struggles to Meld a Governing Coalition," *Congressional Quarterly Weekly Report* (August 7, 1993), pp. 2175–9.

24 George Gallup, *The Gallup Poll 1992*, (Wilmington DE: Scholarly Resources, 1993) pp. 160–1.

25 Ibid., p. 195.

26 Ibid., p. 210.

27 Ibid., p. 198.

28 Paul Starobin, "Time to Get Real," *National Journal* (December 19, 1992), pp. 2879–80.

29 Ibid., pp. 2881–2882.

30 See Louis Uchitelle, "Economists Shifting Priorities," *New York Times* (March 31, 1992), pp. D1, D8: Peter Passell, "Making a Case for a Fiscal Jolt," *New York Times* (July 10, 1992), p. D1; Uchitelle, "Old Ideas Gain New Respect," *New York Times* (October 8, 1992), pp. D1, D8.

31 See David Gordon, "Twixt the Cup and the Lip: Mainstream Economics and the Formation of Economic Policy," *Social Research* 61(1), (1994), pp. 1–33; Also Robert Heilbroner and Peter Bernstein, *The Debt and the Deficit* (New York: W. W. Norton, 1989); Robert Eisner, *The Misunderstood Economy* (Boston: Harvard Business School Press, 1994); Dean Baker and Todd Schafer, "The Clinton Budget Package: Putting Deficit Reduction First? *Challenge* (May–June, 1993), pp. 4–10.

32 Starobin, "Time to Get Real," p. 2879.

33 Ibid., p. 2882.

34 John Cranford, "New Clinton Economic Team Veers toward the Center," *Congressional Quarterly Weekly Report* (December 12, 1992), pp. 3799–803.

35 Ibid., p. 3800.

36 Starobin, "Time to Get Real," p. 2879.

37 Gwen Ifill, "Economic Plan Grew Slowly out of Marathon Debate," *New York Times* (February 21, 1993), I, p. 20.

38 Congressional Quarterly, *Congressional Quarterly Almanac, 1993* (Washington D C: Congressional Quarterly, 1994), pp. 85–8.

39 Ibid., p. 86.

40 Ibid., p. 86.

41 Woodward, *Agenda*, p. 140.

42 For example, Allen Myerson, "Clinton's Aides Sell Message on Trading Floor," *New York Times* (February 19, 1993), p. D16.

43 Woodward, *Agenda*, pp. 141–2.

44 Ibid., p. 144; Robert Hurtado, "Mixed Greeting for Clinton Plan; Bonds Jump," *New York Times* (February 19, 1993), pp. D1, D13.

45 Woodward, *Agenda*, pp. 143–4.

46 *Business Week*, "Business Boards the Clinton Express" (April 5, 1993), p. 53.

47 Ibid., pp. 53–4.

48 *Across the Board*, "CEOs to Clinton: Cut the Deficit. Pronto" (March, 1993), pp. 14–15.

49 Steven Greenhouse, "The Clinton Economic Plan's Winners and Losers," *New York Times* (February 14, 1993), III p. 5; Greenhouse, "Corporations Attack Plans to Lift Taxes," *New York Times* (February 15, 1993), pp. D1, D6.

50 Steve Lohr, "For Business, Ample Pain to Share," *New York Times* (February 18, 1993), pp. D1, D8.

51 Congressional Quarterly, *Almanac 1993*, p. 89; R. W. Apple, "Democrats' Unease may Slow Clinton Economic Plan," *New York Times* (February 21, 1993), I, p. 20.

52 See Ann Reilly Dowd, "How to Get Things Done in Washington," *Fortune* (August 9, 1993), pp. 60–2.

53 Woodward, *Agenda*, pp. 161–3.

54 See Eisner, *Misunderstood Economy*; Gordon, "Twixt the Cup and the Lip."

55 Congressional Quarterly, *Almanac 1993*, p. 103.

56 Ibid., pp. 706–9.

57 Ibid., p. 108.

58 Steven Greenhouse, "Manufacturers and Farmers Oppose Clinton Energy Tax," *New York Times* (May 6, 1993), p. B16.

59 Michael Wines, "Two Business Groups Attack Tax Plan," *New York Times* (May 11, 1993), p. A1.

60 Jackie Calmes, "Rostenkowski Looks to Firms on Tax Plan," *Wall Street Journal* (May 17, 1993), pp. A3, A10; Congressional Quarterly, *Almanac 1993*, p. 109.

61 Calmes, "Rostenkowski Looks to Firms."

62 Congressional Quarterly, *Almanac 1993*, p. 111.

63 Agis Salpukas, "Going for the Kill on the Energy Tax," *New York Times* (June 5, 1993), I, pp. 37, 49.

64 See Dowd, "How to Get Things Done;" Michael Wines, "Tax's Demise Illustrates First Rule of Lobbying: Work, Work, Work," *New York Times* (June 14, 1993), pp. A1, B6.

65 Salpukas, "Going for the Kill."

66 Dowd, "How to Get Things Done," p. 62.

67 Congressional Quarterly, *Almanac 1993*, pp. 114–15.

68 Ibid., p. 119.

69 Ibid., pp. 119, 122.

70 Viveca Novak and Paul Starobin, "Spreading the Money," *National Journal* (August 14, 1993), pp. 2019–22.

71 Congressional Quarterly, *Almanac 1993*, pp. 119–22.

72 George Hager and David Cloud, "Democrats Tie their Fate to Clinton's Budget Bill," *Congressional Quarterly Weekly Report* (August 7, 1993), pp. 2122–9.

73 George Hager, "1993 Deal: Remembrance of Things Past," *Congressional Quarterly Weekly Report* (August 7, 1993), pp. 2130–1; Louis Uchitelle, "How Clinton's Economic Strategy Ended Up Looking Like Bush's," *New York Times* (August 1, 1993), IV, pp. 1, 4.

74 Hager and Cloud, "Democrats Tie their Fate," p. 2129; Jonathan Rauch, "Stage Two," *National Journal* (August 7, 1993), p. 1963.

75 *Challenge Magazine*, "From Stagnation to Renewed Growth," interview with Laura D'Andrea Tyson (May–June 1994), pp. 18, 20.

76 Ibid., p. 20.

77 Ibid., pp. 20–1; emphasis added.

78 Ibid., p. 21.

79 *Fortune*, "Clinton Speaks on the Economy," interview with Bill Clinton (August 23, 1993), pp. 58–60.

80 For example, *Fortune*, "The Job Drought" (August 24, 1992), pp. 62–7, 70, 74; *Fortune*, "When Will the Layoffs End?" (September 20, 1993), pp. 54–6; *Business Week*, "No Help Wanted" (September 21, 1992), pp. 26–9; *Business Week*, "Jobs, Jobs, Jobs" (February 22, 1993), pp. 68–71, 74; Pascal Zachary and Bob Ortega, "Age of Angst: Workplace Revolution Boosts Productivity at Cost of Job Security," *Wall Street Journal* (March 10, 1993), pp. A1, A8; Clare Ansbery, "Hired Out: Workers are Forced to Take More Jobs with Fewer Benefits," *Wall Street Journal* (March 11, 1993), pp. A1, A9.

81 On this point see Jonathan Fuerbringer, "Clinton Plan's Economic Drag Cited," *New York Times* (August 5, 1993), p. D16.

82 Dowd, "How to Get Things Done," p. 62.

83 *Business Week*, "Why Business Hates Clinton" (October 10, 1994), pp. 38–40.

84 See the analysis of the 1996 election by Ruy Teixeira, "Finding the Real Center," *Dissent* (Spring, 1997), pp. 51–9. Teixeira argues that Clinton's victory was due more to his defense of *old* Democrat programs like social security, Medicare, and education than to his moving to the right on social issues.

# 11

# The Failure of Health-Care Reform

## The Role of Big Business in Policy Formation

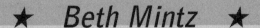

## ★ Beth Mintz ★

## Introduction

The introduction of the Clinton Administration's Health Security Act of 1993, while an historic moment in American history, is likely to remain among the most controversial episodes in President Clinton's first term in office. Under the leadership of Hillary Rodham Clinton, the 500 or so academics, consultants, and government employees on the President's Task Force on Health Care produced a 1,364-page plan aimed at revamping a sector of the economy approaching 15 percent of the GDP and employing millions of workers. Earlier failed attempts at health-care reform – most far less ambitious than this – characterized the terms of some of the most illustrious presidents of the twentieth century, yet in the early 1990s the reform effort seemed ripe for success.

In the public arena continued corporate downsizing, costing millions of Americans their jobs and their health insurance, had made visible a problem that had long been developing. In both government and business circles, health-care costs had been of major concern for decades. This is illustrated by President Nixon's attempt to extend the

Health Maintenance Organization (HMO) model as the service-delivery form of choice for the American public, and in President Carter's proposed moratorium on public subsidies of health construction projects. In the private sector, in the early 1970s, *Business Week* labelled the US health-care system a "$60 billion crisis";[1] soon after, the Business Roundtable created the Washington Business Group on Health as a vehicle for big business participation in health-care policy formation.[2]

The health-care problems that emerged in public debate in the early 1990s, then, had been recognizable – and pressing – for quite some time. Nevertheless, neither the magnitude of the issue nor the public scrutiny of a weakened system was sufficient to carry the reform effort.

Many different analyses have been offered to explain the failure of the Clinton plan, the most common focussing on one or some combination of the following: the lack of public dialogue; the inexperience – or bungling – of the new administration; the effectiveness of the Health Insurance Association of America's (HIAA) "Harry and Louise" advertising campaign; or the Democratic unwillingness to move toward the center. The institutional analysis articulated by Steinmo and Watts provides still another view, suggesting that American political institutions are biased against this type of reform.[3] Other argue that the plan was simply too ambitious. And, indeed, the proposal was so big, so detailed, and so complex that everyone could find in it at least one extremely distasteful component.

While each of these explanations addresses a part of the larger process, they do not offer an effective framework for understanding public policy development and implementation. An important question in understanding policy formation on the general level, which has not been clarified is the role of the business community in the policy process. The Clinton health-care plan offers a particularly interesting opportunity to explore this issue, since health-care costs have been of long-term concern to the American big business community. This chapter, therefore, explores big business's role in the Clinton plan, addressing three questions specifically: (1) What was big business's interest in health care, including its role in the formation of the reform proposal?; (2) What was big business's role in the failure of the plan?; and (3) What implications can we draw for the public policy formation process in general?

## Big Business Interest in the Health-Care Question

The employer-based nature of the United States health-care system has been experienced by big business as enormously expensive, and this has made health care a particularly important issue in the business community. When considered as a group, business purchases health services for a majority of American workers: By 1992, despite severe downsizing and concerted efforts by corporations to reduce their overall health care costs, 62.5 percent of United States employees were still covered by some type of employer-based insurance.[4] In 1991, these costs translated into an average of $3,217 per worker and accounted for more than 25 percent of employers' net earnings.[5] Between 1970 and 1989, when measured in 1989 dollars, employer health-care spending increased by 164 percent.[6]

In recent years, there has been disagreement over the actual impact of these costs on corporate profitability, with some experts arguing that health-care spending is ultimately borne by labor in the form of wage stagnation or job flight.[7] Note, however, that many companies believe that it is their bottom lines, rather than workers' paychecks, that bear the brunt. Chrysler's Walter Maher suggests, for example, that the United States auto industry competes with foreign companies that have a $300–500-per-car health-care cost advantage.[8] With fierce foreign competition, he notes, compensating price increases are not feasible and, given the rates of health-care inflation, even annual wage cuts would not solve the problem.

Thus, while the actual impact of spiraling health-care costs on corporate profitability is under debate, many business perceive employee health-care benefits as critical to long-term performance ratios. And many consider the health-care system to be in extreme difficulty. By the early 1990s, 54 percent of a sample of business executives believed that the United States was "facing a health care crisis."[9] Similarly, 80 percent of those executives believed fundamental changes in health care are needed.[10] Overall corporate concern with health-care costs, then, was the background in which the Clinton plan was introduced.

### Big business and the Clinton plan

The health-reform proposal that President Clinton announced in September of 1993 was carefully crafted by Hillary Clinton's famous task force on health care. The details were developed and refined on the basis of input from over 1,000 different interest groups, but the cornerstone of the scheme, managed competition, was introduced many years earlier as a market-based vehicle for cost control and system efficiency.[11] The fundamentals of the idea were especially attractive to large employers and insurance companies because of its reliance on market forces, with a limited government role.[12]

Managed competition as a vehicle for large-scale system reform was also the preferred plan of the famous "Jackson Hole group," a collection of policy professionals and health-industry representatives that had been meeting for years to develop a viable plan for health reform, hoping "to head off stronger doses of government financing and regulation that would be a threat to big private insurers and private health care delivery systems."[13] Its members included insurance-company executives; drug manufacturers; representatives of major hospitals, physician groups and HMOs; policy experts; administration officials; and members of Congress. Among its financial sponsors were Aetna Life & Casualty, Prudential, and Metropolitan Life; and its work provided the framework for the Clinton proposal.[14] Thus, the Health Security Act of 1993, carefully crafted by policy experts and Washington insiders, was formulated on a series of assumptions and requirements consistent with the needs of a visible and articulate portion of the big business community.

Two points are particularly important about these developments. First, the contours of the health-reform proposal reflected the interests and preferences of the big business community. We see this in the market-based nature of the reform effort and in the relationship between the work of the Jackson Hole group and the Clinton plan. We also see it in the absence of a single-payer plan, an alternative scheme that many experts believed to be highly superior to the introduced legislation and that Skocpol suggests "would be highly threatening to established stakeholders in health care markets."[15]

Second, the contours of the *debate* about health reform excluded a single-payer option. The entire discourse about the reform effort was organized around the strengths and weaknesses of managed competition; the Health Security Act became the left position as countered by the partisan market adjustment message of the Republican Party. This was clear as the US watched the analysis of the proposal on the news following the President's address to a joint session of Congress as he introduced his bill: The networks, in the spirit of balance, gave equal time to counter-positions promptly turning only to the Republican Party's response.

On a more systematic level, data presented in the *Columbia Journalism Review* suggest that the national media embraced managed competition to the exclusion of other options.[16] In the period between May 1991 and July 1993, they report, 35 *New York Times* editorials endorsed managed competition, occasionally blasting the single-payer model with allegation and inaccuracy, leading the authors to suggest that "thanks in part to ... *The New York Times*, managed competition has been elevated from a theory hatched by insurance executives, physicians, and academics meeting at Jackson Hole ... to the leading blueprint for health care reform."[17]

It was for good reason, then, that the Clinton Administration was confident that their proposal would be well received by a big business community that believed that health care was in crisis, and endorsed the model that became the template for reform.[18] And in the immediate aftermath of the plan's unveiling, the most important business lobbies and health-care coalitions – the Business Roundtable, the United States Chamber of Commerce, the National Association of Manufacturers, the Washington Business Group on Health, the National Leadership Coalition for Health Care Reform, and the Jackson Hole Group – gave formal support to the major goals of the Clinton plan.[19] Given this support, then, and the bipartisan pressure that it could generate, the Health Security Act of 1993 looked like a success. Of course, this was not the case. While it is clear that the failure of the plan can be attributed to multiple causes, many agree that the withdrawal of the Business Roundtable was the defining event. How, then, did this support unravel and what are the implications for the policy formation process?

### Business interests reflected in the policy debate

Most students of intercorporate relations agree that the business community is not monolithic and that differences in interests are more common than points of agreement and shared agendas. Indeed it is this observation that has generated a vast literature on intercorporate organization, examining the extent and conditions under which a divided business community can pursue a unified political agenda. In the health-care case, there has been little evidence to suggest that big business as a whole has been able to organize, despite ongoing concern with health-care costs.[20] As a result, recent work has begun examining the divergent interests of business in relation to health-care profitability, and these differences provide an effective map for understanding an important part of business ambivalence about health-care reform.[21]

The lines of division thought to prevent health-care activism in many ways echo standard differences characterizing intercorporate relations in general. These include differences in interest between the large and the small business community, between industrial and service-sector firms, and between financial and non-financial institutions, as well as interindustry variations. What distinguishes health care from other issues, though, is that typical policy questions affect a limited number of corporate sectors, while most United States companies have some stake in the health-care

debate. The movement for reform, then, has implications for the bottom lines of all but the smallest companies and, thus, the types of differences characterizing corporate America in general are brought into stark relief in the health-care example. This explains, in important ways, why the Clinton plan was the "most heavily lobbied legislative initiative in recent U.S history."[22]

## Potential Winners, Potential Losers, and the Middle Ground

Although the Clinton plan for health reform was consistent with the general interests of the large business community and the reform strategy of choice of corporate America, not all companies were equally privileged by the plan. Three components of the proposal were most important in relation to individual corporate profitability, with each component affecting different companies in different ways. They are: (1) managed competition; (2) employer mandates; and (3) insurance premium caps, regional health alliances, and community ratings. In addition, the regulatory nature of the overall plan had potential economic and ideological implications to which the business community reacted.

### Managed competition

Managed competition, the foundation of the health-reform package, was particularly attractive to large insurers since it emphasized an HMO variant of managed care, a development that the biggest insurance companies were well positioned to exploit. Having entered the HMO market in force in the late 1980s,[23] it is not surprising that insurance-owned managed-care companies dominated insurance-industry spending on lobbying and campaign contributions.[24]

Smaller insurers, on the other hand, remained mainly dependent upon traditional indemnity plans and, therefore, were extremely vulnerable to the capitated form of managed care that drove the reform effort. One insurance industry spokesperson speculated that health-care reform could reduce the number of United States insurance companies by 30–50 percent; Himmelstein and Woolhandler predicted the survival of only five or six of the largest firms.[25]

Managed competition in itself, therefore, provided the basis for what developed into a highly visible and effective component of the anti-reform movement. It generated a split within the insurance industry, although this was not evident in the public debate. The largest companies withdrew from the industry's premier trade association, the HIAA, to pursue their own agenda of expanded HMO usage. In the public mind, however, the HIAA remained the voice of the industry and the voice of opposition to Clinton's health-care plan. Their highly effective "Harry and Louise" advertising campaign brought strong public visibility to the debate; this, coupled with behind-the-scenes lobbying of potential insurance "losers," fed the anti-reform posture of the Republican Party.

Note that, even though the largest insurers were extremely well positioned given the managed-care foundation of the Clinton plan, large insurance as a group did not read their interests in identical ways. In the early days of discussion, Aetna, for example, reacted favourably to the bill, while Travelers viewed it as an "extreme government-oriented version" of health reform. This difference suggests that structural location alone cannot account for a company's interpretation of its material interest. As we see below, however, as the debate progressed Travelers' position became more and more typical.

In sum, while some critics of the Health Security Act of 1993 read the proposal as a gift to the insurance industry, the insurance industry itself did not see it quite that way.

The managed-competition framework was a crucial point of division separating large insurers from mid-size and small companies. These differences led to radically different positions vis-à-vis the reform movement and radically different strategies for influencing the debate. Finally even large insurers, the potential victors of the plan, were at odds with some of the specific provisions, and this led to a different set of divisions within corporate American, to be discussed below.

### Employer mandates

The "Harry and Louise" media campaign of the HIAA was the most publicly visible anti-reform effort of the debate on health reform, but the NFIB's well-orchestrated strategy was probably the most effective. Small business as a group had much to lose if required to provide health insurance for its workers, and it was for this reason that the NFIB opposed the bill. Its strong – and early – stand against mandates was so popular among small businesses that the United States Chamber of Commerce was eventually forced to compete for membership by adopting an anti-reform position.

Yet while employer mandates were most articulately and successfully fought by the NFIB, what began as a division between big and small business developed into a more complex mix of diverging and overlapping sets of interests. At the onset, the Clinton reform proposal targeted big business as a powerful force to attract. And, indeed, the initial reception was quite positive. Since a majority of uninsured Americans are workers who are not covered by employer-sponsored health-care plans, the employer-mandate portion of the plan would address the problem of cost shifting: the pricing practice in which the insured subsidize the medical costs of the uninsured. And, thus, big business sentiment toward employer mandates was rather sympathetic. Martin reported that 54 percent of her sample of large business leaders supported the notion;[26] both the Business Roundtable and the Chamber of Commerce accepted the necessity of mandates, and some of their members embraced them with enthusiasm.

Not all large businesses shared this attitude, however. As Judis points out, several different positions were apparent within the Business Roundtable, much of which reflected the individual interests of member companies.[27] While firms like IBM and Eastman-Kodak supported employer mandates, some very large corporations had diversified into sectors characterized by part-time workers and minimal benefit plans. These included such corporate giants as Sears, Pepsico, and Marriott, which were strongly against coverage requirements. An executive of General Mills articulated this group's position well when he noted the need for some minor changes in underwriting practices and universal access: "Beyond that, we felt that the health care market, which has been in rapid change anyway, would develop reasonable alternatives for people."[28]

Some firms took an ideological rather than an economic stand. These included an assortment of companies that insured their employees, believed that health-care reform would bring large savings, but feared the expansion of interventionalist government. Still other companies initially supported employer mandates but found the proposed plan to be overly generous: It required businesses to pay 80 percent of the health-care coverage costs of their workers, to a maximum of 7.9 percent of a company's payroll. Thus, the reform package assumed a universal standard of employer coverage previously available in only the best plans, with these "cadillac" programs themselves becoming fewer and fewer.

As the details of the plan became better understood, then, and the administration's spin on key components developed, the employer-mandate provision became extremely controversial. What had begun as a reform provision that big business conceivably could support developed into an issue characterized by lines of division and points of cleavage reflecting different economic interests, as well as different ideological positions. Some have interpreted this as an example of how business cannot overcome individual interests and organize effectively.[29] Kosterlitz suggests, however, that business's support for employer mandates was always conditional and that many contingencies can be found in formal statements of support.[30]

This suggests that while in theory an employer mandate was in the overall interest of the big business community, the specifics of the proposed mandate were troubling. Coupled with other worrisome provisions of the bill, the Clinton proposal presented a problematic package with too much uncertainty about its long-term ramifications. Thus, we wonder whether the divisions within the business community, thought responsible for the withdrawal of big business's support for the Clinton plan, might obscure a more unified position, one based on the uncertainty of the long-run implications of the proposed reform package.

*Insurance premium caps, regional alliances, and community ratings*

Health-care companies found themselves in a peculiar position amid the reform debate. Earlier, we explored the divisions within the insurance industry in relation to managed care. On the question of employer mandates, insurance's position was not as clear: Requiring employers to provide coverage for their workers was consistent with the material interest of the entire industry. Many feared, however, that such requirements would be accompanied by less attractive government provisions, including insurance premium caps and community ratings. And it is in the question of the role of government intervention that we find the overlap of individual corporate interest and ideological position.

The ideological stand against employer mandates assumed by a small segment of the corporate community was echoed by many firms and industries when insurance premium caps, regional alliances, and community ratings were considered. Health-care companies in general – not only insurers, but hospital corporations and pharmaceuticals as well – actively opposed premium caps out of economic self-interest, and they were represented by the Health Care Leadership Council, a lobbying group of about 55 CEO's.[31] Some firms supported insurance caps but were less clear about the regional alliances that the Clinton plan required. Proposed as a vehicle for reintroducing community ratings – the spreading of risk among large groups of people – the plan called for the formation of regional purchasing cooperatives of about one million people that would negotiate competitive contracts with insurance companies. While the idea was attractive to the same large insurance companies that favored managed care, it was strongly opposed by the HIAA, whose members were too small to compete effectively for these contracts. Businesses employing over 5,000 workers were not required to join these alliances, but many firms still worried about their regulatory nature,[32] and some companies that supported employer mandates were concerned about their ability to continue to self-insure or to purchase insurance nationally on terms they negotiated.[33]

Thus, when we explore the details of government regulation in the context of the Clinton health-care plan, we see a dimension of uncertainty that is shared – in some cases for very different reasons – by a variety of corporations with very different interests vis-à-vis health-care reform. What began as a discussion of splits and divisions within the corporate community based on the economic consequences of the present health-care system can be viewed from another vantage point: the potential costs of a proposal that was seen as overbureaucratized and overregulated.

## Business Withdrawal and the Cooper Plan

Given the uncertainty that developed within the big business community over the Clinton proposal, Representative Jim Cooper's alternative health-care bill became a plausible substitute. Cosponsored by Senator John Breaux of Louisiana, it offered a less regulated version of health reform that was labeled "Clinton lite" by many. It reflected the original market-driven, managed-competition model developed by the Jackson Hole group, offering universal access rather than universal coverage, and including neither employer mandates nor insurance caps. It quickly became the preferred legislation of the five largest insurance companies, which were well positioned under a managed-care model, but feared the prospect of premium caps.[34] The lack of employer mandates helped generate much interest as well.

The official big business position on the Clinton health proposal came from the Business Roundtable when, in February of 1994, it officially announced its support for the Cooper–Breaux bill, arguing that it was "built around market mechanisms rather than mandates".[35] This stand was decisive in crystallizing overall business sentiment and was soon followed by similar positions assumed by the NAM and the Chamber of Commerce.[36]

Note that the Business Roundtable's support for the Cooper bill should not be interpreted as a united front in favor of the actual legislation, since it was, in the final analysis, only cosmetic. The endorsement rejected the financing mechanism central to the plan, and thus the Roundtable's position should be read as a rejection of the Clinton plan, but not as a serious attempt to find an alternative that could actually become law.

Nevertheless, this withdrawal of support for the President's health-reform agenda has been interpreted by many as the final blow.

According to Representative John Dingle, the chair of the important House of Representatives Energy and Commerce Committee, "When the President failed to get the [Business Roundtable], there was a shift in sentiment inside the committee . . . that was a defining event."[37]

Many have argued that this rejection of the Clinton plan was caused by business's inability to overcome its differences and act in concert. Skocpol, for example, suggests that societal groups, including big business, are not organized into peak organizations where leaders can act on behalf of all their members.[38] Similarly, Judis suggests that the health-care example illustrates a fundamental problem within the business community: Inescapable conflicts that typically prevent unity are overcome only under extraordinary circumstances.[39]

The specifics of many of the analyses of the Business Roundtable's decision making on the issue of health-care reform are consistent with these conclusions. The dominance of executives from large insurance companies, coupled with disproportionate representation of both health-care firms and companies that did not fully insure their workers, has been interpreted as demonstrating that the Business Roundtable had been captured by a narrow, but powerful, segment of the big business community. Thus, instead of mediating among the different interests characterizing the corporate world, the Roundtable's position reflected the needs of the few. And, indeed, the composition of the Health, Welfare, and Retirement Income Task Force, the group charged with generating a position on health policy for the Roundtable as a whole, heavily represented those sectors most likely to oppose the Clinton plan. As the group was chaired by the CEO of Prudential Insurance had a strong presence from health-care companies and large restaurant-chain owners, decision making within it has been interpreted as one-sided.[40] Similarly the Washington Business Group on Health was chaired by Mary Jane England, a former Prudential executive, and an active participant in the Jackson Hole group.[41]

Here I offer an alternative explanation: The defection of big business can be viewed as a unified action, based not on the ability of a narrow, self-interested segment to dominate the decision-making process, but on the uncertainty that the Clinton proposal generated for the big business community. What was originally perceived as an opportunity to end cost shifting, to defray some of the costs of health-care coverage for early retirees, and to contain costs on the basis of a market-driven model of reform developed into an extremely complex, overly-regulated plan carrying new financial burdens in the form of premium taxes and restrictions on self-insurance.[42] Thus, while there is much evidence to suggest that the key decision makers within the Business Roundtable were drawn from firms with clearly defined vested interests, it is less obvious that this represents the betrayal of a broader business interest. By the time the business community acted, its confidence in the ability of the Clinton proposal to solve its health-care problems had eroded; it was understandably unwilling to sign on, given the level of uncertainty that had developed. Moreover, many believed that passage of the bill would create an open-ended entitlement program that would ultimately raise taxes and increase the federal deficit.[43] And these fears were exacerbated by a profound distrust of the White House.[44] Given these uncertainties, business's rejection of the Clinton plan is difficult to view as the self-serving agenda of the powerful few.

## The Larger Political Context

Business's actions and reactions, of course, were only one – and in some ways a minor –

part of the larger reform debate. Many different groups had enormous stakes in the final outcome of any health-care system reform attempt, and many made their intentions quite visible in Washington political circles. Citizens for a Sound Economy, for example, formed a loose alliance of conservative special interest groups, including the Christian Calliton and the National Tascpayers Union, that lobbied intensively against the Clinton plan. The largest Political Action Committee (PAC) contributors of 1993 and 1994, with health-related interests, included the following non-business groups: the American Federation of State, County and Municipal Employees; the International Brotherhood of Electrical Workers; the United Brotherhood of Carpenters and Joiners; the Association of Trial Lawyers; the American Medical Association; the American Maritime Officers; the American Dental Association; and the American Chiropractic Association.[45] Add to this the American Association of Retired Persons (AARP), with its 33 million members and a $300-million annual budget; the AFL-CIO, representing 87 unions and 14 million workers; and the non-business component of the more than 1,000 organized lobbying groups that addressed Hilary Clinton's health-care task force.[46] Advocates of the Canadian-style single-payer system, effectively excluded from the debate before it began, represented still another point of view trying to be heard.

The Republican Party's response to the Clinton proposal was obviously crucial. As Johnson and Broder point out, what began as a heavily ideological campaign by powerful right-wing Republicans to paint the plan as a model of big-government inefficiency turned into a strategy that weakened the Democrats in general leading to the "electoral earthquake" of 1994.[47] The success of this campaign, as the environment in which the Republicans introduced their seemingly invincible "Contract With America" is addressed in more

detail elsewhere in this volume; here suffice it to say that the Republicans were quite successful in relation to health-care reform. Given these actors, how important, then, was business in either the formulation of the Clinton proposal or the final outcome?

Two different analyses of the origins of Clinton's Health Security Act come to mind in this context. The first is Skocpol's persuasive argument about the politics of the possible, in which any plan introduced with a serious intention of passage had to please, or at least pass muster with, a wide assortment of other interest groups.[48] Thus, she suggests, Clinton presented a solidly middle-of-the-road proposal designed to alienate the smallest number while attracting the support of some powerful interests. This could not include a single-payer plan, favored by many knowledgeable health economists, a variety of labor unions, and health-care activists, since the Clinton administration believed that: (1) a tax increase, either direct or in the form of a payroll tax, was not possible; (2) such a plan would cause wholesale unemployment in the insurance industry, a major employer; and (3) it would alienate the many Americans who, although rarely visible, were happy with their health-care coverage.

In this view, Clinton's plan was designed to appeal to "New Democrats" who wanted market-oriented reform that included cost control, and who understood the need for universal coverage in preventing cost shifting. It was also crafted with an eye on the public's desire for affordable coverage; and with its emphasis on managed competition, it was believed attractive to the big business community, whose support was seen as important to the plan.

Note that this analysis views big business in particular as a powerful force to attract, and that the formulation of the reform package directly addressed big business's needs. It was only one of many interest groups, however, and therefore its needs – to the extent that it could be considered as a group – were not formative.

Here I would like to offer an alternative scenario. Earlier I emphasized both big business participation in the Jackson Hole group, where the template for the Clinton plan was developed, and the absence of the single-payer alternative in the public debate about reform. This locates business's role in the policy-formation process in a very different place. Rather than one of many interests to be considered, big business preference defined the contours of debate.

In both scenarios, the politics of the possible or business preference, the outcome was the same: The negotiations, the concessions, the trading that characterize the legislative process, in general, took their toll on the Clinton plan. Independent of whether the proposal originated with the needs of big business or incorporated those needs as belonging to one of many actors to be taken into account, the bill evolved into something that big business could not support. This raises an important question: If big business could not control the outcome, does its role in policy formulation matter? And the answer is a decided "yes." Both analyses offer similar conclusions about the future of health reform: Quite possibly, with the defeat of the Clinton plan, we have lost our last chance of achieving universal coverage.[49] The origin of the loss is of issue, however. Skocpol's argument suggests that what many experts viewed as the best option for real reform – a single-payer system – was excluded because it was believed to be unattainable, given the political realities of the 1990s. My argument is very different: The absence of the single-payer plan was the result of business participation in policy formation, and it was this participation that defined the parameters of the debate. While this does not suggest that, if on the agenda, a single-payer plan would necessarily have passed, the discourse about reform would certainly have been different,

as would the boundaries between left and right.

Thus, independent of whether we understand business's official posture on health reform as resulting from its inability to come to agreement, in the way many critics have suggested, or as a united stand in the face of a proposal that carried risks too great to ignore, in the way we have suggested here, the role of business in the overall process remains an extremely important question. The Clinton proposal was soundly defeated. The outlines of the plan, however, with its emphasis on market reform and the role of large insurance, emerged as *the* model of health-care delivery, and the implications of this, we suggest, remain the most important component of the larger debate.

## Legislative Failure, Market Success

The major irony of the debate over health-care reform is that while Congress rejected any sort of national plan, the United States underwent a health-care revolution. This did not begin with the Business Roundtable's statement of support for the Cooper bill or with the official defeat of the Clinton plan. Nevertheless, while Congress argued, private market forces were implementing the type of consolidation and innovation that critics predicted passage would encourage. According to the *New York Times*, "In the two years that Congress wrangled over health care . . . private market forces were acting on their own to transform the country's medical system dramatically.[50]

While managed care did not originate with the Clinton proposal, defeat of the plan did nothing to slow its spread. By the end of 1994, a majority of employer-sponsored health programs were managed-care plans, which – Harry and Louise notwithstanding – greatly limit both one's choice of doctors and available treatments. And, as the *New York Times* notes, a majority of HMOs, the most stringent form of managed care, are now for-profit enterprises in the business of money making, and more than three-quarters of practicing physicians have signed contracts with managed-care companies requiring the physicians to cut their fees and accept direct oversight of their medical decisions.[51]

What this suggests is that the assumptions that framed the Health Security Act of 1993 endured, despite the formal defeat of the plan. Even that portion of the Clinton proposal that sounded the most radical, "mandatory alliances," is familiar to anyone who works for a large organization, with its enrollment periods, choice of networks, and copayment requirements.[52]

What is clear, then, is that, as Skocpol acknowledges, private market forces have been rapidly transforming both health-care delivery and finance, as managed care becomes the normative health-care arrangement in the United States.[53] I suggest that this transformation is fundamentally altering health-care delivery as we know it, and seriously constraining future possibilities for health reform. Many of the provisions that consumers feared with the Clinton plan – limited choice of physicians, limited access to high-tech treatments, for example – are quickly becoming a reality, despite the failure of the reform proposal. What we have, then, is a protracted and highly visible legislative debate about the future of health delivery, and a market system that is implementing the fundamental tenets of a health-reform proposal that was officially defeated in the legislative arena.

What is the outcome for big business? Many segments of the big business community have fared quite well. Large insurers have gotten managed care without premium caps or community ratings. And they have done so in precisely the way that the HIAA feared: with no protection for smaller companies. In fact, the oligopoly of enormous insurers that some

predicted would emerge from the Clinton plan turns out to be the likely result of nonlegislation.

Employer mandates were not implemented, and this has allowed cost shifting – the indirect subsidizing of employees of firms that do not cover their workers by companies that do – to continue. It also allows employers to try to shift their costs to their workers, and this continues to characterize current employer – labor relations strategies in the post-reform period. Thus far, the effort has been extremely successful.

The threat of increased government intervention that many feared disappeared with the plan's defeat: Employers maintained control over their health-care plans with the flexibility prescribed in the Employment Retirement Security Act of 1974, and this should be viewed as an important outcome. Finally, future prospects for a single-payer plan, with its government intrusion into health delivery and its replacement of the private health-insurance industry, look bleak as market forces become the vehicle for system adjustment.

Thus, the failure of the Clinton healthcare plan has worked quite well for big business on the general level. Some companies have fared better than others, but in overview, the defeat of the Clinton health-reform bill has had quite a positive impact.

## Conclusion

To return to the role of the (big) business community in the public policy process, several questions about business's participation in the health-reform debate have been raised. Under the larger questions of big business's interest in health care and its role in the failure of the Clinton plan, a series of other issues about the relationship between the big business and the reform proposal has been addressed.

The first question is about business's role in the formation of the Clinton plan, and many agree that big business, or at least big insurance, was well represented in its formative stages as paid participants in the famous Jackson Hole group. This participation did not produce a final proposal that could be embraced by either the participants or the larger business community, suggesting that even though business was well represented in the (extragovernmental) planning stages, it could not control the larger process. The negotiations characterizing legislative debate created a proposal with too much uncertainty and risk for business support.

Thus, the first conclusion that we draw from the example of the recent health-reform attempt is that even if major segments of the big business community participate in the policy-formation process, they cannot control the larger debate. Ultimately, they become one of many interest groups operating in the legislative arena.

This does not suggest that all groups are equal, however, as illustrated by the most recent developments in health-care delivery. Above we noted that current trends in the growth of managed-care systems are closely following the Jackson Hole group's plan for health reform. Here we suggest that the final outcome, as it looks at the time of writing at least, is the implementation of the most fundamental part of that plan. From this we conclude that even though big business could not shape the policy-negotiation process, its preference was the one that was implemented. And the market-driven, rather than interventionist, nature of that implementation is consistent with the vision of the larger business community.

Moreover, the most interesting results of the debate over health reform include both the manipulation and the absence of public opinion as a force to be considered in the future of the American delivery system. We see this in the omission of a single-payer plan as a viable alternative to managed competition or managed care. And we see it in the implementation of a managed-care model that realizes the public's worst fears: limited choices of physicians and limitations on coverage.

In evaluating the outcome of the debate over health-care reform, then, I draw the following conclusions: While big business was one of many groups influencing the policy-formation process, it fared much better than most. And when we compare the results with the priorities of the American public, it is safe to say that big business won, hands down.

The long-term debate about the relationship between big business and the state has addressed the ability of big business to organize, and recent research has explored the conditions which generate collective action. The Clinton health-care plan offers some insight into this process. Here I take very seriously big business's input into the original formulation and argue that the Business Roundtable's decision not to support the Clinton plan is an example of shared interest, given the specific provisions that the legislative negotiation process generated.

This example of unified action is a weak variant, however, when we consider it in light of what was not done: Why did the Business Roundtable, for example, not lobby more forcefully for the development of a plan that it could support? As we have seen, some analysts argue that this was the result of the inability of the business community to overcome its differences and act in concert in a proactive way. Others suggest that the economic recovery lessened the perceived import of official reform, allowing some crucial actors to withdraw from the debate entirely.

Here I offer a different possibility: I suggest that an inhibiting factor in business's ability to organize on this issue is the level of complexity and uncertainty inherent in any health-reform plan. As we have seen, the individual interests of different segments of the corporate community diverged and cross-cut in multiple ways. While two sectors saw their interests very differently in some components of reform, their economic interests overlapped in others. In still other cases, firms in the same industry with the same economic interest interpreted these interests in different ways.

Martin argues that corporate political capacity – the ability of corporate executives to understand issues and to act on that understanding – influences the degree of business support for policy innovation.[54] I agree, and suggest that both the number of unknowns and the intricacies of health-care financing and health-care delivery – which themselves were in flux – overtaxed the capacity of individual corporations to evaluate the details of the debate. Hence, an important part of corporate inaction was the result of uncertainty about not understanding the consequences of specific proposals. I suggest, then, that one of the conditions required for collective business action is some degree of confidence about the implications of a position.

The uncertainty that developed over the consequences of the Clinton proposal helps explain why corporations in the same structural location can take different positions on policy issues. Earlier I noted that Aetna Life and Travelers, two of the largest insurance companies in the United States, reacted quite differently to the initial draft of the Clinton bill. Theoretically, the reform proposal would have affected both companies in identical ways, but this was not reflected in their response to the bill's provisions. Many non-structural forces may account for these differences, and corporate political capacity is an important notion to consider. Differences in corporate culture or the ideology of the leadership team are other possibilities to explore in our attempts at understanding the conditions that generate collective action within the big business community.

Finally, what does this case tell us about the consequences of business's inability to act forcefully in a proactive way? In some cases, at least, the result is still an outcome consistent with business's larger interests; in this case, the market-driven implementation of a managed-care model of health reform.

## Notes

1 Paul Starr quoted in Theda Skocpol, *Boomerang: Clinton's Health Security Effort and the Turn against Government in U.S. Politics* (New York: W. W. Norton, 1996).

2 Beth Mintz, "Business Participation in Health Care Policy Reform: Factors Contributing to Collective Action Within the Business Community," *Social Problems* 42 (August, 1995), pp. 408–28.

3 Sven Steinmo and Jon Watts, "It's the Institutions, Stupid! Why Comprehensive National Health Insurance Always Fails in America," *Journal of Health Politics, Policy and Law* 20 (Summer, 1995), pp. 329–89.

4 Center for Public Integrity, "Well-Healed: Inside Lobbying for Health Care Reform, Part III," *International Journal of Health Services* 25 (3) (1996), pp. 19–46.

5 Betty Leyerle, *The Private Regulation of American Health Care* (Armonk NY: M. E. Sharpe, 1994).

6 Paul Starr, *The Logic of Health Care Reform* (New York: Penguin, 1992).

7 Uwe E. Reinhardt, "Health Care Spending and American Competitiveness," *Health Affairs* 8 (Fall, 1989), pp. 5–21.

8 Walter Maher, "Back to Marketplace Basics," *Health Affairs* 9 (Spring, 1990), pp. 169–70.

9 Quoted in Cathie Jo Martin, "Mandating Social Change: The Struggle within Corporate America over National Health Reform," paper presented at the annual meeting of the American Political Science Association (1994), p. 10.

10 Joel Cantor, Nancy Barrard, Randolph Desonia, Alan Cohen and Jeffrey Merril, "Business Leaders' Views on American Health Care," *Health Affairs* (Spring 1991) pp. 99–101.

11 Starr, *Logic of Health Reform*.

12 Haines Johnson and David Broder, *The System: The American Way of Politics at the Breaking Point* (Boston: Little, Brown, 1996).

13 Skocpol, *Boomerang.*

14 Center for Public Integrity, "Well-Healed: Inside Lobbying for Health Care Reform, Part II," *International Journal of Health Services* 25 (4) (1995), pp. 593–632.

15 Skocpol, *Boomerang.* Given the role of large insurers in the plan's formulation, it is not surprising that some critics labeled the proposal the "Health Insurance Preservation Act." Note, though, the crucial distinction between the largest and smaller insurance companies, to be discussed below. While the plan favored the very largest insurers, it probably meant the demise of smaller companies.

16 The Kaiser Health Reform Media Monitoring Project, "Newspaper Coverage of Health Care Reform April 1–July 31, 1993: A Content Analysis," *Columbia Journalism Review* 32 (4) (November/December, 1993), p. 1.

17 Ibid.

18 Theda Skocpol, "The Rise and Resounding Demise of the Clinton Health Care Plan," *Health Affairs* 14 (1995), pp. 66–104.

19 John Judis, "Abandoned Surgery," *American Prospect* 21 (Spring, 1995), pp. 65–73.

20 Note that prior to the defeat of the Clinton plan, some students of corporate behavior were still expressing guarded optimism about business's ability to organize. See Linda Bergthold, "American Business and Health Care Reform," *American Behavioral Scientist* 36 (July, 1993), pp. 802–12; Cathie Jo Martin, "Together Again: Business, Government, and the Quest for Cost Control," *Journal of Health Politics, Policy and Law* 18 (Summer, 1993), pp. 359–93.

21 See Bergthold, "American Business and Health Care Reform"; Lawrence Brown, "Dogmatic Slumbers: American Business and Health Policy," *Journal of Health Politics, Policy and Law* 18 (Summer, 1993), pp. 339–57; Martin, "Together Again"; Beth Mintz, "The Role of Capitalist Class Relations in the Restructuring of Medicine," in Scott McNall, Rick Fantasia, and Rhonda Levine, eds, *Bringing Class Back In* (Boulder: Westview Press, 1991); Mintz, "Business Participation."

22 Center for Public Integrity, "Well-Healed, Part III."

23 Beth Mintz and Michael Schwartz, "The Relationship between Public and Private Capital Formation: Lessons from the Development of the United States Health Care System," in Takuyoshi Takada, Beth Mintz, and Michael Schwartz's, eds, *Corporate Control, Capital Formation, and Organizational Networks: Intercorporate Relations in Japan and The United States*, (Tokyo: University of Chuo Press, 1996).

24 In early 1993, prior to the introduction of a formal health-care reform proposal, Cigna owned 42 managed-care plans covering 42 states; Prudential owned 28 plans in 18 states; Aetna owned or managed 28 plans in 19 states; and Metropolitan Life owned 14 in 14 states. Nancy Watzman and Patrick Woodall, "Managed Health Care Companies' Lobbying Frenzy," *International Journal of Health Services* 25 (3) (1995), pp. 403–10.

25 Center for Public Integrity, "Well Healed: Part II"; David Himmelstein and Steffie Woolhandler, *The National Health Program Book* (Monroe ME: Common Courage Press, 1994).

26 Martin, "Mandating Social Change."

27 John Judis, "Abandoned Surgery," *American Prospect* 21 (Spring, 1995), pp. 65–73.

28 Quoted in ibid.

29 Graham Wilson, "Interest Groups in the Health Care Debate," in Henry Aaron, ed., *The Problem That Won't Go Away: Reforming U.S. Health Care Financing* (Washington DC: Brookings Institute, 1996).

30 Julie Kosterlitz, "Interest Groups in the Health Care Debate: Comments," in Aaron, *The Problem That Won't Go Away.* The Public Agenda Foundation makes a similar point about national commitment to health reform in general. They describe the "apparent consensus" as a "house of cards that will fall apart with the first gust of reality" (quoted in Johnson and Broder, *System.*

31 Center for Public Integrity, "Well-Healed: Part II."

32 Johnson and Broder, *System.*

33 Center for Public Integrity, "Well-Healed: Inside Lobbying for Health Care Reform, Part

I," *International Journal of Health Services* 25(3) (1995), pp. 411–53.

34 Ibid.

35 Center for Public Integrity, "Well-Healed: Part II, p. 623."

36 Judis, "Abandoned Surgery."

37 Quoted in Dana Priest and Michael Weisskopf, "Health Reform: The Collapse of a Quest," *Washington Post* (October 11, 1994), p. A6.

38 Skocpol, "Rise and Resounding Demise."

39 Judis, "Abandoned Surgery."

40 Michael Weisskopf, "Health Care Lobbies Lobby Each Other," *Washington Post* (March 1, 1994), pp. A8.

41 Judis, "Abandoned Surgery."

42 Richard Lowry. "The Lost Crusade?" *National Review* 46 (September 12, 1994), pp. 21–2.

43 Priest and Weisskopf, "Health Reform."

44 Johnson and Broder, *System.*

45 Center for Public Integrity, "Well-Healed: Part III."

46 Ibid.

47 Johnson and Broder, *System.*

48 Skocpol, *Boomerang.*

49 Ibid.; Himmelstein and Woolhandler, *National Health Program Book.*

50 Erik Eckholm, "While Congress Remains Silent, Health Care Transforms Itself," *New York Times* (December 18, 1994), p. 1.

51 Ibid.

52 James Fallows, "A Triumph of Misinformation," *Atlantic Monthly* 275 (January, 1995), pp. 26–38.

53 Theda Skocpol, "The Aftermath of Defeat," *Journal of Health Politics, Policy and Law* 20 (Summer, 1994), pp. 485–9.

54 Martin, Cathie Jo, "Nature or Nurture? Sources of Firm Preference for National Health Reform," *American Political Science Review* 84 (December, 1995), pp. 898–914.

# Part III
## Acting Out Conservative Ideology

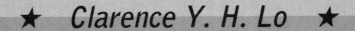

# 12

# The Malignant Masses on CNN

## Media Use of Public Opinion Polls to Fabricate the "Conservative Majority" against Health-Care Reform

## ★ Clarence Y. H. Lo ★

## Introduction

In January 1993, President Bill Clinton was poised to lead the US on a quest to fundamentally change the nation's health-care system with a government guarantee of health insurance for all. But soon the media were full of news stories about opinion polls showing declining public support for Clinton and his health-care plan. Congress failed to pass health-care legislation, and in November, 1994, voters elected a new Republican Congress, which was counterpoised to drastically cut health, welfare, and social-service spending. The American public had rejected the welfare state and had opted for a conservative revolution. Or had they?

In this chapter, I offer a different account of the failure of health-care reform, one that does not assume that press reports of opinion polls are accurate measurements of what the public actually thinks. I first analyze how CNN broadcast opinion poll results, and argue that it reported public rejection of the Clinton plan even before attitudes had really crystallized, and spotlighted the opposition once it did mobilize.

Rather than seeing CNN news stories as evidence of the public's negative judgement of the Clinton health-care plan, I see them as

indicating that media institutions themselves were making negative judgements by selectively highlighting poll results. These judgements, I hypothesize, can be traced back to news sources among political elites in Washington, DC. In particular, conservative Democrats, closely tied to the large business community, strenuously opposed Clinton's health-care reform by arguing that it was costly and bureaucratic, and also unpopular. CNN broadcast these elite arguments, and furthermore, when it emphasized the polls showing opposition to the Clinton plan, it created the impression that it was the people rather than the elites who had rejected universal health insurance.

In addition to both promoting and, ironically, disguising the political elite opposition to Clinton's health-care reform, CNN promoted a style of discourse fostering assumptions that have eroded support of the welfare state. My content analysis of CNN's coverage shows that, at key turning points in the debate, CNN reinforced the notion that public policy should be judged according to the self-interest of individuals rather than the good of society. The individuals who really mattered were upper-middle-class rather than underprivileged. The discourse of individual self-interest helped to shift the goals of health-care reform away from insuring the uninsured, toward preserving the advantages of those who already had insurance.

I thus argue that media reports of public opinion polls were elite-contrived representations of what the public allegedly was thinking. My notion is that elites, not the populace, define and construct public opinion. I sharply differ from the conventional democratic model of public opinion, which asserts that opinion polls provide an accurate gauge of what the public actually thinks about issues and candidates, thereby helping leaders to heed the voice of the people. George Gallup, one of the pioneers of public opinion research in the mid-twentieth century, thought that through polling, the views of Americans could continually influence government, not just during election campaigns.[1]

According to the democratic model, the mass media perform a crucial function when they report on public opinion polls.[2] With the advent of sampling techniques to measure the opinions of an entire population, Philip Meyer and Maxwell McCombs have lauded the use of opinion polls in news stories as "precision journalism." Polling and other instances of precision journalism, such as the use of quantitative data, supposedly increase the accuracy of the news. Thus, according to polling enthusiasts, the citing of opinion polls in the news fulfills two sacred values of the journalistic profession – enlightenment through conveying objective facts, and democracy through fostering civic participation.[3]

Some recent literature on polls and the media, while questioning whether democratic ideals have been fully achieved, nevertheless maintains the assumptions of the conventional model that the United States is basically a democracy. These analysts, whom I call the "improvers," have criticized technical features of polls with an eye to improving their accuracy. Improvers point out that, particularly in telephone interviews, the high non-response rate might compromise poll results, if sub-

jects refusing interviews have opinions markedly different from other respondents. Nuances in the wording of questions and the order in which questions are presented can significantly alter poll findings. Other improvers, notably Everett Carll Ladd, have criticized journalists for failing to adequately report the complexities and methodological underpinning of polls, leading to the misuse of polling data.[4] But despite their criticisms, the improvers expect that refinements in polling techniques and in the quality of journalism will enhance the democratic process.

Some believe that the America of polls and electoral campaigns is the embodiment of the democratic ideal or is, at least, but one small reform away from democracy. By contrast, the skeptics contend that the actual functioning of the American political system is far from approaching democratic ideals. Some skeptics, whom I term skeptics of below, have questioned whether most citizens are even capable of political participation. Philip Converse argued in a pivotal essay that most citizens do not hold meaningful political beliefs, because citizens lack basic information and consistent world views. However, my approach, like that of Stuart Hall, Todd Gitlin, Lance Bennett, and Robert Entman, whom I call skeptics of above, blames the lapses of American democracy on the shortcomings of elites and elite institutions rather than the citizenry.[5]

In my characterization of media coverage, I will depart from the assumption of precision journalism enthusiasts that the media are transmitting objective facts when they report on opinion polls. My approach to the mass media builds upon the sociological concept of social construction, which emphasizes that institutions and the taken-for-granted arrangements of everyday life are the historically specific products of persons with unequal power who interact in society.

Social constructionists have argued that the news is something more than an assemblage of important objective facts. There are far too many facts for the media to use in stories. What is crucial is *which* facts get chosen for inclusion in the news. Tuchman argues that journalists utilize networks of established sources to spin a "web of facticity," composed of statements that appear to be facts verifying each other. Gans, in a detailed analysis of the values, institutions, and interests that shape media decisions to disseminate certain stories, lists the criteria by which executives, editors, and the journalists themselves deem some facts newsworthy but not others. The media's end-product, according to Lance Bennett, simplifies complicated and ambiguous information into potent symbols and images.[6]

Decisions to report certain opinion polls as news are judgement calls that can contribute to important political outcomes. An ABC television news story on October 4, 1988, for example, led off with a survey showing that presidential candidate George Bush was leading Michael Dukakis in states that contained an overwhelming majority of electoral votes.[7] Not emphasized was the fact that Dukakis was only five points behind in a national preference poll. The ABC poll set the frame for an immediately upcoming presidential debate. Many pundits commented that in order to have any chance of winning the election, Dukakis needed to score a decisive win in the debate. Dukakis's failure to meet this expectation added to the unfavorable press coverage that contributed to his falling further behind and losing the election.

The media, then, have considerable discretion in deciding how to interpret and publicize poll results, thereby creating a news story with political ramifications.[8] The more the results differ from poll to poll or fluctuate over time, the more leeway the media has for selectivity, to choose a poll that highlights a specific finding and creates a story different from other possible stories. In a primary election campaign, when the public has relatively

little information about the candidates and expresses only tentative attitudes, one would expect the media to have greater latitude to construct news stories, which would have a strong impact on attitudes or even electoral outcomes. After Gennifer Flowers in 1992 played her tape, allegedly containing evidence of an affair with candidate Bill Clinton, the *Boston Globe* published a poll showing that Clinton's support did not fall appreciably. The poll, however, was conducted too soon after the playing of the tape to fully measure how it impacted on respondents' opinions. Although the *Globe* used polls to minimize the effect of this scandal, at other times a feeding frenzy of press reports about voter concern intensifies scandals.[9]

Opinion polls about issues rather than candidates frequently reveal a public with little knowledge of or interest in the substance of policy. Polls on the issues often show a large percentage of "don't know" responses, and attitudes that differ depending on what information is presented to respondents and how questions are phrased. Opinion polls about health-care reform early in the debate in 1993 had precisely these characteristics, enabling elites and the media to play a major role in characterizing public opinion on this issue.[10]

The media have some discretion to pick which poll numbers to publicize. But the media are more constrained in the types of questions that they can choose from and the concerns the questions address. Questions have been standardized; thinking about issues has been structured. Thus, the media coverage of polls about the Clinton health-care plan can be considered as texts that provide examples of broader patterns of discourse, i.e. basic categories of knowing and acting that have been built into the institutions of society.

Discourses are related to a history of practical activity. The media stories about the polls on the Clinton plan are related to the practices of the professional opinion researchers, who feature certain types of questions – about

popularity and self-interest, for example – in
their survey instruments. Campaign consultants and a host of other institutions and professionals are involved in gathering,
disseminating, and utilizing specialized knowledge about public opinion.[11] Discourses are
not only built into the routine functioning of
these institutions; they also are built into the
routine thought patterns of the persons who
work in those institutions, and may be dis-
cerned through a careful reading of the communications of workers in institutions. Those
politicians and political advisers central to
certain discourses about preserving the middle class, for example, could coordinate their
activities ultimately, as I will argue, to defeat
the Clinton plan, because they could easily
communicate, make sense to each other, and
identify themselves to each other as having
shared interests and concerns about the
Clinton plan and politics generally.

Given the inequalities in the distribution
of political power, economic resources, and
knowledge and technology, many discourses
involve the domination of social groups by
others. Only some groups have access to the
technical and financial means to conduct polls;
media ownership is even more highly concentrated. The institutions involved in the
discourses may well have interests that are
not shared by other segments of the population. This chapter will link the content of
media coverage of polls to the interests of
elites and elite institutions.

I will characterize the media coverage of
polls based on a content analysis of the instances when CNN mentioned an opinion poll
on the subject of health-care reform (see this
chapter's methodological appendix). I seek to
typify the poll questions that were mentioned
in the media, thereby exemplifying different
discourses that pollsters, politicians, pundits,
and the media construct about public opinion. The media, for their part, frequently
mentioned polls purporting to measure the
voters' overall approval ratings of the Clinton

health-care plan. Accordingly, the first type
of discourse that I will examine is what I
term the discourse of popularity.[12]

## The Discourse of Popularity: Acting Out Clinton's Slide in the Polls

The media's focus on the popularity of the
Clinton plan is related to the incessant media
coverage of the popularity of presidents and
political candidates. In covering the Clinton
health-care plan, the media frequently reported
results from poll questions like the following:
"Do you approve or disapprove of the Clinton
health-care plan?" These questions attempt
to fathom whether the public supports the
proposals that Clinton enunciated in the 1992
campaign and that his health-care task force
elaborated. But the queries do not mention
the specific provisions of the plan and hence
could be influenced by Clinton's personal
popularity. The questions are part of a discourse in American politics that personalizes
politics, replacing dialog about issues with the
adulation or vilification of specific persons.[13]
Questions of this type also include other snap-
judgement queries that identify the health-
care reform plan with Clinton personally or
ask about stances of other political actors (e.g.
"Do you approve of how the Democrats in
Congress are handling health-care reform?").

In 1993 and 1994 this type of poll question
showed a declining trend of public support
for the Clinton plan. The margin of those
favorable over those opposed was around 30
percentage points during October, 1993, falling to an even split during January, 1994; the
plan was losing by seven points in August,
1994. A very different impression of public
opinion could be obtained from using other
poll questions. In August, 1994, when describing the plan as Clinton's caused those
polled to reject it, reading a summary of the
Clinton plan to respondents without tagging

it with Clinton's name led those favorable to exceed the unfavorable by 24 points.[14] This question was used in surveys infrequently, however. Instead, the discourse of popularity questions accounted for an increasing percentage of poll questions asked during 1993–4 by the Harris Poll, the Wirthlin Group, the NBC/*Wall Street Journal* poll, and the ABC News/*Washington Post* poll: 19 percent in the first quarter of 1993, 32 percent in the first quarter of 1994, and 44 percent in the third quarter of 1994.

I assessed the media coverage of polls by counting the number of instances when the media cited findings from different types of questions. CNN, with its extensive news, features, and talk-show coverage of politics, provided 145 instances where speakers mentioned public opinion polls on health-care reform during the national discussion between January, 1993, and September, 1994. In 47 (32 percent) of the instances, speakers cited questions measuring the popularity of (i.e. respondent favorability to) the Clinton health-care plan. Twelve of the instances mentioned polls on the respondents' favorability toward congressional action on the Clinton proposals.

During the first part of the debate, from Clinton's inauguration in January, 1993, to his address to Congress on September 22, 1993, CNN coverage of the polls on health-care reform was generally favorable to Clinton. Speakers on CNN cited polls on a total of 44 occasions, mentioned 14 times that the public strongly supported major changes in the health-care system, and stated eight times that the public favored universal-coverage health insurance. In these and other ways, the CNN coverage of polls in this period generally had positive implications for the Clinton plan (50-percent positive in the first quarter of 1993, 73-percent positive in the second quarter, and 85-percent in the third).

In the fourth quarter (October to December) of 1993, most major polls, including many of CNN's own, continued to provide favorable

data for the Clinton plan. However, the tone and framing of the CNN poll coverage dramatically shifted from highly positive to 85-percent negative. For example, in their fourth quarter, 1993, reports on the popularity of the Clinton plan, CNN cast negative implications in four out of five instances (compared with no negative out of four instances the previous quarter). On October 30, 1993, in the program *Capital Gang*, host Mark Shields led off, "Support for the [proposed health-care] law and the plan itself has slipped from 57 percent to 43 percent. Tom Foley, is the president's health plan in serious trouble?" The words "slipped" and "serious trouble" tinge the overall message with negative implications. CNN's report made the 43 percent appear to be only a minority favoring the Clinton plan. However, CNN failed to report the percentage opposed and the percentage with no opinion in its own poll, and did not convey that other polls of the time were showing that those favoring the Clinton plan were a plurality over those opposed and a majority of those expressing an opinion, by margins as large as 34 points in a Harris poll.

A CNN news broadcast on the next day, October 31, did report the percentages both in support and in opposition, but the percentage opposed was much higher compared to polls by other organizations. "A new CNN–*USA Today* poll shows respondents equally divided on the Clinton plan – 45 percent support it, 45 percent oppose it. Support is down from a month ago when 59 percent gave it a thumbs up, and 33 percent thumbs down." Eight days later CNN issued another poll that was more in line with the polls by others, which showed a majority in favor of the Clinton plan:

More poll findings. A new CNN–*USA Today* Gallup Poll shows that President Clinton's plan for health care reform has picked up a little support among the U.S. population. Fifty-two percent of the more than 1,000 people surveyed favor[ed] the reform package when questioned on

November 2, 3, and 4. Forty percent were opposed. In late October, the same poll showed 45
percent in favor of the Clinton plan, with another
45 percent against.

But the CNN anchor framed the story as
Clinton gaining a little support and implied
that a slim majority was not enough. Again,
on November 11, 1993, similar poll numbers
showing a plurality of support were placed at
the bottom of a story with an overall negative
spin on the Clinton plan: "President Clinton
has a way to go in explaining his health-care
reform plan."[15]

Later in the debate, from January through
September, 1994, CNN polls found a single-
digit plurality against the Clinton plan and
reported this with negative implications for
Clinton. Now that the poll numbers were bad
for Clinton, CNN mentioned polls much more
frequently, 37 times (with 25 negative implications), compared to five mentions in the
first three quarters of 1993 (with no nega-
tives). Host Mike Kinsley introduced *Crossfire*: "More bad poll numbers for President
Clinton. A new CNN–*USA Today*–Gallup
Poll paints a bleak picture of the president's
popularity. His favorable rating is down to 49
percent, from 56 percent in April, and 62
percent at the beginning of the year." A CNN
correspondent then tied the decline of support for the Clinton health-care plan to a decline in Clinton's personal popularity:

The president's health-care reform plan may be in
need of emergency treatment, according to a new
CNN–*USA Today*–Gallup Poll. The survey shows
only 46 percent approve of the Clinton approach.
That compares with 57 percent approval for the
plan last month. The public thinks less of the president's overall handling of the health issue. Thirty-
nine percent say they approve versus 51 percent
in January. The slip gave ammunition to those
offering alternate visions of health-care reform.

Then CNN cut to a sound bite from Senator
Phil Gramm, (Republican, Texas): "There is

a clear distinction growing between Elvis and
the president's health-care plan. And the distinction is that Elvis may be out there alive
somewhere."[16]

CNN coverage focussed on the decline in
the polls as the most newsworthy and consequential element of the health-care story. But
the fall in the polls was quite typical and was
not necessarily a compelling reason for Congress to reject the plan. Public support usually stands at high levels just after a president
announces a new policy initiative, but declines
after the details are released, and falls further
with public debate. The fall in support over
time, compared to other policy departures,
was not particularly rapid or steep, and did
not indicate that the Clinton plan was dead
on arrival in Congress. CNN, however, used
the decline in the polls to justify congressional failure to pass the Clinton plan.[17]

In short, when the public approved the
Clinton plan in the spring and summer of 1993,
CNN gave scant coverage; that autumn, when
the public approved the Clinton plan by a
slightly smaller margin, the CNN story was
that Clinton's plan was drastically sinking in
the polls. In 1994, when the public disapproved
of the Clinton plan by a single-digit margin,
CNN declared the plan dead in Congress.

## The sources of media construction
of poll results

What explains why the media covered the
opinion polls on the Clinton plan as they did?
Media assessments of the polls about policies
and judgments of the policies themselves tend
to follow the evaluations of high-level political insiders, who serve as the sources for journalists and who have been deemed appropriate
contributors of newsworthy facts. Political elite
sources are constantly assessing the power of
the president to judge whether they should
cooperate with, criticize, or even go against
the president.[18]

Books by investigative journalists such as

Bob Woodward or Haynes Johnson and David Broder portray the details of the concerns and decisions of these political elites. The books present evidence consistent with my tentative explanation of the negative media coverage of the Clinton plan – that conservative Democrats, some of them with high-level positions inside the Clinton Administration, did not like Clinton's health-care plan, and hence conveyed negative judgements about its content and political feasibility to reporters throughout 1993. By October, 1993, these insiders' judgements had hardened into the conventional wisdom among the Washington press corps – that Clinton's attempt to enact his health-care plan was doomed to failure. The media then promulgated to the audience the declining opinion polls as yet another indication that the plan would fail.

Although candidate Clinton in 1992 had made health-care reform a major campaign theme, and although President Clinton in 1993 had made Hillary Clinton chair of the task force to redesign the nation's health-care system, he was of two minds on the issue. President Clinton's powerful economic advisers – Treasury Secretary Lloyd Bentsen, National Economic Council director Bob Rubin, and Council of Economic Advisors chair Laura Tyson – believed, as did Bill Clinton himself, that deficit reduction should be the major priority of his administration. The economic advisers argued that the federal budget reconciliation bill should be passed as soon as possible. Placing health-care reform in the budget bill, or even mentioning the government outlays or taxes that health-care reform could cost, might wreck the delicate compromises needed to pass the budget bill. White House economic advisers at a key meeting on the health plan voiced criticisms that were leaked to the *New York Times*, as was a chart which the *New York Times* claimed to indicate that the final costs of the Clinton plan would exceed $100 billion.[19]

Even after the budget bill narrowly passed

Congress in August, 1993 (by a single vote in the Senate), Bentsen thought the president's approach to health care was too costly. He and Health and Human Services Secretary Donna Shalala believed it involved too much government regulation of insurance companies, and too many price controls over insurers and medical providers. These sentiments and others detrimental to the Clinton plan found their way into the media. Shalala told *USA Today* that a major tax was being considered to fund the plan; Senator Daniel Patrick Moynihan said the efficiencies that the Clinton plan promised for Medicare and Medicaid were "fantasy."[20]

If key conservative Democratic leaders did not like the president's plan, did not want it to pass, and may have even provided stories to reporters to ensure that it would not pass, then it is plausible that they seized upon and highlighted opinion polls that indicated the Clinton plan was unpopular, and may have done so in their discussions with reporters. Since conservative Democratic leaders were willing to leak and the press was willing to print proposals and economic projections unfavorable to the Clinton plan, then probably these same elites selectively promulgated estimates of public opinion to question the plan's practicality. Both economic projections and opinion polls were presented as objective social science, but actually were potent political arguments. Although key Clinton advisers – Hillary Clinton, Ira Magaziner, Harold Ickes, and David Wilhelm – had established an operation out of the White House with a mission to sell the Clinton plan and publicize favorable poll numbers, there were more powerful conservative Democrats, Republicans, and lobbyists who publicized the unfavorable. Conservative political leaders, as I will argue below, promoted not only a media discourse centered on Clinton's unflattering popularity ratings, but also a fundamentally conservative discourse of self-interest and privilege for thinking about public policy goals.

## The Discourse of Individual Self-Interest and the Social Construction of the Middle-Class Consumer

CNN coverage frequently made use of data from poll questions like the following: "Would you and your family pay more or less out of pocket if the Clinton health-care plan were adopted?" This type of question was a standard one in the Wirthlin, Harris, NBC/*Wall Street Journal*, and ABC/*Washington Post* polls of the time, amounting to 28 percent of the total questions in the third quarter of 1993 and 18 percent in the fourth quarter. CNN too cited poll results based on this type of question, along with findings indicating that the Clinton plan was becoming more unpopular.

Reports of these poll questions about individual interest had a deeper effect than CNN's negative spin on the Clinton plan's approval ratings. Health-care reform was not only a partisan battle between Clinton and his Republican opponents. The political and media institutions promulgating the discourse of individual interest set the assumptions on which people thought about and evaluated government policy. The grounds of discussion shifted from societal, collective concerns toward the economic self-interest of individuals, or of one's self and immediate family. It would end in the triumph of privileged conservatism over the vestiges of the welfare state.[21]

The CNN reporting of polls between April and December, 1993 (a crucial period early in the health-care debate, when the Clinton plan was formulated, announced, and criticized), emphasized questions about individual interests. Among the 35 instances in this period where CNN speakers referred to polls, nine instances (26 percent) were questions asking respondents about their individual interests. In 1993 CNN crafted a changing portrait around those poll questions, from a public in the sec-

ond quarter of 1993 concerned about the common good and favoring universal coverage, to individuals later in 1993 focussing on just keeping their own advantages. Earlier in the health-care debate, CNN commentators had featured polls indicating the public strongly favored health-care reform, not so much because of individual grievances, but because of problems in the larger society. Pollster and CNN commentator William Schneider portrayed Americans as thinking beyond self-interest:

We asked people whether they were satisfied with the cost of health care for themselves and their families. People were split on this – half said yes, half said no, but no less than 90 percent said they were dissatisfied with the cost of health care in the country as a whole. Most people told us they were satisfied with the quality of health care they themselves received. The public split over the quality of health care in the country as a whole. A solid majority, 70 percent, said they're happy with their own health insurance coverage but an even larger majority, 76 percent, say they're unhappy with health insurance coverage in the country as a whole. In each case, we found more dissatisfaction about the country than about people's own personal situations.[22]

Through the first year of the Clinton administration, CNN's opinion polls were still indicating that almost three-quarters of Americans supported universal-coverage health insurance.[23] But on the air, CNN barely mentioned this finding after July, 1993 – only twice in the last six months of 1993. Instead, in this period, CNN emphasized polls (on seven occasions) portraying a public that was asking: "What can the country do for me?" CNN speakers highlighted poll findings that Americans were expecting to pay more, get fewer benefits, and have fewer choices under the Clinton plan. In July, 1993, CNN reported that "Americans appear to be skeptical, doubting that reform will either lower costs or improve quality. A new *Washington Post/ ABC* poll shows 56 percent of those questioned think they will have to pay more. Only

25 percent believe they'll pay less." This poll was taken about three months before Clinton's address to Congress on September 22, 1993, announcing the outline of his plan, and more than two months before a leaked copy of the plan had been publicized in the *New York Times* and the *Washington Post*. Pollsters were pronouncing the public's judgement of the plan even before the plan had been unveiled![24]

After Clinton's September address, CNN stated that those expecting to pay more under the Clinton plan had risen to 61 percent, and then to a two-to-one margin at the end of October, 1993.[25] Poll questions about individual interest were mentioned in such a way that viewers would draw negative implications about the Clinton plan – from 14-percent negative mentions in April–June, 1993, to 57-percent negative in July–December, 1993.

As in the case of popularity polls for the Clinton plan, I can offer only tentative hypotheses about how political elites and judgements affected media presentations of poll data emphasizing individual interests. Senator Daniel Patrick Moynihan, chair of the Senate Finance Committee, believed that Americans were largely satisfied with their health care and would resist any plan that would reduce their own benefits to provide for the uninsured. Johnson and Broder[26] claim that Clinton's 1992 campaign pollster and later White House adviser Stanley Greenberg, along with his associate Celinda Lake, saw the public as individuals who wanted to reduce their own costs, increase their benefits, reject any scheme to lower the quality of their care, and forget those without insurance. The two influential pollsters argued their views at an early meeting of the task force on health-care reform back in January, 1993. This portrait of the public was also the one that CNN, along with other media outlets and their political elite sources, helped construct in mid-1993, as the network departed from its earlier presentations of the public as favoring universal coverage.

"Will you pay more or less" poll questions about the Clinton plan affected the health-care debate in important ways. First of all, the questions reinforced the assumption that health care is a commodity, that is, medical services are bought and sold for money. The polls encouraged people to accept the economic limits on the American welfare state, and to think of improving one's lot in life by making marginal improvements (lower price, better quality) in one's role as a consumer.

But even within the limits of commodified medical goods and services, talk about improving one's material interests could lead in alternative directions. One possibility was the economism of American trade unionism – higher wages and benefits – but fighting together to obtain those wages and benefits for all in a larger group. Economism, as Frances Fox Piven has argued in this volume (Chapter 1), has an electoral component: using the collective state apparatus to provide benefits for all citizens. In this manner, individuals' economistic desires could still lead to universal health coverage, according to Robert Blendon's insightful analyses of poll data. Blendon's reading of the public was that individuals were very concerned about lowering their own high bills for medical care and insurance. These "public views" could lead to support for a program of universal access to health care, which Blendon himself favored.[27]

Blendon was an influential expert (with funding from the Robert Wood Johnson Foundation) and the elite national media felt obliged to use him as a source of facts. But the *New York Times*, for example, did not use his overall thesis that self-interested "public views" for lower out-of-pocket expenses and higher quality ought to lead to the enactment of universal coverage. Instead the *New York Times* made its own argument that the self-interest of middle-class individuals ought to lead them to reject the Clinton plan to cover all the uninsured:

Analysts keep warning that the most important audience for the coming debate is the middle class and its perceptions of the costs and benefits of the Clinton plan. In a paper he helped write in the recent *Journal of the American Medical Association*, Robert J. Blendon, an expert at Harvard on public opinion about health care, argued that Americans were "unwilling to accept more than a modest amount of sacrifice in order to achieve health-care reform." Robert D. Reischauer, head of the Congressional Budget Office, makes a similar point. "Most of the middle class view themselves as pretty well covered and having a good relation with a primary care physician as it now stands," he said. "They might be willing to pay a little more to insure this won't be taken away from them if they switch jobs or change family circumstances, but I don't think they're interested in paying huge bucks to pay for the chronically uninsured."[28]

Blendon was the source for the social science data, but the principal source for the overall argument was Reischauer, an elite Washington insider and Democrat who by then had already judged that the Clinton plan would not pass Congress.

The *New York Times* was upholding not Blendon's "public views" supporting universal coverage, but rather the views of conservative and business elites. Their main interest was to *reduce* the money the US spends on health care, which would have a perverse effect on individuals: *increasing* the amount people pay and/or *reducing* benefits. The conservative agenda is clear in an article later in 1994, astounding for its presumption, in which Robert Pear lectured Clinton on cutting the costs of the welfare state rather than expanding it:

President Clinton's health plan was inspired as much by a desire to control costs as by a passion to guarantee insurance for every American. But the goal of cost control has been eclipsed by the furor over universal coverage. Consumer groups [sic], business executives and labor leaders who joined the campaign for health care legislation in hopes of controlling costs are profoundly disappointed. This spreading sense of unease could have

deep political consequences as Mr. Clinton nears the midpoint of a term in which health care has preoccupied him more than any other policy issue.[29]

The media could have started from individuals' understandable concerns about their own health care, and could have developed public understanding of universal coverage. The media could have emphasized the specific benefits to individuals that the Clinton plan would have provided. But instead CNN in 1994 focussed on the debate among politicians who trafficked in fears about how the public would materially fare under the plan. CNN and the *Times*, as I will argue, were constructing a discourse of individual self-interest to preserve the advantages of the middle class.

Throughout 1994 CNN was reporting that increasing percentages of poll respondents felt not only that they would pay more under the Clinton plan, but also that they would be worse off generally, with lower-quality care and fewer choices. On CNN, pollster and pundit William Schneider was now presenting a very different slice of public opinion than he had presented in May, 1993. In April, 1994, 40 percent said worse off, and only 19 percent better off:

There is a change. The number of people who say they'd be better off has really dropped since last fall. In October it was 28 percent and now we say 19 percent. That's about one in five Americans say they'd be better off under Clinton's plan. I think there's more consciousness of the costs of the plan and for most Americans, the costs either neutralize or outweigh the benefits, which of course would be health care security.

There was a change not only among poll respondents but also in the mind of pollster Schneider, who had bought Robert Novak's vision of the public as shopping mall:

I think what the American people, when they were – when they started to buy into this health care what they thought they were going to get was better health care at less money. Who wouldn't want that? But suddenly, they are saying, am I going to get something worse? And that's the real debate. Is the average Joe American and his wife going to be in worse shape because of this? And that's why the Democrats are losing their argument.[30]

A CNN anchor cited a survey by Republican pollsters the Wirthlin Group concluding that "only 21 percent consider universal coverage the top health-care priority. . . . And the greatest concern, raised by 45 percent, is that health care not be made any worse. And just to give the president one thing more to worry about, Harry and Louise are back."[31]

| | |
|---|---|
| *Woman in commercial:* | This was covered under our old plan. |
| *Man in commercial:* | Oh, yeah – that was a good one, wasn't it? |
| *Commercial announcer:* | Things are changing, and not all for the better. |

Novak's "average Joe American" had been reimagined as a more upscale "Harry and Louise," the couple who starred in the Health Insurance Association of America's attack ads against the Clinton plan. Harry and Louise became a potent symbol that galvanized baby boomers' fears that they might become worse off. The ads (or rather the media discussion promoted by the ads, because the ads ran in only a few markets) resonated among Americans who indeed had something to lose, Americans who already had health insurance and were relatively satisfied with it. From December, 1993, through June, 1994, CNN repeatedly mentioned stories like this: "The polls this week show that 80 percent of Americans are happy with their health care, and for people who have health plans they like and doctors their family relies on, they have a lot to lose under the Clinton bill."[32]

The media discourse promoted a style of health-care politics that I call the preservation of advantage, a mirror of the politics of

tax-cutting Proposition 13 in California that I described in *Small Property versus Big Government*.[33] The media help to define politics as a movement for the haves, who seek to defend their relative privileges. In the case of Proposition 13, the privilege to be maintained was affordable home ownership in the suburbs. In the health-care debate, the privilege was continuous coverage by private health insurance. In the tax revolt, a great fear focussed on the state taxing away property. In health-care reform, the fear became the state taking away another prop of middle-class security: "Several polls have indicated that the biggest concern is giving up what you've got. . . . There's a very strong sentiment and I think it's shared in Congress, that the worst thing that Congress could do would be to take things away from people."[34] The politics of property-tax reduction tended to revolve around the interest of upper-middle-class suburbanites. The discourse of individual interest in health care tended to center on those with well-paying jobs and benefits.[35]

The media discourse about the self-interest of high-end consumers tended to shift the goals of health-care reform from insuring the uninsured to assuring that the insured stayed insured, even if they lost their jobs or developed expensive ailments. At the beginning of the health-care debate in the first quarter of 1993, CNN publicized five poll questions about public support for the goal of universal coverage (31 percent of all questions mentioned that quarter). One year later, at least four different polling organizations, including a Time/CNN/Yankelovich Partners poll, showed continued strong public support for universal coverage, running between 73 and 86 percent in the first quarter of 1994.[36] But on the air CNN did not emphasize these results, instead choosing to mention questions indicating popular support for the goal of insurance reform as an alternative to universal coverage. CNN's mentions of questions about not losing insurance reached a peak of 17 percent of all mentions in the second quarter of 1994:

And yet again in the poll, it sounded as if, from what Bill was saying, from the results, people are not so much interested in universal coverage as they are in making sure their own coverage, that people who have coverage now, that it's not lost and they don't run the risk of losing that.

The media's focussing attention on those already with insurance, and their self-interest and their fears that they might be worse off, tended to undermine the goal of universal coverage and contributed to the unpopularity of the Clinton plan:

The debate on health care has focused on the 39 million Americans who are uninsured, but in fact the vast majority of Americans do have health insurance and polls show that what they're really worried about is losing it. Isn't this more what the Republican idea, the Republican proposal, the Dole proposal would address, which is insurance reform so that working people can keep their insurance if they change jobs or lose their jobs?[37] . . .

Well, people do favor universal coverage but other things are more important than providing coverage for people who don't have it right now. . . . We asked people which is more important – providing coverage for all or making sure that people cannot lose their coverage even if they lose their job or develop a medical problem? The answer is, by majority, make sure people can't lose their coverage. That's a second weapon in the Republican arsenal. More limited health-care reforms are OK. . . .

So we asked people, "What worries you more – that you could end up without health insurance if Congress doesn't pass a bill, or that you could end up worse off if Congress does pass a bill?" The answer is, people are more worried about what will happen to them if the bill passes. The public still wants health care reform, but they want a more moderate version than what President Clinton originally proposed. They're happy with Congress because they believe Congress is moving in that direction.[38]

The media portrayal of polls encouraged the middle class not to make common cause with the uninsured, but to see the uninsured as a group with vastly different interests, and ultimately as an alien economic threat, to be warded off with the Contract for America:

Our polling shows the public now sees health care reform as a typical social welfare program, one that will help the poor and hurt the middle class. Democrats have to use this debate to convince the middle class that they're the ones who will benefit from health care reform. At the outset of this debate, Judy, the middle class just doesn't see it.[39]

The televised message from the discourse of individual self-interest is: Universal coverage is welfare. It is a blank government check for the uninsured, paid for by the middle class. Welfare: Cut it, vote for the Contract with America in 1994. The insurance reform plan that Senator Dole had proposed as a modest alternative was renamed the Kassebaum–Kennedy Bill, was passed by Contract with America 104th Congress, and was signed into law by President William Jefferson Clinton in August, 1996.

## Conclusion: Getting the Right Health Care

During the debate over health-care reform, CNN selectively cited public opinion polls to create two powerful images – a self-interested middle class safeguarding its privileges, and an unpopular plan from an ineffective president. Each of these images was rooted in long-standing discourses and other practices among the media, pollsters, and political elites.

However, neither image, when first promulgated in mid-1993, matched political reality particularly well. In contrast to the image of an obsessively self-interested populace, an overwhelming, decisive majority of citizens, who generally had health insurance already, endorsed its extension to those who did not have it. CNN promulgated the image of the self-interested middle class in summer, 1993, at a crucial time in the health-care debate. Then, Americans had little information and uncertain opinions about the Clinton plan. CNN helped to establish the assumptions and criteria for the judgements that followed. The triumph of the discourse of individual self-interest led CNN in summer, 1994, to high-light poll results indicating that the public wanted insurance reform, rather than polls showing continued strong support for universal coverage.

In contrast to the image of the unpopular Clinton plan, those favoring the plan in autumn 1993 held a double-digit plurality in the polls over those opposed. CNN repeated the unpopular president image particularly often right when Congress was considering Clinton's proposals. The widespread perception that the plan lacked popular support discouraged Congress from acting and over-coming the special interests arrayed against health-care reform.

I have suggested a hypothesis for further study – that the peculiar interpretations of poll data that CNN broadcasted are strikingly similar to the strongly held views among conservative Democratic political elites. These leaders, who had ties to top business elites, worked from their positions inside the Clinton Administration, and did everything short of publicly breaking with and denouncing their president to oppose the Clinton health-care plan, which they saw as leading only to excessive costs and government regulation. In some instances, these conservative Democratic leaders may have directly been a news source for the program segments aired on CNN.

This in turn suggests that the main explanation for the failure of the Clinton plan was a lack of support from the political center of conservative Democrats and moderate Republicans, rather than attacks from the ideological right wing, such as the NFIB,[40] the Christian Coalition, and leaders like William

Kristol. This suggestion differs from the approach of Theda Skocpol, who in *Boomerang* claims that the battle to kill health-care reform was won by the right wing in the spring and summer of 1994.[41] I contend in this chapter that the battle was lost earlier, in 1993, by centrist political elites who were well connected to large business elites.

An implication of this chapter and the previous one by Beth Mintz is that Skocpol does not sufficiently analyze the role that business elites played in the failure of Clinton's plan. Top business elites such as the Washington Business Group on Health were ambivalent about the Clinton plan and then, along with conservative Democratic and moderate Republican political elites, turned against it. John Ong (chair of the Business Roundtable), Robert Winters (chair of the Roundtable's health policy committee and of Prudential Insurance), and Ralph Johnson (Johnson and Johnson CEO) concluded in June, 1993, that the Clinton plan involved too much government regulation. In February, 1994, the Business Roundtable formally voted its opposition. Another key moment in the plan's demise came in June, 1993, when Paul Ellwood and Alain Enthoven, leaders of the influential Jackson Hole study group on health care that included participants from the largest insurance companies, opposed the Clinton plan because of its government price controls and other regulatory features.[42]

The media considered the negative judgements of centrist elites to be significant stories. The media also tended to adopt their sources' judgements that the Clinton plan was not feasible economically or politically. My empirical research on the CNN coverage of public opinion polls has provided an example of how media judgements colored their selection of polling information and its presentation in news stories.

Researchers will disagree as to whether or not media representations of opinion polls actually affected the views of Americans on health-care reform. But regardless of whether or not a media presentation of poll results has a bandwagon or spiral effect upon opinions on that question, I have argued that the media coverage of the polls did contribute to political outcomes. The media focussed on the news that the Clinton plan was falling in the polls, even when the plan commanded majority support. The media spent insufficient time discussing why we might need health-care reform, or what the Clinton plan would do.[43] Rather than examining the plan itself, the media focussed on political judgements about the plan.

I have argued that unfavorable poll results were publicized because they were a proxy for the more influential judgements by centrist elites. The media coverage of such polls was an indicator of the dominance of such elite judgements. Expressed on CNN and in other news stories, the negative judgements of centrist elites did indeed have a powerful effect on policy. Media presentation of their arguments was a justification for their action to kill the Clinton plan. And media presentations of poll data, over and above unfavorable economic data, create the impression that the US is a democracy where the people, not the elites, killed health-care reform.

I take the liberty of concluding with the following sketch, offering my interpretation of how the health-care debate of 1993–4 exemplifies the relationship between the presidency and business elites during the Clinton era.[44] Clinton took the presidential oath of office as a relatively young outsider to Washington politics. He was no business mogul but a person of modest wealth who tried to secure his retirement by making losing investments in Arkansas real estate. This president, even more than Kennedy, was to be tested by foreign affairs crises, by a skeptical business community, and, most important, by old-time Washington insiders – the partners in the top Washington DC law firms, the

congressional leadership, Republican nemeses, the board of directors of the Brookings Institution, former presidential advisers, and the media titans described in Halberstam's *The Powers that Be*.

The agenda was Clinton's, but how the agenda would unwind would in large measure be decided by the Washington establishment. They noted that Clinton had been elected without a majority of the popular vote. They looked askance at appointees Lani Guinier and Jocelyn Elders, but at least Treasury and State, they thought, were safe in the hands of Bentsen and Christopher. Clinton seemed to have gotten the message on health-care costs, but there was too much talk about government-guaranteed health care as a right, and too much criticism of the drug companies. Besides, all the right people from business and the insurance companies had been kept off the task force. Ira who?

The immediate question was to judge whether the new president would succeed in mobilizing popular support and pushing a reform bill through Congress. In the higher circles in the spring of 1993 the distinguished heads shook their answer: no, these Clintons shall learn of the system. This was a political judgement made by the principals, not by the pollsters and campaign technicians. It was like the judgement that big institutional investors make about which businesses will perform the best – a judgement that, once made, tends to produce an upward move in the company's stock price. So too would journalists register a move in the months ahead.

Knowledge of insider judgements was the prize to be teased out by journalists and columnists Bob Woodward, Robert Pear, and George Will over drinks at the elite social clubs of the US Capitol. How the insiders would lean, position, hedge, and play was discreetly mentioned in the *New York Times* and the *Washington Post*, then mirrored on CNN and countless other media outlets. So when it came time to report on health-care reform, stories were peppered with public opinion polls about the declining support for Clinton and his plan. Now the world would know which way to lean, position, hedge, and play. As the big players fell out with health-care reform, the smart money on Wall Street rotated out of health-care stocks, and the major campaign contributors took another look at the Republican National Committee.

## Methodological Appendix

My research involved searching the transcripts of CNN programs, available on Lexis/Nexus, for all airtime segments between January 1, 1993, and September 30, 1994, that mentioned within 50 words of one another the words "health" and "poll" or any five-letter word beginning with the letters "poll." All these segments were read by a graduate assistant coder, Ms Jane Downing (whose efforts are gratefully acknowledged), to see if they actually did refer to public opinion polls on the subject of health-care reform. One hundred and forty-five segments were identified in this manner.

Each use of poll data by a speaker was considered as a mention and was coded for several variables: date, name of speaker, whether the speaker was a CNN host or anchor, and positive or negative implication (negative if the poll data were set in an overall impression or argument that the Clinton plan was undesirable or should not pass).

The coder also recorded the instances of seven major categories of poll questions and results, namely opinions about: the popularity of the Clinton plan; the goals of universal coverage and insurance reform; the importance or urgency of health-care reform as an issue; taxes, employer mandates, and other ways to finance the plan; whether individuals would be better or worse off with the plan; business and politics; and the plan as an example of the problems of big government. Subcategories were also coded for under each of the categories. The subcategories corresponded to questions that were asked in polls by several organizations.

Each mention on CNN of polling data could be coded under several categories and subcategories, but not with the same subcategory more than once. A speaker repeatedly mentioning polls at several different times in the program, interspersed with other speakers, was recorded as several mentions. The mentions of poll data in the different categories and subcategories were tabulated and summed for seven quarter-year intervals.

## Notes

Support for my research from the Research Council of the University of Missouri at Columbia and one year's research leave granted by the Office of the Provost are gratefully acknowledged, as are suggestions from G. William Domhoff, Darlaine Gardetto (whose research on discourse was inspiring), Donald Granberg, Anthony Orum, Michael Schwartz, Richard Wilsnack, graduate students in Sociology 409 in winter, 1997, at the University of Missouri, and those attending my presentations at the University of Hawaii at Manoa, the Humanities Center at the University of Missouri at St Louis, and Temple University, especially Alvin So, Karen Lucas, Dennis Judd, and Magali Sarfati-Larson. I am also indebted to Guy Molliney of Hart Research Associates for an interview, and to a contributor to this volume for suggesting the title to my chapter at a party graciously hosted by Susan Rabinowitz of Blackwell Publishers.

1 George H. Gallup, "Preserving Majority Rule," in Albert H. Cantril, *Polling on the Issues* (Cabin John MD: Seven Locks Press, 1980); Albert H. Cantril, *The Opinion Connection: Polling, Politics, and the Press* (Washington DC: Congressional Quarterly Press, 1991), p. 226,

refers to this as the "town-crier" model.
2 For use of polls in the media, see David L. Paletz, Jonathan Y. Short, Helen Baker, Barbara Cookman Campbell, Richard J. Cooper, and Rochelle M. Oeslander, "Polls in the Media: Content, Credibility, and Consequences," *Public Opinion Quarterly* 44 (1980), pp. 495–513.
3 Arnold H. Ismach, "Polling as a News-Gathering Tool," *Annals of the American Academy of Political and Social Science* 472 (March, 1984), pp. 106–18; Philip Meyer, *Precision Journalism* (Bloomington: Indiana University Press, 1973); Maxwell E. McCombs, Donald L. Shaw, and David Grey, *Handbook of Reporting Methods* (Boston: Houghton Mifflin, 1976).
4 John Brehm, *The Phantom Respondents: Opinion Surveys and Political Representation* (Ann Arbor: University of Michigan Press, 1993); Seymour Martin Lipset, "The Wavering Polls," *Public Interest* 7 (1976), pp. 70–89; Stanley L. Payne, *The Art of Asking Questions* (Princeton NJ: Princeton University Press, 1951); Everett Carll Ladd, "Polling and the Press: The Clash of Institutional Imperatives," *Public Opinion Quarterly* 44 (1980), pp. 574–84.
5 Philip Converse, "The Nature of Belief Systems in Mass Publics," in David Apter, ed., *Ideology and Discontent* (New York: Free Press, 1964); Robert M. Entman, *Democracy Without Citizens: Media and the Decay of American Politics* (New York: Oxford University Press, 1989); W. Lance Bennett, *Public Opinion in American Politics* (New York: Harcourt Brace Jovanovich, 1980); Stuart Hall, "Culture, the Media, and the 'Ideological Effect,' " in J. Curran, M. Gurevitch, and J. Woollacot, eds, *Mass Communication and Society* (London: Arnold, 1977).
6 Gaye Tuchman, *Making News: A Study in the Construction of Reality* (New York: Free Press, 1978); Herbert Gans, *Deciding What's News: A Study of CBS Evening News, NBC Nightly News, Newsweek, and Time* (New York: Vintage, 1979); Bennett, *Public Opinion*, pp. 310, 331. See also Teun A. Van Dijk, *News as Discourse* (Hillsdale NJ: Lawrence Erlbaum Associates, 1988); Murray Edelman, *Constructing the Political Spectacle* (Chicago: University of Chicago Press, 1988).
7 David W. Moore, *The Superpollsters: How they Measure and Manipulate Public Opinion in*

*America* (New York: Four Walls Eight Windows, 1992), p. 229; Cantril, *Opinion Connection*, p. 220.
8 Lawrence R. Jacobs and Robert Y. Shapiro, in "Questioning the Conventional Wisdom on Public Opinion toward Health Reform," *PS: Political Science and Politics* (June, 1994), p. 208, write, "The interpretation of public opinion by the media and other political observers, however, is not a neutral process dictated by scientific methods; it is the product of institutional and political struggles for position and power. . . . Is the conventional wisdom merely a smokescreen established and maintained by powerful institutional and political interests?" Gladys Engel Lang and Kurt Lang, *The Battle for Public Opinion: The President, the Press, and the Polls During Watergate* (New York: Columbia University Press, 1983), p. 131.
9 Christopher Hitchens, "Voting in the Passive Voice: What Polling has Done to American Democracy," *Harper's Magazine* (April, 1992), pp. 45–52; Moore, *Superpollsters*, p. 199; Cantril, *Opinion Connection*, pp. 53, 69.
10 As late as February, 1994, five months after Clinton's major address on his health-care plan, two-thirds of those polled had not heard or read about employer mandates. Kathleen Hall Jamieson and Joseph N. Cappella, *Media in the Middle: Fairness and Accuracy in the 1994 Health Care Reform Debate* (Philadelphia PA: Annenberg Public Policy Center, University of Pennsylvania, February, 1995), pp. 6–7; John Immerwahr and Jean Johnson, *Second Opinions: Americans' Changing Views on Healthcare Reform* (New York: Public Agenda Foundation, 1994).
11 W. Lance Bennett, *The Governing Crisis: Media, Money, and Marketing in American Elections* (New York: St Martin's Press, 1992); Larry J. Sabato, *The Rise of Political Consultants: Ways of Winning Elections* (New York: Basic Books, 1981).
12 For an interesting analysis of press coverage of polls on political figures (albeit pre-election polls rather than approval ratings of office holders), see C. Anthony Broh, "Horse-Race Journalism: Reporting the Polls in the 1976 Presidential Election," *Public Opinion Quarterly* 44 (1980), pp. 522, 525, 527.

13 For politics as personalization and symbolization, see Edelman, *Political Spectacle*.

14 *Gallup Opinion Monthly* (August, 1994), p. 5; see also Jamieson and Cappella, *Media in the Middle*, pp. 6–7.

15 Mark Shields, host, *Capital Gang*, CNN (October 30, 1993); Judy Woodruff, anchor, *News*, CNN (October 31, 1993); *Inside Politics*, CNN (November 8, 1993); Lou Dobbs, host, *Moneyline*, CNN (November 11, 1993).

16 Mike Kinsley, host, *Crossfire*, CNN (July 21, 1994); Jeff Levine, host, *Inside Politics*, CNN (March 1, 1994).

17 Public support for Medicare fell before it was enacted, although the decline was not as great compared to that of the Clinton plan. Sixty-two percent favored "President Johnson's program of medical care for the aged under Social Security" in March 8, 1965. But when asked to choose between Medicare and an alternative private and voluntary plan supported by the American Medical Association, the percentage choosing Medicare fell from 56 to 46 percent between March 1962 and February 1965. See Hazel Erskine, "The Polls: Health Insurance," *Public Opinion Quarterly* 39 (1975), p. 128; Michael E. Schlitz, "Public Attitudes toward Social Security, 1935–1965" (Washington, DC: Government Printing Office, 1970).

   For CNN's use of polls, see Jay Rockefeller, *Inside Politics*, CNN (June 13, 1994).

18 Entman, *Democracy*; Bennett, *Public Opinion*, p. 235. For further research on the hypothesis of agenda building see David Weaver and Swanzy Nimley Elliott, "Who Sets the Agenda for the Media? A Study in Local Agenda-Building," *Journalism Quarterly* 62 (1985), pp. 88–94. In front-page news stories, the most common sources are male federal government executives. Jane Delano Brown, Carl R. Bybee, Stanley T. Wearden, and Dulcie Murdock Straughan, "Invisible Power: Newspaper News Sources and the Limits of Diversity," *Journalism Quarterly* 64 (1987), pp. 45–54.

19 Haynes Johnson and David S. Broder, *The System: The American Way of Politics at the Breaking Point* (Boston: Little, Brown, 1996), pp. 119–28, 141; Bob Woodward, *The Agenda: Inside the Clinton White House* (New York: Simon and Schuster, 1994), pp. 122–3, 199–200.

20 Johnson and Broder, *System*, pp. 115, 137, 140, 161, 167, 172; Woodward, *Agenda*, p. 316. For examples of the power of Moynihan's insider judgements to influence opinions of elite journalists, see the proliferation of his "fantasy" quotation by Jack W. Germond and Jules Witcover, "Getting it Right on Health Care Plan," *National Journal* (October 16, 1993), p. 2497; William Schneider, "A Fatal Flaw in Clinton's Health Care Plan?" *National Journal* (November 6, 1993), p. 2696.

21 Bennett, *Public Opinion*, pp. 304–10, in contrast to the term "agenda setting," uses the term "agenda reinforcement" to refer to the media's functioning to reinforce basic orientations, in which I would include consumerism and individualism.

22 William Schneider, *Inside Politics*, CNN (May 14, 1993). Political scientists Jacobs and Shapiro, in "Questioning the Conventional," pp. 209–10, argue that through October, 1993, the public supported the Clinton plan because it thought "most Americans" and "the country as a whole" would be better off, even though individual respondents felt they would be worse off. This contrasts to media arguments that people opposed the plan because they felt it would make them worse off. See below.

23 See also Immerwahr and Johnson, *Second Opinions*, p. 4.

24 Frank Sesno, anchor, *News*, CNN (July 7, 1993); Jamieson and Cappella, *Media in the Middle*, p. 6, comment that media coverage the next year (1994) of polls on health care shows similar problems: "Reporters presented these polls without analysis, creating 'news' out of opinions which were uninformed."

25 For the 61-percent figure, see Hunt, host, *Capital Gang*, CNN (September 25, 1993); Andrea Arceneaux, anchor, *News*, CNN (September 25, 1993). See also Mark Shields, host, *Capital Gang*, CNN (October 30, 1993).

26 Johnson and Broder, *System*, pp. 152, 353. Adding his voice to the chorus about middle-class self-interest later in the year was Norman Ornstein of the conservative think tank the American Enterprise Institute, in "Who Cares Anyway: Health Care Reform," *New Republic* 209 (August 16, 1993), p. 21: "The insured are

more concerned with their own coverage – retaining it, making sure it is adequate, keeping costs in line – than with the problem of others."

27 Robert J. Blendon, Tracey Stelzer Hyams, and John M. Benson, "Bridging the Gap between Expert and Public Views on Health Care Reform," *JAMA, The Journal of the American Medical Association* 269 (May 19, 1993), pp. 2573–8.

28 Robin Toner, "Changing Health Care: Political Memo, Clinton Facing Reality of Health-Care Reform," *New York Times* (May 21, 1993), section A, p. 14. For Reischauer, see Johnson and Broder, *System*, pp. 117, 282–7. At a key point in the debate over the Clinton plan, Reischauer was instrumental in getting the Congressional Budget Office to declare the mandate that employers would pay for their workers' health insurance was a federal tax and should be counted as such. This gave further credence to the Republicans' attacks on the Clinton plan as big government at its worst.

29 "Cost is Obscured in Health Debate," *New York Times* (August 7, 1994), section 1, p. 1. Consumer groups and labor unions actually had little interest in the conservative agenda of cutting macroeconomic costs of the welfare state.

30 William Schneider, *Inside Politics*, CNN (April 19, 1994); Robert Novak, host, *Capital Gang*, CNN (March 5, 1994).

31 Charles Bierbauer, anchor, *News*, CNN (June 20, 1994). CNN ran part of the ad. as an introduction to a feature, *Inside Politics*, CNN (September 15, 1993).

32 Elizabeth McCaughey, *CNN and Company*, CNN (March 10, 1994). See also Karen Miller, host, *CNN and Company*, CNN (December 17, 1993).

33 Clarence Y. H. Lo, *Small Property versus Big Government: Social Origins of the Property Tax Revolt*, revised paperback edn (Berkeley CA and Los Angeles: University of California Press, 1995).

34 Chip Kahn, anchor, *News*, CNN (June 20, 1994).

35 Benjamin Ginsberg, *The Captive Public: How Mass Opinion Promotes State Power* (New York: Basic Books, 1986), pp. 135–47, discusses how public affairs programming tends to revolve around the interests of affluent consumers.

36 Robert J. Blendon, Mollyann Brodie, Tracey Stelzer Hyams, and John M. Benson, "The American Public and the Critical Choices for Health System Reform," *JAMA, The Journal of the American Medical Association* 271 (19) (May 18, 1994), p. 1539.

37 Judy Woodruff, host, *Inside Politics*, CNN (June 29, 1994); Deborah Marchini, host, *CNN and Company*, CNN (August 12, 1994).

38 William Schneider, *Inside Politics*, CNN (June 29, 1994); Schneider, *Inside Politics*, CNN (August 10, 1994).

39 Ibid.

40 G. William Domhoff, "Who Killed Health Care Reform in Congress, Small Business or Rich Conservatives, and Why Did they Do It?," paper presented to the meetings of the American Sociological Association (August, 1994).

41 Theda Skocpol, *Boomerang: Clinton's Health Security Effort and the Turn against Government in U.S. Politics* (New York: W. W. Norton, 1996), pp. 133–72.

42 Johnson and Broder, *System*, pp. 148, 318–22.

43 For varied views on bandwagon effects, see Elisabeth Noelle-Neumann, *The Spiral of Silence: Public Opinion – Our Social Skin*, 2nd edn (Chicago: University of Chicago Press, 1993); Stephen J. Ceci and Edward L. Kain, "Jumping on the Bandwagon with the Underdog: The Impact of Attitude Polls on Polling Behavior," *Public Opinion Quarterly* 46 (1982), pp. 228–42; Robert Navazio, "An Experimental Approach to Bandwagon Research," *Public Opinion Quarterly* 41 (1977), pp. 217–25; Kurt Lang and Gladys Engel Lang, "The Impact of Polls on Public Opinion," *Annals of the American Academy of Political and Social Science: Polling and the Democratic Consensus* 472 (March, 1984), pp. 129–42. See also Thomas B. Rosenstiel, "Press Found Putting Stress on Politics of Health Reform," *Los Angeles Times* (March 26, 1994), p. A24.

44 Thomas R. Dye, *Who's Running America? The Clinton Years* (Englewood Cliffs NJ: Prentice Hall, 1995). See also David Halberstam, *The Best and the Brightest* (New York: Random House, 1969); Halberstam, *The Powers that Be* (New York: Knopf, 1979).

# 13

# Popular Consensus or Political Extortion?

## Making Soldiers the Means *and* Ends of US Military Deployments

## ★ *Jerry Lee Lembcke* ★

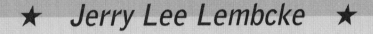

*We may be facing another Vietnam scenario. If our troops start coming home in body-bags and we strike hard at the Bosnians, I hope that no student today will repeat the mistakes of the generation that preceded us – by spitting on Marines.*[1]

## Introduction

In a *New York Times* op–ed piece on October 29, 1995, Elaine Sciolino pointed out the difficulty faced by the Clinton Administration in marketing its military mission to Bosnia to the American people. Drawing a lesson from the Persian Gulf War, she opined that without a villain like Iraqi leader Saddam Hussein to stir the passions of Americans, Clinton would be hard pressed to gain the support of the voting public. Sciolino expressed doubts that, without a Saddam Hussein in the story, Clinton would be able to justify a military commitment.[2]

Sciolino, however, missed important elements in the Bush Administration's campaign to win public approval for its military policy in the Persian Gulf and thereby missed the clue to how it might be done again. The following re-examination of the Gulf War case finds that, essentially, the Bush Administration paralyzed rational discourse by putting forth one reason after another for the deploy-ment of troops to the point where reasoning within a means–end framework was rendered impossible. At that point, public decision making defaulted to emotion and symbolism, and the administration, ably assisted by the highly orchestrated yellow-ribbon campaign, used the soldiers in the Persian Gulf as the reason war should be supported. The means of war became the ends of war.

By situating the Persian Gulf case histori-cally between precedents and antecedents that bear similarity to it, we can discern a pattern cutting across the lines of Republican and Democratic administrations which has con-tinued through the first Clinton Administra-tion.

## Reasoning Paralyzed

In early January, 1991, the US Congress de-bated the question of going to war against Iraq. By votes of 250 to 183 in the House and 52 to 47 in the Senate, Congress authorized

George Bush to use armed forces to expel Iraq from Kuwait. But for many Americans, the reasons for war in the Gulf had more to do with support for the US men and women already stationed in the Gulf than it did with Iraq or Kuwait. By the time the US went to war on January 16, the US soldiers in the Gulf had become the reason for the war. How did it come to pass that the means of war, the soldiers themselves, became, in the popular mind, the ends of the war?

Although a military response by the US was immediately down played as a possibility after Iraq's August 1, 1990, incursion into Kuwait, the Bush Administration soon began spinning events in ways intended to justify the use of US military force. In the fuller version of this story I reconstruct the history of those five months, showing how the Bush Administration put forth one reason and then another for why the US should intervene militarily in the Gulf.[3] Those reasons constituted the *ends* that would, or would not, justify the extraordinary *means* of war.

I contend that the Bush Administration put forth each of its six reasons for war in a way that constituted a story or narrative in which Americans would understand their own relationship to the war. These narratives framed the events for people, providing contexts within which to interpret and make sense out of their government's unprecedented action.[4] I argue that, in the end, by putting forth one reason after another, the Bush Administration created a collage of rationales that rendered absurd the means-and-end decision-making calculus, thus forcing the body politic to make the decision to go to war on purely emotional and symbolic ground. The constituent elements of that ground were the image of the spat-upon Vietnam veteran – used as a "perfecting myth" to give the American people a non-rational framing for the war – and yellow ribbons, traditional symbols for prisoners and hostages, turned into a symbol of support for soldiers in the Gulf. In January

of 1991, mere days before the bombing actually began, the administration exploited a confusion between support for the troops and support for the war – a confusion it had helped to create – and swept American public opinion into support for the war.[5]

The first reason was the *defense of Saudi Arabia*,[6] which was supplanted in news headlines about a week later by the second reason, *military teeth for the economic blockade of Iraq*.[7] Both of these reasons, being relatively benign sounding, had the effect of keeping opposition to the US move frozen for most of August.[8]

The third reason, *freedom of the hostages*, would ultimately prove to be the keystone of the Bush Administration strategy to muster domestic support for the Gulf War, and for that reason it deserves greater elaboration. The hostage issue was a transitional one that allowed the Bush Administration to begin recasting the crisis from "this is about 'them' " – the defense of Saudi Arabia and the sovereignty of Kuwait – to "this is about us." It was a prelude to fuller discussions of what US "vital interests" were at stake in the region. Given the history of US hostages in the Middle East and the vague associations that many Americans made between hostages and Arab terrorists, it was easy to create a public perception that hostages *were* the vital interest that justified a military response.

Moreover, by writing the role of hostages into the script, any Americans who were in the Gulf region, including military personnel, could be cast in the role and used as a reason for war. The hostage issue, in other words, paved the way for means and ends to be conflated and, ultimately, for the troops in the Gulf to be both the reasons for the war and the means of war. During late August there was an unbroken string of hostage stories about Americans confined to hotels in Baghdad, the Bush Administration's fears that Saddam Hussein might be holding American hostages, and the saga of the US children who were stranded in Kuwait when their British Airways flight was unexpectedly grounded by the crisis. Sometimes the stories were about hostages being taken, sometimes about hostages being released; sometimes just speculation about who was or was not a hostage. Regardless of their content, the stories managed to tell Americans that this crisis was about hostages.

George Bush played the hostage card deftly. So deft was he that he played it by not playing it. He simply held the card, let everyone see it, and let the work of newscasters, right-wing social movements, and public imagination do the rest. Doing the rest meant commingling the hostage story with troops-in-the-Gulf stories during the months of September and October.

The commingling began with George Bush's choice for an occasion to declare, officially, the beginning of the "hostage crisis" – the Veterans of Foreign Wars (VFW) convention on August 21.[9] My conclusion is that in this case, the message was in the medium and the medium was the venue: by declaring the hostage crisis at the VFW convention and commingling the national anxieties about hostages and soldiers, the association between soldiers, veterans, and hostages had been made.

The ultimate commingling of hostage and troop-support symbolism was the use of yellow ribbons. Never before the Gulf War had this quintessential hostage-support symbol been used as a symbol of support for soldiers, much less for war. Its first use during the fall of 1990 came near military bases and was explicitly linked to troops, not civilians. The yellow-ribbon campaign was not spontaneous, and it was not simply organized – it was, in fact, an organization. "Operation Yellow Ribbon" was founded in the fall of 1990 by Gaye Jacobson, a manager for a Silicon Valley, California, defense contractor. Later incorporated in the state of California, Operation Yellow Ribbon claimed 27 chapters with 5,000 members in six states. Jacobson, who initially

volunteered her time to the organization, was eventually voted a $4,000-a-month salary.[10]

Reason four was the *liberation of Kuwait*, which took over the headlines in mid-September and extended the hostage narrative to include the Kuwaitis. In late September Kuwait-related hostage stories dominated the news. We now know that many of those stories, including the widely reported story about Iraqi soldiers dumping 312 Kuwaiti babies out of hospital incubators, were concocted by a Washington public relations firm, Hill and Knowlton, which was headed by Craig Fuller, a former chief of staff for then Vice-President Bush.[11] For five straight days, from September 25 to 30, the liberation of Kuwait was the headline story of the Gulf crisis; and then it faded, like the others, to be periodically returned to prominence as events and administration needs dictated.

Of the last two reasons for intervention, *Hussein the Hitler* and *jobs*, only the former deserves comment. The demonization of Saddam Hussein was a logical extension of the hostage issue. If there were hostages to be liberated, they would have to be liberated from someone or something. The hostage narrative required a hostage taker/holder. The campaign to demonize Saddam Hussein is already a textbook case of propaganda and the Hitlerizing of him was, supposedly, a lethal analogical construct. Replete with scary gas stories, the Hitler analogy also helped the US government recast the conflict as one with global dimensions. Hitler was, after all, out to conquer the world so, as George Bush put it, this was not about the United States against Saddam Hussein, this was Saddam Hussein against the world.[12]

On the surface, the administration's demonization of Hussein and resort to "jobs" as a reason for military intervention appeared to be acts of desperation. The administration had, after all, frantically constructed one after another reason for its buildup toward military action in the Gulf. Yet none of those reasons had convinced the American people that war was necessary. A *New York Times/CBS* poll reported on November 20 that 56 percent of respondents said restoring the government of Kuwait and defending Saudi Arabia were not good enough reasons to go to war, while 62 percent said the protection of the world's oil was not a good enough reason. The administration had failed.

Or had it? In the end, the putting forth of one reason after another functioned to paralyze rational discourse. Could anyone make sense of what this looming conflict was all about? No; and that was the point. The administration had succeeded in making it impossible to reason about the rightness and wrongness of this war. With reason neutralized, opinion about the war defaulted to the levels of emotion, symbolism, and myth. It was the myth of the spat-upon Vietnam veteran that galvanized the sentiments of the American people sufficiently to discredit peace activists and give George Bush his war.

In early fall there were only scattered reports of opposition to the buildup, but after the November 8 announcement of increased troop deployment, opposition grew, and by early December church organizations, students, and in-service soldiers were voicing their objections. This rising anti-war movement, dubbed the "Coalition Against the U.S." by the *National Review*, was ominous in the administration's eyes and had to be engaged.[13]

A conservative group calling itself the Coalition for America at Risk began running a series of paid television commercials and newspaper ads that made the soldiers themselves the reason for the war.[14] The full-page ads in major papers such as the *New York Times* and the *Wall Street Journal* featured a large photo of barren ground with a curvy line running across it. Beneath the photo, in mid-sized type justified to the left margin, was the caption: "It's not just a 'line in the sand' . . . it's . . ." Then, in large block type beneath the caption and centered on the page,

was the single word: "PEOPLE." The bottom half of the page addressed itself to "all the men and women participating in Operation Desert Shield," with the words "we are behind you and support you 100%!" Reading down, the ad passed along a "special hello from home" to 63 nicknamed soldiers in a unit identified as HMLA-367: Slick, Max, Rooster, Elvis, Bilbo, Badfinger, Fuzzy, The Dakota Kid, etc.[15]

In no sense, however, was this ad a greetings message to the troops in the Gulf. Its audience was the American people. The construction of the ad asked us to make a distinction between material and human reasons for war. It gave us, the readers, permission to choose. But the choice was about more than what the war was about. The choice was about how to make choices about support or nonsupport for the war. To choose the "line in the sand" as a reason for what "it's" about was to choose a materialist framework within which logical propositions about the ends and means related to the defense of national boundaries could be debated and adjudicated. It was in effect a choice to make one's decision within the mode of discourse chosen, up to that point, by both the Bush Administration and the anti-war theologians. To choose "people," on the other hand, was to choose to make decisions about the war on different, largely emotional, grounds. But which people should this war be about? Who are the people in this ad? Not Kuwaitis, not Saudis; this war is about Fuzzy and Bilbo, the boys from down the block. The war is about the soldiers who have been sent to fight the war.

In other words, the ad conflated the objectives of war with those who had been sent to fight the war. By thus dissolving the distinction between ends and means, the framework within which people could reason about the war was destroyed. In place of a discourse of reason, the ad gives us a discourse of emotion and identity: We should not think about what this war is about, we should feel.

*What* we should feel was mediated by the symbols mobilized for the occasion, and the image of the spat-upon Vietnam figured prominently in the rhetoric of those supporting the Gulf War. The idea that members of the anti-war movement spat upon soldiers just returned from Vietnam and cursed them as baby killers and murderers had been cultivated by *Rambo*-type movies during the 1980s. But the link between that Vietnam-era issue and support for the Gulf War was not spontaneously made by masses of people. In fact, the link was first made by Senate and House members, Vietnam veterans, who were interviewed for a story in the *New York Times* on September 16. Representative John Murtha, who had served as a Marine in Vietnam, said that on a recent visit to the Gulf "troops repeatedly asked whether 'the folks back home' supported them. 'The aura of Vietnam hangs over these kids,' the Pennsylvania Democrat said. 'Their parents were in it. They've seen all these movies. They worry, they wonder.' "[16]

The "aura of Vietnam" – what the war in Vietnam was about, as framed by this story, was the level of support that soldiers and veterans received from the American people. To make sure that nobody missed the point, the media fed us dispatches like the following from James LeMoyne:

One soldier asked that his name not be used and also asked that an officer step away to permit the soldier to speak freely to a reporter. . . . "When we deployed here, people cheered and waved flags," he [said], "but if I go back home like the Vietnam vets did and somebody spits on me, I swear to God I'll kill them."[17]

These sentiments, brought to the surface during the middle weeks of the Gulf War buildup, were then played upon by Operation Yellow Ribbon in December.

Operation Yellow Ribbon carried out its campaign through state and local organizations that claimed the support of all branches of the military. It collected material items that

it claimed were needed by soldiers in the Gulf and carried out a propaganda campaign in the public schools. In the context of the times, Operation Yellow Ribbon's foray into the schools was an act of provocation, and when parents objected, Operation Yellow Ribbon, with the help of the press and grassroots conservatives, construed their objections to be anti-soldier. Before long, local papers were flooded with letters that parroted the themes of soldiers, hostages, Vietnam, and the anti-war movement that the Bush Administration had so ably commingled during the previous weeks. Most of those letters took the form of the following, which was printed in the Worcester, Massachusetts, *Telegram and Gazette* on December 12: "Some of these peace activist groups have been around since the Vietnam war. What I find interesting is that we haven't heard any thing of them since then . . . are these the same people that spit on the GIs when they came home?"[18]

That the pro-war movement carried out a two-pronged mission of supporting the troops while attacking the anti-war movement is clear from the words of one of its supporters, interviewed at a protest rally in February, 1991. When asked by the interviewer why she was at the rally, she said:

The first reason, the first time I came out, the reason was, is because of what happened to the Vietnam vets. I felt that they were treated so badly and they fought for their country and they were treated so bad that I tried to make up for it in this way. . . .

I heard *they* [motions to peace vigil] were going to be here. And I didn't know anybody else was going to be here but I came down to protest the protesters. That's the only reason I came. Was to protest the protesters. I want the boys over there to know that there *are* people over here who are behind them and they're not gonna have to come home ashamed of their uniform; they're not gonna be having to take their uniform off at the airport so they can sneak into their own country and not be called murderers and everything.[19]

But how real is the image of the spat-upon Vietnam veteran? While there is evidence that conservative veterans' organizations like the American Legion were hostile to anti-war Vietnam veterans, there is virtually no evidence that anti-war activists were hostile to veterans. And while it is difficult to prove a negative – in this case, to prove that Vietnam veterans were not spat upon – there is plenty of evidence of real solidarity between Vietnam veterans and the anti-war movement. Anti-war activists set up coffee houses around military bases and offered counseling services to in-service GIs. Near Fort Hamilton, New York, on the Brooklyn end of the Varazzano Bridge, soldiers leaving the fort were regularly leafleated by members of the anti-war movement and offered sanctuary in a nearby church if they chose to leave the service. Soldiers were never attacked or harassed by anti-war people.[20] A Nielsen poll of GIs returning from Vietnam in 1971 showed that 50 percent approved of the peace demonstrations.[21]

But in the war of words being waged by the Bush Administration in the fall and winter of 1990–1, proof mattered little, if at all, and truth itself became what the people believed. What mattered is that lots of Americans believed that the image of anti-war protesters spitting on Vietnam veterans was true and allowed it to frame their thinking about the Gulf War.

## Armed Propaganda

To say that millions of Americans supported the Gulf War because they thought that to do otherwise would be a disservice to the US soldiers in the Gulf is to say that the Bush Administration had successfully made the means of war, soldiers, also the ends, or the reason for the war in the minds of the American people.

By this reading, the dispatching of troops to the Gulf was an exercise in what is some-times called "armed propaganda" and the war was really a propaganda war against the American people. Armed propaganda is a way of arguing through action. In this case, rather than going to the American people first and explaining why intervention in the Gulf was necessary, Bush sent the troops and then sought approval. Not getting the approval he wanted by November, he sent more troops – then asked again. In part it is the audacity of the actor, George Bush in this case, that is intended to be persuasive – who would dare oppose? And who would get hurt if opposition was successful? Why, the troops, of course. It was policy by extortion, blackmail.

### The Nixon legacy

Although honed to perfection by the Bush Administration, the use of armed propaganda during the Gulf War was hardly original. Richard Nixon used the same technique to counter the credibility of the anti-war movement and prolong the war in southeast Asia. Nixon had won election as a peace candidate with a commitment to not being the first American president to lose a war. It was a contradictory agenda and when the Vietnamese supplied a fresh offensive against Saigon from sanctuaries in Cambodia in February, 1969, Nixon began bombing that neutral country. Fearing that the US peace movement would use the bombings to build opposition to the war to new heights, Nixon tried to keep the bombings secret. But in May, with the US taking heavy losses on "Hamburger Hill" in the A-Shau valley, news of the bombings leaked out. It was time to change the subject, time to redefine what the war was about.[22]

From the spring of 1969 on, the war was going to be about the men who were sent to fight the war and, in the first instance, this meant POWs. The administration's campaign to muster public opinion around the POW issue was launched on May 19 at a press conference held by Defense Secretary Melvin

Laird. Enthusiastically promoted by the media, the POW issue soon dominated war news to the point where, as Jonathan Schell observed, "many people were persuaded that the United States was fighting in Vietnam in order to get its prisoners back."[23]

The POW issue created new visions of the war for Americans. As H. Bruce Franklin wrote, "The actual photographs and TV footage of massacred villagers, napalmed children, Vietnamese prisoners being tortured and murdered, wounded GIs screaming in agony, and body bags being loaded by the dozen for shipment back home were being replaced by simulated images of American POWs in the savage hands of Asian Communists."[24] But with the revelations of US army atrocities against civilians in My Lai in the fall of 1969, the vision blurred again. Hundreds of thousands turned out for the Moratorium Days in October and November of 1969, making it clear that, while the POW issue would animate a certain amount of pro-war sentiment, it was not enough.

The POW issue had an undeniable humanitarian appeal to it, however, which, if extended, could be applied to all soldiers in Vietnam. The Nixon Administration made the extension. Our boys in Vietnam, be they in prison or in the field fighting, could not be abandoned. Funding for the war would have to be continued lest the safety of the troops in the field be undermined; rhetoric against the war would have to be curbed lest the enemy be encouraged and our boys feel betrayed. The 30,000 GIs who had already died in Vietnam would have been sacrificed for nothing if we quit now. The war had to go on for peace with honor if not for victory. As long as there were US soldiers in Vietnam the war had to be supported because to do otherwise would mean abandonment and betrayal. In the soldiers themselves, Nixon had the perfect reason to continue the war.

Formally, the US role in the war ended with the signing of the peace accords in January of 1973. By spring of that year the draft had ended and the last US troops left Vietnam. The middle 1970s was a period for forgetting about the war. Those who fought the war and fought against it turned to other matters. Some tried to restart lives interrupted by the war, others started their careers and families. The reality of the war faded.

But pre-war rumblings stirred in the postwar quietude of the declining empire. In the wake of the United States' defeat in Vietnam a wave of Third World revolutionary movements swept into power in Africa, Asia, and South America. The Soviet incursion into Afghanistan signaled a heating up of the Cold War, and the success of the Sandinista Revolution in Nicaragua during 1978–9 made visions of communism lapping at the north shore of the Rio Grande seem real. In this climate, the Carter Administration floated a proposal to reinstate draft registration and lost its reelection bid to Ronald Reagan, who promised to bring the US hostages home from Iran.

### Reagan and Bush perfect the technique

Vietnam loomed large in the calculations of policy makers heading into the 1980s. The American people, having answered anti-communism's clarion call to the jungles of southeast Asia, would likely strangle the next bugler playing that tune. America's will to war, if there was any left, would have to be summoned through appeals to different sentiments. What had carried over from Vietnam, though, was the emotional imperative to protect American lives, safeguard American bystanders, free or account for American hostages and POWs, and support the fighting troops. If an electoral campaign could be mobilized around American hostages, why not an entire foreign policy?

What began with Reagan's invasion of Grenada in 1983, and continued into the 1990s, was a pattern of US military engagements around the world that had most, or all, of the following elements:

- US troops are dispatched to the area with little or no prior public discussion.
- The US commitment is wrapped in the flag of some larger regional or international organization, such as the Organization of American States or the United Nations.
- After the troops are there, peacekeeping or humanitarian objectives are announced as the reason.
- The local state is alleged to be inadequate for purposes of political order and economic development.
- US civilian or military personnel whose safety is at stake are said to be in the area.
- There is a strong local leader who can be demonized.
- No local military force is able to offer effective resistance to US military presence.
- There is the ostensible threat that an "outside superpower" might intervene in the situation.
- News coverage is tightly controlled.

Grenada had all of the above. It was a tiny, peaceful nation whose people allegedly longed for modernization and liberation from the despotic Maurice Bishop's cultist New Jewel Party. There were US medical students on the island whose safety was a concern. Although the virtual absence of a local military ensured the low cost of the operation, rumors of Cuban military presence on the island created sufficient drama to keep the US press and public interested. The invasion was launched with no public discussion or political approval at a time when public anxiety over international terrorism was very high.

On October 23, 1983, a truck bomb killed 300 Marines at their barracks in Lebanon. Two days later troops who were supposedly sailing for Lebanon to relieve the battered Marines were diverted to Grenada. With no prior notice, the American people were simply told that a landing on Grenada was under way. Grenada's close proximity to Cuba, the mysterious nature of the operation, plus the fact that few Americans knew anything about the island, all dovetailed with the emotionalism surrounding the losses in Lebanon. Timed as it was to follow so closly on the Lebanon incident, the Grenada operation had no trouble galvanizing the concern of Americans for the welfare of their boys there. Whatever was lacking in the administration's political and economic rationale for the mission was made up for by the rationale that "our boys are there, support them." With Thanksgiving and the religious holidays approaching, that was enough.

The invasion of Panama in the fall of 1989 followed a modified version of the same script. In this case there was somewhat more public awareness of US governmental concerns about the leadership of Panamanian dictator Manuel Noriega and the security of the Panama Canal. But the sending of troops in December of 1989 took most people by surprise. The pre-emptory nature of President George Bush's action, coupled with the regional threat of Nicaraguan Sandinismo and questions about our boys being home for Christmas, kept opposition muted for several weeks. Less than a year later Bush began the series of actions outlined above that led to war with Iraq, and in December of 1992 he sent Marines to Somalia.

## Clinton continues the practice

President Clinton inherited the Somalia commitment when he took office early in 1993. He also inherited the well-rehearsed Republican Party technique for leveraging public support for overseas military missions. Indeed, so leveraged was the public emotion for the series of mini-wars waged during the Reagan/

Bush administrations that the country was in a state of near chronic excitation by the time Clinton took office. What will to resist was still alive was clearly fatigued after Central America, Grenada, Panama, Iraq, and Somalia. It appeared that presidents, Republican or Democratic, could send troops wherever for whatever, with little worry about the domestic political repercussions – as long as the script was followed. And, with some modifications, Clinton followed the script.

Clinton's first use of the military portended his continuance of Republican past practice. On June 26, 1993, he launched Tomahawk cruise missiles against Iraqi intelligence headquarters in Baghdad in response to allegations that the Iraqis had plotted to assassinate George Bush when Bush had visited Kuwait months earlier. As a reason for military action, the supposed plot against Bush seemed very contrived, the action itself a kind of limp signal to the American public that Clinton's foreign policy would be shaped by inertia more than imagination.

Haiti was Clinton's next chance to put his own mark on foreign policy. Jean-Bertrand Aristide, a radical priest, had been elected president in Haiti's first democratic elections. Inaugurated in February, 1991, he was ousted by a military coup in September of that year. In June, 1993, the United Nations imposed sanctions on Haiti's military dictatorship led by Lieutenant Raoul Cedres. Negotiations over Cedres's departure and Aristide's reinstatement continued for several months, and in early May, 1994, the UN imposed broader sanctions. The sanctions increased the severity of economic conditions in Haiti, causing thousands of Haitians to flee to the United States.

One way in which the Clinton Administration's approach to Haiti differed from that of his Republican predecessors was that he did not send troops first and ask for permission later. In a way reminiscent of Bush's approach to Iraq, however, he did initially rule out us-

ing military force and then begin a campaign to win public and congressional approval to do just that.[25] The press knew its lines. On May 20 the *New York Times* ran "Clinton Spells Out Reasons He Might Use Force in Haiti" on its front page.[26] Adjacent to it was a story headlining Vietnamese "missing in action" (MIAs), which carried the subheading "Vietnam Revisited." This subheading and the juxtaposition of the two stories infused the reading of the story on Haiti with the subtext of soldiers' welfare and the sentiment that many Americans carry with them from the Vietnam era. Moreover, read in the post-Persian Gulf War period as it was, the packaging of the two stories clearly exploited the linkage that the Bush Administration had created between means and ends of war. Clinton did not spell out s-o-l-d-i-e-r-s as a reason why Americans should support military action in Haiti. He did not have to. The emotional embers from the Gulf War propaganda campaign were still glowing, making only a suggestion of the link between Vietnam and support for the troops necessary. If and when Clinton sent troops, the *Times* had cued up the rhetorical imagery necessary to make sure the support would be there.

"Americans in harm's way" as a reason for military force has options, of course. Recall that the Bush Administration toggled between civilian and uniformed "hostages" as a reason for war. If soldiers as a reason to support a military venture in Haiti were the subtext in Clinton propaganda, "civilians in harm's-way" were the text. Along with the "in our backyard" and "stemming the flow of refugees to our shores" reasons offered in the May 20 story, Clinton pointed to the several thousand Americans living in Haiti as a reason for the troops. By July 4, the protection of Americans in Haiti had grown to a major concern. In words that evoked memories of the Iranian embassy hostages and Saddam the hostage taker, William Gray, Clinton's special envoy on Haiti, said:

The President has a responsibility to protect American lives, and we have an embassy there with staff, and in light of the escalating human rights violations and the repression, which is really the driving force behind these refugees leaving, there is great concern that we must be prepared to protect American citizens.[27]

Again, public opinion mustered to support the protection of civilians could be easily transferred to support for the troops once they were sent.

But protection of Americans (civilian or military), stemming the flow of refugees, and policing our backyard were not the only reasons. There were others and, through the summer and early fall of 1994, the administration cited one or another as the chief reason. American citizens were the main reason in early July, removing the junta was the main goal in August.[28] On September 15, when Clinton announced his plan to invade and call up military reserves in support, he reiterated most of the reasons that had accumulated in the previous months. By that time, though, reason was irrelevant. Clinton had already made clear that with or without congressional approval, he would send troops if he wanted to. " 'I would welcome the support of the Congress and I hope that I will have that,' " Mr. Clinton said, " 'But like my predecessors in both parties, I have not agreed that I was constitutionally mandated to get it'."[29] Wrapped in the higher authority of the United Nations and the precedents of Panama and Grenada, US troops sailed for Haiti – just in time for Americans to worry about them being home for Christmas.[30]

President Clinton continued the pattern in Bosnia. From June, 1993, when the United Nations Security Council passed a resolution to create six "safe areas" for Bosnian Muslims and deploy 25,000 UN soldiers, the US government and press worked the Bosnian issue relentlessly. Day after day, major stories about Bosnia ran on the front page of the daily papers. Yet, for all the interest it

drummed up, the detailed nature of the reports about places and people that Americans found incomprehensible left most readers thoroughly befuddled. Even normally opinionated academics were wont to ask, "What is this conflict about?" Was it a religious war? An ethnic struggle? A Cold War remnant? A contest for power between Croat, Muslim, and Serbian warlords? As in the run-up to the Persian Gulf War, the more we heard, the less we knew. Indeed, many of the stories told us that "these people" have been fighting for centuries, they are irrational, their actions defy understanding – so do not try. What we were given were very emotion-evoking images that demonized the Serbs: rape camps, mass graves, and the Hitlerian Radovan Karadzic, leader of the Bosnian Serbs. The American people's decision to support the dispatch of US troops to Bosnia had to be made on the basis of these images, not reason.

On November 13, 1995, two explosions ripped through an American-run military training center in Riyadh, Saudi Arabia, killing four Americans and wounding over 30. Two radical Islamic groups claimed responsibility for the bombings. The New York Times reportage of the event emphasized the large number of Americans in the area where the bombing took place and linked the attack to Islamic radicalisms, the bombing of Pan Am Flight 103 over Lockerbie, Scotland, in 1988, and the bombing of the Marine Corps barracks in Lebanon in 1983.[31]

To the casual news reader, the story of the Riyadh bombing appeared unrelated to events in Bosnia. But read as a piece of the pattern identified in the foregoing paragraphs, it was to Bosnia what the bombing of the Marine Corps barracks was to Grenada. It was the precipitating event for a US military commitment. The day after reporting the terrorist attack on the US installation in Saudi Arabia, the New York Times announced Clinton's intention to put still more Americans in harm's way. The Yanks were coming, albeit not to Saudi Arabia. Clinton would put 20,000 troops in Bosnia as part of an international peace keeping force. And they would not be home for the holidays.

## Clinton: After but Not Beyond the Republicans

The Clinton Administration practices a domestic propaganda technique that was perfected by his Republican predecessors. It is a technique that replaces reason and rational argument with appeals to the emotions. It communicates through a discourse of military symbolism, not words and logical propositions.

Obscured by this discourse-through-symbolism are the more substantial reasons behind the lengthening series of US military deployments dating back to the early 1980s. Base-building is among the most obvious but least talked about accomplishments of this policy. Wherever the US military goes, it leaves behind an infrastructure – air strips, roads, sanitation facilities, and communications networks – that can be easily utilized at a future date. In most cases a skeletal crew is left behind to maintain equipment, serve as a listening post for intelligence, and act as a liaison with the local population.

Troop training has also been well served through the successive deployments from Grenada to Bosnia. At no other time in modern history has one country deployed troops in so many and such diverse settings, in such a short period of time, as the US has since 1983. The rapidity and diversity of the deployments has honed a generation of soldiers in the techniques of invasion and occupation to an unprecedented level. While less than full-blown warfare, operations like Somalia, Panama, and Haiti are also more than training exercises. They are the real thing under carefully chosen and controlled condi-

tions and they have produced a military more practiced in the arts of warfare than most armies in history.

State building, of the type seldom seen in this century, has also returned under the guise of US peace keeping missions. What distinguished twentieth-century imperialism from colonialism was that the former installed its own political apparatus in the "host" country, through which it directly controlled the native population while exploiting the country's land, labor, and resources. Imperialism intensified the economic exploitation within a framework of foreign-owned manufacturing operations and political independence. Today, the United States continues the practices of imperialism while installing state structures that are only nominally independent. From choosing who the political leaders will be, to running the elections and training the police, the United States is outfitting ostensibly stateless people with everything except a flag. Like a political McDonalds, the US government is cloning itself and building a franchise empire.

The pattern identified here is, finally, as much about how our knowledge of US military ventures is constructed as about the timing and logic of the policy decisions themselves. The role of the press in this endeavor cannot be overestimated. At first glance, the fact that one *New York Times* reporter like Elaine Sciolino can credibly write on events as disparate as terrorist bombings in Saudi Arabia and the restoration of democracy in Haiti, and then write a major opinion piece on the Bosnian situation, might suggest her remarkably global breadth of knowledge. Examined more critically, however, we find that there is a subtext to all these stories that makes them, essentially, the same story. Beneath their surface, all of them weave a single narrative telling the American people why they should support the troops being dispatched.

The particulars of a case, be it Iraq, Haiti,

or Bosnia, are merely the vehicles for the conveyance of the lesson of Vietnam. Vietnam was lost because the mission was betrayed on the home front. Our soldiers paid the price for that betrayal, and the only way to right the wrong done them is to renounce that chapter of our history and write a new one. The wrong done must be avenged, and we do that by repudiating the anti-war movement that stabbed them in the back and by continuing the mission. Stories of "Americans under siege," whether in Grenada, Saudi Arabia, or Haiti, tap our collective subconscious, reminding us of our forgotten POWS and spat-upon veterans of Vietnam. Once tapped, that emotional reservoir pours forth, flooding the powers of reason. Bosnia is far removed from Vietnam in both appearance and reality. Yet, as the epigraph to this chapter attests, the image of spat-upon Vietnam veterans can still be counted on to evoke support for the mission. Like a kind of "Remember the Alamo!" for late-twentieth-century America, the spat-upon veteran has become an icon of the American myth.

Unfortunately most of our analyses still focus on the government's ability to censor the press. That is not unimportant. But the analysis made here is more in keeping with that of Neil Postman, who points out that control over *how* we know is more important than control over *what* we know. While it is true that the government controls the content of news about military missions, it is more important that it is able to enormously influence how the American people think about – or do not think about – those events. Its control is more Huxlian than Orwellian, its problematic more epistemological than empirical.[32] And the task of envisioning counter-strategies to this brave new world is every bit as daunting at the end of the first Clinton Administration as at its beginning.

## Notes

Portions of this article were first published in the journal *Vietnam Generation: A Journal of Recent History and Contemporary Culture* 6 (3–4, 1995), pp. 24–36.

1 John Thomson, *Bay of the Wolf 4 (December, 1995)*, self-published newsletter, Holy Cross College, Worcester MA.
2 Elaine Sciolino, "Soldiering On, Without an Enemy," *New York Times* (October 29, 1995), p. E1.
3 Jerry Lee Lembcke, "The Myth of the Spat-Upon Vietnam Veteran and the Rhetorical Construction of Soldiers as Means and Ends in the Persian Gulf War," *Viet Nam Generation: A Journal of Recent History and Contemporary Culture* 6 (3–4) (1995), pp. 24–36.
4 Good discussions of "framing" can be found in D. A. Snow and B. Benford, "Ideology, Frame Resonance, and Participant Mobilization," *International Social Movement Research* (1988), pp. 197–217; M. Kanjirathinkal and J. Hickey "Media Framing and Myth: The Media's Portrayal of the Gulf War," *Critical Sociology* (1) (1992), pp. 103–12.
5 I am using the term "Bush Administration" in the broad sense, to include not just the president and his Cabinet, but also the governmental apparatus, private political consultants, and the press establishment that was responsible for the formulation, execution, and selling of the Gulf War policy. J. R. MacArthur, who was publisher of *Harper's Magazine* at the time, writes an excoriating account of collaboration between the government and the mainstream press during the Gulf War in *Second Front: Censorship and Propaganda in the Gulf War* (New York: Hill and Wang, 1992).

In presenting the six reasons sequentially, in the order they rose to prominence during the fall months of 1990, I do not mean to imply that they did not overlap with one another temporally and thematically. In real time, during the fall of 1990, they blurred together, sometimes being conjoined in administration press statements in packages of two or three.

Not always able to distinguish one reason from another, the public was less able than it otherwise might have been to engage political leaders in meaningful debate on the issues surrounding US intervention in the Gulf.

6  R. W. Apple, "Iraqis Mass on Saudi Frontier," *New York Times* (August 4, 1990); p. A1; T. L. Friedman, "Battle for the Saudi Soul," *New York Times* (August 4, 1990), p. A1.

7  J. Kifner, "Iraq Proclaims Kuwait's Annexation," *New York Times* (August 9, 1990), p. A1.

8  The real truth was that there probably had never been a threat to Saudi Arabia. As former US Attorney General Ramsey Clark put it in his book *The Fire This Time: U.S. War Crimes in the Gulf* (New York: Thunder's Month Press, 1992), p. 28, "the U.S. Government [had] lied to justify placing 540,000 troops in the Saudi Arabia to attack Iraq." News stories revealing the truth on this issue began surfacing in late 1990 but the mainstream news media ignored them.

9  "Excerpts from President's Remarks to V. F. W. on the Persian Gulf Crisis," *New York Times* (August 21, 1990), p. A12.

10  J. DeParle, "Despair, Calm and Disdain Greet Mobilization at Bragg," *New York Times* (August 13, 1990), p. A1; L. Belkin, "Crisis Hits Home: 'Everything is Different,' " *New York Times* (September 15, 1990), p. A1; Anon., "Gaye Jacobson," *People* (Spring/Summer, 1991), p. 44.

11  MacArthur, *Second Front*; D. K. Kellner, *The Persian Gulf TV War* (Boulder: Westview Press, 1992).

12  M. W. Brown, "To Baghdad, Poison Gas is 'Poor Man's A-Bomb.' " *New York Times* (August 9, 1990), p. A1; A. Molnar, "If My Son is Killed . . ." *New York Times* (August 23, 1990), p. A23; F. Protzman, "Germans Arrested on Iraqi Exports," *New York Times* (August 18, 1990), p. A23; J. Brinkley, "Israelis' Fear of a Poison Gas Attack is Growing," *New York Times* (October 24, 1990), p. A8.

13  D. Horowitz, "Coalition Against the U.S.," *National Review* (February 15, 1991), pp. 36–8.

14  M. Tolchin, "TV Ads Seek U.S. Support on Gulf Stand," *New York Times* (December 17, 1990), p. A12.

15  See *New York Times* (December 17, 1990) p.

B14, for an example of the ad.

16  R. W. Apple, "U.S. Set to Blockade Baghdad's Shipping," *New York Times* (August 10, 1990), p. A1.

17  J. LeMoyne, "President and the G. I.s: He will Get Respect," *New York Times* (November 22, 1990), p. A23.

18  S. Greenlaw, Letter to the Editor, Worcester, Massachusetts, *Telegram and Gazette* (December 12, 1990).

19  J. Porter, interview with Carolyn Howe (February, 1991). Cassette recording in possession of the author.

20  I was stationed at Fort Hamilton during the summer and fall months of 1968.

21  J. Neilson, "Survey of American Veterans," *Congressional Record – Extension of Remarks* (May 17, 1971), p. E4471: 73.

22  Stanley Karnow, *Vietnam: A History* (New York: Viking Press, 1983), p. 591, 601.

23  Schell is quoted by H. Bruce Franklin in *M.I.A. or Myth Making in America: How and Why Belief in Live POWs has Possessed a Nation* (New York: Lawrence Hill Books, 1992), p. 60. Franklin's book is an excellent debunking of the POW/MIA myth.

24  Ibid., p. 54.

25  Gwen Iffil, "White House Not Ruling Out Force in Haiti," *New York Times* (May 3, 1994), p. A1.

26  Douglas Jehl, "Clinton Spells Out Reasons He Might Use Force in Haiti," *New York Times* (May 20, 1994), p. A1.

27  Elaine Sciolino, "Haiti Invasion Not Imminent, Envoy Says," *New York Times* (July 4, 1994), p. A2.

28  Douglas Jehl, "Clinton Addressed Nation on Threat to Invade Haiti; Tells Dictators to Get Out," *New York Times* (September 16, 1994), p. A1.

29  Sciolino, "Haiti Invasion Not Imminent."

30  No byline, "In the Words of the President: The Reasons Why the U.S. May Invade Haiti," *New York Times* (September 16, 1994), p. A10.

31  Elaine Sciolino, "Blasts Wreck U.S. Military Aid Installation – 35–40 are Wounded in Attack," *New York Times* (November 14, 1995), p. A1.

32  Neil Postman, *Amusing Ourselves to Death: Public Discourse in the Age of Show Business* (New York: Penguin, 1985).

# 14

# Theorizing and Politicizing Choice in the 1996 Election

## ★ *Zillah Eisenstein* ★

## Introduction

Today's politics is a mix of amnesia and anesthesia.[1] "We" sleep walk through it acting as though we are awake. And the "we" here is a slim majority of the public that still votes. The rest do not even pay attention. They have been effectively shut out of the entire process – even the limited and passive activity of voting.

There has been a continual closing down of politics – the arena of debate and its liberal democratic language of "choice" – for the past quarter of a century. The early 1970s marks the visible beginnings of global capitalism and its brother, neo-conservatism. This is not to set up some imaginary loss of real democracy in the US. Instead I see important shifts to the right – away from liberal democracy's promise of equality of opportunity and individual freedom of choice, which have always only been a symbolic of capital's possibility – toward a privatized rhetoric which narrows expectation.

"Choice," like the term "liberal," is hollowed out of its meaning and vaporized. Those who still vote accept that alternatives are limited, and choose to pretend that their vote still means something. They make a choice even if they think it does not "really" make much of a difference.

It used to be radicals, or malcontents, or feminists of different varieties that wrote off the electoral arena as lacking any real choices or alternatives. The 1996 election has orchestrated the normalization and acceptance of "no-choice" discourse as part of the electoral arena itself. By the time we arrive at the "virtual" debates in October, 1996, election rhetoric has cleansed itself of all controversy – about abortion, welfare reform, health care, and global competition. There are "choiceless choices" to be made.

The public – whoever that precisely is – is supposed to watch, and listen, and pretend to "choose." Polls repeatedly confirm the statement: There is really no difference, "but I'll still vote." I wonder what has happened to make this process so normalized for the mainstream voter. This dumbing-down is not insignificant. It reveals an acceptance that "real" choice is not central to the democratic pro-cess. This authoritarian model of democracy smooths the way for global capital.

Variations of capital's sexist and racist policies cover over the lack of "real," substantive choosing. So Dole says he does not favor family leave, and Clinton says he does. Neither one says the leave should be with pay, which is the only way to give it any punch, especially for women.

There has been no simple linear process which has landed us here. Rather, there has been a complicated process of: delegitimizing the role of government as a major player in creating a cohesive nation; a rhetorical unifying of the globe post-1989 as capitalist with no real alternative or choice; a focus on the sexual/private side of elected officials as though this were the entirety of politics; a numbing of the mind through continual scandal; and the neutralizing of conflict by a president who is always looking for a compromise.

So it is politics as pretend, as performance, as chimera, as sound-bite. But this screen is not one and the same as its symbol, so the 1996 election is not about nothing. There are real needs not being met. There are real people who are homeless, and hungry, and in need of health care, and seeking abortions that cannot be gotten.

I want to make a record here and create a collective memory. I want to politicize the 1996 election by naming/theorizing abortion and reproductive rights, the destruction of welfare rights, the manipulation and misuse of feminist discourse, the privatization of public responsibilities, and the outrageous excessive wealth of transnational corporations alongside unbearable poverty inside the US as well as elsewhere in the globe.

The 1996 election silences these concerns and instead presents two main candidates, neither of whom embraces public debate and dialogue. Both are neo-conservatives. One swings to the right, the other to the center, of neo-conservatism. Neither is anywhere close to a moderate position of liberal democrat, though Clinton is ironically smeared with this label even after his open capitulation to right-wing demands.

Liberalism has become hyper-real.[2] It is a code-word for (pseudo-socialism). The label, as code, no longer relates to any actualized meaning. It has taken on its own significance and political history, and is used to smash democratic imaginings that were once aligned with it.

## Global Capitalism and the Privatization of the Public

Neo-conservatism has been attacking/downsizing the social welfare part of the US nation state for about a quarter-century now. Not much is left, especially since the signing of the welfare reform/destruction act. This privatization of the public arena – the rejection of the symbolic community with its tired and its poor – underlies a new crassness of corporate excess.

Privatization takes many forms. In one meaning, what used to be done by the government will now be done by private corporations. In another meaning, it defines individual responsibility as the core of the opportunity society. In yet another meaning, it means that what was once thought of as public is now private. The society is privatized by corporate greed and by individual loneliness/aloneness.

Yet one more side of this privatization of publicness reduces the private realm – be it corporate interests or sexual privacy – to public life. In this privatized reductionism, sex scandal stands in for knowledge. Instead of connecting private/personal life to a public set of meanings, personal/private stories, like the hooker foot fetish of Dick Morris, parade as information in the disinformation society. Supposedly we know it all, even the sexual underside; and instead we have never known so little.

Maybe one reason the public seem so ready to embrace and embroil themselves in sexual scandal is that it seems like the only "real" thing left in politics. Or as Russell Baker says, thank heavens for sex, "thank heavens for politicians who never learn. At last, life!"[3] So sex is not irrelevant here and it is not simply image making either. It rather reveals the "realness" of image making as part of the deception itself.

## Gender Gaps/Canyons

Women support Clinton by anywhere from 12 to 25 percent more than men. This is true for middle-aged women more than younger women, and for black women more than white women. Clinton is said to be more caring than Dole; more in touch with the world; raising a daughter; gentler and kinder. Dole is skewered as the nasty husband women are dumped by. So angry white men are ready to vote for Dole and "anxious white women," especially so-called soccer moms who live in the suburbs, are courted by Clinton's campaign.[4] These mainly white, married, college-educated women, who work part-time, become the symbol of the struggling middle class.[5]

The news media are too much: They can not treat women seriously even when they are trying. So stressed and hard-working white women who live in the suburbs become soccer moms, and this group stands in for the diverse women's vote. What about the rest of the women's vote: women of color, poor women, professional women, pro-choice women, etc.? Well, they have nowhere to go, other than hang with the Clinton camp, so they need not be courted. Women just have to swallow the way Clinton dumped Zoe Baird, Johnnetta Cole, Lani Guinier, and Jocelyn Elders. And we are supposed to forget about Paula Rice and Gennifer Flowers, etc.

Progressive women are not really excited about Clinton or the Democrats but they are stuck with them, while white men, excited or not, move toward the Republican Party. Polls show that the real gap between men and women is about the social-welfare state, its existence and expansion of health care, social programs, affirmative action, etc. This explains white men favoring the Republican Party in 1994 by 26 percentage points while unmarried women – of all colors – backed democrats by a 32-point margin.[6]

Women are said to be concerned with family issues like health care and education; but they are also twice as concerned as men about the insecurity of their finances.[7] Many more women than men still believe in an activist government providing a social safety net.[8] This should be no surprise given that women have the smallest safety net and yet most of the responsibility for children.[9]

As for abortion, Clinton will keep it legal, but no more than that. He will stand by it – and a woman's right to choose – but forget creating access to abortion for the women in this country. Abortion has been privatized like much else: It exists for those who can get it, and the government has no role to play in creating access in terms of either available services, or funding for the poor.

Abortion has been largely silenced in the election, except for the mess Dole created by first saying that he would not accept the Republican anti-abortion platform stance and then reneging on his promise. Otherwise, Clinton has utilized his pro-abortion record and his support for the abortion pill RU-486 to capture the women's vote. His pro-choice stance covers up much of his centrism/neo-conservatism. Many of his federal court appointees are pro-choice but otherwise not "liberal."[10]

I cannot help feeling uncomfortable about women being a decisive factor in the election of a man who clearly loves "the" sexual politics of conquest. How strange: He feels our pain and gets off on the cheap; his stance on abortion allows him lots of room to maneuver. As Faye Wattleton, former president of Planned Parenthood, says of abortion: It has become a proxy for a lot of other issues women care about.[11] It makes him look like a moderate when he is overseeing the orchestration of the neo-conservative state. Women can have the right to decide about their bodies while the safety net is pulled out from under them. Children and their mothers on AFDC will be forced off welfare even when there is no child care or job available to them.

In this whole process things are not what they seem.[12] Clinton is feminized – he diets and worries about his weight – and Hillary is masculinized as the ball-busting policy wonk. In the beginning, in 1992, there was much upset about Bill's philandering, his lack of discipline, his endless waffling. Hillary was an asset then. She spoke on his behalf and defended their marriage for all to see, and he used her unspoken feminism to shield himself.[13] They mimicked a fashionable adrogyny.

Four years later the public seems exhausted or anesthetized by it all, and women, more than men, side with Clinton as the choiceless choice. This is quite a sorry state. Women prefer someone who at least mouths a rhetoric of care, even if he does little to enact it, to someone who does not know how to look as though he cares.

Meanwhile Hillary is out of favor; she absorbs the attacks and leaves Bill free to seem more presidential. Hate Hillary, as we are often directed to hate the mother and wife. But who really hates Hillary, and why? Is the hatred because she is corrupt like most people in power? Or is it because she is a strong woman and she is just supposed to be a wife? This all mixes up a messy brew from which to inhale.[14]

In this surreal arena of politics Dole casts about looking for female voters and the two parties seem to be gender swapping. The Republican convention appeared quite feminized with Lizzie Dole working the crowds and Susan Molinari with baby underfoot. Those of us watching are not supposed to pay any attention to the fact that Molinari's vote matches Newt Gingrich's over 90 percent of the time. Columnist Maureen Down calls the convention an "estrogen festival to woo women,"[15] and the Democrats act tough, like the stern father, and clean up welfare.

Of course, by 1996, everyone knows that political conventions are made for TV. They are orchestrated and rehearsed, and the media analysts even keep telling us this is the case; so we know they are a chimera, but we are supposed to act as though it all matters anyway. Inevitably, however, fewer and fewer are listening and watching.

Politics is said to be the activity of image making by the image makers themselves. TV expects the public to pretend, and the voting public acquieces. By the time Dole takes center stage at his convention all controversy is left behind. This was most true of the mess he made of the abortion issue: Pre-convention he got hammered by reporters for dropping the tolerance plank for pro-choice Republicans, and was furious; but then this passed and abortion was silenced for the remainder of the campaign.[16]

Abortion is clearly important and unimportant electorally, and it is not taken to the convention. Both pro-choice and anti-choice voices were quieted; only Colin Powell uttered the word.[17]

And what about abortion for the Democrats? It becomes a foil and operates as a mask for the destruction of the social-welfare state. This is not to say that abortion is a mask; after all, reproductive rights are essential to democratic practices. But in the 1996 presidential election abortion is used as a mask and allows Clinton to otherwise pander to the angry white male vote.[18]

Abortion, family leave, affirmative action, welfare reform, and immigration law have been silenced as an entire package.[19] The real issues lie here, and open dialogue and conversation would uncover the limited choice between Clinton and Dole. The orchestrated silences promote a listlessness with the public(s). A choiceless vote authorizes the narrowed, privatized politics of neo-conservatism, and small differences retheorize the justification of politics for global capital. With no alternative vision – like the former Soviet Union – around, the discourse of liberal democracy vanishes. Liberalism, in its demonized form, is now fully in place, and instead of choice, there is acquiesence and despair.

Abortion, as a discourse of liberalism and the freedom of choice, takes on new significance within the choiceless global economy.[20] It remains as one of the few sites where the language of choice still has enormous pull. As such, as a demand central to women's lives, it locates women in an ambivalent relation to its use as a mask for centrist politics.

## The Politics of Choice and Global Capital

The economic nation is under assault from global capital, or, as Clinton's adviser Robert Reich makes clear, corporate power has new viability today. It can move around at whim; unlike the displaced laborer. Labor is stuck where it is and within national borders that are being redefined away from multiple publics, like the poor and unemployed, and toward the tax needs of the richest.

Anti-tax rhetoric is all of a piece with anti-government jargon. Capitalist universalism negates multiple particularisms, and Clinton says he will end government as we have known it. Government tax structures, along with deregulation of land rights, pollution, patents, etc., will give capital a free hand, and in the process political discourses are closed down. Meanwhile, anti-tax rhetoric is used to seduce struggling middle-class workers.

This anti-tax, anti-government stance is a tough place to be as a politician. Neither Clinton nor Dole can speak of a government which entitles people to what they need without challenging the business interests that back them; and this is no small consideration when the presidential campaign costs $800 million. It is no surprise that even one of Dole's advisers finds it hard to clarify how the two differ. He says of the Clinton camp, "they're running to the right of us."[21]

The presidential debates institutionalized the "no-choice" discourse of global capital for all to see, and the extreme right- wing poli-

tics of the militias keep the neo-conservatives looking centrist. These are not happy alternatives: neo-conservatives at the center, and radical rightist anti-abortionists and right-wing militias in the wings.

## Welfare Reform and the Destruction of Publicness

I do not single out the welfare-reform package as completely extraordinary, although it has devastating consequences. Clinton's attitudes toward welfare are an intrinsic part of his privatized "New Democrat" stance: to end government's public responsibility as we have known it. This is continuous with his days in Arkansas as governor.

The destruction of social welfare as it has existed involves the cutting of $56 billion from its budget.[22] Clinton justifies his support: "On balance this bill is a real step forward for our country, our values, and for people who are on welfare." He also admits disappointment that "the bill contains provisions that will hurt legal immigrants in America, people who work hard for their families, pay taxes, serve in our military." But, in the end, he says this will help those who are "trapped on welfare."[23]

Clinton's welfare legislation, derived largely from Newt Gingrich's Contract with America, ends the government's guarantee for cash assistance for poor children. The head of every family on welfare will have to work at a job within two years; lifetime welfare benefits will be limited to five years; payments to unmarried teeange parents under 18 will be allowed only if the mother stays in school and lives with an adult; and eligibility standards for disabled children will become stricter.[24] All of this is being done to an already downsized social-welfare state which accounts for less than 1 percent of GNP.

The welfare bill ends *any* right to assistance for needy children and families. For the first time since the New Deal, no guaranteed help from the government exists for the poor, and states are free to develop their own drastic measures. This takes us backward to pre-New Deal times.[25] Little is said of the fact that creating enough entry-level jobs for the poor at the current rate they are developing would take 21 years.[26] Little is said of the tax breaks given to corporations and wealthy individuals in 1996 amounting to $440 billion, which is more than 17 times the combined worth of state and federal spending on AFDC.[27]

Welfare functions as the imaginary of failed government, and poor women of color are the scapegoats here. Most families who need welfare usually need it for less than two years at a time. About 40 percent of these families are on welfare for one year at a time; another 28 percent leave welfare within two. As such welfare is not a trap but an assistance for those who work jobs at poverty wages.[28]

The "typical" family on AFDC is a mother and one child. The birth rate among AFDC women is lower than among the rest of the population. This stands in stark contrast to the imaginary welfare woman who has babies at the expense of the government. And more to the point, the welfare payments themselves have become more imaginary (as a handout) than real, because benefits have considerably shrunk in the last ten years.[29]

Making social welfare look bankrupt is part of the bankrupting of the "idea" of governmental public responsibility. Make the poor look irresponsible and lazy and take away their entitlements; the government is blamed for creating the very problem of poverty it is supposed to address. Senator Patrick Moynihan is clear about how corrupt this all is. This is the author of the infamous Moynihan Report of 1965, which attacked the government's role in maintaining the deviancy of single-parent black families. Today he stands against the abolition of social welfare, as it will create at least another 2.6 million people living below the poverty line; 1.1 million of those being children. He muses: "Just you wait until there are a third of a million children in the streets."[31]

This destruction of welfare for the poor – named as reform and as an end to government as we have known it – leaves the way wide open for new business "opportunities of a lifetime," as private companies compete to take over the administration of welfare. Leading the way is Ross Perot's Electronic Data Systems, a $12.4-billion information-technology company.[31]

## Clinton's Neo-Conservatism

Sound-bites are the communication form of transnational capital. Politics appears dispersed, fragmented, and disconnected, and there is a series of important issues that are made into non-issues. The Clinton record never coalesces as a coherent neo-conservative agenda but instead is depicted as liberal and pro-government by Dole and the Republican Party.

Memory requires that we remember that Clinton was elected in 1992 promising health care for all. In his 1994 State of the Union message, Clinton held up a pen and told congress that he would veto legislation that did not guarantee every American health insurance that could never be taken away. He said health care was "our most urgent priority."[32] This stance is all but dropped in the 1996 campaign, when, at best, Clinton says he needs to figure out "ways to give more people access to health insurance,"[33] and is reduced to promising new moms an extra day in the hospital.

Neither candidate speaks about the crisis of health care, or the way it has a stranglehold on the US economy and the 40 million people who remain without health insurance at present. Instead, medical insurance companies have won big and now orchestrate the movement toward managed/mangled care.

The private market is reforming and remaking the health-care system, instead of the government doing it;[34] and this anti-government rhetoric will most probably lead to the destruction of social security during Clinton's second administration.

Clinton supports both the Marriage Act denying spousal social security and pension benefits to gays and the V-Chip and Communications Decency Act; all to protect children and family life from porn on the one hand, homosexuality on the other. He says he is against discrimination against gays in the workplace and clearly sees this as an utterly different issue than discrimination by marriage law. Instead of carrying through on an end to the ban on gays in the military, Clinton instituted the "don't ask, don't tell" policy.

While Clinton polices porn on the information highway, he leaves in place the unequal jail time for crack and cocaine use. He has overseen a crime bill which creates dozens of new death penalties, he supports the idea of random drug testing for welfare recipients, and his welfare bill denies assistance to anyone convicted of a drug felony. He uses wire taps quite regularly in his administration. In sum, this neo-conservative supports net censorship, wire tapping, and file gathering in his war on privacy.[35] And Clinton clearly believes that civil liberties will have to be amended in the fight against terrorism.

He supported a minimum wage increase to $5.15 an hour even though this still leaves a family of four below the poverty line. He has allowed a weakening of the Delaney Clause, which monitors the carcinogens in food. He has lessened the effects of the Endangered Species Act, pushed to privatize public lands, continued to allow the devastation of western forests, and overseen the exacerbation of chemical pollution.[36]

Clinton and Dole do not look too different here. Yet Clinton is still seen as a liberal by 37 percent of those polled, and another 43 percent see him as a moderate.[37] He nurtured his moderate/liberal identity as he stood up to the gun and cigarette lobbies at the Democratic convention, and he also has retained, so far, a committment to affirmative action. He says we must "mend, not end" it, although the process of mending may undermine its initial integrity. It is true too that Clinton has appointed more white women and members of minorities to high-level positions than has any other president.[38] These "little differences" sustain the "moderate/liberal" rhetoric.

Transnational corporations want a downsized government. They, however, simultaneously support a corporatist version of multiculturalism and feminism which replaces government programs with old-style rugged individualism. This transnational/capitalist politics can abide opportunity for all; just not equality. Clinton is out there trying to figure out how to negotiate the necessary moves towards what he calls the "center" in order to maintain what is left of the US nation state. No surprise, then, that legal immigrants are on their own to fend for themselves; and workers need to find their own health care; and poor women who cannot afford abortions do not get them.

To conclude when there is really nothing left to say: I cannot vote for Clinton again. This is made easy for me because it is clear he will win.

## A Post-Election Query

Clinton and Dole leave a legacy of imaginaries and images that look more different than similar, even though they are more similar than different. But if politics is as much imagery as "real," political discourse matters. When Dole and the Republican Congress are symbolized as conservative and Clinton is described as a moderate New Democrat seeking the center, this should matter somewhat. We will have to wait and see whether Clinton's message of moderation holds any sway with his rightward drift.

It is hard to imagine the next four years. Neither candidate ran with a serious agenda. Clinton pretty nearly repudiated all the important ideas of the Democratic Party, so now that he's re-elected it is not clear what the Democrats will do. Newt is said to be "gentler and kinder" and willing to compromise.

In 1992 when Clinton won there was a lot of hope that he could/would make a differ-ence. I was one of those who believed that he might turn back the "Reagan/Bush" decade of privatization. In 1996 it would be irresponsible to hope. Instead, progressive, feminist, civil rights, pro-choice, labor, gay, immigrant, and child voices must be organized and heard as loud as, or louder than, the selfish voice of transnational capital. We must be vigilant at pressing and pushing our waffler of a president beyond his center.

# Notes

This chapter was first delivered as a pre-election guest lecture at Cornell University, Ithaca NY, October 21, 1996. My thanks to Rosalind Pollack Petchesky and Asma Barlas for helpful comments on the present revisions.

1 Susan Buck-Morss, "Aesthetics and Anaesthetics: Walter Benjamin's Artwork Essay Reconsidered," *October* 62 (Fall, 1992), pp. 3–41.

2 Jean Baudrillard, trans. Charles Levin, *For A Critique of the Political Economy of the Sign* (St Louis: Telos Press, 1981); Baudrillard, trans. Mark Poster, *The Mirror of Production* (St Louis: Telos Press, 1975).

3 Russell Baker, "Sex to the Rescue," *New York Times* (August 31, 1996), p. A21.

4 Elaine Sciolino, "As Clinton Gains With Women He Falls in Eyes of Many Men," *New York Times* (October 6, 1996), p. A1.

5 Neil Mac Farquher, "What's A Soccer Mom Anyway?," *New York Times* (October 20, 1996), p. E1.

6 Steven Stark, "Gap Politics," *Atlantic Monthly* 278(1) (July, 1996), pp. 71–80.

7 Taken from a poll in *Good Housekeeping* 223(3) (September, 1996), p. 14.

8 Gail Collins, "Wooing the Women," *New York Times* Magazine (July 28, 1996), pp. 32–5.

9 Elinor Burkett, "In the Land of Conservative Women," *Atlantic Monthly* 278(3) (September, 1996), p. 29.

10 According to Nat Hentoff in "Bill Clinton's Judges", *Village Voice* XLI (44) (October 29, 1996), p. 25, judges appointed by Clinton have written liberal decisions 35 percent of the time, whereas Jimmy Carter's did so 52 percent, Gerald Ford's 39 percent, and Richard Nixon's 37 percent.

11 Stated in Frank Rich, "Dole's Pregnant Silence," *New York Times* (October 19, 1996), p. A23.

12 Roger Morris, *Partners in Power* (New York: Henry Holt, 1996); Bob Woodward, *The Choice* (New York: Simon and Schuster, 1996).

13 Erica Jong, "Hillary's Husband Re-Elected!," *Nation* 263 (17) (November 25, 1996), p. 14.

14 Todd Purdham, "Advisers See Bright Side to Criticism of First Lady," *New York Times* (August 25, 1996), p. A1. See also Zillah Eisenstein, *HATREDS: Racialized and Sexualized Conflicts in the Twenty-first Century* (New York: Routledge, 1996), Ch. 5, for a full analysis of Hillary Clinton.

15 Maureen Dowd, "Plowshares into Pacifiers," *New York Times* (August 16, 1996), p. A27.

16 Katherine Seelye, "Under Pressure, Dole Reconsiders Abortion Plank," *New York Times* (July 13, 1996), p. A1; Seelye, "Moderates in G.O.P. Vow Fight On Platform Abortion Language," *New York Times* (August 7, 1996), p. A1.

17 Sam Howe Verhovek, "With Abortion Scarcely Uttered, its Opponents are Feeling Angry," *New York Times* (August 15, 1996), p. A1.

18 Russell Baker, "In the Attic? Hillary?," *New York Times* (August 3, 1996), p. A19.

19 Adam Nagourney, "On Volatile Social and Cultural Issues, Silence," *New York Times* (October 9, 1996), p. A1.

20 See Susan Faludi for an interesting discussion about the conflicts surrounding abortion in the Republican Party, in "The G.O.P.'s Back Stairs," *New York Times* (August 18, 1996), p. E15.

21 Stated in John Heilemann, "Netizen: Big Brother Bill," *Wired* 4 (10) (October, 1996), p. 199.

22 Peter Kilborn and Sam Howe Verhovek, "Clinton's Welfare Shift Reflects New Democrat," *New York Times* (August 2, 1996), p. A1.

23 "President Clinton's Announcement on Welfare Legislation," *New York Times* (August 1, 1996), p. A24.

24 Robert Pear, "Clinton Says He Will Sign Welfare Bill to End U.S. Guarantee," *New York Times* (August 1, 1996), p. A22.

25 Women's Committee of One Hundred, "Update" 2 (June, 1996), 750 First Street, N.E., Suite 700, Washington DC 20002.

26 Alan Finder, "Welfare Clients Outnumber Jobs they might Fill," *New York Times* (August 25, 1996), p. A1.

27 Randy Albelda, Nancy Folbre, and the Center for Popular Economics, *The War on the Poor* (New York: New Press, 1996), p. 20.

28 Ibid.

29 "Welfare Myths: Fact or Fiction," prepared by the Center on Social Welfare Policy and Law (1996), e-mail HN0135@handsnet.org.

30 R. W. Apple Jr, "His Battle Now Lost, Moynihan Still Cries Out," *New York Times* (August 2, 1996), p. A16.

31 Nina Bernstein, "Giant Companies Entering Race to Run State Welfare Programs," *New York Times* (September 15, 1996), p. A1.

32 Michael Wines and Robert Pear, "President Finds he has Gained Even if he Lost on Health Care," *New York Times* (July 30, 1996), p. A1.

33 Alison Mitchell, "Despite his Reversals, Clinton Stays Centered," *New York Times* (July 28, 1996), p. A1.

34 For a discussion of the initial Clinton healthcare proposal see Theda Skocpol, *Boomerang: Clinton's Health Security Effort and the Turn against Government in U.S. Politics* (New York: W. W. Norton, 1996).

35 Heilemann, "Netizen," pp. 52–3.

36 James Ridgeway, "Green All Over," *Village Voice* XLI (41) (October 8, 1996), p. 26.

37 Reported from a *New York Times* News Poll, June/July, 1996, noted in Mitchell, "Despite his Reversals."

38 Steven Holmes, "On Civil Rights, Clinton Steers Bumpy Course Between Right and Left," *New York Times* (October 20, 1996), p. A16.

# 15

# The Right Family Values

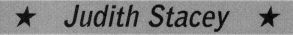

## ★ *Judith Stacey* ★

*The way a male becomes a man is by supporting his children. . . . What [the Democrats] cannot accept is that government proposals have failed. It is the family that can rebuild America. . . . The dissolution of the family, and in particular, the absence of fathers in the lives of millions of America's children is the single most critical threat [to our future].*

Dan Quayle (September 8, 1994)

*That is a disaster. It is wrong. And someone has to say again, "It is simply not right. You shouldn't have a baby before you're ready, and you shouldn't have a baby when you're not married."*

President Clinton (September 9, 1994)

## Introduction

In November of 1992, there seemed impeccable cause to imagine that the US family wars were about to abate. The extent and irreversibility of family change, assisted by Murphy Brown, the Republican Convention fiasco, and the Year of the Woman, seemed to have vanquished the family-values brigades, while "the economy, stupid" lured many Reagan Democrats back from their costly supplyside fling. Who would have predicted that even the liberal media would scramble to rehabilitate Dan Quayle's image before Bill and Hillary had survived their blistering first 100 days?

Yet that is exactly what happened. "Dan Quayle was Right," blared the April, 1993, cover of the *Atlantic* monthly,[1] a magazine popular with the very "cultural elite" whom the former Vice-President had blamed for the decline of western civilized family life. Far from withering, a revisionist campaign for family values flourished under Democratic

skies. While Clinton's job-stimulus package suffered a silent demise, pro-family-values stories mushroomed in magazines, in newspapers, on radio and TV talk shows, and in scholarly journals. The *Atlantic* cover story by Barbara Defoe Whitehead ignited "the single strongest public response to any issue ever published by the *Atlantic* since at least 1981," and was recycled from sea to rocky sea.[2] A *New York Times* op–ed, "The Controversial Truth: The Two-Parent Family is Better," by Rutgers University sociologist David Popenoe, also enjoyed acclaim, with retreads and derivatives appearing from the *Chronicle of Higher Education* to the Santa Rosa, California, *Press Democrat*.[3] In the winter 1992–3 *American Scholar*, Senator Daniel Patrick Moynihan, a founding father of post-World War II family crisis discourse in the US, added to his hefty inventory of family-values jeremiads, while James Q. Wilson, the Collins Professor of Management and Public Policy at UCLA, earlier proponent of racial theories of criminality, weighed in with a featured family-values essay in *Commentary*.[4] From *This Week with David Brinkley* to the *MacNeil-Lehrer News Hour* television followed suit, featuring guests like Popenoe chanting kaddish over an idealized family past.

Less a revival than a creative remodel job, the 1990s media blitz on "family values," which coincided with the Clinton administration's rapid conversion to its credo, signals the considerable success of a distinctively new political phenomenon. Because the rhetoric of family-values discourse seems so numbingly familiar, most progressives have failed to recognize, or to respond appropriately to, what is dangerously novel here. To comprehend the cultural politics of the Clinton Administration, one must understand how and why a revival of the family-values campaign coincided with the changing of the political guard that appeared to spell its decline.

## Pseudo-Scholarly Cultural Combat

Old-fashioned family-values warriors, like Jerry Falwell, Dan Quayle, and Pat Buchanan, are right-wing Republicans and fundamentalist Christians, overtly anti-feminist, anti-homosexual, and politically reactionary. Their "pro-family" campaign, which provided zeal and zeitgeist for both of Reagan's victories, enjoyed its heyday in the 1980s and suffered a major setback during the 1992 electoral season – from Quayle's infamous "Murphy Brown" speech, through the ill-advised "family-values" orgy of the Republican Convention, to defeat at the polls. By 1996 this highly mobilized, zealously Christian pro-family movement had secured such a firm grip on the Republican Party that "moderate" candidates, such as Senators Arlen Specter and Pete Wilson, who failed its anti-abortion or anti-gay litmus tests, could not seriously contend for their party's presidential nomination.

In contrast, the revisionist family-values campaign to which the Clinton Administration succumbed has an explicitly centrist politics, rhetoric, and ideology. A product of academicians rather than clerics, it grounds its claims in secular social science instead of religious authority, and eschews anti-feminism for a post-feminist family ethic.

While the right wing may prove the prime beneficiary of current family-values discourse, it is not its primary producer. Rather, an interlocking network of scholarly and policy institutes, think tanks, and commissions began mobilizing during the late 1980s to forge a national "consensus" on family values that soon shaped the family ideology and politics of the Clinton Administration and his "new" Democratic Party. Central to this effort are the Institute for American Values, of which David Blankenhorn is president and Barbara Dafoe Whitehead (author of the *Atlantic* article) vice-president, and its offshoot, the Council on Families in America, cochaired by Popenoe and Jean Bethke Elshtain. The former, which Popenoe describes as a "nonpartisan public policy organization," sponsors the latter, whose 18 members depict themselves as "a volunteer, nonpartisan program of scholarly research and interdisciplinary deliberation on the state of families in America. We come from across the human sciences and across the political spectrum."[5]

"This is an attempt to bring people together who could convince the liberal intelligentsia that the family was in trouble and that this was a big problem," Popenoe explained to me in an interview. "Most of us are neoliberal – you know, New Democrats, affiliated with the Progressive Policy Institute. We try to keep to the middle of the road."[6] The political networks, and the funding sources, of these center-laners merge with those of the "communitarians" – a movement which its founder, sociologist Amitai Etzioni, characterized as "struggling for the soul of the Clinton Administration."[7] They are linked as well with those of the Democratic Leadership Council's Progressive Policy Institute. Political scientist William Galston, who was Clinton's chief domestic policy adviser until he resigned in June of 1995 (citing his paternal responsibilities as reason for his decision), is a communitarian as well as a member of the Council on Families. Blankenhorn, Popenoe, and Elshtain all are communitarians, as is Henry Cisneros. Al Gore spoke at a 1991 communitarian teach-in.

Galston co-authored a family-policy position paper for the Progressive Policy Institute,[8] which echoed themes from a conference cosponsored by the Institute for American Values at Stanford University in 1990. The conference volume, *Rebuilding the Nest*, edited by Blankenhorn, Elshtain, and Steven Bayme, helped guide the deliberations of the National Commission on Children, which issued the 1991 "Rockefeller Report," *Beyond Rhetoric: A New American Agenda for Children and Families*.[9] Governor Bill Clinton of Arkansas was a member of that commission.

These groups share the same benefactors, like the Randall, Smith Richardson, Scaife, and Mott foundations, and the Brookings and American Enterprise institutes, according to Popenoe, more of which are conservative than liberal, he conceded.[10] With such support, revisionists are self-consciously waging a cultural crusade, one modelled explicitly after the anti-smoking campaign, to restore the privileged status of lifelong, heterosexual marriage. Declaring that "the principal source of family decline over the past three decades has been cultural," Whitehead urged the Institute for American Values readership to join a cultural mobilization to restore nuclear family supremacy.[11] Wilson's *Commentary* essay went further, calling "this raging cultural war" over family values "far more consequential than any of the other cleavages that divide us."[12] *Newsweek* columnist Joe Klein, now notorious as the anonymous author of *Primary Colors*, the best-selling novel based on

Clinton's campaign to become the 1992 Democratic Party presidential candidate, applauded revisionist proposals for, "a massive anti-pregnancy [sic] and proselytizing campaign similar to the anti-smoking and -drug crusades of recent years. 'Those *worked*,' says presidential adviser William Galston. 'They really changed behavior patterns, and this might, too.' "[13] Likewise, when Blankenhorn addressed a corporate-sponsored, invitational public forum on crime that I attended in San Francisco in the fall of 1995, Blankenhorn made the remarkable claim that "there is one main thing going on out there in this country – the absence of fathers," and argued that in order to address it, "the most important thing to change is our minds."[14]

If the effects of this campaign on sexual and conjugal behaviors in the "private" sphere remain to be seen, it quickly achieved an astonishing, and disturbing, impact on the public behavior and policy priorities of the Clinton Administration. It took scarcely a year to convert Clinton from representing himself as a proud icon of an independent, single-mom's glory into a repentant Quayle acolyte. "Hurray for Bill Clinton. What a difference a year makes," Quayle gloated in December 1993, right after *Newsweek* had published the president's revised family credo: "Remember the Dan Quayle speech? There were a lot of very good things in that speech," Clinton acknowledged. "Would we be a better-off society if babies were born to married couples? You bet we would."[15] The rhetorical means through which Clinton's family-values makeover occurred merit close scrutiny.

## Feigning Iconoclastic Courage

In one of the more effective rhetorical ploys of the revisionist campaign, these mainstream social scientists, policy lobbyists, and prominent political officeholders and advisers ride the coat tails of the anti-political correctness crusade by positioning themselves as dissident challengers of a formidable, intolerant, ideological establishment. Popenoe, for example, is Associate Dean of Social and Behavioral Sciences at Rutgers University, as well as co-director of the Council on Families in America. Wilson occupies an endowed professorship of management and public policy at UCLA, and Elshtain an endowed professorship of theology at the University of Chicago. Etzioni was the 1994–5 President of the American Sociological Association. And Senator Moynihan, well . . .

Yet Wilson characterizes those scholars who reject a nostalgic view of 1950s families as "policy elites."[16] During a radio debate over the superiority of the two-parent family, Popenoe portrayed me and other feminist sociologists as part of the "liberal social science establishment."[17] Whitehead laments, "it is nearly impossible to discuss changes in family structure without provoking angry protest,"[18] citing as evidence enraged responses in the mid-1960s to Moynihan's *The Negro Family: The Case for National Action*, which had labeled the rising percentages of black single-mother families a "tangle of pathology." She attributes to ideological pressures some of the "caution" exercised by researchers who do not support the claim that single-parent families are deficient. "Some are fearful that they will be attacked by feminist colleagues," Whitehead claims, "or, more generally, that their comments will be regarded as an effort to turn back the clock to the 1950s – a goal that has almost no constituency in the academy."[19]

Wilson predicted that were President Clinton to exercise leadership in condemning unwed child bearing, he would elicit, "dismayed groans from sitcom producers and ideological accusations from sociology professors, but at least the people would know that he is on their side."[20] Exploiting popular resentment against "PC" cultural elites builds upon

a tradition of disingenuous populism honed by former Republican vice-presidents Spiro Agnew and Dan Quayle. At the same time, it pays tribute to the considerable, albeit precarious, influence over gender and family discourse which feminism has achieved during the past quarter-century. Inside the academy, many centrists probably do feel threatened and displaced by feminist scholars. They are fighting back.

## Constructing Social-Scientific Stigma

While the right-wing family-values campaign appeals to religious and traditional patriarchal authority for its family vision, centrists are engaged in an active, indeed an entrepreneurial, process of transmuting into a newly established, social-scientific "truth" one of the most widely held prejudices about family life in North America – the belief in the superiority of families composed of married, heterosexual couples and their biological children. Revisionists argue that the presence or absence of two married, biological parents in the household is the central determinant of a child's welfare, and thereby of our society's welfare. They identify fatherless families as the malignant root of escalating violence and social decay, claiming such families generate the lineage of unemployed, undomesticated, "family-less fathers," as John Gillis aptly puts it,[21] who threaten middle-class tranquility.

Through the sheer force of categorical assertion, repetition, and cross-citation of each other's publications, these social scientists seem to have convinced most of the media, the literate public, and Clinton himself that a fault-free bedrock of social science research validates the particular family values that they and most Americans claim to favor, but fail to practice. "In three decades of work as a social scientist," asserted Popenoe in his *New York Times* op–ed, "I know of few other bodies of data in which the weight of evidence is so decisively on one side of the issue: on the whole for children, two-parent families are preferable to single-parent and stepfamilies."[22] In the *Atlantic* story three months later, Whitehead quoted these very lines as authority for a similar assertion: "The social arrangement that has proved most successful in ensuring the physical survival and promoting the social development of the child is the family unit of the biological mother and father."[23] Whitehead also relied on Moynihan's "Defining Deviancy Down," which blamed "broken families" for almost all of our current social crises. Moynihan, in turn, had quoted an earlier essay by Whitehead in support of a similar argument.[24] Moynihan, Whitehead, and Popenoe all cited the National Commission on Children Rockefeller Report, and the report returned the favor with frequent citations to essays by Popenoe and his associates in the Institute for American Values and the Council on Families in America.[25]

Then, when in April, 1993, Popenoe defined the "ideal family" in the *Chronicle of Higher Education*, he paraphrased views that he and Blankenhorn both had expressed in *Rebuilding the Nest* and that Whitehead and the Rockefeller Report had endorsed:

What are the characteristics of an *ideal* family environment for childrearing? The Council believes they are an enduring family with two biological parents that regularly engages in activities together; has many of its own routines, traditions, and stories; and provides a great deal of contact between adults and children.[26]

With minor editorial revisions, the council reprinted this definition as one of eight propositions on the family in America.[27]

It is not often that the social construction, or more precisely here the political construction, of knowledge is quite so visible or incestuous as in the reciprocal citation practices of these cultural crusaders. Through such means they have convinced the president and

most of the public that "it is a confirmed empirical generalization," as Popenoe maintains, that non-traditional families "are not as successful as conventional two-parent families."[28] Yet the current status of social-scientific knowledge of the success of diverse family structures is far more complex, and the views of family scholars far more heterogeneous, than revisionists pretend. Social scientists continue actively to debate whether family form or processes determine diverse family outcomes and whether the family or socio-economic crisis has generated its counterpart.[29] For example, in a judicious, comprehensive review essay of the cumulative research on changing parent–child relations, prominent family sociologist David Demo concluded that "the consequences of maternal employment, divorce, and single-parent family structure have been greatly exaggerated, and that researchers need to investigate processes more directly influencing children, notably economic hardship and high levels of marital and family conflict."[30] In fact, according to Demo, "the accumulated evidence is sufficiently consistent to wonder whether we, as researchers, are asking the most important questions, or whether we, like the families we are trying to study, are more strongly influenced by traditional notions of family normality".[31]

Revisionist social scientists suppress these debates by employing social-scientific sleights of hand. For example, they rest their claims on misleading comparison groups and on studies, like Judith Wallerstein's widely cited research on divorcing parents, that do not use any comparison groups at all.[32] While it is true that, on average, children whose parents divorce fare somewhat worse on several measures than those whose parents remain in intact marriages, this reveals little about the impact of divorce on children. To address that question, one must compare children of divorce not with all children of married parents, but with those whose unhappily married parents do not divorce. In fact, research indicates that high-conflict marriages harm children more than do low-conflict divorces. "There is abundant evidence," David Demo concludes, "that levels of family conflict are more important than type of family structure for understanding children's adjustment, self-esteem, and other measures of psychological well-being."[33] Unhappily married parents must ask themselves not whether divorcing or staying married is worse for children in general, but which would be worse for their particular children in their particular unhappy marriage.

Centrists use additional statistical tricks to exaggerate the advantages some children from two-parent families enjoy over their single-parented peers. For example, they pretend that correlation proves causality, they ignore mediating variables, or they treat small and relative differences as though they were gross and absolute. In fact, most children from both kinds of families turn out reasonably all right, and when other parental resources – like income, education, self-esteem, and a supportive social environment – are roughly similar, signs of two-parent privilege disappear. Most research indicates that a stable, intimate relationship with one responsible, nurturant adult is a child's surest track-lane to becoming the same kind of adult. In short, the research scale tips handily toward those who stress the quality of family relationships over their form.[34]

Once dissenting scholarly views on the pathology of single-parent families had been muffled or marginalized, only a rhetorical baby-step was needed to move from the social to the moral inferiority of such families; ergo the remarkably respectful public response which American Enterprise Institute scholar Charles Murray received in November, 1993, to his overtly punitive quest to restigmatize unwed child bearing via Dickensian welfare policies. "My proposition is that illegitimacy is the single most important social problem of our time – more important than crime,

drugs, poverty, illiteracy, welfare or homelessness because it drives everything else," Murray declared in defense of his proposal "to end all economic support for single mothers." Forcing single mothers on welfare to go cold turkey would slash non-marital child bearing, Murray reasoned, because "the pressure on relatives and communities to pay for the folly of their children will make an illegitimate birth the socially horrific act it used to be, and getting a girl pregnant something boys do at the risk of facing a shotgun."[35] Instead of receiving timely visits from the Ghosts of Christmases Past, Present, and Future, Murray was soon the featured guest on *This Week with David Brinkley*, and even in liberal San Francisco, an op–ed by a supporter of his proposals from the right-wing Hoover Institute upstaged the more charitable Christmas-week commentaries aired on the local affiliate of National Public Radio.[36]

By then, revisionists had deftly paved the yellow brick road to Murray's media coronation. "Bringing a child into the world outside of marriage," Blankenhorn had asserted three years earlier, "is almost always personally and socially harmful."[37] In December of 1992, Moynihan congratulated himself on having predicted both the epidemic of single-parent families and its calamitous social consequences nearly 30 years earlier. "There is one unmistakable lesson in American history," he had written in 1965; "a community that allows a large number of young men to grow up in broken families, dominated by women . . . asks for and gets chaos."[38] In April, 1993, just as Whitehead's *Atlantic* essay hit the stands, Wilson explicitly advised President Clinton that, to honor his populist pretensions, he should "say that it is wrong – not just imprudent, but wrong – to bear children out of wedlock."[39]

Thus, by the time the 1993 holiday season began, the ideological mortar had dried firmly enough to encourage *Newsweek* columnist Joe Klein's view that "the issue is so elemental, the question so basic, the answer so obvious" that one should not have to ask a president, as the magazine just had done, whether it is "immoral for people to have children out of wedlock." Klein applauded when President Clinton, himself possessed of dubious parentage and out-of-wedlock half-siblings who seem to surface intermittently, answered, "much as Dan Quayle, to whom he gave considerable credit, might have: 'I believe this country would be a lot better off if children were born to married couples.'" After all, Klein lamented:

It's a measure of our social fragility and moral perversity that the president's statement will be controversial in certain circles even though there's now a mountain of data showing illegitimacy to be the smoking gun in a sickening array of pathologies – crime, drug abuse, physical and mental illness, welfare dependency. Bill Clinton's morality will, no doubt, be seen as hopelessly retro – or worse, as cynical politics – in Hollywood, where he was off raising money over the weekend and where out-of-wedlock births are quite the fashion.[40]

Indeed, by then, the revisionist cultural onslaught had been so effective that even Donna Shalala, the token feminist progressive in Clinton's cabinet, felt politically compelled to recite its moralist mantra: "I don't like to put this in moral terms, but I do believe that having children out of wedlock is just wrong." And "a dyed-in-the-wool, but curious, White House liberal" confided, off the record, to *Newsweek*, "I'd like to see the Murray solution tried somewhere – just to see, y'know, what might happen."[41] In June, 1994, *before* the right-wing Republican mid-term electoral rout, Clinton sent a "welfare-reform" proposal to Congress with caps on child-bearing and benefits that threatened to satisfy such liberal curiosity. He signed a more diaconian assault on welfare at the height (or depths) of the 1996 electoral campaign.

## The New Postfeminist Familism

Despite inflated claims to iconoclasm, revisionists promote family values that seem, at first glance, tediously familiar. Sounding like card-carrying conservatives in academic drag, they blame "family breakdown" for everything from child poverty, declining educational standards, substance abuse, homicide rates, AIDS, infertility, and teen pregnancy to narcissism and the Los Angeles riots. They attribute family breakdown, in turn, to a generalized decline in family values, which, in its turn, they often associate with feminism, the sexual revolution, gay liberation, excessively generous welfare policies, and escalating demands for social rights.

While orthodox and revisionist family preachers share obvious affinities, centrists take wiser note of present demographic and cultural terrain than do their right-wing counterparts. Because they claim to decry rampant individualism, they tend to acknowledge greater public and corporate responsibility for family decline and redress than is palatable to family-values hardliners. Many used to claim to support the Progressive Policy Institute's call for a "guaranteed working wage" that would lift families with full-time workers out of poverty. Most also claim to favour family-friendly workplace reforms like flextime, family leaves, and flexible career paths.[42] Disappointingly, however, they and the Clinton Administration have devoted far less of their political energies to these more progressive goals than to the cultural campaign which has done much to undermine them.

Perhaps the most significant distinction between the traditional and neo-family-values campaigns is in gender ideology. Departing from the explicit anti-feminism and homophobia of a Jessie Helms or Pat Buchanan, family centrists accommodate their family values to postindustrial society and postfeminist culture.[43] They temper their palpable nostalgia for Ozzie and Harriet with rhetorical gestures toward gender equality. "The council does not bemoan the loss of the traditional nuclear family," with its strict social roles, distinguishing between male breadwinners and female homemakers," Popenoe maintains. "Recognizing," instead,

the importance of female equality and the changing conditions of modern society, we do not see the previous model of lifelong, separate gender roles within marriage as either desirable or possible on a society-wide scale. But we do believe strongly that the model of the two-parent family, based on a lasting, monogamous marriage, is both possible and desirable.[44]

Blankenhorn has been developing a more reactionary gender ideology in the course of his mounting crusade against fatherlessness, but just a few years ago he too espoused postfeminist ideology:

Strengthening family life in the 1990s cannot and should not mean the repeal of the past 30 years of new opportunities for women in the workplace and in public life. Just as today's cultural ethos of individualism affects men just as much as women, so must a revived ethos of family life affect the behavior and priorities of both sexes.[45]

Revisionists place great emphasis on reviving paternal commitment. Wilson lauds efforts by the National Center for Neighborhood Enterprise "that try to encourage men to take responsibility for their children."[46] Whitehead praises a high-powered Boston attorney who "left his partnership at a law firm and took a judgeship that gave him more manageable hours," so that he could spend more time with his children and his wife, also an attorney, who left trial law for more family-friendly work.[47] Similarly, Galston cited his paternal priorities when he resigned as Clinton's chief domestic-policy adviser to attend to his own domestic concerns, and his university professorship, in June 1995: "I told the president,

'You can replace me and my son can't.' "[48]

Blankenhorn has turned combatting fatherlessness into his overarching mission. Joining forces with Don Eberly, a former aide to Jack Kemp, he formed a national organization of fathers to "restore to fatherhood a sense of pride, duty and reward."[49] Combining a massive promotional tour for his 1995 book *Fatherless America* with a campaign for the National Fatherhood Initiative, which Blankenhorn chairs, he is actively crusading to counter "excesses of feminism," like the belief that "men will not become new fathers unless they do half the diaper changes or bottle feedings." Instead, his campaign promotes a neo-traditional model of fatherhood, in which "the old father, with some updating in the nurturing department, will do just fine."[50]

Such postfeminist ideology appeals to many conservative feminists and to many liberals. It builds upon a body of thought I once labeled "new conservative feminism," to which family centrists Elshtain and Sylvia Hewlett made formative contributions.[51] One of the defining features of this ideology is its weak stomach for sexual politics. Centrists offer tepid support, at best, for abortion rights, often supporting restrictions like spousal and parental notification, partly with the claim that these could hold men more paternally accountable.[52] And as communitarian founder Etzioni put it, "there are some issues, such as abortion and gay rights, that we know communitarians cannot agree on, so we have completely avoided them."[53]

Rather than confront the internal contradictions, unjust power relations, and economic reorganization which underlie the decline of lifelong marriage, revisionists promote what Whitehead terms a new familism, in which postfeminist women willingly, admirably, and self-consciously *choose* to place familial needs above the demands of "a life defined by traditional male models of career and success." "In the period of the New Familism," Whitehead exults, "both parents give up something in their work lives in order to foster their family lives. The woman makes the larger concession, but it is one she actively elects and clearly sees as temporary."[54] Popenoe explicitly proposes "revising the cultural script" for modern marriages by making such "temporary," asymmetrical gender concessions a normative feature in his model of the "modified traditional nuclear family."[55] Blankenhorn's bio-evolutionary view of parenthood explicitly scorns feminist or androgynous family values. "Ultimately, the division of parental labor is the consequence of our biological embodiment as sexual beings and - of the inherent requirements of effective parenthood." His vision of rehabilitated paternity embraces only slightly modified forms of traditional paternal authority and responsibility:

Historically, the good father protects his family, provides for its material needs, devotes himself to the education of his children, and represents his family's interests in the larger world. This work is necessarily rooted in a repertoire of inherited male values . . . These values are not limited to toughness, competition, instrumentalism, and aggression – but they certainly include them. These "hard" male values have changed and will continue to change. But they will not disappear or turn into their opposites. Nor should we wish them to.[56]

## . . . And Other Euphemisims for Injustice

### The "stability" of gender inequality

One need hardly be a paranoid feminist to penetrate the shallow veneer of revisionist commitments to gender equality. Defending a lengthy lament by Popenoe about American "family decline," family sociologist Norval Glenn, for example, conceded that there is "a rational basis for concern that attempts to put the family back together' may tend to erase

recent feminist gains." Likewise, Wilson acknowledged that "what is at stake, of course, is the role of women."[57]

Of course. Few feminists were confused when Quayle lashed out at Murphy Brown. Perhaps a few more will be misled by the higher-toned, centrist retread of his views. Yet, despite lip-service to gender equality, the revisionist campaign does not redress marital inequities or question that women bear disproportionate responsibility for their children and families. Rather, in the guise of rejecting "male models," it adds to the unjust burden of guilt, anxiety, and marginality that divorced, unmarried, and unhappily married mothers already suffer. That Wilson and Glenn recognize the gender stakes in this discursive game underscores how much more the communitarian rhetoric of "family values" impugns the individualism of women than that of men.

Postfeminist familist ideology appropriates feminist critiques of conventionally masculine work priorities while appealing to those conventionally feminine maternalist values that feminist scholars like Carol Gilligan and Deborah Tannen have made popular. This ideology also exploits women's weariness with the incompatibility of postindustrial work and family demands, as well as their anxiety over the asymmetrical terms of the heterosexual courtship and marriage market and of women's vulnerability to divorce-induced poverty.

Centrists often blame excessive divorce rates as well as unwed motherhood on a general rise of selfishness – gender unspecified. To curb such indulgence they advocate measures to restrict access to divorce, such as mandatory waiting periods and counseling and the reinstatement of "fault" criteria in divorces that involve children. Typically they present their proposals for these restrictive measures under a child-centered mantle that taps women's all-too-ready reservoirs of guilt about failing to serve "the best interests" of their children. In It Takes A Village, Hillary Clinton follows this suit. She supports mandatory "cooling-off" periods and counseling for parents considering divorce, explaining, "with divorce as easy as it is, and its consequences so hard, people with children need to ask themselves whether they have given a marriage their best shot and what more they can do to make it work before they call it quits."[58]

The backlash against no-fault divorce is gaining popularity among politicians in both political parties. Republican Governor Terry Brandstad of Iowa denounced no-fault divorce in his 1996 State of the State Message. In February, 1996, Michigan became the first state to consider a bill to revoke no-fault divorce in cases where one spouse opposes the divorce, and several other states are considering following Michigan's lead. Arguing that people "must begin to see the connection between divorce and other problems, especially poverty and juvenile delinquency," Jessie Dalman, the Republican sponsor of the Michigan bill, augmented the child-protection rationale with a direct appeal to women's fear of impoverishment.[59] Likewise, Dan Jarvis, director of the Michigan Family Forum policy group that has campaigned vigorously for this bill, portrayed it as protecting women: "Let's say a homemaker has a husband who cheats on her. Under the proposed law, she would have the upper hand. She can say: "All right, you want your divorce? You can have it. But it's going to cost you.' "[60]

Many women – especially homemakers – and their children indeed have been impoverished by the unfair effects of current no-fault divorce property settlements, as feminist scholars and lawyers have documented.[61] The current unjust economic consequences of no-fault divorce laws are a serious problem in need of serious legislative and judicial reforms. It is a postfeminist sleight-of-hand, however, to pretend that repeal of no-fault divorce is the only or best possible remedy, or that it will promote greater gender equality in marriage. The rhetoric against no-fault erroneously implies that men seek a disproportionate number of contemporary divorces and that women have greater interests than men in sustaining their marriages. Unfortunately, the reverse is closer to the truth. Women seek a disproportionate number of contemporary divorces, despite the unjust consequences they risk in doing so, often because they find the injustices and difficulties of their marriages even harder to bear.[62]

Whether revisionist efforts to affix a tepid norm of gender equality to family-values rhetoric are well intentioned or disingenuous, their marriage seems ill-fated. Principles of egalitarianism and stability frequently collide, and, as in too many traditional marriages, the former are sacrificed to the latter. Revisionists, unlike both orthodox family-values advocates and feminists, rarely confront a disturbing contradiction at the heart of the western ideal of a fully volitional marriage system: Historically, stable marriage systems have rested upon coercion, overt or veiled, and on inequality. Proposals to restrict access to divorce implicitly recognize this unpleasant contradiction, one which poses a thorny dilemma for a democracy. If, as many feminists fear, a stable marriage system depends upon systemic forms of inequality, it will take more than moralistic jeremiads bemoaning family decline, or even mandatory waiting and counseling prerequisites to divorce, to stanch our contemporary marital hemorrhage.

This bleaker, feminist analysis of contemporary marital fragility, rather than the "family optimism" which revisionists attribute to social scientists, like me, who do not share their views,[63] explains some of the political passions at stake in our dispute. Without coercion, as Wilson concedes, divorce and single motherhood rates will remain high. Indeed, I agree with Popenoe that women's capacity to survive outside marriage, however meagerly, explains why both rates rose so sharply in recent decades. Marriage became increasingly fragile as it became less economically obligatory, particularly for women. These developments expose the inequity and coercion that always lay at the vortex of the supposedly voluntary "companionate marriage" of the traditional nuclear family. It seems a poignant commentary on the benefits to women of that family system that, even in a period when women retain primary responsibility for maintaining children and other kin, when most women continue to earn significantly less than men with equivalent "cultural capital," and when women and their children suffer substantial economic decline after divorce, in spite of all this, so many regard divorce as the lesser evil.

I do not dispute Glenn's judgement that "male–female equality in a society in which the quality of life is mediocre for everyone is hardly anyone's idea of utopia."[64] However, because I am far less willing to sacrifice women's precarious gains on the chimerical altar of social stability, I am more motivated to find alternative, social responses to our misdiagnosed familial ills.

## The "biology" of heterosexism

Homophobia also plays a closeted role in the centrist campaign, one that could prove more insidious than right-wing gay bashing. Wilson includes popular discomfort with same-sex marriage in his sympathetic inventory of the family values of "reasonable people."[65] Popenoe makes one foray at a definition of "the family" broad enough to encompass "homosexual couples, and all other family types in which dependents are involved," only to retreat instantly to the linguistic mantra favoring "two biological parents" that pervades revisionist rhetoric.[66] Moynihan's conviction that children need to grow up in families that provide them with a "stable relationship to male authority" is echoed by Whitehead's undocumented claim that research demonstrates "the importance of both a mother and a father in fostering the emotional well-being of children."[67] Blankenhorn, once again, goes even further by explicitly condemning lesbian child bearing. Indeed, his book *Fatherless America* formally proposes restricting access to donor sperm and alternative insemination services exlusively to married couples with fertility problems. "In a good society," Blankenhorn maintains, "people do not traffic commercially in the production of radically fatherless children."[68]

Elshtain unapologetically concedes that when she and her colleagues affirm a heterosexual family model, "we are privileging relations of a particular kind in which certain social goods are at stake."[69] Doing so panders to popular heterosexist prejudice. Despite consistent research findings that lesbians and gays parent at least as successfully as heterosexuals,[70] the Council on Families in America refuses to advocate equal marriage, adoption, or child-bearing rights for the former. If neo-family-values fans were faithful to their stated goals of promoting lasting familial bonds and committed, two-parent families, they should actively endorse what former *New Republic* editor Andrew Sullivan calls "a conservative case for gay marriage."[71] Yet no such sermons issue from their bully pulpits. Rather, these challengers of "ideological constraints" remain faithful to Etzioni's credo, quoted above: "there are some issues, such as abortion and gay rights, that we know communitarians cannot agree on, so we have completely avoided them."[72] Similarly, even though First Lady Hillary Clinton claims that she wrote *It Takes a Village* in order to challenge "false nostalgia for family values," the book pursues this centrist strategy of evasion by failing even to mention the subject of gay marriage or gay families, let alone to advocate village rights or resources for children whose parents are gay.[73] Likewise, in the 1995 fall pre-election season, when President Clinton sought to shore up his flagging credibility among gays and lesbians by announcing his administration's support of a bill to outlaw employment discrimination against gays, he specifically withheld his support from gay marriage.[74]

This evasion abetted the social agenda and political strategy of organized reactionaries. Homophobia has become the latest "wedge issue" of the New Right family warriors, and served this function in the 1996 Republican electoral strategy. When Republicans sought to scuttle passage of the Family Leave Act in January 1993, newly inaugurated Clinton's own first family-values offering, they did so by attempting to saddle it with a rider to prevent lifting the ban on gays in the military. Likewise, Falwell seized upon Clinton's nomination of a lesbian, Roberta Achtenberg, to an undersecretary post as an opportunity to flood the coffers of his Liberty Alliance. Urging readers to send donations of $25 with a "Stop the Lesbian Nomination Reply Form," Falwell warned that, "President Clinton's nomination of Roberta Achtenberg, a lesbian, to the Department of Housing and Urban Development is a threat to the American family . . . Achtenberg has dedicated her life to winning the 'rights' of lesbians to adopt little babies. Please help me stop her nomination."[75] The Traditional Values Coalition, based in Anaheim, claims to have sold 45,000 copies of the videotape *Gay Rights, Special Rights* that they designed expressly to mobilize anti-gay sentiment among African Americans.[76] However, gay marriage, precisely the issue that Clinton and his centrist advisers sought to evade, emerged as the family-values centerfold of the 1996 Republican electoral strategy. At a Saturday-night church service and "marriage-protection" rally on the eve of the Iowa primary caucuses, "Republican presidential hopefuls declared war on the notion of same-sex marriages."[77] Promising to pursue the culture war he had waged at the 1992 GOP convention, Pat Buchanan declared: "We cannot worship the false god of gay rights. To put that sort of relationship on the same level as marriage is . . . a moral lie." Follow-

ing the service, candidates Phil Gramm and Alan Keyes joined Buchanan in signing a pledge to oppose same-sex marriage.[78] One month later, Randall Terry, director of Operation Rescue, the extreme right-wing anti-abortion group, flew to Hawaii to wage a direct-action campaign against the state court's anticipated legalization of gay marriage.

On May 8, 1996, gay marriage galloped onto the nation's center political stage when congressional Republicans introduced the Defense of Marriage Act (DOMA), which defines marriage in exclusively heterosexual terms as "a legal union between one man and one woman as husband and wife." The last legislation that Republican presidential candidate Bob Dole cosponsored before he resigned from the Senate to pursue his White House bid full throttle, DOMA exploited homophobia in order to defeat President Clinton and the Democrats in November, 1996. With Clinton severely bruised by the political debacle incited by his support for gay rights in the military when he first took office, but still dependent upon the support of his gay constituency, the president indeed found himself "wedged" between a rock and a very hard place. Unsurprisingly, he first tried to waffle. Naming this a "time when we need to do things to strengthen the American family," Clinton publicly opposed same-sex marriage at the same time as he tried to reaffirm support for gay rights and to expose the divisive Republican strategy. However, he also tried to finesse the Republican strategy by quickly promising he would sign the bill if it reached his desk.[79] It did, and Clinton kept his promise.

Ironically, the identification of Republicanism with such intolerance alarms many party moderates. However, a forum they convened in May of 1993 to reorient the party foundered on just this faultline, with conservatives supporting Buchanan's view that "traditional values is the last trump card the Republican Party possesses."[80] Clinton's capitulation to the centrist family-values ideology colluded with a homophobic, right-wing agenda at a dangerous moment.

## Making a "career" of class bias

Less obvious than the gender and sexual stakes of family-values rhetoric, perhaps, are ways it also serves as a sanitized decoy for less reputable prejudices of class and race. Having studied working-class families struggling to sustain body, soul, and kin ties in the economically depressed Silicon Valley during the mid-1980s, I cannot help but wonder what sort of bourgeois, bubble world revisionists like Whitehead, Popenoe, and the communitarians inhabit. Perhaps their moralistic images of selfish, individualistic, hedonistic adults, who place their own emotional and sexual pleasures and "career" ambitions above the needs of their vulnerable children, derive from observations of some who reside in a professional – corporate social cocoon.

Such caricatures bear little resemblance to 20-something Carole, a layed-off electronics assembler and fotomat envelope stuffer, a wife and mother of four, who left and returned to her abusive husband before she died of cancer. Nor do they apply to Lanny, another 20-something, layed-off drafter, who divorced the substance-abusing father of her young daughter after discovering he had "snorted away" the down payment she had laboriously accumulated to purchase a house. They do not fit Jan, a 40-year-old lesbian, social-service worker, who continues to contribute time, resources, and love to the son of a former lover. They do not adequately depict the tough choices or the family realities that confront any of the women I studied, nor, I would venture, those of the vast majority of citizens. The idiom of "careers" that family-values enthusiasts employ suggests ignorance of how few adults in the postindustrial USA enjoy the luxury of joining "a new familism" by choosing to place their children's needs above the demands of

their jobs. They could win much more respect for their cause, and enhance its prospects, if they would spend nearly as much time badgering public and corporate leaders to provide citizens with the kinds of jobs, incomes, schedules, and working conditions that might make the practice of any reasonable sort of "familism" viable as they have devoted to persuading individuals that "the most important thing to change is our minds."[81] Ironically, it is the failure of the Clinton Administration's 1992 employment and health-care agenda that fostered its retreat into the rhetorical politics of family values. In June, 1996, for example, "seeing no immediate prospect of an agreement with Congress on welfare," as one reporter put it, "President Clinton announced yesterday that he was taking steps on his own to increase child-support collections and track down fathers who violate child-support orders."[82] Yet this in turn buttresses the very assaults on welfare that now threaten to devastate millions of the nation's poorest children and families.

## Willie Horton in whiteface

Wherever class bias flourishes in the US, race can seldom be far behind, for, in our society, these two axes of injustice are, always already, hopelessly entangled. Quayle's 1992 attack on Murphy Brown was an ill-fated attempt to play the Willie Horton card in whiteface. Without resorting to overtly racist rhetoric, the image conjured up frightening hordes of African-American welfare "queens" rearing infant fodder for sex, drugs, and video-taped uprisings, such as had just erupted in Los Angeles. As Elizabeth Traube points out, "shadow traces of African-American family practices are inscribed in postfeminist visions of the family," and the *Murphy Brown* program directly exploits semiotic effects of this ancestry with Motown music on its opening theme soundtrack.[83] Lurking in Murphy's shadows were descendents of the pathological "black matriarchs" Moynihan permanently etched into the collective consciousness nearly three decades ago.[84]

In case anyone in the fin-de-siècle USA remained ignorant of the racial coding of family-values discourse, Charles Murray used a megaphone to give them a crash course. His *Wall Street Journal* op–ed, reprinted by the *Philadelphia Enquirer* under the title "The Emerging White Underclass and How to Save It," warned whites that their family patterns now resemble that malignant "tangle of pathology" which Moynihan presciently diagnosed in 1965 among African Americans. Displaying greater honesty than most revisionists, Murray concluded by speaking the unspeakable: "the brutal truth is that American society as a whole could survive when illegitimacy became epidemic within a comparatively small ethnic minority. It cannot survive the same epidemic among whites.[85]

Racial anxiety runs as subtext to the entire history of family-crisis discourse in the US, a history which long predates Moynihan's incendiary 1965 report. It reaches back a century to xenophobic fears that, in the face of high fertility among "inferior" eastern and southern European migrants, the "selfishness" of native white women, whose birth rates were declining, threatened their tribe with "race suicide." It reaches back much further into the history of colonial settler fears of the diverse sexual and kinship practices of indigenous cultures, as well as to rationales that esteemed white scholars offered for African American slavery–that it helped civilize the heathen by teaching family values to a species which lacked these. Consider that, until E. Franklin Frazier published *The Negro Family in the United States* in 1939, most social scientists subscribed to the view of Howard Odum that "in his home life, the Negro is filthy, careless, and indecent, . . . as destitute of morals as many of the lower animals . . . [and with] little knowledge of the sanctity of home or marital relations."[86] And this about a

system that denied slaves the right to legal, or permanent, conjugal and parental bonds.

If marriage was a form of racial privilege under slavery, it is rapidly becoming so again today. William Wilson's chauvinistic, but still stunning, "marriageable Black male index" graphs the increasing scarcity of African American men who are neither unemployed nor incarcerated. His index indirectly demonstrates that male breadwinning and marriage are becoming interactive badges of race and class status.[87] Indeed, the greatest contrast in family patterns and resources in the US today is between two-steady-earner and single-mother households, and these divide notably along racial lines. No doubt this is why presidential voting patterns in 1992 displayed a "family gap" more pronounced than the gender gap. Married voters heavily favored Bush, while the unmarried shored Clinton's precarious margin of victory.[88] A campaign that sets couple- and single-parent families at odds has political consequences. During the 1996 campaign, Clinton strategists set out to erode the advantage Republicans enjoy among the largely white, middle-class, heterosexual, two-parent family set. According to Democratic National Committee pollster Stanley Greenberg, by June, 1996, married mothers were favoring Clinton over Dole, and Clinton had reduced Dole's strong support from married fathers to a margin of only 5–6 percentage points. "It's a very big deal," Greenberg enthused, "that the President is running very well with married mothers and, to some extent, married men.[89] The disproportionately white, middle-class character of that constituency appears to have escaped Greenberg's and the public's notice.

## The Emerging Conservative Cultural "Consensus"

Whether or not the centrist family-values strategy successfully enhanced Clinton's re-election prospects, it succeeded in promoting a conservative political agenda. As leaders of the right-wing Christian "pro-family" movement recognize, with delight, family-values ardor furthers their reactionary goals. Gary Bauer, president of the right-wing Family Research Council and editor of the fundamentalist *Focus on the Family Citizen*, gloated over "signs that a pro-family consensus, which has been forming for several years, is continuing to gel," despite the election of Clinton. Identifying the *Atlantic* as the premier organ "of smug, elitist, knee-jerk liberalism," Bauer aptly read Whitehead's vindication of Quayle as the most prominent of increasing "signs that the traditionalist revival among policy experts has not been snuffed out."[90]

Bauer understands the political implications of revisionist discourse better than do its propagators. Despite the collectivist aspirations of communitarian ideology, the political effects of identifying "family breakdown" as the crucible of all the social crises that have accompanied US postindustrialization and the globalization of capitalism are privatistic, and profoundly conservative. Clinton's own "welfare-reform" proposals, which differed from those of the Republican right wing only in their lesser degree of severity rather than in their ideological presumptions about family breakdown and welfare dependency, should be persuasive on this score.

Particularly troubling, and ironic, has been the success of recent appeals to homophobic family values among many African American ministers and the electorate they influence. In November, 1993, the religious right succeeded in winning support for repeal of a local gay-rights protection ordinance from 56 percent of the voters in traditionally liberal black precincts in Cincinatti. Effectively portraying the gay and lesbian movement "as a group of well-off whites fighting for 'special rights,' " their right-wing family-values campaign convinced a majority of African American voters that the interests and constituencies

of the two movements are antagonistic.[91] Similar strategic alliances of right-wing family-values activists and African American clergy had blocked the passage of the first referendum for domestic partners legislation in San Francisco in 1989.

Thus the rush to consensus on family values is not only premature; it is undemocratic. The idea that we should all subscribe to a unitary ideal of family life is objectionable on social-scientific, ethical, and political grounds. I had hoped, and Bauer and his associates had feared, that Clinton's 1992 electoral defeat of the right-wing family-values campaign would signal an opportunity for democratic initiatives on family and social reforms, initiatives that would begin with a recognition of how diverse our families are and will continue to be. Instead, under the Clinton Administration, we witnessed the startling resurrection of family-values ideology. Beneath its new, velvet gown is an old-fashioned, confining, one-size-fits-all corset. But US families come in many shapes and sizes, and will continue to do so. A democratic family politics must address diverse bodily and spiritual desires in rhetoric people find at least as comfortable as the ever-popular combat uniform of "family values."

## Toward Reconfiguring Feminist Family Politics

No sound-bite rebuttal can convey the complex, contradictory character of family and social turmoil. Still, we must disrupt the stampede to premature consensus on family values. To wage a viable counter-cultural campaign for *social* values, progressives need to confront the impoverishment of our national capacity to imagine human bonds beyond familial ones that can keep individuals safe from our "heartless world." So atrophied is this cultural muscle that "family" impulses overcompensate, a voracious floating signifier for all manner of social ties, as is "family breakdown" for all manner of social disarray.

Two media items illustrate the depressing ubiquity of this ideological translation. An op–ed by China scholar Franz Schurmann that lauded the cooperative, cultural traditions that have generated phenomenal economic growth in China concluded that "creating new *social power* is the key to reversing the United States' decline" (my emphasis). Not once did Schurmann use the ubiquitous "F" word, but the editorial page editor affixed the title "Families that Work are Helping China."[92]

More predictable was the photo caption, "The post-nuclear family," which the *New York Times* ran over a picture of young black "doughnut men" (joyride car thieves) in Newark, New Jersey. The photo accompanied a story identifying family decline as the source of delinquency, as well as the impetus for parental appeals to "government, schools and whatever communal vestiges remain in a mobile and complex society," for help in rearing law-abiding youth.[93]

We cannot counter the flawed, reductionist logic of family-values ideology, however, unless we resist using knee-jerk, symmetrical responses, like a feminist bumper sticker Whitehead cited effectively to mock feminism: "Unspoken Traditional Family Values: Abuse, Alcoholism, Incest."[94] Portraying nuclear families primarily as sites of patriarchal violence, as some feminists have done, is inaccurate and impolitic.[95] It reinforces a stereotypical association of feminism with anti-familism, which does not even accurately represent feminist perspectives on the subject. Certainly, protecting women's rights to resist and exit unequal, hostile, dangerous marriages remains a crucial feminist project, but one we cannot advance by denying that many women, many of them feminists, sustain desires for successful and legally protected relationships with men and children. We must steer a tenuous course between cultural warriors who blame public violence on (patriarchal) family decline, and

those feminists who blame family decline on (patriarchal) domestic violence.

A better strategy is to work to redefine family values democratically by extending full rights, obligations, resources, and legitimacy to a diversity of intimate bonds. We might take our lead here from the, only partly, parodic family-values campaign currently blossoming among gays and lesbians.[96] Progressives could appeal to the rhetoric of the revisionist family-values crusade to advocate full marital, reproductive, and custody rights for gays and lesbians. Such a strategy requires bridging the rift between gays and blacks, first by disputing the erroneous notion that these are distinct communities, and second by addressing racism among white gays and black homophobia at the grassroots level. African American heterosexuals and all homosexuals, supported by a full-spectrum "rainbow coalition," must come to recognize mutual interests in democratizing family rhetoric, rights, and resources.

Exposing the "PMC" (professional middle-class) bias of communitarian ideology, as Charles Derber has done, offers another opportunity to identify with the actual family needs of the vast majority of citizens.[97] However, we must first acknowledge that full-time homemaking, like the male family wage on which it depends, has become a form of class privilege in the fin-de-siècle US that eludes increasing numbers of women to whom it appears, often legitimately, far preferable to the unsatisfying, poorly paid work to which they are consigned.[98] Until feminism can shed its well-earned reputation for disdain toward the world of the full-time, cookie-baking mom, revisionists will effectively exploit feminist class prejudices.

Another way to reconfigure family values is to up the ante in the revisionist bid to elevate the cultural status and responsibilities of fatherhood. Here I agree with Blankenhorn that the sort of family-values campaign we most urgently need is one to reconfigure popular masculinities. "Family-less fathers," be they married or single, do seem to be disproportionately harmful to women, children, and civil society, as well as to themselves. Normative masculine behavior among the overpaid ranks of greedy, power-hungry, competitive, corrupt, corporate and professional, absent fathers, and also among more overtly macho, underpaid, underemployed, undereducated, volatile "boyz in the hood," can lead women, as well as men like Blankenhorn, to idealize cinematic visions of Victorian patriarchy. We sorely need cultural drives to deglamorize violence, predatory sexuality, and sexism, such as one announced in 1994 by an organization of black professional women, as well as efforts to combat the destructive androcentric logic behind "the clockwork of male careers."[99] Unfortunately, currently the most prominent inititatives of this sort – the Christian men's movement, Promise Keepers, and the 1995 African-American Million Man March called by Farrakhan – seem to share with Blankenhorn a nostalgic affection for a world of "Father Knows Best." The democratic challenge is to find ways to affirm the laudable sentiments these movements tap while enticing them to follow Patricia Williams's call for a more egalitarian "different drummer please marchers."[100]

Progressive might try to go further than revisionists in efforts to domesticate men. Why not promote full-time homemaking and child rearing as a dignified alternative to over-, under-and unemployment for men, as well as for women? Although the percentages remain small, increasing numbers of men have begun to find this a rewarding and challenging vocation. Popenoe, citing both James Q. Wilson and George Gilder and echoing even feminist Sherry Ortner, maintains that "men need the moral and emotional instruction of women more than vice versa, and family life, especially having children, is a considerable civilizing force for men."[101] If that is correct, then giving men full-time domestic obliga-

tions should prove a potent curriculum.

Rethinking family values requires dodging ideological corners into which revisionists deftly paint feminists and other progressives. First, we should concede that the best familial interests of women (or men) and children do not always coincide. While research demonstrates that high-conflict marriages are at least as destructive to children as is parental divorce, there *are* some unhappy marriages whose adult dissatisfactions harm children less than do their post-divorce circumstances. Some divorces *are* better for the adults who initiate them than for the children who must adjust to them. Ironically, joint-custody arrangements often impose a particularly unfair burden on the children of divorce. Joint-custody preferences were adopted by many-states along with no-fault divorce not only to foster greater gender equality for parenting adults, but also to serve children's interests in maintaining intimate relationships with both parents after a divorce. Unfortunately, the consequences have been far less benevolent. At their best, even amicable joint-custody arrangements typically force children, rather than parents, to become residential commuters between two different households, neighborhoods, or even communities. At their worst, antagonistic joint-custody situations extend indefinitely the exposure of children to the damaging effects of parental hostility and conflict. In consequence, so many women have bargained away economic support in order to retain primary custody of their children that some feminist lawyers are proposing to revise the custody standard applied in divorce-custody conflicts. For example, University of California family law professor Carol Bruch is promoting legislation to replace the state's current judicial presumption in favor of joint-custody awards with one that grants primary custody to the parent who actually had served as a child's primary caretaker prior to the divorce.

Likewise, just as there are His and Her

marriages, so too divorce is often better for one spouse (not always the male) than the other, as are many remarriages and the stepfamilies they create. When the best interests of the genders collide, it is not easy to say whose should prevail. However, it is also not easy to say whether or not the genders actually do have incompatible interests in making all marriages harder to leave. The vast majority of women, men, and their children derive clear benefits from living in loving, harmonious, secure relationships, but men and women in marriages like these rarely choose to divorce. What is really at issue in the great divorce controversy is the extent to which easy access to divorce encourages individuals to indulgently throw in the towel on marriages that are not too wet to be saved. In other words, how many marriages that now end in divorce could have been saved, and would have been better off for all parties if they had been?

Research does not, and probably cannot, shed much useful light on this question. No doubt "divorce culture," as critics call it, does foster some undesirable instances of capricious divorce. But how large is that incidence, and at what cost do we deter it? Contrary to the claims of the anti-divorce campaigners, there is little evidence that many parents regard divorce as a casual, impulsive, or easy decision. Nor is there evidence that divorce restrictions are likely to achieve their intended effect of buttressing marital commitment. They are at least as likely to deter people from marrying in the first place, and more likely to encourage unhappily married individuals to resort to extra-legal forms of desertion and separation. These practices have become so widespread in Roman Catholic countries that even Ireland has taken measures to legalize divorce. For better and worse, governmental attempts to socially engineer the quality, as opposed to the legal form, of intimate relationships have an abysmal historical track record.

The campaign against single mothers calls for an analogous response. We do not need to defend single mothers from the open season of cultural bounty hunters by denying that two compatible, responsible, committed, loving parents generally *can* offer greater economic, emotional, physical, intellectual, and social resources to their children than can one from a comparable cultural milieu. Of course, if two parents are generally better than one, three or four might prove better yet. A version of Barbara Ehrenreich's Swiftian proposal, that to lift their families out of poverty black women should wed "Two, Three, Many Husbands,"[102] is unlikely to win popular affection. Still, we might draw upon communitarian sentiments to foster much more collective responsibility for children. Spontaneously, many childless and child-free adults are choosing to become unofficial "para-parents," by forming nurturant, long-term relationships with the children of overburdened parents (a category from which few parents would exclude themselves). Children's advocates might actively promote and seek social protection for these voluntary extended kin relationships, which, as the *New York Times* put it, treat "children as a collective commitment that is more than biological in its impulse."[103] No doubt such proposals would prove more appealing and constructive than polyandry.

Similarly, we should not feel obliged to reject the claim that in industrial societies, teenage motherhood often does not augur well for the offspring. Without disputing the view that most teens today lack the maturity and resources to parent effectively, we might point out that this is at least as true of those whom Murray would shame and starve into shotgun marriages as of those who lack daddies or whose daddies lack shotguns. The rising age of marriage since the 1950s is a positive rather than a negative trend, but one which leads to more non-marital sexuality and pregnancies. Yet countries like Sweden, which do not stigmatize unwed births but make sex education, contraception, and abortion services widely and cheaply available to all, witness few unwanted births and few births to teen mothers. The miguided drive in the US to restigmatize "illegitimacy," with which the Clinton Administration collaborated, demands renewed struggle to destigmatize abortion among both the populace and health providers and to vastly increase its accessibility. A reinvigorated campaign for comprehensive reproductive rights, perhaps reviving that old Planned Parenthood slogan, "every child a wanted child," should promote a full panoply of contraceptive options, like RU–486. It might include a "take back our bodies" drive to wrest exclusive control over abortion provision from doctors, particularly when so few of these in the US have proven willing to subject their professional status, personal safety, perhaps even their lives, to the formidable risks that the anti-abortion movement imposes on abortion providers.[104] At the same time, we should resist the misrepresentation of feminism as hostile to motherhood or "life" by continuing the struggle for genuine, humane workplace and welfare *reforms* (rather than repeals) that make it possible for women to choose to mother or to reject maternity.

Feminists are well placed to promote this humane brand of progressive family values. Unlike the centrists, we understand that it is not "the family" but one, *historically specific*, system of family life (the "modern nuclear family") that has broken down. We understand that this has had diverse effects on people of different genders, races, economic resources, sexual identities, and generations. Some have benefitted greatly; others have lost enormously; most have won a few new rights and opportunities and lost several former protections and privileges. The collapse of the former US national consensus on family values, like the collapse of our prosperous economy to which it was intricately tied, has not been an "equal opportunity" employer. Indeed, women, especially poor and "minority" women, have been some of the biggest winners, and most of the biggest losers. Those who do not want to count feminism, liberalism, and human compassion casualties of the Clinton Administration's conversion to the politics of neo-family values had better disrupt the mesmerizing, but misguided, centrist campaign.

## Notes

This is an updated version of an essay originally published as "Scents, Scholars and Stigma: The Revisionist Campaign for Family Values," *Social Text* 40 (Fall, 1994) pp. 51–75. A related version appears as chapter 3 in my *In the Name of The Family: Rethinking Family Values in a Postmodern Age* (Boston: Beacon Press, 1996).

1 Barbara Dafoe Whitehead, "Dan Quayle was Right," *Atlantic* 271 (4) (April, 1993), pp. 47–84.
2 Barbara Dafoe Whitehead, "Was Dan Quayle Right?," *Family Affairs* 6 (Winter, 1994), p. 13. For sample retreads, see Mona Charen, "Hey, Murphy, Quayle was Right," *Orange County Register* (March 29, 1993), B9; Suzanne Fields, "Murphy's Chorus of Enlightened Celebrities," *Orange County Register* (March 29, 1993), p. B9.
3 David Popenoe, "The Controversial Truth: The Two-Parent Family is Better," *New York Times* (December 26, 1992), p. 13; Popenoe, "Scholars Should Worry about the Disintegration of the American Family," *Chronicle of Higher Education* (April 14, 1993), p. A48; Joan Beck, "What's Good for Babies: Both Parents," *Santa Rosa Press Democrat* (March 7, 1993), pp. G1, G6.
4 Daniel Patrick Moynihan, "Defining Deviancy Down," *American Scholar* (Winter, 1993), pp. 17–30; James Q. Wilson, "The Family-Values Debate," *Commentary* 95 (4) (1993), pp. 24–31.

5 Popenoe, "Scholars Should Worry," p. A48. For the statement and list of council members, see Council on Families in America, "Family and Child Well-Being: Eight Propositions," *Family Affairs* 6(1–2) (Winter, 1994), p. 11.

6 Personal interview conducted in Oakland, California (April 6, 1994).

7 Quoted in Karen Winkler, "Communitarians Move their Ideas Outside Academic Arena," *Chronicle of Higher Education* (April 21, 1993), p. A7.

8 Elaine Ciulla Kamarck and William A. Galston, "Putting Children First: A Progressive Family Policy for the 1990s," Progressive Policy Institute pamphlet (September 27, 1990).

9 David Blankenhorn, Jean Bethke Elshtain, and Steven Bayme, eds, *Rebuilding the Nest: A New Committment to the American Family* (Milwaukee: Family Service America, 1990); National Commission on Children, *Beyond Rhetoric: A New American Agenda for Children and Families* (Washington DC: Library of Congress, 1991).

10 Personal interview (April 6, 1994).

11 Barbara Dafoe Whitehead, "A New Familism?" *Family Affairs* 5(1–2) (Summer, 1992), p. 5.

12 Wilson, "Family-Values Debate," p. 31.

13 Joe Klein, "The Out-of-Wedlock Question," *Newsweek* (December 13, 1993), p. 37.

14 Blankenhorn made these remarks during his presentation to "Safe Communities: A Search For Solutions," a 1995 California Public Affairs Forum sponsored by Hitachi, Ltd, held at the Sheraton Palace Hotel, San Franisco (September 28, 1995).

15 Quoted in Michael Kranish, "In Bully Pulpit, Preaching Values," *Boston Globe* (December 10, 1993), p. 17.

16 Wilson, "Family-Values Debate," p. 24.

17 The debate took place on an ABC radio call-in program, "*The Gil Gross Show*," (broadcast on January 18, 1993).

18 Whitehead, "Dan Quayle was Right," p. 47.

19 Ibid., p. 80.

20 Wilson, "Family-Values Debate," p. 31. Syndicated columnist Suzanne Field abridged Whitehead's *Atlantic* story, charging that Dan Quayle was punished like a messenger in a Greek tragedy when he attacked Murphy Brown, "knocked about for delivering bad news that contradicted the biases of the media, the morality chic of the beautiful people, and the scholarship of ideological feminists, among others." After ridiculing media stars who spoke up for Murphy Brown, Field remarked, "We can't expect wisdom from celebrities, but feminist academics at good universities peddle similar claptrap. Sociologist Judith Stacey of UC, Davis, describes a post-modern future for women in which none of us are oppressed by the nuclear family." Field, "Murphy's Chorus," p. 89.

21 Gillis suggested the term during a discussion of an early draft of this chapter with the "family-values" seminar at the Center for Advanced Studies in the Social and Behavioral Sciences (November 29, 1993).

22 Popenoe, "Controversial Truth," p. 13.

23 Whitehead, "Dan Quayle was Right," p. 48.

24 Whitehead, "The Expert's Story of Marriage," quoted in Moynihan, "Defining Deviancy Down," p. 24.

25 *Beyond Rhetoric* cites essays by Blankenhorn, Elshtain, Popenoe, Sylvia Hewlett, and other contributors to Blankenhorn, Elshtain, and Bayme, *Rebuilding the Nest*.

26 Popenoe, "Scholars Should Worry," p. A48.

27 Council on Families in America, "Family and Child Well-Being," p. 11.

28 Popenoe, "Controversial Truth," p. 13.

29 To sample the diversity of scholarly views, see a careful evaluation of the inconclusive findings of research on the impact of divorce on children, Frank Furstenberg and Andrew Cherlin, *Divided Families: What Happens to Children When Parents Part?* (Cambridge MA: Harvard University Press, 1991). For a review of the research on gay and lesbian parenting, see Charlotte Patterson, "Children of Lesbian and Gay Parents," *Child Development* 63 (1992), pp. 1025–42. Indeed, even Sara McLanahan, whom Whitehead's *Atlantic* essay portrayed as recanting her earlier views on the benign effects of single parenting, provides a more nuanced analysis of the sources of whatever disadvantages the children of single parents experience than Whitehead leads readers to believe. McLanahan acknowledges that research does not demonstrate that children of "mother-only" households would have been better off if

their two biological parents had married or never divorced. See McLanahan and Karen Booth, "Mother-Only Families: Problems, Prospects, and Politics," *Journal of Marriage and the Family* 51(3) (August, 1989), pp. 557–80.

30 David Demo, "Parent–Child Relations: Assessing Recent Changes," *Journal of Marriage and the Family*, 54 (February, 1992), p. 104.

31 Ibid., p. 110.

32 Judith Wallerstein and Joan B. Kelly, *Surviving the Breakup: How Children and Parents Cope with Divorce* (New York: Basic Books, 1980); Wallerstein and Blakeslee, *Second Chances: Men, Women, and Children a Decade after Divorce* (New York: Ticknor and Fields, 1989).

33 Demo, "Parent–Child Relations," p. 110. For an even more comprehensive, balanced survey of research on the impact of divorce on children, see Furstenberg and Cherlin, *Divided Families*.

34 See Furstenberg and Cherlin, *Divided Families*, for a summary of this research.

35 Charles Murray, "The Time has Come to put a Stigma Back on Illegitimacy," *Wall Street Journal* 29 (October, 1993), Forum.

36 Murray appeared on *"This Week with David Brinkley,"* (November 29, 1993). The op–ed by Hoover Institute scholar John Bunzel aired on *Perspective*, KQED-FM, San Francisco (December 21, 1993).

37 Blankenhorn et al., *Rebuilding the Nest*, p. 21.

38 Quoting from an essay he wrote in 1965; Moynihan, "Defining Deviancy Down," p. 26.

39 Wilson, "Family-Values Debate," p. 31.

40 Klein, "Out-of Wedlock Question," p. 37.

41 The quotations from Shalala and the unidentified liberal appear in Klein, "Out-of-Wedlock Question."

42 See Kamarck and Galston, "Putting Children First," p. 9.

43 Many feminists fear that even employing the concept "postfeminism" cedes important political ground to the backlash. I disagree and use the term to indicate a culture that has both assimilated and tamed many of the basic ideas of second-wave feminism. For a fuller discussion of this use of this term, see Deborah Rosenfelt and Judith Stacey, "Second Thoughts on the Second Wave," *Feminist Studies* 13 (2) (Summer, 1987), pp. 341–61.

44 Popenoe, "Scholars Should Worry," p. A48.

45 Blankenhorn et al., *Rebuilding the Nest*, p. 19.

46 Wilson, "Family-Values Debate," p. 31.

47 Whitehead, "New Familism?" p. 2.

48 Sue Shellenbanger, "Bill Galston Tells the President: My Son Needs Me More," *Wall Street Journal* (June 21, 1995), p. B1.

49 Jay Lefkowitz, "Where Dad Belongs," *Wall Street Journal* (June 18, 1993), p. A12.

50 Susan Chira, "Push to Revamp Ideal for American Fathers," *New York Times* (June 19, 1994), p. 10. Blankenhorn presents an extended, polemical exposition of his neo-traditional fatherhood ideology in his *Fatherless America: Confronting Our Most Urgent Social Problem* (New York: Basic Books, 1995).

51 For my earlier critiques of Elshtain, Friedan, and Hewlett, see Judith Stacey, "The New Conservative Feminism," *Feminist Studies* 9 (3) (Fall, 1983), pp. 559–83; Rosenfelt and Stacey, "Second Thoughts."

52 Blankenhorn, for example, is interpreted approvingly by a *Wall Street Journal* columnist as providing intellectual justification for "laws that mandate spousal notification prior to all abortions. Today laws in most states consider fetuses the property of pregnant women. Unfortunately, this posture leads to the view that children are the sole responsibility of mothers." Lefkowitz, "Where Dad Belongs," p. A12.

53 Quoted in Winkler, "Communitarians Move their Ideas," p. A13.

54 Whitehead, "New Familism?" p. 2.

55 Popenoe, "Modern Marriage: Revising the Cultural Script," Council on Families in America, Working Paper 17 (New York: Institute for American Values, August, 1992), p. 2.

56 Blankenhorn, *Fatherless America*, p. 122.

57 Norval Glenn, "A Plea for Objective Assessment of the Notion of Family Decline," *Journal of Marriage and the Family* 55(3) (August, 1993), p. 543; Wilson, "Family-Values Debate," p. 25.

58 Hillary Rodham Clinton, *It Takes a Village: And Other Lessons Children Teach Us* (New York: Simon and Schuster, 1996), p. 43.

59 Dirk Johnson, "No-Fault Divorce is Under Attack," *New York Times* (February 12, 1996), p. A8.

60 Ibid.
61 The most influential treatment of no-fault divorce has been Lenore J. Weitzman, *The Divorce Revolution: The Unexpected Social and Economic Consequences for Women and Children in America* (New York: Free Press, 1985). However, Weitzman's data have since been challenged, and she has acknowledged errors in coding and analysis.
62 Constance R. Ahrons, *The Good Divorce* (New York: HarperCollins, 1994), p. 35.
63 Popenoe applies this term to me and other critics of "family-values" ideology in "Scholars Should Worry."
64 Glenn, "Plea for Objective Assessment," p. 544.
65 Wilson, "Family-Values Debate," p. 29.
66 David Popenoe, "American Family Decline, 1960–1990," *Journal of Marriage and the Family* 55(3) (August, 1993), p. 529.
67 Moynihan, "Defining Deviancy Down," p. 26; Whitehead, "Dan Quayle was Right," p. 70.
68 Blankenhorn, *Fatherless America*, p. 233.
69 Jean Bethke Elshtain, "Family and Civic Life," in Blankenhorn et al., *Rebuilding the Nest*, p. 130.
70 See, for example, Patterson, "Children of Lesbian and Gay Parents"; Joan Laird, "Lesbian and Gay Families," in Froma Walsh, ed., *Normal Family Processes*, 2nd edn (New York: Guilford Press, 1993), pp. 282–328.
71 Andrew Sullivan, "Here Comes the Groom: A Conservative Case for Gay Marriage," *New Republic* (August 28, 1989), p. 10.
72 Quoted in Winkler, "Communitarians Move their Ideas," p. A13.
73 Clinton, *It Takes a Village*, book jacket copy.
74 Clinton, according to his senior adviser George Stephanopoulos, "thinks the proper role for the government is to work on the fight against discrimination, but he does not believe we should support [gay] marriage." Quoted in Marc Sandalow and David Tuller, "White House Tells Gays it Backs Them," *San Francisco Chronicle* (October 21, 1995), p. A2.
75 John Batteiger, "Bigotry for Bucks," *San Francisco Bay Guardian* (April 7, 1993), p. 19. For primary evidence of the prominence of homophobic appeals in right-wing organizing, see, for example, James C. Dobson, "1993 in Review," *Focus on the Family Newsletter* (January, 1994).
76 Evelyn C. White, "Christian Right Tries to Capitalize on Anti-Gay Views," *San Francisco Chronicle* (January 12, 1994), p. A6.
77 Susan Yoachum and David Tuller, "Right Makes Might in Iowa," *San Francisco Chronicle* (February 12, 1996), p. A1.
78 Quoted in ibid., pp. A1, A3.
79 Carolyn Lochhead and David Tuller, "Clinton Attempts to Strike Balance on Gay Marriages," *San Francisco Chronicle* (May 15, 1996), pp. A1, A11.
80 Robin Toner, "Republican Factions Gather Under One Tent, Then Argue," *New York Times* (May 11, 1993).
81 See n. 14 above.
82 Chronicle News Services, "Clinton Cracks Down on Deadbeat Dads," *San Francisco Chronicle* (June 19, 1996), p. A2.
83 Elizabeth Traube, "Family Matters," *Visual Anthropology* 9(1) (1995), pp. 56–73, esp. p. 63.
84 Daniel Patrick Moynihan, *The Negro Family: The Case for National Action* (Washington DC: US Department of Labor, 1965).
85 Charles Murray, "The Emerging White Underclass and How to Save It, *"Philadelphia Enquirer* (November 15, 1993), p. A15.
86 Howard Odum, *Social and Mental Traits of the Negro* (New York: Columbia University Press, 1910) quoted in Gutman, "Persistent Myths about the Afro-American Family," *Journal of Interdisciplinary History* 6(2) (Autumn, 1975), p. 184.
87 Wilson defines this index as the ratio of employed black males per 100 black females in the same age group. He charts a decline in this ratio from 70 in 1960 to 40 in 1986, and the disparity is reflected in the decline of black marriage rates. William J. Wilson, *The Truly Disadvantaged: The Inner City, the Underclass, and Public Policy* (Chicago: University of Chicago Press, 1987).
88 Married voters aged 18–34 with children voted 48 percent for Bush, 39 percent for Clinton, and 22 percent for Perot; singles (with and without children) in that age group voted 58 percent for Clinton, 20 percent for Bush, and 19 percent for Perot. Poll data were reported

in a *Washington Post* story by Barbara Vobejda, reprinted as "Family Gap' Found in Post-Election Poll," *San Francisco Chronicle* (November 27, 1992), p. A4.

89 Quoted in Allison Mitchell, "Banking on Family Issues, Clinton Seeks Parents' Votes," *New York Times* (June 25, 1996), p. C19.

90 Gary L. Bauer, "Family Values Matter!," *Focus on the Family Citizen* (May 17, 1993), p. 16.

91 Donald Suggs and Mandy Carter, "Cincinnati's Odd Couple," *New York Times* (December 13, 1993), p. A11.

92 Franz Schurmann, "Families that Work are Helping China," *San Francisco Chronicle* (December 23, 1993).

93 Ronald Smothers, "Tell it to Mom, Dad and the Authorities," *New York Times* (November 14, 1993), Week in Review, p. 2. For an astute analysis of media treatment of the Newark car theft panic, see Steven Gregory, "Time to Make the Doughnuts: On the Politics of Subjugation in the 'Inner City,' " paper presented at American Anthropological Association Meetings, Washington DC (November, 1993).

94 Whitehead, "Dan Quayle was Right," p. 55.

95 Some academic feminists indulge this impulse as well. For a recent example, see Elspeth Probyn's otherwise incisive critique of postfeminist TV family fare, "Television's *Unheimlich* Home," in Brian Massumi, ed., *The Politics of Everyday Fear* (Minneapolis: University of Minnesota Press, 1994).

96 I discuss the politics of the gay and lesbian family-values campaign at length in Judith Stacey, *In the Name of The Family: Rethinking Family Values in a Postmodern Age* (Boston: Beacon Press, 1996), ch. 5.

97 Charles Derber, "Coming Glued: Communitarianism to the Rescue," *Tikkun* 8(4) (July–August, 1993), pp. 27–30.

98 For example, in a 1985 Roper poll, 51 percent of women claimed that, given the choice, they would prefer a paid job to full-time home-making, but in 1991 only 43 percent of women expressed that preference, while 53 percent said they would rather stay home. Nancy Gibbs, "The War Against Feminism," *Time* (March 9, 1992), p. 55.

99 Arlie Hochschild, "Inside the Clockwork of Male Careers," in Florence Home, ed., *Women and the Power to Change* (New York: McGraw-Hill, 1975), pp. 47–81.

100 Patricia J. Williams, "Different Drummer Please, Marchers!," *Nation* (October 30, 1995), p. 493.

101 David Popenoe, "The Family Condition of America: Cultural Change and Public Policy," in Henry J. Aaron, Thomas E. Mann, and Timothy Taylor, eds, *Values and Public Policy* (Washington DC: Brookings Institute, 1994), p. 98. See also Wilson, "Family-Values Debate," p. 30: "marriage is in large measure a device for reining in the predatory sexuality of males." While, according to Gilder, "Men without women frequently become the single menace, "often destined to a Hobbsean life – solitary, poor, nasty, brutish, and short." Gilder, *Men and Marriage* (Gretna LA: Pelican, 1986), pp. 6–7, 10. For a feminist reading of the social evolutionary domestication of men, see Sherry Ortner, "The Virgin and the State, "*Feminist Studies* 4(3) (October, 1978), pp. 19–35.

102 Barbara Ehrenreich, "Two, Three, Many Husbands," in *The Worst Years of Our Lives: Irreverent Notes from a Decade of Greed* (New York: Pantheon, 1990), pp. 183–7.

103 Pepper Schwartz, "Children's New Bonds: Para-Dads, Para-Moms," *New York Times* (November 9, 1995) pp. B1, B4.

104 For an astute and moving account of the experiences of some of the heroic doctors who have paid these costs, see Carole Joffe, *Doctors of Conscience* (Boston: Beacon Press, 1996).

# 16

# Welfare Reform and Reproductive Politics on a Collision Course

## Contradictions in the Conservative Agenda

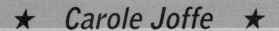 ★ *Carole Joffe* ★

## Introduction

In the 1990s conservatives have been the dominant force in US domestic social policy. In two of the signature issues of contemporary conservativism, abortion and social welfare, they have won significant victories. While abortion remains legal, the cumulative effects of unceasing conservative attacks – in the legislative, judicial, and cultural arenas – have dramatically affected access to it, and by the early 1990s, some 84 percent of US counties were without an abortion provider. Opponents of abortion have launched an effective campaign to ban a controversial abortion procedure (so called "partial-birth abortions") in a move that many see as the opening round in an assault on all procedures after the first trimester.[1] In the realm of welfare, the victory has been even more substantial. With their victory in the 1994 election, Republicans controlled both branches of Congress for the first time in over 40 years, and they pushed the debate on welfare reform sharply to the right. By the summer of 1996, Bill Clinton, yielding to pressure from the right, signed a welfare bill that overturned 60 years of social policy in the United States.[2] The bill elimi-

nated the entitlement of poor children to government support through the AFDC program that had first been established in the Social Security Act.

But these political victories also reveal serious contradictions within contemporary conservatism. The story of the welfare-reform bill of 1996 is not simply an ideological triumph of the right over liberalism; it is also a revealing instance of the sea change in US conservatism that has occurred since the rise of the "New Right" in the late 1970s. The distinctive feature of the New Right is its focus on "social issues," as opposed to the old right's concern with foreign policy and economic issues.[3] In fact, the recent welfare reform can be seen as another sign of the dominance of "social-issue" conservatives over the older, economic conservatives. In the division of labor that had obtained until recently, welfare had been the province of the economic right, while the social conservatives focussed on the "hot-button" issues – preeminently abortion, but also teen pregnancy, homosexuality, AIDS, school prayer, and so on. The decision by social conservatives to claim ownership of welfare and the corresponding dramatic rhetorical transformation of welfare from an "economic" issue to a "moral" one has been a brilliant political manuever. However, this change reveals some vexing contradictions within the conservative movement. The two dominant issues that now preoccupy social conservatism – social welfare and reproductive politics – are fundamentally in conflict with each other, in terms of the policy choices that each issue suggests. The collision course between these two issues has important ramifications for the future of the conservative movement's ability to hold the various strands of its coalition together, and to attract a broader base.

## Conservatives and Welfare Before 1980

The forerunners of what eventually came to be known as AFDC were a series of programs known as "mothers' pensions" or "widows' pensions," which were approved by nearly all state legislatures around the time of World War I. These were quite small financial grants made to women (almost exclusively white) who were raising children without the benefit of a male breadwinner, because their husbands had either deserted them or died. These pensions were promoted at the first White House Conference on Children, convened by President Theodore Roosevelt in 1909. As the conference concluded, in a famous document of US social policy: "Home life is the highest product of civilization . . . children of reasonably efficient and deserving mothers who are without the support of the normal breadwinner, should, as a rule, be kept with their parents, such aid being given as may be necessary to maintain suitable homes for the rearing of the children."[4] These pensions, advocated by the first generation of women social-welfare activists gathered in the newly created Children's Bureau, are emblematic of the creation of national social policies that took place during the progressive era.

When debated in the individual state legislatures, the mothers' pensions did generate some conservative opposition. Consistent with the type of objection that has appeared since the earliest historical attempts at governmental cash transfers to the poor, opponents questioned the practice of giving public funds to those who did not work. As one opponenent fumed about the prospect of giving money to non-workers, "Widowed mothers present the strongest sentimental appeal and the very best case for the entering wedge toward state socialism. The battle cry is not alms but the right to share . . . It [state assistance] . . . represses the desire for self-help, self-respect and independence . . . it is not virile."[5]

By and large, however, the conservative opposition was fairly muted and the pensions enjoyed broad support across political lines. The major opponents, in fact, were not political conservatives, but rather officials associated with private charity organizations who feared that governmental involvement in charity would threaten their organizational interests.[6]

To be sure, this early form of state assistance was not without its moralistic elements. The presumption that mothers could not also be "breadwinners" reveals a conservative social outlook that is all the more striking because this historical period, in fact, is one in which child-care programs for working women were quite common in the settlement houses.[7] Furthermore, as the two different names of the programs suggests, one had to either be married (with an absent husband) or widowed to qualify. Moreover, the programs involved some degree of behavioral monitoring by the charity workers who administered them. For example, recipients of pensions who tried to generate extra revenue by taking in boarders were threatened with loss of their stipends.[8] In general, though, the major legacy of the mothers' pensions of the early part of the twentieth century is that they set a precedent for governmental financial support of dependent families with children – and in light of all that would come later, there was remarkably little political opposition to these programs.[9]

These small state pension programs were the foundation for the New Deal program of Aid to Dependent Children (ADC, later changed to AFDC). Governmental support of women and dependent children was now expanded to include more recipients, with joint administration between the states and the federal government. But ADC was not an especially controversial part of the New Deal. Throughout the 1940s and 1950s, ADC went on as a fairly small, relatively uncontested program that continued to have white widows as its primary constituency.[10]

The 1960s definitively changed both the composition of the AFDC rolls and the public perception of the program. As Frances Fox Piven and Richard Cloward have demonstrated persuasively in their classic work on that period, the social protests that swept through most American cities led to a dramatic explosion in welfare rolls – between 1960 and 1969, 800,000 families became AFDC recipients, an increase of some 107 percent. Many of those now being added to the rolls, in contrast to earlier periods, were African American mothers who were often unmarried or divorced.[11]

Along with the expansion of the rolls came the politicizing of the identity of welfare recipient. By the mid-1960s, there was extensive organizing by AFDC mothers, both in local groups and in the National Welfare Rights Organization. Welfare recipients routinely sat in at AFDC offices, demanding more resources and better services. Sympathetic poverty lawyers achieved a number of key legal victories for AFDC recipients, such as the striking down of the infamous "midnight raids," in which welfare case workers would visit recipients' homes unannounced, to see if they were harboring male visitors.[12]

The 1960s also saw the first signs of the demonization of the AFDC mother that was to reach full flower in the 1990s. The militance of many welfare recipients, as shown by their participation in various protests, tied welfare inextricably in the public's mind to the racial conflicts of the 1960s. AFDC was increasingly perceived as a "black" program, and was closely linked to other Great Society programs that were often reviled as failed social experiments.[13]

The 1960s also saw a foreshadowing of the focus on the moral behavior of welfare recipients that was to greatly intensify in the years ahead. In 1965, Daniel P. Moynihan, then an adviser to President Lyndon Johnson, issued his controversial "Moynihan Report," in which he attempted to relate black economic status to family structure. In particular, Moynihan struck a nerve when he spoke of the "tangled pathology" associated with the households headed by single black females.[14] Additionally, many conservatives of the period began to voice criticism of AFDC because of the program's incentives for "family breakup": most states during that period did not allow AFDC to be granted to households where there was a married couple, even if both were unemployed. And social scientists – liberal and conservative alike – began to increasingly speak of the "culture of poverty" in which many welfare recipients were allegedly trapped.[15] But even though some in this period began to speak of the "promiscuity" of the welfare recipient, the main objections drawn from the Moynihan report and from the family breakup critics was that AFDC weakened the work ethic of black males and created "economic dependency" among black women (and of course heightened costs for taxpayers). Thus, a major development of welfare policy during this period was a renewed call for work requirements tied to welfare, and the creation of various job-training/job-readiness programs.[16]

Additionally, in the late 1960s and into the 1970s, conservatives began to link welfare and other social programs to negative imagery of "big government." As Barbara Ehrenreich has effectively traced out, first George Wallace in his 1968 campaign and then Spiro Agnew, while Richard Nixon's vice-president, by their invocation of the "pointy headed bureaucrats" and "effete snobs" in Washington, laid the groundwork for what would later become a full-scale attack by conservatives on virtually all federal social programs.[17] It is worth noting, for our purposes, that this phase of the ideological attack on welfare was on the "liberal elites" designing these programs, not on the recipients themselves.

## Conservatives and Social Welfare After 1980

With the election of Ronald Reagan in 1980, and the corresponding rise of the New Right as a force in American conservatism, the portrayal of the AFDC recipient began to change in important ways. Reagan himself had the habit at his news conferences of frequently citing anecdotes of "welfare queens" and cheaters – AFDC recipients who allegedly were bilking the system of hundreds of thousands of dollars. Most significantly, the distinctive focus of the New Right on social issues, including those pertaining to sexuality and reproduction- -abortion, sex education, teenage pregnancy, and so on – made it inevitable that conservatives would turn to more explicit consideration of the moral breakdown associated with AFDC.

This transformation in conservative discourse about AFDC recipients can be seen clearly in the work of two of the most influential conservative intellectuals of the Reagan era, George Gilder and Charles Murray. In his bestselling book *Wealth and Poverty*, published in 1981, and in several lesser-known works, Gilder laid out a case against welfare. In contrast to the frank racism of some conservatives of that period, Gilder's tone was one of deep sympathy for the black poor, and especially the black male. His social theory basically posits that young urban men are being

"cuckolded by the compassionate State." As he puts it, "Civilized society is dependent on the submission of the short-term sexuality of young men to the extended maternal horizons of women who will marry them. This is what happens in monogamous marriage."[18] But the civilizing opportunities of marriage are not available to the black urban male because of the availability of AFDC. The existence of this program will either cause present marriages to break up, or cause some to never take place at all. In short, Gilder's argument is that AFDC not only does not solve the problems of the urban minority poor, it makes things worse. It is welfare itself that leads to the pathologies associated with the ghetto, as men who perceive they are not needed in families join together in male groups that engage in destructive behaviors.

This theme of the destructive aspects of welfare was continued in Charles Murray's 1984 book, *Losing Ground*. In this widely discussed book (which received massive promotion by a conservative think tank)[19] Murray purported to offer definitive proof of the "failure" of social programs, especially AFDC. He too focussed not only on the futility of such programs in terms of dollars wasted but, like Gilder, on the social dimensions of such programs, especially their promotion of immoral lifestyles. In this book, he first proposed as a "thought experiment" what a decade later he and other conservatives would propose as concrete social policy: to simply get rid of AFDC.

Murray's preoccupation with the moral dimensions of AFDC reached its height in fall, 1993, with an op–ed in the *Wall Street Journal* on "The Coming White Underclass." Stating that the 22 percent illegitimacy rate among whites in the US now was about what the black rate was when Moynihan issued his warning about the black underclass in 1965, Murray asserted that illegitimacy is "the single most important social problem of our time – more important than crime, drugs, poverty, illiteracy, welfare or homelessness because it drives everything else." Arguing that AFDC is the chief cause of this rise in illegitimacy, he called forcefully for the "end of all economic support for single mothers."[20]

Murray's op–ed electrified social conservatives, both in Congress and out. After the 1994 Republican takeover, the reconstruction of welfare as a predominantly moral issue, focussing on the sexual behavior of underclass women and their allegedly inadequate parenting, increasingly dominated the ongoing welfare-reform debates. Newt Gingrich drew national attention for his suggestion that the children of the welfare poor be raised in orphanages. On the floor of Congress, right-wing representatives unflatteringly compared the parenting behaviors of AFDC recipients with those of wolves and alligators. But above all, the social conservatives focussed on the link between welfare and illegitimacy.[21] Remarks during the debate on welfare reform by Congressman Norwood of Missouri, a stalwart of the Christian Right, give a flavor of his group's appraisal of the stakes in this battle:

I hear the other side wail and whine that we are hurting the children. Perhaps they are so busy defending the status quo that they fail to see the dismal failure our system has become. Perhaps they think it is compassionate for our system to encourage illegitimacy. Perhaps they think it is OK for 1 in 3 babies in this Nation to be born out of wedlock.

Similarly, Congressman Chambliss pointed out, "Illegitimacy rates in this country have quadrupled in 25 years . . . In 1970 the proportion of teen mothers who were unmarried was 30 percent. By 1992, it was 72 percent . . . this cycle need not continue. Our welfare reform package provides tough love for welfare recipients."[22]

Thus a struggle broke out within Republican ranks over the eventual character of the welfare-reform bill. Encouraged by such influential figures as Robert Rector of the Heritage Foundation, the social conservatives made clear that they were not going to be content merely with financial cutbacks or even work requirements – they wanted a welfare-reform bill that would punish illegitimacy.[23]

Certainly, this focus on illegitimacy had a certain resonance with many Americans anxious about a host of related issues – divorce, family breakup, teenage pregnancy, and so on. Furthermore, casting the welfare "problem" as, above all, an issue of personal irresponsibility about sexual matters rather than lack of a work ethic resonated beautifully with the anti-governmental fervor of the moment; namely, if the problem facing the underclass is a lack of income and jobs, then it is logical to expect government to do something about it. But this, of course, raises the spectre of job training and job creation that had become so problematic, once it had become clear to all players in the welfare debate that such job-related measures indeed would be *more* costly than simply resting with the existing AFDC program. On the other hand, if the core problem is promiscuity and moral degeneration, then the solution is not government spending but moral exhortation.

To be sure, the welfare-reform bill of 1996 did ultimately contain work requirements, as well as sanctions against illegitimacy, as I shall shortly discuss. However, as has become increasingly evident in the months since the bill's passage, it is utterly unrealistic to expect successful job placement of the millions of welfare recipients that will be required to work.[24] The lack of any commitment to job training or job creation in the legislation is confirmation of the triumph of the social conservatives. But as we shall see, this ideological coup has its problematic aspects as well.

## Conservatives and Reproductive Issues

The relation of conservatives to reproductive issues – abortion, contraception, sex education, condom distribution – is a complex one that has undergone significant changes in the last 15–20 years. All the above issues were vigorously opposed by leading conservative groups by the mid-1990s[25] but historically, conservatives had made crucial distintions between contraceptive services and other reproductive issues. In fact, until fairly recently, birth control was typically *more* likely to be promoted by those who called themselves conservative (with the exception of the Catholic church) and distrusted, because of the possibilities of coercion, by sectors of the liberal/left, including the feminist health movement. The earliest days of birth-control activism in the US were marked by the opportunistic alliance that Margaret Sanger – certainly no conservative herself – made with various eugenic groups. And an undeniable eugenic element has hovered over many of the family-planning initiatives in the US since Sanger's time, leading to massive criticism from feminists.[26]

The 1960s and 1970s contain numerous examples of birth-control measures pushed by old-line conservatives. The first substantial federal involvement in family-planning services – Title X of the Public Health Act of 1970 – occurred during the Nixon presidency, and is commonly understood to have occurred as a response to the recent explosion in the welfare population. Indeed, the first federally funded birth-control clinics were denounced by many progressives because of their disproportionate location in many minority communities.[27] A few years before the passage of Title X, AFDC recipients were "mandated" to receive counseling on family planning as part of an expansion of social services to this group. During this same period, evidence of widespread sterilization abuses were revealed; poor women – in many cases, AFDC recipients – were being coerced to agree to sterilization when they entered hospitals for obstetrical services.[28] Though, as I will argue below, the ascendancy of social conservatives

in the 1980s largely muted old-line conservatives' calls for population-control measures, the Norplant controversy was a striking exception. After the long lasting contraceptive implant Norplant was introduced in the US in 1990, several state legislatures considered making this method mandatory for welfare recipients, various right-wing political candidates campaigned on a platform urging mandatory Norplant, and virtually all states announced that they would subsidize Norplant insertion for AFDC recipients.[29]

In short, there had long existed support for publicly supported family-planning programs among conservatives – often, as I have indicated, with the little-disguised intent of reducing child bearing among the welfare population. Throughout the 1970s, after the *Roe* v. *Wade* decision legalizing abortion led to repeated votes on various abortion-related measures in Congress, the conventional understanding in American politics for many old-line conservatives was to support family planning "in order to make abortion less necessary."

This understanding broke down quite rapidly after the Reagan election of 1980. Many of the domestic policy slots in the first Reagan administration were granted to individuals politically tied to the New Right. Hitherto relatively obscure policy positions, typically granted to career bureaucrats, such as the deputy assistant secretary for population affairs, and the largely symbolic role of surgeon general, were made to individuals on the basis of anti-abortion credentials. This contributed to the Reagan Administration's high-profile stance against abortion, but it also meant the politicization of many issues that had previously been non-controversial.[30]

The Reagan/Bush era, from 1980 to 1992, saw not only unyielding assaults on abortion, but a fusion of the opposition to abortion with opposition to contraception. Family planning programs were no longer seen as a logical way to *prevent* abortions, but rather as "supportive of the abortion mentality." Conservatives made this claim in part because many of the facilities that offered birth-control services also offered either abortion counseling or abortions themselves. In the much-heralded campaign to "defund the Left" announced by the New Right early in the Reagan years, the Planned Parenthood Federation of America was listed as a prime target; though Planned Parenthood clinics received no federal funds for abortion services, various of the federation's clinics were Title X contractees. Throughout the Reagan/Bush era and continuing into the present, conservatives attempted an outright abolition of Title X; though not successful to date, they have succeeded in substantially weakening that program and others that provide contraceptive services. A recent study reveals that in the years from 1980 to 1994, federal funding for family-planning services decreased by more than one-quarter, nearly $100 million.[31] At the international level, anti-abortion forces in the Reagan White House were successful in pushing through the "Mexico City Policy," meaning that US population assistance could not go to overseas groups which supported abortion, even if the US funds were to be targetted only to family-planning services.

Besides assaults on abortion and family-planning services, sex education in schools and especially AIDS education programs also became highly contested during this era. Starting in the 1980s, and continuing through to this day, local boards in many localities have been torn apart by conflicts over appropriate sex-education curriculums, by the issue of school-based clinics which would offer contraceptive services or referrals, and by the question of condom distribution in schools.[32] Though at the national level, the election of Bill Clinton as president in 1992 could salvage legal abortion, because of his ability to appoint Supreme Court judges, much of the sexual agenda of the Reagan/Bush era – that is, the hostility not only to abortion, but to

birth control and sex education – stayed in place locally, because of the efforts of grassroots activists tied to the larger efforts of groups such as the Christian Coalition.

## The Collision of Welfare and Abortion

In spite of the right's considerable victories in the realms of both abortion and welfare, these victories have not been without cost. Social conservatives' taking on and recasting of welfare as a moral issue has put the movement on a collision course with its stand on abortion. As the following examples will show, there is a fundamental incompatibility in advocating both the abolition of abortion (and related reproductive services) and the elimination of public support for dependent children.

The grassroots anti-abortion movement is one arena where this contradiction is evident. Anti-abortionists across the country have established a network of "pregnancy crisis centers," institutions where pregnant young women can find "alternatives" to abortion. The creation of these centers was partly a response to the accusation that those opposed to abortion were also opposed to the social services needed by pregnant women – as the taunt of the pro-choice movement put it, "for pro-lifers, life begins at conception, but ends at birth." These centers were established to give moral support to help the pregnant women through their pregnancies, and then to aid either in adoption or in keeping the child. But only a tiny number of unmarried pregnant women give up their babies for adoption – about 3 percent in one estimate. Therefore, a major activity in many of these centers (though a fact not widely broadcast by the pro-life movement) has been to help these young women become enrolled in AFDC. Hence the abolition of AFDC poses a tremendous challenge to the ability of pregnancy crisis centers to follow through on their promises to their clients.

The contradictions inherent in the welfare–abortion link may also jeopardize social conservatives' abilities to hold on to some of their most important coalition partners. One of the potentially most significant dissenters is the Catholic church. The church has been a valued component of the conservative coalition because of its leading role in the anti-abortion movement. But the church has a long-standing tradition of support for the poor, and broke with its usual allies in the abortion struggle on the issue of welfare reform.[33] How profound this break over one issue will be is difficult to forecast.

This collision between the two agendas of social conservativism was very evident in the wrangling over the 1996 welfare legislation. A case in point is the conflict that developed over the issue of "family caps" – the prohibition on additional funds being received by a welfare recipient for any children born while she is already on welfare. These family caps were strongly supported by various key organizations in the conservative coalition, such as the Family Research Council and the Christian Coalition. But this policy was deeply opposed by the National Right to Life Committee (NRTLC) because of the belief that such caps would encourage poor women to have abortions they otherwise would not seek.[34] Indeed, the clash between the anti-abortion beliefs of the NRTLC and the anti-illegitimacy sentiments of the other conservative groups were so unbridgeable (at least on the family cap provision) that in a rare (and admittedly temporary) alliance, the NRTLC and NARAL, the pre-eminent pro-choice group in the US, gathered at the same microphone to condemn such caps – the latter arguing that this policy would interfere with the reproductive freedom of poor women.

These differences were papered over in the welfare legislation through an ingenious but probably unstable compromise. First, the question of family caps was left as an option that states could decide to pursue, creating the potential for fratricidal conflict among conservatives in state legislatures. Second, the bill established "illegitimacy bonuses" for those states that were most successful in reducing out-of-wedlock births, but this required the further qualification that states would not be eligible if their abortion rates rose. The bonuses consisted of $20–25 million to be distributed to the five states that have the largest reduction in out-of-wedlock child bearing for the years 1999 through 2002. The already daunting technical challenge of data collection on illegitimacy rates is made even more complex because there are numerous problems in accessing reliable data on abortion – several states simply do not collect such data, many women who receive abortions cross state lines to do so, some doctors do not report the fact that they perform abortions, and so on.[35]

In short, the unprecedented inclusion of "illegitimacy bonuses" and "abortion indexes" in a welfare bill show how far social conservatives have come in defining and controlling the issue. However, such measures may have unintended consequences. One likely outcome is that states will respond to these incentives by spending more on family-planning services. Another is that the battles over shaping new welfare regimes at the state level might intensify the divisions within the conservative coalition.

## Conclusion

One of the mixed blessings of achieving success in the political mainstream is that a movement's positions come under greater public scrutiny. Beyond creating tensions within the conservative orbit, the welfare-reform campaign succeeded in making highly visible to the American public some of the more unpopular stands associated with contemporary conservatism. By their very success in recasting the welfare "problem" as one of underclass women having babies out of wedlock, social conservatives were narrowing policy to one alternative – exhorting poor women to practice sexual abstinence. But most of the public finds the notion of urging chastity on adult women not only unrealistic but unfair.[36]

Thus a price that may have to be paid for the conservative victory on welfare is further confirmation of the movement (and the Republican Party by extension) as meanspirited in relation to the poor, and "extreme" and out of touch with respect to the sexual values held by most Americans. The electoral consequences of an unyielding anti-abortion policy have already caused much soul searching among Republicans. The harshness toward the poor in evidence during the welfare debate led a prominent Republican senator several months later to announce his sponsorship for a children's health bill, to show, in his words, "that Republicans don't hate children."[37]

Conservatives who thought they were furthering their movement's agenda by turning welfare into a referendum on immorality will likely find, as many have predicted, that abortion rates among the very poor will increase as a result of the new legislation.[38] They may also find that an unanticipated effect of this legislation will be to *increase* public support

for reproductive services, especially family-planning programs. That is, the hypocrisy involved in demanding that welfare mothers go to work, receive welfare for only a limited time, and not receive additional funds for children born while on welfare will make it increasingly untenable to also oppose state support of birth-control services.

This is not to suggest, of course, that only conservatives will be held accountable for the social miseries caused by the Personal Responsibility and Work Opportunity Act of 1996. After all, a Democratic president signed this bill, and many Democratic law makers voted for it. (Certainly the assertions of Bill Clinton and other politicians who supported such measures as work requirements and time limits because these would "lift AFDC recipients out of dependency" increasingly ring hollow to many, as the evidence mounts on the inadequate supply of entry-level jobs.)[39] My point, rather, is that in speculating about the future prospects of conservativism in American politics, the welfare-reform campaign suggests the inherent contradictions of the social right's attempt to address issues of underclass poverty – which are deeply rooted in the contemporary global economy – through a moralism that is impractical, and to many Americans, simply unacceptable.

## Notes

I am grateful to Fred Block for his help with this chapter.

1 Stanley Henshaw and Jennifer Van Vort, "Abortion Services in the United States, 1991 and 1992," *Family Planning Perspectives* 26 (1994), pp. 100–6, 112. The House and Senate have already once passed legislation banning such procedures – termed "intact dilation and extraction" in the medical community – which was then vetoed by President Clinton. As of the time of writing, in April, 1997, a ban has

once again been passed by the House, and is expected to be passed again by the Senate.
2 The full name of the bill signed in August, 1996, is the Personal Responsibility and Work Opportunity Reconcilement Act of 1996. Besides abolishing the AFDC program – replacing it with a Temporary Assistance for Needy Families (TANF) block grant to the states – the bill also made a number of significant cutbacks in other major social-welfare programs, including the food stamp program and the Supplemental Security Income (SSI) program.

3 On the New Right (now more commonly called the "Christian Right") and its preoccupation with social issues, including social welfare, see Barbara Ehrenreich, "The New Right Attack On Social Welfare," in Fred Block, Richard A. Cloward, Barbara Ehrenreich, and Frances Fox Piven, *The Mean Season: The Attack on the Welfare State* (New York: Pantheon, 1987), pp. 161–96. In *Abortion and Woman's Choice* (New York: Longman, 1984), pp. 241–85, Rosalind Petchesky effectively shows how the abortion issue was used as a "battering ram" by New Right leaders in the late 1970s and 1980s as a means of mobilizing a massive grassroots movement against a range of social issues, including welfare. Lucy Williams offers a comprehensive account of evolving right-wing strategies to attack welfare in "The Right's Attack on Aid to Families with Dependent Children," *Public Eye* (Fall/Winter, 1996) pp. 1–18.

4 Quoted in Theda Skocpol, *Protecting Soldiers and Mothers: The Political Origins of Social Policy in the United States* (Cambridge MA: Harvard University Press, 1992), p. 425.

5 Quoted in Robert H. Bremner, *Children and Youth in America: A Documentary History. Vol. II: 1866–1932* (Cambridge MA: Harvard University Press, 1971), p. 383.

6 On the opposition to pensions, see Skocpol, *Protecting Soldiers and Mothers*; Mark Leff, "Consensus for Reform: The Mother's Pension Movement in the Progressive Era," *Social Service Review* 47 (September 1973), pp. 397–419.

7 Margaret O'Brien Steinfels, *Who's Minding the Children? The History and Politics of Day Care in America* (New York: Simon and Schuster, 1973).

8 On the moral surveillance of pension recipients, see Leff, "Consensus for Reform;" Linda Gordon, *Pitied but Not Entitled: Single Mothers and the History of Welfare* (New York: Free Press, 1994), pp. 37–66.

9 Writing, in 1973, of his appraisal of the legacy of the mothers' pensions, Leff's words have an ironic ring today, in the aftermath of the abolition of AFDC that took place in summer 1996: "The legacy of the mothers' pension movement, though, went beyond the passage of one unique piece of child welfare legislation. It laid a foundation for later contentions that government had the responsibility to establish welfare as a right. ... The United States had reached a preliminary recognition of poverty as a public program requiring governmental remedies." Leff, "Consensus for Reform," p. 415.

10 Mimi Abramovitz, *Regulating the Lives of Women: Social Welfare Policy from Colonial Times to the Present* (Boston: South End Press, 1988), pp. 313–45.

11 Frances Fox Piven and Richard Cloward, *Regulating the Poor: The Functions Of Social Welfare* (New York: Vintage, 1993), p. 183. By 1961, even before the surge described by Piven and Cloward, widowed families represented only 7.7 percent of the ADC caseload. Abramovitz, *Regulating the Lives of Women*, p. 321.

12 To be sure, this phenomenon of "midnight raids" (described in Abramovitz, *Regulating the Lives of Women*, pp. 324ff) that were a commonplace feature for AFDC recipients in many places suggests that moral preoccupation with the personal lives of welfare recipients was present long before the triumph of social conservatism in the 1990s. My point is not that welfare recipients were not under moral surveillance before then. Indeed, from the time of the mothers' pensions onward, this population was always subject to various kinds of behavioral monitoring by social service authorities, as amply documented by authors such as Abramovitz and Gordon. But this monitoring was largely a feature of internal social-service culture. My point in this chapter rather is that the behavior – especially the sexual behavior – of AFDC recipients did not became a major feature of conservative discourse, and a major influence on social policy, until the rise of the New Right in the Reagan years.

13 In 1992, the most recent year for which data are available, nearly 39 percent of AFDC families were non-Hispanic white, nearly 18 percent were Hispanic, and 37.2 percent were African American – an actual reduction by about 10 percent of the figure for African Americans since 1961. Williams, "Right's Attack," p. 3; Abramovitz, *Regulating the Lives of Women*, p. 321.

14 Daniel P. Moynihan, *The Negro Family: The*

*Case for National Action* (Washington DC: US Department of Labor, Office of Policy Planning and Research, 1965).

15  For a review and critique of the "culture-of-poverty" thesis as it was deployed in the 1960s see Michael Katz, *The Undeserving Poor: From the War on Poverty to the War on Welfare* (New York: Pantheon, 1989), pp. 17–43.

16  Jill Quadagno, *The Color of Welfare: How Racism Undermined the War on Poverty* (New York: Oxford University Press, 1994), pp. 121–31.

17  Ehrenreich, *Mean Season*, p. 162.

18  George Gilder, *Wealth and Poverty* (New York: Bantam, 1981), esp. pp. 83–4. See also Gilder, *Naked Nomads: Unmarried Men in America* (New York: Quadrangle/New York Times Books, 1974).

19  Charles Murray, *Losing Ground: American Social Policy 1950–1980* (New York: Basic Books, 1984). Michael Katz, in *Undeserving Poor*, describes the massive promotion of this book by the conservative Manhattan Institute, including the hiring of a public relations specialist to manage the "Murray campaign," p. 152. Among the most persuasive critics of Murray's claims about the failure of social programs has been Christopher Jencks, "How Poor are the Poor?" *New York Review of Books* 32 (May 5, 1985).

20  Charles Murray, "The Coming White Underclass," *Wall Street Journal* (October 20, 1993), p. A14.

21  The campaign among social conservatives to assure that illegitimacy would be a major target of any welfare reform legislation is exhaustively documented in Williams, "Right's Attack", esp. pp. 14–18.

22  *Congressional Quarterly's Washington Alert*, "Welfare Reform," (March 24, 1995), p. H3736; ibid. (March 22, 1995), p. H3421.

23  Robert Rector, "Welfare Reform and the Death of Marriage," *Washington Times* (February 23, 1996), p. A20.

24  Christopher Jencks, "The Hidden Paradox of Welfare Reform," *American Prospect* 32 (May–June, 1997), pp. 33–41.

25  Christian Coalition, *Contract with the American Family* (Nashiville TN: Moorings Press, 1995).

26  On Margaret Sanger and her dealings with the eugenicist movement, see Ellen Chesler, *Woman of Valor: Margaret Sanger and the Birth Control Movement in America* (New York: Simon and Schuster, 1992). Two of the strongest critiques of the coercive possibilities of the "population establishment" that have emerged from feminist political circles are Linda Gordon, *Woman's Body, Woman's Right* (Baltimore: Penguin, 1977); Petchesky, *Abortion and Woman's Choice*.

27  Thomas Elwood, in *The Politics of Population Control* (Notre Dame: University of Notre Dame Press, 1977), gives a detailed account of the family-planning controversies during the Nixon years, including conservatives' impulses toward population control, and the angry responses of many minority activists.

28  On mandated family-planning counselling, see Abramovitz, *Regulating the Lives of Women*, p. 337. On sterilization abuse, see Claudia Dreifus, "Sterilizing the Poor," in Dreifus, ed., *Seizing Our Bodies: The Politics of Women's Health* (New York: Vintage, 1978), pp. 105–20.

29  Barbara Feringa, Sarah Iden, and Allan Rosenfield, "Norplant: Potential for Coercion," in Sarah Samuels and Mark Smith, eds, *Norplant and Poor Women* (Menlo Park CA: Henry J. Kaiser Family Foundation, 1992), pp. 53–63.

30  The extraordinary extent to which abortion became the defining issue of domestic policy during the Reagan presidency is vividly recounted in Michelle McKeegan, *Abortion Politics: Mutiny in the Ranks of the Right* (New York: Free Press, 1992). A celebrated case of such an appointment that backfired was that of Everett Koop, who was appointed surgeon general, with New Right backing, because of his anti-abortion activity. However, once in office, he enraged his right-wing supporters because of his principled stands on AIDS education and his refusal to supply "proof" of the existence of a "postabortion stress syndrome." Everett Koop, *Koop: The Memoirs of America's Family Doctor* (New York: Random House, 1991).

31  A recent example of the long-standing right-wing battle against Title X is the Christian Coalition's call for an end to funding for this program (*Contract with the American Family*, pp. 68–9). On the decline in public funding for family planning since Reagan took office,

see T. Sollom, R. B. Gold, and R. Saul, "Public Funding for Contraceptive, Sterilization and Abortion Services, 1994," *Family Planning Perspectives* 28 (1996), pp. 166–73.

32 For a discussion of how abortion politics at the local level constrains teenage pregnancy-prevention efforts, see Carole Joffe, "Sexual Politics and the Teenaged Pregnancy Prevention Worker," in Annette Lawson and Deborah Rhode, eds, *The Politics of Pregnancy: Adolescent Pregnancy and Public Policy* (New Haven CN: Yale University Press, 1993), pp. 284–300.

33 Catholic church opposition to welfare reform has been voiced both in terms of support for the poor, and because of fears of increased abortion. On the former, see Elizabeth Shogren, "Religious Groups Attack GOP Welfare," *Los Angeles Times* (November 9, 1995), p. 35: "[T]he bishops issued a report decrying poverty in America as a 'social and moral scandal' and calling for government as well as private action to combat it." On the latter, see Judith Havemann, "Women in Congress, Others Appeal to Welfare Conferees," *Washington Post* (October 17, 1995), p. A10: "[T]he U.S. Catholic Conference asked the lawmakers to reject any 'simple and dangerous fixes' that could pressure poor women into having abortions."

34 For two conservative accounts of the family cap dilemma, see Suzanne Garment, "Loss of Predictable Moorings Makes for Political Misalliances," *Los Angeles Times* (May 21, 1995), p. M2; Cheryl Wetzstein, "Abortion Tops 'Family Cap' Debate," *Washington Times* (May 1, 1995), p. A6.

35 Mark Greenberg and Steve Savner, "A Brief Summary of Key Provisions of the Temporary Assistance for Needy Families Block Grant of H.R. 3734" (Washington DC: Center for Law and Social Policy, August 13, 1996), p. 6. To suggest just some of the difficulties ahead in calculating the "abortion index," in 1995, five states had no mechanisms to collect abortion data, and many others had imperfect systems. Stanley Henshaw, personal communication (March, 1997).

36 Measures which would regulate and punish teen sexuality and child bearing evoke a greater consensus within the general public--but teenage women head only 7.6 percent of AFDC families (and most of these teenagers are 18 or 19 years old). US Department of Health and Human Services, "Aid to Families with Dependent Children: Characteristics and Financial Circumstances of AFDC Recipients" (Washington, DC: US Government Printing Office, 1992), p. 42.

37 Robert Pear, "Hatch Joins Kennedy to Support a Program to Provide Health Insurance for Children," *New York Times* (March 14, 1997), p. A10. Predictably, however, this attempt at "Republicanism with a kinder face" has, at the time of writing in spring, 1997, been put in jeopardy by the anti-abortion politics of the right-wing of the party (as well as the party's anti-tax sentiment). One Republican senator has been distributing literature against the bill arguing (rather misleadingly) that it would "mandate abortion funding for teens." Adam Clymer, "G.O.P. Fights a Health Plan for Children," *New York Times* (April 12, 1997), p. A8.

38 As Charles Murray in "The Coming White Underclass" acknowledged, in discussing the likely effects on young women of the abolition of AFDC: "It will lead many young woman who shouldn't be mothers to place their babies for adoption. This is good. It will lead others . . . to take steps not to get pregnant. This is also good. Many others will get abortions. Whether this is good depends on what one thinks of abortion."

39 In March, 1997, several months after signing the welfare- reform bill, President Clinton called for government agencies to hire welfare recipients – but in 1996, according to the *New York Times*, "the Federal Government hired 31 people in the Boston area, 27 in Dallas, 8 in Kansas City . . . Nationwide, the Government lists only 11 openings for nursing assistants, 6 for clerk typists, and 9 for mail and file clerks." Robert Pear, "President Orders Agencies to Train those on Welfare," *New York Times* (March 9, 1997), pp. A1, A22.

# Conclusion: Business Action, Ideological Acting, and Institutional Enactment

## Economic Constraints on Social Policy

### ★ Clarence Y. H. Lo ★

## Introduction

In the last quarter of the twentieth century, business interest groups and right-wing politicians and think tanks have sought selectively to reduce government spending in social programs. The reductions in the 1990s took the form of cutting welfare programs for the poor, lowering health-care costs, and trimming social security and Medicare benefits, while maintaining military spending at slightly less than Cold War peaks, reducing taxes, and lowering the budget deficit.

The chapters in this volume have examined the major social and economic policy issues during the years of the Clinton presidency. Yet the chapters go beyond the controversies surrounding Clinton to analyze how it is that austerity has been the staple of American social policy for the last quarter-century. We have argued that economic limits, sometimes real, sometimes exaggerated, have constrained social policy and have made for a conservative agenda. Sometimes business decisions amount to their own social policy. Sometimes policy is driven by the rhetoric that the social policy of America is business. And sometimes changes in political institutions create situations where businesses and their priorities will govern.

In this concluding chapter, I argue that the conservative agenda prevails because of economic constraints which sometimes are clear business *actions*, but increasingly involve *acting* and *enactment*. It is obvious that conservative policies are imposed when large businesses take direct action in the private-sector economy, for example, by driving interest rates up to force a president to reduce the deficit and cut social programs. But even if businesses do not take action, conservative elites through their public statements can act out a drama that portrays how economic constraints necessitate austerity. And even if politicians remain silent about the economic imperatives on policies, they can enact changes in the rules, processes, and structure of institutions, thereby imposing economic constraints on future policies.

Thus, this volume has pursued three related lines of analysis. We have examined how business action restructures economic inequalities, how elites transform meanings through acting out ideologies, and how leaders reshape the state institutions which enact policy. The chapters have drawn upon the intellectual currents of neo-Marxism, social constructionism, and historical institutionalism. Rather than trying to argue that policy is mainly driven by business elites, ideology, or the government, the chapters have, for different policies, illuminated the varied interrelationships between the three forces. I will begin to untangle the interrelations between action, acting, and enactment[1] by elaborating upon each, in turn.

## Business Action: The Not-So Invisible Hand in the Global Economy

Large business institutions through their day-to-day actions – hiring and firing workers, buying materials, borrowing money, marketing goods, and locating production facilities and corporate headquarters – exert a powerful impact on society, often overpowering the effect of government programs. Such business actions materially constitute social policy. Furthermore, business actions can pressure governments to change policy. This pressure is leveraged when business action is accompanied by speculation. Nowadays speculation occurs less through the actual material transfer of gold or the physical hoarding of goods than as computerized trading in a virtual market of electronically recorded assets. In this era of speculation, as I argue in this section, conservatives interpret market gyrations as calls for imposing their agenda, which hypersensitive presidents heed for fear of losing their political fortunes.

Perhaps the most important business action is to control flows of money. Mintz and Schwartz's path-breaking work, *The Power Structure of American Business*,[2] analyzes a form of business action which was significant around 1980. The major New York banks exercised control over capital flows, constraining the decisions of even big industrial firms. Occasionally investment banks took action directly

in financial markets, for example, by dumping the stock of a corporation whose managers no longer had the confidence of the finance capitalist community. At other times, banks took administrative actions to impose economic constraints and intervened directly in specific managerial decisions or dictated that a client firm restructure. Finance capitalists, however, preferred to act in a quieter manner to constrain firms, by managing a regular but conditional pattern of loans to subject corporations.

Such business actions are social policy. The principal New York banks took action and lowered the credit ratings of New York City bonds, bid the bond prices down, refused to underwrite additional debt, and thereby precipitated the financial crisis of New York City in 1975, leading to cuts in city budgets and services.[3] Furthermore, business decisions not to invest, locate in, or service inner-city minority neighborhoods have produced the intractable social problems of poverty for the urban underclass. Major corporations not investing in basic manufacturing within the United States have resulted in deindustrialization and hardship in many cities of the midwest. With the globalization of economic activity, business actions have imposed constraints shaping economic life throughout the globe. Large corporations have taken action to expand abroad, resulting in low-wage jobs with few benefits in the United States, declining living standards, and upward redistribution of wealth to benefit the few, thereby limiting what government social policies can accomplish.

Business actions such as capital flows are made even more potent by speculators who try to anticipate future economic turns and take actions creating swings in financial markets. The booming value of junk bonds and commercial real estate unleashed powerful speculative forces that ultimately resulted in the demise of many savings and loan institutions and hundreds of billions of dollars in government bailouts. Orange County, California, and other localities invested billions in speculative investments that were profitable when interest rates fell but caused bankruptcy when rates rose, with catastrophic effects on county social services.

These speculative swings sometimes occur in charged political circumstances and therefore have overt repercussions on nation states. One of the most dramatic examples in the twentieth century occurred after the election of Leon Blum's socialist government in France in 1936. Businesses expected that Blum's concessions to militant unions would ruin France. Anticipating these trends, speculators sold French stocks and francs and moved money out of France, causing a foreign-exchange crisis and the downfall of the regime the next year.[4] Business actions had become a political drama of epic proportions and an integral part of world ideological conflict. Business action, in short, was ideological acting.

Business action and ideological acting are thus related because of the speculative component of business action. Speculation, a phenomenon that involves the spread of mass beliefs, is fertile ground for sociologists to analyze how groups construct reality and, in particular, bizarre perceptions with little empirical validity. But even if an economic move is unlikely and is only a feared imaginary, speculators can believe a trend is imminent and, with enough market power, can act to shift market prices, alter capital flows, or merely threaten action, with devastating results.

Although capital and market movements were not cataclysmic during the Clinton Administration, they did have continuing political repercussions. Clinton promoted the actions of American corporations that trade and invest overseas, pushing the North American Free Trade Agreement through Congress, and extracting trade concessions from Japan and China. In fact, a major priority for the Clinton administration was to help US-based firms that operated globally with deterimental

consequences for poor and working Americans.[5] Why did Clinton adopt austerity as a priority? Was it because of corporations moving money or otherwise taking direct action in the economy to force Clinton's hand? Frances Fox Piven[6] argues that transnational capital mobility, by itself, does not prevent the United States government from spending on social programs. When American business leaders pursued their agenda of austerity during the first months of the Clinton Administration, they did not take action like their brethren in France in 1936, who caused cataclysmic capital flows out of France. American business leaders did not need to. But they and conservative politicians did proclaim and act out the ideology that global competition and maintaining the confidence of financial markets were ironclad constraints upon the state of domestic welfare.

After the 1993 Clinton inauguration, businesses did not move capital out of the US or drive stock prices down or interest rates way up. The US stock market was rising and long-term interest rates, while not at historic low levels, had fallen substantially from double-digit peaks in the early 1980s. Nevertheless, bond traders remained suspicious of the new president and his promises of reform, especially universal health-care coverage. Traders did not need to make an actual speculative move. Conservatives merely had to make news and speculate about the speculation in the bond market, much as Alan Greenspan would do for the stock market in 1996 when he spoke of "irrational exuberance" and was widely quoted. The bond markets, by slightly foreshadowing possible upward moves in interest rates, were part of a process that eventually empowered former business leaders, serving inside the Clinton Administration, to demand that Clinton adopt austerity as a priority.

Business and conservative leaders exerted political pressure and argued that in the bond market long-term interest rates would move upward further unless Clinton decisively reduced the federal budget deficit. Big business leaders, along with many leading academic economists, insisted that it would take a $500-billion deficit reduction over five years to bolster bond and stock markets and to reassure the financial community and Federal Reserve Board Chairman Alan Greenspan.[7] These leaders proclaimed fiscal conservative ideologies, as I will argue below, and acted out an elaborate public ritual that unnecessarily established stock prices, bond prices, the deficit, price stability, and international competitiveness as economic constraints on social policy.

In his first term, Clinton sometimes privately cursed the linkage between Wall Street fortunes and his own political fortune, but by 1996, he (and his campaign adviser Dick Morris) had decided the linkage was an embrace. Clinton chose to run his re-election campaign in 1996 based on a growing economy, symbolized by a soaring stock market. His political capital had become even more directly tied to any fall in the market. Even though he was re-elected in 1996, he was vulnerable to business's arguments that in order to keep the stock market soaring, it was necessary to further implement the conservative agenda and resolve to balance the budget, cut taxes, and cut Medicare.

## Conservative Ideology and the Acting Out of Economic Constraints

The power of the conservative agenda thus stems not only from business taking direct action in the economy, but also from business and the right wing acting out a drama highlighting economic constraints on social policy. Sometimes conservatives win when they act as if, and then convince us that, economic necessities compel them to eliminate high-paying jobs in the US, move production to low-wage foreign nations, balance the budget, and cut expenditures for social programs.

The retirement system will go bankrupt, so the conservatives argue, if social security and Medicare expenditures are not restricted. Manufacturers will have to relocate production elsewhere, so the conservatives chant, if wages are too high. If the federal budget is unbalanced, the government must finance the national debt by selling a mountain of bonds, driving interest rates higher, choking off consumer and business credit, and thereby causing a recession. It is indeed ironic that the most simple kind of economic determinism, falsely attributed to Marxists on the left, is the battle cry of conservative revolutionaries, who now are the ones seeking to smash the state.[8] Where conservatives see ironclad economic constraint, the authors of this volume see conservative elites arguing and acting to ensure that alleged economic constraints become reality.

By using the words "act" and "acting," I do not wish to imply that every constraint on public policy is non-existent and merely fabricated. The capitalist economy, banks, and large businesses do indeed constrain workers, consumers, and governmental institutions. However, I maintain that in order to advance their agenda, conservatives have at times selectively highlighted, exaggerated, and publicized certain constraints, occasionally creating what can only be described as mass illusion.

Social programs, higher wages, and environmental measures may slightly reduce the profit margins of some corporations. But rarely are the effects so compelling that it is the life-or-death factor business alleges, especially for the largest corporations, which can make market forces rather than succumbing to them. But business and political elites can construct a crisis in the hopes of imposing their agenda by making it seem economically necessary.

### Economic constraints as ideology

Conservatives argue that the need to maintain growth and price stability should constrain social policy because, they claim, too much welfare-state spending causes slow growth and high inflation. Gosta Esping-Andersen counters by demonstrating that research has not clearly demonstrated these claims. Block argues that spending for social programs and higher wages, in fact, do not necessarily make a nation's exports too costly or otherwise destroy a nation's competitiveness, which depends on many complex factors.[9] Social programs are not necessarily wasteful but can increase the overall productivity of a nation. The notion that welfare spending occurs at the expense of economic prosperity must remain an ideology, i.e. a set of beliefs conveying a political agenda, argued but not proven.

Conservatives argue that if we want prosperity and jobs, we must forego environmental regulations. However, government regulations to clean up the environment in the 1970s did not lead to business bankruptcies or unemployment. Businesses closed plants because they were old and inefficient, not just because they failed to meet environmental standards. Many new jobs were created in resource and waste management and in environmental technology and facilities construction.[10]

But even though the arguments that we cannot afford social programs or environmental regulation are of dubious validity, to the extent that elites promulgate them in the media and other "responsible" sources confirm them, high government officials are more likely to pursue the conservative agenda. If fiscal conservatives present a predominant argument that a continuing federal budget deficit will cause inflation and high interest rates, government priorities will be constrained by the conservative agenda. Constraints are more effective if they are presented as bona fide market or economic trends. If conservative arguments prevail among politicians and the media that capital flow out of a country is the economic law of the gold standard, rather than

manipulation by powerful bankers, a regime committed to the welfare state can better be scuttled.[11] Economic constraints are more than the invisible hand of market forces, operating automatically and impersonally through business decisions. Rather, it takes experts with a learned hand, with specific knowledge, ideologies, and power to act out publicly so that economic realities confirm their prejudices.

The first to act out economic ideologies as constraints are often business lobbyists and elites. Economic elites formed the American Energy Alliance and argued that Clinton's proposed Btu energy tax would kill American jobs. This notion resonated among those concerned about the lingering effects of the 1991 recession. The alliance successfully organized grassroots pressure on Congress to replace the Btu energy tax with a small increase in the gasoline tax.[12] Other successful ideological acts involving business, experts, the media, and politicians are the campaigns by the Concord Coalition to reduce the budget deficit, and by Peter Peterson and the Association for Generational Equality to trim social security.

Elite business policy groups played a major role in developing ideologies emphasizing global trade, international competitiveness, and high technology – ideologies that have defined fundamental constraints on economic policy for the past quarter-century. J. Kenneth Benson and Nick Paretsky[13] trace these ideologies from the 1980s, when the Council on Foreign Relations argued for increasing American competitiveness in high technology, to the moment when president-elect Clinton adopted versions of the ideas that had spread to the Democratic Leadership Council and his economic advisers.

Business and conservative elites have sought to trim social security and have acted out ideologies about economic constraints on spending. Jill Quadagno[14] analyzes the arguments of social-security opponents that entitlement spending is rising out of control, that revenues raised through social-security taxes are used to offset deficit spending, and that the social-security trust funds will be bankrupt in 30 years. Quadagno finds all of these arguments to be based on questionable projections and data.

The arguments of conservative social-security critics are accepted in part because of the power of the disseminating groups. But in addition, politicians and the media have an easy time because the arguments are cleverly built upon the public's deep-seated perceptions, common sense, and fears. Americans believe less and less that one's social security benefits are funded from one's own past contributions, held in trust over the years. The conservatives' arguments resonate with the public's fears that social security is leading to cuts in other worthwhile social programs.

In short, social policy results from a process of political argumentation which defines, publicizes, and thereby acts out economic constraints. The most successful constraints prevail because they operate as potent political symbols, lavishly financed and produced by the top political-consulting studios using celebrities as actors to sell through multiple media outlets. My use of the word "act" emphasizes these dramaturgical and socially constructed aspects of economic constraint, aspects highlighted in the qualitative tradition of sociology.

*The social crisis and acting out the ideology of family values*

In short, business elites argue that economic trends compel the government to adopt the conservative agenda. Academic economists of the same mind sometimes portray economic tendencies as a crisis – a crisis of greedy entitlements, a crisis of ballooning deficits, a crisis of over-regulation. Karl Polanyi pointed out that when crises actually do occur in world history, they are not merely economic crises but, more importantly, social crises, involving disruption and transformation of human relations. Great crises are also moral crises, since they upset expectations of the good life, the good society, and the proper obligations to others.[15] This lesson of history is not lost on those who would act out crises to push the conservative agenda.

The so-called crisis in the contemporary American family is just such an ideological construction. It guided the policies of the Clinton Administration and in turn, profoundly affected economic inequalities and constraints. Pro-family values contain assumptions about gender and class inequality, heterosexual couples, and racial prejudice, and therefore turned the welfare state even further away from benefitting the poor, racial minorities, and women, making the state even more a racialized state, a capitalist state, and a patriarchal state.[16]

Clinton turned away from his 1992 campaign talk about diversity among families, and instead adopted the pro-family rhetoric of neo-conservative and neo-liberal intellectuals. Judith Stacey argues that social scientists such as David Popenoe and Jean Elshtain, who constructed ideologies about the crisis of family values, were just as instrumental in pushing policies to the right as were the economists who publicized the doctrines of the supply side, monetarism, and the free market.[17]

The Clinton Administration combined a pro-family rhetorical foundation with an articulation of economic constraints to consolidate a turn to conservative policies. In Clinton's 1996 campaign, the family that needed help was imagined as a white, middle-class, two-income-earner suburban family, complete with a soccer mom – the legendary independent swing voters. These were the families to whom Clinton promised tax credits and deductions from the first year of college on.

## A critique of acting out, ideology, and discourse

The chapters in this volume offer different analytical methods to criticize the prevailing ideologies claiming that the economy constrains policy. Quadagno criticizes economic data on its own terms, questioning the accuracy of the fiscal projections conservatives use to argue that the social-security system will go bankrupt. Quadagno estimates social security will only increase by less than 2 percent of GDP by the year 2010. Stacey challenges the assertions of family-values advocates that single-parent families cause social problems. Stacey argues that pro-family advocates simplify social-science findings, use misleading or no control groups, and exaggerate the effects of divorce on children. She goes on to examine the social position, interests, and affiliations of the family-values academics, and the implications of their arguments. The chapters by Lembcke and myself are concerned not only about the truth value of specific arguments, but also more generally about what is talked about, the categories used to discuss it, and the domination that is thereby maintained. Both Lembcke and I critically evaluate the extent to which contemporary patterns of discourse can be judged to be rational.

Jerry Lee Lembcke investigates arguments supporting the Persian Gulf War, which have become the rhetorical foundation justifying the Clinton Administration's military incursions into Somalia, Haiti, and Bosnia. Presidents explaining military interventions have spoken repeatedly of the need to support troops that had already been sent. Those who back the troops frequently contrasted their support to the largely mythical vilification of Vietnam-era troops, allegedly spat upon by anti-war demonstrators. These rhetorical devices evoke powerful emotional symbols, making it impossible for the public to have a reasoned discussion about whether committing US troops is a rational means to accomplish foreign policy objectives. Rather than the troops being considered as means to an end, the troops become an end in themselves, to be supported at all costs.[18]

Specific types of discourse were crucial in constructing economic constraints during the debate over Clinton's health-care plan. I argue in chapter 12 that the Clinton plan died when the terms of the debate shifted from how universal coverage would benefit society to how individuals who already had insurance would lose under the Clinton plan. This individual, cost-benefit language underlay public debate and was conveyed by the media to the public as common sense, profoundly affecting the future of social policy.

I argue that another major reason for the defeat of the Clinton plan was the news reports that public opinion had turned against the Clinton plan. I contend that this reading of public opinion was a highly selective interpretation of disparate and contradictory opinion poll results. The news that public opinion had rejected the Clinton plan was actually a judgement call that conservative Democratic politicians and experts, some with top positions inside Clinton's own administration, had made at the beginning of the debate. Journalists in the national media echoed these judgements and promulgated them until they became the political facts of life.

Sometimes, business and political elites used conservative discourses against Clinton, as was the case in health-care reform and social security. Other times, it was President Clinton himself who used conservative ideology to justify a right turn in policy, as in the family-values controversy. In the case of balancing the budget, Clinton served the important function of publicly authenticating the arguments of business and conservative elites.

Business elites and groups begin an ideological act by arguing that a balanced budget is an inviolate economic constraint. Part of a convincing performance can be a public drama, whereby a president who is supposedly a liberal comes to terms with and eventually endorses key constraints that business advocates. If the act is to be credible, it is important for the president to maintain a pose that he has not completely abandoned liberal principles when he accepts the economic constraints. The president must act as if he believes the constraints to be true.[19]

The drama of President Clinton's first term was to authenticate many of the limitations that fiscal conservatives asserted. Clinton's actions sent the message that the deficit was indeed a compelling constraint; he cut the deficit immediately upon taking office in 1993, vowed to reduce the US's health-care costs, and agreed with congressional Republicans over the need to balance the federal budget within a decade.

Although Clinton built a consensus that the deficit was an intermediate-term problem, Republicans went further and presented the deficit as an immediate crisis. In winter, 1995–6, Republicans refused to approve increases in the national debt, leading to a federal government shutdown. Acting as if the deficit were a direct constraint, conservatives hoped to convince the public to support the Republican deficit-reduction plan. However, the strategy failed when the public began to see the winter budget crisis not as economic reality, but as a Republican partisan ploy.

### Necessity, freedom, and the ideologies of economic constraint

Where conservatives see constraints, the authors in this volume see freedom to implement policies broadening welfare-state entitlements. Ann Markusen in chapter 7 of this volume argues that social programs and investments can be expanded and military production further reduced, because government can implement the proper incentives to encourage military contractors to diversify,

increase non-military exports, and plan for lower budgets. Piven also contends that the US can increase social welfare expenditures; she notes that German workers receive twice as much in salary and benefits as do American workers. Since German businesses continue to be globally competitive, the US can afford adequate social provision for its workforce. Molotch argues that despite the ideology that cities must grow to ensure their prosperity, it is possible for localities to decide to stop using tax money to finance private developers, and to more effectively use the environmental review process and growth limits to get developers to pay for public services and amenities.

The task of critical social scientists, when confronted with ideologies arguing that economic necessity should govern public policy, is to analyze the appearance of necessity to uncover the essential realm of freedom, the freedom for a democracy to choose policies that meet human social needs. Perhaps what progressive intellectuals must do today is adopt the opposite approach to Karl Marx's criticism of the ideologies of freedom to reveal underlying necessity. The prevailing ideologies of Marx's day proclaimed that markets were the realization of human freedom – the freedom to choose one's employer and the freedom to decide what consumer products to purchase. Where Adam Smith saw freedom, Marx saw constraint – the necessity of workers who lack land and other means to produce for themselves and who must labor for an employer to earn wages for a living.

Today, shrill conservative ideology heightens and misrepresents economic constraints. In actuality, the federal government does not face an immediate problem of bankruptcy. Neither does the social security system, even 15 years from now. Nor has the United States lost its competitive edge in high-tech products and processes. The ideologies of the conservative agenda falsely see economic constraint as dictating the immediate decisions of public policy.

The economic constraints so heralded in conservative ideology can only be dealt with not as immediate phenomena, but rather as evidence of deeper economic contradictions. Economic problems can only be analyzed as Marx analyzed them, by abstracting concepts such as commodities, socialized production, and exchange from immediate economic appearances and then developing theories analyzing the interrelationships and dynamics between the abstract concepts.

In this manner, some important literature treats surface economic phenomena as manifestations of root problems. Budget shortfalls, as James O'Connor argues, reflect the underlying problem that the government spends more and more to subsidize infrastructure and labor costs needed by private businesses, while those businesses reap the profits from public subsidies. Behind the crisis in the social security system, according to Claus Offe and Gosta Esping-Andersen, is an underlying tension between maintaining the labor market that corporations need and workers' resistance to being treated as a commodity on that labor market.[20] Trade rivalries are symptoms of the fundamental problem that, after the collapse of the gold standard, the world has yet to develop an adequate system for the flows of international economic exchange.

A major theme of this volume, then, has been that business and political elites act out the apparitions of economic necessity as a morality play, thereby increasing the economic constraints on social policy. Politics is thus a class act that can be analyzed using the tools that qualitative sociologists have devised to study the presentation of the self and the formation of the taken-for-granted in everyday life.[21]

In dramatizing the specter of economic constraints, leading roles go to institutions such as the presidency, business interest groups, the Congress, and, as I show in my chapter on health-care reform, the media acting as public opinion pollsters.

In the acting out of the trials and tribulations of social security, the key institutional players have been the business press and organizations such as the Americans for Generational Equality. In the first years of the Clinton presidency, the Bipartisan Commission on Entitlement was center stage, but the conservatives gave an unconvincing performance. Part of the reason was an institutional factor – the rules governing operations of the commission, reflecting the deep stalemate between the Democratic and Republican parties. Institutional factors help determine how economic constraints are dramatized. I now turn my attention to these important institutional arrangements and their larger role in imposing austerity.

## Enacting the Conservative Agenda: Political and State Institutions as Economic Constraint

Political institutions are the means by which the economic constraints of austerity are enacted. I use the word "enact" in the same sense as we speak of legislation being enacted through institutions such as congressional committees and caucuses and the House and Senate. But I also use the word "enact" more broadly to refer to the processes of policy making and change in a range of institutions, not just legislatures.

Institutional leadership, resources, and power in the Executive branch, as well as the legislative, help to determine the enactment of policy. When Clinton staffed key agencies with staunch fiscal conservatives, those leaders placed their imprint on the entire spectrum of policy. The new Clinton Administration took up deficit reduction as the major priority, leading to the demise of Clinton's proposals to stimulate the economy and provide jobs, which had been promised in his campaign document, "Putting People First."

If characteristics of political institutions affect policies, then changes in institutions are sometimes the prerequisite for policies, as conservatives who advocate austerity agendas well know. Congressional Republicans in 1995 thus sought to accomplish their Contract with America not only by legislating specific policies, but also by enacting or attempting major changes in the political rules of the game, such as a constitutional amendment requiring a balanced federal budget, the line-item veto (giving the president the power to cut specific spending items out of a larger appropriations bill), and legal reform (making it difficult for consumers to win large settlements of lawsuits).

Political institutions change, but not only at the stroke of leaders who directly change rules. Over time, the weight of policies pursued helps to shape the development of institutions, networks, structures, and groups, which then can have a further effect on policy. The establishment of the social-security system and its increased importance in the lives of seniors increased the strength of the American Association of Retired Persons. Government policy on home mortgages contributed to a suburban pattern of economic growth. The seniors' lobby and suburban constituencies are powerful institutions seeking to perpetuate some social programs.

In their chapter about science policy, Gregory Hooks and Gregory McLauchlan[22] provide another compelling example of how policies lead to the growth of institutions that develop vested interests in the continuation of those policies. Despite Clinton's 1992 campaign rhetoric – about developing dual-use technologies beneficial to the civilian economy, about downsizing the military, and about the peace dividend – the federal government has continued to pay top dollar to develop advanced technology, both for weapons and for the surveillance of hostile nations to detect

any development of mass-destruction weapons. Large military projects as far back as the Manhattan Project have produced institutions and a structure of American science and technology that have inexorably made Clinton's high-tech policy a continuation of the policies of previous administrations.

Institutions which promoted military spending and science constrained the development of industrial policy in the civilian economy. Many industrial policy ideas, such as innovations in labor-management relations and large investments in infrastructure and job training, fell by the wayside. Only those policies that could be connected to existing national-security-oriented programs gained modest budgets.[23]

In the military sector, high spending levels build institutions that continue further spending, whereas for welfare, decreases in budgets destroy institutions, leading to further reductions in the welfare state. The spectacle of Clinton and the Republicans both campaigning against welfare indicated that politicians were competing with each other to worsen the economic conditions of lower-income citizens rather than uplift them. Politicians can no longer deliver a better economy for working people just in time for the next election – what Piven in chapter 1 calls "electoral economism." Recent cuts have been destroying the very capacity of government institutions to improve economic conditions, thereby destroying any faith that citizens can better their lives by engaging in politics. The failure of the politics of electoral economism could lead to the politics of fundamentalist irrationalism – an angry popular reaction against clients of the welfare state. As Ronald Walters reminds us (Chapter 2), anti-welfare sentiment has been anti-black sentiment throughout American history, and such sentiments have been institutionalized in the Democratic as well as the Republican Party.

## Devolution as enactment of constraint

Thus, the rise of the military-industrial complex and the collapse of the Keynesian welfare state are hotly contested institutional changes involving huge flows of money and other economic trends of consequence. Another important institutional change has been brought about by the 1996 welfare-reform law (Public Law 104–93), which gave the 50 states the power to set welfare benefits and decide how to spend their allotment of federal welfare funds. These changes in political institutions are important, not just to those studying federalism. The enactment of the Clinton–Republican welfare reform is significant because institutional reform will bring powerful economic forces into play below the federal level. States will be under further economic constraints to cut welfare spending and taxes, for example, as states compete aggressively for businesses to locate within their borders.

Harvey Molotch continues the argument that institutional changes must be seen in the context of overarching class inequalities.[24] Clinton's rhetoric, following the lead of conservative urban-policy experts, emphasized "local empowerment." With much of Clinton's urban policy involving "devolution" to the local level, policy will be determined by the economic forces operating at that level. Kicking decisions back to the localities is not a victory for grassroots democracy, or for the poor and moderate-income earners supposedly served by the Department of Housing and Urban Development. Once policy is at the discretion of city and town government, it will be at the mercy of a local land-power complex – the growth machine.

Growth machines consist of local landowners, corporations headquartered downtown, and other institutions with a stake in a particular locality and its growth, such as media outlets, utilities, and elite cultural institutions. In order to gain in the competition with other localities, a growth machine seeks to enact pro-development government policies, such as lower business taxes, reduced spending for the poor, and police protection of property.[25] Handing over welfare policy to the growth machine can only result in folded programs, spindled services, and mutilated lives.

Some of the austerity of the conservative agenda was accomplished by the 1996 welfare-reform law and the devolution it enacted, which activated powerful economic constraints at the local level. In order to accomplish a cutback of spending (or any other policy, for that matter), it is often easier to enact an institutional reform and let numerous, highly constrained, lower-level authorities opt for the cuts. This is easier than attempting to get a definitive decision at the national level and then trying to compel many subordinates to abide by the decision.

Definitive decisions are impractical because they are predicated upon a system of sovereign power unlikely to exist today. Stuart Clegg[26] argues that authoritative power, in the classic image of Hobbes's Leviathan, has been replaced with localized strategizing and bargaining amid complex organizations and multiorganizational fields. By their policy of devolution and local constraints, conservatives have admitted that it is politically difficult to obtain a clear decision to gut popular social programs: better to let a thousand growth machines do it. And rather than a federally determined health-care paln, better to set the incentives to grow a hundred health-maintenance organizations and five insurance companies.

## Flexible economizing

Economic constraints can thus be enacted by political institutions – local government units constrained to economize because of their inadequate resources and because of pressures from local business constituencies. Decentralized units have only the discretion of creative finance, to economize in their own way – a pattern which I call "flexible economizing."

Flexible economizing is strikingly parallel to cost-cutting in the private-sector economy, now characterized by, in Mingione's terms, flexible specialization. By contrast, the Fordist period of the first part of the twentieth century according to Mingione, Harvey, and other theorists, was characterized by centralized mass production, relatively well-paid and unionized production workers, and a welfare state.[27] This has been replaced in the last quarter of this century with a post-Fordist economy. Depending on the vagaries of economic conditions, capitalists now scatter production sites throughout the world and hire workers in smaller enterprises producing for market niches. Today's capitalists demand flexibility from their employees – long hours of work if market conditions demand it, otherwise no work at all, and not even a safety net.

The parallel trend in the public sector, flexible economizing, entails a multiplicity of decentralized governmental units selectively cutting and redirecting programs, adapting to economic constraints. The 104th Congress and President Clinton enacted those constraints by decentralizing welfare provision. The 50 states will cut welfare further in future regional-level fiscal crises caused by dislocations in the world economy. One would expect the cuts to be hastily considered measures to achieve the desired bottom-line figures. Flexible economizing involves short-term financial calculations and only in that sense may be considered rational. But in the long run, flexible economizing is socially irrational, causing lost opportunities, stunted development, and the compounding of future costs.

A further implication of the concept of flexible economizing is that policy making involves a historical sequence of implementation that continually creates and reshapes economic constraints. To study the making of housing and urban policy is to analyze not only insti-

tutional enactment, but also the related business actions and ideological acting that construct economic constraints. The first constraint is acting out the drama of keeping interest rates down and the deficit under control, thereby limiting federal resources and hence housing-policy options. The second constraint is the enactment of devolution. This sets up the third set of constraints, which operate at the local level – actions by local business in real estate, acting out the ideology that localities must grow, and enacting changes in government administration that foster urban growth.

Similarly, policy for the homeless is also the successive implementation of economic constraints. The Reagan Administration's implacable hostility to social spending was the first economic constraint, an ideological act that severely constrained later policy. Homeless shelters could only exist if they were financed by several existing federal programs like Medicaid and treatment for substance abuse. Such service-intensive homeless shelters, pioneered in Westchester County, New York, by Andrew Cuomo, were the second constraint, an administrative enactment establishing patterns of resource acquisition. These institutionalized enactments became the third generation of economic constraints during the Clinton Administration, as Cuomo became Clinton's assistant secretary and later secretary of housing and urban development.[28]

Furthermore, the policy of service-intensive shelters, once implemented and justified, reinforced the ideology that homeless families were broken families, in need of a broad range of training, counseling, and other rehabilitative services. Such rhetoric may have helped the homeless gain funding under a pro-family rubric, because homeless shelters could be presented as rebuilding entire families who had suffered misfortune. But this policy also stigmatized homeless families as pathological. In the Clinton period, and indeed throughout the twentieth century, social-welfare policy has been dominated by institutional programs that dramatized the values of the patriarchal family and the moral uplift of the poor. This acting out of ideology in the public arena was an integral part of the institutional enactment of the conservative agenda.

Thus, in social policy, ideological acting and institutional enactment are closely related. Definitive research on policies for the homeless and other social policies must include analysis of both acting and enactment. More generally, it is fruitful to combine theories of changes in institutions with an understanding of the ideological and mythic notions that accompany the changes. To implement budget cuts, conservatives call for non-partisan commissions, expert panels, emergency decision makers (czars), and control boards composed of business, labor, and civic leaders. These measures are perhaps not the ones that actually are effective, but rather are the ones that are thought to be so. What is deemed appropriate administration thus depends on ideological and cultural factors.

The widespread use of these mechanisms to impose austerity is an example of what Powell and DiMaggio[29] have termed "institutional isomorphism." Sometimes the mechanisms are enacted through coercion, imposed by bankers or other powerful decision makers. Austerity mechanisms can also be enacted because of professionalism, when managers are trained in the same techniques to handle economic crises. Finally, austerity mechanisms are sometimes mimicked – copied because the practices become customary and legitimate.

Powell and DiMaggio's "new institutionalism" brings an analysis of social construction and myth back into the study of organizations and is useful for those analyzing institutions. An understanding of how features of the economy are defined as desirable will help scholars who historically study institutions and the limits to the welfare state at the end of the twentieth century.

In the next section I will discuss historical institutionalist scholars and their attempts to analyze austerity. A complete explanation of the power of the conservative agenda involves examining the interrelations between not only institutions and ideologies, as I have done above, but also state institutions and the structures of class inequality in capitalist societies. I begin with a sketch of the concerns that launched historical institutionalist theories.

## Theories of historical institutionalism

The most prominent theory of the state in the past decade has been historical institutionalism, exemplified by the work of sociologist Theda Skocpol and political scientists Peter A. Hall, Paul Pierson, Margaret Weir, and Peter Katzenstein.[30] In their view, the most important determinant of state policy is the evolution of political institutions.

Historical institutionalists argue that, beginning in Europe in the fifteenth century, the growth of state bureaucracies and state capacity to raise taxes crucially affected the economic development of nations competing and fighting in the world arena. State officials and bureaucracies often developed outlooks and interests distinct from other elites in society. In addition, constitutions and other political rules of the game often had a decisive impact, because they set the patterns by which groups influenced outcomes.

Historical institutionalists have also analyzed contemporary policy by emphasizing the importance of institutions such as the system of political parties. Skocpol,[31] for example, attributes the failure of Clinton's health-care reform to American political leaders and parties, and the Democratic Party in particular, which was not sufficiently issue-oriented. Political parties in the United States are weak coalitions put together for winning elections, not for proclaiming agendas to govern as they are in the parliamentary systems of Europe.

Theories of historical institutionalism were developed with particular reference to time periods when the state was increasing the resources it controlled, multiplying the numbers of its bureaucrats and clients, and otherwise extending its authority to new areas of society. Such was the case in early modern Europe, when states took up the tasks of nation building, as Charles Tilly describes in detail.[32] The progressive era in the early-twentieth-century United States, the New Deal of the 1930s, and the Kennedy–Johnson liberalism of the 1960s were times when major expansions of welfare programs built up the capacities of the nation state. Can historical institutionalist theories explain policy during periods when state bureaus, employees, and budgets are being cut? Yes, I argue, but only if historical institutionalism is combined with an analysis of class inequality.

## Historical institutionalism on austerity

Paul Pierson applies historical institutionalism to analyze what he terms "retrenchment" i.e. the cuts made in the welfare state by Prime Minister Margaret Thatcher in England and President Ronald Reagan in the United States. Pierson argues that policy makers succeeded in cutting certain programs because of institutional factors such as "traceability." When hardships can be directly traced back to politicians' decisions to cut budgets in relatively centralized political systems, then politicians will seek to avoid blame and will be less likely to cut deeply. Pierson applies another historical institutionalist concept, shifts in the political rules of the game, when he argues that granting the 50 states the power to set policy can have a profound effect on outcomes. Furthermore, reducing state fiscal capacity (another institutionalist notion) through tax cuts can be an effective way of slashing many programs and producing "systemic retrenchment."[33]

Pierson's arguments have been extended by the arguments of several authors in this volume. For example, although Pierson notes that decentralizing can have important consequences, it remains for Molotch to definitively analyze the economic context of the local level that will become a significant influence with the devolution of policies. Furthermore, Pierson's notion of systemic retrenchment becomes in Piven's hands the theory of the end of electoral economism, which elaborates how reducing state capacity will have broad consequences on the American political system and political ideology. Theories of historical institutionalism can provide useful beginning concepts for building a synthetic understanding of organization and class inequality in social policy.

## The limits of historical institutionalism: a synthesis with class analysis

Some historical institutionalists, however, in their rush to bring the state back into the forefront of analysis, have been too eager to throw class out. They have been insisting on explanations relying too heavily on institutional factors, with only passing reference to the capitalist economy and major class actors such as organized business groups. Pierson's analysis of retrenchment for example, specifically denies the importance of class power and resources. Skocpol argues that the passage of the Social Security Act of 1935 had little to do with the support from some top executives of large business firms. Similarly, Skocpol's analysis of the 1994 failure of Clinton's health-care plan does not adequately discuss the role of organized big business groups, like the Washington Business Group on Health, and the role of corporate leaders in policy-planning networks like the Jackson Hole Group (see chapter 11 in this volume).

However, other scholars affiliated with historical institutionalists have hinted at a fruitful integration of institutional and class analysis, emphasizing business actors and economic structures in their research. Some have mentioned causal arguments about class at key points in their largely institutionalist thesis. Gourevitch[34] argues that international economic competition has led many businesses with global markets to lower costs by reducing wages, taxes, and social programs. Furthermore, Hall[35] has noted the economic constraints on the state; he points out that banks and other private financial institutions have leverage over government Keynesian policies, because of the state's need to find buyers for government bonds. Others bring class back into historical institutionalism by arguing that differences in political rules affect how classes can organize to influence the state.[36]

Furthermore, institutional and class analysis can be combined in studies of economic organizations. Peter A. Hall's and Peter Gourevitch's analysis of Keynesian policies discusses how organized labor and other economic groups form the social base of governing political parties. The organization of labor and the organization of business are crucial factors affecting the state's economic policy. Katzenstein makes much the same point when he argues that the policy network between capital and the state is an important determinant of policy.[37] Campbell, Hollingsworth, and Lindberg's institutional analysis is noteworthy because it focusses not on the state, as do most historical institutionalists, but rather on the private sector. Campbell, et al. examine how businesses in an industrial sector institutionalize patterns of coordination which affect economic performance.[38]

Other scholars, critical of the historical institutionalists and focussed more on the large-scale structures of class inequality, have nevertheless shown greater appreciation of institutional factors and have argued that the power of labor and capital depends upon how they are organized and how their influence is channeled through political institutions. Esping-Andersen elaborates how the working class and other groups organize and make alliances in political parties, thereby affecting the type of welfare state "regime" that develops. In an earlier volume, I analyze how small property owners and small businesses organized themselves and formed alliances to oppose metropolitan administrative institutions that had been unresponsive to taxpayers' concerns. The class basis of political organization explains how an apparently populist tax revolt in the United States in the 1970s developed a pro-business program.[39]

Bob Jessop summarizes recent developments in theories of the state that combine an analysis of fundamental economic determinants with a newer concern with state institutions, political conflict, ideology, and political action. Jessop sees state policies as composing overarching hegemonic projects, i.e. political activity that tends to support a specific form of capitalism (a "regime of accumulation") at a particular point in history.[40] The contemporary conservative agenda of austerity is just such a hegemonic project.

The chapters in this volume have argued that a combination of the best features of historical institutionalism and class analysis can yield a promising approach to a study of the imposition of austerity. Our analysis of economic constraints, class structures, and the dominance of business priorities was enhanced through an institutionalist analysis of how specific business groups and sectors organize to wield power and how forms of organization shape the trajectory of government policy.

Historical institutionalism directs our attention to how policies build or destroy state institutions that will make future social policy. But only if the analysis of class inequality is made central can we fully understand how the interrelations between state institutions and the economy can dictate austerity. Austerity policies which channel funds toward private investment and military technology, and away from public services, can have a profound effect on institutions – threatening to undermine welfare provision completely. And institutional changes such as the devolution of welfare create effects that ripple past immediate political quicksands to activate new sets of economic constraints.

In this conclusion, I have drawn upon the chapters of this volume to argue that the agenda of austerity stems from the business *actions* of corporations and certain definitions of economic interests that have been *acted out* and promoted by elites. Those seeking to impose austerity have also *enacted* changes in institutions which may have locked in austerity policies for times far beyond the Clinton presidency.

By the very coining of the concepts of business action, ideological acting, and enactment of economic constraint, I indicate the value of a three-fold analysis of how right-wing groups seek to shape class inequalities, define

the construction of reality, and transform the institutions making policy. The concept of economic constraint is fundamental for the analysis of capitalism as an economic system. I have developed it by adding the concept of "acting," connoting a political performer who dramatizes. I have further developed the concept of economic constraint through the notion of "enactment," denoting the passage of laws and connoting the varieties of institutionalist theorizing.

The concepts of action, acting, and enactment enable us to critically analyze the ideologies of economic constraint in social policy debates. Some constraints are truly limits, and others are mere justifications for domination. A theoretical critique of what passes nowadays as economic constraint can recover the freedom we have to change our conditions. It is essential that we continue to analyze the future of social policy by such theorizing, and imagination.

## Notes

The author wishes to thank Darlaine Gardetto, Michael Schwartz, Maurice Zeitlin, and especially Fred Block for their perceptive suggestions and comments on drafts of this conclusion.

1 Business action which changes the value of the dollar compared to other currencies, for example, depends upon previous institutional enactments that facilitate global capital flows and weaken the regulatory powers of government central banks.
2 Beth Mintz and Michael Schwartz, *The Power Structure of American Business* (Chicago: University of Chicago Press, 1985).
3 Roger E. Alcaly and David Mermelstein, eds, *The Fiscal Crisis of American Cities* (New York: Vintage, 1976). Business actions make health policy by creating for-profit health-maintenance organizations, no matter what the government's health-care policy is. See ch. 11 by Beth Mintz in this volume.
4 My concept of international business action as

an economic constraint on the nation state builds upon the work of Fred Block, whose analysis of international monetary policy provides important theories about how the state acts in the capitalist world order. See Block, "Political Choice and the Multiple 'Logics' of Capital," in Sharon Zukin and Paul DiMaggio, eds, *Structures of Capital: The Social Organization of the Economy* (Cambridge: Cambridge University Press, 1990), pp. 293–309; Block, *Origins of International Economic Disorder: A Study of United States International Monetary Policy from World War II to the Present* (Berkeley CA: University of California Press, 1977).
5 See ch. 6 of this volume by Morris Morley and James Petras.
6 See ch. 1 of this volume.
7 See ch. 10 of this volume by Patrick Akard.
8 For a trenchant critique of these economic myths, see Fred Block, *The Vampire State: And Other Myths and Fallacies about the U.S. Economy* (New York: New Press, 1996).

9 Gosta Esping-Andersen, "Welfare States and the Economy," and Fred Block, "The Role of the State in the Economy," in Neil J. Smelser and Richard Swedberg, eds, *Handbook of Economic Sociology* (Princeton NJ: Princeton University Press, 1994); Block, "Political Choice."

10 Richard Kazis, *Fear at Work: Job Blackmail, Labor, and the Environment* (New York: Pilgrim Press, 1982).

11 Block, "Political Choice," p. 303.

12 See ch. 10 of this volume by Akard.

13 See ch. 9 of this volume.

14 See ch. 5 of this volume.

15 Karl Polanyi, *The Great Transformation: The Political and Economic Origins of Our Time* (Boston: Beacon Press, 1944).

16 See ch. 2 of this volume by Ronald Walters, ch. 14 by Zillah Eisenstein, and ch. 16 by Carole Joffe.

17 See ch. 15 of this volume.

18 See ch. 13 of this volume.

19 Peter M. Hall, "Asymmetric Relationships and Processes of Power," *Studies in Symbolic Interaction* Supplement I, "Foundations of Interpretive Sociology: Original Essays in Symbolic Interaction" (1985), pp. 309–34.

20 James O'Connor, *The Fiscal Crisis of the State* (New York: St Martin's Press, 1973); Claus Offe, *Disorganized Capitalism: Contemporary Transformations of Work and Politics*, ed. John Keane (Cambridge MA: MIT Press, 1985); Gosta Esping-Andersen, *Politics against Markets* (Princeton NJ: Princeton University Press, 1985).

21 See, for example, the work of Irving Goffman, such as *The Presentation of Self in Everyday Life* (Garden City NY: Doubleday, 1959).

22 See ch. 8 of this volume.

23 See ch. 9 of this volume by Ken Benson and Nick Paretsky.

24 See ch. 3 of this volume.

25 John R. Logan and Harvey Molotch, *Urban Fortunes: The Political Economy of Place* (Berkeley CA: University of California Press, 1987). In my terminology, these local economic constraints are exaggerated and hence involve acted-out ideology. Local economic constraints also involve business actions – e.g. speculation in increasing land values. They are politically enacted through the institutions of the growth machine.

26 Stuart Clegg, *Frameworks of Power* (London: Sage, 1989).

27 Michael J. Piore and Charles F. Sable, *The Second Industrial Divide: Possibilities for Prosperity* (New York: Basic Books, 1984); Enzo Mingione, *Fragmented Societies: A Sociology of Economic Life Beyond the Market Paradigm*, trans. Paul Goodrick (Oxford: Blackwell, 1991); David Harvey, *The Condition of Postmodernity* (Oxford: Blackwell, 1989).

28 See ch. 4 of this volume by Cynthia Bogard and J. Jeff McConnell.

29 Walter Powell and Paul DiMaggio, eds, *The New Institutionalism in Organizational Analysis* (Chicago: University of Chicago Press, 1991).

30 In addition to the works cited below, see Theda Skocpol, *Protecting Soldiers and Mothers: The Political Origins of Social Policy in the United States* (Cambridge MA: Harvard University Press, 1992); Skocpol, *Social Policy in the United States: Future Possibilities in Historical Perspective* (Princeton NJ: Princeton University Press, 1995); Peter Evans, Dietrich Rueschemeyer, and Theda Skocpol, eds, *Bringing the State Back In* (Cambridge: Cambridge University Press, 1985); Margaret Weir, *Politics and Jobs: The Boundaries of Employment Policy in the United States* (Princeton NJ: Princeton University Press, 1992).

31 Theda Skocpol, *Boomerang: Clinton's Health Security Effort and the Turn against Government in U.S. Politics* (New York: W. W. Norton, 1996), pp. 74–106.

32 Charles Tilly, *Coercion, Capital, and European States, AD 900–1900* (Oxford: Blackwell, 1990).

33 Paul Pierson, *Dismantling the Welfare State? Reagan, Thatcher, and the Politics of Retrenchment* (Cambridge: Cambridge University Press, 1994), pp. 35, 38, 46.

34 Peter A. Gourevitch, "Keynesian Politics: The Political Sources of Economic Policy Choices," in Peter A. Hall, ed., *The Political Power of Economic Ideas: Keynesianism across Nations* (Princeton NJ: Princeton University Press, 1989), p. 105.

35 Peter A. Hall, "Conclusion: The Politics of Keynesian Ideas," in Hall, *Economic Ideas*, p. 381.

36 Robert Hanneman and J. Rogers Hollingsworth, "Refocusing the Debate on the Role of the State

in Capitalist Societies," in Rolf Torstendahl, ed., *State Theory and State History* (London: Sage, 1992), pp. 38–61, which draws on Erik Wright, "States and Classes in Radical Theory," unpublished paper (1986). See especially Ira Katznelson, *City Trenches* (Chicago: University of Chicago Press, 1981).

37 Hall, "Conclusion," pp. 376–7; Gourevitch, "Keynesian Politics"; Peter A. Hall, "The Movement from Keynesianism to Monetarism: Institutional Analysis and British Economic Policy in the 1970s," in Sven Steinmo, Kathleen Thelen, and Frank Longstreth, eds, *Structuring Politics: Historical Institutionalism in Comparative Analysis* (Cambridge: Cambridge University Press, 1992), p. 91; Kathleen Thelen and Sven Steinmo, "Historical Institutionalism in Comparative Politics," in Steinmo et al., *Structuring Politics*, p. 6; Peter Katzenstein, *Between Power and Plenty* (Madison WI: University of Wisconsin Press, 1978).

38 John L. Campbell, J. Rogers Hollingsworth, and Leon N. Lindberg, *Governance of the American Economy* (Cambridge: Cambridge University Press, 1991).

39 Clarence Y. H. Lo, *Small Property versus Big Government: Social Origins of the Property Tax Revolt*, 1st paperback edn (Berkeley CA and Los Angeles: University of California Press, 1995); Esping-Andersen, *Politics against Markets*.

40 Bob Jessop, *State Theory: Putting the Capitalist State in its Place* (University Park PA: Pennsylvania State University Press, 1990), pp. 248–71.

# Index